Developing
Object-Oriented
Software

An Experience-Based Approach

IBM Object-Oriented Technology Center

To join a Prentice Hall PTR internet mailing list, point to

http://www.prenhall.com/register

Prentice Hall PTR
Upper Saddle River, New Jersey 07458
http://www.prenhall.com

Library of Congress Cataloging-in-Publication Data

Developing object-oriented software: an experience-based approach / IBM Object-Oriented Technology Center.

     p. cm.

    Includes bibliographical references and index.

    ISBN 0-13-737248-5 (alk. paper)

     1. Computer software—Development.   2. Object-oriented methods (Computer science)   I. IBM Object-Oriented Technology Center.

QA76.76.D47D49   1997

005.1'17--dc21   96-46938

                                  CIP

Editorial/production supervision: *Kathleen M. Caren*
Manufacturing manager: *Alexis R. Heydt*
Acquisitions editor: *Michael E. Meehen*
Marketing manager: *Stephen Solomon*
Editorial assistant: *Kate Hargett*
Cover design director: *Jerry Votta*

Published by Prentice Hall PTR
Prentice-Hall, Inc.
A Simon & Schuster Company
Upper Saddle River, New Jersey 07458

The publisher offers discounts on this book when ordered in bulk quantities.
For more information, contact:

    Corporate Sales Department
    PTR Prentice Hall
    One Lake Street
    Upper Saddle River, NJ 07458

    Phone: 800-382-3419, Fax: 201-236-7141
    E-mail: corpsales@prenhall.com

Printed in the United States of America
10 9 8 7 6 5 4 3

ISBN 0-13-737248-5

Prentice-Hall International (UK) Limited, *London*
Prentice-Hall of Australia Pty. Limited, *Sydney*
Prentice-Hall Canada Inc., *Toronto*
Prentice-Hall Hispanoamericana, S.A., *Mexico*
Prentice-Hall of India Private Limited, *New Delhi*
Prentice-Hall of Japan, Inc., *Tokyo*
Simon & Schuster Asia Pte. Ltd., *Singapore*
Editora Prentice-Hall do Brasil, Ltda., *Rio de Janeiro*

Contents

Part 4. Work Product Construction Techniques 361

Part 5. Video Store Case Study 477

Figures

Tables

Foreword

The atmosphere surrounding object-oriented software development approaches in the mid-1990s can best be described as Darwinian—survival of the fittest. During this turbulent period, different approaches have struggled for critical mind share among mainstream developers. A small number of approaches have generated sufficient market momentum to advance the evolution of object-oriented software development approaches into a phase of consolidation. In this phase, the approaches that have been employed successfully and have garnered the strongest market support are being amalgamated into more comprehensive, and hopefully better, development approaches.

IBM has been an active participant in the evolution of object-oriented software development approaches. In 1992, IBM established the Object-Oriented Technology Center (OOTC) to assist IBM product groups in the successful application of object technology. Since its inception, members of the OOTC have worked with IBM software development groups on over 70 projects at 20 different IBM sites throughout the world. Over the years, many different approaches to object-oriented software development have been employed. The resultant, best practice approach, has been consolidated and is described in this book—written by the experienced professionals of IBM's OOTC.

What differentiates the software development approach described in this book from the majority of books on object-oriented development is its focus—work product oriented and workbook-centered. Most contemporary object-oriented development approaches focus on methods and notations for developing object systems. This book focuses on the artifacts or work products that are produced during a software development project, and the manner in which the work products are logically organized (i.e., the project workbook).

The good news is that the approach advocated in this book is complementary to other method- and notation-based approaches. In particular, the methods and notations of other approaches can be used as a means of creating and representing the work products described herein. So, if your object-oriented software development approach provides a substantial assortment of techniques and notations, but leaves you wondering exactly what artifacts you need to produce to reach end of job, you will find this text a useful complement for developing object-oriented software. If you are a newcomer to object technology, you will benefit from the clarity of thought that the work product/workbook approach brings to developing object-oriented software.

Kenneth S. Rubin
Director and Managing Principal
IBM North America Object Technology Practice

September 1996

Preface

ABOUT THIS BOOK

This book describes an approach to object-oriented software development that has been created, used, improved, and proven throughout the five years of existence of the Object-Oriented Technology Center (OOTC), a team of object technology experts that provides mentoring on the use of object technology at the International Business Machines Corporation (IBM).

The book details the OOTC's philosophy of focusing on the creation of a "Project Workbook" that spans the object-oriented development process and includes various "work products," which are planned, concrete results, either the final deliverable or intermediate ones, created at the various phases of the process.

This approach results in a highly tailorable and flexible baseline process that can be easily adjusted to fit the needs of projects whatever their size, object technology skills, or problem domain.

The book presents advice, guidance, and techniques for the use of this approach and for the development of the various work products.

The book's point of view is the project. It is based on the experiences of the IBM OOTC in assisting IBM product development groups in their efforts to effectively use object technology, and thus it is intended to be used as a reference guide by members of project teams that are using object technology. It provides very specific information on particular aspects of object-oriented development that can be used to build or refresh knowledge on how to approach a certain phase of object-oriented development.

The book presents information on:

1. *The work product oriented and workbook-centered approach to object-oriented software development*

   - Discusses the advantages of focussing on the work products that need to be created at each phase of the development process.

   - Describes the project workbook and why successful object-oriented projects consider it a critical tool for driving the object-oriented development process.

2. *The object-oriented development process*

   - A discussion of the development process that is recommended for use with the approach to object-oriented development described in this book.

   - Topics covered include project structure, iterative and incremental development, typical shapes of object-oriented projects and variations on those shapes, and the development phases of an object-oriented project.

3. *Work products produced in each phase of the object-oriented development life cycle*

   • The book contains detailed descriptions of 48 work products.

   • Each work product description provides information on what the work product is used for, who constructs it, techniques for constructing it, advice and guidance on the construction and use of the work product, examples of the work products, and more.

4. *Techniques for developing various work products*

   • A set of techniques that are useful for developing the work products and utilizing the approach described in this book are presented.

   • Each technique description provides detailed advice and guidance

5. *A Case Study of a project using this approach*.

   • The book provides an example project workbook for a project to develop a Video Store Administration system using the approach described in this book.

   • The book also provides example templates that can be used as a guide for developing your own project workbook.

INTENDED AUDIENCE

This book presents an approach that can be used by teams of varying sizes in the development of object-oriented software. It provides advice and guidance on the full range of the object-oriented development life cycle from initial requirements gathering and planning through analysis, design, implementation, and testing. It provides techniques that can be used by technical personnel and project managers.

Therefore, this book contains something of value for people filling a wide variety of roles:

Project Managers and Team Leaders can use this book to gain an understanding of the work products that can be expected in an object-oriented development project and how to customize, measure, and track an iterative and incremental development process that is based on those work products.

Team Leaders, Analysts, Architects, Designers, Domain Experts, and Developers will see how the work products that they will create in their roles interrelate in an object-oriented development process. This book will provide them with some valuable insights, both from the detailed description of the work products and from the advice and guidance that can be of assistance in the development of specific work products.

Human Factors Engineers, Information Developers, and Testers can gain an understanding of the object-oriented development process and the opportunities it presents to them for earlier involvement in the project than perhaps was possible using traditional processes.

Planners and Customers can use this book to enhance their understanding of object technology and the iterative and incremental development process, and to gain insight into how the characteristics of the technology and the process can be exploited to achieve early customer involvement in product development and to shorten time-to-market of critical product function.

Librarians can begin to get a feel for the types of work products that they will likely have to process in an object-oriented software development project.

Finally, ***everyone*** can benefit from the fact that this approach provides for standards for documentation of project workbooks. These workbooks drive the development process in a powerfully intuitive manner, provide a focal point for communication between people working on the project, and can facilitate reuse within and between projects by establishing a common ground for easier sharing.

BOOK ORGANIZATION

This book is organized into six major parts:

Part 1, "Key Messages" on page 13, is a discussion of the three critical attributes of object-oriented software development described in this approach: *Work Product Oriented and Workbook-Centered Development, Iterative and Incremental Development,* and *Scenario-Driven Development.*

Part 2, "Development Process" on page 51, describes the sequencing of activities in an object-oriented development project.

Part 3, "Work Products" on page 75, describes the work products that are produced at each phase of an object-oriented development process including advice on how to build them.

Part 4, "Work Product Construction Techniques" on page 361 , discusses some additional, alternative techniques that can be used to produce some of the work products.

Part 5, "Video Store Case Study" on page 477, is an example of an "in progress" project workbook for a project being implemented with this approach.

Part 6, "Appendixes" on page 599, contains project workbook templates, a glossary, and a bibliography.

HOW TO USE THIS BOOK

There are likely many ways to use this book depending on your role, your knowledge of object technology, and your particular need at any particular point in time. Reading the entire book is, of course, an option. Three other possible approaches for using this book are described below.

1. **The Basic Path:** Recommended for those people who are new to object technology, are in a management position, or who want to get an in-depth view of the approach presented in this book:

   a. The "Glossary," page 617, to ensure understanding of the terminology used in this book.

   b. The introductory chapter in Section 1.0, "Introduction" on page 1, to get some background on the evolution of this approach.

   c. The "Key Messages," section in Part 1, page 13.

   d. The description of the object-oriented development life cycle in Part 2, "Development Process" on page 51.

   e. Section 8.0, "Information About Work Products" on page 77 for a description of what work products are.

   f. The "Video Store Case Study," in Part 5, page 477, to get an example of a project workbook implemented with this approach

   g. Particular work products that are of interest to you in your role. The Summary of Work Products Table on page 84, can be used to get an overview of the work products that are described in the book.

   h. Particular techniques that are of interest to you in your role in Part 4, "Work Product Construction Techniques" on page 361.

2. **The Fast Path:** This path is recommended for those people who are experienced with object technology:

   a. Part 1, "Key Messages" on page 13.

   b. Section 8.0, "Information About Work Products" on page 77 for a description of what work products are.

   c. Particular work products that are of interest to you in your role. The Summary of Work Products Table on page 84, can be used to get an overview of the work products that are described in the book.

   d. Particular techniques that are of interest to you in your role in Part 4, "Work Product Construction Techniques" on page 361.

3. **The Reference Guide Path:** Recommended for those who want to use the book as support material to aid in their use of object technology:

    a. Part 1, "Key Messages" on page 13.

    b. Particular work products that are of interest to you in your role. The Summary of Work Products Table on page 84, can be used to get an overview of the work products that are described in the book.

    c. Particular techniques that are of interest to you in your role in Part 4, "Work Product Construction Techniques" on page 361.

METHODOLOGY WITHIN IBM

Object technology is widely used inside IBM, and a variety of commercial object-oriented methods have been employed in the company. The methods of James Rumbaugh, Grady Booch, Sally Shlaer and Stephen Mellor, Ivar Jacobson, and Peter Coad and Ed Yourdon have been among the more popular. However, as experience has deepened and the use of object technology has become more mature, the trend has been toward hybridization. In other words, published methods have been adapted and customized based on project experiences. The approach described in this book has evolved in exactly that way and is being used extensively in the company. It is also influencing the direction of other IBM methodology efforts.

The IBM Consulting Group has the corporate mission to define methods for use by the IBM consulting community in the services they provide to IBM customers. System development methods are described in the *Worldwide Solution Design and Delivery Method (WSDDM)*. WSDDM contains coverage of object technology.

The material presented in this book was a primary building block for the object-oriented portion of WSDDM and many of this book's authors participated in the definition of the WSDDM object technology content. In its description of object technology, WSDDM also takes a work product oriented view of system development. Work products are described in much the same way in WSDDM as they are in this book. The majority of the work products described in this book are contained in WSDDM.

The key difference between this book and WSDDM is that the latter is more prescriptive in describing a process model and the specific tasks that generate work products. WSDDM also goes into more detail in areas such as project management, engagement management, and deployment and describes additional work products in support of those areas.

WSDDM is used by IBM Consulting during the delivery of services to their customers and is available only through that mechanism.

In addition to its value as a stand-alone text describing an experience based, widely used approach to object-oriented software development, this book can be used to gain an insight into WSDDM because of the many similarities between the two approaches.

AUTHORS

This book is the result of a group effort by many past and present members of the IBM Object-Oriented Technology Center (OOTC). The contributing authors are:

- John Barry (IBM Poughkeepsie, New York)
- Tom Bridge (IBM Toronto, Canada)
- Paul Fertig (IBM Manchester, England)
- Tom Guinane (IBM Santa Teresa, California)
- Geoff Hambrick (IBM Austin, Texas)
- Daniel Hu (IBM Poughkeepsie, New York)
- Tom Kristek (IBM Austin, Texas)
- Dave Livesey (IBM Poughkeepsie, New York)
- Guillermo Lois (IBM Lidingö, Sweden)
- Mike Page (IBM Toronto, Canada)
- Branko Peteh (formerly of IBM Oslo, Norway)
- Frank Seliger (IBM Böblingen, Germany)
- Thomas Wappler (IBM Böblingen, Germany)
- Brian Watt (IBM Austin, Texas)
- Martin West (IBM Hursley, England)
- George Yuan (IBM Raleigh, North Carolina)

ACKNOWLEDGMENTS

The members of the OOTC have had a unique opportunity to work in a group that was put in place with the express purpose of gaining deep understanding of object technology and how to effectively apply it to real software development projects. This book is a direct result of the investigation, mentoring, and support activities that these jobs have allowed us to undertake.

We would like to thank the International Business Machines Corporation, and in particular, its software development divisions for having the foresight to fund and support such a group.

We would also like to thank all of the project teams that have afforded us the opportunity to work and learn with them. This book would not have been possible without those experiences.

Further thanks go out to all of readers of the previous internal versions of this book who have provided us with constructive feedback based on their experiences using the approach described herein.

And finally, numerous people have provided in-depth reviews of the book, have been tremendous supporters of the IBM OOTC, or in other ways have provided us with invaluable professional guidance and support. We are indebted to Michael Branson, Allan Dickson, Dan Douglas, Guenter Fehrenbach, Michael Florentino, Eric Herness, Achim Huebner, Pat Janasak, Astrid Kreissig, Gerald Kreissig, Susan Lilly, Slavko Malesevic, Ken McCauley, Chris Newlon, Donna Prime, Christer Rehnström, Bonita See, Chuck Smith, Anders Stange, and John Vlissides.

TRADEMARKS

The following terms, which are used throughout this book, are trademarks or registered trademarks of the IBM Corporation in the United States and/or other countries:

AIX	AIX/6000
BookMaster	CICS/ESA
CMVC	CMVC/6000
CUA	DATABASE 2
DataJoiner	DB2
DB2/2	DB2/6000
DRDA	DSOM
ES/9000	ESA/9000
IBM Foundry Blueprint	IBMCLASS
LAN Distance	LE/370
MVS	MVS/ESA
Open Blueprint	Open Class
OS/2	PowerPC
Presentation Manager	PS/2
RISC System/6000	RS/6000
SDE Workbench/6000	SOM
SOMobjects	SP
VisualAge	VisualAge C++
VisualInfo	VMT

The following terms, which are used throughout this book, are trademarks or registered trademarks of other companies:

Apple

Bento

Digitalk

Fusion

Lotus

Microsoft

Motif

ObjectStore

OMG

Open Scripting Architecture

Oracle

Postscript

Rational

Select OMT

SunSoft

Taligent

VisualC++

VisualWorks

WordPerfect

OSF/Motif

Apple Events

CodeCheck

Freelance Graphics

Hypercard

Macintosh

Microsoft Project

Novell

ODMG

OMT

OpenDoc

Paradigm Plus

ProLint

Rational Rose

StateChart

SuperProject

VisualBasic

VisualSmalltalk

Windows

Word Pro

1.0 Introduction

There are numerous critical success factors associated with the use of object technology for software development. These include, but are not limited to:

- Management support for the use of object technology in a particular project

- Assessing team needs for training in object technology and supporting tools and making the needed investments in training and tools

- Ensuring that the development team has access to the knowledge of experienced practitioners of object-oriented software development either as team members or as mentors

- Understanding of the object-oriented software development life cycle by all members of the project's management, technical, and support teams

    - Understanding the differences between object-oriented development and whatever approach to software development is currently being used in the organization

    - Understanding the impacts that those differences have on the steps used in building software

- Understanding the artifacts that need to be produced at each phase of the development life cycle in order to support successful use of object technology

    - Understanding the various choices of methods and techniques that exist for producing these artifacts and how to select the approach best suited to a particular project

This book focuses on the critical areas of "understanding the object-oriented software development life cycle" and "understanding the artifacts that need to be produced." It presents the approach to object-oriented software development that the IBM Object-Oriented Technology Center (OOTC)[1] uses and advocates in its day-to-day activities supporting object technology use in IBM.

The OOTC has been in operation since 1992 with a mission to provide information and support on the use of object technology within many of IBM's software development laboratories. The three primary means of providing this support are:

1. Mentoring IBM software development projects on how best to apply object technology to their projects

2. Providing short-term assistance such as technical presentations and seminars, pointers to technical information, and design and code reviews

---

[1] The IBM OOTC and object technology centers are described in [Korson96].

3. Developing documents that provide information on various aspects of object technology and its usage.

The OOTC is staffed by people with expertise and experience in the use of object technology and has supported the use of object technology in 70 projects at 20 IBM locations worldwide. It has produced 15 internal documents on various aspects of object technology and its usage and more than 22,000 copies of those documents are in circulation. The OOTC has also provided short-term assistance to over 2,000 people.

This book is a direct product of that body of work and of the collective experience of the OOTC's members. It is reflective of our current understanding of the approaches to object-oriented software development that have been most successful for us and our clients.

The approach presented in this book was developed over a period of five years and has evolved to its present state on two paths:

1. Evolution: This book presents an approach to object-oriented software development at which OOTC members have arrived at philosophical agreement despite some differing preferences on specific object-oriented methods and techniques. The approach has been documented and enhanced through numerous cycles of use in OOTC mentoring engagements and solicitation of feedback from readers.

2. Genealogy: This approach is based on the aspects of many other methods and approaches to object-oriented software development that we have found to be of the most practical value in our work with object-oriented development projects.

These paths are discussed in the following three sections.

1.1 THE EVOLUTION OF THIS APPROACH

The mentors who comprise the OOTC, typically about 14 in number, are recruited from throughout the IBM software community. The staff is diverse in terms of professional background and areas of object technology expertise and has included members with backgrounds in research, marketing and services, tools development, product development, and education and training with expertise in a variety of domains including operating systems, engineering software, class library development, networking software, and databases.

The staff's areas of object technology expertise have covered areas such as analysis, design, C++, Smalltalk, Java, metrics, testing, reuse, tools, databases, and object request brokers.

The customer set that the OOTC exists to support, IBM's Software Development Laboratories, is also widely diverse in terms of problem domains, approaches to software development, development tools and platforms, target platforms, favorite object methodologies and notations, and object technology skills.

Further, in the early days of the OOTC, object technology was evolving rapidly and there were few standard approaches, processes, methods, or tools.

When the OOTC began providing mentoring services, not much was thought was given to the potential problems of diverse mentors and clients working with an evolving technology. The advice that the OOTC's mentors gave their clients during engagements was based on "what they knew" and was not formed into a consistent, repeatable documented approach.

This was because while each OOTC mentor had developed a high degree of expertise and experience relative to their clients, it was typical that this expertise and experience was different. Typically, two mentors would be assigned to an engagement and it was common that they had not worked with each other previously. This meant that either there was no common ground from which to work, or that any common ground that might exist was not readily apparent.

This approach worked for the OOTC and its clients during the OOTC's first year, but it was clear that this approach would not be adequate for long. There were several reasons for this:

1. The OOTC's clients began to demand documentation of the advice and guidance that they were receiving in the mentoring sessions. There was a need for documents that the clients could refer to in the absence of the OOTC's mentors.

2. The client base was becoming more sophisticated and experienced. Object technology was growing in usage and importance inside IBM and the knowledge and expectations of the OOTC clientele were growing with it. The clients were beginning to expect well-thought out answers to increasingly complex questions. Additionally, many of the projects had made preliminary choices of methods and notations that the OOTC needed to work with. So, the OOTC's advice and guidance on best practices for object-oriented software development needed to fit well with these differing notations and methods in order to be effective.

3. Consistency was a problem. Sometimes a project follow-up visit might have to be performed by different mentors because of scheduling conflicts. A mentor new to a project would often be puzzled by what they found their predecessors had advised.

4. There was no basis for quality control of the OOTC mentoring offering. Because each mentor used their own particular approach, and the mentoring process was not documented, it was difficult to judge what approaches were meeting with the most success.

The OOTC team agreed that to continue to be successful it was important to reach some consensus on the approach to be used in mentoring engagements and on the important advice and guidance that the OOTC was giving its clients. The benefits expected from this were:

1. A consistent and repeatable approach. This would provide a baseline, agreed approach from which change could be discussed and negotiated.

2. A documented approach with documented advice and guidance. This would allow mentoring clients to have a reference guide to use when OOTC mentors were not at hand.

3. A handbook for OOTC mentors. It would provide a reference document for new OOTC mentors to master, support, and help evolve.

4. A vehicle for exchanging approaches, experiences, successes, and failures amongst OOTC members. This would be critical for creating a cohesive team of mentors and for ensuring that the overall process could continue to evolve in a positive direction.

Reaching consensus was not easy. This was largely due to the fact that each OOTC mentor had strongly held opinions about the relative merits of their favorite methods, approaches, and techniques.

The starting point for attempting to develop consensus was for each OOTC mentor to present the team with an overview of their approach to object-oriented development including examples of the artifacts that they normally produced throughout the development cycle. At the end of this exercise it was clear that consensus was a long way off.

It was soon observed, however, that, while the flow through the development process and the specific techniques used to create artifacts were different, the artifacts (or work products) themselves were quite similar. For example, everyone was using a Rumbaugh-like Object Model and producing something similar to Jacobson's Object Interaction Diagrams. This insight caused the team to begin to focus on what they produced rather than how they produced it. The "what" turned out to be fairly standard.

The team also considered two particular OOTC mentoring engagements that were very successful in their use of object technology. These completely different projects had some strong similarities in approaches: They produced similar work products at the same phases of the development life cycle; they were dedicated to maintaining these work products; and they consolidated the work products into a project workbook.

This led the us to concentrate on work products in the context of a project workbook. It was decided that an approach that standardized on work products but allowed for individual choices on particular techniques used to produce work products was the best fit for the OOTC. It would help us to gain the benefits of a standardized approach while not sacrificing the strengths that each mentor possessed in applying individual techniques.

Thus this book began to take the form of work products described in the context of a workbook, accompanied by a tool kit of techniques producing those work products.

It soon became apparent, though, that what began as a necessity had turned into a virtue. Providing mentoring within the context of a well-defined project workbook structure turned out to be a good decision independent of OOTC history. Focusing on work products instead of on process permits standardization and structure without sacrificing the flexibility demanded by projects that typically differ very widely and many of which have already chosen particular methods, notations, and techniques.

Since this approach was first documented in early 1995, it has been enhanced regularly based on feedback derived from its usage:

- In OOTC mentoring engagements

- By other object-oriented projects inside IBM

- As the basis for material presented in IBM education courses on object-oriented software development

- By IBM marketing and services personnel in engagements with IBM customers

- By more than 2,000 IBM employees as a general reference guide on object-oriented development

These enhancements include:

- Improvement of work product descriptions and advice and guidance

- The addition of new work products which were found to be useful

- The addition of techniques that had proven useful in the OOTC mentoring practice

- Crisper definition of the object-oriented development life cycle that works best with this approach

- The addition of a complete case study that demonstrates how the work products described in this approach flow from phase to phase in the development life cycle.

So, the evolution of this approach did not end with the first attempt at defining, documenting, and using it successfully. Rather, it has been continuously improved since then through a process of use, feedback, and enhancement.

1.2 THE GENEALOGY OF THIS APPROACH

This approach is not identical to any published method such as those described in books by James Rumbaugh, Grady Booch, or Ivar Jacobson, although it borrows concepts and notations from these and others. It has been our experience and observation that mature practitioners of object-oriented software development do not follow any standard method exactly as it is published. Most seasoned veterans of object-oriented development wind up hybridizing their approach—they use what they find works from a base method and extend it by borrowing from other approaches and experiences that they find useful. This was the case with the OOTC, as is shown in Figure 1-1. This figure shows some of the influences of the approach described in this book.

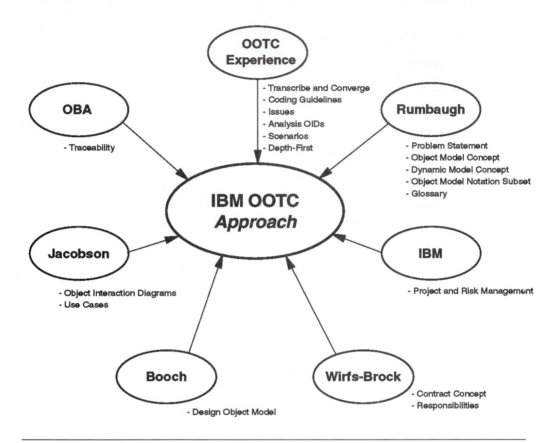

Figure   1-1. Sources of the IBM OOTC Approach.

The methods referenced above are considered to be "established methods." (Sometimes called First Generation Methods.)   Hybrids, such as Fusion [Coleman94], [Malan96]   or SOMA [Graham95] (sometimes referred to as "Second Generation Methods" in the literature) have combined ideas from more than one of the established methods.   There are a whole range of emerging methods evolving at this time in the object-oriented community (for example, KISS [Kristen94], BON [Walden95], OORAM [Reenskaug96], ROOM [Selic94], et cetera).   As they become better known and more experience is gained, they will undoubtedly influence the evolution of our approach.

We have incorporated various aspects, such as techniques and notations, from long established and second generation methods. As Figure 1-1 shows, our approach has not been developed from scratch, but incorporates several aspects from other methods, such as notations and various work products for requirements, analysis, and design.

1.2.1 Notation

The Object Modeling Technique (OMT) [Rumbaugh91a] is one of the more popular methods in the object technology field. It is well adapted within the community; it has extensive tool support; and there are many training courses available. Several books and articles ([Derrer95], [D'Souza95], [D'Souza94], [Rumbaugh91b], et cetera) discuss modeling with OMT. For these reasons we decided to adapt the OMT notation style as a base for our notation.

In our experience OMT strengths are:

- Flexibility and extensibility of the method

- Easy to learn and somewhat intuitive

- Strong treatment of relationships.

Having said that, the key messages of this book are entirely independent of notation, and the ideas that we present in this book can be used with other notations, for example Grady Booch, James Rumbaugh, and Ivar Jacobson's "Unified Modeling Language" notation [Booch96].[2] This is also confirmed by our own experience where approximately 40 percent of the projects we have been involved in have used other notations such as Booch, and Shlaer and Mellor).

1.2.2 Work Products

Many of our requirement work products are taken straight from standard software development practices (such as *Business Case* and *Acceptance Plan*). The same is true of our project management work products (*Resource Plan*, *Schedule*, et cetera). These have been included in this book for completeness, and not because they are novel.

The *Glossary* work product is maintained through all development phases beginning with requirements gathering. It is based on OMT's Data Dictionary ([Rumbaugh91a], pages 156-157).

The Object Behavior Analysis (OBA) approach ([Gibson90], [Rubin92], [Wirfs-Brock92]) has as its primary emphasis the modeling, representation, and communication of the requirements of a system through the use of a consistent vocabulary and by maintaining full traceability of the resultant artifacts to the stated business goals and objectives [Rubin94]. OBA includes an interesting feature called a *traceability model*. This model shows the interdependencies of the various work products. The traceability concept of our approach is based on this model.

---

[2] The Unified Modeling Language is a merging of the models and notation from the Booch, OMT, and Objectory methods by Grady Booch, James Rumbaugh, and Ivar Jacobson.

In common with many other emerging object-oriented development approaches, we make use of the great contribution to the field made by Ivar Jacobson, namely Use Cases. A Use Case is defined as "... a special sequence of transactions in a dialogue between a user and the system. Each use case is thus a specific way of using the system. A Use Case may have one basic course and several alternative courses." ([Jacobson92], page 510). Our use of Use Cases differs from the above definition. Our Use Cases are not sequences of transactions but statements of externally visible system behavior. We refine Use Cases into *Scenarios* each of which elaborates a Use Case with a set of assumptions and a set of outcomes. Each of our Scenarios may have an Object Interaction Diagram (OID) that shows graphically in terms of interactions between objects how a particular Object Model can support its Scenario. Ivar Jacobson incorporates the function of all three of these work products: Use Case, Scenario, and OID into his concept of Use Cases. There is scope, of course, for both sets of ideas to be used in parallel, but we believe that our approach is frequently helpful, as it encourages developers to focus on one concern at a time. The idea of a Scenario as we have defined it, in terms of assumptions and outcomes, turns out to be exactly what is required when system behavior has to be defined rigorously. The idea of defining behavior in terms of assumptions (preconditions) and outcomes (postconditions) comes from software engineering. This view has also been used by Syntropy [Cook94].

We have found state modeling to be a useful means of gaining insight into the lifecycle of objects (as in [Rumbaugh91a] and [Shlaer92]), although applied on a very selective basis.

The static aspects of our approach are specified using an entity centric object model (such as OMT or Booch), with modeling constructs such as classes, attributes, and associations. The *Analysis Object Model* and *Design Object Model* work products are based on OMT's object model concept [Rumbaugh91a], [Rumbaugh95a]. The *Design Object Model* is augmented with directionality and many of Grady Booch's adornments [Booch94].

In the Unified Modeling Language, a notation framework is introduced to present the design information "for an object-oriented system under construction" [Booch96]. The notation covers the modeling aspects for static class relationships, use cases, message tracing, state modeling, and system organization. Our approach is an enhancement of OMT (and by the way these aspects have not been resolved in the Unified Modeling Language) by (1) simplifying the notation for the practical usage, (2) adding development processes and emphasizing how to utilize the notation and modeling in each development phase, and (3) separating the notation for the business modeling (object-oriented analysis) that is independent of technology from the one for solution modeling (object-oriented design) that is dependent of underlying technology.

OMT's Dynamic Model Concept [Rumbaugh91a], [Rumbaugh95b], and Jacobson's Interaction Diagrams [Jacobson92] have leveraged our dynamic modeling work products: *Object Interaction Diagrams* and *State Models* at both the analysis and design levels of abstraction.

From the Responsibility-Driven Design (RDD) method by Rebecca Wirfs-Brock ([Wirfs-Brock89]) we have incorporated the concept of responsibilities during analysis and

RDD's Contract concept in our *Subsystem Model*. In RDD the examination of collaborations and responsibilities is the central part of the method. RDD regards an application very much in a client-server fashion where objects collaborate and provide services for each other. These services are described in a contract between the service provider and a client requesting the service.

Our *Subject Areas* work product is inspired by Sally Shlaer and Steve Mellor's Domains [Shlaer92] and Peter Coad's Subjects [Coad90]. Both Domains and Subject Areas are mechanisms for permitting developers to focus on one logically independent topic at a time. Subject Areas differ from Domains (and Subsystems), however, because they are identified at analysis time. Subject Areas partition the *problem domain* that relates directly to the business problem and that is the subject matter of analysis.

Much of our project management work products derive from the project management techniques, processes, and approaches that have been long employed by software development groups inside IBM. Some have been modified for use with an object-oriented approach. Some are used in much the same way as they have always been. This is one of the strengths of the approach as far as our ability to have it accepted by the managers and technical leads of project development groups. They don't have to throw away everything they have done in the past and, in particular, in the important area of project management; much of what they have done in the past can still be effectively employed in the object-oriented world.

And finally, many of the key components of our approach such as coding guidelines, our use of issues, and our approach to analysis object interaction diagrams, as well as techniques such as Depth-First (see Section 17.1) and Transcribe and Converge (see Section 18.3) have evolved from our work with software development projects in our mentoring practice.

1.3 ROLES IN AN OBJECT-ORIENTED PROJECT

The authors hope that this book has something of interest to almost everyone involved with object-oriented software development whatever their specific role. Throughout this book (particularly in Part 3 and Part 4) there are references to who does certain things in the process. When using this book it is important to understand what we mean by a certain role. The major roles of interest for purposes of this book follow. You may also see elsewhere in this book some off-shoot of a role described below or some slightly different terminology used. We hope that with an understanding of the following, that those slight variations will not be confusing or misleading, and we will continue to strive toward consistency in future releases.

When trying to relate these roles to those you may see on your team, it is important to note that in some cases one person may fill more than one role. For example, an architect might also be the team leader.

Customer
> The real-life external or internal customer for whom the product is intended, or some representative of the external customer (such as a marketing representative or a "typical" end user), or any other receiver of the project deliverables.

Planner
> Acquires and coordinates project requirements and also develops and tracks the Project Schedule.

Project Manager
> Owns overall responsibility for the development of a project. Ensures that proper personnel and resources are available and tracks tasks, schedules, and deliverables.

Team Leader
> Provides technical direction for the project. Leads team through the development process. Of course in large projects, you may have an overall team leader and leaders of smaller teams.

Architect
> Responsible for overall design/architecture of the project. Manages the interfaces to other development activities related to this project.

Analyst
> Takes user requirements and generates project specifications. Interprets user intention and defines the problems that need to be solved. Responsible for developing domain analysis model with users and other team members.

Designer
> Responsible for the design of a subsystem or category of classes. Directs implementation and manages interfaces to other subsystems.

Domain Expert
> Understands a particular business area. Keeps project focused on solving problems with relationship to the domain.

Developer
> Implements the overall design; owns and designs specific classes and methods, codes and unit-tests them, and builds the product. Developer is a broad term and specialization is possible, such as a Class Developer.

Information Developer
> Creates the documentation that will accompany the product when it is released. Includes installation material as well as reference, tutorial, and product help information in both paper and machine readable form.

Human Factors Engineer

Responsible for the usability of the product. Works with customers to ensure that user interface requirements are met.

Tester

Validates the function, quality, and performance of the product. Develops and executes Test Cases for each development phase.

Librarian

Responsible for creating and maintaining the integrity of the project library, that is comprised of the project work products. Is also responsible for enforcing work product standards.

1.4 METHOD AND LANGUAGE INDEPENDENCE

An object-oriented application development method should be implementation language-independent. That is to say that it should not make a significant difference in your development approach whether you are going to be building the application in Smalltalk, C++, or Java. The approach described in this book is language-independent and has been used in C++, Smalltalk, and Java projects.

The work products described in this book are language-independent. For example, an Analysis Object Model (see Section 11.3) has no language-specific requirements.

This is not to say there are no differences between individual work products depending on the language of implementation. Naturally, there are differences, particularly in low-level design and implementation work products. However, the same overall process is followed and the same work products are produced.

1.5 ADAPTING THIS APPROACH FOR A SPECIFIC PROJECT

This approach has been used in many software development projects both inside and outside of IBM. In some cases it has been used more or less as described in this book and in other cases has been used as a baseline and adapted to the particular needs of projects.

Many organizations have an existing methodological approach to systems development and wish to preserve as much of that approach as possible while defining a standard methodology to be used on object-oriented projects in their organizations. Rather than introduce a completely new approach, there is a desire to take an evolutionary approach and preserve as much as possible of their current development process.

Our experience has shown that many elements of standard development approaches are applicable to the object-oriented development world. Elements such as user documentation requirements, deployment, user training, and system testing tend to survive relatively unchanged in the move to the object-oriented world.

The areas that are impacted the most are planning, requirements, analysis, and design.

Planning is impacted due to the iterative and incremental nature of object-oriented development.   Many standard approaches to development are based on a waterfall approach.   Planning incremental and iterative development is much different from traditional styles.

The key differences in the area of requirements, analysis, and design are that when using object technology they should be expressed in terms of collaborating objects.   Thus, existing techniques that express the world in terms of processes or entities must be changed.   These are the areas that will be most impacted by a transition to objects.

It is possible to integrate the approach in this book with an existing development process.   To do this, each work product in this book should be evaluated in light of an existing process.   Where you find equivalency, feel free to substitute existing work products that you are more comfortable with.   You may also wish to extend this approach in areas that you prefer to cover in more detail.   You may also choose to cut back in areas of coverage that you find overly detailed.   However, be careful as it isn't as simple as you might think.   Two of the more common problems we have seen are:

- *Eliminating an object-oriented work product in favor of a nonobject equivalent* - We have seen projects eliminate Object Interaction Diagrams in favor of some form of process modeling.   Unfortunately, process models do not express the world in terms of objects and therefore do not meet the requirements of object analysis or design.

- *Assuming an object is an entity* - Many organizations have some form of entity modeling in their existing processes and try to adapt an entity-based work product into an object-based work product.   This should not be done.   An entity is not an object and the manner in which entity-based work products are developed is not the same as object-based work products.

A standard approach should be defined in light of real systems development needs. Once defined, any process should be modified in the light of experiences.   Therefore, it is essential that a "continuous improvement process" be defined.   Getting feedback on how the approach is working or not working on projects must be part of the process.

In addition, object technology methodology is still an evolving field so it is necessary to keep an eye on developments within the industry in order to take advantages of important advancements.

Part 1. *Key Messages*

The key messages we wish to convey in this book are that we believe that the development of object-oriented software should be:

1. Work Product[3] Oriented and Workbook-Centered

2. Iterative and Incremental

3. Scenario-Driven

These key messages are derived from insights gained by the authors during object-oriented project mentoring engagements and are founded on an evolved philosophy rooted in two fundamental principles:

- Separation of Concerns

- Management of Risks

Together, these messages and principles form a framework for object-oriented software development that is largely independent of the specific notations and languages in that you might choose to develop, and independent of the specific techniques that you might use for development. We consider that this separation of process, notation, and techniques is very important, because it allows you to tailor each independently to the needs of your problem and development context. We don't think that one shape of development method should or could fit all development projects.

---

[3] A *work product* is a concrete result of a planned project-related activity such as analysis, design, or project management. Work products include items delivered to customers and items used purely internally within a project. Examples of work products are Project Schedules, Object Models, Source Code, and even executable software products.

In the following chapters we describe what we mean by each of the key messages, why we think that these ideas are so important, and how the remainder of this book is related to them. But first, let's look at the fundamental principles and how they affect our approach.

Separation of Concerns

Modern software development is a complex, expensive, and risky endeavor. Adding an object technology transition to it does not immediately ease the endeavor, but it does add confusion. The confusion comes from many sources, including competing and overlapping: technologies, middleware products, experts and advice, CASE tools, analysis and design methods, notation and even "war stories." All of these ingredients are blended together into an assortment of enticing soups and given exotic, popular, or misleading names. Not until you recursively analyze the ingredients of the different soups can you see the familiar, the common, and the unique elements and how they interact when called for in the different "recipes."

From our own experience, as well as from studying object-oriented analysis and design methods from renown experts, we have come to the understanding that certain products of object-oriented analysis and design are essential and that their necessity and value have little to do with the notation, tool, method, technique, process, or technology used to develop them. This led us to a guiding principle of *Separation of Concerns*. Just as software systems need to be analyzed[4] before they are designed[5], so too do we need to analyze the software development problem before we design development approaches (strategies).

After our analysis of this problem, and through our work with object-oriented software development projects, we designed an approach that maintained separation of certain concerns in order to maximize applicability of the approach, allowing it to support different methods, processes, and tool environments. We chose to separate:

- Tools and Notation from Work Products

- Work Products from Development Process and Techniques

- Analysis from Design from User Interface Design from Implementation

- Project and Risk Management from Work Product Development

Although we have separated these topics, we have also described how they relate to each other. So, you will find work product descriptions providing possible notations, advice on tool usage, references to techniques, and hints of traceability (method). Multiple tech-

---

4 Analysis is the act of exploring the problem domain to gain a better understanding of the problem.

5 Design is the process of planning construction of a solution to a problem.

niques and methods are related to the work products that they yield. Project and Risk Management are planning activities that result in their own work products.

More importantly, the work product orientation itself allows us to focus on one concern at a time. For example, our Use Case work product focuses on basic functionality, whereas our Scenario work product expands on functionality by enumerating the different outcomes implied by different starting conditions.

By separating the concerns here, we hope you get to understand them more easily, as individual topics. By relating them in multiple ways, we hope you learn to combine them in your own situations to solve your unique problems most appropriately.

Management of Risks

In his *Mythical Man-month*, Fred Brooks quipped,

How does a project get to be a year late?
...One day at a time.

This should not only remind us of the importance of maintaining and following a plan but also remind us of how lightly we consider risks. It is as if "risk" had the connotation of imminent and complete failure only. In fact, there are many small risks that arise, accumulate, and feed on each other on a daily basis that are equally pernicious. Nearly everything we profess in our approach is based on managing risk:

Separation of concerns
> Addresses the risks of mental overloading, confusion, losing touch with fundamentals, and unnecessarily tying the fate of one concept, facility, or work product to another less suitable one.

Separating analysis from design
> Addresses the risk of designing a solution for the wrong problem by allowing us to understand the users problem and its domain before we set out to create a solution.

Separation of user interface design from system design
> Addresses the risks of creating a developer oriented (vs. user oriented) system and of letting the user interface get locked into the design by allowing us to involve experts (users and human factors) in an asynchronous cycle of user interface design and prototyping while the development team addresses design model and system environment issues.

Work product orientation
> Addresses the risk of losing ground when tools, notations, techniques, method, or process need to be adjusted by allowing us to vary them while maintaining the essence and value of completed work.

Workbook-centered

> Addresses the risk of clumping too much and too varied work products into hard to manage phase review documents by allowing us to work in parallel teams, incrementally, and iteratively adjusting our tools and methods while continuing to track the completeness and consistency of our tangible development artifacts.

Prototyping

> Addresses the risk of waiting too long before knowing essential information by allowing us to minimize schedule and effort investments while resolving risks that require knowledge only achievable through direct experience.

Incremental development

> Addresses the risk of "putting all our eggs in one basket" by allowing us to "learn as we go and apply what we learned," thereby minimizing the impact of misconceptions and suboptimal decisions.

Iterative development

> Addresses the same risk as incremental development and of excessive schedule dependency by allowing us the freedom to try different alternatives and not get hung up on getting it right the first time.

Scenario-driven development

> Addresses the risk of designing a system that does not satisfy the requirements by allowing us to focus on the traceability of functional requirements while casting our designs into objects.

If you look at the techniques sections you should be able to recognize how each of them addresses some risk too.

Perhaps (if we're successful), you will be able to quip:

> How did this project manage to complete on schedule?
> ...By addressing each and every risk, one at a time.

2.0 Work Product Oriented and Workbook-Centered Development

We refer to our approach as "work product oriented" and "workbook-centered," since a prime focus of the way in which we do object-oriented development is to focus on the development of work products and carefully manage them in a logical entity called the "Project Workbook" that spans the development life cycle. We have observed that our more successful mentoring engagements have been with those projects that have taken a serious, rigorous approach to the development and maintenance of such a project workbook.

This is not a conceptual or theoretical approach to object-oriented development. The approach has evolved out of the mentoring engagements led by the authors since 1992 and is reflective of our experiences during those engagements.

During the evolution of our approach, there was general agreement on appropriate work product content and workbook structure, but we found differing opinions when it came to techniques for producing the work products. This is one reason why we have separated the presentation of the work products from a presentation of the techniques that might be used to build them. You could think of the techniques we list as a toolkit to be applied (and extended) as appropriate. They are offered for the reader to review and consider.

2.1 WHAT DOES WORK PRODUCT ORIENTED MEAN?

The object-oriented paradigm shift allows software developers to view the problem domain and their projected solutions to problems as a set of collaborating autonomous objects, each with their own attributes, relations, and behaviors. This view creates a natural framework, based on real-world and conceptual objects, in which analysis, design, and implementation take place. Though the characteristics of objects are normally hidden, they form the basis for classification (via commonalities and differences) within the framework. This allows for the conceptual and constructive efficiencies of inheritance and reuse, the flexibility of substitution, and the robustness of limiting the scope of changes. Unlike the procedural paradigm, which views software problems and solutions as a hierarchy of procedure invocations, an object-oriented approach yields a network of connected active building blocks.

This type of paradigm shift is not limited to the domain of software structure (i.e., programming). It can also be applied to the domain of software development (i.e., development process). In the same way that we shifted from the procedural view of software having phases, actions, tasks, and processes to thinking of software in terms of objects with encapsulated and, possibly inherited, attributes, relations, and behaviors, so too can we make the shift in thinking about *how* we develop software. Instead of thinking of the development *process* having phases, activities, tasks, and processes, we can think of software development as a network of collaborating objects (called work products or deliverables) which have unique and common attributes, relationships with other work products, and methods for developing, verifying, and presenting themselves.

Just as the object-oriented paradigm shift allows flexibility and robustness, so too does the work product oriented paradigm shift. Rather than specifying a prescriptive, step-by-step, procedure for creating working software from incomplete requirements, we can, instead, think of the facets and views of the problem we need to understand and the types of specifications we need to design that software. In essence, we need to identify the real world objects *from the software development domain* and develop them in an object-oriented way. We call these *work products*.

Which of these work products you need to develop and in which order they should be developed depends on the characteristics of your problem domain and your project. Factors that influence which work products you produce and the order in which you develop them depends on several factors:

- The size of the project

    Projects with more requirements, more people, or longer schedules tend to need more project management work products, a greater emphasis on subsystems, reuse, portability, testing, and packaging.

- The complexity of the problem

    Complex projects tend to have more risks that need to be managed via creative project management, which includes prototyping and use of iterative and incremental processes, and a more detailed treatment of system architecture.

- The degree of technical uncertainty involved

    Concerns such as performance in a networked or client-server environment, performance of large or heavily queried databases, intuitiveness and usability of systems oriented towards casual users, et cetera, require more emphasis on risk management, prototyping, and creative project management (iterative and incremental), as well as more emphasis on domain and requirements analysis.

- The nature of the givens and requirements

    The existence of legacy systems, data, and conceptual models as well as open versus closed sets of functional requirements and reuse intentions affect the precedence (relative importance and traceability) among work products.

The general and specific characteristics of work products are discussed in Part 3 and sample work products can be found in the workbook in Part 5.

2.2 WHAT DOES WORKBOOK-CENTERED MEAN?

Focusing on the production of work products is not enough. Since they comprise the primary means of project communication, they must be available and organized for easy access by the entire project.

To manage the independent development of numerous work products of varying types by many teams or individuals, successful projects create and manage a central depository, the *Project Workbook*, for all work products developed in support of the project. The "care and feeding" of this project workbook becomes the unifying characteristic of the project.

At its lowest level the workbook is organized by work product types. Depending on the project characteristics, higher levels of organization might be based on the subsystems that comprise the product, the releases that incrementally satisfy the requirements, development phases, or some other prime characteristic. In practice, what this requires is early agreement on what the structure of the project workbook will be, the specific work products it will contain, and the format of these work products.

This approach results from the observation that projects that have been successful have produced and used good project workbooks. We have also seen projects fail, due to poor requirements gathering, an almost total lack of analysis, ad hoc design, or no documentation. These failures could have been avoided had the team followed a workbook-driven approach.

2.3 WHAT IS A PROJECT WORKBOOK?

A project workbook is a *logical* book containing all project *work products*. The workbook is *logical* in the sense that its physical medium is not relevant, and it may refer to some of its constituent work products instead of containing them directly. Work products are the result of planned project activities such as project management, analysis, design, et cetera. Work products include items delivered to customers and items used purely internally within the project. Project Schedules, Analysis Object Models, Source Code files, and even the executable software product are all work products.

An important facet of a project workbook is that all the work products that contribute to the workbook have a common structure, at least conceptually. The common work product structure that we suggest is described in Section 8.1. See Part 3 for descriptions of each of the work products that we recommend for inclusion in a project workbook, and Part 4 for a collection of techniques that may be used to build these work products.

Note: Do not confuse the template that we have used in this book to describe each kind of work product with the structure that we suggest you use when constructing real work products for a project.

Ideas for the structure of your Project Workbook are presented below.

2.4 WORKBOOK STRUCTURE

The following lists the major chapters of a project workbook. Each chapter can be viewed as a different perspective on the project and acts as a "logical" container of the work products associated with that perspective.[6]

1. **Requirements** represent the application requirements from the customer's view.

2. **Project Management** is information required for the successful management of the software development effort.

3. **Analysis** work products are a formal representation of the problem domain from the customer's point of view.

4. The **User Interface Model** documents the design of the application's user interface.

5. **Design** describes the structure of the software to be built.

6. **Implementation** is the working application and all work products required to build it.

7. The **Test** chapter contains work products associated with the validation of the software.

8. Typically the **Appendix** is the repository for historical (old) work products.

We have chosen to organize the workbook by these perspectives, rather than chronologically, in order to support iterative and incremental development as well as other life cycle variations, which will be discussed later in this book. The purpose of the workbook is to emphasize that all work be documented as work products and be organized for ready access by the whole project team.

While we discuss the workbook as if it were a single, unified artifact, in reality, it may consist of a number of separate things: for example, current analysis and design products may be kept in a single document; historical analysis and design work may be kept in a file folder in a drawer somewhere; a project plan may be maintained as a separate document; and the code may reside on the hard drive of a team server.

---

[6] By "logical," we mean that each chapter might actually contain the work products, might just refer to the work products residing elsewhere, or might refer to other workbooks.

2.4.1 Composite Structure Workbook

Workbooks are a logical structure to organize and hold work products. The typical high-level structure of a workbook is organized by development phases or perspectives as shown earlier. This looks very simple and is an intuitive structure for a single development cycle of a monolithic system.

Physical Workbook Structure for Complex Systems

Large systems are often divided into subsystems to afford parallel development, application of specialized skills, and planned reuse. Also, large subsystems are often subdivided further into smaller subsystems for the same reasons. Since we recommend using the same the same workbook outline structure for each system and subsystem, we envision the complete system being described by a set of workbooks which reference each other. Logically, the system contains subsystems and the system workbook contains subsystem workbooks. Physically, though, each subsystem could be documented in a whole separate workbook or in whole major sections of a single physical workbook as shown in 2-1.

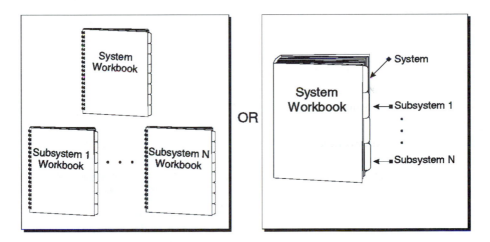

Figure *2-1. Physical Workbook Schemes for Subsystems.*

System Phases or work products shared by subsystems can simply be referred to by the subsystems, for example:[7]

---

[7] We use the HyperText Markup Language (HTML) for general familiarity. You should be able to map this concept to GML, SGML, et cetera.

```
<h1>Subsystem D
<h2>Project Management
<p>Subsystem D will comply with the same Project Management
decisions as System X (see "System X, Project Management...").
```

For systems or subsystems with significant releases and/or internal integration check-points, we advise organizing the Workbook around those releases. It is probably best to keep the subsystem organization foremost, but keep all the phase/work-product material together in document parts. For a single physical workbook, a subsystem organization would be:

```
<TITLE>System X: Project Workbook>
<! Introductory preface, ToC, ...>
<hr><!---------------------->
<h1> System Release 1
<h2> Requirements
...
<h2> Testing
<hr><!---------------------->
<h1> Subsystem A Release 1
<h2> Requirements
...
<h2> Testing
<hr><!---------------------->
<h1> Subsystem A Release 2
<h2> Requirements
...
<h2> Testing
<hr><!---------------------->
<! Appendices, Glossary, et cetera.>
```

If each subsystem has its own workbook, then simply use document parts (for example, HTML's <hr><h1> tags) to separate the releases:

```
<TITLE>System X: Project Workbook>          <TITLE>Subsystem A: Project Workbook>
<! Introductory preface, ToC, ...>          <! Introductory preface, ToC, ...>
<hr><!---------------------->               <hr><!---------------------->
<h1> System Release 1                       <h1> System Release 1
<h2> Requirements                           <h2> Requirements
...                                         ...
<h2> Testing                                <h2> Testing
<hr><!---------------------->               <hr><!---------------------->
<h1> Subsystem A Release 1                   <h1> Subsystem A Release 1
<h2> Requirements                           <h2> Requirements
...                                         ...
<h2> Testing                                <h2> Testing
<hr><!---------------------->               <hr><!---------------------->
<h1> Subsystem A Release 2                   <h1> Subsystem A Release 2
<h2> Requirements                           <h2> Requirements
...                                         ...
<h2> Testing                                <h2> Testing
<hr><!---------------------->               <hr><!---------------------->
<! Appendices, Glossary, et cetera>         <! Appendices, Glossary, et cetera>
```

Internal releases (integration checkpoints) can be kept as deltas over the previous release. External releases should be organized as complete workbooks (show all the work products that make up that release). This is not too difficult when using a word/document processor that supports imbedding files. For these, the common work products can be kept in common files and imbedded unchanged into all releases that use them. When a work product changes, future workbooks can refer to the correct version of the imbed file. A configuration management and version control system should be used to manage the versions of the source files (just as you would for source code files).

Composite Structure of Workbook

When a system is decomposed into subsystems, there is a "composite pattern" [Gamma95] among the system and subsystems, and also between their corresponding workbooks. In this pattern, a "component" can be a "leaf component" (complete) or a "composite" (defined by one or more subcomponents). See Figure 2-2.

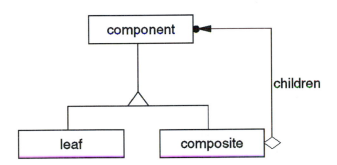

Figure *2-2. Composite Pattern.*

Translating to system terminology, a system or subsystem is either complete or is composed of other subsystems. Likewise, a system or subsystem workbook is either complete (self-contained) or refers (defers) to lower level subsystem workbooks. The subsystems' run-time dependencies might be represented as a directed graph; however, the subsystems' definition is a simple containment hierarchy (see Figure 2-3.)

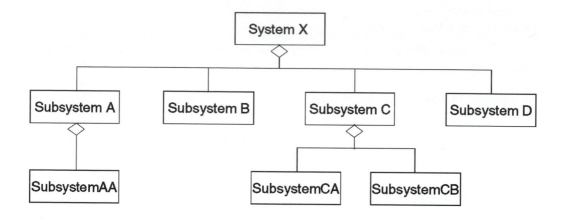

Figure   2-3. System/Subsystem Workbook Structure.

The relationship between a composite workbook and its component workbooks is defined by the Subsystem Model, see Section 13.5. The enclosing workbook can simply define and coordinate the relationships among its subsystem workbooks. In this case, some of enclosing workbook sections will be thin (or empty) since the content has been divided among (and deferred to) its subsystems. This will be more likely when the subsystem boundaries are sufficiently clear and stable or when the subsystems are not dependent on each other for definition (a reuse potential indication). It is less likely when the subsystems are more dependent on each other.

In the independent subsystem case, it is best to defer as much work (analysis, design, et cetera) as possible as early as possible. That is to say, identify the subsystems and their responsibilities and divide the work among parallel development teams as soon as you can.

In the dependent subsystem case, spend more time in the composite workbook, coming to a common analysis, high-level design, et cetera, so that there are fewer decisions (and potential for inconsistency) when the subsystem teams are formed and turned loose.

Workbook Strategy

The work products described in this book are those that we have found useful for medium and large development projects. Small projects might be expected to use only a subset of the work products. The goal of a project workbook is to act as a vehicle for coordinating, directing, and communicating development effort. While there are many ways in which project size may be measured, the characteristic that is of interest to us in this book is the amount of effort that must be put into coordination, direction, and communication between members of the development group.

One simple measure of gauging project size is the number of parallel development teams (where a team typically consists of four to six people).

Pick a strategy that matches the characteristics of your project:

- Small project (one or two teams)

    - Use single monolithic workbook

    - Separate logical workbooks for each major release

- Medium (three or four teams) and large (five or more teams) projects

    - Separate logical workbooks for each subsystem and release

    - If subsystems are independent/reusable

        — Defer as much work to subsystems workbooks as soon as possible

    - If subsystems are interdependent

        — Limit the work in subsystem workbooks by addressing it in common (composite-level) workbooks.

Spending the effort to keep information in the workbook current is essential to a project's success. Things can't just exist in someone's head—they must be written down somewhere so they can be reviewed and understood by others.

2.5 TERMINOLOGY

Workbook	A *logical document* containing all the *work products* of a project.
Logical document	A collection of machine-readable and other material that is considered to be a single, conceptual whole, even though its physical representation may be distributed across media, tools, and location.
Work product	A concrete result of a planned project-related activity such as analysis or project management. Work products include items delivered to customers and items used purely internally within a project. Examples of work products include Project Schedules, Object Models, Source Code, and even the executable software product.

For additional terms see the "Glossary" on page 617.

3.0 Iterative and Incremental Development

The approach that we describe in this book is iterative and incremental in the sense that we believe that an iterative and incremental development process is beneficial for most (not all) projects. What that means will be described in this chapter.

A variety of development process models have been proposed. These include waterfall, spiral, iterative, incremental models, and others. This chapter will discuss some of these, including the advantages and disadvantages of each. The chapter will then relate these to the needs of real projects, in particular project risks, and present a process model that we call the "iterative and incremental" model.

Note that many overlapping and conflicting definitions exist in the vocabulary of process models. This chapter does not attempt to be definitive but instead it should be read partly as a clarification of terminology for the purpose of later discussions in this book, and partly as an attempt to explain our understanding and interpretation of the terms. The particular terms used here are not necessarily standard in the literature. They are used here because they are considered the most appropriate.

3.1 DEVELOPMENT PROCESS MODELS

3.1.1 The Waterfall Process Model

The waterfall model of development was the first attempt to discuss the software development process in semiformal terms. The waterfall model consists of a sequence of "phases" whereby in each a particular (and unique) kind of development work is done.

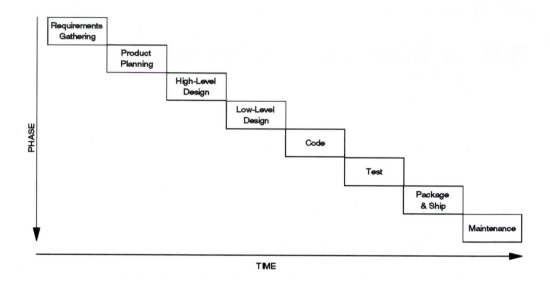

Figure   3-1. Waterfall Process Model.

The specific phases identified by Boehm [Boehm88], in Figure 3-1, are not relevant here; what is important is the sequential nature of the activities: All requirements are gathered before the next phase begins, et cetera. The essence of the model is that project phases are identified, ordered, and then carried out in this order without ever revisiting previous phases. That at least is the theory.

   In reality, the model is usually contaminated by schedule pressures and downstream decisions:

- Successor phases often start before their predecessors end due to the pressure to shorten development schedules and sometimes due simply to early staffing of people with the special skills to carry out the successor activity. One might think of these as "leaks" in the waterfall.

- Earlier phases are often revisited, creating "gravity defying eddies" in the waterfall metaphor, in order to reconcile details with discoveries and decisions made in later phases.

The early appearance of "leaks and eddies" signaled the naivete of the model.

Advantages:

- *Simplicity.* The main advantage of the waterfall model is that it is the simplest possible model. Everyone can understand it, provided of course that everyone agrees on the definition of each project phase and its relationship to all the other phases.

- *Ease of management.* A corollary of the simplicity of the model is the ease of managing a project run along these lines, provided of course that the model is appropriate to the project. When managing a waterfall project, tracking progress against a plan is straightforward, as there is only one planned pass over each work product that is, therefore, either complete or incomplete.

Disadvantages

- *Incomplete or unknown requirements.* The model assumes that it is possible to gather all project requirements before analyzing the problem and designing a solution. In practice, requirements are very rarely all known in advance in this way. Even if complete requirements are written as an initial step, requirements frequently change as the project proceeds as both developers and potential users or customers of the software understand the problem and the solution better. If requirements do change during a waterfall project, the process model has no way of taking this into account. The result is frequently a crisis.

- *Incomplete design experience.* Assuming that complete, correct, and unchanging requirements can be gathered in one sweep, it may still not be possible to design a solution to the problem in one go. Design occurs at many levels from architecture down to low-level design and coding. It frequently happens in practice that lower-level design activities shed light on the implications of higher-level design statements. The issues raised in this way are usually foreseeable in advance, if only sufficient thought and experience had gone into the design. The fact remains, however, that complete design attention to detail and complete design experience are rarely available in practice, for whatever reason. In such a case it is difficult or impossible to design a complete solution and expect it to be successful without any feedback from developers, testers, users, et cetera. A waterfall project has no way of addressing a need for redesign if one arises. The result, once again, is predictable.

- *Scheduling.* Scheduling a waterfall project requires a great deal of confidence in the relative resource required for each project phase. A serious mistake in project planning is very hard to recover from, because the waterfall process makes it difficult to deliver partial solutions: It is all or nothing. This is partly a result of the fact that the waterfall process does not partition work in time except by phase, and partly because the planning of a waterfall project is itself one of the initial project phases that (in waterfall style) is carried out once and not expected to change.

Applicability

All published process models are appropriate to some kinds of project. The waterfall model is appropriate to projects that are very similar to projects that have already been completed by the same development team, or projects that involve relatively minor extensions or modifications to existing software components. In such cases the requirements, design, and resources can probably all be anticipated and a sequential planning and stepping through the project phases is probably the simplest and best solution.

3.1.2 The Incremental Component Process Model

By "incremental component process" we mean the building of components one by one. This process is simply the composition of a "Divide and Conquer" approach and the waterfall process. The process requires the system to be decomposed ("Divide") into components that are each developed using the Waterfall Process ("Conquer"). Conceptually, the waterfall process is repeated sequentially by the development team, but in practice parallel development teams would realize some concurrency. The components might be as fine grained as objects, but they are more likely to be coarser grained.

Advantages

- *Simplicity*. This process is only slightly more complicated than the waterfall process. The fewer the components, the simpler it is.

- *Ease of management*. The incremental process has the same ease of management as waterfall. The only difference is that there are a series of waterfalls.

- *Scheduling*. Since each increment is smaller than the whole project, management sees finer grained scheduling, checkpoints, and reporting of progress. It is much more informative to say "75 percent of the components are complete" than to say "We're two-thirds through high-level design."

- *Benefit of Experience*. Later increments benefit from the knowledge, skills, and resources developed during earlier increments. Confidence and quality levels normally increase for later increments.

Disadvantages

- *Incomplete or unknown requirements.* The incremental process has the same disadvantage as the waterfall process in that it only addresses each phase (of each component) once. If requirements change, or are not understood in the first place, the process cannot deal with it.

- *Incomplete design experience.* The incremental process is slightly better than the waterfall process here in that experience gained from developing one component can sometimes be transferred to later ones. But again, this process does not account for insight gained in later phases of a component's development affecting decisions made in earlier phases.

Applicability

The incremental component process model is appropriate for projects that have readily identifiable components that are relatively independent of each other or build upon each other. It is especially useful where there are many similar components, since later components are more likely to benefit from the knowledge and experience gained during earlier development. It is also appropriate when fine grained schedule tracking is indicated to manage development cycle time risks.

3.1.3 The Iterative Process Model

The iterative model describes a process where an initial set of work products evolves into the production system by reworking the work products iteratively. In a sense it is similar to the incremental process in that it employs the waterfall process repetitively, but it differs in that it reworks the same (monolithic) component each time. It is often characterized by having monthly or weekly internal "drivers," "code drops," and alpha, beta, and early-ship releases.

Advantages

- *Simplicity.* Conceptually, the iterative process is quite simple: Just run through the waterfall process repeatedly on the same scope until it is correct. If, based on previous experience, you know how many passes it will take to "get it right," then it is not hard to set up and explain.

- *Incomplete or unknown requirements.* With this process you have several chances to deal with late discovery of requirements. When you discover a requirement that affects phases previous to the one you're working on, just schedule it to be handled on the next pass.

- *Incomplete design experience.* Similarly, as design, implementation, testing, and packaging experience is gained during early iterations, they can be factored into earlier phases (e.g., nonfunctional requirements, scenarios, state models, subsystem models, et cetera) of later iterations. This provides a "second chance to do it right."

Disadvantages

- *Ease of management.* Determining the number and duration of iterations can be difficult. Since requirements and architecture are allowed to be open-ended, tracking progress against a plan is difficult.

- *Scheduling and resource planning.* In addition to the confidence required in understanding the resource requirements for each phase of waterfall development, the iterative process also requires confidence in understanding the relative resource requirements of each iteration. Statements such as "We've just completed the second of six planned iterations" only have meaning as a measure of progress toward project completion if the schedule duration and resource requirements for all iterations are understood since one iteration is likely to be different from the next.

Applicability

Despite the disadvantages, the iterative model is widely used and is appropriate for projects working in new domains or environments where requirements and technical difficulties cannot be foreseen. It works best with established development groups where the project manager has some experience with the resource and scheduling needs and characteristics of the group.

3.2 PROJECT RISKS

When discussing different development process models, two things become clear. Firstly, no one process is the right one for all projects. Radically different projects require different development processes. Whether or not this is desirable is not the point; it is inevitable. Secondly, the decision of which process to use is risk-driven. If there are no risks associated with your development project, then there is no need to adopt anything other than a waterfall development process. Anything else would be unnecessarily complicated. For good or for bad, it is almost never the case that a project has no risks.

The presence of risks implies a need to test and to answer technical questions sufficiently early in the life cycle of a project so that there will be time to act on the information obtained. The nature of your project risks will determine the process model that is most appropriate to you. By understanding the relationship between risks and process it is possible, and profitable, to tailor your development process to your needs, which might involve using a process that is different from any of the published variations. This should not be a cause for undue concern. Greater concern should be reserved for the unthinking application of development processes.

The relationship between risk and process is precisely the one mentioned above: *The scheduling of any project activity that carries risk must take that risk into account.* This is not, of course, to say that all bets must be hedged; many, for example, the collapse of the building in which development is being carried out, might be too expensive for the probability of the risked event occurring. A decision must be made of which risks to take into account.

There are many kinds of project risk. Section 10.7 provides examples and a discussion of risk management in general. Risks associated with development are frequently managed appropriately by arranging the project timetable so that risky development activities are scheduled with adequate time for review, testing, rework, re-review, et cetera. When this principle is applied to whole categories of development risks, it leads to some form of iterative and/or incremental schedule, but one which is tailored to the needs of a particular project and not just uniformly iterative or uniformly incremental. This topic will be explored further in the following section, and again in Section 5.0.

3.3 THE ITERATIVE AND INCREMENTAL PROCESS MODEL

Having said that no one process is appropriate for all projects, we cannot now claim to present the ultimate process, and it is not our intention to do so. It has, however, been our experience that almost all projects fall into the category of those requiring at least some incremental aspect and at least some iterative aspect. Furthermore, it has also been our experience that projects typically benefit from a development process that is strongly incremental.

At this point some clarification of terminology is required. By "incremental" we refer, here and subsequently, to *incremental by requirements*. That is, an incremental process builds executable drivers or products each of which satisfy successively more end-user requirements. The portion of a project that aims at developing a particular driver or product is termed an "increment." By "iterative" we refer, here and subsequently, to a process in which *iterative rework* is performed within increments.

Thus, when we say that most projects would benefit from a development process that is strongly incremental, we are observing that most projects:

- have requirements that are uncertain and incomplete,
- employ technologies with which the development team are not entirely familiar,
- are reasonably large and complex.

The first two points imply obvious risks that are most directly addressed by some form of iterative and/or incremental schedule, as mentioned in Section 3.2. The last point, however, rules out a development process that is predominantly iterative, for the reasons discussed in Section 3.1.3, principally design instability. The answer would seem to be some form of hybrid process.

Development may be thought of in terms of a matrix of requirements vs. components as shown in Table 3-1.

Table 3-1. Requirements Versus Components Matrix.										
Components	**Requirements**									
	R1	**R2**	**R3**	**R4**	**R5**	**R6**	**R7**	**R8**	**R9**	**R10**
A	A1	A2								
B		B2			B5		B7		B9	
C	C1		C3			C6		C8		C10
D			D3	D4						
E		E2			E5	E6			E9	
F				F4			F7			F10
G	G1					G6		G8		
H					H5				H9	
I			I4				I7		I9	
J						J6		J8		J10

Development may proceed either horizontally or vertically in terms of this matrix. Vertical development, constructing the application a row at a time, is essentially an *incremental by component* process. Of course, to test (vertical) end-user functionality, all the rows that contribute function will by then have to be in place. Horizontal development, constructing the application a column at a time, is essentially an *incremental by requirement* process that implements only that piece of the design at each stage to support the requirements in question. Both vertical and horizontal development processes are incremental in some sense, but in the former it is components that are delivered incrementally while in the latter it is end-user requirements that are being satisfied incrementally.

The advantage of an incremental by requirements process is that it permits the system to be built slowly and with focus (as in the incremental by component process), and hence with attention to quality, while still permitting tests of end-to-end functionality to be performed early in the project (like the iterative process).

Envisaged, then, is a cyclic process in each cycle of which particular end-to-end requirements are designed and implemented (see Figure 3-2)

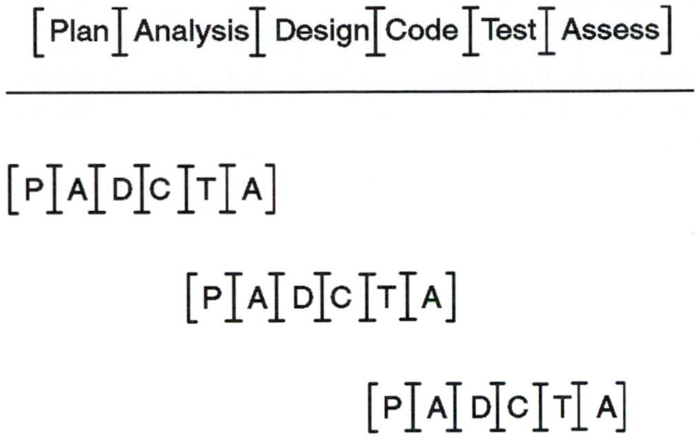

[Plan ⌉ Analysis ⌉ Design ⌉ Code ⌉ Test ⌉ Assess]

[P ⌉ A ⌉ D ⌉ C ⌉ T ⌉ A]

[P ⌉ A ⌉ D ⌉ C ⌉ T ⌉ A]

[P ⌉ A ⌉ D ⌉ C ⌉ T ⌉ A]

Figure   3-2. Overlapping Iterative Development Process.

To address project risks each development cycle must not only satisfy the new requirements on that cycle but it must also budget resources to rework existing functionality in the
light of reviews, tests, user responses, et cetera, stemming from the previous cycle. The
element of rework in each cycle will vary from cycle to cycle, but it should dominate
development. To remind us of the fact that each development cycle is driven by the need
to satisfy the particular requirements that define that cycle, and not by rework, each development cycle is called an "increment." Each increment includes a certain proportion of
iterative rework. When planning the increments it will not be possible to anticipate which
particular parts of the design will require the rework, but a certain proportion of each increment should nevertheless be set aside to anticipate the inevitable fact that rework of some
kind will be necessary. Iterative rework might be necessary to correct errors, increase
performance, increase modularity, or increase extensibility. Some of these issues will be
anticipated; others will arise only during reviews and tests.

Increments can overlap in time, but functional dependencies between increments and
the need to plan the rework content of an increment imposes constraints on the degree of
overlapping that is possible in practice.

We call this development process an "iterative and incremental" process. Note that
while the iterative and incremental process defines the large-scale structure of a project, it
does not prescribe the way in which the development of each increment is to be carried
out. That is, it does not prescribe the internal structure of an increment. The discussion of
the iterative and incremental development process is continued in Section 5.0.

Advantages

- Focus on high risk project activities
- Early feedback on key design points
- Tangible deliverables at every stage of development
- Establishment of an end-to-end software development framework
- Overlap of development activities
- Incremental product release
- Rapid operational capability
- Efficient use of resources
- Reduced risk of product disaster
- Flexible in the face of changing requirements and environments
- Permits rework of architecture and design
- Developers can learn as they go
- Reduction of risk by reducing uncertainty
- Improvement of quality by continuous testing during development
- More visible reuse opportunities

Disadvantages

- Additional project management and process complexity
- Difficulties in identifying the requirements for each iteration
- Difficulties in prioritizing risks
- Subsequent increments may affect the work done in the earlier ones
- Coordination of teams working in different stages
- Additional change-control management required
- Possible ignoring of long-term architectural and usage considerations
- Lack of an initial complete specification to aid early estimation

Applicability

The iterative and incremental process is not universally applicable. It is appropriate to medium and large projects with end-to-end requirements that can be partitioned conveniently and that face uncertainties. These uncertainties might take the form of:

- Unknown, uncertain, or incomplete requirements
- Design risks
- Unfamiliar application domains
- Unfamiliar technologies (such as object technology)

Because the iterative and incremental process combines both iterative and incremental aspects, it can be used as a generic template for a project. Projects that lend themselves more to a waterfall or iterative approach simply have few increments or a greater proportion of iterative rework in each increment respectively. Thus waterfall and iterative processes can, if one wishes, be considered as "degenerate" forms of the iterative and incremental process model. That might be a useful point of view because the iterative and incremental process forces the planner to think about risks and about scheduling. Adoption of a purely waterfall or iterative approach preempts or constrains such considerations.

The iterative and incremental process model is further discussed in Section 17.2.

3.4 TERMINOLOGY

Waterfall development
> A process model for software development in which development is partitioned into unique phases, each characterized by a particular kind of activity such as planning or analysis. The phases are strictly ordered and carried out in that order with each phase being performed exactly once.

Iterative development A process model for software development in which the system evolves by iterating over its work products during a sequence of iterations. Each iteration results in executable system code.

Incremental by requirements development
> A process model for software development in which the project is divided into a sequence of increments. The work products of each increment satisfy successively more end-user requirements. Each increment results in executable system code.

Incremental by components development
> A process model for software development in which the project is divided into a sequence of increments. During each increment a particular set of components of the final product is constructed. Each increment results in executable code for one or more subsystems.

Iterative and incremental development
> A process model for software development in which the project is divided into a sequence of increments. During each increment a combination of incremental by requirements development and iterative rework is performed. Each increment is principally driven by the end-user requirements that define that increment, but a certain proportion of the increment is set aside for iterative rework of existing work products to take reviews, tests, experience, and other feedback into account.

For additional terms, see the "Glossary" on page 617.

4.0 Scenario-Driven Development

The approach that we describe in this book is scenario-driven in the sense that there is very strong traceability from requirements right through to Source Code and Test Cases, and that a key work product in this chain of traceability is the Scenario.

4.1 THE TRACEABILITY GAP

The overly simplistic object technology hype is that you take a set of requirements; build an object model that identifies classes relevant to the problem and the relationships between the classes; add design classes relevant to the solution; code the classes; and that's about it. Unfortunately, this hype is believed by many people.

There are a number of flaws in this argument. It ignores the fact that requirements are rarely complete or correct, and the fact that design involves much more than the adding of classes. The former is discussed in Section 3.0; the latter is addressed in Sections 7.5 and 13.2. A more subtle problem is that the hype does not indicate how the classes of the object model are to be identified, and how the object model is to be validated against the requirements. In other words, there is a traceability gap between requirements and the object model. This applies equally to the analysis object model and to the design object model.

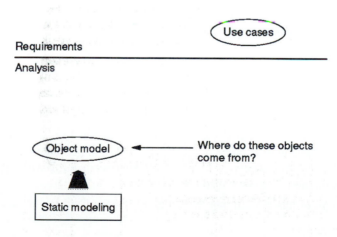

Figure **4-1.** *The Traceability Gap.*

Using purely *static* modeling, the construction of an object model, it is impossible to bridge the gap between requirements and either analysis or design (Figure 4-1). What is missing is any reference to the *dynamic* modeling: That is, the construction of models that describe how the system works to satisfy its requirements. Dynamic modeling is not relevant solely to real-time systems; it is a vital part of the mainstream development process. Dynamic modeling fills the traceability gap, whether or not the system is real-time (Figure 4-2).

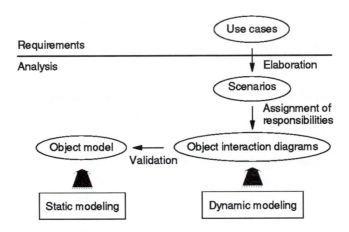

Figure **4-2.** *Static and Dynamic Modeling.*

4.2 USE CASES

In order to understand requirements traceability, we should first look at the work product designed to capture the functional requirements. It is called the *Use Case Model* and you can read all about it in Section 9.2. For now, though, it is sufficient to describe it as the set of:

Actors   People and other external objects that use the system or interface with it.

Use Cases What the actors do with the system.

In this book we treat Use Cases as the definition of all externally visible, end-to-end behavior of the system. To keep things manageable and focused, we don't concern ourselves with all the variations of outcome due to the possible permutations of assumptions. For example, "Fax machine Receives Fax" does not concern itself with "out of paper," "incomplete transmission," "power disruption," et cetera.

You might think of this as outlining the Quick Reference Card for the system.

4.3 SCENARIOS

Scenarios are the work products intended to elaborate Use Cases by enumerating all the variations of outcome due to the possible sets of assumptions. If it helps, think of the set of assumptions as the possible starting states the system can be in when a Use Case is enacted and the outcomes as the resultant ending states. The Scenario need not concern itself with *how* it is to be implemented in the target system or which other objects it needs to collaborate with to accomplish the task, unless it is part of the required outcome. For details, see Sections 11.4 and 13.7.

By following this *separation of concerns* and by using a workbook organization (with naming conventions), we have taken the first step toward requirements traceability. There is a thread now from each actor to its set of Use Cases and from each Use Case to its set of Scenarios. The Scenarios can be checked for completeness and consistency and also used in early project estimation metrics.

You might think of this as outlining the Principles of Operation manual for the system.

4.4 OBJECT INTERACTION DIAGRAMS (OIDS)

The Object Interaction Diagram is the next work product of interest in scenario-driven development, see Sections 11.5 and 13.8. Its purpose is to divide the responsibility of attaining the outcome specified by a Scenario amongst the objects indicated by the:

Use Case - the actors (especially when acted on or prompted)

Scenario - assumptions and outcomes are really states of participating objects

Domain (from an evolving Object Model) - real or conceptual objects that help in this environment

During analysis, identification and division of responsibilities among the objects are the prime goals. During design, the responsibilities take a more detailed form indicating method names, parameter types, data flow, et cetera, for all the participating objects.

At this point you should be able to see how the requirements can be traced from Use Cases down to services (methods) that need to be implemented in the set of collaborating objects. You might think of this as tracing the internal events resulting from the enactment of the Use Case within a particular Scenario.

4.5 A CHAIN OF TRACEABILITY

We have seen how Use Cases are a convenient way of defining the system boundary and expressing the top-level functional requirements of the system. We have also seen how Scenarios can be used to expand the Use Cases into detailed functional requirements. It has then been shown how OIDs can be used to demonstrate how objects obtained from an object model can interact in order to perform a scenario. Put together, this is a recipe for closing the traceability gap. A continuous chain of traceability now runs as follows.

- Use Cases
- Scenarios
- Object Interaction Diagrams (OIDs)
- State Models
- Class Descriptions
- Object Model

Thus far, the list holds for both analysis and design sets of work products separately, although there is obviously analysis/design traceability too.

- Source Code
- Test Cases

Each of these work products, and their interrelationships, is explained in Part 3. A complete table of traceability between work products is presented in 8.6. In a scenario-driven approach, all development activity is derived from the need to satisfy functional requirements expressed as scenarios. Furthermore, the work products on this main line are linked by a strong concept of validation.

- Fundamental functional requirements are recorded as Use Cases.

- Each Use Case is expanded into multiple Scenarios by listing possible combinations of assumptions and outcomes.

- Scenarios are elaborated into Object Interaction Diagrams (OIDs) by depicting object collaborations and the assignment of responsibilities to classes.

- The state-dependent behaviors of certain objects is explored through State Models that show the possible states and state transitions of an object.

- The Object Model characterizes the classes identified by the OIDs in terms of their key attributes, their operations, their states, and their relationships.

- The Class Descriptions collect all the information associated with a class from the Object Model, OIDs, and State Models.

- The Source Code for each class is developed from the specifications found in the Class Descriptions.

- The Scenarios are used as specifications for Test Cases that validate the classes, subsystems, and systems implemented via their Source Code, which closes the development loop.

Many variations on this theme are possible and desirable depending on circumstances. What is important is that each of these work products are produced, and that they have certain relationships with each other. It is primarily the order in which the work products are produced, updated, and validated with respect to each other that can and should vary depending on the development context. This is the link between the scenario-driven and work product oriented concepts.

The connection between the iterative and incremental and scenario-driven ideas is that the requirements of each increment should, we believe, be defined in terms of scenarios. This enables Test Cases derived from requirements to close the development loop of each increment. This idea is explored further in Section 6.0.

An important aspect of defining increment requirements in terms of scenarios, and using the traceability between work products described above, is that we do not advocate designing complete classes and then building them. Instead, only those methods that a class requires in order to carry out a scenario of the current increment are designed and built in that increment. Thus while classes are used to structure analysis, design, and implementation work products, it is scenarios that scope this work and are used to decide which classes and which methods are to be included.

The links between Use Cases, Scenarios, OIDs, and Object Models in particular can be exploited in many ways. For example, during development many Issues will arise. These Issues frequently take the form of a question: how should we implement a particular Scenario bearing in mind certain factors? The obvious way to express the various design options for the problematic Scenario is by means of OIDs, each OID demonstrating a different way of assigning responsibilities to objects of the Object Model in order to carry out the Scenario. Resolution of the Issue consists of selecting one of these design options. Scenarios and OIDs can therefore be used as a basis not only for documenting completed designs but also as a vehicle for expressing design problems and options.

For more details on this technique, see Section 18.7.

4.6 SCENARIO-DRIVEN DEVELOPMENT VARIATIONS

Although we recommend the Scenario-driven approach for most projects since it validates the purpose and need for each object and its features, there are situations when alternate approaches are more appropriate. We present them here so that you will understand the nature of the exceptions that justify these variations.

We should also note that these variations should be consciously considered for each subject area, subsystem, and even each increment of development, so that the best approach is used in every situation. All of these approaches are valid and interoperable—you can "mix and match."

Before we dive into the variations, let's present the core sequence of work products to be developed for the Scenario-driven approach (see Figure 4-3).

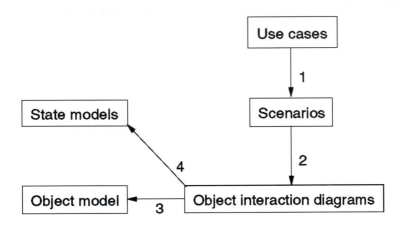

***Figure   4-3.** The Scenario-Driven Sequence of Work Product Development.*

In this sequence, functional requirements, in the form of Use Cases, are elaborated into Scenarios, which enumerate the assumption and outcome pairs associated with each Use Case. Then each Scenario is elaborated into an Object Interaction Diagram which distributes the system function to the objects by assigning class responsibilities and identifying object collaborations. The classes and their OID-implied attributes, associations, and operations are next organized by class and transferred to an Object Model. When a significant amount of class behavior varies due to an object's state, the operation sequences identified in the OIDs referring to that class are collected and reorganized into a State Model (e.g. a State Transition Diagram). This will ease the culling out of method descriptions that are part of the Class Description work product.

The Scenario-driven approach is most appropriate for the following situation:

Given   Rich set of functional requirements (use cases)
Not Given Legacy data domain structure
Goals   Functionality, conformance to agreed functional requirements, strong traceability through development process

4.6.1 Data-driven approach

The data-driven approach is a natural one for designers who have been involved in data modeling or database oriented programming. It should not be used as the standard approach, but is appropriate when working with a rich pre-existing data domain *and* an *open-ended* set of functional requirements. That is, data-driven is often appropriate when striving for evolutionary stability, longevity, and extensibility, since the data and their organization are more important than the functional requirements for each increment of development.

The sequence of work product development (modeling) starts with the Object Model (data model) that has prime significance. Other work products (models) are subordinate to it and their development follows the same sequence as the scenario-driven approach (that's why we call this a variation of scenario-driven). Traceability of functional requirements therefore is secondary to development of a strong data model.

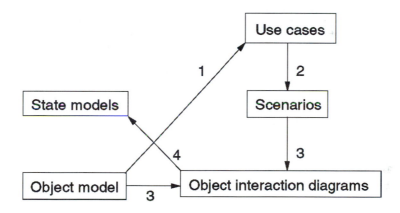

Figure   4-4. *The Data-Driven Sequence of Work Product Development.*

In this sequence, the Object Model is developed first. It is usually derived from a pre-existing entity-relationship (ER) diagram, database schema, or legacy data structures. Although classes, attributes and most associations (relationships) can be harvested this way, it is not so easy to identify the responsibilities and operations for each class. So, after the data portion of the Object Model is developed, the normal scenario-driven process is used to identify Use Cases, Scenarios, Object Interactions, and State Models. The Object Model acts like a design constraint. It is updated from the OID with the assignment of operations and possibly new attributes and associations that became evident during the dynamic modeling.

The data-driven approach (see Figure 4-4) is most appropriate for the following situation:

Given   Rich pre-existing data domain (e.g., Object Model)

Not Given *Closed set* of functional requirements
Goals   Extensibility, longevity, stability

4.6.2 State-driven approach

The state model-driven approach is a natural one for designers who have been involved in "real-time" system design and those involved in business process re-engineering. It should not be used as the standard approach, but is appropriate when working with a rich pre-existing behavioral domain *and* an *open-ended* set of functional requirements. That is, a state model-driven process is often appropriate when striving for emulation of real-world behavior in distributed control applications, since object state transitions, actions, and collaborations are more important than simply satisfying the functional requirements for each increment of development.

Don't think of state modeling as something reserved for real-time manufacturing process control systems and traffic control systems. *Orders*, *Order items*, *Invoice*, *Customer Account*, *Catalog Item*, et cetera, all have significant real-world state models which define the very meaning of what we call business.

The sequence of work product development (modeling) starts with the state models for stateful objects. These have prime significance. Other work products are subordinate to it, and their development follows the same sequence as the data and scenario-driven approaches (we still call this a variation of scenario-driven). Traceability of functional requirements and the structure of the data model are secondary to development of a state models that closely model the real-world.

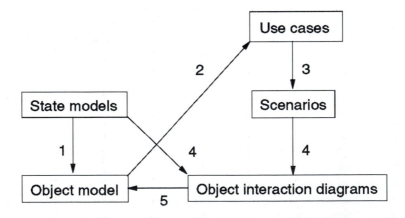

Figure *4-5. The State Model-Driven Sequence of Work Product Development.*

In this sequence, the State Models are developed first. They are usually derived from pre-existing State Models from legacy systems. Although state attributes, transition operations (actions), and some associations (relationships) can be harvested this way, only a limited portion of a system's classes and their characteristics can be identified like this. So, after the few State Models are developed and transferred to the Object Model, the Data-driven variation of the Scenario-driven process is used to identify Use Cases, Scenarios, and Object Interactions. The State Model acts like a design constraint when developing the Object Interaction Diagrams. Finally, the Object Model is updated with all the additional classes (and their attributes, relations and operations) that became evident during the dynamic modeling.

The state model driven approach (as shown in Figure 4-5) is most appropriate for the following situation:

Given   Rich behavioral model (e.g., State Models)
Not Given   *Closed set* of functional requirements
Goals   Distributed control, emulation of real-world behavior

4.7 TRACEABILITY FOR SCENARIO-DRIVEN DEVELOPMENT

An extremely important concept to developing object-oriented software is the concept of traceability. This is recognition of the fact that there exist interdependencies between various work products and should the content of one work product change, there may be a ripple effect impacting other work products in the project workbook.

For any work product we need to understand what other work products it can be "impacted by," and what other work products it "impacts."

The benefit of traceability is that it can dramatically lessen the impact and risk associated with changes to the project. Of course to gain the benefits of traceability does not come for free. It is vital that documentation be kept current, and this involves effort and rigor on the part of the team. Documentation cannot be an afterthought.

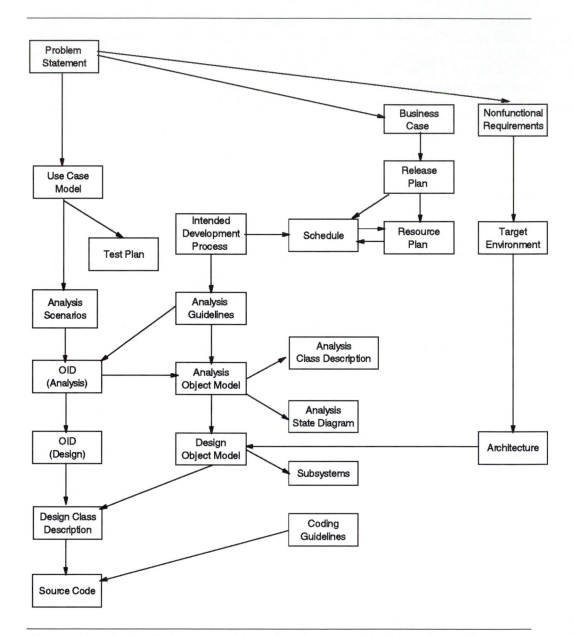

Figure   4-6. *Partial Work Product Traceability Using Scenario-Driven Approach.*

Figure 4-6 shows some of the traceability dependencies among some of the work products described in this book. Note that this is only a partial traceability model intended to illustrate the traceability and scenario-driven development. In this figure, we can see that the Analysis OIDs are impacted by scenarios and in turn impact Analysis Object Model and Design OIDs.

Traceability Example

Imagine you have developed an application to support a Life Insurance company's sales agents. The application is in production and involves 200 classes and about 40,000 lines of code. Now a change occurs to the way a policy is processed. With traceability the changes required to the application are easier to manage. Traceability allows us to:

- Identify affected Use Cases (and if required generate a new Use Case)
- Identify impacted scenarios and their Object Interaction Diagrams (analysis)
- Revise the Analysis Object Model (adding any new classes, attributes, behaviors, and relationships)
- Review and alter the associated Design Object Interaction Diagrams (OIDs) as required
- Identify classes and methods impacted by relationship between the Design OIDs and code files
- Update code

Object-oriented analysis, design, and implementation support traceability, because of the manner that Use Cases and Scenarios can be traced through the entire project life cycle. Rather than having to go through thousands of lines of code and determine which of it is impacted by changes, traceability presents a structured, manageable, methodical approach to maintenance and change control. This is one of the reasons that so many object-oriented applications report improved productivity on object-oriented application maintenance.

4.8 TERMINOLOGY

Use Case   A statement of top-level functional system requirements. A Use Case is usually defined textually, but for convenience it may also be represented in a *Use Case Model*. A Use Case may represent a way that the system is to be used by external *Actors*, or a way that the system is to use its *Actors*. See Section 9.2.

Actor   An agent external to the system, with which the system interacts. See Section 9.2.

Use Case Model   A representation, often graphical, showing the boundary of a system, the *Actors* external to the system, and the *Use Cases* internal to the system. See Section 9.2.

Scenario   An externally-visible system behavior. A Scenario is a *Use Case* plus a set of assumptions plus a set of outcomes. Assumptions and outcomes can be specified formally or informally as appropriate to the project and the development status. A Scenario can be thought of as a detailed functional system requirement.   See Sections 11.4 and 13.7.

Object Interaction Diagram (OID)

An OID is a graphical depiction of the way that objects interact to carry out a *Scenario*.   An OID is frequently depicted as vertical time lines representing the participating objects, and horizontal arrows representing object interactions.   See Section 11.5 and 13.8.

Scenario-driven development

A developmental focus on a continuous chain of traceability from *Use Cases* through *Scenarios*, *OIDs*, to *Object Models* and the other analysis and design work products.

For additional terms, see the "Glossary" on page 617.

Part 2. *Development Process*

We describe the work products that we have found to be effective in many object-oriented software development projects in Part 3, Work Products. This might be thought of as the "what" of a project. Part 4, Work Product Construction Techniques, describes a toolkit of techniques to help build these work products. This might be thought of as the "how" of a project. A vital and (relatively) independent dimension to project development is the development process, which might be characterized as the "when" of a project. Process is about "when" in the sense that it is concerned with the sequencing of the various project activities.

Although in a work product oriented approach there is no concept of a fixed development sequence, work products are still developed in a nonrandom order. Work products don't just happen, they are the result of planned activities. The order in which they are developed is determined by their increment and phase associations as well as by their supportive relationships with each other within a phase.

It is appropriate to discuss the sequencing of activities at a number of different levels of granularity. In Section 3.3, The Iterative and Incremental Process Model, we considered the usefulness of an iterative and incremental process in which a project is divided into a sequence of increments, each of which adds functionality to the system, and also incorporates an element of iterative rework. This is the level at which process is usually discussed. Each increment, however, constitutes a miniprocess of its own, and the sequencing (and definition) of the phases that make up each increment must also be addressed by a development process. Lastly, each phase focuses attention on a particular set of work products. How is effort on these work products to be sequenced?

There are, therefore, three levels of granularity at which it is appropriate to discuss process. These might be characterized by the following questions.

* What is a project (in terms of increments)?
* What is an increment (in terms of phases)?
* What is a phase (in terms of work products)?

This part of the book sets out to answer each of these questions in turn.

It was mentioned in Section 3.0, Iterative and Incremental Development, that no one process is applicable to all projects. Although there is no such thing as a "typical" project, it is useful to describe a model project that can serve as a reference point when attempting to discuss the constraints that one can encounter when trying to develop in the real world. Most projects will not employ this process precisely, but will bear some resemblance to what is described. They will all be "variations on a theme."

Variation itself is actually a theme of this book. The principal reason for separating the presentation of work products in Part 3, from the presentation of development techniques in Part 4, is to emphasize the prime importance of focusing on work products when deciding upon a development strategy. One should fit development techniques around the work products, and mix and match the techniques to fit the project and application context. The same applies to process. The process that is concentrated upon has been found to be appropriate to many projects. Every project is different, however, and deserves thought in its own right at the level of process. You should treat what is written here in the spirit of a reference model from which variations will inevitably have to be made to tune the model to the needs of your project. Even within the process presented here, there are many possible minor variations.

The lowest level of development activity that is described in this part of the book is the *phase*. In each phase, focus is placed on a particular set of work products. For example, during the analysis phase we are most concerned with constructing the analysis group of work products such the Analysis Object Model. The particular work products that we recommend are produced in each phase are described in Part 3, Work Products. Think of *phase* not as a single portion of time within the development process but rather as a recurring period of focus on a particular facet of development. For instance, in an iterative and incremental process, the developer "visits" the design phase several times.

Project increments and the project as a whole can be thought of as containers or packages of phases. In that sense it seems logical to start the discussion of process with phases and then to proceed to package the phases into increments and then projects. We have not opted to do that. Instead, we have chosen a top-down approach to describing process. The reason for this is that the top-level process of a project defines the relationship between increments, and hence provides context for the discussion of increments. An increment, similarly, has a certain structure, and it is within the context of this structure that it is appropriate to discuss the phases that constitute each increment.

5.0 Overall Project Structure

The highest level of process granularity is the entire project. This chapter considers how this top level of process concerns can be addressed. The two following chapters address themselves to the lower-level concerns of how increments are put together and how an increment is composed of phases that the "real" development work is done.

5.1 OVERALL PROCESS

As mentioned in Section 3.3, The Iterative and Incremental Process Model, most projects that we have seen are of the following form:

- Ill-defined, incomplete, or uncertain requirements
- Use technologies (such as object technology) or components with which the development team is not completely familiar
- Large and complex

As discussed in Section 3.0, Iterative and Incremental Development, such requirements do not lend themselves to waterfall, pure iterative, or incremental component development processes. The problem with a waterfall process is that the project risks are far too high for all development strands only to be brought together near the end of the project. There is no time budgeted for the inevitable rework. The trouble with a purely iterative approach is that while time is allowed for considerable rework, in fact this is the structure of the process. The rework required for a project of significant size is likely to result in an unacceptable amount of *design churn*. That is, a process based solely on iteration will tend to be unstable if the project is reasonably large. An incremental component process will not suffer from the problem of instability because of size, but it permits component integration, and hence testing of the overall design, too late for test results and other kinds of feedback to be incorporated. One answer is to combine the end-to-end early testing advantages of an iterative approach with the stability of an incremental component process. The resulting iterative and incremental process is the one that is described in Section 3.3, The Iterative and Incremental Process Model.

It is this rationale that leads us to recommend the iterative and incremental process as a "default" process. It will not fit all projects but it does very well for most. We suggest that it is used unless it can be demonstrated that it is inappropriate for a particular project. Section 5.4, Variations on Project Shape considers factors that might influence a project and that might indicate that a top-level process variation is required.

An iterative and incremental project consists of a sequence of increments whereby in each increment time is allowed for reworking existing software in the light of test results, feedback from end users, design reviews, et cetera. The effect of an iterative and incremental process is to bring forward in time all the testing phases of the project. It is based on the assumptions that we probably don't know all the system requirements in advance, that the requirements will change, and that we will both understand the problem domain better and discover better ways of solving problems as we go along.

5.2 PROJECT SHAPE

In practice, the number of iterations and increments to be performed on a particular set of work products will vary depending on the risk associated with that work product. For example, a project may do requirements gathering, analysis, and architectural design in a single increment, but the remaining design, implementation, and testing work in several increments and iterations. This would be appropriate for a large project where architectural design churn is considered a much greater risk than misunderstanding requirements. Many other combinations are possible. Each combination is appropriate to a particular development context; in addition, each combination determines a particular shape that the project will have.

Activities that are scheduled for the initial increment and for which no subsequent iterative or incremental effort is budgeted may be considered to belong to an initial, waterfall part of the project. A purely waterfall project is a special case since *all* activities are of this low-risk nature. (Having said that, waterfall projects usually end up with iterative and incremental development cycles for product maintenance and enhancement, even if they were not initially conceived in this way.)

As mentioned above, many variations are possible, but a project shape that is appropriate to many projects follows (see Table 5-1).

Table 5-1. Typical Project Shape.

Increment	Purpose	Activities
1	Get project started	Develop all planned work products for the Requirements and Project Management phases. Review Analysis work products with the customer. Concurrently, analysts, designers, and implementers develop guidelines for their phases. Designers can also start the System Architecture, Target Environment, and Subsystem Model work products.
2	Familiarize team with process and environment	Using the Depth-First technique [8] with a few Use Cases, develop all planned work products for the Analysis, User Interface, Design, and Implementation phases.
3..n-1	Complete project development	Taking a few Use Cases at a time, develop all planned work products for each phase through Implementation. As new work products are developed, old ones may need to be extended or amended.
n	Package, test, and deliver the product	Implement the Physical Packaging Plan and conduct the Installation, System, and Acceptance test plans.

5.3 WORK PRODUCTS RELATED TO PLANNING PROJECT SHAPE

The work products that are most relevant to planning the overall development process and the project shape are discussed in:

- Section 10.1, Intended Development Process
- Section 10.3, Resource Plan
- Section 10.4, Schedule
- Section 10.5, Release Plan
- Section 10.7, Risk Management Plan
- Section 10.11, Project Dependencies

Those sections include further information, including examples and suggestions for how to construct the work products.

5.4 VARIATIONS ON PROJECT SHAPE

Table 5-1 suggests a shape for a "normal" project. Real-life risks and situations usually force variations to be made. The following list identifies some common conditions that impact real projects and usually cause a project to deviate from the typical project shape described above.[9] After each condition, we have listed some project shape variations to consider when addressing these conditions.

Weak Requirements

- Iterate on Problem Statement and Use Case Model with Customer before doing any Project Management work products.

- Jump ahead into Analysis Scenarios or Screen Flows or even a User Interface Prototype to ferret out unforeseen requirements and complexities.

- If this is a competitive situation, try developing a Use Case Model based on the competition's capabilities. Then reduce the model to what your customer needs and what you are capable of delivering.

---

8 See Section 17.1, "A Depth-First Approach to Software Development" on page 363 for a description of the technique.

9 To learn more about this topic, we suggest reading Chapter 5 in [Goldberg95].

Complex/Unfamiliar Domain

- Engage domain experts.

- During project management phase schedule more iterations and increments for the analysis phase.

- Use the scenario-driven process to define the domain from the functional requirements.

- Seek customer "buy in" with the analysis phase work products.

Complex/Unfamiliar Target Environment

- Engage technical area experts and consultants.

- Schedule education in key areas for developers immediately before design or implementation phases.

- During project management phase, identify technical risks, assign to key developer, and track resolution.

- Schedule, track, and implement as many technical prototypes as are needed to resolve the risks before it is too late.

- Schedule more iterations and increments in design or implementation phase (whichever has risks).

Complex/Unfamiliar Development Environment

- Prioritize the Development Environment work product and schedule its review and iterations to start long before the rest of the development team depends on it.

- Schedule education in key areas for analysts and developers immediately before attempting object-oriented analysis, object-oriented design, or object-oriented programming.

- Schedule more Depth-First[8] approach increments so that team gets more experience using the techniques and tools of the development environment with smaller increments of function (less risk).

- If there are many early concerns, perform a Depth-First increment for a trivial problem (perhaps unrelated to the planned product).

Parallel Development

- During project management phase, focus more attention on Resource Plan and Schedule. Iterate on these when Subsystem Model is available so that contracts with earliest or riskiest dependencies are prioritized.

- During analysis phase, focus early attention on Subject Areas work product to identify potential parallel analysis and development of subsystems.

- Start System Architecture work product early to start capturing intent to structure system for parallel development (nonfunctional requirement).

- Start Subsystem Model work product early to focus on intersubsystem (intergroup) contracts.

- During the design phase, emphasize the Subsystem Model and API work products.

- Other than these coordinating activities, treat the development of each subsystem as if it were a complete system. That is, develop a separate project workbook for each subsystem and use the complete process on each subsystem allowing tailoring as needed.

- Use an iterative and incremental approach that requires periodic integration testing to validate subsystem APIs and contracts.

- Be especially vigilant if subsystems are to be subcontracted out.

Short Schedules

- Don't plan too many increments. Limit it to two or three.

- Favor prototyping over formal increments to address risks.

- When developing the Project Workbook Outline, focus on those work products that are most effective in attaining your goals.

- When developing Analysis, Design, and Coding Guidelines, consider the cost and benefit of each given your schedule.

Long Schedules

- Long schedules don't mean lax schedules. Long schedules require more details and attention to risks than shorter ones.

- Pay special attention to scheduling risk-resolving prototypes.

- Take advantage of the opportunity to fit in more meaningful increments and iterations.

- Allow time for injecting additional increments especially midway and near the end of the development.

- Early and periodically in the project management phase, look for parallel development opportunities. If you were offered another team or ten more developers, how would you use them?

- If you lost a team, how would you adjust? Plan for contingencies before they are needed.

Reverse Engineering and Re-engineering Projects

- Here's a case when the Waterfall approach, a single increment of development, may work the best.

- If risks are low, plan to use the simple, efficient Waterfall approach.

- Be selective when considering work products for Project Workbook Outline and when considering guidelines for each phase.

- Produce all the work products that you planned to do.

6.0 Project Increments

A project increment is a miniproject, so it should be no surprise that planning one is like planning a miniproject. You should consider all the possible work products that can be developed in light of the constraints implied by the increment. Here are some things to consider:

Purpose   Each increment is planned to accomplish a specific set of goals. They should be documented so that the participants can share a common vision. The reasons for this are the same as those that require the whole project to have a Problem Statement. But here, inside an increment, the purpose should be simpler since its goal is to focus a small part of the project for a shorter time.

Scope   Each increment should be limited by the selection of a specific set of:

- Use Cases and Scenarios
- Subject Areas or Subsystems
- Development phases that will be carried out
- Work products that will be produced
- Completion dates (Schedule)

Guidelines A project should decide whether the work products and guidelines that govern them should evolve throughout the product's development, or whether they should address the final criteria from the start.

Process   Besides the criteria implied by guidelines, each increment may employ a variation on the process used for its duration. For example:

- Will there be iterations within the increment?

- In which order will the work products be developed? (Which are the prime and which are the subordinate models?)

- How often will work products be reviewed or verified? (as soon as they are completed, at end of phase within the increment, or at the end of the increment, et cetera.)

- Besides work product verification, how will any product deliverables be tested? Will there be an independent test team to integrate and test new and extended components (exercise the scenarios specified in the scope)?

6.1 TYPICAL PROJECT INCREMENTS

We address the preceding considerations for the typical project increments identified in Table 5-1 in the following four tables.

Table ***6-1.*** *Project Initiation Increment.*

Purpose	Get the project started, fully understand the requirements and the problem domain, lay the foundation for design and implementation to begin.
Scope	Develop all intended Requirements, Project Management, and Analysis work products. Concurrently develop (or select) User Interface, Design, and Coding Guidelines. Develop first pass of System Architecture, Target Environment, and Subsystem models. Allocate 25 percent of schedule for this increment.
Guidelines	All Requirements, Project Management, and Analysis work products should comply with predetermined guidelines right from the start.
Process	All work products will be verified as they are completed. Their owners should allow for a couple of iterations within the scheduled completion dates. The phase review should simply verify that all critical Issues have been closed and others assigned to owners with appropriate due dates. The Acceptance Plan and Use Case Model will be verified with the customer at the end of the phase.

Table ***6-2.*** *Developer Familiarization Increment.*

Purpose	Familiarize the development team with the new processes, techniques, and tools that they will need to use in this project. Shake down the process and development environment.
Scope	Using the Depth-First technique with a small number of simple Use Cases, develop all the planned work products for the Analysis, User Interface, Design, and Implementation phases. Excluding education and training, only allocate a couple of weeks for this.
Guidelines	Try to comply with the guidelines developed for each phase, but don't get stuck trying. If the guidelines need adjustment, this is when that should be determined.
Process	All work products will be verified as they are completed. Their owners should allow for a couple of iterations within the scheduled completion dates. There will be no phase reviews, but the increment review will focus on identification of Issues associated with the development process, environment, and tools.

Table **6-3.** *Normal Development Increment.*

Purpose	Complete the development of the product.
Scope	Selecting a significant number of related Use Cases, develop all the planned work products for the Analysis, User Interface, Design, and Implementation phases. Allocate 50 percent of the schedule for several increments of this type.
Guidelines	All Analysis, Design, and Implementation work products should comply with predetermined guidelines right from the start.
Process	All work products will be verified as they are completed. Their owners should allow for a couple of iterations within the scheduled completion dates. The phase review should simply verify that all critical Issues have been closed and others assigned to owners with appropriate due dates. The User Interface Prototype will be verified with the customer at the end of User Interface design phase.

Table **6-4.** *Release Increment.*

Purpose	Package, test, and deliver the product.
Scope	Implement the Physical Packaging Plan and conduct the Installation, System, and Acceptance Test Plans. Allocate 20 percent of the schedule for several iterations of these activities.
Guidelines	All Implementation and Test work products should comply with predetermined guidelines right from the start.
Process	All work products will be verified as they are completed. Their owners should allow for a couple of iterations within the scheduled completion dates. The phase review should simply verify that all critical Issues have been closed and others assigned to owners with appropriate due dates.

6.2 WORK PRODUCTS RELATED TO PLANNING INCREMENTS

The work products that are most relevant to planning increments are:

- Section 10.1, "Intended Development Process" on page 127
- Section 10.3, "Resource Plan" on page 135
- Section 10.4, "Schedule" on page 139
- Section 10.5, "Release Plan" on page 144
- Section 10.6, "Quality Assurance Plan" on page 147
- Section 10.7, "Risk Management Plan" on page 152
- Section 10.9, "Test Plan" on page 164

Those sections include further information, including examples and suggestions for how to construct the work products.

6.3 VARIATIONS ON INCREMENTS

6.3.1 A Set-Up Increment

Set-up increments are similar to Depth-First increments except that the *purpose* of the former focuses more on shaking down and learning the development process, techniques, environment, and tools. The *scope* is limited to only those phases, work products, tools, and techniques that are new to the development team. The Use Cases and Scenarios don't have to come from real requirements. The Schedule is usually very tight unless this is being run concurrently with the Project Initiation phase. The *guidelines* are usually slackened and the *process* is aimed at finding development environment and process problems.

6.3.2 A Depth-First Increment

A Depth-First increment differs from a Set-up increment in that its *purpose* is to do a small amount of real development (it counts) while learning the development process, techniques, environment, and tools. The *scope* can go from analysis scenarios through implementation or it can start from design scenarios. It should use real Use Cases and Scenarios. The Schedule is usually short but not as short as a Set-up increment. The phase *guidelines* are respected but can be questioned. The *process* should be as close to normal development as the initiates can bear.

6.3.3 Release 1.0 Increment

It may sound strange to have a *Release 1.0 Increment*, but considering that it usually follows a *Beta* release of the product, it is a special type of increment.

Its *purpose* is to finish the development that didn't make it into the Beta release and to clean up the many problems often discovered with the Beta release. The *scope* is usually limited to implementation and test work products, but can occasionally go back as far as design scenarios. There are often Target Environment assumptions and outcomes that were not considered before the product entered the real world. The Schedule is usually very short since a published *ship date* is usually at risk. The phase *guidelines* are respected but are occasionally deferred when "missing the date" is a possibility. The *process* should be as close to normal development as the weary developers can bear.

6.3.4 Release 1.1 Increment

Sometimes software products "ship by definition"; that is, before they are ready. Release 1.1 is what the product developers usually intended to ship and what the customer expected. The Schedule for Release 1.1 is usually chosen so that the customers will automatically receive it before they put Release 1.0 into production (hopefully, before the customer dared to install it).

Release 1.1's *purpose* is usually to fix "known bugs" that could not be addressed in Release 1.0 without impacting the ship date. Therefore, the *scope* is limited to implementation and test work products. No new requirements or "features" are allowed into this increment. The Schedule is always very short. The phase *guidelines* are respected but are occasionally deferred when "missing the date" twice is a possibility. The *process* should be as close to normal development as the ready-to-quit developers will tolerate.

6.3.5 Release 2.0 Increment

For Release 2.0, development should be back to normal. The only difference is that there is a base legacy to protect and improve upon. All work products from previous releases are now assets to work from (though some may seem like liabilities). Release 2.0 usually incorporates significant new function or changes in design to better address Nonfunctional Requirements (e.g., performance or usability).

Release 2.0's *purpose* is to significantly extend or change the design of Release 1.x. If the risks are small and the process, Development Environment, Target Environment, and Architecture are well understood, this can be developed in a single, waterfall, increment. Otherwise use the increments defined for the typical project shape described earlier.

In any case, these increments should clearly enumerate all goals it is expected to attain. Therefore, the *scope* will include all phases, but will concentrate on Requirements and Analysis work products if the main purpose is to *extend* function of the product, and will concentrate on Prototyping and Design work products if the main purpose is to *change* the design of the product. The Schedule is usually shorter than the original release. The phase *guidelines* are respected and often improved as the veterans gained religion since their first project. The *process* is an experience-based improvement of what was normal development during the first release.

7.0 Development Phases

A development phase is a state of product development that focuses on making progress on a particular aspect or facet. In this book we have chosen to focus on the following development phases:

- Requirements Gathering

- Project Management

- Problem Analysis

- User Interface Design

- System Design

- Implementation

- Testing

We realize that there are other phases that may precede or follow these such as market analysis, project initiation, marketing, deployment, maintenance, withdrawal, and harvesting reusable components, but we have chosen to limit our scope to those phases of interest to *software developers*.

Although the list of phases may remind some of the waterfall approach to development, we strongly recommend that you view them as periodic phases. They may be entered repeatedly to add new functionality to the system (incremental development) or to rework previous work products to correct or improve them (iterative development). In general, the phases discussed below are presented in the order that you will encounter them in a normal project, but there will always be reasons to delay or accelerate development of certain work products normally associated with a particular phase.

The following diagram provides a pictorial overview of the development phases and their relationships with each other and with key development repositories. It is intended to show that:

- Requirements Gathering and System Test are pre and post-iterative phases, respectively.
- Analysis, Design and Implementation phases occur in an Iterative and Incremental process.
- Analysis needs to be performed before Design.
- User Interface and System Design can be done concurrently.
- Design precedes Implementation.
- Project Management is an on-going activity.

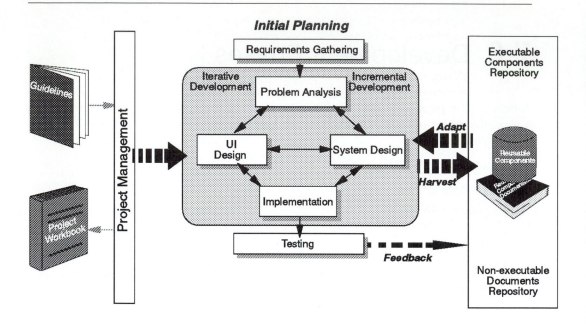

Figure   7-1. *Development Life Cycle Overview.*

The following sections provide a description of the development phases discussed in this book.

7.1 REQUIREMENTS GATHERING

Requirements are crucial because they provide a scope and a boundary for later activities, especially planning, analysis, and design.

Poorly understood requirements can severely impact the development efforts of the project team. There are two major kinds of requirements that are important to the object-oriented development process:

- *User Requirements* describe what the needs of the intended users are. User requirements drive analysis. Our approach to object-oriented development strongly recommends that these requirements be expressed by Use Cases.

- *Nonfunctional Requirements* that address concerns such as:

  - *Performance:* requirements that clarify the space, time and other system resource constraints the customers require of the application. The performance requirements drive activity during the design phase.

- *Platform:* requirements that detail the desired "delivery vehicles" for the system, such as hardware and target language, et cetera. Platform requirements drive both the interface specification and implementation activities.

Nonfunctional Requirements drive design. If Nonfunctional Requirements are not known during the early phases of a project, they can be deferred provided they are known at design time. Design time commences when design decisions need to be taken as a precursor to development. At this time, the Nonfunctional Requirements must be nailed down in order to permit the development team to get started.

7.2 PROJECT MANAGEMENT

Project Management is ongoing throughout the life of a project. As a practice, its concerns are not much different from a traditional effort. Some of the differences are:

- Managing iterative development that is new to some managers.

- Understanding the object-oriented work products across analysis, design and implementation.

- Coming up with initial sizing of a software development effort.

- Bringing people up the object-oriented learning curve.

These will all improve as our experience deepens with object-oriented technology.

7.2.1 Initial Project Planning

This aspect of the project management phase usually occurs before the requirements gathering phase. Its purpose is to identify the need and objectives for the project. The development organization must decide whether or not to proceed with the project and a decision must be made as to whether or not to use object-oriented technology.

Initial sizings will usually be done at this time and used for purposes of beginning the pursuit of funding.

The process of staffing will get under way as well. In a project using object technology, particularly for the first time, a critical activity will be to do a skills assessment (or technology maturity assessment) of the likely time. This assessment should determine the skills needed to do the project (including object skills, domain skills, development environment skills et cetera). You should then begin to make plans to fill any gaps through staffing, education, and consideration of the use of mentors or consultants. If outside expert help will be used in the form of consultants, this is the best time to bring them in.

The nature of initiating a project can vary widely depending on the culture and processes of the organization doing the development. During initial planning, most of the work products developed are business as usual and are not specific to object-oriented technology. The biggest challenge most organizations face at this time is overcoming the challenge of estimating effort. Because object-oriented projects are built iteratively and incrementally, sizing the total effort required often proves a serious challenge. The best advice to follow on a first-time project is to size it using your business as usual approach (i.e., as if you were using your traditional, non-object-oriented development approach). Use this as a strawman and revise it as you proceed.

7.2.2 Organize Project Plan

To some, the question "Which comes first, the requirement or the plan?" is much like the chicken and the egg problem. Since gathering requirements is an activity that requires project resources, it should be planned. However, the project plan is driven by the requirements, because its main purpose is to:

- Group the requirements into releases that will be delivered as a unit;
- Define the development processes and activities; and,
- Allocate project resources to the activities.

A lot more goes into a project plan, the gory details of which are described in the associated workbook (Section 10.0, Project Management Work Products). The challenge is to complete it quickly without getting in the way of the real work to be done! Unfortunately, this pressure to get things moving to avoid "plan paralysis" (similar to analysis paralysis) can cause "plan churn" to occur. Plan churn can cause everything to come to a screeching halt while the details change again and again, or worse, create the need to throw away work that has been done and start over.

Solving these two problems is where the iterative and incremental development process comes in. Just as "time prevents everything from happening at once," an iterative and incremental development process eliminates the need to plan everything at once.

The use of planned iterations, where discoveries made during later activities cause changes to the work products of previous ones (with a subsequent "ripple" effect), can relieve most of the pressure of having to create a perfect plan (or analysis/design model, et cetera) up front.

7.2.3 Maintain Project Workbook

Quality documentation is a critical success factor for large-scale object-oriented development. Although it may be arguable that a small one-person software development effort can be done in a person's head, any nontrivial project requires accurate and timely documentation at every stage. Documentation is the key to technical project communication. Without it there is no project.

The project workbook communicates to the project its plans, its decisions, and its progress.   Timely and accurate work products consolidated in the project workbook are vital.   An up-to-date project workbook allows for movement of personnel in, out, and around the project.   A project workbook is tailorable to any size and type of project, but it all starts out by defining a Project Workbook Outline.

Good project workbooks make for successful projects.

7.3 PROBLEM ANALYSIS

Analysis is about domain understanding and is essential to good object-oriented development.   Object-oriented analysis tells us what objects are part of a domain as well as their attributes and behaviors.   Object-oriented analysis consists of techniques and work products that identify objects that are relevant to the problem being solved.   The process includes classifying the objects and finding relationships among them.

During object-oriented analysis we apply techniques to understand, develop, and communicate user requirements for an application.   The analysis phase focuses on clarifying and representing requirements in a concise manner at a more detailed level than during requirements gathering.   Many object-oriented analysis techniques are graphical in nature and involve work products that contain diagrams.

To summarize then, object-oriented analysis is concerned with understanding the problem domain.   This involves:

- Identifying objects and their attributes

- Learning about how objects behave and their responsibilities

- Understanding how objects interact with each other

Analysis must be done with persons who know the domain: for example, if building an application for Insurance Underwriters, then an Insurance Underwriter should be involved in the analysis process.

Analysis should be done in a constraint-free fashion.   Avoid letting implementation constraints impact analysis.

1. Constraints can and do impact domain understanding.

    Knowing that a database will be implemented in a relational database like DB2 should not affect analysis, but often developers will build relational data models during analysis as a short-cut to implementation.   They then come to think about the world in terms of tables that they will be building eventually.   This is a mistake.   Do not let the final design or implementation influence the way you think about, discuss, or model the domain.

2. Design detail clutters and obscures analysis.

3. Adding design detail to analysis would make it difficult for users to understand and validate.

4. Adding design or implementation detail into an analysis model makes it less generic and thus less reusable.

5. Implementation constraints can change (for example, platform or database).

   These changes should not invalidate your analysis.

Analysis must be independent of the delivery environment. If the planned deployment changes from MVS to OS/2 in a client-server environment, the analysis work products should not change. The objects that are meaningful to users in their domain will not change if the implementation environment changes. This is important if there is any hope of reusing the analysis work products. The benefits are great if this approach is adopted. Deployment decisions such as hardware platform or development software can change over time. By keeping the analysis independent of these considerations, the analysis work products can be reused, regardless of the production system. There is a risk that deployment decisions can affect the application analysis. It is tempting during analysis to say, "it is a given that we are going to represent our data in DB2, so let's just represent things in tables." Also, there is a danger that this may impact on the analysis by leading to the attitude that "we can't do that in DB2, so let's ignore it." These considerations mitigate against achieving a true understanding of the application domain, which is the purpose of analysis. Analysis should be constraint-free.

7.4 USER INTERFACE DESIGN

User Interface design is concerned with planning the construction of software that has an intuitive and standardized human-machine interface. Today, this usually means the layout, appearance, and flow of control involving a graphical video display with "windows."

While it is possible to consider the User Interface design as being part of system design, it is treated in isolation to allow for a separation of concerns that is frequently exercised in real-world software development. User interface work is usually done before and independent of the system design phase, often by a team of user interface specialists within the project.

Often, User Interface design is done in parallel with the analysis phase. In such cases, coordination between the user interface and analysis teams is important.

When the "friendliness" (easiness, intuitiveness, and lack of surprises) of a user interface is critical to the success of the products, a User Interface Prototype is built to get user feedback on that friendliness and to better understand the user's conceptual model of how it should work.

7.5 SYSTEM DESIGN

While during analysis we focused on problem-domain objects, during design we focus on solution domain objects. Some of the classes that existed in the analysis model will disappear (as they won't be implemented) and new ones will appear specific to the System Architecture and Target Environment (e.g., a DB2 interface class).

Many teams have difficulty discerning between analysis and design and want to skip the analysis phase and go straight to design. In an object-oriented project, it is essential that analysis not be bypassed.

Design is concerned with how an application will be built and involves factoring in Nonfunctional Requirements such as:

- Platforms
- Languages
- Performance
- Interoperability
- Persistence
- Maintainability
- Use of standard components and subsystems
- Reuse
- Cost
- Time

Much of design is involved with addressing these constraints. It often involves weighing trade-offs, as many of the design considerations are mutually exclusive (for example, high functionality with small memory).

By separating analysis and design we are able to make the analysis more generic and reusable, so that when design decisions change, the analysis model will still hold. For example, in the banking industry, the way that a Bank Loan is decided upon should be the same regardless of the software tools used to implement a lending application.

If we construct hybrid analysis/design work products, it is difficult to identify what represents business requirements and which are introduced at design time for implementation reasons.

7.6 IMPLEMENTATION

Implementation involves the transformation of design work products (detailed plans for solution) into compilable software (Source Code) and other product deliverables. In object-oriented development, the bulk of implementation effort is concerned with creating class implementations in an object-oriented programming language that supports the specifications recorded in the Design Class Descriptions. Although the Design Class Descriptions focus on external characteristics, they often include information concerning the internal states, operations (method descriptions), and representation. When they don't, the implementer need only access other design work products, especially the Design Object Model and the Design Object Interaction Diagrams.

In a scenario-driven approach, the implementer will benefit from following the traceability of functional requirements as Use Cases lead into Design Scenarios and Design OIDs. The results are organized into classes that are described by the Design Object Model and the Design Class Descriptions.

In an iterative and incremental process these work products evolve, so the implementer's task is to match that evolution in the class's Source Code. The incremental implementations can be tested by applying the Design Scenarios (with their assumptions) and verifying the outcomes. This completes a typical development increment.

As a scenario takes a thin slice of the problem and represents an end-to-end solution, at the end of an iteration a subset of the application has been developed. After a number of iterations, the functionality builds up gradually to encompass more and more of the requirements.

A benefit of this approach is that the developers can work from the Object Interaction Diagrams (OIDs) that directly convey requirements in a form that is usable during implementation. This still gives a developer a fair amount of latitude—the OID represents a form of contract between the collaborating classes. The messages being passed back and forth tell the implementer of a class what its responsibilities are, but not how to fulfill them—the class remains a black box.

Another interesting aspect of this approach is that it results in "just-in-time programming." Classes and their methods are implemented to fulfill the requirements of a set of scenarios, but no more.

7.7 TESTING

Testing within object-oriented projects is a bit different from testing traditional software. Unlike traditional development, testing is not a phase that occurs only after the completion of development.

In object-oriented projects discrete testing phases, similar to traditional software development, still occur. Depending on what sort of testing you are used to doing, you may still perform System Test, Integration Test, User Acceptance Test, Stress Test, and Performance Test. The difference is that you may perform some of these more frequently on subsets of the system. For example, at the end of each development increment, the executable code produced by the increment must be unit and function tested by running Test Cases that test the function specified by the scenarios designated to be developed in that increment. After *implementing the entire application*, traditional function and system tests can be run using executable "white" and "black" box Test Cases developed from Scenarios.

Thus testing is much more of an ongoing activity. This is one of the strengths of object-oriented application development and greatly lessens the risk of building the wrong application (by virtue of the ongoing feedback coming back from the testing).

In addition to the normal (but more frequent) testing of executable code, there are other activities that must occur within each phase of the development process that might be considered to be testing activities. We refer to these activities as *validation* and *verification* of work products. Validation consists of establishing that the right work product has been built. Verification consists of checking that the work product has been built correctly. Validation and Verification are so important to the object-oriented development process that they are a fundamental part of each work product's development in our approach.

For purposes of this book, we will consider testing to mean the traditional testing of product executable code, and we will treat validation and verification as an integral part of developing a work product. This is discussed in Section 8.3, Validation and Verification of Work Products. You will also find advice on verification of work products in each work product description.

7.8 SUMMARY OF DEVELOPMENT PHASES

The following table shows a summary of the life-cycle phases.

Table   7-1 (Page 1 of 2). Development Phase Summary.

Phase	Activity	Work Products
Requirements Gathering	Group requirements into Use Cases and prioritize by importance, window of opportunity, and technical complexity.	Problem Statement, Use Case Model, Non-functional Requirements, Prioritized Requirements, Business Case, Acceptance Plan
Project Management	Allocate requirements to releases and/or increments and plan activities that manage resource availability and other project constraints.	Intended Development Process, Project Workbook Outline, Resource Plan, Schedule, Release Plan, Quality Assurance Plan, Risk Management Plan, Reuse Plan, Test Plan, Metrics, Project Dependencies, Issues
Problem Analysis	Develop solutions to scenarios in terms of active objects that group related tasks and communicate with other objects in order to complete them.	Analysis Guidelines, Subject Areas, Object Model, Scenarios, Object Interaction Diagrams, State Models, Class Descriptions
User Interface Design	Document how users will interact with the application.	UI Guidelines, Screen Flows, Screen Layouts, UI Prototype
System Design	Plan a solution to the problem examined during analysis in terms of interacting objects, within the constraints specified by the Nonfunctional Requirements.	Design Guidelines, System Architecture, APIs, Target Environment, Subsystem Model, Object Model, Scenarios, Object Interaction Diagrams, State Models, Class Descriptions, Rejected Alternatives

Table   7-1 (Page 2 of 2). Development Phase Summary.

Phase	Activity	Work Products
Implementation	Systematically code the classes specified as a result of design in a programming language according to documented public/private interfaces so that they can be built and installed on the target platforms.	Coding Guidelines, Physical Packaging Plan, Development Environment, Source Code, User Support Materials
Testing	Insure that the application meets the requirements set forth in the Problem Statement and Requirements.	Test Cases

Part 3. *Work Products*

Project workbooks contain work products. This section of the book describes work products that we recommend be built during the course of an object-oriented software development project. They are grouped according to the sections described in Section 2.4, "Workbook Structure" on page 20.

8.0 Information About Work Products

A **work product** is a concrete, planned result of the development process. A work product might be a final deliverable, or it might be an interim item such as a Design Object Model. Examples of work products include a Project Schedule, an Analysis State Model, and Source Code. The work products described in this book are those that we have found useful in practice. This part of the book lists each kind of work product, grouped according to the phase of a project during which attention is likely to be focused on this work product.

The headings in this part reflect those that we would expect to see in a project workbook: a logical repository of work products. There is, therefore, a heading called "Analysis Scenarios" and another called "Design State Models." This, however, merely reflects the divisions that we would expect to see in a workbook. It does *not* imply that all your Analysis Scenarios together *must* form a single work product to be owned by one person. The same is true for Design State Models, and all the other work products. The appropriate granularity of work products must be decided separately for each project. In this part of the book we define a format for each kind of work product, and this format necessarily says something about work product clustering. This should, however, be taken as a baseline to be adapted to the needs of your project. You might find it appropriate to combine work products that we have defined separately, or to split work products. The decision should be based on what seems an appropriate unit of responsibility for your project. It is possible that information that we say some work product should cover might appear in some other form in your project. In that case the work product can simply point to that other source of the information. Of course, you may wish to tailor the work products that we describe in other ways too.

In this particular section we:

- Describe the common attributes of work products

- Explain the format we will use for describing each work product presented in the remaining sections of this part of the book

- Discuss the information flow between work products

- Summarize, in tabular format, all of the work products presented in this book and indicate those work products that we consider to be essential

- Summarize, in tabular format, traceability between work products. That is, for each work product, you will see what other work products this work product is impacted by and which work products it impacts.

8.1 COMMON ATTRIBUTES OF WORK PRODUCTS

Each work product described in this book contains different information and has a different structure. There are, however, certain characteristics shared by all work products. This section describes those attributes.

If we were to define a class hierarchy to describe a model of object-oriented development, **work product** would appear at the top. All of the work products described in this book would **inherit** the attributes described here. No matter what kind of work product you are building, therefore, your team should document the following "attributes":

- Identifier
- Date
- Author
- Owner
- Status
- Issues
- Metrics
- Traceability
- History

These attributes support the common Plan-Do-Review-Iterate cycle that is fundamental to the development process of every type of work product. We recommend that each work product that you write includes each of these attributes, in addition to attributes containing the "real" content of the work product. A suggested format for "real" content is described in the Notation part of the template used to describe the work products in this book. The other parts of the description template used in this book are used only to motivate and describe each kind of work product; they should not appear in the actual work products that you write.

The remainder of this section will discuss in turn each of the common work product attributes.

Identifier

It is vital that each work product have a unique identifier (usually a number). This is a requirement for traceability and for general tracking and management.

Date

While this may seem simple, it is important to date all work products. Over time you may have multiple copies of the same work product, and if they are not dated you may have difficulty determining which copy is the most recent.

You may also wish to track major enhancements to work products through the use of version numbers for work products.

Author

This is the name of the author of the work product.

Owner

Every work product needs an owner to drive it along to completion. The owner is responsible for the overall integrity of the work product even if she doesn't actually build it. More complex work products, like analysis models, may be broken into subsystems that are considered to be separate work products and have their own owners. In this case, the overall owner is responsible for integrating all the components. She usually serves as the "decision maker" in reviews of the lower level components and the "presenter" in reviews of this work product.

Status

A terse statement of the current state of the work product. Sample values might be *unstarted, estimated, in_progress, under_review, and completed.*

Issues

This is the list of issues related to this work product. It should include both outstanding problems and alternatives under consideration. The owner of a work product is responsible for tracking and resolving issues specific to the work product. Note that besides this common work product attribute, there is a separate Issues work product that is used for global issues that may impact many work products.

Metrics

This is the set of metrics and corresponding measurements relevant to this work product. (A metric is a rule for measuring.) Depending on the kind of work product, it might include effort, productivity, and quality metrics. For each metric, both estimated and actual measurement values should be provided. Note that besides this common work product attribute, there is a separate Metrics work product that provides summary estimations and data.

Traceability

In the approach to object-oriented software development described in this book, each work product can be impacted by, and have an impact on, other work products. This we refer to as work product traceability.

See Table 8-2 for a discussion on traceability and a complete work product traceability table.

History

Over time work products change and evolve. Sometimes, especially when issues are raised, it is very important to go back and see why things happened. As a result, it is important to keep previous versions of the work product available for future reference. This attribute can either include the Historical Work Products directly, or just references, for example to a workbook appendix.

8.2 OUTLINE FOR A WORK PRODUCT DESCRIPTION

This book describes a number of work products that are developed in typical object-oriented software development projects. Information on each work product is presented in the following format:

- **Description:** a general description of the work product.

- **Purpose:** the purpose served by developing this work product.

- **Participants:** who is involved in the creation of the work product.

- **Timing:** at what stage in a project the work product is normally produced.

- **Technique:** a general description of how the work product can be built. Some alternative techniques for building work products are discussed in Part 4, Work Product Construction Techniques.

- **Strengths:** what the advantages are of building this work product.

- **Weaknesses:** what the weaknesses of this work product are.

- **Notation:** a description of the notation the authors use when building this work product.

- **Traceability:** there are two kinds of traceability:
  - **Impacts:** describes work products that are dependent on this work product and that may be impacted should this work product change.
  - **Impacted by:** describes work products on which this work product is dependent. This identifies which work products could have an impact on this work product should they change.

- **Advice and Guidance:** describes experiences and rules of thumb that a practitioner may find useful.

- **Verification:** describes guidelines for verifying the internal correctness of a work product. See Section 8.3.

- **Example(s):** we try to illustrate as many work products as possible with real-world examples.

- **References:** these are citations of books and/or articles that describe the work product in further detail.

- **Importance:** this is our subjective view on how important the work product is to the object-oriented software development effort. We classify a work product as being either "Essential" or "Optional."

  We view "Essential" as meaning that the work product's existence (or the existence of similar material in some other form) is crucial to the success of a project following our approach.

  Of course, we recognize that all projects are different and what is essential in one may not be needed at all in another. For example, if your project has no Application Programming Interfaces (APIs), then the API work product is obviously not needed, but if you do, then it would be essential.

  There are also numerous differences caused by project size. A large project would find essential many of the Project Management Work Products that a small project might find completely unnecessary. Please see the Workbook Strategy discussion on page 24 for more information on the relationship between project size and the use of this approach.

  In summary then, the importance we assign to a specific work product should only be taken as a guideline.

8.3 VALIDATION AND VERIFICATION OF WORK PRODUCTS

The role of testing in the development approach presented in this book is discussed in Section 7.7, Testing. and Section 15.0, Test Work Products. Those sections point out that in an object-oriented approach to software development, and particularly when using the approach advocated in this book, there are important activities, beyond the normal testing of executable code, that need to occur throughout the development process. These items are the validation and verification of work products:

- *Validation.* Validation consists of checking that the right work product has been built. That is, validation determines whether a work product satisfies its specification. For example, validating an Analysis Object Model might involve checking that it is possible to write Analysis Object Interaction Diagrams that demonstrate that the object model is capable of supporting the required scenarios. Validation is done by checking the information flows implied by the diagram in Figure 8-1. For each flow, the consistency of the relevant information at each end of the arrow must be checked. The traceability attribute of each work product description should provide a consistency checklist.

- *Verification.* Verification consists of checking that we have built the work product correctly. That is, verification determines whether a work product is internally consistent. For example, verifying an Analysis Object Model might involve checking that cycles of associations are necessary and consistent. It is principally verification that is addressed during reviews.

Taking a "validation and verification" view, we can summarize the kind of test activities that are possible during various phases in the typical process.

- After *gathering requirements*, a team should validate the requirements by reviewing them with the appropriate customer sets.

- When *organizing the project plan* is complete, there should be a review with the management team to validate the Business Case and approve the resource allocations. Customers may need to be consulted to double check the release structure.

- Once *analyzing the problem* is finished, the customers can review the proposed solution by validating the scenarios. Periodic reviews with users can also be done before 100 percent completion (and in fact are highly desirable). Consistency checking can be automated or be done internally via inspection.

- After *specifying the interfaces*, the customers can actually work with the look-and-feel of the application.

- Once *designing the architecture* is completed, the team can simulate the application to verify that it meets performance requirements.

- At the end of an *implementation iteration*, results are shown to users for feedback. This feedback is acted on by making corrections to the application or recording as Issues.

Apart from that, each work product, Source Code or not, must be checked for correctness *as an integral part of the process of constructing that work product*. The review of a work product might address issues other than correctness, for example design style, but it is correctness that is the concern here.

Note that testing techniques specifically for object-oriented technology are being researched (see [Binder94]).

For each work product described in Part 3, Work Products, there is a verification section that discusses how one can verify that particular work product.

8.4 INFORMATION FLOW AMONG SELECTED WORK PRODUCTS

This part of the book covers the key work products of an object-oriented development project. It describes each one in detail and shows how they may be documented in a project workbook. Figure 8-1 depicts a simplified flow of information among selected requirements, object-oriented analysis (OOA), and object-oriented design (OOD) work products. This is intended to be a birds-eye view of how core work products support each other.

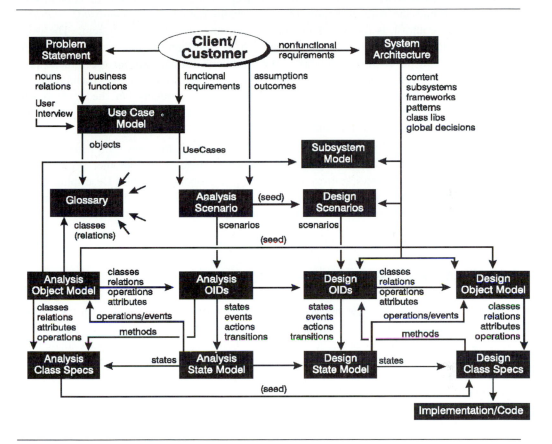

Figure   8-1. *Information Flow Among Core Requirements/OOA/OOD Work Products.*

Work products do not exist in isolation. Each is dependent on others and is constructed from information that flows from other work products. Figure 8-1 also shows the typical information flows between work products. Other flows are possible, but the ones shown will almost always be present in significant development efforts. As you will see from the diagram, it is impossible to develop these work products in any purely sequential order. There are cycles of dependencies, and these dependencies can only be satisfied by an iterative style of development, at least within the analysis and design phases.

Within the constraints of these dependencies between work products there are several possible strategies for development. Each strategy uses a slightly different pattern of "navigation" through the above figure as work products are built, validated, and iterated on, exploiting the synergies expressed in the information flows between the work products.

No one of these strategies is the right one; different strategies may be appropriate for different application domains and different development contexts. For example, an *administrative* application is likely to focus on the object model to arrange the functionality of the system around the data structures of the problem domain. An *embedded real-time* application, by contrast, is likely to focus instead on state models of the system. The work product oriented and workbook-centered approach to development that we advocate supports variations in development strategy. The workbook format that we recommend provides for the documentation of work products and their interdependencies. Techniques are suggested in this book for the construction of these work products but the development strategy that you use (which techniques you use and in which order) is up to you. That has to be the case because no one strategy fits all projects.

From the "bird's-eye" view in Figure 8-1 we can also see the flow symmetry between the corresponding analysis and design work products. There is also another symmetry of sorts between the static views, portrayed in the Object Models and Class Descriptions, and the dynamic views portrayed in the Scenarios, OIDs, and State Models. Together, the work products provide a medium for recording all viewpoints and the traceability ties them all together.

8.5 SUMMARY OF WORK PRODUCTS

Table 8-1 shows a summary of the Work Products described in this book. An "X" in the "Es" column indicates that we consider the work product to be essential for all projects following the approach described in this book. This is based on our own experiences. Any user of this approach should certainly weigh their own circumstances to determine which work products are needed on a particular project. Please be aware that while some work products are not considered essential in all cases, they may well be considered essential in particular cases, such as in large projects. These cases are described in the *Importance* section of each individual work product description.

Table   8-1 (Page 1 of 4). *Summary of Work Products.*

Phase	Name	Es	Description
Requirements	**Problem Statement**	X	Description of the problem being solved in non-technical terms.
	Use Cases	X	An object-oriented formalization of functional requirements specifying usage of the application by external agents.
	Nonfunctional Requirements	X	Requirements that do not relate to user function, such as performance, integration, platform.
	Prioritized Requirements		Defines the relative priorities of system requirements covering both functional and nonfunctional requirements.

Table   8-1 (Page 2 of 4). Summary of Work Products.

Phase	Name	Es	Description
	Business Case	X	Justification for the project.
	Acceptance Plan		Criteria and/or process for verifying the project meets its targets.
Project Management	Intended Development Process		Outlines the general approach to be adopted in terms of techniques, work products, standards, et cetera.
	Project Workbook Outline	X	An organized list of work products that are expected to comprise the project workbook.
	Resource Plan	X	Analysis of resources required for the successful completion of the project. Often focused on Human Resources (skill type, level, and quantity).
	Schedule	X	Time line showing dates, milestones, critical path, et cetera.
	Release Plan		For a multirelease project, this shows what functionality will be delivered in what release of the project (for example, in a Bank Loan Processing application, Loan Approval will be in Release 1 and Electronic Funds Transfer is planned for Release 3).
	Quality Assurance Plan		Documents quality assurance activities for topics such as Defect Removal.
	Risk Management Plan		Describes the plan for minimizing project risk.
	Reuse Plan		Describes what approaches will be followed to achieve the desired level of reuse.
	Test Plan	X	Outlines the project's plans for testing the application.
	Metrics		Lists the planned and actual measurements for the project. Used to determine whether a project is on schedule.
	Project Dependencies		Describes what dependencies or assumptions the project is relying on (for example, a deliverable from a vendor).
	Issues	X	A list of all outstanding issues, questions, and concerns that are reviewed on a regular basis.
Analysis	Guidelines		Records the details on the analysis approach being followed.
	Subject Areas		A distinct business domain of interest that can be identified at analysis time perhaps allowing it to be analyzed and developed as a separate unit.

Table 8-1 (Page 3 of 4). *Summary of Work Products.*

Phase	Name	Es	Description
	Object Model	X	A consolidated model of objects' data (attributes), behavior, and relationships. Gives a high-level overview of the domain being analyzed.
	Scenarios	X	Use Case plus assumptions plus outcome.
	Object Interaction Diagrams	X	A working out of a scenario, showing interactions between objects to accomplish a task.
	State Models		Show the life cycle of an object—its possible states and how it can change states.
	Class Descriptions		A detailed description of each class.
UI Model	**Guidelines**		Describes user interface standards.
	Screen Flows		Documents user navigation through the application's user interface.
	Screen Layouts		Documents screen details.
	UI Prototype		A prototype built to show users "look and feel" often used to solicit feedback.
Design	**Guidelines**		Records the details on the design approach being followed.
	System Architecture	X	Description of the high-level components/structures of the implementation and the design principles guiding the implementation.
	APIs		Describes programming interfaces to the product.
	Target Environment	X	Describes hardware and software environment in which the software will run.
	Subsystem Model		Partitioning of the system into smaller pieces (subsystems).
	Object Model	X	A consolidated model of objects' data (attributes), behavior, and relationships. Gives a high-level overview of the solution being designed. Contains only implementation classes.
	Scenarios	X	Scenarios that are only visible at design time.
	Object Interaction Diagrams	X	A working out of a scenario, showing interactions between objects to accomplish the implementation of a task.
	State Models		Shows object's possible states and state changes.
	Class Descriptions	X	A detailed description of a class.
	Rejected Design Alternatives		Details of designs considered but rejected.
Implementation	**Coding Guidelines**	X	Guidelines for developers.

Table	8-1 (Page 4 of 4). Summary of Work Products.		
Phase	**Name**	**Es**	**Description**
	Physical Packaging Plan		Documentation about deliverables that will be shipped with the product.
	Development Environment		Describes the Development Environment.
	Source Code	X	Actual implementation of the product.
	User Support Materials	X	Documentation, delivered in various forms, which support the customer's use of the product.
Testing	**Test Cases**	X	Testing work products.
Appendix	**Glossary**	X	Definitions of terms.
	Historical Work Products		Back-level work products.

8.6 WORK PRODUCT TRACEABILITY

Table 8-2 shows the traceability among work products; that is, which work products impact others and which work products are impacted by others.

The table shows the general paths of impact between different types of work products. Real work products are individual instances of information. They impact and are impacted by other specific instances, for example: a single Design Scenario probably impacts a single Design OID, but a single Use Case may impact many derived Analysis Scenarios.

Table 8-2 (Page 1 of 2). Work Product Traceability.

IMPACTS / IMPACTED BY

IMPACTS \ IMPACTED BY	Problem Statement	Use Case Model	Nonfunctional Requirements	Prioritized Requirements	Business Case	Acceptance Plan	Intended Development Process	Project Workbook Outline	Resource Plan	Schedule	Release Plan	Quality Assurance Plan	Risk Management Plan	Reuse Plan	Test Plan	Metrics	Project Dependencies	Issues	Analysis Guidelines	Subject Areas	Analysis Object Model	Analysis Scenarios	Analysis OIDs	Analysis State Models
Problem Statement																		●						
Use Case Model	●																	●						
Nonfunctional Requirements	●																	●						
Prioritized Requirements	●	●	●															●						
Business Case	●																	●						
Acceptance Plan		●		●														●						
Intended Development Process										●	●							●						
Project Workbook Outline										●	●							●	●					
Resource Plan				●	●				●	●			●	●	●	●	●	●			●			
Schedule				●	●	●		●		●	●		●	●	●	●	●	●						
Release Plan				●	●	●		●	●	●			●	●			●	●						
Quality Assurance Plan						●										●	●	●						
Risk Management Plan				●													●	●						
Reuse Plan				●														●						
Test Plan		●			●								●			●		●						
Metrics																		●						
Project Dependencies														●				●						
Issues																								
Analysis Guidelines							●	●				●		●	●			●						
Subject Areas	●	●																●	●	●		●		
Analysis Object Model																		●	●			●		
Analysis Scenarios		●																●	●					
Analysis OIDs																		●	●	●		●		
Analysis State Models																		●	●	●		●		
Analysis Class Descriptions																		●	●	●		●		
User Interface Guidelines			●															●						
Screen Flows		●	●															●						
Screen Layouts		●	●															●						
UI Prototype		●	●															●						
Design Guidelines							●	●				●		●	●			●						
System Architecture		●	●											●			●	●						
APIs			●															●						
Target Environment			●															●						
Subsystems			●											●			●	●						
Design Object Model			●															●			●			
Design Scenarios			●															●				●		
Design OIDs			●															●					●	
Design State Models			●															●						●
Design Class Description																		●						
Rejected Design Alternatives																		●						
Coding Guidelines							●	●					●		●			●						
Physical Packaging Plan												●					●	●						
Development Environment														●				●						
Source Code														●				●						
User Support Materials	●	●	●															●						
Test Cases															●			●						
Glossary	●																	●			●	●		●
Historical Work Products																		●						

Table 8-2 (Page 2 of 2). Work Product Traceability.

IMPACTS

IMPACTED BY

- Analysis Class Descriptions
- User Interface Guidelines
- Screen Flows
- Screen Layouts
- UI Prototype
- Design Guidelines
- System Architecture
- APIs
- Target Environment
- Subsystems
- Design Object Model
- Design Scenarios
- Design OIDs
- Design State Models
- Design Class Description
- Rejected Design Alternatives
- Coding Guidelines
- Physical Packaging Plan
- Development Environment
- Source Code
- User Support Materials
- Test Cases
- Glossary
- Historical Work Prodcuts

Note:

- Subsystems impact to subsystem workbooks install procedures.
- Historical work products should relate to their ancestors and descendants.
- Subject Areas work product impacts the workbook of each Subject Area.

Legend:

Work products listed at left impact work products listed at top when a ◆ appears at the intersection, for example:

- Problem Statement impacts Use Case Model, Nonfunctional Requirements, Prioritized Requirements, Business Case, Subject Areas, User Support Materials and Glossary.
- Alternatively, Analysis Object Model is impacted by Issues, Analysis Guidelines, and Analysis OIDs.

9.0 Requirements Work Products

The requirements chapter of the workbook represents the specification of the project. As such it is an important part of the contract to which both customer and development team bind themselves. The term "customer" is used here in its accepted sense, even though it is understood that many development projects may not have a direct customer. In this case the term should be understood to mean someone who is acting on behalf of customers of the product in order to determine and validate requirements. This might in practice be a potential user of the system, a domain expert, or a development team member nominated to represent the technical interests of customers.

Customer involvement in some form or other is an important part of object-oriented development, and a central part of requirements gathering in particular. The contract between the development team and the customer may be formal or it may be informal but the concept of an agreed contract is nevertheless important. Whether formal or informal, it is obviously important that all parties agree in advance on the task to be performed. It is vital that the requirements are expressed clearly, simply, and unambiguously. Both customer and development team must understand the requirements, and it must be obvious that their understandings are identical. Poorly understood or constantly changing requirements are a frequent cause of project failures. Achieving a common understanding of requirements gives a project a much better chance of success.

The requirements section of the project workbook consists of the following work products:

- Problem Statement

- Use Case Model

- Nonfunctional Requirements

- Prioritized Requirements

- Business Case

- Acceptance Plan

These work products all "inherit" the common work product attributes described in Section 8.1, in addition to which they have specialized attributes of their own. The work products and their specialized content are defined and commented upon in the following sections.

The first step towards a complete, formalized set of requirements is a Problem Statement, which is a succinct statement of the problem that the system is intended to solve.

A complementary work product is the Business Case, which presents the commercial (or some other) justification for the project from the point of view of the development organization.

The Problem Statement and Business Case together act as important points of focus for the subsequent requirements-gathering activity.

There are many aspects to the requirements themselves. Broadly, requirements are divided into functional requirements, which specify what the system is to do, and Nonfunctional Requirements, which specify constraints on the system. Examples of nonfunctional constraints are reliability and performance.

The work products of the requirements project phase are not directly related to the use of an object-oriented software development approach at all. By their nature, they concentrate on the system interfaces, which after all, is how the system is going to be judged. How the system will work internally is not of direct concern to the customer. Having said that requirements are not directly related to the use of object technology, some forms of requirements specification turn out to be more convenient starting points for object-oriented development than others. One form that is very useful in practice for capturing functional requirements is the Use Case Model. Other forms of requirements work products may additionally, however, be necessary in order to conform to organizational development standards. For example, what is traditionally known as a functional requirements document is a list of the features that the system will support. This kind of document usually duplicates material presented in a Use Case Model. If possible, the two should be brought together, for example by using the Use Case Model work product as the format for the functional requirements document.

The Prioritized Requirements work product defines the overall priorities of the system requirements by looking at both the functional requirements, represented by the Use Case Model, and Nonfunctional Requirements.

The final requirements work product is the Acceptance Plan, which is the way in which the customer agrees to decide whether the system does indeed satisfy the requirements. The Acceptance Plan closes the contractual loop and binds the technical requirements to the contract of which it is a part.

Of course, the set of requirements work products described above is not necessarily sufficient to satisfy a development team that the project is feasible within the constraints. Only by actual development or prototyping effort, and other means such as adopting and exploiting an iterative and incremental schedule, may the risks of commitment to a set of requirements be reduced; almost certainly they cannot be eliminated entirely. The point being made is that the existence of particular requirements work products in this chapter does not mean that *only* these should be produced prior to a developing team committing to develop a solution that addresses the requirements. How much development or prototyping effort should be expended before commitment is as much a political and economic question as a technical one.

Similarly, a customer may require that considerable analysis is performed before agreeing to a requirements document. There may also be projects that are so complex that much analysis is needed to gain a good understanding of the requirements work products. The requirements chapter of this book contains only those work products that are unique to requirements gathering. The process of requirements gathering may in addition necessitate the production of work products that are normally associated with other project phases, and hence documented in other chapters of this book.

9.1 PROBLEM STATEMENT

Description

A Problem Statement should describe the *business* requirements of the application to be developed. These are not functional requirements but a short description of the business problem that the application should solve. The Problem Statement does not say what the application should be or do, but instead concentrates on why it is needed at all.

It should be written by people familiar with the domain and the focus should be on the business needs of the intended users. Design and implementation topics should not be present; however, it is valid to address needs such as integration with an existing environment.

Purpose

This is done to communicate to everyone involved what the project objectives are. By writing a Problem Statement, you ensure common understanding and agreement. While it may surface issues or areas of disagreement, the sooner this is done the better.

Participants

The customer writes the Problem Statement. It may be written by an executive, or a project manager, or someone paying for the development effort.

Timing

Preferably before any work on a project begins.

Technique

Have the customer write a brief text answering:

1. What are we trying to accomplish?

2. Why are we making this effort?

   Do not be concerned with how the problem will be solved.

Strengths

- A Problem Statement provides a way of determining whether everyone connected with the project agrees on its objectives.

- It can put the project into context for the development team.

- Problem Statements help to identify candidate objects (nouns) and behaviors (verbs).

- They are good for determining application boundaries.

- They usually generate questions about scope, function, et cetera.

Weaknesses

- Problem Statements are rarely complete and are often incorrect.

- Achieving consensus on the Problem Statement can be challenging.

- It can be difficult to write for a project that is aimed at creating something new, rather than automating or improving some existing process or service. If new roles are being created, it is often difficult to find someone able to articulate what the new world will look like.

Notation

Free format text.

Traceability

This work product has the following traceability:

Impacted by:	**Impacts:**
• Issues (p. 176)	• Use Case Model (p. 96)
	• Nonfunctional Requirements (p. 106)
	• Prioritized Requirements (p. 111)
	• Business Case (p. 115)
	• Subject Areas (p. 187)
	• User Support Materials (p. 341)
	• Glossary (p. 355)

Advice and Guidance

1. The Problem Statement should be reviewed at the first team meeting when the project is initiated.

   It is important that the team have a shared understanding of what the business purpose of the project is. Look for and record issues.

2. Completeness and correctness

   Note that a Problem Statement is rarely complete or correct. It may be written by someone who may not have a working knowledge of the day-to-day operations of a particular area. Therefore, you should always review the Problem Statement with people working in the domain.

3. Avoid things like "be best of breed" unless competitive analysis is an aspect of the project (i.e., it can be clearly articulated what it means to be "best").

4. Consensus

When the project is started, there may be a lack of consensus or even disagreements on the accuracy of the Problem Statement. This may happen because the sponsor is not familiar with the day-to-day operations of the business problem being addressed. If this is the case then a consensus must be achieved. The team may wish to rewrite the Problem Statement and then review it with the project sponsor(s).

It may also be that there is not a consensus within a business area and this must be addressed and addressed. While this can be time consuming, the alternative (nonconsensus) is not desirable.

5. Additional information this work product should contain:

- Objectives
- Highest priority problem (may be useful when weighing trade-offs)
- Intended users

6. The typical Problem Statement is between one-half and two pages in length.

Verification

- Check that the problem and not the solution is described.

- Check that the Problem Statement includes an explanation of why a solution is needed (preferably from a business perspective).

Example(s)

The following is a Problem Statement from an object-oriented project to develop an Education Administration application:

> Our company spends over $5 million a year on education for our employees, but we don't know where the money is going or if it is being spent effectively. We are not sure if we are getting value for our money (for example, is the education being purchased helping us to meet our company's strategic objectives?).
>
> There is a concern in management that some employees are getting too much or too little education. Some staff are required to maintain their professional standing by completing certain courses. Others are expected to attend courses as part of their career development.
>
> We are looking for some means of tracking and measuring the effectiveness of our education spending. It has been suggested that a means of doing this might involve creating a catalogue and tracking staff's education and doing evaluations and follow-ups.
>
> An external consultant has suggested that this education tracking system should be tied in to our Human Resources system.

References

See [Rumbaugh91a] for discussion and an example of a Problem Statement.

Importance

Essential. It is critical for the entire team to understand the reasons for the project. If you can't articulate this, then the project could be in serious trouble.

9.2 USE CASE MODEL

Description

A Use Case Model is a convenient form in which to express top-level functional requirements. A Use Case Model consists of a set of actors (representing external agents), Use Cases (representing usages of the system by the actors or vice versa), and links between the actors and the Use Cases.

A Use Case Model is the central part of a requirements document for the object-oriented development approach recommended in this book. It states what the proposed system is to do. This is in contrast to the Nonfunctional Requirements that impose constraints on the system: performance, reliability, availability, et cetera.

A Use Case describes a particular, observable, system behavior. An observable behavior is one that is visible externally via a system interface. The set of observable behaviors define the functional system requirements. Use cases are guaranteed to be observable by the fact that they must be connected to one or more actors. Examples of Use Cases are *Query bank account* and *Aircraft enters controlled airspace*. Examples of actors are *Customer* and *Radar*. Actors may be human users or other systems such as database management systems.

A Use Case Model and the Analysis Scenarios (see Section 11.4) which are derived from it together constitute a complete set of functional requirements. Particularly if the same person or team is responsible for both the Use Case Model and the Analysis Scenarios, as is often the case, the Use Case Model, itself, need not be particularly detailed. Detail can be added during analysis. The degree of detail required is, of course, related to the formality of the requirements document as a legal contract. Use case models are initially highly informal, but through iterative analysis phases they become more formal and more complete. Actors and Use Cases are usually documented using a combination of diagrams and text.

Some development organizations require functional requirements to be captured using a particular format, usually a flat list of system features. Such a functional requirements document is no replacement for a Use Case Model, although it can be used as a good source of information from which to construct one if the document already exists. If not, then the Use Case Model should be written first and the functional requirements document derived from that.

Purpose

A Use Case Model captures the customer's expectations of the functionality of the system. This must be expressed clearly so that both sides can commit themselves to the project requirements, so that misunderstandings can be avoided.

It is vitally important that the requirements document, in general, and the Use Case Model, in particular, are written so that it can be easily understood by customers, domain experts, and end users. If customers cannot understand the functional requirements, they will not feel committed to them. If users or domain experts cannot understand the functional requirements, they will not be able to check that the requirements are correct. The intuitive and simple form of a Use Case Model helps to achieve this common understanding.

A Use Case Model, as opposed to any other format, is used to represent top-level functional requirements, because it emphasizes interfaces and end-to-end functionality. When you identify an actor in a Use Case Model, you are making a statement about where the boundary of the system is, and about what interfaces the system will need. When you identify a Use Case in a Use Case Model, you are describing how the system will be used by one or more of the actors, or how actors will be used by the system.

There is no chance of falling into the common trap of making internal design statements because only observable behaviors can be Use Cases. This is so because they must be linked directly to actors. This helps the Use Case Model to ensure that it concentrates on the system boundary, and not on internal structure, mechanisms, or algorithms. If internal details such as these are allowed to creep into requirements documents, the document will become unwieldy, it will not be understandable by potential users, and it may constrain design unnecessarily.

Participants

Who defines the Use Case Model depends on the context of the project. Whoever defines the requirements, it is the responsibility of the project manager to ensure that they are formalized appropriately, that they are adequate, and that the customer understands them.

If possible, the Use Case Model should be written by a small team which represents both the customer and the development team (analysts) and includes the project manager and the team leader. At least one domain expert should be included, as well as one end user, if possible. As mentioned in the introduction to this chapter, it is important that customer interests are represented. If the development team has no direct customer, a potential end user should take this role.

Timing

The Use Case Model forms part of the contract between the customer and the development team; it is written before any commitment is made on either side.

Technique

A starting point for the Use Case Model is the Problem Statement. This is a succinct statement of the problem that the system is to solve. Turning the Problem Statement into a Use Case Model involves discovering exactly where the boundaries of the system are, who the users of the system are, and what each type of user expects from the system. This is usually done by interviewing or observing users and domain experts. Involving these people in regular reviews of the Use Case Model is very important.

Naturally, not all user expectations can be met, and the authors of the Use Case Model must bear in mind that requirements have costs. The Problem Statement and the Business Case together help to decide which expectations are reasonable.

Strengths

A simple, clear Use Case Model capturing functional requirements encourages commitment and enthusiasm by customers and end users, as well as the project team. This is a prerequisite for success. Vague or ambiguous functional requirements virtually guarantee problems later in the project life cycle.

Weaknesses

The Use Case Model is not typically a standard format for a functional requirements document. If feasible, consider adjusting your development process to bring it into line with planned object-oriented development deliverables by using a Use Case Model as the format for the functional requirements document. If that is not possible and you need to do both a Use Case Model and a business as usual functional requirements document, try to do it in such a way as to avoid confusion and redundancy of information. While a Use Case Model is not a conventional format, it covers conventional needs and should be a more than adequate replacement.

Notation

A Use Case Model of functional requirements is best documented using a combination of diagram and text.

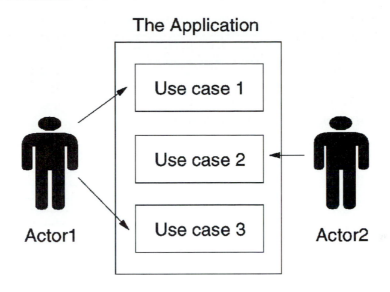

Figure *9-1.* *The Form of a Use Case Diagram.*

Figure 9-1 shows how a Use Case Model may be shown in a diagram. The box represents the system to be constructed. Inside the box are the named Use Cases that are to be supported by the system. The Use Cases are shown with their links to the external, named actors. One could imagine using different graphics to represent different kinds of actors, for example external systems as opposed to humans, although this is by no means necessary. A very small system might be shown on one diagram such as this. A larger system might use several. While little by way of concrete requirements are shown on this kind of diagram, it is very good at indicating the nature of the system interfaces in an intuitive manner.

Links between actors and Use Cases are directional, with the direction indicating which of the two (the system or the actor) initiates communication. An actor may be linked to many Use Cases, and a Use Case may be linked to many actors.

Other forms of notation can be added to a Use Case diagram to express, for example, inheritance between actors, and *uses* or *extends* relationships between Use Cases. See [Jacobson92] for a full description of the possibilities. These extensions should only be used if they aid understandability of the Use Case Model in practice.

In addition to the Use Case diagram, textual descriptions of each Use Case and actor should be provided. For each Use Case, a template of the following form may be completed.

```
┌─────────────────────────────────────────────────────────────────────┐
│                                                                       │
│     Use case name        _____  │
│     Definition           _____  │
│     Notes                _____  │
│                          _____  │
│                          _____  │
│                                                                       │
└─────────────────────────────────────────────────────────────────────┘
```

For each actor, a template of the following form may be completed.

```
┌─────────────────────────────────────────────────────────────────────┐
│                                                                       │
│       Actor              _____  │
│       Definition         _____  │
│       Notes              _____  │
│                          _____  │
│                          _____  │
│                                                                       │
└─────────────────────────────────────────────────────────────────────┘
```

The names of the actors and Use Cases connect their textual descriptions to their representations in the Use Case diagram. The *Definition* slots provide space for the actors or Use Cases to be described in whatever detail is considered appropriate. The templates also contain slots to enable notes to be recorded. Design or interfacing ideas, suggestions, and/or constraints will arise during requirements gathering. The *Notes* slots enable these comments to be noted while still separating requirements from design detail. Interfacing notes may consist of or refer to sketches of Screen Layouts, GUI Prototypes, or relevant standards such as CUA or RS-232C.

The pictorial representation shown in Figure 9-1 is often a very convenient way of showing the links between actors and Use Cases. An alternative format for representing the same information, which may be more suitable for large systems, is a two-column table of actors and Use Cases. Yet another way of representing the actor to Use Case links would be to augment the textual actor and Use Case templates with a *Links* slot. It is vital that the links between actors and Use Cases are defined. The method of representation can be chosen to suit the tools available for the size of project.

Traceability

This work product has the following traceability:

Impacted by:
- Problem Statement (p. 93)
- Issues (p. 176)

Impacts:
- Prioritized Requirements (p. 111)
- Acceptance Plan (p. 119)
- Test Plan (p. 164)
- Subject Areas (p. 187)
- Analysis Scenarios (p. 203)
- Screen Flows (p. 237)
- Screen Layouts (p. 242)
- UI Prototype (p. 247)
- User Support Materials (p. 341)

Advice and Guidance

- Involve customers, domain experts, and end users in the formulation and review of the Use Case Model.

- Drive all development activity from the Use Cases—analysis in particular. All development activity should be traceable back to the Use Cases. This ensures that only the required system is built. A practical way of doing this is the scenario-driven approach to development described in Section 18.7.

- Drive the system acceptance tests from the Use Cases, thus closing the project loop.

- If a particular format of functional requirements document has to be written, build the Use Case Model first and derive the functional requirements document from that. This is the preferable way round as the Use Case Model is a good vehicle to use for communicating with customers and users, and hence it is appropriate to agree on the Use Case Model first. If a functional requirements document already exists, then the information contained in it should be used as input to a Use Case Model which should still be reviewed in its own right with customers, domain experts, and users.

- Consider the Use Case Model and the Analysis Scenarios as a complementary pair of work products. The Use Case Model identifies system boundaries, external agents, and top-level system requirements; the Analysis Scenarios elaborate on the requirements and tease out the behavioral variations of the system. Together they constitute the functional requirements of the system. They may also be considered to be the abstract functional specification of the system. The specification is abstract in the sense that it omits interfacing details. These details are added during design; the Design Scenarios may be considered for the concrete functional specification of the system.

- If the system being defined is large, then there may well be a large number of Use Cases. In this situation the Use Cases must be organized in some manner. The organizing principle chosen should be consistent with the way that the requirements will subsequently be analyzed, in order to simplify that analysis.

  For example, if the system is a real-time one, and the analysis is largely driven by state models, then it will be appropriate to organize the Use Cases according to the possible states of the system. If the system is more static, then the analysis is likely to be driven more by the object model, and it will be more appropriate to organize the Use Cases according to the parts of the system that they affect. This process is eased if a domain analysis has already been performed (see Section 18.1) and problem domain classes have already been identified. Use cases can then be grouped according to the classes to which they relate.

- A Use Case Model should not be avoided because of the amount of detail that is apparently required. A minimal Use Case Model would consist of a list of actors, a list of Use Cases, and a representation (pictorial or otherwise) of the links between them. A minimal Use Case Model such as this would be well worth doing and maintaining.

- Do not duplicate information between the Use Case Model and the Analysis Scenarios. Only document the Use Case Model sufficiently to enable the Analysis Scenarios to be written.

- Don't forget to include external systems as actors.

- If the Use Case Model is part of a workbook describing a subsystem, then the other subsystems will appear in the Use Case Model as actors.

- Feel free to record design or interfacing notes in the *Notes* slot of a Use Case or actor template, but be sure that these are not confused with requirements.

- Each Use Case and actor should be documented textually using no more than one page unless it is exceptionally complex. As a rule of thumb, it will take about one day to define each Use Case, but this will depend on familiarity with the domain and the degree to which the system boundaries and the system requirements are "obvious."

- To estimate the total number of Use Cases, spend an hour drawing a Use Case diagram. Count the Use Cases identified and add 25 to 50 percent depending on how familiar you think you are with the domain.

- If the estimated number of Use Cases exceeds 50, either your Use Cases are too small (closer to Scenarios, see Section 11.4) or you should consider splitting the project into subprojects.

- Large numbers of Use Cases need to be grouped in some way for convenience and clarity. This can either be done by subject area or by Actor. Grouping by Actor consists of asking each Actor, in turn, which Use Cases that Actor is involved in, and then documenting these Use Cases as a single group. These groups will naturally overlap as some Use Cases are related to more than one Actor. When this happens, simply document each Use Case once fully, somewhere, and reference this documentation from each duplicate. If the lists are simply of names, with each Use Case being described more fully in a separate, flat list, then the problem of duplication is not important.

- Grouping by subject area consists of first identifying distinct areas of concern. These might follow an already completed partitioning of the system into subsystems, or they may stem from a natural decomposition in terms of business domains, for example, Administration, Accounts, Security, et cetera. Each subject area is then visited in turn, and the Use Cases in the subject area listed. Duplicate entries in multiple lists are unlikely in a grouping by subject area.

- Use the Use Case Model as an important vehicle of communication with customers, users, and domain experts. The intuitive nature of the model will facilitate this. Use the model to check both completeness and correctness with customers. This is most easily done by explaining each group of Use Cases, whether grouped by subject area or by Actor, and trying to find gaps, misplaced system boundaries, additional Actors, errors, and the like.

- The Use Case Model can also be used as the basis for interviewing customers to determine requirements. Such an interview would consist of asking which people are to use the system, which reports are to be generated, and with which external systems the system is to interact. This information results in a draft list of Actors. The Use Cases related to each Actor can then be teased out by asking the different roles of each Actor, and how each Actor is to use (or be used by) the system in each role. It may be that it is the roles that form the Actors, instead of the Actors that were originally identified. Actors should be logically distinct agents rather than physical people or systems. As the Use Cases are listed, or subsequently, they can be marked to indicate their subject area. All the identified Use Cases in a particular subject area can then be extracted and examined for completeness. Almost certainly this cross checking will find omissions. Many variations on this kind of interview are possible.

Verification

- Check that actors and Use Cases are connected appropriately. This can be done by considering all possible *roles* of each actor, and all *tasks* of each actor in each role, and ensuring that every task is enabled by adequate connections to the appropriate Use Cases. If the system uses the actors, instead of the other way round, the analysis should also be reversed: Ask about the roles and tasks of the system, and whether they are adequately covered by connections to actors.

- Check that the Use Case Model includes a representation of the system boundary.

- Check that the descriptions of each Use Case focus on visible system functionality and not on the internal behavior of the system.

Example(s)

Figure 9-2 shows a Use Case diagram for a fax recognition and forwarding application. The application has interfaces to three actors: users, administrators, and fax devices.

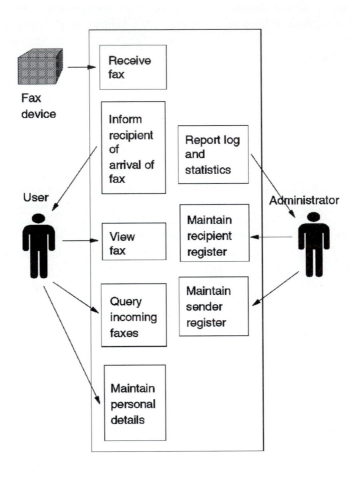

Figure   9-2. *An Example of a Use Case Diagram.*

The description of the *Receive fax* Use Case might look like the following:

Use case name	Receive fax.
Definition	The action of receiving an incoming fax, determining its intended recipient user if possible, and notifying that person. When a fax is received, the fax sheet images are stored. Optical character recognition is performed to determine the recipient, sender, and subject of the fax. If a recipient is discovered, she is notified of the fax arrival. In any case, the fax is added to the incoming fax list.
Notes	• Use a list of known cover page patterns to aid cover page interpretation.
	• Maintain a database of known senders and recipients, and the mapping from senders to the cover page patterns that they use.
	• Think about notification by voice mail in release 2.

The description of the *User* actor might look like the following.

Actor name	User.
Definition	A human user of the fax recognition application. Users must be known to the application; their details are defined by an administrator and maintained by the user herself.
Notes	Users using the fax application are notified of the arrival of a fax message by a dialog window that appears on their workstation. The dialog box has a button so that the user can ask to view the fax.

References

See [Jacobson92] for a full presentation of Use Cases and their role in driving the development process. Jacobson uses Use Cases in a different way to that proposed in this book. Jacobson positions Use Cases as the centerpiece around which all development activities are structured. In this book we advocate placing Scenarios in that role instead of Use Cases. Our reasons are the following.

- Scenarios describe end-to-end behaviors that connect requirements, development work, and test cases in an intuitive and straightforward manner. We use Use Cases to determine system boundaries and to serve as the roots from which Scenarios are subsequently derived. The Use Cases that flow from a Jacobson Use Case Model are not necessarily end to end; many of the Jacobson Use Cases are *components* of the top-level, initial Use Cases.

- Introducing Scenarios allows a useful separation of concerns: a Use Case Model is used to determine the system boundaries and the top-level system behaviors. Scenarios are then used to tease out the assumptions, outcomes, and variations of each of these. The Jacobson form of Use Cases cannot be conveniently used in this way.

- A focus on Scenarios yields a *declarative* description of a system in terms of visible behaviors and what these behaviors mean. This leaves the designer maximum freedom to structure the system as she wishes. A Jacobson Use Case analysis tends to encourage a much more *operational* style of system description that might lead to premature design.

Importance

Functional requirements are essential in some form. We recommend that functional requirements be represented as a Use Case Model and Scenarios.

9.3 NONFUNCTIONAL REQUIREMENTS

Description

Nonfunctional Requirements are the collection of system requirements that are not directly related to what the system should do. Examples of Nonfunctional Requirements include statements of reliability, availability, performance, and details of components (hardware and software) that are to be used or reused. Nonfunctional Requirements usually take the form of constraints on how the system should operate.

Nonfunctional Requirements involving constraints on hardware and software components are often represented pictorially.

Purpose

The Nonfunctional Requirements are a vital component of the requirements document. While the functional requirements drive the analysis process, the Nonfunctional Requirements drive the design. For example, performance constraints will be one factor determining the application Architecture, but they do not affect the analysis of the problem. Another example is the Nonfunctional Requirement that distributed clients and servers should run under OS/2 using TCP/IP sockets for communications. Once again, this affects system design, but not problem analysis.

There is one sense where Nonfunctional Requirements can impact problem analysis: Nonfunctional Requirements may shed light on the external agents with which the system must interact. These agents may well then become *actors* in the Use Case Model that documents the system's functional requirements, see Section 9.2.

Like all other aspects of system requirements, it is essential that Nonfunctional Requirements are expressed clearly and understood by all parties.

Participants

The planners, project manager, and team leader set the Nonfunctional Requirements with customer representatives.

Timing

Nonfunctional Requirements are identified and agreed on as part of the requirements gathering phase.

Technique

One way to generate or to check the coverage of Nonfunctional Requirements, is to pass over the Use Case Model that represents the top level of functional requirements, see Section 9.2. For each Use Case and for each Actor to Use Case link, ask what are the appropriate constraints. For each such interface, the Nonfunctional Requirements related to some predefined set of headings should be listed. The set of headings should include:

- Reliability
- Availability
- Security
- Performance
- Standards
- Look and Feel.

Also, any components, hardware or software, that the system must, or should, use should be listed or depicted graphically.

Strengths

Clear statements of Nonfunctional Requirements are vital to avoid surprises later in the development process. Design churn is one symptom of indecision over Nonfunctional Requirements.

Weaknesses

None.

Notation

Free format text augmented by diagrams, if appropriate, showing constraints on hardware and software configurations. Nonfunctional Requirements may be grouped under headings such as those mentioned above.

Traceability

This work product has the following traceability:

Impacted by:
- Problem Statement (p. 93)
- Issues (p. 176)

Impacts:
- Prioritized Requirements (p. 111)
- User Interface Guidelines (p. 234)
- Screen Flows (p. 237)
- Screen Layouts (p. 242)
- UI Prototype (p. 247)
- System Architecture (p. 257)
- APIs (p. 265)
- Target Environment (p. 272)
- Subsystems (p. 274)
- Design Object Model (p. 281)
- Design Scenarios (p. 293)
- Design OIDs (p. 298)
- Design State Models (p. 306)
- User Support Materials (p. 341)

Advice and Guidance

- Use a set of standard headings, such as those listed above, to organize and to check the completeness of Nonfunctional Requirements.

- Consider prototyping activity to determine realistic constraints.

- Ask "What if?" questions to check the completeness of the Nonfunctional Requirements.

- Some constraints will be on the border between functional and Nonfunctional Requirements, such as user interface constraints. Document them in one place and reference them from the other.

- Include Nonfunctional Requirements that refer to how the system might be expected to change in the future. This will be very valuable when it is decided what flexibility to build into the design.

- Include Nonfunctional Requirements that refer to the hardware and software environment in which the system must run, but include only those environmental constraints that are truly requirements and not just design expectations. Design *decisions* about the software environment, as opposed to *imposed requirements*, should be documented in the Architecture work product, see Section 13.2. Use the Target Environment work product, see Section 13.4., to document hardware environment decisions.

Verification

- Check for coverage by preparing a list of the broad areas that are appropriate to be covered by Nonfunctional Requirements. (This list will vary depending on the type of application and Development Environment.) For each of these areas, check that adequate Nonfunctional Requirements have been produced.

- Check that each Nonfunctional Requirement is in fact nonfunctional, that it is a constraint on system behavior and not a description of new behavior.

- Check that each Nonfunctional Requirement is really required. In particular, check that it is not an attempt to do some premature design.

- Check for contradictions between Nonfunctional Requirements.

- Check for tensions between Nonfunctional Requirements and record these as Issues.

Example(s)

Nonfunctional Requirements for an application with a GUI might include the following.

- All queries must be completed within 0.5 second.

- All updates must be completed within 1 second.

- The system should support up to 20 concurrent users.

- MTTF (Mean Time to Failure) should be at least three months.

- Object technology should be used as a development technology to ease future maintenance and enhancement.

- The IBM Open Class collection class library should be used to represent all collection classes.

- Distributed System Object Model must be used for interprocess communications.

- User interfaces must conform to IBM's Common User Access (CUA '91) standards.

- The hardware architecture shown in Figure 9-3 is to be used as a customer requirement.

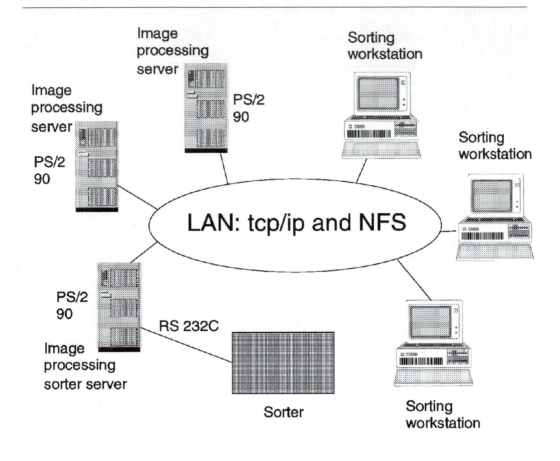

Figure 9-3. Example Environment Requirements Diagram.

References

None.

Importance

Essential. Clearly understanding the Nonfunctional Requirements for a system is critical to ensuring that the system built satisfies the full breadth and depth of customer requirements.

9.4 PRIORITIZED REQUIREMENTS

Description

The Prioritized Requirements work product defines the relative priorities of system requirements: both the functional requirements that are represented by the Use Case Model and the Nonfunctional Requirements. The prioritization can be formal or informal as appropriate and should reflect the views of the customer and users.

Note that a Prioritized Requirements primarily represents input from the customers and users. By itself it cannot dictate the priorities of the development team as these are also affected by dependencies between requirements, development risks, et cetera. This information must be factored in before scheduling decisions are made.

Purpose

Whether the customer and potential users have been involved in the writing of the Use Case Model and the Nonfunctional Requirements, these two work products alone do not contain sufficient information to permit planners to begin to construct a Release Plan. Two further kinds of information are required: the *importance* of each requirement, and the *urgency* of each requirement.

It is very easy, when interviewing customers or users, for requirements to take the form of "wish lists" of functionality that would be nice to have but which are not necessarily essential. It is clearly important for a development team to be know which requirements are vital and the ones that are wishes. Similarly, and particularly if delivery of the system is to be phased over a long period, the relative urgency of requirements is very relevant. Customers cannot necessarily have all their requirements satisfied. Both when constructing the initial Release Plan and subsequently during development, trade-offs will have to be made. Requirement X will take longer than we thought: Should we slip it or hit that deadline at the expense of requirement Y? In such situations it is obviously necessary for the priorities of the customer and the development team to be in tune. Disappointment and surprise will be the results otherwise. Customers might be willing to accept a slippage in the overall schedule if certain key features are provided early. You need to find out what those key features are.

Participants

The customer, project planner, project manager and team leader are the people most directly involved in writing this work product.

Timing

Prioritized Requirements is written as part of the process of requirements gathering. If it is necessary for requirements to be prioritized in great detail, then it may continue into the analysis phase.

Technique

The basic technique for prioritizing requirements is very simple: The requirements are listed, and customers and users are asked to evaluate the relative importance and urgency of each. The role of the planner, manager, and team leader is to ensure that the customers and users understand the costs and other implications of each requirement.

The degree of detail appropriate for a Prioritized Requirements will vary from project to project. For example, a small project with a "friendly" customer can afford to be fairly informal in its prioritization. On the other hand, a large, complex project must be prioritized in greater detail. You will have to decide the appropriate level of detail for your project.

Detail is introduced in two ways: when listing requirements and when prioritizing them. When listing requirements, one can be content with working at the Use Case level only. Alternatively, one might wait till Analysis Scenarios are available and prioritize at that level (similarly for priority levels). When deciding the relative urgency and importance of each requirement, at whatever level of detail the requirement is described, a coarse or a fine grain spectrum of options might be used. No one level of granularity will fit all projects.

Strengths

Making the priorities of the customers and users explicit in this way reduces the risk of surprises and shocks later. It also helps the development team to make the inevitable trade-offs that arise in design in a consistent and hence effective way.

Prioritization is the language of negotiation. It is both natural and vital to prioritize when faced with project risks.

Weaknesses

In a very small development effort with few requirements and where no incremental releases are planned, prioritization of requirements may not be needed.

Asking customers to prioritize requirements might seem inappropriate for someone who is trying to present a "can do" image. Why ask about priorities if I want to create the impression that I can do anything? If you can in fact do anything then you can forget about prioritization; the rest of us need a way of knowing how to deal with resource constraints, with unseen design difficulties, and with all the other kinds of project risks, in ways that will be acceptable to the customer.

Notation

The precise format of a Prioritized Requirements will depend on the size and nature of the project, as suggested above. In general, however, the project requirements are listed, and each requirement is assessed for both urgency and importance. For most projects it is adequate to list functional requirements at the Use Case level; it is probably not necessary to descend into the detail of Analysis Scenarios. It will probably be necessary to prioritize each Nonfunctional Requirement separately.

For each requirement, its urgency and importance can be specified in greater or lesser detail. For many projects a three-value scale for each is probably appropriate.

Importance   1 (vital), 2 (important), 3 (would be nice)

Urgency   1 (immediate need), 2 (pressing), 3 (can wait)

Requirements can either be listed by name, by numerical or other identifier, or the prioritization can be added to the Use Case Model and Nonfunctional Requirements work products directly. If the prioritization is separate from these other work products, then a simple three row or column table is adequate.

Traceability

This work product has the following traceability:

Impacted by:
- Problem Statement (p. 93)
- Use Case Model (p. 96)
- Nonfunctional Requirements (p. 106)
- Issues (p. 176)

Impacts:
- Acceptance Plan (p. 119)
- Resource Plan (p. 135)
- Schedule (p. 139)
- Release Plan (p. 144)
- Risk Management Plan (p. 152)
- System Architecture (p. 257)

Advice and Guidance

- Involve customers, users, development team members, and management in prioritizing requirements.

- Once you have drawn up the Prioritized Requirements table, go back to the Acceptance Plan, which should identify the acceptance tests that are most important to the customer. If you meet 95 percent of the customer's requirements and the customer tests first the 5 percent you didn't meet, you will have failed in the customer's eyes. On the other hand, if you meet the most important 5 percent of customer requirements (those that the customer will test first), you will probably have earned the customer's willingness to tolerate some lower priority fixes if needed.

- Start with a coarse-grained set of urgency and importance values as suggested above. Only if these result in too little information should you then use a more fine-grained spectrum of possibilities.

- Start with prioritizing Use Cases and only if this is problematic, or if you estimate that particular, individual Use Cases involve great effort, should you switch to prioritizing functional requirements at the Analysis Scenario level.

- The Prioritized Requirements framework can be extended to deal with more than just input from customers and users. Additional columns or rows could list estimates of risk, complexity, et cetera. This information, in addition to dependencies between requirements, can then be used as direct input to the scheduling process. An additional row or column, a "scheduling prioritization index" might be added as a rough numerical aggregate of the rest of the information accumulated for each requirement.

- Adding the prioritization information directly to the Use Case Model and Nonfunctional Requirements work products makes sense, if they do not fragment the information unacceptably. If the prioritization information is not entered as a separate table then it must be possible to extract this table from the other work products. This depends on tool support.

- Be sensitive to the statements of the customer and users. If they seem to imply that part but not all of the functionality of a Use Case is vital, then explore this further with Analysis Scenarios, if only informally by asking about different situations.

- It may well be that it is appropriate to prioritize at the level of Scenarios instead of Use Cases, but be selective; do not do this automatically and uniformly.

Verification

- Check that writing the Prioritized Requirements has yielded real information. Having all requirements listed with importance "2" is not useful. In such cases either use a finer-grain set of values and/or force the issue by asking questions such as "What if I could only supply this or that. Which would you choose?"

- Check that prioritization has been adequately detailed for listing requirements. If you anticipate that particular Use Cases will be refined into many Analysis Scenarios then try prioritizing a few of the Scenarios to see whether their priority values differ from those of their Use Case.

- Present the prioritization table to the developers and ask for their feedback. They may have insights into risks and complexity that warrant additional questions being asked about priorities.

- Small projects might well make do with an informal statement of priorities. A few lines of text might be sufficient to say what is most important and pressing, and what can be slipped or dropped if necessary.

Example(s)

The following is a simple example of a Requirements Prioritization. The scale of urgency and importance values is as suggested in the Notation section earlier in this work product description.

Table   9-1. An Example of a Requirements Prioritization.

Requirement	Importance	Urgency
Export to spreadsheet	2	3
Determine net worth	1	1
Get detailed changes	1	2
Purchase securities	1	2
Transfer funds	1	2
Make loan application	1	3

References

There are no references for this work product.

Importance

Optional, but very important for projects that may have more requirements than available resources can reasonably handle.

9.5 BUSINESS CASE

Description

A Business Case provides a justification for the undertaking of a project. The Business Case is complementary to the Problem Statement: The Problem Statement states the problem to be solved whereas the Business Case justifies the effort. There are two kinds of Business Case that one encounters: quantitative, which is based on hard measurements (e.g., cost-benefit analysis); or qualitative, which is based on something less tangible and not necessarily measurable (here, the move to objects may be based on a sponsor's vision and may not be subject to a cost-benefit analysis).

Besides providing the justification for a project, a Business Case is important as a focus for requirements. For example, if a Business Case rests on the project feeding certain reusable parts into a parts center then this commitment must be taken into account during all development phases.

A Business Case has to justify a project from a business perspective. It often takes the form of a cost/benefit analysis. The cost of the project is an estimation of the resources that it will consume. The benefits of the project have many possible sources including the following:

- Revenues

- Productivity

- Customer goodwill

- Accomplishment of organizational mission statement

- Development experience gained, for example the project will result in three developers sufficiently trained in C++ design and coding that they can work independently in future projects

- Reusable components, for example, a telephony domain analysis and a framework for simple telephony applications that can be reused in a future application.

Purpose

Too many teams begin projects without knowing why. Or perhaps each senior team member knows why but the reasons differ from person to person. This is obviously undesirable. The Business Case assists with achieving a shared vision and understanding of the project's value.

Participants

It is usually the project manager who is responsible for articulating a Business Case, though planners and financial analysts typically play a major role.

Timing

Either before or during requirements gathering.

Technique

Standard business techniques for justifying a project should be used.

Strengths

- A Business Case ensures that expectations are explicit and constant.

- The Business Case helps to focus attention on why the project has been undertaken. Surprisingly many projects are started without any clear idea about why they have been undertaken.

- Agreeing on a written Business Case is a good test of common commitment and direction. This is obviously vital during the planning phase of a project, but it is also very helpful during development. For example, when selecting an Architecture, various alternatives with different trade-offs may be considered. Understanding the justification for a project can at times assist with making decisions during the project.

- Depending on the circumstances, a Business Case may be essential to obtaining project funding.

Weaknesses

Business Cases can be unreliable in their forecasts and it is often difficult to accurately quantify the benefits of a project. Having to develop, sell, and defend a Business Case is also hard work at a time when it might be more interesting to refine requirements and begin to build project plans.

It is, however, essential and projects are much more likely to fail, or be perceived to have failed, without one.

Notation

Free format text.

Traceability

This work product has the following traceability:

Impacted by:
- Problem Statement (p. 93)
- Issues (p. 176)

Impacts:
- Resource Plan (p. 135)
- Schedule (p. 139)
- Release Plan (p. 144)
- Reuse Plan (p. 158)

Advice and Guidance

- Include a description of the analysis, design, and code assets that the project is expected to accrue. This might include a domain analysis, architectural or utility frameworks, or reusable code.

- Include reference to the skills that will be acquired as a result of carrying out the project.

- Use the Business Case as input into design decisions to ensure that design trade-offs are consistent with each other and with the overall project objectives.

- Understanding the justification for the effort can be a major benefit in assisting the team to make decisions relating to functionality.

Verification

- Check that the Business Case focuses on why the project should be undertaken by the development team, rather than on why the customer needs the system.

Example(s)

Below we present examples of qualitative and quantitative Business Cases. We have chosen to show examples that are different in scope from others presented in this book in that they are not specifically related to a project employing object technology. Rather, they are examples from two companies of the Business Cases for the deployment of object technology in their software development communities.

We have chosen this approach since Business Cases for software development is really a business as usual work product but for many projects, the question of how to justify the deployment of object technology is a harder question. These are examples of how two companies that we have had some involvement with approached this problem.

The first example is based on an actual Business Case but has been modified for reasons of confidentiality. In making these changes, the arithmetic may not stand up, but it is intended as an illustration only.

Initial plan outline for a move of 100 people to object technology:
- Our company has an Information Technology group consisting of 200 programmers.
- It is estimated that going to objects will improve productivity by 50 percent over time.
- Within the first three years we plan to convert at least 50 percent of our development staff, roughly 100 persons, to using objects.
- It is estimated that the cost of training will average three months per person. The investment per person is a rather complex calculation, bearing in mind that after some initial training, programmers will be productive but at a lower productivity rate than usual.
- Assume productivity improvements achieve their target levels in year two of the transition.
- There will be an additional cost of six full-time mentors at a cost of $900,000 per year (planned for 2 years).
- Administrative and infrastructure costs of the transition are a net cost of $1 million (rather complex accounting comes into play here, and there are tax benefits that will not be covered here).
- Software acquisition costs are not factored in as they are covered by usual budget.
- Costs:
  - 25 person years of effort (100 persons for 3 months) for a total cost of $2.5 million (assuming a $100,000 internal cost for a person year)
  - Mentoring Costs = $1.8 million (for 2 years)
  - Infrastructure Overhead = $1 million (for 2 years)
  - Total Costs = $5.3 million (for 2 years)
- Benefits
  - Starting in year 2, the 100 programmers will be 50 percent more productive.
    - Yielding a benefit of $5 million per year (100 programmers will produce the work of 150 programmers).
    - Because of the current application development backlog, the productivity gain will be applied to reducing the backlog (i.e., there is no plan to reduce the workforce).
  - The investment will be recovered early in year 3 of the transition.
  - Some internal object technology mentors will emerge from the group of 100 programmers.

Figure 9-4. Example of a Quantitative Business Case.

The following example outlines an actual Business Case for a company piloting the use of object technology. While some of the benefits could be measured (for example, the time to introduce a new product), the company did not produce a quantitative Business Case.

The following represents a qualitative Business Case—the benefits were not subjected to hard measurement.

The company plans to adopt object technology hoping to achieve the following objectives:
- Deliver software that better meets our users' needs.
- Improve our ability to deliver new products to the marketplace in a timely fashion.
- Improve programmer productivity.
- Develop an infrastructure to support software reuse and lessen software development time.
- Involve users more in the software development process via Object-Oriented Analysis techniques.

Figure *9-5. Example of a Qualitative Business Case.*

References

- Chapter 4 of Goldberg and Rubin [Goldberg95] has some advice on how to make the business case and obtain management commitment to use object technology.

- Chapter 1 of Malan [Malan96] offers advice and a case study on getting management buy-in.

Importance

Essential. All projects need some level of justification before any significant amount of resources are expended on them.

9.6 ACCEPTANCE PLAN

Description

The Acceptance Plan is a description of the sequence of steps by which the customer, or a potential end user playing the role of the customer, will verify that the constructed system does indeed satisfy its requirements. Each step of the plan should be clearly and fully described in terms of how to set up the test, and the acceptable system behaviors in response to the test. These behaviors should be stated in such a way that it will be obvious whether or not the test is passed.

The contract with the customer should include a clause to the effect that the system will be accepted formally if the acceptance tests are all successful. If there is no direct customer, the contract and the Acceptance Plan will be informal, but their existence is still relevant.

Purpose

Requirements documents are often long. Verifying that a given system satisfies every statement of the requirements document can take a prohibitive length of time, and can be open to interpretation, particularly if the customer is looking for excuses not to accept. Furthermore, the burden of proof that the requirements are satisfied lies with the development team. Proving correctness is notoriously difficult, at best. For example, the requirements document may state that a particular interface should use a particular protocol. Proving that the code correctly generates the protocol is almost certainly not feasible. Running tests is the only alternative, but which tests and how many? The scope for disagreement is considerable. Bearing in mind that disagreement might mean lack of payment, it is up to the development team to ensure that this situation does not arise.

The Acceptance Plan is an integral part of the requirements document, and as such is agreed to by both parties when the project is started. If requirements change during the lifetime of the project then both new statements of requirements and a new Acceptance Plan will have to be negotiated.

Participants

The Acceptance Plan will typically be developed and agreed to by a team made up of representatives with decision-making responsibilities from the project team (perhaps the project manager and/or the team leader) and the customer (or someone representing the customer set).

Timing

The Acceptance Plan is written after the rest of the requirements document but before commitment to the project is made by either side. If there is no direct customer, and hence no formal contract or commitment, this timing can be relaxed and the Acceptance Plan written in parallel with development work.

Technique

The Acceptance Plan should be designed to demonstrate in a positive manner that the project requirements have been met. It should be driven by the functional requirements of the system, that is, the set of Use Cases, see Section 9.2. The Use Cases each summarize one way in which the system is to be used. For each of them, the Nonfunctional Requirements must be applied and an adequate set of tests decided upon. The tests should all be closed. That is, it must be guaranteed that each can be determined to be either successful or unsuccessful within a definite period of time. Sometimes this means that time-limits or other bounds must be applied to tests.

Strengths

The existence of an adequate Acceptance Plan ensures that the customer is committed to a definite way of determining whether or not to accept the system.

Weaknesses

The writing of an Acceptance Plan is time-consuming. In particular, it consumes scarce resources at the start of the project that are also required for project planning. The temptation exists to claim that an Acceptance Plan is not urgent and can be constructed as the project proceeds. Once the contract has been signed, however, the negotiating power of the development team is considerably lowered, and there is no compelling reason for the customer to commit to the plan at all. If there is no direct customer, of course, there is less justification for writing an Acceptance Plan early.

Notation

The format of the plan is a grouped sequence of individual steps of the following form.

Test group name	_____
Test number	_____
Prerequisites	1. _____
	2. _____
Set-up instructions	1. _____
	2. _____
Test instructions	1. _____
	2. _____
Acceptable behavior	1. _____
	2. _____
Test performed on date	_____
Test performed at time	_____
Name of customer signatory	_____
Name of project signatory	_____
Test result (pass/fail)	_____
Signed for customer	_____
Signed for project	_____

The Acceptance Plan should include instructions for the repetition of tests in the event of failure. For example, it might be stipulated that if a test fails, then the development team is permitted a given length of time to make corrections before the group of tests of which that test is a part is repeated; the rest of the Acceptance Plan does not need to be repeated.

Traceability

This work product has the following traceability:

Impacted by:
- Use Case Model (p. 96)
- Prioritized Requirements (p. 111)
- Issues (p. 176)

Impacts:
- Test Plan (p. 164)

Advice and Guidance

- Review each test, asking under what circumstances it could fail. If any of these circumstances depend on the environment of the system, for example, they depend on system loading, then add set-up or test instructions to ensure that a limit is not exceeded.

- Set-up and test instructions should be constructive. That is, they should specify a definite sequence of steps for achieving the test. They should not, for example, say that system loading must not exceed some specified value, because this does not state how the permissible loading is to be achieved. Instead, they should specify the user actions to be performed by a definite number of users. This can be achieved and controlled precisely.

- Place time-limits on tests. No test should be allowed to drag out with no predetermined time-limit.

- Link tests together by means of prerequisites to save complex test set-up instructions.

- If there is no direct customer, the need for strict criteria for determining release is still valid.

Verification

- Check that each use case of the Use Case Model is covered by adequate acceptance tests.

- Check that each Nonfunctional Requirement is covered by adequate acceptance tests.

Example(s)

The following is an example of an Acceptance Plan from a group which is testing that an application can be installed successfully as per specifications:

Table **9-2.** *Example of an Acceptance Plan.*

Test group name	Installation
Test number	1
Prerequisites	1. Hardware as specified in user guide
	2. Software as specified in user guide
Set-up instructions	1. OS/2 running
Test instructions	1. Execute "A:\INSTALL" from OS/2 command line.
	2. Follow installation instructions in dialog boxes, using all provided defaults.
	3. Reboot.
	4. Execute "PPP" from OS/2 command line.
Acceptable behavior	Successful completion of installation procedure within 10 minutes. The PPP command results in the application sign-on dialog appearing.
Test performed on date	_____
Test performed at time	_____
Name of customer signatory	_____
Name of project signatory	_____
Test result (pass/fail)	_____
Signed for customer	_____
Signed for project	_____

References

None.

Importance

Optional. An Acceptance Plan is certainly a good idea and a good way to ensure that the project team and the customer have the same understanding as to what will be delivered and in what state. But, it is possible to have a successful project without such a plan.

10.0 Project Management Work Products

The Project Management chapter of the workbook describes work products that are important to the successful control and management of the project.

Many software development projects are large and complex. Throw in the possibility of unclear and unstable requirements, dependencies on other organizations, and the use of new technologies and processes (such as with object technology) and the difficulty of successfully completing a project grows enormously. The management team and the project's technical leaders must deal with staffing the project, scheduling it, selecting development processes, managing risk, setting quality goals, and identifying and resolving risks, issues, and dependencies.

The projects that succeed in that kind of environment are those on which the team has a strong commitment to applying good Project Management principles to the project throughout its life.

The project management section of the project workbook consists of the following work products:

- Intended Development Process

- Project Workbook Outline

- Resource Plan

- Schedule

- Release Plan

- Quality Assurance Plan

- Risk Management Plan

- Reuse Plan

- Test Plan

- Metrics

- Project Dependencies

- Issues

These work products all "inherit" the common work product attributes described in Section 8.1, and have specialized attributes of their own.

Many of these work products are just as necessary in projects not using object technology as in those that are following an object-oriented software development approach. In most cases, the changes to these work products caused by a move to object technology are subtle. Yet, they should still be treated as essential work products in the project workbook for any object-oriented project.

The Intended Development Process provides a broad outline of the development process that the development team will be following. The general principles for development set forth in it will be used in other work products that set specific schedules and plans.

The Project Workbook Outline may in some sense be particular to those projects using a workbook-centered approach to development, but if seen as documentation of the act of specifying what work products will be produced during each phase of a particular project, it is important to all projects. An understanding of what work products will be built certainly impacts most of the other Project Management work products.

The Resource Plan identifies the resources needed, and the timing of when they are needed, to produce a solution that addresses the requirements laid out in the Requirements work products on the necessary Schedule. The Resource Plan must be coordinated with Schedule, Release Plan, Project Dependencies, Issues, and various others work products.

The Schedule is a means for understanding the work that needs to be completed and when in order for the project to complete successfully. Like many of the Project Management work products it needs to be closely coordinated with the other work products described in this chapter.

The Release Plan is used to place Requirements into manageable units of work reflected by project releases, versions, iterations, and increments and is closely aligned with the Schedule and Resource Plan.

The Quality Assurance plan sets project goals for quality, which usually have a lot of customer input, and outlines the activities that will take place throughout the life of the project to meet those goals.

Most projects involve some level of risk. The Risk Management Plan is used to identify potential risks and details plans to address them. Risks can impact Prioritized Requirements which in turn can affect the Schedule and the Release Plan.

The Reuse Plan work product recognizes the fact that reusing existing components, and producing new components that can be reused by others, are often integral parts of an object-oriented approach to software development. It also recognizes that reuse will not happen unless it is planned in advance and the necessary time and resources are allotted for it.

A Test Plan is a critical part of any software development project as testing is typically needed to ensure that the project's Requirements are being met, and testing is usually a large piece of any Quality Assurance Plan.

Metrics can be a very useful tool in projecting necessary resources, setting schedules, and identifying issues and risks.

The Project Dependencies work product is an important tool for understanding those items that your project requires, perhaps from other organizations, to successfully complete a solution that addresses the project's requirements on the required schedule.

Finally, the Issues work product is an important tool for capturing, understanding, and addressing the inevitable issues that will occur throughout the life of the project.

The following sections provide more detail on each of these work products.

10.1 INTENDED DEVELOPMENT PROCESS

Description

The Intended Development Process work product documents the broad outlines of the development process that is to be used for this project. By itself it is not a plan; other parts of the project workbook apply the information of this work product to the particular project to form plans, schedules, workbook guidelines, et cetera. For example, this work product may decree that the project will be incremental, with increments lasting approximately six weeks. The project manager will then use this information, and much more, to generate a work schedule. The process documented in this work product is project-independent, although it has obviously been selected for its appropriateness to deal with the problems and constraints of the current project. The Intended Development Process should be thought of as a development process template.

This work product is broad but shallow. That is, it addresses the entire project life cycle, but only at a very high level. The work product should address the development process itself, the techniques and notations to support the process, and the tools to automate some of the development activities.

There are two aspects to the Intended Development Process that may be described. First, the overall project profile, and secondly, the individual project life cycle phases. The overall project profile describes the large-scale shape of the project. That is, whether it is to be iterative, incremental, waterfall, or some combination of these. Each of these profiles has parameters that must be set for a project, for example, the length of each increment, and the phases that constitute each increment and their durations. All of these parameters have their approximate "ideal" values that consider the requirements to manage complexity, communications, and change. These issues are common to all projects, and their solutions are to a certain extent independent of the details of any particular project. External and organizational constraints and project peculiarities are, however, significant influences. A presentation in this work product of both the ideal and the actual Intended Development Process will help the issues to be thought through and will make the work product more reusable in future projects.

Besides the overall project profile, the individual phases of the project life cycle may be described in outline in this work product. The phases and their definitions will vary from organization to organization, but they must encompass the chapters of the workbook described in this book.

For each of the life cycle phases, the techniques to be used, the notations to support the techniques, and the tools to automate the techniques should be described, as far as is reasonable at this early stage. The goal is to define a development process, leaving the localized details of the steps to be dealt with later as appropriate. For each development phase, the following issues may also be addressed.

- The process by which the work products are to be validated for correctness and verified for internal consistency.

- Version and change control.

- The way that the size of the activities may be estimated, and both progress and quality monitored.

- The technology and techniques to be used to construct and use various kinds of prototypes.

For the project planning phase, the planning work products may be described, along with planning and scheduling tools that may be useful in producing and maintaining these.

For the requirements phase, the format of the requirements document may be presented, along with tools that are capable of assisting the gathering and sorting of requirements. The way that customers and end users can be involved in the process may be discussed.

For the analysis and design phases, the modeling notations may be specified, for example Booch or OMT. Modeling notations tend to be neutral to the development process used, but they influence tool and education choices, and may be controlled by organizational rules. If possible, tools should be selected for their appropriateness to the Intended Development Process and techniques, and not for their support of a particular notation. The global impact of development tools, and hence of development techniques and notations, makes them a proper subject of discussion in this work product although they do not strictly fall under the heading of "process."

For the implementation phase, the target programming language may be specified, if this is appropriate, along with code generation, programming and programming support tools. The principles of code integration should be presented.

For the code testing phases, the testing principles may be established, along with any testing or test generation tools that are relevant.

The Intended Development Process work product is used as the basis from which to write the guidelines work products of each chapter of the workbook. The difference between these is that the Intended Development Process work product is aimed at project managers and leaders, whereas the guidelines work products of the workbook are aimed at the team members responsible for completing the work products covered by the guidelines.

Purpose

The Intended Development Process work product enunciates the principles behind the process to be followed, and some of their details. This is done to separate these principles from their application within the context of a particular project. This in turn is for three reasons.

- Documenting principles separately from their application helps the project manager to separate them mentally.

- The principles represent a body of project management techniques that are independent of a particular project, and hence they can be reused from project to project, provided of course that they are applicable. It is difficult to reuse something unless it is documented separately.

- This work product can be reviewed at the end of the project to judge what worked, what didn't work, and why. Reviewing in this way a project-independent statement of development process principles makes the lessons learned more reusable than simply reviewing the various project-specific plans.

Participants

The project manager must approve the Intended Development Process. It will probably be written jointly by the team leader and the project manager.

Timing

The Intended Development Process is input to the other project planning steps. As such it is a very early deliverable, at least in draft form. It is probably one of the first project management work products to be completed.

Technique

Reuse the documented development process of a previous, successful project. If no such process is available to be reused, use the process given in the example below as a starting point.

Strengths

A well-documented Intended Development Process can prevent later confusion and unnecessary discussions about how the project is to be tackled. It represents the reusable portion of the project management chapter of the project workbook. Thinking through and documenting the complete development process at a very early stage permits tool and education requirements to be anticipated.

Weaknesses

It is difficult to document an Intended Development Process if this is a first-time project for the team. Giving guidance and still giving the team necessary flexibility is a difficult balance to strike. A well-documented Intended Development Process takes considerable time to produce.

Notation

Free format text, but you might use one heading for the overall project profile, and one for each of the phases of the project life cycle. Under each life cycle step there should be subheadings for techniques, notation, tools, metrics, et cetera.

An alternative, more formal approach would be to represent the Intended Development Process as a complete, idealized process. If that approach is followed, this work product would contain, in summary form, a complete project management document. Such a document would be generic, because it would be independent of the details of any particular project. These details are instead supplied in parametric form: the total effort of the project, the project "profile," staffing, et cetera. The actual project management details could then be supplied by "filling in the blanks," which would obviously have great advantages. This is an approach similar to that used by automated project estimation and scheduling packages.

An advantage of this more formal approach is that it makes explicit the parametric dependencies of the plan, and hence provides more guidance (for example) on how to estimate effort and track progress. Furthermore, standardizing in this way on process not only makes projects more repeatable, but means that metric data is more widely applicable.

A compromise can be reached. For example, an informal approach can be used for an initial project, after which the project management workbook chapter of that project can be summarized and abstracted to form the Intended Development Process for later projects.

Traceability

This work product has the following traceability:

Impacted by:
- Quality Assurance Plan (p. 147)
- Test Plan (p. 164)
- Issues (p. 176)

Impacts:
- Schedule (p. 139)
- Release Plan (p. 144)
- Analysis Guidelines (p. 183)
- User Interface Guidelines (p. 234)
- Design Guidelines (p. 253)
- Coding Guidelines (p. 322)

Advice and Guidance

- Where appropriate and when time permits, note the reasons for selecting a particular process. This will help when this work product is reused by other projects, or assessed for its reuse potential.

- It should be clear that the development team can deviate from the intended process if there are good and well-documented reasons for so doing.

- The Intended Development Process work product should not duplicate material presented in the Analysis, User Interface, Design, and Coding Guidelines work products. Use references to those work products to provide information on how the Intended Development Process is to be applied.

Verification

- Check that all reusable process management material is included in or referred to from this work product.

- Check for balance of release process documentation and development process documentation.

- Check that tool support, if covered in the Intended Development Process, ensures that manually-entered information needs to be entered only once.

Example(s)

An Intended Development Process might include details such as the following:

- Use the workbook and basic techniques described in the book *Developing Object-Oriented Software: An Experience-Based Approach* (that's this book!).

- Use a combination of a waterfall and an iterative and incremental process. Requirements gathering, initial project planning, analysis, and architectural definition phases are performed in a waterfall manner, followed by a series of incremental development cycles. The work products of these initial phases, like all others, are subject to iterative improvement during the life cycle of the project.

- Use conventional estimation techniques to provide initial project sizing estimates. From the end of the analysis phase, estimate total classes (including utility and graphical user interface) in the ratio of 1:6 analysis classes to final implementation classes. Use an initial estimate of one person-month (PM) per implementation class for all project phases through to delivery. (This is an estimate for experts. For intermediates, use 2 PM's per implementation class; for novices, use 3 PM's per implementation class.) Use these figures to update the original estimate of project size.

- The incremental part of the development process follows a seven-month release schedule. Each release consists of three eight-week increments, followed by a four-week system test cycle, culminating in the release.

- Each increment has three distinct phases of two weeks each:
  - design and interface development
  - implementation and documentation
  - integration, final verification test (FVT), metric data analysis, process adjustment, and plan adjustment.

  Further, the activities associated with the first two phases include a week of developing the work products followed by a week of review and iterative rework. As an estimate, a person can design, implement, and document the solutions to five scenarios throughout the two week cycle (including the review and iteration).

- The very first development increment follows a depth-first approach (Section 17.1), consisting of a series of four minicycles of two weeks' duration each. The goals of these minicycles are to establish the Development Environment, to give all team members a taste of all development phases, and to establish the basic Architecture.

References

Succeeding with Object Technology by Goldberg and Rubin [Goldberg95], in particular the chapters on "Strategies for Developing with Objects," and "What is a Process Model."

Importance

Optional but important. All projects should have an understanding of what their approach is going to be before starting. But, it is possible that this understanding can be gained through some of the other work products such as Schedule and Resource Plan.

10.2 PROJECT WORKBOOK OUTLINE

Description

The Project Workbook Outline is an organized list of work products that will comprise the project workbook. As the name suggests, it takes the form of an outline. The key items in the outline are work product types (e.g., Problem Statement). It is recommended that those items be grouped by the phase or facet of work to which they belong (e.g. Project Management, Requirements).

The outline shows not only the intended content of the workbook but also the order that the items will appear in the workbook. It represents a commitment by the development team to produce that set of work products and to record them in the workbook.

Remember that a project workbook is a logical container of concrete work products. The workbook needs to have a place for every agreed to work product, though the actual work products may physically be stored in a database managed by a CASE tool or a configuration and version management tool. In fact a physical work product might even be stored in a file drawer.

Not all work products are "deliverables," as in "customer deliverables," but all that the team agrees to produce do need to be kept and be made accessible to the development team via the project workbook.

Purpose

The Project Workbook Outline is needed to find agreement among the development team members about the set of work products to be created for the project. It is also needed to establish a commitment from the development team to record each of the identified work products in the project workbook.

There is no reason not to create a Project Workbook Outline. The mere existence of a project workbook implies a de facto structure or outline. Establishing the outline first forms a plan for consistency and completeness.

If an outline is not created first, development team members will not know which work products to create and record for the project. A good development team will question the lack of a Project Workbook Outline. A team less experienced will probably set off creating the work products that they used in their last project. If there is more than one team, there will be several different outlines.

Participants

The Project Workbook Outline should be developed by the team leader and the project manager.

Timing

The Project Workbook Outline should be decided and recorded during the project management phase, but it will be retroactive to the requirements phase.

Technique

Start your outline with the essential work products listed in Table 8-1. Add other work products to the outline depending on the size and risks of your project. Review the work product list with the project manager and team leaders to ensure that each work product in the outline is suitable for the project.

Strengths

If you have a published Project Workbook Outline, everyone in the project will know which work products they need to create and which they can expect to find and work with from other team members.

Weaknesses

None.

Notation

Since the outline will only be used to establish the workbook, any form (numbered or not) of two level outline will suffice.

The recommended structure for a project workbook is one major section per phase or facet of work and one subsection for each work product type associated with that phase. Intuitively, the order of phases and work product types within the phase should approximate the chronological order in which they are normally produced.

The Project Workbook Outline should match the intended workbook structure.

Traceability

This work product has the following traceability:

Impacted by:
- Quality Assurance Plan (p. 147)
- Issues (p. 176)
- Analysis Guidelines (p. 183)
- User Interface Guidelines (p. 234)
- Design Guidelines (p. 253)
- Coding Guidelines (p. 322)

Impacts:
- Quality Assurance Plan (p. 147)
- Analysis Guidelines (p. 183)
- User Interface Guidelines (p. 234)
- Design Guidelines (p. 253)
- Coding Guidelines (p. 322)

Advice and Guidance

Especially for new projects with teams who have not worked together before, create and distribute the Project Workbook Outline early. It helps the team to see the scope of work that they will be performing and the work products they will be expected to create and record.

During team orientation meetings make sure that the entire team understands the nature of each work product and the relationships that exist among them (i.e. the common facets).

Ensure that the team agrees with the necessity of each work product in the outline.

Verification

Use either the complete development team (for a small project) or the team leaders (for a large project) to review the Project Workbook Outline. Ensure that the review group understands what each work product is and how it is related to others. Seek consensus from the review group that each work product is necessary and that the list is sufficient for the success of the project.

Example(s)

For a small project, the following outline would be a reasonable starting point, with other things like User Interface Model work products or the Application Programming Interfaces work product added if applicable to the application.

- Requirements
  - Problem Statement
  - Use Case Model
  - Nonfunctional Requirements
  - Business Case
- Project Management
  - Project Workbook Outline
  - Resource Plan
  - Schedule
  - Test Plan
  - Issues
- Analysis
  - Analysis Object Model
  - Analysis Scenarios
  - Analysis Object Interaction Diagrams
- Design
  - System Architecture
  - Target Environment
  - Design Object Model
  - Design Scenarios
  - Design Object Interaction Diagrams
  - Design Class Descriptions
- Implementation
  - Coding Guidelines
  - Source Code
  - User Support Materials
- Testing
  - Test Cases
- Appendix
  - Glossary

Figure 10-1. *Example of a Project Workbook Outline.*

References

Just this book!

Importance

Essential. If you are going to create a project workbook, you need an outline. There's no way around this.

10.3 RESOURCE PLAN

Description

A Resource Plan identifies requirements of the project in terms of staff, training, equipment, services, and budget. It should state the types and quantities of the resources, and when they are required. This item is a normal project management deliverable.

Purpose

Early in a project's life it is essential to identify all of the resources that will be required during the life of a project for its successful completion. During the life of the project the Resource Plan needs to be updated and reviewed periodically to manage resource exposure risk.

Participants

The project or resource manager would normally perform this task. To acquire the necessary resources it will require negotiation with the resource owners.

Timing

A basic Resource Plan should be completed as early as possible. The plan should then be updated and refined as the project proceeds and more details of the project are available. It should be reviewed regularly to identify risks.

Technique

A possible approach to building a Resource Plan is:

- Choose and obtain a project management tool. A site or development organization will normally have standardized on one, and there are numerous choices. Example tool sets that have been used with the approach described in this book can be found in Appendix C.

- Estimate the resources needed for each phase of the project. The estimates for later stages are likely to be less accurate than the initial ones; therefore, they should be reevaluated as the project progresses.

- Enter this data into a project management system.

- As resource requirements and timings change, update the data in the project management tool.

- Pay heed to warnings about resource exposures that the tool gives.

- Do not underestimate time and effort associated with activities such as installing tools, educating staff on object technology and the tools to be used, and ramping up staffing.

There is little difference in resource planning between traditional development and object technology-based development.

Strengths

It ensures that the project identifies the resources needed for successful completion. It helps in the management of risk.

Weaknesses

It requires effort and discipline to establish and maintain but is a good investment in all but the smallest projects.

Notation

Many available tools support PERT charts, time lines, and critical-path analysis. These capabilities are essential to good project management.

Traceability

This work product has the following traceability:

Impacted by:
- Prioritized Requirements (p. 111)
- Business Case (p. 115)
- Schedule (p. 139)
- Release Plan (p. 144)
- Reuse Plan (p. 158)
- Test Plan (p. 164)
- Metrics (p. 169)
- Project Dependencies (p. 173)
- Issues (p. 176)
- Subject Areas (p. 187)

Impacts:
- Schedule (p. 139)
- Release Plan (p. 144)

Advice and Guidance

Building a Resource Plan is difficult, but it really needs to be done to have control of a project and to minimize the risks of not having enough resources to successfully complete the project. Some simple advice and guidance follows:

- If this is your first project using an object-oriented software development process and have no idea how to estimate resources, it might be useful to start by estimating the resources as you would if this were not an object-oriented project. You can then add some appropriate buffer (say 10 to 25 percent) to cover the fact that you are using a new approach, and it will likely cost some time and resources during this initial attempt to use it.

- Factor in costs for training, mentors, tools installation and support, process definition and deployment, and other factors related to the move to the use of object technology.

- Revisit the Resource Plan often (certainly after each iteration of your project) and make adjustments based on the new knowledge you will have at hand.

- Keep a history of Resource Plans and adjustments to them to build a base of data from which to estimate resource needs for future object-oriented development projects.

Verification

- Check that all appropriate kinds of resource have been addressed.

- Check that the plan identifies when and for how long each resource is needed.

- Check that the timing of each resource is appropriate; not too early and not too late.

- Check that resources are not overcommitted in the sense that the same resource is required to do too much at once.

- Check that resources specified are adequate for each task.

Example(s)

The following example demonstrates that a Resource Plan should cover specific project activities as well as things like vacations and other "absences" in order to be truly useful:

Activities	1997				
	Jun	Jul	Aug	Sep	Oct
--Holidays, etc			▬▬▬	▬▬▬	
----Vacation CF		▬▬▬			
-------CF (CF)		▪			
-------CF (CF)			◈		
-------CF (CF)			▬		
----Vacation (AMW)				▭	
----Conference (AMW)					▫
----Vacation (STH)				▭	
--Development	▬▬▬▬▬	▬▬▬▬▬	▬▬▬		
----Inc 6A Build		◈			
----Inc 6B Build			◈		
----Inc 6C Build				△	
----Increment 6C		▬▬▬			

References

Succeeding with Object Technology by Goldberg and Rubin [Goldberg95], in particular the chapter "Plan and Control a Project."

Importance

A Resource Plan is essential for ensuring that the appropriate resources are available to a project at the proper times. While a very small project might choose to document its Resource Plan informally, it still needs to have some idea of resource needs and availability.

10.4 SCHEDULE

Description

The schedule is a set of:

- Activities
- Start dates and durations for each activity
- Work assignments
- Milestones

It is closely allied to the Resource Plan. At the start of a project a schedule will be created based on the functions to be delivered and the deadlines that have to be met, using project estimation Metrics, comparisons to similar projects, and general experience.

Purpose

The schedule is produced to understand the work completed and the work needed to be completed for the project. It is used to plan and measure project progress.

Initially it will be a feasibility exercise to see whether the project can deliver the required functions on the desired deadlines. During the life of a project, it provides a view of the progress of the project.

Comparison of the actual dates achieved for the items in the schedule to the planned dates provides feedback to the project managers on the progress of the project and whether it is on track. If the project is behind schedule, it provides a driver for corrective action to bring the project back on schedule. The reasons for the differences between planned and actual have to be analyzed to determine their causes so that remedial action can be taken as appropriate. If appropriate, metric data used for project estimations should be updated to reflect actual schedule data.

Participants

The project manager and planner(s) share responsibility for the schedule with help from the project team leaders.

Timing

A basic schedule should be completed as early as possible. The schedule should then be updated and refined as the project proceeds and actual details of the project become available. It should be reviewed regularly to identify divergence from the plan so that corrective action can be initiated as appropriate.

Technique

- Obtain a project management tool. Example tool sets that have been used with the approach described in this book can be found in Appendix C.
- Build an initial schedule by entering milestones, tasks (with durations), resources, and work assignments.
- Often, initially, the minimum task duration is a week. As the project plan is refined, activities can be broken up into more detail and shorter duration activities.
- Link dependent activities together. Group related activities together under a hammock (an abstract superactivity). This helps to avoid micromanagement by hiding small items from the project plan.
- Examine critical path(s) to see if plan alternatives can be found to reduce the criticality. A critical path is a set of linked tasks within a project that have no float (gap between the end of one task and the start of the next task) and end with some deliverable of the project. This means that if any one task in this critical path slips, that deliverable slips and possibly the entire schedule slips.
- Critical paths in a project should be flagged as high-risk elements during risk management planning.

Strengths

It ensures that the project identifies the critical activities that the project team has to achieve on time for successful completion of the project. It alerts project management when the project is slipping behind the plan.

Weaknesses

It requires effort and discipline to establish and maintain but is a good investment in all but the smallest projects.

Notation

There are a variety of notational styles for schedules and they are typically tool-dependent. Please see the example section of this work product description for a look at one possible notation.

Traceability

This work product has the following traceability:

Impacted by:
- Prioritized Requirements (p. 111)
- Business Case (p. 115)
- Intended Development Process (p. 127)
- Resource Plan (p. 135)
- Release Plan (p. 144)
- Risk Management Plan (p. 152)
- Reuse Plan (p. 158)
- Test Plan (p. 164)
- Metrics (p. 169)
- Project Dependencies (p. 173)
- Issues (p. 176)

Impacts:
- Resource Plan (p. 135)
- Release Plan (p. 144)

Advice and Guidance

Building a schedule is not easy, but it is critical to the success of the project. Some simple advice and guidance follows:

- If this is your first project using an object-oriented software development process and have no idea how to build a schedule, it might be useful to start by estimating time needed as you would if this were not an object-oriented project. You can then add some appropriate buffer (say 10 to 25 percent) to cover the fact that you are using a new approach and it will likely cost some time and resources during this initial attempt to use it.

- Factor in time for training, mentors, tools installation and support, process definition and deployment, and other factors related to the move to the use of object technology.

- Revisit the Schedule often (certainly after each iteration of your project) and adjust it based on the new knowledge you will have at hand.

- Keep a history of Schedules and adjustments to them to build a base of data from which to estimate resource needs for future object-oriented development projects.

- Keep initial iterations small both in time and content. This will allow you to begin to shake out your development process and environment and give the team some early experience with object-oriented software development. This can be a valuable tool for getting an early assessment of how good your schedule is and for making any needed adjustments.

Verification

- Check that the schedule takes account of technical dependencies implied by the Subsystem Model.

- Check that the critical part through the schedule is marked.

- Check that the milestones are adequate.

- Check that all identified risks have been addressed in the schedule.

- Check that adequate buffers of time exist in the schedule.

Example(s)

The following example is the initial plan for a three-month feasibility study:

Activities	1995					
	Mar	Apr	May	Jun	Jul	Aug
Setup		▭				
--refine plan		▣				
--Assign resources		▣				
-----hardware		▣				
-----software		▣				
-----people		▣				
-----Space planning		▣				
--Project KO			▣			
3Months			▭			
--Get scenarios			▭			
----Scenario 1			▣			
------Get			△			
------Analyze			▣			
----Scenario 2			▣			
-------get			△			
-------Analyze			▣			
----Scenario 3			▣			
-------get			△			
-------analyze			▣			
----Scenario 4			▣			
-------get			△			
-------analyze			▣			
----Scenario 5			▣			
-------get			△			
-------analyze			▣			
----Scenario 6			▣			
-------get			△			
-------analyze			▣			
--Learn Visual Age			▣			
--Review requirements			▣			
--Define API			▭			
----Baseline OOD			▣			
----baseline API			▣			
----OO Design				▭		
----API Def Doc					▭	
----Main team review						▣
--Perform. Proto			▭			
----define scope			▭			
----create Bus Vol DB			▣			

Activities	1995					
	Mar	Apr	May	Jun	Jul	Aug
-------Rand DB generate				▫		
-------Build DB				▫		
---hand bld PP1T1			▫			
----hand bld PP1Tn				▫		
-----hand bld PP2T1				▫		
-----hand bld PP2Tn				▫		
-----investigate patterns			▫			
-----refine products				▫		
-----Create Harness			▫			
----Run tests				▭▭▭▭		
-------test PP1T1				▫		
-------test PP1Tn				▫		
-------test PP2T1				▫		
-------test PP2Tn				▫		
-------test refinements					▫	
-------batch test				▫		
-----Produce perf rpt					▫	
--Workshops		▭				
----Prod Decomp ws			▫			
-------DP1			▫			
----Contract Adm WS				▭		
-------DP1 all scenario				▭		
----Prod Dev WS			▫			
-------DP1 Scenario			▫			
--User Interface				▭▭▭▭▭		
----Product def				▭▭▭▭▭		
------DP1 -def				▭▭▭▭▭		
-------Testing & Valid.					▭▭	
--Documentation					▭▭▭	
----Product API						▫
----promotion proces					▭▭	
-------Product knowledge					▭▭	
-------DB knowledge					▭▭	
----Quality Plan				▭		
----Full Proj plan				▭		

References

Succeeding with Object Technology by Goldberg and Rubin [Goldberg95], in particular the chapters "Plan and Control a Project" and "Case Studies of Process Models."

Importance

Schedules are essential for planning the project and its resources and for tracking progress against that plan.

10.5 RELEASE PLAN

Description

The Release Plan maps the requirements gathered in the Requirements section of the workbook into the releases, versions, iterations, and increments during which the system will be developed (or changed) to handle them.

At the lowest level of granularity, the plan will group the phases and activities that are scheduled. These phases and activities are derived from the Intended Development Process that serves as the model to be followed during the development of the release.

Purpose

The Release Plan is essential to set the scope of the project and divide the work up into manageable units. Having the scope of a release, version, iteration and increment helps to avoid the various forms of paralysis that can stall the project. For example, analysis activities can often result in the identification of additional desired function, the exploration of which can lead to "analysis paralysis" (i.e., the inability to determine when to stop and move on to the next phase). By clearly setting the scope of the requirements to be addressed in each increment, new function that is identified should be allocated to another increment unless its development is certain not to affect the current schedule. New functions that are deemed to be high priority should displace lower priority requirements into later increments if necessary to maintain the plan integrity.

Participants

The Release Plan is the responsibility of the project manager in conjunction with the planners and team leaders. Marketing representatives will also be involved to the extent that they are representing the customers and their requirements. Together, they insure that the overall plan delivers an application that meets the requirements within the window of opportunity and is cost-acceptable to the customers.

Timing

An initial Release Plan is built early in the project cycle; however, it is not a static document. Using an "iterative and incremental" approach, one starts the Release Plan after the requirements have been prioritized and the dependencies between them noted. Customer priorities may change—also technical challenges may arise that require retuning of the plan. After each increment is completed, the plan is adjusted to reflect any changes that have occurred that could affect delivery of the releases.

Technique

Usually, it is best to work first on the highest value, most complex requirements with a near-term window of opportunity. This will make it easier to adjust to problems and/or cancel the project altogether (the latter might occur if it turns out that the problems are insurmountable). It is always better to find the problems sooner than later, so do not put the hard stuff off until later.

To avoid plan "paralysis" do not try to plan the entire project in detail up front. Instead, break the project into 6 to 12 week increments per release, allocating the high priority requirements to the first increments. You might put fewer requirements in the early increments to allow room to adjust for learning curves and other changes to the team productivity "model."

To avoid plan "churn" do not stop work to change the plan for the current increment. If for some reason a work product is not going to be finished on time, decide whether to:

1. "Stretch" the phase to allow it to be completed as planned as part of the current increment. Do this when a high-priority requirement that many others depend on is in jeopardy.

2. "Shift" the work product in question to the next increment to keep the date intact. Do this with lower priority requirements or in early increments where a learning curve (or other forms of "paralysis") may be involved. Moving to the next increment as scheduled can get your team "over the hump."

3. "Share" the work by allocating additional resources to keep both the date and the deliverables of the current increment intact. Do this for a complex work product that can easily be decomposed into two subsystems and worked on separately. Of course, this solution assumes that some resources have been left "in reserve" for this purpose.

Plan some time after each increment to adjust the plan for the later increments and releases. During this period, the complexity measurements of the work products should be used to revise productivity estimates and facilitate Release Plans that are more and more accurate as the project unfolds.

Strengths

- As discussed above, two of the strengths of this approach are that a team can avoid "plan paralysis" and "plan churn." It allows a team to get going in the face of uncertainty and build up a baseline of knowledge to reduce that uncertainty within the lifetime of the project.

- This work product allows the development team and, more importantly, the customer, to see what functionality will be delivered in what time frame.

Weaknesses

This approach makes it more difficult for inexperienced teams to commit to the exact content of any increment or release ahead of time because of the lack of good productivity estimates to apply to the plan. However, the ability to identify problems early and adjust in a systematic fashion without disrupting development more than makes up for the uncertainty at the beginning.

Notation

Free format text is sufficient.

Traceability

This work product has the following traceability:

Impacted by:
- Prioritized Requirements (p. 111)
- Business Case (p. 115)
- Intended Development Process (p. 127)
- Resource Plan (p. 135)
- Schedule (p. 139)
- Risk Management Plan (p. 152)
- Reuse Plan (p. 158)
- Project Dependencies (p. 173)
- Issues (p. 176)

Impacts:
- Resource Plan (p. 135)
- Schedule (p. 139)

Advice and Guidance

Releases normally are planned with the customer. Usually functionality is prioritized and this is a key driver of releases. It is also impacted by the schedule, the resources available, the technology available, and costs.

Verification

- Check that the functionality of each release can be tested.

- Check that the plan is risk-driven.

Example(s)

While the following is not a complete plan, it should give you some idea of what a Release Plan contains. It is based on a recent banking project:

Release 1 will include (to be released 12/95):

- Customer opening an account

- Automatic notification of overdrawn accounts to Client representative

Release 2 will cover (planned for 3Q96):

- Collection of data for management reports

Future Release Content, not yet scheduled:

- Management report generation

Figure 10-2. *Example of a Release Plan.*

References

None.

Importance

Optional for a project with only a single release. Essential for projects planning multiple releases.

10.6 QUALITY ASSURANCE PLAN

Description

The Quality Assurance Plan in some form is a traditional part of most software development processes and is not unique to the use of an object-oriented development process.

The Quality Assurance Plan involves:

- Establishing quality goals, defining success criteria, and defining expected results

- Validation and tracking

- Removing defects

- Addressing global quality aspects

A Quality Assurance Plan is a required item in the development processes of many companies. The details of the Quality Assurance Plan should be specified in terms of the measurements that will be taken and the expected results. This will help drive the review part of the process in a much more objective and systematic fashion.

An organization may have a common Quality Assurance Plan that is a template for all development projects. Based on that template each project will have a project specific Quality Assurance Plan. The specific form that a Quality Assurance Plan takes may vary by organization. This section will, therefore, only address Quality Assurance Plans generally.

Quality Assurance Plans generally include:

- Customer Satisfaction goals: overall satisfaction and satisfaction for areas such as usability, capability, and performance

- Code Quality Goals: typically, still, some ratio of "Total Valid Unique Problems per Thousand Lines of Shipped Source Instructions"

- Tools and approaches: some specification of the tools or methods that will be used to track customer satisfaction and code quality

- Defect removal models: showing the number of defects that are to be uncovered at each phase of the development cycle

- A Quality Management section: describing processes for change control and defect management, how quality will be tracked and assessed, and specific quality improvement line items or actions that will be taken

Purpose

A Quality Assurance Plan forces a focus on quality and defect removal throughout the development process and is a valuable tool for ensuring that quality is built into the product from the beginning. If the quality goals are realistic and based on past product results, then the Quality Assurance Plan can allow managers to quickly assess whether the current product is going to achieve its quality objectives.

Additionally there may be other reasons why a Quality Assurance Plan is useful:

- There may be organizationwide quality activities, processes, goals, et cetera, that are best captured in a separate document.

- Quality data is input to future planning (for example, code quality influences maintenance costs, usability influences user support costs).

- ISO 9000 or other processes may require a plan to track quality related aspects of a project separately.

Participants

The project manager owns the Quality Assurance Plan, but typically, many people in related groups such as testing, usability, performance, and service will contribute to the development and implementation of the plan.

Timing

- Quality goals and their verification criteria are one kind of Nonfunctional Requirement. They are defined at the beginning of the project. These quality-related requirements are either given by the organization as cross-project quality goals or are set by the customer. They are quite often based on previous versions of the product or on the results of similar products.

- Quality Plans typically have activities and goals that are performed and tracked throughout the life cycle during the development of the work products.

- Overall results are reported when the project is shipped and they continue to be modified as customer problem data is reported.

Technique

The four aspects listed previously in the Description Section are discussed here in more detail:

1. Establishing quality goals, success criteria, and defining expected results:

    As stated above quality goals and criteria are part of Nonfunctional Requirements. There may be different requirements that address specific aspects such as usability, performance, or code quality. Each product may, because of its nature, place a different importance on different aspects. All functional and Nonfunctional Requirements are addressed and validated in the appropriate work product. For example:

    - Usability may be addressed in the user interface design work product, which is validated through usability tests. For this, the overall quality goal is likely defined with the user.

    - The Acceptance Plan described in Section 9.6, also defines quality criteria that need to addressed in the Quality Assurance Plan.

    - Performance is addressed during design and architecture and validated in a prototype or early drivers.

    - Code quality is an aspect of implementation and will be validated by tests or code inspections.

    A Quality Assurance Plan may then select a few key quality-related requirements and assign priorities. (For example, there may be an organization-specific focus on code quality, which may receive higher priority than usability or a product may have to achieve certain performance measurements in order to be competitive in the market place.)

    These key quality criteria need to be defined together with the customer of the product (or with the funding organization).

2. Validation and tracking

    - Each work product described in this book has advice and guidance on how to validate the work product.
    - Causal analysis and defect prevention are concepts used to improve the quality beyond single projects.
    - Tracking design changes (and errors found during validation activities and testing) will give quantified feedback about quality levels.

- Metrics need to be established that define what is tracked. Section 10.10 introduces various metrics relevant for an object-oriented project.
- The Test Plan, described in Section 10.9 will be used to plan the detailed activities needed for validating and tracking various quality metrics.

3. Removing defects

- As stated above, most Quality Assurance Plans include defect removal models. They normally describe the number of defects that are expected to be uncovered during each phase of the development process.

    The Quality Assurance Plan should also define the steps that will be taken to uncover and remove these defects. These actions can range from reviews (i.e., of analysis or design work products) to testing (of the code at various iterations).

    The object-oriented development process described in this book is very front-end intensive. This suggests that with the proper reviews of analysis and design work products, many defects should be removed early in the development cycle. Additionally, we recommend an iterative and incremental process which, among its other benefits, provides for testing of functional code far earlier in the product development process than would occur using a waterfall approach.

4. Addressing global quality aspects.

    There are various technical or organizational decisions that can be made early in a project life cycle that can have a positive impact on the overall quality of the project. Some examples of these kinds of decisions include:

- Using proven class libraries, such as IBM's Open Class Library, allows the reuse of important functions provided in code of exceptional quality. The Open Class Library has the added advantage of being available on multiple platforms. The library reuses a large, common, platform independent code base. This ensures common quality on all platforms.
- Solutions aimed at a particular customer or set of customers can (and should) include the customer(s) to identify required functions and to help define quality criteria and quality assessment plans.
- Agreeing on a specific object-oriented development approach for the project or across projects will allow you to reap the benefits of object-oriented development.
- Most products can adapt an iterative and incremental development process as described in this book. This allows for early verification of particular implementations of functions.
- Larger development areas can benefit from common quality procedures across multiple product development efforts.

Strengths

A Quality Assurance Plan defines a formalized approach to delivering a product of high quality and demonstrates an organizational commitment to quality. A thorough Quality Assurance Plan can help a project to judge quality and react to any problems throughout the development cycle.

Weaknesses

A Quality Assurance Plan can take a lot of time to develop and execute and as such requires a very strong organizational commitment to a planned approach to quality.

Another pitfall to be aware of is that overemphasis of one or a few quality aspects (too often code quality) can often lead to overlooking other potential quality problems (for example, performance).

Notation

English text or graphics, showing customer feedback or error removal rates, can serve as notation for this work product.

Traceability

This work product has the following traceability:

Impacted by:
- Project Workbook Outline (p. 132)
- Test Plan (p. 164)
- Metrics (p. 169)
- Issues (p. 176)

Impacts:
- Intended Development Process (p. 127)
- Project Workbook Outline (p. 132)
- Test Plan (p. 164)
- Analysis Guidelines (p. 183)
- User Interface Guidelines (p. 234)
- Design Guidelines (p. 253)
- Coding Guidelines (p. 322)

Advice and Guidance

- Ask customers to define key quality requirements
- Follow the Quality Assurance Plans defined for your organization
- Use the Advice and Guidance that are listed for each work product

Example(s)

Please refer to the case study for an example (page 508).

References

- *Succeeding with Object Technology* by Goldberg and Rubin [Goldberg95], in particular the chapter "What is Measurement?"

- The Defect Prevention Process (DPP), found in [Mays90], discusses improving quality by preventing defects from getting into a product.

- Chapter 7 of [Malan96], discusses metrics and defect tracking.

- The International Standards Organization (ISO) has a standard for quality management called ISO 9000. The document: *'ISO 9000 International Standards for Quality Management'* is available from the ISO Central Secretariat.

- [Schulmeyer90] proposes statistical controls over the development process to produce quality software.

- [Kaplan95] discusses 40 innovations that have lead to improved quality software.

- The Total Quality Management (TQM) approach to improving software quality is discussed in [Arthur92].

Importance

Each work product described in this book has a description of how to verify it. This helps to build quality into every aspect of the process recommended herein. A Quality Assurance Plan is therefore optional, unless the organization where the project is performed requires the use of a separate Quality Assurance Plan.

10.7 RISK MANAGEMENT PLAN

Description

A *risk* is anything that may jeopardize the success of the project. Risks in a software project do not relate only to technical matters. Developers must also deal with things like politics, competition, window of opportunity, credibility, reputation, shrinking market, unproven target environment, fuzzy requirements, fickle clients, et cetera. For example, the possibility that a key project architect may leave the company midproject may be a risk that has to be addressed.

A Risk Management Plan identifies risks associated with a project and provides plans to manage them. Risk management is important in any type of software development project, but the use of object technology does introduce certain risks of its own.

A risk, once identified and assessed for probability and impact, may be managed at the following levels.

1. **Elimination of risk**. Some risks can be eliminated entirely. For example, the risk that a particular key architect may leave midproject may be eliminated by bringing into

the project someone else with comparable skills. If the architect leaves, the second architect could step in. The event under discussion (architect leaving) may still occur during the project, but it is no longer a risk. Of course, most risks cannot be eliminated in this way.

One particular form of risk elimination is risk transference, which involves transferring the risk to another party. For example, a project might be concerned about not being able to recover its expenses to develop a product that has questionable market value. This risk could be transferred by having the customer pay expenses up front, the expenses being recoverable if the project is successful. This kind of strategy, of course, only eliminates the risk for the development team.

2. **Risk reduction**. If a risk cannot be eliminated, the next form of risk management to be considered is to try to lower the probability that the event identified as a risk will occur in practice. An example of this in the case of the architect who may leave might be to improve that person's working conditions. Depending on the anticipated reasons for leaving, this strategy may make it less likely that the architect will actually leave.

Another example of risk reduction is reducing announced release requirements to reduce the probability of schedule slip.

3. **Damage control**. If it has proved impossible to lower sufficiently the probability of the event associated with the risk, then the possibility that the event will actually occur must be faced. If it does, then by definition the project will be harmed in some way. Steps must then be taken to limit this damage as far as possible. As an example, if the architect leaves midproject, an adequately qualified person from elsewhere in the company must be found as a replacement. Before the replacement is found and up-to-speed, the project leader will provide cover.

Other examples of damage control are car bumpers, sprinkler systems (for fires), circuit breakers (for electrical overload), and running tasks in separate processes (OS/2).

4. **Contingency planning**. If damage control steps are planned, their implementation must be effective as soon as possible after the risk event has occurred. For this to happen, contingency plans must be laid to remove obstacles from the critical path to damage control. For example, if the architect leaves, then the finding of a replacement will be speeded up by preparing in advance a list of qualified people who might be available. Another contingency plan might be to provide time for the project leader to familiarize herself with the application Architecture.

Other examples of contingency planning are spare parts, backup systems, and archiving.

For each identified risk, the Risk Management Plan should address each of these levels as appropriate. A risk management strategy for handling a particular risk may combine elements of more than one of the risk management levels. This does not matter; the above list should serve as a checklist only.

Purpose

Innovative projects inherently involve risk. It is important for people to recognize and deal with all facets of the risks that they face. Awareness breeds readiness, competence, and confidence. Not recognizing and managing risks will lead to unpleasant surprises that in turn lead to budget and schedule overruns, or noncompetitive products.

Some projects suffer because of factors outside the control of the project, while others are harmed by internal factors. Analyzing and managing the risks in your project can limit damage and reduce wasted investments.

With an iterative and incremental development process, criteria must be agreed upon for deciding how to sequence development work. Probably the most important criterion is risk. Requirements should be partitioned between development cycles to minimize risk to the project. This is impossible without knowing what the risks are, and without a plan to manage them.

Participants

Risk management should be part of the way all project members do business. Of course, broader and more expensive risks should be coordinated by the project management, but everyone should be aware of risks, thereby documenting, and planning for them.

Timing

Risk management is a continuing activity throughout the project life cycle. Obviously, a concentrated focus on risk assessment and planning occurs while the initial project plan is being constructed. Risk management should be done, however, throughout the project life cycle.

Technique

For each project phase (requirements gathering through to maintenance) and for every release and development cycle, all the risks for that phase, component, release, or activity should be identified, weighed, prioritized, assigned ownership, and scheduled for resolution. Risk resolution is the process of determining how to manage a particular risk. The likelihood of failure (the undesirable event identified by the risk actually occurring) compounded by the cost of that failure should be used to rank the risks. Those with the highest rank should be resolved first and assigned to the most competent people for the earliest completion.

Doing this involves looking at nearly everything as a potential risk:

- If we start too late, we will never get done.
- If the network delay is too great, the product won't perform well.

- If the user interface isn't more intuitive and powerful than the competition, the product won't sell.

- If we miss the window of opportunity we will have to be xx percent better to catch up, and we will have yy percent less money to do it.

- If the product is buggy, we will lose our reputation.

- The users are fickle; we don't know what they want.

Besides analyzing each risk directly as it is recognized, groups can run brainstorming sessions to develop checklists of risk management strategies that might be appropriate for different kinds of risk.

Strengths

A risk is anything that may jeopardize the success of the project. Anticipating them and laying plans to manage them is vital for any form of project management. A formal Risk Management Plan helps a manager track risks and acts as a management checklist.

Weaknesses

Risk management requires effort at times when project resources are probably already stretched.

Judgment must be exercised when deciding what is a risk worth managing formally. Categorizing everything as a potential risk will grind the project to a stop.

Notation

A template of the following form can be used to document each identified risk:

Test group name _____
Description _____
Owner _____
Deadline _____
Dependencies (on other risks) _____
Likelihood of occurrence _____
Cost of occurrence (without applying strategy) _____
Cost of applying strategy _____
Cost of occurrence (when strategy is applied) _____
Priority [1 to 10 (max)] _____
Management strategy _____

Traceability

This work product has the following traceability:

Impacted by:
- Prioritized Requirements (p. 111)
- Project Dependencies (p. 173)
- Issues (p. 176)

Impacts:
- Schedule (p. 139)
- Release Plan (p. 144)

Advice and Guidance

- Assess the probability of Project Dependencies being met. Some of these may be risks.

- Technical risks may frequently be managed effectively through prototyping. It is usually employed as a risk elimination strategy. Technical risks often take the form of not knowing in advance whether something is technically feasible or efficient. Prototypes are experiments designed to answer these questions and hence eliminate the risk.

- Another technique for managing technical risks is the judicious use of an iterative and incremental development process. Early development cycles may be used to implement a component with which some form of risk is associated, such as low performance. If this implementation is judged to be unacceptable, later development cycles may be used to rework its design and implementation. The use of the development process in this way is damage control. The damage of an unsatisfactory design is controlled by redesign. The contingency planning required is to advance the implementation of this component to a sufficiently early development cycle so that there is adequate time for the subsequent rework if it proves necessary.

- The use of object technology and object-oriented development can introduce some specific risks into a software project where each must be managed. The risks of the use of object technology include the following:

  - The learning curve might swamp the project.

  - Inexperience with the object-oriented approach might result in a low-quality design.

  - The immaturity of object-oriented tools might affect development productivity.

  - An iterative and incremental development schedule might lead to design churn and/or unnecessary development.

  - The emphasis sometimes placed on object-oriented analysis and a lack of experience with object-oriented design may lead developers to try to implement the analysis directly, without adequate consideration of the many design Issues.

  - Uncertainty about the problem or how to proceed might lead to "analysis paralysis."

- An initial checklist for use in brainstorming sessions to identify risk management strategies might include the following:

- Prototype to eliminate a well-defined technical risk. If the risk can be phrased as a well-defined technical question, for example: Is it efficient to use a relational database to store image objects; the answer can frequently be obtained by constructing a prototype. See Section 17.4 for a discussion of the use of prototypes in risk management.

- Schedule work in an early development cycle to manage technical risks arising from the uncertainty of untried designs. This differs from prototyping because a prototype is targeted at answering a specific question whereas a development increment is a check of the complete design, albeit a design with reduced functionality.

- Reduce risks associated with productivity uncertainty by estimating effort using a parameterized formula and comparing the estimated and actual productivity and effort values. Use updated estimates in later development cycles.

- Reduce the risk that the user interface may not be as the customer wants by involving the customer in user interface prototyping activity.

- Reduce the risk of external drivers not arriving in time by omitting this functionality from early development cycles, or by building scaffolding to simulate the driver. For example, a project dependent on a database interface to be supplied by another project may omit persistence from the requirements of the first development cycle.

- Each subsystem should have its own Risk Management Plan that should be reprioritized during each development cycle. The highest ranked items, based on whatever realistic weighting scheme the project chooses, should be addressed in the current or imminent cycle.

  Leaders of projects involving the parallel development of multiple subsystems should have an integrated Risk Management Plan for the entire system. Subsystem and system plans may be connected either by *delegating* a risk item from the master plan to a particular subsystem, or by *promoting* a risk item from a subsystem plan to the master. Risk promotion may be effected by having the project manager personally weigh and integrate the subsystem risk plans or by having the subsystem team leaders prepare an update to the master plan for the project manager to review.

Verification

- Check that all appropriate kinds of risks have been addressed. This can be done by producing a list of the risks that are appropriate to your project (which varies from project to project), and checking for coverage under each of these headings.

Example(s)

The following is a Risk Management Plan for a project that is under threat of budget cuts:

A project manager is concerned that her budget may be cut mid-project.

- Risk will be managed at two levels:

    1. Risk Reduction

        - Project Plan heavily incremental to allow early product-level deliverables

        - Allows reduced function deliverable prior to likely date of a budget decision

    2. Damage Control and Contingency Planning

        - Work staged through an iterative and incremental approach

        - Allows for a sequence of smaller releases

        - Any design investment is only to satisfy requirements of the current release

        - Helps to ensure that the most recent product-level deliverable represents a large proportion of the development effort up to that point in time

---

Figure 10-3. Example of a Risk Management Plan.

References

- See [Rakos90] for a discussion of risk management in general

- See [Boehm88] on the use of risk management to guide the development process.

- [Boehm89] is a collection of papers on Software Risk Management.

Importance

Optional. But, many projects would find it essential. You must assess the level of risk your project has and decide whether you need this work product. Understanding and planning for risks is an important part of successfully completing software projects.

10.8 REUSE PLAN

Description

A Reuse Plan is a statement of which existing software parts are going to be reused, which reusable parts are to be built, and the costs and benefits of doing this. In the case of building reusable parts, the Reuse Plan must include a business justification and details of how the parts are to be supported.

Effort, costs, and the schedule of a project greatly depend on the amount of "reuse" the project will be doing. This may include savings if the project can reuse existing reusable parts. It also may include additional effort if the project decides to build reusable parts.

So, a Reuse Plan is very intertwined with the Business Case and the overall project plan (Schedule, Resource Plan, and concrete actives such as Design).

A Reuse Plan might also explain why parts of the projects had to be written from scratch and why parts of the project could not be made reusable.

Purpose

Both reusing existing parts and building reusable parts will affect a project plan and have to be taken into consideration.

There are two major items that are affected by reuse:

1. The Business Case (for example, development costs): Saving through reuse will affect the Business Case and may be the decisive factor for an investment decision. Any costs from reusing parts or building parts have to be taken into account as well.

2. The Project Plan (for example Schedule, Resource Plan, and concrete activities such as design): Reusing parts can lead to savings in time and effort and creating reusable parts can increase the required time and effort on a project. Thus effective planning of project activities requires an understanding of what reuse activities are planned.

Development for reusable parts has to be justified, planned, and tracked separately from the rest of the project, so this has to be documented as a separate item in the project plans.

In general, additional efforts have to be planned and there has to be management commitment to these efforts. Otherwise a project under short-term pressure may stop reuse efforts in which the value is not seen until much later in the project or perhaps not until subsequent projects.

If a project does not exploit the benefits of reuse, it may want to document which steps were made to try reuse, which reuse options were considered, and why the reuse options were rejected. Reuse is one of the best ways to improve productivity and quality so it is important to understand impediments to doing it.

Participants

The project planner, the architect, team leaders, and the manager all have input on the project's reuse efforts.

Timing

Planning for reuse should be done when:

- Preparing the Business Case
- Preparing a detailed project plan
- Reviewing project plans after each development cycle

Technique

- Analyze opportunities for reuse (what could be reused and what could be built).
- Use previous experience (your own, or that of other projects), use prototyping, and make estimates for costs and savings based on experience or prototyping.
- Step through all development phases and consider activities, efforts, and savings.
- Make appropriate sizings.
- Factor results into the appropriate plan documents.

Strengths

Reuse requires concerted effort and planning outside of what is "normal" for a development project. Committing those efforts in a written plan will encourage the allocation of the proper time and resource to ensure the necessary activities are done.

Listing reused components will document increased Project Dependencies.

Weaknesses

If reuse is not a strong commitment of the entire project team, including management, the investments needed to identify reuse opportunities and to build reusable parts may be the most likely to be cut when the project experiences schedule pressure. Actual opportunities for reusing existing parts may not be known during project planning. Unless you have past experience and/or a very clear understanding of your technical requirements and the technical capabilities of the reusable part, you may discover during development that you can't use a particular part. Take this into consideration and refine your plan for each development cycle.

Notation

Free format text.

Traceability

This work product has the following traceability:

Impacted by:
- Business Case (p. 115)
- Issues (p. 176)

Impacts:
- Resource Plan (p. 135)
- Schedule (p. 139)
- Release Plan (p. 144)
- Project Dependencies (p. 173)
- Analysis Guidelines (p. 183)
- Design Guidelines (p. 253)
- System Architecture (p. 257)
- Subsystems (p. 274)
- Physical Packaging Plan (p. 326)
- Source Code (p. 334)

Advice and Guidance

For reusing existing parts:

- Reusing existing parts is not free. Plan for the "costs of reuse." If your people are not familiar with the parts you must allocate time to scan available reusable parts, to evaluate the reusable parts early in the project cycle, to "look for reuse opportunities" during inspections, et cetera.

- Plan for the savings, including savings for design, development, test, and maintenance.

- Understand what's available.

- Understand your needs. Depending on the kind of project, this may be easy ("we need just the same as last time") or hard ("we never worked in this domain, so we don't know what we really need").

- Before you commit yourself to use a reusable part, know your requirements and understand if they are met.

- Reusing existing parts creates an additional dependency. You have to manage this dependency. You may have to make compromises in order to be able to use a generally reusable part.

- Consider giving a team member time and responsibility for driving reuse in the project much as you would give someone responsibility for other line items.

For building reusable parts:

- There is no firm requirement to develop a reusable part completely within your project. But ideally you should make a complete analysis and design including aspects outside your immediate need. Otherwise the parts may be too project specific and not reusable in other projects.

- After a (relatively) complete analysis and design you may still decide to implement only the pieces that you need in your project. Any future extensions then should not require changes to the existing code.

- If there is no time to make at any parts fully reusable, you should at least make some effort to enable future projects to "harvest" pieces from your project.

- Building reusable parts increases the short-term costs. There is a rule of thumb that reusable software costs three times as much as "normal" software. These costs may be spread over several projects or iterations, but the actual savings may only occur after the third usage. The decision to spend extra effort and how much will be spent has to depend on usage projections. For example, if parts are only going to be reused a couple of times, extensive documentation will be unnecessary. It may be more effective to get direct help from the owner. On the other hand for parts that are expected to be reused hundreds of times it becomes essential to reduce the cost of reuse by providing good documentation, examples, usage patterns et cetera.

- Be aware that others will become dependent on you.

- Strongly consider building a small separate team responsible for building the reusable parts.

- Get support from a management "sponsor." Usually projects will face schedule pressure. You need strong management support to keep the investment for the reusable parts in your schedule.

- Understand what's available; for example, don't build what's already available.

- Do a domain assessment to select where to invest. A domain assessment helps to decide whether parts are needed in the domain, if the domain is mature enough to invest in parts, or if this is a domain where your organization will work in the future.

- Include the necessary efforts in your plan. For example, make sure there is appropriate time allocated for analysis, design, development, et cetera. for the reusable parts. They don't just "happen."

- Be aware that even after the project is finished, somebody has to maintain the reusable part.

- Consider adding reuse topics to your local process guidelines.

Verification

- Check that all intended reuse work tasks have been planned and appropriate staff assigned.

- Check that effort is being made to search for reusable work products.

- Check that a minimum of new development is being undertaken.

- Check that reasonable effort is being made to enable the work products of the project to be reusable.

Example(s)

The following example shows a potential Reuse Plan of a client-server application. The application is supposed to deal with archiving data.

Reused Assets:

Open Class
> The project will use the class libraries that are shipped with VisualAge C++ (Open Class).

> *Effort:* Three members of the development team need training for the use of the class libraries early in the project so that design can be done with those class libraries in mind.

> *Justification:* Rewriting Graphical User Interface classes or collection classes would destroy the Business Case for the project.

DSOM
> Distribution will be done through the Distributed System Object Model (DSOM).

> *Effort:* Two members of the team need training for SOM/DSOM.

> *Justification:* Developing a mechanism for distributing objects from scratch would destroy the Business Case for the project.

No application specific reusable parts
> After a brief survey we couldn't find any reusable parts in the application domain.

Building Reusable Assets:

Reusable Classes for Archiving Data
> The project will not be able to build fully reusable classes or class libraries, but since archiving data is a common problem, there will be an attempt to make this service reusable. The goal will be to have classes that can be easily extracted and made reusable in a separate project.

> *Effort:* To make classes reusable an additional person month will be spent during design.

> *Justification:* The common need for an archive function will offset the small investment needed to make the classes for this function easily extractable.

Domain Model
> Although the concrete classes will not be fully reusable, we plan to have a complete model for archiving data.

> *Effort:* To make the domain model as complete as possible, two person months of effort will be spent to interview domain experts and to review the domain model with domain experts.

> *Justification:* It is important that the model for this critical function be complete and accurate.

Figure 10-4. *Example of a Reuse Plan.*

References

- Chapters 9 through 11 of Goldberg and Rubin [Goldberg95] offer a good introduction on issues related to reuse.

- [Tracz95] provides a good overview of a number of reuse topics.

Importance

Optional, but, for projects doing reuse it is important that any major reuse activities are explicitly documented and committed and would therefore be essential for them.

10.9 TEST PLAN

Description

A Test Plan is a document answering the *who*, *when*, *what* and *how* of testing. It specifies which kinds of tests should be performed and in what order. If any specific environment is needed (hardware, software) it is also described there.

Here the term "testing" refers only to the testing of code. Any noncode testing, such as the validation and verification of work products other than code, can be put either into the Quality Assurance Plan, the Intended Development Process, or the various Guidelines work products.

Planning for testing must take into account the acceptable quality level of the product, as defined in the Quality Assurance Plan, that the project is delivering with given resources, because that is the ultimate requirement that governs the testing. For example, a drawing program might be quite acceptable if it has fewer than one error reported per week of exploitation, while such a rate would clearly not be acceptable for a life-support machine's software. Depending on the required quality level that the product must fulfill, the amount of resources dedicated to testing will be different.

If an iterative and incremental development process is being used, testing is done both as an integral part of each development phase of each increment, and also as a distinct phase in its own right in order to function test the executable deliverables produced by the increment. A Test Plan should refer to both increment function testing as well as testing the whole deliverable.

Purpose

It is produced to ensure that testing is complete, feasible, and successful, and that adequate resources for testing are identified and planned for. A Test Plan ensures that the testing strategy is agreed to in advance.

Participants

A testing team, in cooperation with the team leader, planner, developers, human factors, and information developers build and maintain the plan. Coordination between the testers, the team lead, and the project planner is necessary in order to ensure that development and testing activities are synchronized (in the Test Plan). This is especially important when the development process is incremental and iterative.

Timing

This typically happens at the same time that the project and iteration plans are made. Like any other planning activity, it is impossible to make a final plan before the beginning of the project, but that should not be an excuse for not having a plan. An initial Test Plan, as complete as possible, with clearly identified dependencies on the Resource and Release Plans and Schedules, offers a good document that should be updated as the project progresses from iteration to iteration.

Technique

For each activity identified in the iteration plan, an appropriate testing period needs to be allocated in the Test Plan. What the appropriate time is depends on the particular project, iteration, and work products concerned:

- Projects new to object-oriented technology may want to allocate more time for testing to allow for thorough testing of all work products, while projects already experienced in object-oriented technology can plan to focus more on testing those work products that in their previous engagements were identified as not being at the required quality level.

- Every iteration consists of analysis, design and implementation work products, only their ratios are different from iteration to iteration. This results in different times being required for testing code in different iterations.

- Implementation work products (code) can be reviewed, but are largely tested by running Test Cases that test different aspects of their quality (function, performance, usability, et cetera). Planning to complement code reviews with code testing will yield the best results, as those activities are complementary and used to discover different categories of problems. When planning for testing of code, one must plan resources for Test Case development, execution, and maintenance. If the projected number of Test Cases turns out not to be sufficient (for example, because during development the code was discovered to be more complex than was initially anticipated), the Test Plan should be revisited and updated accordingly. The best approach is to plan to review the Test Plan on a regular basis.

Strengths

- Identifies potential bottlenecks of testing resources.
- Enables planning of resources.

Weaknesses

- If the project and/or iteration plan is incorrect, the Test Plan will likely be wrong as well.

- Not knowing the required quality level of the product may lead to too little testing (potentially dangerous), or too much testing (unnecessary).

Notation

The same syntax used for project and iteration plans can be used. Typically, management tools have scheduling possibilities, the output of which can be printed and included in the Test Plan document.

Traceability

This work product has the following traceability:

Impacted by:
- Use Case Model (p. 96)
- Acceptance Plan (p. 119)
- Quality Assurance Plan (p. 147)
- Metrics (p. 169)
- Issues (p. 176)
- Screen Flows (p. 237)

Impacts:
- Intended Development Process (p. 127)
- Resource Plan (p. 135)
- Schedule (p. 139)
- Quality Assurance Plan (p. 147)
- Analysis Guidelines (p. 183)
- Design Guidelines (p. 253)
- Test Cases (p. 346)

Advice and Guidance

1. Determine the required quality level for the product.

2. Identify all software and hardware dependencies and when they are needed (for example: before the first iteration, after the second iteration, et cetera).

3. Based on the projected size of the project, required quality level, and initial number of iterations, allocate the resources accordingly. The higher the required quality level, the more time is needed in testing. As a very rough estimate, for projects with a required quality level that is:

   - **High**: Plan for 95 percent or more of overall project resources for testing (no errors are acceptable, for example, a nuclear power-plant management system).[10]

---

[10] From a talk given by Nancy Leveson on "System Safety and Software Design" describing experiences about designing software for safety-critical systems, delivered at OOPSLA '94, Portland, Oregon, on October 26, 1994.

- **Medium**: Plan for between 20 to 50 percent of overall project resources for testing (a few errors are fine, providing the fixes are available quickly, for example a customer solution for assisting bank managers in granting loans);
- **Low**: Plan for up to 5 percent of overall project resources for testing (a few errors are fine, even if the fixes are not available until the next release, for example a general-purpose text editor).

Verification

- Check the testing process: Test Case generation, testing, test result logging, and analysis of testing must be as automated as possible.

Example(s)

A project is developing a customer solution for an investment company. It will need to be able to handle information pertaining to about 10,000 customers from several different countries and to process any of their transactions (transfer, buy, and sell) in no more than five seconds. The customer's hardware is one RS/6000® 990, as a central server, and five RS/6000 590's, as local servers for each country. The operating system of all machines is AIX 4.1.2, with TCP/IP communication over fiber-optic cables between the servers. The contract states that the solution provider will provide 24 hour on-line help, and will find and fix any reported problem within 24 hours from notification, otherwise a penalty of $20,000 per exceeding day is due.

The initial analysis model consists of 20 classes and 7 Use Cases that expand into 16 scenarios. The design model is likely to add 20 new classes, bringing the total to 40 classes. DB2/6000 will be used for storing all the customer and transaction data. The development is planned as four iterations of six weeks, as follows:

1. User management scenarios
2. User transactions on a local machine
3. Concurrent user transactions
4. Backup and recovery procedures.

Given information about the project, we note the following:

1. The required quality level for the product is medium to high.
2. The hardware requirements are:
   - One RS/6000 990 with 30GB disks for data and 512MB of RAM (needed before iteration 4)
   - Five RS/6000 590 with 6GB disks for data and 512MB of RAM (one needed before iteration 1, the rest needed before iteration 3)
   - Fiber-optic communication boards (needed before iteration 3)
3. The Software requirements are (needed before iteration 1):
   - AIX 4.1.2
   - TCP/IP
   - DB2/6000

As this is a project with a medium to high required quality level, the testing time should take between 50 to 70 percent of resources, as follows:

- Before iteration 1:

    - Get the testing hardware and software (note that this is different from the Development Environment).

    - Prepare the testing environment.

- During iteration 1:
    - Plan for four days for review of analysis and design models.
    - Based on accepted design model, plan for designing, implementing, and executing five Test Cases per class and five Test Cases per scenario for code being developed during this iteration.
- During iteration 2:
    - Plan for three days for review of analysis and design models.
    - Based on accepted design model plan for designing, implementing, and executing five Test Cases per class and five Test Cases per scenario for code being developed during this iteration, and an additional 40 Test Cases that explicitly test the integration with code developed during iteration 1. Re-execute all the Test Cases that failed during iteration 1.
- During iteration 3:
    - Plan for two days for review of analysis and design models.
    - Based on accepted design model plan for designing, implementing, and executing five Test Cases per class and five Test Cases per scenario for code being developed during this iteration, and an additional 20 Test Cases that explicitly test the integration with code developed during iterations 1 and 2. Also plan for design, implementation, and execution of 30 performance and 10 stress Test Cases. Do the usability testing with at least 10 people. Re-execute all the Test Cases that failed during iterations 1 and 2.[00]
- During iteration 4:
    - Plan for a day for review of analysis and design models.
    - Based on accepted design model plan for designing, implementing, and executing five Test Cases per class and five Test Cases per scenario for code being developed during this iteration, and an additional 20 Test Cases that explicitly test the integration with code developed during iterations 1, 2, and 3. Continue with performance and usability testing. Do the regression testing based on a random selection of 40 Test Cases in addition to all that have failed before.[00]
- After iteration 4:
    - Plan three days for installation test.
    - Plan two weeks for system test in conditions as close to real life as possible.
    - Plan three days for "internal" user acceptance test.

Note that in every iteration, the test plan addresses reviewing the analysis and design models. This is done to obtain an understanding of how the application will be used as well as how it is being designed in order to build the necessary test cases for that iteration.

References

- See [Pressman92] for a general discussion of software testing strategies.

- For a general review of object-oriented software testing, see [Siegel96].

- For an overall review of quality processes, see [Whitten89].

Importance

A Test Plan is an essential means for projects to ensure that their products achieve and maintain the required quality levels.

10.10 METRICS

In order to understand and control a project or activity it is necessary to understand the critical factors that will influence its successful delivery. These factors should then be expressed as Metrics that can be estimated and tracked.

Description

Metrics are measurements of essential elements of the development project that enable successful planning and tracking of projects. A measurement is a particular value of a metric at some time. For instance the value of the average lines of code per class metric might be 200 at the end of the first iteration of a project. Metrics fall into four general categories.

Size Metrics	Metrics that measure the dimensions of a project and its components. This will include things like number of classes and number of people.
Productivity Metrics	Metrics that measure the rate at which project members are able to produce project deliverables.
Quality Metrics	Metrics that provide a measure of the quality of the design and implementation.
Reuse Metrics	These Metrics focus on the exploitation of existing assets, both internal and external to the project.

There are two distinct uses of these Metrics that are related to the separate tasks of planning and tracking the project. In performing these tasks, estimates must first be made of the size of the project, and of the productivity that will be achieved. This provides the information to do schedule planning. Other Metrics, for example related to quality, must also be selected and estimated as part of the planning process. The chosen set of Metrics should then be tracked during the project. Estimation of metric data is an essential part of project planning; the tracking of the same Metrics is vital for determining progress and conformance to plan. The actual project size may vary from the estimate; it usually grows by a factor of two to three due to poor estimation, poor understanding of the requirements, and the expansion of project scope. Productivity assumptions, like all other metric data estimates, should be validated against the actual productivity being achieved.

Note that, like good objects, individual development work products are responsible for their own metric data. For example, the Design Object Model work product should contain the metric data relevant to it, perhaps total class count and total method count. For each of these, the estimated and actual values should be included. The *Metrics* attribute common to all work products is used to do this. The Metrics work product presented in this section is used to document which Metrics are to be used in the project and to contain summary estimated and actual measured metric data.

Purpose

The definition, collection, and analysis of metrics can be very useful in building project plans and schedules, tracking projects, managing project risks, and providing benchmarks for process improvements. Metrics can:

- Provide data on which to produce a project plan.

- Provide a baseline for tracking project progress.

- Manage risk, which includes schedule and quality.

- Provide benchmarks for development process improvements.

Participants

Many people are involved, but there are two main types of people, users, and collectors of Metrics. Ideally the tools being used in the development process will provide Metrics collection. The project managers, planners, and team leads will be users of the Metrics. The project manager and planner in conjunction with team leaders also select the Metrics to be used.

Timing

During the planning of the project, existing metric data should be used to estimate the resources required for the project. During the life of the project the Metrics should be collected and tracked against the planned values.

Technique

- Decide on the way in which the project will be estimated and tracked in terms of size, schedule, resource expenditure, and quality.

- Choose an appropriate set of Metrics. The following basic Metrics are recommended by the authors:

  - Number of Use Cases (if used).

  - Number of Scenarios for each Use Case.

  - Number of events for each scenario.

  - Number of classes and instances for each scenario.

  - Number of classes at analysis, design, and implementation.

  - Number of methods for each class at analysis, design, and implementation.

  - Lines of code (LOC) for each method.

  - Development effort per class at analysis, design, and implementation.

- Make a projection of the values that will be expected during the development iterations, increments, and phases.

- Collect the actual measurements of the chosen Metrics and review them against the planned values.

- Analyze variations to determine reason, evaluate risk to project, and take remedial actions as appropriate. For example if LOC per method is predicted to be in the range 15 to 40 and a method is found to have 150 LOC, investigate why this is the case. It may be found that there is a rational reason, the method is implementing a complex algorithm for instance.

- Complexity Metrics can also be collected. These Metrics measure things like class coupling, cohesion, and method complexity.

See the references section of this work product description for references that can provide more complete sets of possible metrics.

Strengths

A set of Metrics by which a project is planned and tracked is essential for a successful project. They help to make the assumptions of the project plan explicit, and provide a means to measure conformance to the plan. Metrics from previous projects enable better use of resources and more accurate planning.

Weaknesses

Getting developers to collect Metrics is a difficult task. Automatic collection by tools should be strongly considered.

Notation

If using a tool, it will have a particular format for collecting data.

Traceability

This work product has the following traceability:

Impacted by:
- Issues (p. 176)

Impacts:
- Resource Plan (p. 135)
- Schedule (p. 139)
- Quality Assurance Plan (p. 147)
- Test Plan (p. 164)

Advice and Guidance

- Determine which set of metrics are most important to your ability to plan, run, and track your project.

- Using tools, basic Metrics can be collected for tracking purposes and for subsequent use in estimating. Tools can be very useful in monitoring Metrics that seem to be out of line.

Verification

- Check that the parameters of heuristics or algorithms used to estimate the project size are being tracked.

- Check that the measurement data needed to improve the process of estimating your next project are being gathered.

- Check that the data required to check quality targets are being gathered.

Example(s)

Here is a very brief example from a project that was piloting object technology and the use of C++. It is provided only as an example of the types of metrics that could be interesting and useful to collect.

Metric	Actual Values
Table 10-1 (Page 1 of 2). Example of Project Metrics.	
Number of Classes Implemented (total)	24
Root Classes (total)	11
Number of Classes Reused	3
Lines of code	13423
Number of Methods	194
Maximum depth of hierarchy	3

Table 10-1 (Page 2 of 2). Example of Project Metrics.

Metric	Actual Values
Analysis Person Days	180
Design Person Days	100
Implementation Person Days	75
Test Person Days	30
Documentation Person Days	40
Education Person Days	240
Methods Per Class	8.1
LOC/Class	559.3
Lines of Code Per Method	69.2

References

- [Lorenz94] discusses specific metrics for objects.

- [Henderson-S96] provides a detailed discussion on various metrics.

- Chapter 20 of Goldberg and Rubin [Goldberg95] offers a good introduction on issues related to metrics and measurement.

Importance

Optional. Our experience indicates that metrics are essential to the efficient planning and tracking of medium and large projects, but we also understand that many projects have managed to complete projects without doing this. Even if they are not needed at a project level, an understanding of metrics can have a great benefit organizationally. The more metrics on hand, the easier to estimate and plan future object-oriented development efforts.

10.11 PROJECT DEPENDENCIES

Description

Project Dependencies are items that your project requires for successful completion. You identify these items and build assumptions that these items will be provided at specific times during the course of your project. If they are not, then the project is at risk of failure. Anything is valid as a Project Dependency, but it most often involves prerequisite artifacts, personnel, skills, hardware, or software function to be delivered by a group outside of the management scope of your project.

Purpose

If you could assume everyone had a memory like an elephant, you would never need to write anything down. Since this is not the case, you need to track the important items that might kill your project. Keeping a record of these items and periodically reviewing them to ensure completeness is essential.

Many times dependencies are not under your span of control. These items need to be watched carefully, since their owners may not have the same priorities as you. Should a dependency default, you need to know as quickly as possible to be able to react.

Participants

The planner is responsible for maintaining the list. Everyone in the project is responsible for identifying dependencies and assumptions. The project manager may need to get involved to resolve issues with organizations that own specific dependencies.

Timing

The list should be created when the project and iteration plans are made. At this time only global assumptions may be identified. Dependencies may only be flushed out during low level design or implementation, so a checkpoint during each iteration must be created to review status of existing dependencies and assumptions. Any fallout from this review should be addressed and new items should be added. This checkpoint can be placed at the end of each iteration.

Technique

Each dependency should be documented separately and tracked. These items should also be integrated into the project plan. Any dependency that is in the critical path must be flagged and tracked tightly as a key plan item.

Dependencies on other organizations should be discussed with that organization. If critical, a document of understanding may be created to ensure both parties understand the agreement. At a minimum, for critical dependencies, they should have in their project plan a reference to your dependency date.

Dependencies should be kept in a database of sorts for tracking, updating, and reporting.

Strengths

If dependencies can be integrated into the project plan, you should be able to know if they are being met, and if there are any problems, you can react quickly. Maintaining a list and reviewing it frequently will help in keeping the project on track and possibly identifying other assumptions or dependencies.

Weaknesses

In the past, this type of activity was documented very poorly, if at all. Most of the time, assumptions existed in the heads of the architect or developers and were forgotten or not shared with the rest of team. Building a worthwhile list is dependent on the team's participation and commitment to help to identify, document, track, and resolve dependencies.

Notation

Each dependency should have the following information provided:

- Short description of dependency
- Full explanation of dependency
- Organization responsible for dependency and responsible contact
- Date dependency required/committed
- Person in your team who is tracking this dependency
- History of activity and current status

Traceability

This work product has the following traceability:

Impacted by:
- Reuse Plan (p. 158)
- Issues (p. 176)

Impacts:
- Resource Plan (p. 135)
- Schedule (p. 139)
- Release Plan (p. 144)
- Risk Management Plan (p. 152)
- System Architecture (p. 257)
- Subsystems (p. 274)
- Physical Packaging Plan (p. 326)

Advice and Guidance

- Make sure the owner of what you are dependent on is aware of your dependency. If possible, have them document a date in their plan to provide the deliverable to you.

Verification

- Check that the people and projects on which you are dependent are aware of your dependency.
- Check that a process is in place for tracking each dependency.

Example(s)

The following example is for a project with a dependency on receiving a class library in stable, working order:

```
Dependency #:    7

Abstract:        Transaction Class Library (TCL)

Explanation:     We need a stable TCL to validate our interaction with
                 the register input.

Responsible:     Joe Benjamin, TCL Development manager

Date required:   April 1, 1996

Tracker:         Marie Russell

History/Status:
                 1/19 - TCL scheduled for a 3/23/95 delivery (Joe)

                 3/12 - Schedule has slipped one month to 4/24 (Tom Junior,
                        TCL team lead)

                 4/2  - Verified required portion of TCL is still on target
                        for 4/24 (Joe/Marie/Tom)
```

Figure 10-5. *Example of a Project Dependency.*

References

None.

Importance

Optional. But, you should assess whether your particular project does have dependencies. If it has a number of them then you might find this work product to be essential. Your project should record dependencies in some manner and periodically review their status and effect upon your schedule.

10.12 ISSUES

Description

During the software development process, it will often occur that there are disagreements, areas of uncertainty that require clarification, or questions requiring answers or decisions by users or a sponsor. These should be recorded as issues to ensure that they are not forgotten. All resolved issues or decisions made should be recorded and remembered. Recording decisions is an important aspect of this activity.

Note that the issues being discussed here are global, project impacting issues (ones that a project manager or team lead would want to be aware of). We have said elsewhere in this document that an individual work product may have issues associated with it. Those issues should be considered private to the work product owner.

Purpose

Issues are worth their weight in gold. It is vital that issues are surfaced, recorded, tracked, and resolved in order to keep the project moving forward as planned.

Identifying and resolving issues is a major objective of the application development process. The earlier in a project that issues can be identified, the better.

Participants

The collection of all issues has an owner who is responsible for ensuring that all issues are resolved in a timely fashion. The project manager has the ultimate responsibility for ensuring issues are tracked and resolved. This responsibility is often shared with team leaders. Anyone can identify and submit an issue.

Each issue is assigned to someone who is responsible for its resolution.

Timing

Throughout the duration of the project.

Technique

Gathering issues is a natural part of the application development process and they should be actively solicited. Any area of disagreement should be recorded and added to the issues list. As part of the project management process, issues should be reviewed on a regular basis. They should be prioritized, assigned, and due dates for resolution determined.

Strengths

Tracking issues is simple and a powerful means of ensuring that the correct application is built.

Weaknesses

For the effort involved when compared with the risk of not recording and tracking them, there is no downside.

Notation

Issues should be dated, numbered, and kept in a list or a book or even on-line in a Lotus Notes® database. The general form for an issue is:

- Number or identifier
- Title
- Owner
- Assignee
- Status (such as unassigned, assigned, or closed)
- Description
- Priority (such as High, Medium, or Low)

- Open date
- Close date
- Due date (used when there are activities dependent on resolution of this issue)
- Action plan
- Activity log
- Decision (record rejected alternatives)

There are many possible outlines for an issue and it should be structured to meet the project's needs.

Note that some of these attributes are inherited from the common work product attributes already defined (Section 8.1) and so are redundant. They are reiterated here for emphasis.

Traceability

This work product has the following traceability:

Impacted by:
- None.

Impacts:
- All Other Work Products

Advice and Guidance

- It is best to have someone on the team assigned the responsibility of managing the issues list.

- The transcribe and converge technique described in Section 18.3 is a terrific source of issues. You will frequently observe differences of opinion when using this technique. These differences often merit recording for subsequent review.

- Watch out for emotional arguments during analysis and/or design. It is best to record them as issues and move on. The assignee can then do whatever fact-finding is best and present findings to the team.

- If you ever encounter a situation where there is consensus but an individual still holds out for his or her position (often identifiable by the phrase "Yes, but ..."), suggest recording as an issue for later investigation. Often, over time, the issue goes away.

- Issue resolution: OIDs (see Section 11.5) are a useful means of working out a resolution. Either find or invent a scenario that covers the area of dispute, construct an OID that addresses the concern, and see how it works out.

- Issues should be reviewed on a regular basis by management.

- Closed issues should be retained for future reference, and they should include proper detail to ensure that the reasoning can be recalled.

- Note that decisions made, even if made on the spot, normally represent identification and closure of an issue.

For example, during a planning session someone asks, "What UI standard are we following?" and after a very brief discussion, it is decided that the CUA89 standard will be adopted. This should be documented as the issue, "What UI standard will be adopted" and then the reasons for the decision should be recorded.

- The use of Lotus Notes, or some similar mechanism, for managing an Issues database is recommended.

Verification

- Ensure that the issue list has an owner.

- Check that all issues are being tracked. During most project-related meetings, someone should be responsible for recording issues.

- Check that the status of all issues is correct.

Example(s)

The following issue is from a project to develop a tool for host database management:

Table 10-2. Example of an Issue.

Issue: 29

Title: Resolve Alert Management Process

Owner: Charles

Assignee: Mary

Status: Closed

Description: It was recorded in the requirements that alerts would be sent to an Operator's console or proxy. However during analysis, the domain expert (Mike) recommended that the notification should go directly to the Data Base Administrator.

Priority: Urgent (Alert design cannot proceed until resolved).

Open date: Feb. 23, 1996

Close date: Mar. 11, 1996

Action Plan: Resolve by asking the expected users of the application

Activity log:

- 2/25 - Mary asked our second expert (Sheila) her opinion. She suggested this should be a programmable option that would be specified at install time.

- 3/1 - Mary asked User Council. After much discussion, they favored the programmable option.

- 3/3 - met with design team leads to discuss cost. Determined that this would be a costly addition as install program development has already begun.

- 3/4 - asked sponsor who concurred with the decision below.

Decision: While the suggestion has merit, due to the impact on the project, it has been decided that this will not be built into the first release—especially as the User Council did not express strong views. It will be closed and recorded as a suggestion for Release 2.

References

None.

Importance

Essential. Identifying and resolving issues drive the software development process.

11.0 Analysis Work Products

The Analysis portion of the project workbook details those work products that are created during the analysis phase of the project.

Analysis is the separation of a whole into its component parts; an examination of a problem, its elements, and its relationships.

Object-oriented analysis is the process of identifying objects that are relevant to the problem to be solved and their relationships. The process includes classifying the objects and finding relationships among the classes.

During object-oriented analysis, we apply object-oriented methods and techniques to understand, develop, and communicate the functional requirements of an application.

From the modeling viewpoint, we model the problem domain by focusing on both the static and the dynamic aspects of a problem. The static and dynamic work products are separate, but tightly coupled, as is their development.

The *static* aspects are best described in an object model, which shows the objects in the system and how they relate to other objects.

The *dynamic* aspects, the transition between object states and the interaction between objects, are best explored by analyzing the behavior of objects as they collectively fulfill the goals set up by the Use Cases. Use Cases and their Scenarios provide the input to the dynamic modeling process in the form of object interaction diagrams. Such diagrams also provide sample test cases for the system.

Analysis is focused on the *problem domain*, and not on the application. Thus, as far as possible, the only classes that should be included in an analysis are those that an end user would recognize. An area that is problematic is the system boundary. On the one hand the analysis is restricted by the boundaries of the application; on the other hand the design of the system interfaces is not an analysis concern. A solution that works in practice is to produce *a problem domain analysis that covers the application.* That is, it is aimed squarely at the problem domain (and not at the application *per se*), and it ignores as far as possible all the details of the system interfaces. The analysis *covers* the application in the sense that it includes the abstractions mentioned in the Use Case Model, but is not much broader in scope.

According to this viewpoint, the Actors of the Use Case Model become analysis classes with responsibilities and collaborations like any other analysis classes. After all, they are first-class entities in the problem domain. This enables communications across the system boundary to be described in abstract terms during analysis, deferring their design till design time.

One of the problems many teams have to deal with is to decide how detailed the analysis should be and/or for how long one should perform the analysis activities. *Analysis paralysis* is the name given to the phenomenon of a team being extremely reluctant to leave the analysis phase. The analysis phase as a result consumes much more resource than planned. The following is a list of rules of thumb for avoiding analysis paralysis.

- Adopt an iterative and incremental development process. This means accepting, among other things, that the analysis of early cycles is provisional and subject to change following feedback from developers and customers.

- If an iterative and incremental approach is used, define the requirements of each development cycle as a series of scenarios. Only perform enough analysis to enable the scenarios of the current cycle to be expressed.

- Obtain feedback from customers and domain experts. One cause of analysis paralysis is a lack of confidence in the domain. Ask the experts.

- If analysis discussion is getting bogged down, make a working assumption and record the matter as an Issue to be checked off-line.

- Use predefined, although maybe rotating, roles during each analysis session. Roles should include a leader, a timekeeper, and a scribe. The role of leader should not rotate.

- Do not use modeling CASE tools until the central analysis work products have stabilized.

- Consider using a depth-first approach (see Section 17.1) to development. One of the causes of analysis paralysis is uncertainty in the boundary between analysis and design. Depth-first development ignores this boundary for a small, initial set of scenarios.

- Beware of introducing design detail into analysis. If in doubt, err on the side of minimal analysis. Design details are characterized by constraints. If an analysis team finds itself worrying about efficiency or performance, then it has crossed the border into design.

- Try using transcribe and converge (see Section 18.3) to achieve consensus.

The analysis section of the project workbook consists of the following work products:

- Guidelines

- Subject Areas

- Object Model

- Scenarios

- Object Interaction Diagrams

- State Models

- Class Descriptions

These work products all "inherit" the common work product attributes described in Section 8.1, and they have specialized attributes of their own.

Analysis Guidelines are documented rules on how analysis will be performed in the project. The intent is to ensure that process for developing the other analysis work products and the format in which they will be delivered is consistent and well-understood across the development team.

Subject Areas allow a large system to be partitioned into smaller and distinct business domains allowing for a more effective divide and conquer approach to analysis.

The Object Model, a static model of the problem domain, is a critical work product that provides a decomposition of the system into classes of objects.

Analysis Scenarios provide refinements of the Use Case Model and are necessary for building Analysis Object Interaction Diagrams that provide a graphical representation of the interactions between objects.

State Models describe the life cycle of classes in graphical form and can lead to better understanding of the nature of a class.

Analysis Class Descriptions provide a summary of information about classes.

Much more detail is provided on these work products in the following sections.

11.1 ANALYSIS GUIDELINES

Description

Analysis Guidelines are the set of rules intended to document the way in which analysis is to be performed on a particular project. There are, in general, two kinds of Analysis Guidelines: work product guidelines and process guidelines.

Work product guidelines describe the nature of the analysis work products that are to be produced by this project. This includes both the range of work products expected and the nature of each. This information will, in general, depend on both application and team, although many guidelines will be common. In addition to describing standard notations that should be used, the analysis work product guidelines should add project-specific rules, if any, for documenting analyses. These additional rules often fall into the following categories.

- Boilerplate conventions, which describe the overall format of the analysis work products. This information can be provided most simply by a set of templates. Documentation templates too should be provided, for example to describe the information to be provided per class, per association, et cetera.

- Naming conventions, if relevant.

- Diagramming conventions. If any variations on the basic notation are to be used then they should be documented here.

Process guidelines provide guidance on the process by which analysis is to be performed. These guidelines may take the form of a list of suggested techniques, or may be more prescriptive. The guidelines might also include tools advice and recommendations for the usage of the tools.

Purpose

The point of Analysis Guidelines is to ensure that the analysis deliverables and process are planned in advance, and that team members are consistent in their application of the process to achieve the deliverables. This does not mean that analysis must necessarily be planned in a step by step manner, but that thought is put into the analysis procedures and are made publicly available. The last thing that a team needs is to be involved in procedural discussions when it should be doing the analysis itself. The existence of guidelines also acts as insurance that there will be relatively few surprises when the analysis deliverables come to be reviewed. The reviewed analysis work products may contain mistakes, but their format should be as expected.

Participants

The team leader and analysts are the people most likely to document the Analysis Guidelines. The guidelines must be written by someone with considerable experience in software engineering, and object-oriented analysis in particular.

Timing

The guidelines must obviously be in place before any analysis activity is started. If there is to be any analysis education then this must be consistent with the guidelines. If the education is just-in-time then the guidelines should be established before the education is delivered, and the education should take them into account, if this is possible. This involves the educators being flexible, and giving them sufficient time to tailor their material. The alternative is to adopt the set of guidelines taught by the educator provided that these are appropriate and well documented.

Technique

Beg, steal, or borrow some existing guidelines. Interview experienced developers to check that the guidelines are reasonable and complete. Consider asking a mentor for advice on Analysis Guidelines, or to comment on those that have already been assembled.

Strengths

Ensures that analysis time is spent doing analysis, as much as possible, and not in meta-discussions on what analysis is, or how to do it.

Weaknesses

A potential problem is that the guidelines may be overly restrictive or prescriptive. The author of the guidelines should only provide rules for cases in which, if they were not followed, it would be difficult to understand or review the work product, or the work product would be hard to use subsequently.

Another potential drawback is that the writing of guidelines will be seen as a distraction from the real work. The guidelines should be minimal, within the constraint that they are sufficient to ensure that the analysis work products are understandable, usable, and consistent.

Notation

Free format text augmented by work product templates or examples.

Traceability

This work product has the following traceability:

Impacted by:
- Intended Development Process (p. 127)
- Project Workbook Outline (p. 132)
- Quality Assurance Plan (p. 147)
- Reuse Plan (p. 158)
- Test Plan (p. 164)
- Issues (p. 176)

Impacts:
- Project Workbook Outline (p. 132)
- Subject Areas (p. 187)
- Analysis Object Model (p. 192)
- Analysis Scenarios (p. 203)
- Analysis OIDs (p. 208)
- Analysis State Models (p. 219)
- Analysis Class Descriptions (p. 227)

Advice and Guidance

- Group the guidelines into lists of guidelines by work product.

- Use work product templates where relevant.

- Use standard guidelines where they are available and appropriate. Modify these only as necessary.

- If they are novel, publish your guidelines for others to comment upon and to use.

- Harvest good templates from the workbooks of other projects.

- Use the guidelines as entry criteria to analysis reviews.

- If the project team consists largely of object-oriented novices, guidelines that are more prescriptive might be appropriate.

- Briefly review the guidelines at the end of each iteration to check their adequacy and completeness.

- Change or add to the guidelines during the project if this is considered necessary.

- Include statements about what analysis is and what it is not. These statements should be backed up by some criteria for deciding when to stop analysis. For example, it might be stated that if analysis modeling activity has started to discuss alternative ways in which the system may be designed or implemented, then it has strayed too far towards design.

Verification

- Check for coverage of each analysis work product. That is, use the list of analysis work products as a checklist of headings under which to add guidelines.

- Check that adequate guidance is provided for the usage of all tools, where appropriate.

- Check that the guidelines provide for maximal integration of analysis work products. For example, are the Analysis Class Descriptions being generated automatically from the Analysis Object Model and other models?

Example(s)

Analysis Guidelines for a particular development team or site might include the following:

- Use Object Modeling Technique (OMT) as a modeling notation and Select OMT as a modeling tool. The tool should be used for documentation only; during modeling sessions use white boards, post-it stickers that double as Class Description cards, and a flip chart for Glossary entries.

- All classes, as soon as they are proposed, should be defined with a Glossary entry.

- Glossary entries, when stable, should be transferred to Select OMT®.

- The analysis process is highly iterative, but the following cycle should broadly be followed.

  - From each of the requirements Use Cases generate a set of Scenarios by considering the different sets of assumptions under which the system would behave in an essentially "straight-line" (unconditional) manner.

  - Generate an initial object model, possibly preceded by a semantic net brainstorming session to generate ideas. Focus on the essence of the business in question and ignore infrastructure and peripheral concerns. Do not worry about cardinality or aggregation at this point. Use transcribe and converge to achieve consensus on the key concepts and relationships. Do not worry for the moment about whether the classes are strictly required, or about identifying generalizations.

  - Produce an object interaction diagram for each scenario. This involves identifying responsibilities and assigning them to classes. As this is done, add the responsibilities to the class descriptions. Distribute responsibilities evenly throughout the model as far as possible. Where helpful, but only then, identify data attributes. Iterate between OID modeling and object modeling in order resolve any tensions that arise. Do not iterate after each OID, as the model will be too unstable if this is done. Wait till a critical mass of OIDs, perhaps five, are available before returning to the object model.

- Document the outcomes of each scenario in terms of objects created, destroyed, and modified.

- Optimize the object model by pruning disconnected classes, identifying generalization/specialization hierarchies, and promoting responsibilities and relationships up the hierarchies if appropriate.

- Avoid including design detail in analysis models. Design detail is characterized by constraints: if proposed detail is included only to satisfy a constraint, omit it.

- Be sure not to do more modeling work than necessary: Only do a sufficient amount to understand how the object model can support the scenarios, without introducing concerns about constraints or other Nonfunctional Requirements.

- For those classes with important and significant dynamic aspects, such as transactions, units of work, or some real-time interfacing classes, draw state transition diagrams to capture their dynamics. Use the OIDs to produce an initial diagram, which is then completed manually.

References

None.

Importance

Optional, but it is our opinion that Analysis Guidelines are important. The existence of these guidelines can keep analysis focused on analysis issues and ensure that time allotted to analysis is spent productively.

11.2 SUBJECT AREAS

Description

A Subject Area is a distinct domain of interest that can be identified at analysis time. It is a recognizable part of the problem domain that can be analyzed as a separate unit. Subject Areas are to Analysis what Subsystems are to Design. Subject Areas might or might not become Subsystems at design time—that is a design issue.

In an object-oriented approach, Subject Areas tend to be defined as clusters of analysis classes that are closely related to each other by inheritance ("is-a"), aggregation ("has-a"), and other ("uses") associations. So it is common (and useful) to associate key classes with a primary Subject Area—the one with the most closely related classes.

Note, however, that it is unlikely that classes only have relations with other classes in their own Subject Area. Subject Areas are usually not self-contained and it is common to have some classes within a Subject Area interact with classes in other Subject Areas. It is useful to promote these "uses" relations from the class level to the Subject Area level. Thus, Subject Areas will "use" or depend on each other.

Purpose

The use of Subject Areas permits a large system to be partitioned very early in its development cycle. It encourages a separation of analysis concerns, and provides a means of organizing work products. Without Subject Areas, or an equivalent organizing concept, analysis work products can become unmanageable due to their size and quantity. Subject Areas provide a means of breaking the analysis into manageable chunks.

Many large applications have natural Subject Areas that may usefully be explored separately at analysis time. This allows different domain experts to be used for (say) an Account Subject Area and a Audit Subject Area, or it might simply allow parallel development in an organization.

Partitioning an analysis using Subject Areas facilitates reuse as it is then easier to examine and to extract information or whole work products related to a common Subject Area shared by applications.

Participants

The analysts, in consultation with customers, domain experts, and end users partition the analysis into Subject Areas.

Timing

Subject Areas are identified during the analysis phase and used to organize the analysis work.

Technique

Subject Areas are either defined "up front," as a way of getting into the analysis of a large application, or they are introduced during analysis as a means of organizing the evolving analysis work products.

If Subject Areas are defined up front, then a very early analysis step is to identify the general categories of objects suggested by the Problem Statement and Use Cases. Identify the *objects*, especially the indirect objects, in *actor-verb-object* statements of functional requirements. Then cluster them into their natural Subject Areas. This will probably, but not necessarily, take the form of a partitioning of an early version of the Analysis Object Model.

Don't be influenced by Nonfunctional Requirements: "User Interface" may be a great idea for a Subsystem (design), but it's probably not a Subject Area (analysis) from the problem domain. Subject Areas should be structured along lines that domain experts would recognize. Thus, things such as Customer Management or Account Maintenance, but not User Interface or Persistence, would make useful Subject Areas.

If Subject Areas emerge as an organizing principle *during* rather than *before* analysis work, then it will probably be as a result of the realization that the quantity and size of the analysis work products is getting unmanageable, and that some way of organizing them must be found. The primary way to discover Subject Areas once analysis has started is to partition the Analysis Object Model into a few clusters that are essentially independent of each other, but which are closely related internally. The remaining analysis work products can then be allocated to these Subject Areas according to their prime focus. But how do you find the "prime focus"?

Since Use Cases (see Section 9.2) are specified in the form of *actor-verb-object*, we can use the *object* part of each Use Case to associate it with its Subject Area. For example, if an analysis of a banking problem has identified Subject Areas: *Accounts, Journals, Audits, Operations, ...*, then the Use Case: "Customer deposits funds to savings account" would, most likely, be assigned to the *Accounts* Subject Area (We are assuming here that *savings account* is a class in the *Accounts* Subject Area). Note that the direct object of the Use Case ("funds") is rather passive (often an attribute of the verb, e.g., *deposit-funds*) and the indirect object ("savings account") is the active receiver. Also note that the other Subject Areas (e.g., Journal, Audit) will eventually be used by the Account Subject Area, probably during the development of the Analysis Object Interaction Diagram (see Section 11.5).

Strengths

Just as the design of large systems needs organization, so does their analysis. Structuring the analysis work products according to Subject Areas allows each aspect of the application to be examined and understood in isolation. It also facilitates checking for consistency and completeness among the closely related classes within a Subject Area.

Weaknesses

Identifying and maintaining Subject Areas takes some time and organization. Partitioning an analysis into Subject Areas erects barriers that might result in inconsistencies between Subject Areas. Effort must be put into communication and reviewing to ensure that this does not happen.

Notation

A simple table of the Subject Areas is sufficient. For each Subject Area, the following is relevant:

- Name of Subject Area
- Brief description
- Key Classes
- Dependencies (Subject Areas used by this one)
- Workbook

The last item refers to the fact that each Subject Area may be given an entire workbook of its own. This workbook might be a part of the overall system workbook or a distinct book or file. Obviously, a Subject Area (like a Subsystem, see Section 13.5) need only include those work products that are relevant to it. It will probably include most of the analysis work products. At design time it will be decided whether to proceed with design at the Subject Area level by adding design work products to each Subject Area workbook, or to proceed with design at the system level by adding design work products to the main workbook. Subject Area workbooks, like Subsystem workbooks, are logically part of the overall project workbook.

Alternatively, most object-oriented CASE tools support the concept of Subject Areas via *views* or hierarchical *layers*. They take the form of named boxes connected by dependency ("uses") arrows. They often show the key member classes as attributes but hide the description in a "properties" panel. See Figure 25-5 on page 554 for an example of "Category Diagram" generated by Rational Rose.

Traceability

This work product has the following traceability:

Impacted by:
- Problem Statement (p. 93)
- Use Case Model (p. 96)
- Issues (p. 176)
- Analysis Guidelines (p. 183)
- Analysis Object Model (p. 192)
- Analysis OIDs (p. 208)

Impacts:
- Resource Plan (p. 135)

Advice and Guidance

- Ensure that Subject Areas partition the analysis and not the design work products. Subject Area descriptions should refer to the business domain and not to design artifacts.

- Use Subject Areas as candidate Subsystems, but ignore this use of Subject Areas at analysis time.

- Be prepared to adjust Subject Area boundaries, or even to split or merge Subject Areas, as analysis proceeds.

- At design time, each Subject Area may form the basis for one or more Subsystems that may be described and developed in their own workbook.

Verification

- Check that definitions and glossary entries are consistent across Subject Area boundaries.

- Check the completeness of the set of Analysis Scenarios in each Subject Area independently.

- Check the dependencies between Subject Areas implied by the Analysis OIDs.

- Ensure each analysis class is represented in one and only one Subject Area.

Example(s)

The following demonstrates a nongraphical presentation of Subject Areas for a banking application:

Accounts

Description	The various types of accounts managed by the bank.
Key classes	Account, Savings Account, Checking Account, Loan
Uses	Journals
Workbook	BANKACCT

Journals

Description	Transaction recording facets of the bank.
Key classes	Log, Transaction Log, ATM Log, EFT Log, Teller Tally
Uses	Operations
Workbook	BANKJRNS

Audits

Description	Error and fraud detection mechanisms of the bank.
Key classes	Audit, Teller Audit, Branch Audit, ATM Audi, EFT Audit, Account Audit
Uses	Journals, Accounts
Workbook	BANKAUDT

Operations

Description	Personnel and scheduling facets of the bank.
Key classes	Schedule, Bank Schedule, Personnel Schedule, Employee, Manager
Uses	(none)
Workbook	BANKOPER

Figure 11-1. Example of Subject Areas.

References

- Our notion of Subject Areas is similar to the "layers" discussed by Grady Booch [Booch94].

- The concept of "domains" of Sally Shlaer and Steve Mellor [Shlaer92] is similar to Subject Areas.

- The concept of "Subjects" of Peter Coad [Coad90] is similar to Subject Areas.

- James Rumbaugh discusses "subsystems" in OMT [Rumbaugh91a]

Importance

Optional in small and medium-sized projects but essential in large projects. Subject Areas provides an important means for dividing analysis work products into more manageable, more understandable pieces.

11.3 ANALYSIS OBJECT MODEL

Description

The Analysis Object Model is a static model of the part of the problem domain relevant to the Problem Statement. In common with the Design Object Model, it consists of classes and relationships between classes. Three kinds of relationships are normally used: associations, aggregations, and generalizations/specializations (inheritance). The Analysis Object Model is a key object-oriented analysis work product.

Purpose

An object model is the fundamental way to document the static aspects of objects in the problem domain. Object modeling is what makes object-oriented development different from traditional development. The basic idea is to decompose a system down into classes of objects that cooperate by passing messages to get the job done.

The power of object modeling, as opposed to data flow or control flow modeling, is that by focusing on modeling complete abstractions (objects), which encapsulate both function and data, it is possible to use the same basic concepts during all development phases from analysis to code. By contrast, one might analyze a problem conventionally in terms of data and then design a solution in terms of function.

Participants

Object modeling is the task of architects and analysts. It is essential to get the active participation of clients and/or domain experts in this modeling activity. Since the real-world objects represented in this model belong to the problem domain; clients, end users, and domain experts are the right audience to give inputs and to validate the model. With their participation, the problem can be better understood, and less mistakes will happen in the analysis.

Timing

The Analysis Object Model is developed primarily during the analysis phase but it needs to be maintained during design or implementation if domain understanding changes.

Technique

- Identify key problem domain abstractions that satisfy the criteria of objects: identity, state, and behavior

- The behavior of objects at analysis time can be activities and/or services

- Define each identified candidate class using a short glossary entry

- Connect the candidate classes by identifying relationships between classes: associations and specializations/generalizations

- Add responsibilities

  - Key attributes
  - Behavior
  - Aggregations

- Check consistency with OIDs and state diagrams

- Iterate until model is stable

- Update class descriptions

- Restructure and refine as required over time

After the Analysis Object Model is complete, if the domain is large enough, you may choose to partition the model into *Subject Areas* (cf. *Class Category* in Booch [Booch94] or *subsystem* in OMT [Rumbaugh91a]). Large models require internal organization [Rumbaugh95a] and partitions help us to group classes and concentrate our attention on a subset of the model at a time. Partitioning borders between analysis and design. The boundary between object-oriented analysis and object-oriented design is not as clear as it was between structured analysis [Demarco79] and structured design [Stevens81]. The clustering of classes can already begin during analysis as is proposed in [Nerson92]. Dividing the analysis into Subject Areas facilitates parallel development by various teams.

Subject Areas are decided by logical criteria aimed at producing a clear and simple analysis. The goal of partitioning a design into Subsystems (Section 13.5) is different. While analysis Subject Areas and design Subsystems might be aligned in some systems, that is incidental and not inherent in the definition of the work products.

Strengths

A key deliverable for capturing and communicating problem domain understanding.

An effective means of communication between team members, customers, and domain experts.

Weaknesses

Only shows the static relationships.

Maintenance of the Analysis Object Model is often neglected. This stems from the (incorrect) assumption that the design supersedes the analysis. This weakness is shared by all analysis work products.

Notation

An Analysis Object Model is a specialized form of work product whose purpose is to capture the relationships between classes of objects in a system or an application. An Analysis Object Model is best represented visually as a class diagram. The following information is usually shown in a class diagram:

- Classes
- Relationships
  - Generalization/specialization (IsA)
  - Association (KnowsAbout)
  - Aggregation (HasA)
- Attributes
- Behavior

Instance objects can also be added if this aids domain understanding.

Some forms of documentation show these aspects separately while others combine them all on one diagram. The choice is up to you and your team members, but our recommendation is that you document all of them in the single diagram described below.

Each of these aspects is discussed in detail below:

Classes: A class can be drawn as a 3-part box, with the class name in the top part, a list of attributes (with optional types) in the middle part, and a list of services or operations (see Figure 11-2).

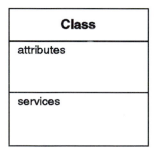

Figure 11-2. *Class Notation.*

Generalization/specialization: Generalization/specialization is usually shown as a hierarchy of super/sub type relationships where the sub types inherit the properties (both attributes and services) of the supertypes. Figure 11-3 shows the notation for class inheritance hierarchy. A Truck, a Car, or a Van are considered to be specializations of Vehicle.

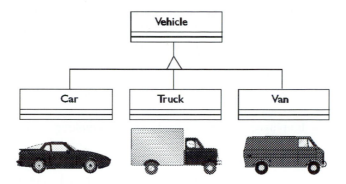

Figure 11-3. *Inheritance Notation.*

Association: Association is the simplest form of relationship. It represents knowledge of the existence of other objects. An association can be thought of as a class in its own right, so that it can support attributes, services and other relationships to enforce the details of the contract. Different notations handle this in different ways, but the basic idea is that associations are the fundamental way to describe how one object uses another to complete a task.

If two classes have an association between them, then instances of these classes are, or might be, linked. These links between instances can be thought of as instances of the association between the classes. Often it is useful to model these links with state and behavior and not just identity. That is, associations can be classes in their own right. For example, the Student-Course association in Figure 11-4 might have the attribute "grade" (*link attribute* in OMT [Rumbaugh95a]).

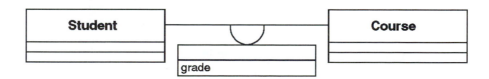

Figure 11-4. *Associations Notation.*

Associations have cardinality. The cardinality shows how many instances of the class can be associated with one instance of the other class. Cardinality can be 0 or 1 (hollow ball), 1 (no marker), 0 or many (solid ball), or some other integer range. Cardinality is important if it is so for the problem domain, for example, a customer can only place one order, et cetera.

An association is, figuratively speaking, the connection through which messages will be passed to access the attributes and services of other model components.

An association is a binary relationship at the analysis level. It reflects *conceptual or physical links* between objects of associated classes [Rumbaugh91a]. At the analysis level, no determination is made whether an association represents conceptual or physical links. This distinction becomes more important at design time and will be discussed later in Section 13.6, Design Object Model. It is sometimes useful to tag associations on an object diagram with a name. These names are often verbs, as the associations usually exist so that instances of one class can "do something" to or with instances of another. For example, Factory and Employee classes might have an "employs" association between them.

Aggregation: Aggregation is a special form of association and shows another view: namely the part-whole hierarchy relating object classes in the model. For example, when a car is decomposed into body and engine (see Figure 11-5), it is thought to "contain" the components, i.e. body and engine; they are its parts. Aggregation often means ownership: The lifetime of the whole encompasses that of its parts. If you are not sure whether a relationship is an association or an aggregation then leave it as association.

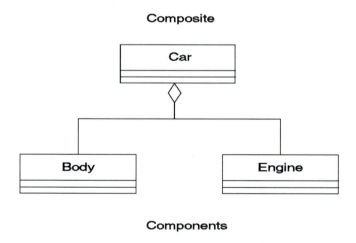

Figure 11-5. Aggregation Notation.

During analysis, aggregations are used to model type composition in a domain. Aggregations can be classified by the cardinality or multiplicity of the aggregate:

- Assembly or container; where a component cannot be part of more than one whole or aggregate (cf. *Aggregates* in [Civelo93])

- Collection; where a composite can have many components [Civelo93]

- Catalog; a component can be used in more than one composite (cf. *Catalog aggregation* [Rumbaugh95a])

Attributes: Attributes represent the structural properties of a class. For example in Figure 11-6 the static properties of the class *Car* are *Make*, *Model*, and *Year*. Each instance of that class will contain its own set of values (for example, "Porsche," "Carrera," "1987") for the attributes.

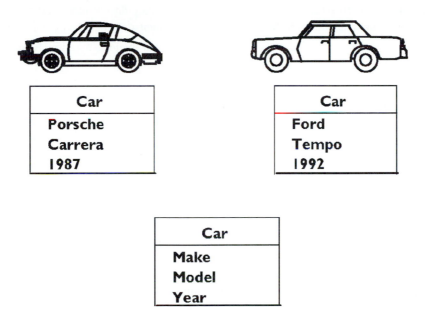

Figure 11-6. *Attributes Notation.*

Behavior: The behavior of a class, often documented as services or operations, is a statement of the responsibilities of the class. Behavior is what separates object modeling from traditional forms of data modeling (such as data models that result in Entity-Relationship-Attribute diagrams). The fundamental aspect of an object class is to encapsulate both data and function into one package and exploit inheritance, polymorphism, and contracts to get a high degree of reuse. Services encapsulate this function.

During analysis we model real world objects that can be physical or conceptual. The representation of a physical object such as a customer is modeled if it exhibits interesting behavior from the model point of view, in other words, if it carries out activities that influence or communicates with the model. For example, a *member* object (Part 5, Video Store Case Study) could perform the activity: *cancel membership*.

The differences between activities and services are that activities are not invoked. They are performed by objects by their own initiative. However, we treat activities and services in the same way. Conceptually, we could think of an object sending a message to itself. We have a different situation with view class, for example, *CustomerView*. One should not include view classes in an Analysis Object Model, because they do not influence the model classes, and only communicate with the model classes for their own benefit.

The operations or services of a class can have formal parameters, a return type, and a textual description.

Traceability

This work product has the following traceability:

Impacted by:
- Issues (p. 176)
- Analysis Guidelines (p. 183)
- Analysis OIDs (p. 208)

Impacts:
- Subject Areas (p. 187)
- Analysis OIDs (p. 208)
- Analysis State Models (p. 219)
- Analysis Class Descriptions (p. 227)
- Design Object Model (p. 281)
- Glossary (p. 355)

Advice and Guidance

- Don't overburden the modeling notation with unnecessary complexities. The simpler, the better. Object models must be readable by the expert and the beginner.

- The model should not contain any design decisions. Design, not analysis, is driven by the system's Nonfunctional Requirements that represent constraints in the way that the system works; for example, performance or availability constraints. Do not add detail to an analysis model simply to satisfy a Nonfunctional Requirement. Leave it for the design work products.

- Objects in the Analysis Object Model should relate to problem domain objects and mean something to the end user.

- Avoid being overly abstract; use the names that people familiar with the domain use (for example, in the bank-lending domain, name objects and services as a Loans Officer would).

- Name objects and services consistently and meaningfully.

  - Name object classes with common noun phrases (for example, customer)
  - Name services that modify objects with active verbs
  - Name services that query objects with verbs indicating queries

- Watch out for objects like computers or databases that may represent implementation constructs. Ask the user what the function is that they provide and try to name accordingly (for example, call a customer database a customer repository).

- Avoid controller objects that control the rest. One (slightly tongue-in-cheek) test for controller objects: Ask all developers which object they would not like to implement. If they all agree on one then you have a controller. Controller classes are often characterized by names such as "controller," "manager," and the like. A goal of using an object-oriented approach is the distribution of function in the system. Controllers act against this trend.

- Avoid multiple inheritance (inheriting from more than one superclass) unless following this guideline would result in a clumsy model.

- Eliminate unconnected objects from the object model.

- Decompose objects to the most primitive components that have meaning to the user.

- Keep any inheritance trees as shallow as possible to reduce the impact of any changes in superclass methods on lower-level subclasses. Most designs can be captured in three or less levels.

- When determining operation ownership, the service should be associated with the provider (server), not the requester.

- It is generally better to have many simple objects than a few complex ones. An overly complex object with too many attributes may be a sign that the object can be split into smaller objects. In other words, ensure that each class represents only one abstraction. One sign that this rule is being violated is an inability in find a good name for the class. Another danger sign exists if a glossary entry cannot simply be phrased in the form "An instance of this class is a ...." Avoid glossary entries that simply list attributes or services: concentrate on the entire abstraction.

- Don't worry about efficiency or minimization of classes in the analysis object model.

- Associations at analysis time are bidirectional, as it is too early to decide which of the two objects will have the responsibility to keep the information about the other or neither object may actually know about the other. During design we may decide to invent a third object that will keep this information (relating to the link between two objects).

Associations should be labeled. Some people insist on labeling both ends of associations, others are comfortable with only one end being labeled (since the inverse associate can be derived).

- Watch out for processor and data objects

    Data objects superficially have behavior but only access functions. Focusing on the abstract responsibilities of a class instead of its concrete services and attributes helps to clarify whether an object is there only to encapsulate data.

- When in doubt, use association instead of aggregation; it is more general.

- When a class is identified, record a short definition of it in some form of Glossary. With the help of a tool the object model and the class descriptions could probably be different representations of the same information.

- If the model is large (more than what fits in a diagram), consider breaking it up into Subject Areas

Verification

- Check that class names are appropriate. Names should convey intent. Be suspicious of names such as *Controller* and *Manager* as these often indicate a centralization of control.

- Check each class against the criteria that a class should have identity, state, and behavior.

- Check necessity and consistency of cycles of associations.

- Check for symmetry of associations, for instance, that related associations are at related levels in the inheritance hierarchies.

- Check that all aggregations imply lifetime encapsulation.

- Check for an absence of overlapping aggregations such as aggregations with the same components might be owned by multiple aggregates at the same time.

- Check the correctness of all unitary cardinalities.

- Check for absence of design artifacts and bias.

- Check that inheritance always implies specialization.

Example(s)

The following requirements describe a library system containing accounts of those users who want to access library documents. A document can be contained either directly in a library, or in a folder. A folder can be contained inside another folder or inside a library. Each account has an associated capability. When a user wants to access a document or a folder, her account's capability is checked against the threshold required by the document or folder. A user can logon the library, if the user has an account. The user with the right capability can open, delete, and copy a folder or a document. A document can be edited also by the user.

Based on the system requirements and using the approach described in the technique section of this work product description, the project team has made the following observations:

- Class *User* has an *m:1* association with class *Library*, called *Logon*;

- Class *User* has an *1:m* association with class *Account*, called *Own*;

- Class *User* has an *m:n* association with class *LibraryItem*, called *Access*, and the association class is *Library*;

- Class *User* is not within the system to be developed;

- Class *Library* has an *1:m* aggregation relation with class *Account*; It also serves as an association class between *User* and *LibraryItem*;

- Classes *Folder* and *Document* have common behaviors which can be generalized into a class called *LibraryItem*;

  1. Their objects have the behavior of checking capability through the *Security* objects.
  2. Their objects have the behavior of being contained by a *Library* object, or a *Folder* object directly.
  3. Their objects also have the behavior of being opened, deleted, and copied by a user object.

- Class *Library* has an *1:m* aggregation relation with class *LibraryItem*;

- Class *Account* has an aggregation relation with class *Capability*;

- Class *LibraryItem* has aggregation relations with class *Security*;

- Class *Security* has an association with class *Capability*, called *VerifiedBy*, and the association has an association class *Threshold*.

The object diagram at the analysis level for this example, rendered as a Class Diagram, is shown in Figure 11-7.

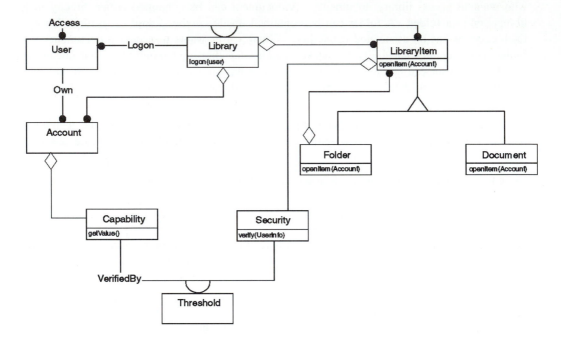

Figure 11-7. *Class Diagram Representation of the Object Model at the Analysis Level.*

References

How to build an object model is well documented in *Object-Oriented Modeling and Design* [Rumbaugh91a] and in various papers by James Rumbaugh.

Importance

An Analysis Object Model is absolutely essential. Decomposing the system into classes of objects that encapsulate data and functionality allows the use of the same concepts throughout the development cycle.

11.4 ANALYSIS SCENARIOS

Description

A Scenario is an elaboration of a Use Case. Use Cases are statements of high-level functional requirements; Scenarios add more detail and describe factors that may result in behavioral variations of a given Use Case.

A Scenario can be defined as follows:

Scenario = Use Case + Assumptions (initial conditions) + Outcomes

A Scenario describes the behavior of the system in a particular situation. The Use Case Model and the set of all Scenarios together constitute the functional requirements of a system. These requirements may be stated as formally or informally as considered appropriate.

Purpose

Use Cases are statements of user needs; however, they are not sufficiently detailed to enable the development of analysis models. Scenarios are refinements of Use Cases and are used to develop Object Interaction Diagrams. A single Use Case can generate multiple Scenarios, and Scenarios derived from the same Use Case can involve the interplay of different classes.

It is very effective to define the requirements of each cycle of an iterative and incremental development schedule in terms of the Scenarios that must be implemented in that cycle.

Participants

An analysis team, led by a qualified analyst who is knowledgeable in object technology should create the Scenarios. It is essential that domain experts or people familiar with the domain participate.

Timing

Start in analysis, after some Use Cases have been identified, and continue throughout the analysis phase.

Technique

Scenarios can be generated directly from Use Cases. They are constructed by taking a Use Case and identifying possible different outcomes (for example, loan granted vs. loan rejected) and different conditions that might result in different kinds of collaborations (for example, the loan requiring a cosigner that in turn results in different kinds of interactions with different classes). At times, this is not as simple as it sounds—sometimes it is hard to imagine different outcomes or assumptions. There will be times when you will have to watch for these happenings while building Object Interaction Diagrams.

There are other sources of information to augment the Use Cases:

- The brains of people with domain knowledge

  A brainstorming session is a useful means of doing this

- Problem Statement

- Reviewing or walking through case studies

- Functional requirements (if a separate functional requirements document exists)

- Variations of other Scenarios

  It is possible to generate new Scenarios by varying the assumptions and outcomes

- Working out Object Interaction Diagrams.

Scenarios are generated by considering each Use Case in turn. For each Use Case the possible behavioral variations of the Use Case are considered. Each variation is documented as a separate Scenario. The behavior of the Scenario is captured by describing the assumptions that the Scenario makes, that is, the initial conditions that must be true, and the outcomes (results) of the Scenario. No information on *how* the Scenario is to be performed is provided, only the conditions before and after the Scenario. The conditions may be informal, textual statements, or they may be formal preconditions and postconditions of the Scenario stated in terms of the states and attribute values of the participating objects.

To generate Scenarios while building Object Interaction Diagrams, watch for questions that will determine what the next request will be or where it should be directed (for example, when processing a loan application, it may make a difference if the customer is known to the financial institution or is a new client). When making an assumption to process an OID, make sure it is explicit and added to the corresponding Scenario. Once this is done, it is easy to generate variations by altering the assumptions (change an existing customer to a new customer, change good credit rating to bad, et cetera).

Like all work products, analysis Scenarios are subject to iterative rework. For example, if state modeling discovers new states of a class, then the language of Scenario assumptions and outcomes has effectively been enriched. It may then be possible to restate the assumptions and outcomes of Scenarios more precisely, or it might be possible to identify new Scenarios.

Strengths

One cannot overstate the importance of Scenarios. They are vital to identifying ways in which the system must respond to real-world situations, or initiate activity in the real world. By identifying assumptions and outcomes we are better able to get a handle on variations that may occur, which may in turn drive out different responsibilities and participants.

Weaknesses

It can be difficult to identify underlying assumptions, as they are often implicit in the situation. One needs to be quite rigorous in searching for assumptions.

Notation

Scenarios are recorded textually; see the examples for a suggested format. The key Scenario attributes to record are its assumptions and outcomes. If doing so would help, then lists of participating objects and parameters may also be added as Scenario attributes.

Traceability

This work product has the following traceability:

Impacted by:
- Use Case Model (p. 96)
- Issues (p. 176)
- Analysis Guidelines (p. 183)

Impacts:
- Analysis OIDs (p. 208)
- Analysis State Models (p. 219)
- Design Scenarios (p. 293)
- Glossary (p. 355)

Advice and Guidance

1. Keep in a list and assign each one a permanent number (even if it is retired or abandoned).

2. Assign a Scenario the same number as its corresponding Use Case.

   As one Use Case may generate many Scenarios, it is useful to extend the Scenario number scheme. Thus Use Case #7 corresponds to Scenario #7.x (that is to say 7.1, 7.2, ...).

3. Watch out for implicit assumptions: Try to make all assumptions explicit.

   This makes it easier to vary Scenarios and identify potential situations that may involve different participants. For example, when a customer applies for a loan (in a banking domain) it makes a difference whether or not they are "known to the bank" (for example, an existing customer). If a customer is new to the bank and applying for a loan, a quantity of background information will be requested. On the other hand, if an existing customer, this step will be bypassed; however, the service person will likely get current account information (for example, existing loan and credit card balances, previous loan history, et cetera).

4. New Scenarios are often developed by finding variations of old ones. When this happens, make sure that the discriminating assumption is added to the original Scenario.

5. Present a Scenario in terms of generic parameters and participating objects, that is, in terms of formal parameters. When the formal parameters are not obvious, document

them explicitly. A Scenario should not refer to specific data values or objects unless doing so is a necessary part of the Scenario. Scenario attributes that document the participants and parameters of the scenarios are particularly useful if there are many participants and/or parameters.

6. If multiple instances of the same class participate in a Scenario, then role names should be given to each. Both role names and class names can be defined in the participant's Scenario attribute, if these are used. If only one instance of a class participates then no role name is necessary, unless it would be helpful to indicate it.

7. If a Scenario participant's attribute is used then only include in it those objects that are mentioned in the assumptions and outcomes lists, not any additional objects that might appear on the object interaction diagram for the Scenario.

8. If doing so would be helpful, use the names of possible states of objects to express the assumptions and outcomes.

9. If a formal style of Scenario presentation is used, Scenario assumptions and outcomes will "feel" more like preconditions and postconditions, and can be labeled as such.

10. If preconditions and postconditions refer to object attributes, they will need to distinguish between the values before the Scenario is performed, and the values after. A useful convention is that all references to after values use the attribute name decorated with a prime symbol. For example a postcondition stating that the new account balance minus the old account balance equals AmountToBeTransferred (a Scenario parameter perhaps) might be written:

```
Account.balance' - Account.balance = AmountToBeTransferred
```

Verification

- Check that each scenario description is as generic as possible. Scenarios must refer to instances, but the description of each instance should be as generic as possible, and not unnecessarily referring to specific instances such as account_512678.

  Instance data is sometimes useful as a means of communicating with users during analysis sessions (for example, Mary the Clerk rather than Clerk).

- To ensure coverage of scenarios, vary all of the assumptions that have been identified and try different combinations and permutations of assumptions and outcomes.

Example(s)

The following are some Scenarios from a banking application that are derived from the Use Case of "customer applies for loan":

```
Use Case 1: Customer applies for loan

Scenario 1.1: Customer Applies for Loan (Granted)

Assumptions:
 • Customer is known to bank (an existing customer)
 • Applied for amount is within Loans Officer's lending authority
 • Customer is employed
 • Customer has a good credit rating
Outcomes:
 • Loan is granted to customer

Scenario 1.2: Customer Applies for Loan (Declined)

Assumptions:
 • Customer is unknown to bank (not an existing customer)
 • Applied for amount is within Loans Officer's lending authority
 • Customer is employed
 • Customer has a bad credit rating
Outcomes:
 • Loan application is declined

Scenario 1.3: Customer Applies for Loan (Marginal Case - approved)

Assumptions:
 • Customer is known to bank (an existing customer)
 • Applied-for amount is within Loans Officer's lending authority
 • Customer is employed
 • Customer has a marginal credit rating
 • Bank requires marginal applications to supply a cosigner
 • Customer provides cosigner
Outcomes:
 • Loan is granted to customer
 • Cosigner is bound by loan contract
```

Figure 11-8. *Analysis Scenario for Customer Loan Application.*

The following is a scenario from a DB performance monitor project:

```
Use Case 1: Monitor Database

Scenario 1.1: Data Collection—First Sample (successful)

Assumptions:
 • User has defined expression (page activity = page read + page write)
 • All objects have been created
 • Only shows the capture of the first sample
 • Only shows collection for 1 database (there could be many)
Outcome:
 • Successful
```

Figure 11-9. *Analysis Scenario for Monitor Database.*

References

- [Jacobson92] has extensive discussion on Use Cases.

- [Spivey88] defines behavior in terms of assumptions and outcomes.

Importance

Absolutely essential. Scenarios allow the refinement of Use Cases necessary for building a complete analysis model.

11.5 ANALYSIS OBJECT INTERACTION DIAGRAMS

Description

An Analysis Object Interaction Diagram (OID) is a graphical representation of an Analysis Scenario, expressed in terms of the interactions between real-world or analysis objects. An Analysis OID presents the dynamics of an Analysis Scenario by showing how the objects that participate in the Scenario collaborate in order to achieve its desired outcomes. Bearing in mind that Analysis Scenarios are derived directly from Use Cases, Analysis OIDs complete the link between the requirements and the Analysis Object model. Although Analysis OIDs present the dynamics behind a Scenario, they stay at the analysis level of abstraction. The key for developing effective Analysis OIDs is to focus on the real-world objects only for understanding and abstracting the problem and business, instead of defining solutions.

Purpose

Analysis OIDs provide a high-level view of how objects or instances of those classes defined in the Analysis Object Model interact in order to carry out the Scenarios that are the requirements in the system. The graphical medium shows the end-to-end execution flows in a simple and sufficient way. Analysis OIDs are used to discover responsibilities that are needed to carry out Scenarios, and to assign those responsibilities to classes. As Analysis OIDs link Scenarios to the Analysis Object Model, they may be used either to help derive the Object Model or to validate an existing Object Model.

The expressiveness of Analysis OIDs in showing the dynamics of real-world objects from the user's perspective makes this work product essential to the object-oriented software development, especially in a scenario-driven process.

Participants

Developing Analysis OIDs is the task of a development team led by an analyst. The team consists of analysts, designers, domain experts, and developers. It is very important for clients and domain experts to participate in this modeling activity. It is vital that the Scenarios and their Analysis OIDs that refine those Scenarios should represent their views, business, and requirements. With their participation, the problem will be better understood, and fewer modeling errors will be made.

Timing

Analysis OIDs should begin to be developed early in the analysis phase. As soon as a primitive Analysis Object Model is ready, relevant Analysis OIDs may be developed to drive the analysis object modeling, such as, enlarging the model with more analysis classes, validating its model, and assigning responsibilities and behaviors to its classes. In an iterative process, it will be performed continuously and incrementally throughout the development to represent the evolving understanding of the problem domain objects.

Technique

An Analysis OID is created for a Scenario by recording how objects in the classes from the Analysis Object Model could cooperate in order to perform the Scenario. The record takes the form of a sequence of messages sent between objects. Writing an Analysis OID forces one to take decisions about which classes are to have what responsibilities, or to validate previous decisions. It is expected that Analysis OID writing and Object Modeling take place jointly and iteratively. Analysis OID's frequently "break" the Object Model that must then be modified.

   Writing an Analysis OID with a primitive Analysis Object Model involves the following:

- Deciding which objects need to participate in the Scenario. These objects are inserted into the Analysis OID as named vertical lines. Instance names should suggest the roles that the objects play in the Scenario, for example, "sourceAccount" or "destinationAccount."

- Deciding the class of each of these participating objects. Unless the Analysis OID breaks the Analysis Object Model, which frequently happens, the class will be one that has already been identified in the model. If no appropriate class exists in the model, it must be added. As a result, the Analysis Object Model is enhanced.

- The question "what happens now" is asked repeatedly, preferably of a domain expert, in order to carry out the Scenario. The object behaviors modeled in Analysis OIDs are presented as *messages* and *internal activities*. Both must be explicitly represented in an Analysis OID with regard to their occurring sequences. Use the responsibilities identified for the classes of the participating objects as menus from which to select messages. If no appropriate responsibility exists, or if it is assigned to an inappropriate class, then the Analysis Object Model is broken, and needs to be fixed. For each message, it must be decided which object sends it, which one is to receive and carry it out, and which parameters are appropriate.

Analysis OID modeling is an iterative process that includes a parallel development of the Analysis Object Model. Whether the Analysis OID modeling drives the Analysis Object Modeling or vice versa will depend on the problem to be modeled, as well as the modeling style. For a behavior-centric problem such as real-time systems, Analysis OID modeling often drives the analysis. On the other hand, for a data-centric problem such as information system applications, Analysis Object Model often plays a more important role in analysis. In either case it is expected that information will flow in both directions as the Analysis OID and Analysis Object Model are developed and made consistent and robust.

Strengths

The strengths of Analysis OIDs can be summarized as dynamics, intuitiveness, and expressiveness. The notation of time lines is intuitively appealing and simple but very powerful in expressing what will happen to objects when the Scenario is in progress. An Analysis OID is a very succinct way of expressing the dynamic and functional aspects of a system through the interactions among objects. It should be noted that the notation of Analysis OIDs is not novel to object-oriented software development, but their application within it is highly effective.

Weaknesses

Each Analysis OID can only describe at most one Scenario of a system. A system can consist of hundreds of Scenarios under different conditions and status; Therefore, the amount of work can be too big to accomplish in a short period of time. One solution proposed in this approach is to model only the key Scenarios of a system or to combine several Scenarios into one.

Another weakness is that using Analysis OIDs might lead developers into premature object design. Sometimes it is better to determine object interaction sequences only at design time. Focus on problem domain objects, but even that rule will not always guarantee that an Analysis OID overspecifies a Scenario into the design level. The only real solution is to use your judgment to avoid design decisions, and reflect your clients' point of view, instead of developers'.

Notation

The notation for the Analysis OIDs is mostly straightforward. We will give a complete description of all the concepts, although only a few may be used for any particular Analysis OID.

1. **Object**: Objects or instances involved in the current Scenario are listed. Each object is identified by a name identifying its class and a name indicating its role in the Scenario, in the format: *<object name>:<class name>*. These names are usually placed at the top of the time line for that object. Role names can be thought of as instance

names, except that an attempt is made in an Analysis OID to refer to generic rather than specific objects.

2. **Time Line**: Time lines are the vertical lines representing each object. They are used as sources and targets of the time-ordered sequence of messages sent between objects.

3. **Message**: Messages represent object interactions. Every message in an Analysis OID has one sender and one receiver. Sometimes the sender can be omitted if objects from more than one class will send the message. Messages can either request information from an object, or change its state. A message sent to *self*, that is, the current object, is represented by a message whose source and destination is the current object. A message can be either a synchronous or asynchronous one.

   - **Synchronous Message**: The sender of a synchronous message expects a returning one represented by a message line with *return(parameter)*. The sender of the message waits for the return before proceeding.

   - **Asynchronous Message**: The sender of an asynchronous message does not wait for an explicit return message before proceeding. This is the only distinction between synchronous and asynchronous messages.

   Incoming messages to a time line represent sync-points.

4. **Message Parameter**: A message can carry parameters in an interaction.

5. **Condition**: A condition within a pair of square brackets represents a decision point in the message sender object. If the condition is true, the message attached will be sent. In any case the object continues with its time line. Using the condition notation can help make the Analysis OID more general, with weaker assumptions. The alternatives to using conditions (and loops) are to use several Analysis OIDs to present the options for a single Scenario, to split up the Scenario, or to omit certain details. Each of these may be the best choice depending on circumstances.

6. **Loop**: In order to perform repeated actions, a loop can be attached to an object's time line. A loop is also associated with a loop condition, which is the condition under which the loop is performed again.

7. **Internal Activity**: An internal activity is any internal behavior that is relevant to a time line, but whose internal details are either not appropriate to provide, or not yet known. An internal activity is represented by the name of the activity in curly brackets appearing at the appropriate point on a time line. Internal activities might be entirely local to that object, or they may involve communications. The internal activity can be further specified in an attached note. An example of an internal activity might be "*{Identify the right account}*." A description of an internal activity can be provided as a footnote to the Analysis OID.

The notation of an Analysis OID is shown in Figure 11-10. We understand that the notation we use is not completely supported by every CASE tool. Users are encouraged to tailor the notation, based on the CASE tool they use. Most commonly supported concepts are *objects, messages*, and *time lines*.

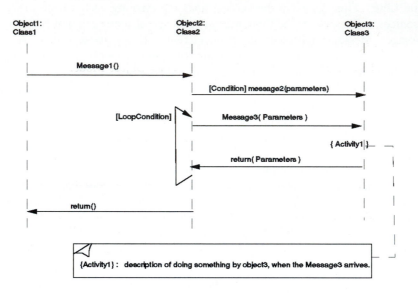

Figure 11-10. *Format of Analysis Object Interaction Diagram.*

Traceability

This work product has the following traceability:

Impacted by:
- Issues (p. 176)
- Analysis Guidelines (p. 183)
- Analysis Object Model (p. 192)
- Analysis Scenarios (p. 203)
- Analysis State Models (p. 219)

Impacts:
- Subject Areas (p. 187)
- Analysis Object Model (p. 192)
- Analysis State Models (p. 219)
- Analysis Class Descriptions (p. 227)
- Design OIDs (p. 298)

Advice and Guidance

- Make Analysis OIDs consistent with the business logic. Analysis OIDs are used for recording what happens in the real world. Any design and architectures related to the system solution should be kept out of it.

- Keep Analysis OIDs as simple as possible. It can help avoid mixing in any design objects and decisions.

- Focus on object general behaviors, instead of methods. Methods are only meaningful under the design, and should be created at the object-oriented design phase. The messages sent between two objects in an Analysis OID help model the behaviors, and these messages are not the methods for the message receiver (but they could be so in the Design Object Interaction Diagram discussed later in this document).

- Make Analysis OIDs consistent with the Analysis Object Model. If object A sends a message to object B, A's class should have a certain relationship with B's class in the Object Model.

- Due to the fact that hundreds of OIDs can be developed, it is important to capture only the major ones that drive out the principal problem features. Do not explore every exceptional condition unless it is significant to the users.

- Avoid Analysis OIDs overspecifying their Scenarios. One common mistake is for analysts to descend into unnecessary detail. If this happens, design objects and decisions creep into the analysis model, resulting in clutter and overspecification. Avoid this by focusing on using the problem domain objects in the Analysis OIDs, instead of implementing the Scenarios. Internal activities in the OIDs can be used to defer low-level object interactions that lead to possible overspecification.

- An important step ignored by many developers is the detailing of assumptions before developing an Analysis OID for a Scenario. Check hidden assumption and outcomes.

- Avoid both overly passive objects (pure data objects), and overly active objects (managing and controlling objects). Distribute the responsibilities throughout all objects.

- Identification and dating are very important. In the case of Analysis OIDs it makes sense to assign to them exactly the same identification as their corresponding Scenarios (as they have a 1:1 relationship).

- The object role names and parameters, or formal arguments, in a Scenario should be consistent with its Analysis OID.

- Write an Analysis OID in terms of specific objects such as "*anAccount*" or "*Account1*," if this promotes clarity. The goal of Analysis OID modeling is not for completeness, but an end-to-end understanding that is missing in the Analysis Object Modeling.

- Make Analysis OIDs general and independent of technology, design, and constraints. There are some situations in which the detail of object interactions is necessarily a design Issue. In such cases leave the Scenario without a corresponding Analysis OID, or leave the problematic interactions as internal activities in the Analysis OID. Postpone the resolution of the design issue to modeling of Design Object Interaction Diagrams.

- Watch out for implicit assumptions and make them explicit.

- Make sure that assumptions are proven in the Analysis OID. For example, if we are processing a customer change of address with the assumption that there is no territory change, we still need to show the object that makes the decision related to territory and its sale representatives in that Analysis OID.

Verification

- A walk-through of Analysis OIDs is an effective technique to check whether the model reflects the reality.

- Check for an even distribution of system intelligence and control.

- Check for an absence of overly passive objects.

- Check that an Analysis OID does not overspecify its Scenario in the sense that it introduces decisions which can better be made at design time.

- Check that Scenario assumptions are necessary and sufficient for each Analysis OID.

- Check that Scenario outcomes indeed occur in each Analysis OID.

- Check for hidden assumptions and outcomes in an Analysis OID.

Example(s)

This example is simplified from a real project. It deals with users accessing the items in a library system. The example presents two scenarios as well as a modification to the second scenario.

A user has an account associated with the library system. The account has security levels associated with each library item. Each library item's security object will check whether the user is permitted to access that library item.

The first scenario shows the business logic for the *access* process for the library file system.

This example is also explored at the design level in Section 13.8, Design Object Interaction Diagrams.

- **Analysis Scenario 1**: A user wants to access a library item.

- **Assumption**: The user has already logged into the library, and a unique identity, *current user*, is established.

- **Outcome**: A library item is permitted to be viewed, if the user passes the security check for that particular library item.

- **Description**: When a library item receives a request for access from a user it first passes the user's identity (account) to its own security object to check whether the user is permitted access. If the user has the clearance to access this library item, the item will display its own content. Otherwise, the request is rejected.

- **Analysis OID**: The Analysis OID for this scenario is shown in Figure 11-11

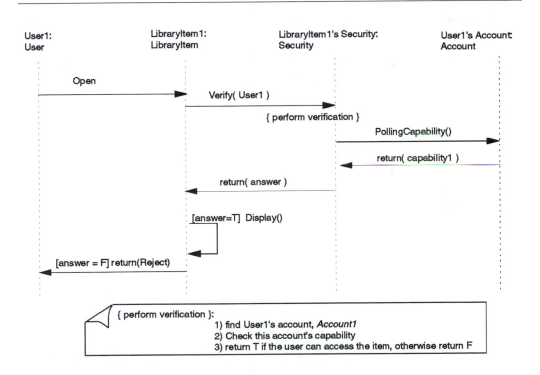

Figure 11-11. *Analysis OID for User Access to Library Item.*

Our understanding of requirements can change over time. Analysis OIDs can facilitate this process. Consider the following example of the Use Case "Customer Changes Address" in a marketing company. The Scenario being addressed is:

- **Analysis Scenario 2**: Customer Changes Address

- **Assumptions**:
  - Caller is an existing customer
  - Address change is immediate (not in the future)

- **Outcome**: Customer's address successfully changed

- **Description**: A customer's address change usually involves an update of the customer's file and notification to the customer's agent.

This could be a situation of a Help Desk (Clerk) for an Insurance Company receiving a phone call from a customer who wishes to notify the company that he or she has moved.

Figure in Figure 11-12 shows a possible Analysis OID for this Scenario.

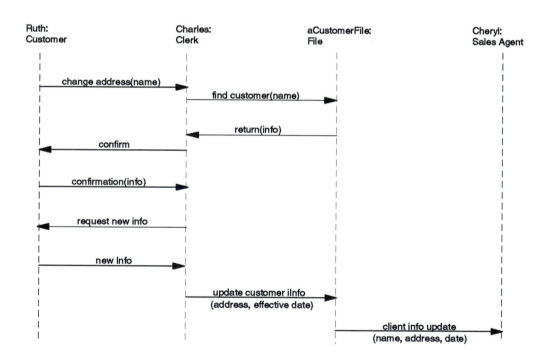

Figure 11-12. Initial Analysis OID for Change of Address.

The basic Scenario is that a customer calls the Help Desk, to notify the company of an address change. The customer's file is found in the customer filing cabinet, its identification is confirmed and the sales agent is notified. This OID satisfies the requirement - at least at first glance. However, later during analysis, we learn that agents have territories, and we must revisit this OID.

With this new information, we can modify the Scenario as follows:

- **Analysis Scenario 2 (modified)** : Customer Changes Address

- **Assumptions**:
  - Caller is an existing customer
  - Address change is immediate (not in the future)
  - Move involves change of territory and new agent must be notified

- **Outcome**: Customer's address successfully changed

- **Description**: A customer's address change usually involves an update of the customer's file and notification to the customer's agent.

We are faced with a problem - who (which object) knows about sales agents' territories. Certainly it would be outside the responsibility of the customer's file. This is an important question as we may be discovering the need for a new object. Figure 11-13 shows a possible solution to the modified Scenario. It only shows the portion of the OID which would be modified.

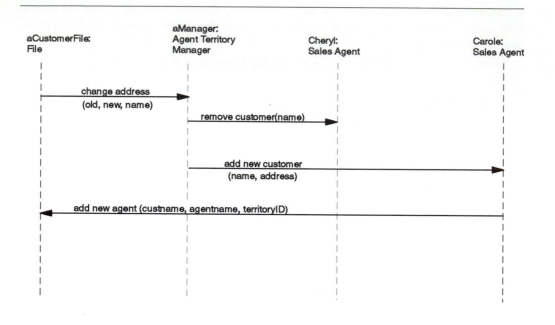

Figure 11-13. Modification to Part of the Analysis OID for Change of Address.

In the modified OID, the customer's file delegates the task of territory management to the Agent Territory Manager object. This object knows about and understands the company's approach to territory management (it can get quite complex). This object will apply current business policies and determine who needs to be informed of the address change (in this case the old and new Sales Agents). If the address change had not involved a change of territory, it would simply have notified the existing agent of the address change and then sent a no change notice back to the customer's file. Otherwise, the customer will be removed from his/her current agent, and forwarded to another agent who is in the territory that the customer moves to. The customer's file is also updated for the change.

This example illustrates a number of points:

1. Analysis OIDs assist with the discovery process and understanding a business area;

2. Always present the business knowledge and logic in Analysis OIDs;

3. Delegation of responsibilities can change with our understanding of the business area;

4. We must always be prepared to learn new information.

References

- Jacobson *et al.* [Jacobson92] were the first group employing Use Cases and OIDs in dynamic modeling.

- OMT [Rumbaugh91a] has its own name for OIDs, that is, "event trace diagrams."

- [Booch94] also has interaction diagram.

- The Unified Modeling Language [Booch96] also utilizes the OIDs under the name "Sequence Diagram" for dynamic modeling.

Importance

Essential. Analysis OIDs are a powerful tool for showing the dynamics of the real-world objects being modeled.

11.6 ANALYSIS STATE MODELS

Description

A state model, as used in object-oriented analysis, describes the life cycle of a class. It describes states that a class may attain and transitions that cause a change of state. The state transitions, representing external stimuli or events, show an object's state changes. A state model is represented by a *state diagram* or a state transition table.

Purpose

A state model represents an object's life cycle in graphical notation or in a tabular form. It gives an overview of how an object reacts to external events without getting into code details. A state model is much easier to develop and understand in comparison with high-level textual descriptions. It is useful because of the insight it can yield about the nature of a given class.

Participants

At the analysis level, state models should be developed by the analysis team. Customers should participate in this activity, so that the modeling can be as accurate as possible based on clients' requirements and knowledge of objects in their domain.

Timing

Analysis State Modeling is done after an initial Object Model and a dynamic model with scenarios and Object Interaction Diagrams (OIDs) have been completed. It is performed for those classes whose OIDs show that they have significant dynamics. This is indicated by incoming messages whose arrival order is vital to the class.

Technique

- Select a class to model.

  During analysis, we look for classes with an interesting or unclear interesting life cycle (for example in a lending application the Loan class is quite interesting).

- Identify how the object comes into being. This will be a state transition leading to an initial state.

- From the initial state, add all transitions that can occur and the states that they lead to.

- Repeat this process for all identified states until complete.

- Note that it is valid to include transitions that lead back to the same state (i.e. loops).

  For example, a Loan is in an active state, a customer makes a payment, is shown as a transition leading back to the active state.

- For completeness, it is advisable to probe whether or not there are transitions leading between various states in the model.

Strengths

A state model provides a complete picture of the life cycle of a class. It is another way of looking at an object, and object behaviors can be clearly presented through such a model.

Weaknesses

The weakness of state models is that one model can only show information limited to one class. It can be difficult to show simultaneous changes of state that occur between multiple, collaborating classes.

Notation

The graphical notation of a state diagram representing the state model is shown in Figure 11-14.

The key elements of the notation are:

- A class's states are shown in circles (or boxes).

- Transitions are shown as directed arcs between states.

- Transitions should be labeled as doer-action tuples (for example, customer makes loan payment).

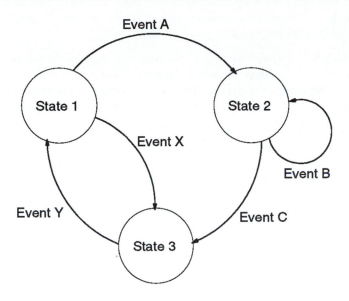

Figure 11-14. *State Diagram Notation.*

Traceability

This work product has the following traceability:

Impacted by:
- Issues (p. 176)
- Analysis Guidelines (p. 183)
- Analysis Object Model (p. 192)
- Analysis Scenarios (p. 203)
- Analysis OIDs (p. 208)

Impacts:
- Analysis OIDs (p. 208)
- Analysis Class Descriptions (p. 227)
- Design State Models (p. 306)
- Glossary (p. 355)

Advice and Guidance

- One of the best ways of building a state diagram is to go through a role playing exercise. This can be quite effective. Pretend that you are the object being examined, assume a state and ask "what can happen to me now?"

- Examine the state chart and ponder whether it is possible to get from one state to any other state. This sometimes uncovers behaviors or actions that otherwise might not be anticipated.

- In analysis, it is important to avoid representing design decisions in the state models; we observed that it is quite easy to fall into this trap.

- Watch that you don't wind up building flowcharts. The best way to avoid this is to ensure you keep a consistent point of view. If you are the "Loan," then you only concern yourself with the "Loan's" point of view.

- When working with "naive" users (i.e., noncomputer people) do not use terms such as finite state machine or state transition diagram. Just say you are going to build a picture of the life cycle of the object, how it gets created, what things can happen to it, what causes it to go away, and so forth. Say that the reason for doing this is in order to achieve a deeper understanding of the domain.

- State diagrams are built on a very selective basis during analysis. In a typical domain, maybe one or two per 100 classes. This will increase dramatically in domains that have a real-time aspect about them (like manufacturing, process control, monitoring, et cetera).

Verification

- At every state close your eyes and ask "what can happen to me now?" and ensure that all state transitions (and their respective states) are represented.

- From every state ask if it is possible to visit every other state in the model (for example, "can I possibly get from here to there?" where "there" is every other state in the model).

- If two states exhibit the same behavior, then collapse them into one provided they exhibit the same behavior (i.e., have same entry and exit conditions).

Example(s)

Figure 11-15 presents a possible state diagram for an Account class for a bank application with our basic state model notation. The life cycle for an *Account* object from creation through being closed is demonstrated in the diagram.

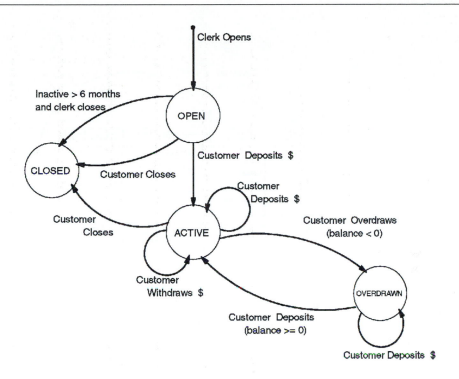

Figure 11-15. *State Diagram for the Account class.*

Figure 11-16 shows another example of a state diagram, this time for a loan class. This was built with the help of a Loans Officer from a bank. If this process is presented to users as being an inquiry about the life cycle of a loan object, users have little difficulty assisting with producing such a diagram (i.e. it is best to avoid describing the process as finite state machines or state modeling when speaking to users).

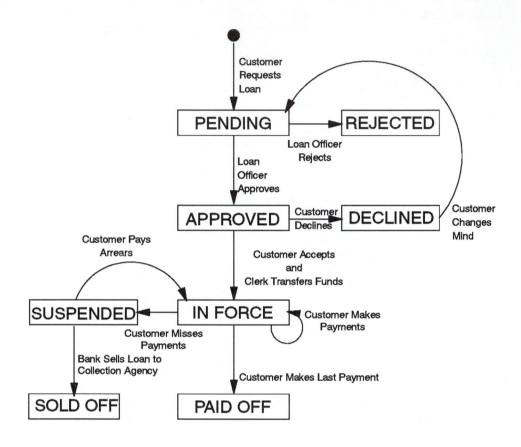

Figure 11-16. *State Diagram for a Loan.*

State Transition Tables: State Transition Tables are useful when State Transition Diagrams (or Statecharts) are not feasible; for example, they must convey state model in an ASCII medium, say e-mail; drawing tools are missing, limited, or not standardized in the development (or documentation) environment.

There are at least two types of state transition table formats that show the same information in different ways.

State Transition Matrix (STM):   Has one row per state and one column per event. The content of the cell is the Next state.   (See Table 11-1)

State Transition Table (STT):   Has three columns labeled *Current State*, *Event*, and *Next State*.   (See Table 11-2)

STMs work well when there are few states and events but have a rich set of possible transitions. They force one to address completeness and consistency.

Table 11-1. *State Transition Matrix for Account Class.*

Event-> State	Clerk Closes	Customer Closes	Customer Deposits [bal+amt >=0]	Customer Deposits [bal+amt <0]	Customer Withdraws [bal-amt >=0]	Customer Withdraws [bal-amt <0]
Open	Closed	Closed	Active	(can't happen)	(can't happen)	(can't happen)
Active	Closed	Closed	Active	(can't happen)	Active	Overdrawn
Overdrawn	(can't happen)	(can't happen)	Active	Overdrawn	(can't happen)	(can't happen)
Closed	(can't happen)	(can't happen)	(can't happen)	(can't happen)	(can't happen)	(can't happen)

STTs work well when there are many states and/or events but sparse transitions; that is, when very few states are sensitive to each event. These are less cluttered and easier to create, but hide incompleteness.

Table 11-2. *State Transition Table for Account Class.*

State	Event	Next State
Open	Clerk Closes	Closed
Open	Customer Closes	Closed
Open	Customer Deposits	Active
Active	Customer Closes	Closed
Active	Customer Deposits	Active
Active	Customer Withdraws [bal-amt>=0]	Active
Active	Customer Withdraws [bal-amt<0]	Overdrawn
Overdrawn	Customer Deposits [bal+amt<0]	Overdrawn
Overdrawn	Customer Deposits [bal+amt>=0]	Active

Using the full Statechart notation [Harel87], events can be elaborated with attributes, conditions, and actions. States can also have entry and exit actions as well as internal activities.

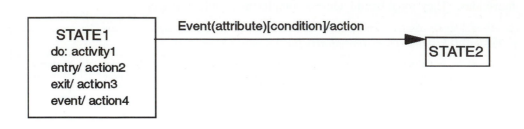

Figure 11-17. *Extended Notation for State Diagrams.*

STMs and STTs can be annotated (extended) with adornments from the underlying modeling technique. For example, the entry/exit actions above can be associated with the Event entry for the transition. Table 11-3 is an elaboration of Table 11-2 that shows event attributes and actions.

Table 11-3. *Elaborated State Transition Table for Account Class.*

State	Event(attribute)[condition]/action	Next State
Open	[6 months inactive]/send notice	Closed
Open	Customer Closes	Closed
Open	Customer Deposits(amt)/bal:=amt	Active
Active	Customer Closes/send check for balance	Closed
Active	Customer Deposits(amt)/bal:=bal+amt	Active
Active	Customer Withdraws(amt) [bal-amt>=0]/ bal:=bal-amt	Active
Active	Customer Withdraws(amt) [bal-amt<0]/ bal:=bal-amt	Overdrawn
Overdrawn	Customer Deposits(amt) [bal+amt<0]/ bal=bal+amt	Overdrawn
Overdrawn	Customer Deposits(amt) [bal+amt>=0]/ bal=bal+amt	Active

References

- Rumbaugh et al [Rumbaugh91a], and Booch [Booch94] recommend using state diagrams to model the dynamic behaviors of objects.

- Statechart, a diagramming notation for states, was developed by Harel in 1987 [Harel87].

Importance

Optional, although as a rule it is extremely useful to use in business domains such as banking where *Loan* would be very interesting or in insurance where an *InsurancePolicy* can be very interesting.

In real-time domains this becomes essential as there will be objects with strong state-dependent behaviors, such as the *Connection* class in a telephony application.

11.7 ANALYSIS CLASS DESCRIPTIONS

Description

Analysis Class Descriptions are summaries of all the information known about a class at the analysis level.   They are similar to the CRC cards of Wirfs-Brock et al [Wirfs-Brock89].   Class-related information exists in several places in the analysis chapter of the project workbook, for example in different parts of an object model, in scenarios, and in state models.   For each class, a class description provides a concentrated summary.

Class descriptions are not intended to overlap or conflict with object or dynamic models.   Good tool support should enable class descriptions to be updated automatically whenever other model views are modified, for example to add a new responsibility to a class in an object model view.   Much of the information of a class description should be generated automatically from the data of the various development models.   Similarly, Class Descriptions and Glossary entries (see Section 16.1) may in practice be generated from the same source data.

Purpose

Analysis Class Descriptions are provided for two reasons.

1. To provide a place to put class-specific information, such as a short description, key attributes, responsibilities, and the like, which might otherwise slip down cracks between the other analysis work products.

2. To provide a single point of contact for analysis information regarding a particular class.

3. To provide a place to record information that won't fit on other diagrams (Object Model, OIDs, et cetera).   This may take the form of pictures, descriptions, standards, related documents, and the like.

Participants

The analyst who owns a class has the responsibility to maintain the Analysis Class Description for that class.   Tools that automatically derive the Class Description information from other work products (for example, the Object Model and the State Model) significantly reduce the effort needed to maintain Class Descriptions.

Timing

Class descriptions are provided at analysis, design, and implementation levels. (Implementation class descriptions are used only if they are needed as a repository for new information about the class.) Thus a particular class may have several class descriptions, one for each level of abstraction in which it is involved: analysis, design, and implementation. These multiple class descriptions may refer to each other, but they are different work products. The reason for this apparent redundancy is that the definition of a class may be subtly different at each level of abstraction.

The Analysis Class Description serves as a repository for summary information as the analysis modeling activity proceeds, and is completed in time to be reviewed along with the remainder of the analysis work products. A class description is opened as soon as there is a need to summarize the properties of a class.

Technique

The creating or updating of class descriptions should be one of the activities performed after each analysis modeling session.

Exactly how the class description is filled in will depend on its format. A class description will (obviously) have a name and it should have a short textual definition. Names are very important and should be chosen to reflect the nature and intent of the class. A vague or ambiguous name is often a sign that the abstraction named is insufficiently understood or inappropriate. The abstraction might be inappropriate because it refers to more than one concept, in which case it is a candidate for splitting into multiple classes (each with more precise names). Another problem that often surfaces with names is that an abstraction is actually a function and not an object. Class names that are verbs like *Connect* or *Initiate* might indicate this. Names such as *Controller* or *Manager* are often hints that the system is too centralized; its intelligence has not been distributed in an appropriate manner. This is a common mistake among experienced developers who are new to object technology. Names should, therefore, be taken seriously.

Even if a modeling team agrees on a name, it frequently happens that they find out later that they do not agree on what the class actually represents. This problem can be solved by insisting that modeling sessions that propose new (or modified) classes also agree on a short textual definition. The shorter the definition the better; one line is perfect although sometimes inadequate. The definition cannot and should not define all aspects of the class. It should, however, capture enough of the meaning of the class to ensure that all developers are thinking along the same lines, and that newcomers to the project can gain an immediate understanding of why the class exists in the model. Agreeing on definitions is often difficult, but if it is not done then the outstanding inconsistencies will dig themselves into the model, requiring considerable excavation work subsequently.

Names and textual class definitions are most conveniently captured initially as Glossary entries, and then incorporated into Class descriptions as the need to summarize information about the classes arises.

Strengths

Class descriptions are an important part of all published development methods. If properly used, they can also significantly improve the readability of a workbook by providing cross-references.

Weaknesses

An appropriate format must be chosen. There are many published formats for class descriptions. It is important that a format is fitted around a development method and not vice versa. Tools complicate the issue by providing support for Class Descriptions, but not necessarily the ability to tailor the format.

Notation

Beyond names and definitions, the format of class descriptions should serve the selected analysis, and not the other way around. If a responsibility-driven approach [Wirfs-Brock90] is being used, then class descriptions should resemble CRC cards. If OMT [Rumbaugh91a] is being used, then the class descriptions will concentrate more on attributes and operations. Whatever the method, it is important that the class description format is decided in advance. Although there will be close correspondences between the analysis and design class descriptions of particular classes, they may each have different formats to support the different nature of the modeling work at each level.

While Analysis Class Descriptions are very important, they do not tend to be as structured as those at the design level, for less emphasis is placed on documenting interfaces at the analysis level. The following template is adequate for Analysis Class Descriptions, although it should be modified to suit the development method if required.

Name	_____
Definition	_____
Operations	_____
	_____
	_____
Key attributes	_____
	_____
	_____
Relations	_____
	_____
States	_____
	_____
Documentation	_____
	_____
	_____

In the above box, "Name" identifies the class name. Under "Definition," a sentence or two describing the class should be provided. "Documentation" is a place holder for any materials related to the analysis of the class that cannot be expressed in the structured forms of the other work products, such as the Analysis Object Model, the Analysis OIDs, et cetera. An example of this might be an existing customer document describing part of the problem domain.

It is useful to note specific key attributes as these often contribute significantly to an understanding of the class. They are, however, to be understood as *logical* attributes, and not attributes that will necessarily appear in the design. An example of a logical attribute might be "Age." The presence of this attribute in an Analysis Class Description should not be taken to imply that a corresponding attribute will exist in the design. The design might, for example, employ a "dateOfBirth" attribute instead.

Attributes and responsibilities that appear in Class Descriptions should include those inherited from other classes, and they should be marked as such.

Traceability

This work product has the following traceability:

Impacted by:
- Issues (p. 176)
- Analysis Guidelines (p. 183)
- Analysis Object Model (p. 192)
- Analysis OIDs (p. 208)
- Analysis State Models (p. 219)

Impacts:
- Design Class Description (p. 311)

Advice and Guidance

- Do not manually duplicate all class-related information in the class descriptions. For example, do not copy association information manually from the object model into the class descriptions. Good tool support will help to store the analysis work products in a nonredundant fashion.

- Class descriptions should be consistent with the information specified in other analysis work products. Thus, if the Analysis Scenarios have Object Interaction Diagrams (OIDs) which specify messages between objects as operations with parameters and results, then the class descriptions should record these operations, parameters and results. If the OIDs specify only message names, then the class descriptions should record only message names, et cetera.

    There is obviously tension between this piece of advice and the one above. Judgement must be used to decide how best to document a model. It is reasonable to summarize operations from scenarios as the class-centered view will otherwise be missing. It is probably unreasonable to include associations, because the graphic object model will do a better job of that, and no summarizing value-add is provided by the class descriptions.

- When initially opening class descriptions to document modeling sessions, don't worry too much about whether it is correct to include a class. If a class turns out not to be relevant to the model, then it will be isolated in the object model and, more tellingly, it will not participate in any scenarios. The class description can be removed at that point. It is often quicker to define classes that *may* be relevant and to proceed with the modeling, than to worry prematurely about the relevance of classes. However tentatively a class is included, though, it should be well defined.

- Design the class description formats and do not simply accept the format that a particular tool provides.

Verification

- Check that the class descriptions are being maintained.

- Check that the descriptive text accompanying each class description describes the intent of the class, and not its internal structure.

- Check for the completeness of class responsibilities, namely, that there are no missing responsibilities.

- Check attributes and relations for completeness, for relevance to the problem domain, and for relevance to analysis.

Example(s)

The following is an example of a class description from a banking application:

Name	BankAccount
Definition	An agreement between a bank and a customer that enables the customer to deposit funds in the bank and, within certain limits, to withdraw funds.
Operations	• Withdraw funds • Transfer funds to and from account • Query creditworthiness • Maintain customer details • Query balance
Key attributes	• Customer details (such as name and address) • Balance
Relations	• Subclasses: CheckingAccount, SavingsAccount • Associations: ownedBy (Customer)
States	• Open • Active • Overdrawn • Closed
Documentation	The rules for withdrawing funds will depend on the nature of the account. An inward funds transfer can only be done with the authorization of the account owner.

Figure 11-18. Example of Analysis Class Description.

References

- Class Specifications in [Booch94] is for the same purpose as the class description.

- [Wirfs-Brock90] uses CRC cards (class, responsibilities, collaborations) which are an alternative form of class description.

Importance

Analysis Class Descriptions are optional, although very helpful. They need not be written independently. Instead they may be summaries of the other analysis work products generated by an analysis tool.

12.0 User Interface Model Work Products

The user interface model describes how users of the system will invoke the functions specified as part of the analysis model. The analysis model assumes external users can communicate directly with the problem domain objects to invoke their services, and concentrates on the object-oriented semantics of the services themselves. The user interface model assumes that the detailed semantics of the services are specified (and managed) elsewhere, and it focuses on simplifying the communication required to invoke them.

There are many reasons to treat the user interface model as a separate chapter of the workbook. An important reason to keep the interface separate from the analysis model is that there is often more than one interface to a system. For example, it is not uncommon to see a command line interface, an application programming interface (API), and a graphical user interface (GUI) associated with the same system. Further, on different platforms, there may be distinctly different interface models, even within the same "class." For example, a VisualAge GUI will have a different look and feel than one that uses Motif®. The Model-View-Controller(MVC) pattern in Smalltalk-80 is another example of separating user interface from its underlying model.

To summarize these differences, it should be clear that:

- Analysis models document function in an implementation and language independent manner.
- User interface models document how to invoke specific functions given a specific language/platform, but independently of implementation.
- Design models document how to carry out specific functions.

The main goals of this approach are to maximize the reuse of analysis, user interface, and design work products, and to provide a logical separation of concerns to ease maintenance and to promote understanding.

Another benefit is that customers can be brought in as soon as the interface is specified not only to test the interface itself but also to validate the analysis model using an executable work product (UI Prototype). Some end users find the analysis level work products too abstract to validate properly.

Also, after the user interface specifications are completed, the "pubs" teams have enough information to start developing the user's guides and help (such as tutorials), as the implementation details are almost always hidden. There is no need to wait until design is done to begin this effort.

Once the externally-visible user interfacing aspects of a system (the work products described above) have been defined, they must be incorporated into the system design. This involves selecting the view classes that are to interact the model classes that have been identified during analysis, and using Object Interaction Diagrams (OIDs) to show how the view and model classes communicate. This is design work, but it is logically separate from the rest of design because it is driven by user interfacing requirements. So, the ideal solution would be to maintain two distinct design models: one that incorporates user inter- facing concerns only, and one that also addresses the remainder of the design issues. This would involve extending the user interfacing work products with Object Model and OID work products that then form the basis for the design work products. In practice, however, the overhead of maintaining these separate models may be prohibitive, in which case the user interfacing Object Model and OIDs may evolve into the design model proper, and only documented there. It is useful, however, to bear in mind that design for user inter- facing is a logically distinct activity. In particular, its traceability and its techniques differ from those used in the remainder of design. The user interface section of the project workbook consists of the following work products:

- Guidelines
- Screen Flows
- Screen Layouts
- User Interface Prototype

These work products all "inherit" the common work product attributes described in Section 8.1, and they have specialized attributes of their own.

User Interface guidelines are used to ensure that interfaces are consistent and meet the needs of the users of the system.

Screen Layouts define specifically what screens will look like and Screen Flows defines the sequences in which screens will be displayed to the user. Together these work pro- ducts can help to assure that the project will meet the needs of the users.

User Interface Prototypes can be used to model, validate, and change the system's user interface at various points during the development cycle.

The work products and their specialized content are defined and commented on in the following sections of this chapter.

12.1 USER INTERFACE GUIDELINES

Description

The guidelines section of the User Interface part of the workbook consists of a set of guidelines to assist developers in constructing work products related to user interfaces. These are typically, but not exclusively, graphical user interfaces (GUIs). Such guidelines might refer to some relative standard such as IBM's Common User Access standard. Such guidelines might refer to any relevant standards and might augment these standards by guidelines specific to the development organization or project. The guidelines may require or suggest the use of a particular tool, for example, a specific GUI-builder.

Purpose

The construction of user interfaces is not purely a matter of applying good design principles. Aspects of the design of these interfaces are often dictated directly by the project requirements due to their external nature. It is the task of this section to help developers meet these requirements in a consistent manner.

Participants

The user interface design team leader, if there is such a separate team, is responsible for writing the guidelines. Important contributors to the guidelines will be human factors advisors and end users or customers.

The guidelines should be considered part of the Nonfunctional Requirements and should be reviewed as such with the appropriate audience.

Timing

The activity of defining the user interfaces will begin during the requirements gathering project phase. The guidelines must be completed before the start of the design phase of the first development cycle.

Technique

The Nonfunctional Requirements will define which standards apply to the construction of user interfaces. This section must specify any additional project constraints on construction; subsequently, a set of positive guidelines to help developers satisfy these constraints must be written. Where possible, tools to simplify and guarantee compliance with these constraints should be found, and their usage described here.

In addition to addressing the issue of standards, the guidelines should include advice on a *process* for producing the user interfaces.

Good sets of guidelines may be developed iteratively over time as different projects are forced to address similar user interfacing constraints.

Strengths

The concentration of user interface construction advice in one place saves duplication of effort by the developers who will need this advice. The focus of the requirements chapter of the workbook is on contractual issues; by itself it does not provide positive guidance as to how user interfacing constraints can be met. Explicit guidelines also assist reviewers to determine whether user interfacing constraints have indeed been met.

Weaknesses

None.

Notation

Free format text.

Traceability

This work product has the following traceability:

Impacted by:
- Nonfunctional Requirements (p. 106)
- Intended Development Process (p. 127)
- Project Workbook Outline (p. 132)
- Quality Assurance Plan (p. 147)
- Issues (p. 176)

Impacts:
- Project Workbook Outline (p. 132)
- User Interface Guidelines (p. 234)
- Screen Flows (p. 237)
- Screen Layouts (p. 242)
- UI Prototype (p. 247)

Advice and Guidance

- Use examples where appropriate, to demonstrate styles of user interface.

- List any tools that can be used to help satisfy interface constraints.

- Comply with user interfacing constraints even in the first development cycle. Only in this way will user interfaces grow incrementally and iteratively during the project in a relatively painless manner.

Verification

- Check that all guidelines are either very explicit or have references to documents or standards.

- Check whether there is a means to extend the user interface standards, and to inform the relevant parties, where appropriate.

Example(s)

Sample User Interface Guidelines might be:

- Use VisualAge for C++ to build UI Prototypes, and extend these to the production UI work products.

- Use the Use Case Model and Analysis Scenarios as starting points for UI design. Develop Screen Layouts and Screen Flows on a white board, in story board fashion, before adding "view objects" to your Design Object Model.

References

- For IBM's Common User Access (CUA) guidelines, see [IBM94b].

- For Motif guidelines see [OSF93].

- For guidelines on Windows® see [Microsoft92].

- General advice on Human Interface Design is offered in [Apple92] by Apple® Computer. So it is useful even if you are not doing the GUI design for Macintosh®.

- See [Fowler95] for general discussions on GUI style.

- A discussion of principles and guidelines for Graphical User Interface (GUI) design in general can be found in [Mayhew92].

Importance

Optional but important if your project has a user interface that is critical to the project's customer acceptance. User Interface Guidelines can help ensure that a consistent interface that meets user requirements is created.

12.2 SCREEN FLOWS

Description

The User Interface (UI) Screen Flow describes the sequence of screens (windows, dialog boxes, prompts, et cetera) the user expects to see from the desired software system as it furnishes the required functions. One can think of the UI Screen Flow as a "story board" that depicts the software system's visual responses and prompts based on the task-oriented actions of the end user.

The actual Screen Layouts are defined in the UI Screen Layout work product, see Section 12.3. The UI Screen Flow work product demonstrates how these screens are invoked in a task-oriented manner.

The UI Screen Flow is usually limited to "main line" functionality of the system, describing all of the user interface presentations relating to tasks expected to be performed by the users without getting into all the exceptional cases (error reporting).

Screen Flows are also used for designing "Help Screens," a sequence of on-line information about using the system. Here, they not only show the information sequence, but they also show where they "hook into" the functional Screen Flow.

Purpose

UI Screen Flows are needed to design user interfaces that match the intended user's conceptual model of the domain and to ensure efficient user interaction with the software. The former implies that Screen Flows steer development towards a user-oriented, or "user friendly," system as opposed to a developer/programmer oriented system (this assumes that developers are not, nor will they be regular users of the system).

Screen Flows also interact with Use Cases by detailing how the information flows from the user to the system, and visa versa, for each functional transaction.

Participants

UI Screen Flows are usually designed and documented by a human factors staff (or others versed in direct manipulation interfaces), by analysts, and by end-user (customer) representatives.

A human factors or UI expert might create the Screen Flows based on their expertise and interpretation of the analysis work products. In this case, the user representative or client would review the Screen Flows for compatibility with their conceptual model of the system.

Alternatively, an analyst might capture the client's prescriptive (how) description of what the system needs to do and translate that into Screen Flows that he could verify with the user (or representative). This could be done iteratively and incrementally with the development of the Use Case Model.

Lastly, the client might provide Screen Flows to the analyst as a concrete specification of what he wants. The analyst could derive the Use Case Model from it. In the latter two cases, a human factors or UI expert might review the Screen Flows and make suggestions for improvement.

Timing

The activity of defining the flow of screens can start at early stages of the project as described above (before, during, or after analysis). In general, Screen Flows are developed before Screen Layouts, but this by no means precludes Screen Flows from referencing existing Screen Layouts. The pair will, of course, be refined through the various development increments.

In some cases, it might be possible to defer development of Screen Flows to the design phase. This is possible in systems that have a rich "Model" domain and few demands on the user interface. Note that in this case, the Screen Flows would still occur before the design of the "View" or "Controller" portions of the system [Krasner88]. It is just that the "Model" design could overlap the Screen Flow development. The "View" and "Controller" design classes then tie the Screen Flow and Layout to the "Model" classes.

Technique

There's more than one way to develop UI Screen Flows, but here's one:

1. From a list of the Analysis Scenarios, select those that are "main line" functions, that is, not dealing with exceptional cases.

2. Organize these by the task being performed or by the subdomain of focus.

3. Organize these groups of Scenarios into what might be typical usage "sessions."

4. For each session, draw a simplified (thumbnail) view of the screen that depicts the starting screen's state before the associated scenario is triggered.

- Add new thumbnails that depict the next screen (or window, dialog, prompt) that the user would see, and connect this to the previous thumbnail with a line.

The result will be a series of "story boards" that are part of a hierarchy or web that describes the whole external behavior of the system.

Strengths

The simple yet concrete representation of the system and its response to user interactions is easy for the client to understand and for the analyst and UI designer to communicate.

Screen Flows work with Screen Layouts (just the content aspect) to identify design criteria (operations, relations, attributes, and states) for view objects. This information does not exist in any of the analysis work products.

Screen Flows are a distinct aspect of design. Breaking them out of design allows a logical separation of concerns that supports parallel development with specially skilled resources.

Weaknesses

Screen Flows have very few weaknesses. Only when they are abused by overuse or underuse, do they cause problems. Overuse leads to voluminous vapid diagrams where interesting user tasks are lost. Underuse makes the system seem simplistic and does not provide the input to view object designers that they need.

Notation

The common notation for Screen Flows is a tree or web of named (labeled) thumbnail screen images connected by sequencing arrows. A less vibrant variation might be a tree or web of screen labels connected with sequencing arrows where the labels refer to accompanying Screen Layouts.

Traceability

This work product has the following traceability:

Impacted by:
- Use Case Model (p. 96)
- Nonfunctional Requirements (p. 106)
- Issues (p. 176)
- User Interface Guidelines (p. 234)
- Screen Layouts (p. 242)
- UI Prototype (p. 247)

Impacts:
- Test Plan (p. 164)
- Screen Layouts (p. 242)
- UI Prototype (p. 247)
- Design Object Model (p. 281)
- Coding Guidelines (p. 322)
- Design OIDs (p. 298)
- Design State Models (p. 306)
- User Support Materials (p. 341)

Advice and Guidance

Use UI Screen Flows to:

- Solicit input from users for analysis and design:
  - Use cases
  - Scenarios
  - State Model
  - Object Model

- Reflect analysis work products back to client in a semidesigned user-oriented form

- Locate and compare UI Screen Layouts in your workbook

- Measure the complexity of your application

Verification

- Is the flow and return of control between screens obvious?

- Are there any ambiguities concerning when flow goes to a screen or where and when and if it returns? Are the connections between the screens directed (arrows)?

- Are all screens labeled?

Example(s)

The following shows an example Screen Flow for a library system:

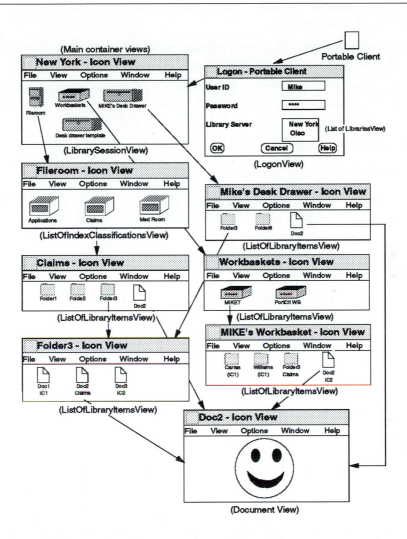

Figure 12-1. *Library System Screen Flow.*

Upon starting the Portable Client application, the end user will be provided a logon window where a User ID, Password, and Library Server (ListofLibrariesView) selection are specified (see Figure 12-1). Upon logging onto the system, the end user will be provided a main window (LibrarySessionView) showing them four main objects:

- Fileroom: provides a look at the index classes (IndexClassView) or the ability to directly search the fileroom. Upon opening an index class object or as a result of a search, a list of library items are displayed in another window (ListofLibraryItemsView).

- Workbaskets: provides a look at the workbaskets (WorkbasketView). Upon opening a workbasket, a list of library items are displayed (ListofLibraryItemsView).

- User ID Desk Drawer (i.e., Mike's Desk Drawer): provides a working area in which users can copy/move documents or folders, resulting in a window listing its library items (ListofLibraryItemsView).

- Desk Drawer Template: provides the user the ability to create new folders.

References

- Dave Collins describes Screen Flow as Rough sketches in "Sequencing View Design" and "Task Interaction Sequencing" in his book *Designing Object-Oriented User Interfaces*[Collins95]

- A general discussion of principles and guidelines for Graphical User Interface (GUI) design can be found in [Mayhew92].

- [Krasner88] is a good introduction on the Model-View-Controller paradigm.

Importance

Optional, although an important way to ensure that the user interface being developed is friendly to the intended users.

12.3 SCREEN LAYOUTS

Description

The User Interface (UI) Screen Layouts depict the actual appearance of screens (windows, prompts, dialog boxes, et cetera) that the user will see during the operation of the system. Usually, the Screen Layouts are only prepared in advance for the main- line tasks performed by the application and not for exceptional conditions. They show the actual text, labels, and icons intended for that screen as well as detailed spatial arrangement of text, icons, controls (buttons, sliders, fields, et cetera).

Purpose

UI Screen Layouts are needed, along with Screen Flows, to validate the functional completeness and usability of the user interface to the intended system. Conformance to UI standards, application conventions, terminology, and even color schemes can be established and checked with Screen Layouts. They are the communication media among users, human factors experts, and designers. So much of the usability of a system is determined by well designed, consistent, and efficient user interfaces. If Screens Layouts are not done during the UI phase, they will eventually be done by the implementation team who might not have the human factors expertise or user understanding, thus jeopardizing the effectiveness and usability of the resultant system.

Participants

The UI Screen Layout work products should be designed and documented by Human Factors experts, User Interface designers, or others versed in direct manipulation interfaces. The Screen Layouts should be reviewed by intended end users in order to get feedback on the usability (comprehension, intuitiveness, and efficiency) of the intended system.

Timing

UI Screen Layouts should be completed before the design of the software components that are directly driven by or control the user interface (*view objects* and *controller objects*). Usually, Screen Layouts are developed after the UI Screen Flows, since they identify the need for individual screens. Together, though, Screen Flows and Screen Layouts can be developed before, during, or after the analysis phase.

When done after analysis, the UI designer has the benefit of the completed analysis work products as the basis of his UI design. This should mean that the UI designer can understand the problem, its conceptual domain (Analysis Object Model), its functional (Use Case Model), and Nonfunctional Requirements, the interaction of the conceptual objects in the domain (Analysis OIDs), and any life-cycle behavior (Analysis State Model) of the conceptual objects.

When done before analysis, Screen Flows and Layouts help discover functional (Use Case Model) and Nonfunctional Requirements. You might think of this as "UI-driven requirements gathering." Although this is not a preferred technique, it sometimes aids communication with clients who have strong ideas about the appearance of the "to be" system.

When done concurrently with analysis, Screen Flows and Layouts help identify conceptual objects, their states, and interactions among the objects (Object Model, State Model, and OIDs). Again, though not too popular, this might be called "UI-driven analysis."

Technique

Working from UI Screen Flows and analysis work products (or user interviews), a UI or human factors expert determines:

- The information to be presented to user

- The information that needs to be solicited from the user

- The actions that can be performed from that view

Using the benefit of UI experience, UI standards, UI facilities, and analysis work products, the expert then designs the screen by addressing:

- Selection of metaphor

These are the set of analogies we use to realize the user's model.

- Selection of a mechanism

    A good metaphor has to be visible to the user. A mechanism is a UI object that helps the system designer to make the system concepts visible. Examples of mechanisms are: button, entry field, menu, prompt, scroll bar, et cetera

- Selection of presentation facilities (titles, labels, fixed text, scrolling text, hidden/detail text, images, icons, et cetera)

- Selection of input facilities (fields, option lists, sliders, spin buttons, radio buttons, and the like).

- Arrangement of UI groups, ("floor planning").

- Arrangement within groups (for example: menu bar order, pull-down order, radio button arrangement, field arrangement, and so forth).

- Font face, style, and size for all text.

- Color for normal and highlighted or grouped information/controls.

- Aesthetics.

UI Screen Layouts are best developed with a GUI builder application, since they can automate many of the mundane tasks (for example: layouts, fonts, drawing of controls, color/texture). Examples of such tools are: VisualAge, X-Designer/XVT, Microsoft VisualBasic®, and possibly Apple's Hypercard®. They also provide an obvious lead into UI Prototyping.

Screen Layouts are reviewed with user for feedback and recommendations.

Strengths

UI Screen Layouts are very concrete work products for addressing external design with users and clients. They give the project a sense of reality that precedes the availability of prototypes or even "alpha" versions of the intended system.

Having Screen Layouts designed by experts before the software is designed aids analysis, increases confidence of the client, and removes a large burden from the default UI designer, and the implementation team (who might not be qualified to create something so subtly intricate and significant to the customer).

Weaknesses

If one does not use UI builder tools, the detailed creation of potentially hundreds of screens, could be a very time consuming proposition.

Trying to depict too much detail too early could be a waste of time.

Notation

Any format that shows the layout of the screens can be used. Usually projects use a visual programming tool or UI builder to draft the layout of the screens and document the work product using a screen capture tool. Hand-drawn figures are sometimes an efficient means of communication of the Screen Layout, especially at early stages in the project.

Traceability

This work product has the following traceability:

Impacted by:
- Use Case Model (p. 96)
- Nonfunctional Requirements (p. 106)
- Issues (p. 176)
- User Interface Guidelines (p. 234)
- Screen Flows (p. 237)
- UI Prototype (p. 247)

Impacts:
- Screen Flows (p. 237)
- UI Prototype (p. 247)
- Design Object Model (p. 281)
- Design OIDs (p. 298)
- Design State Models (p. 306)
- User Support Materials (p. 341)

Advice and Guidance

- Employ human factors or UI experts to develop the Screen Layouts.

- Use a visual programming tool or UI builder tool to create and edit the Screen Layouts.

- Start simple. Use an incremental and iterative approach to Screen Layout development and get frequent feedback from the intended users.

- Focus on the few screens that the users will spend 90 percent of their time with—proportion your effort on UI Screen Layouts according to the importance that interface has to the user (see Figure 12-2).

Verification

- Do all screens identified in UI Screen Flow have Screen Layouts?

- Does each UI Screen Layout appear in a Screen Flow? Is it labeled?

- Are all transitions between screens identified in the Screen Flow enabled by requestable actions in the Screen Layouts?

- Have all applicable UI standards been followed?

- Has the terminology and arrangement been validated by users?

Example(s)

The following is a very simple example of what a Screen Layout might look like:

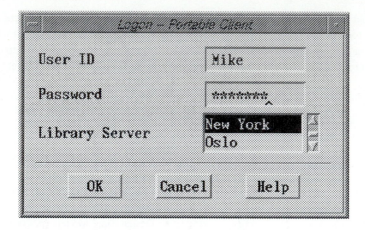

Figure 12-2. *Example of a User Interface Screen Layout.*

References

- Dave Collins describes Screen Layout as "Content View Design" in his *Designing Object-Oriented User Interfaces*[Collins95] .

- For IBM's Common User Access (CUA) Guidelines, see [IBM94b].

- For Motif Guidelines see [OSF93].

- For Guidelines on Windows see [Microsoft92].

- Good advice on Human Interface Design can be found in [Apple92].

- See [Fowler95] for general discussions on GUI style.

- A general discussion of principles and guidelines for Graphical User Interface (GUI) design can be found in [Mayhew92].

- [Krasner88] is a good introduction on the Model-View-Controller paradigm.

Importance

Optional, although very important. For systems with significant User Interfaces, some form of distinct UI design is needed, if not Screen Flows and Screen Layouts, then perhaps a UI Prototype should be developed.

12.4 USER INTERFACE PROTOTYPE

Description

The User Interface Prototype is a small application program which models the look, feel, and sequencing of the intended application's user interface. It should focus on:

- Screen/window layouts, arrangement of
  - Fields
  - Buttons
  - Visual Cues
- Terminology/Semantics, meaning of
  - Icons
  - Field and Button Labels
  - Static Text, Instructions
- Screen Focus
  - Window/DialogBox sequence (GUI-style)
  - Screen/Menu sequence (full-screen video style)

The User Interface Prototypes should try to emulate the intended visual behavior of the application and should not be concerned with anything else (for example: using real persistence, communication, distribution, data model, and DBMS mechanisms). It can be implemented with the intended GUI facilities (for example: VisualAge, X-Designer/XVT, PM, OSF/Motif) or it can be implemented with surrogate UI generating facilities (for example: MS-VisualBasic, Apple Hypercard) or it can be done on paper. Anyway, the point is to invest in validating the application's visual behavior while avoiding as much as possible the other facets of the application.

User interfaces are primarily visual, but other interfaces involving sound, touch, et cetera, should also be included if your application interacts with the user via those cues.

Purpose

The purpose of the UI Prototype is to model and validate the application's user interface (visual, audio, et cetera). Creating a user interface that does not match the user's conceptual model of the domain, or that is not intuitive (for example, consistent with standards) is a major risk that application developers face. To address that risk, many development groups create a User Interface Prototype to demonstrate and tune the user interface to the user's expectations by using feedback from users. See Section 17.4, Prototyping as a Risk Management Technique for a general discussion of how and why to do prototyping.

By using a streamlined process, specialized tools, and by focusing on a narrow set of concerns, the prototype developers can determine the best UI design long before the rest of the application is designed or implemented. A "live" UI Prototype is more engaging and revealing than a "paper" model consisting of Screen Layouts and Screen Flows.

The UI Prototype also raises analysis issues by identifying visual objects, relations, attributes, behaviors, interactions, and states. Starting assumptions and expected outcomes of scenarios are often verified with the user via the UI Prototype.

Participants

The UI Prototype is usually designed and documented by a Human Factors staff or other experts versed in direct manipulation interfaces and GUI standards. This group normally works with the application development group to understand the nature of the intended application (for example: concepts, terminology, functionality). They should also be aware of predecessor and competing applications and their UI strengths and weaknesses. The UI group usually has expertise with specialized tools (for example, GUI builders) and techniques that streamline the development of the UI Prototype.

Timing

The UI Prototype should be developed after the analysis phase and before or concurrent with the design phase. From analysis, the UI Prototype developers need to know domain concepts, terminology, and the function of the intended application. The UI Prototype needs to provide input to the application designers (in design phase), including the sequence of events and parameters that will be sent to the rest of the application and what is expected in return.

Technique

UI Prototype developers should start their activity by studying the following:

- Requirements work products

    - Problem Statement
    - Use Case Model

- Analysis work products

    - Scenarios (with assumptions and outcomes)
    - Object Model (conceptual attributes, relations)

- User Interface

    - UI Guidelines (standards)
    - Screen Layout (if available)
    - Screen Flows (if available)

From these, the developers should use the most efficient tools to generate a working model (test application) of the user interface. If Screen Layouts (Section 12.3) and Screen Flows (Section 12.2) have already been designed on paper, they will provide an advanced starting point for the scaffolded implementation of the UI prototype. Otherwise, the same techniques used to generate them can be used to incrementally design and implement the UI Prototype. Whether Screen Layouts and Screen Flows were developed it should be noted that the UI Prototype is derived from, and should be consistent with, the analysis model.

Strengths

The advantage of creating a UI Prototype over creating Screen Layouts and Screen Flows is that the UI Prototype is more engaging and revealing to the people who exercise it (for example: customers, human factors experts). If the developers use a GUI generator/builder to create the UI Prototype, the effort is less than using drawing tools, and the results are more realistic.

The advantage of creating a UI Prototype over having no UI design work products at all is that, for UI-intensive and general public oriented applications, the significant risk of developing a nonintuitive or unfriendly user interface will be largely eliminated.

The UI Prototype also raises analysis issues and provides an active means of verifying other analysis work products.

Weaknesses

The cost of developing a UI Prototype may be significant if:

- The application is complex

- The application is graphical (2D/3D editors)

- Good UI Builder tools are not available

- There is too much senseless rework (for example, rearranging screens)

If UI Builder tools do not produce results close enough to intended style (for example: missing features, different look and feel) the prototype might not be valid or as valuable than if it did.

If the UI Prototype and its results are not available when the application developers need it, there will develop schedule and resource problems.

Notation

Not applicable, since UI Prototype is an executable program.

Traceability

This work product has the following traceability:

Impacted by:
- Use Case Model (p. 96)
- Nonfunctional Requirements (p. 106)
- Issues (p. 176)
- User Interface Guidelines (p. 234)
- Screen Flows (p. 237)
- Screen Layouts (p. 242)

Impacts:
- Screen Flows (p. 237)
- Screen Layouts (p. 242)

Advice and Guidance

If you have a UI-intensive application or a general public-oriented application, create a UI Prototype to resolve the risk of unintentionally creating a nonintuitive or unfriendly user interface for your application.

- Use a specialized UI team (or human factors team) to do the prototype for you if you can, it will save time.

- Use specialized UI Builder tools to create and exercise the UI Prototype.

- Limit the scope of the prototype to UI issues and concerns (don't overload the prototype with other issues like performance, persistence, distribution, communication, et cetera).

- Develop the UI Prototype in stages (incrementally) and test them with customers before tuning (iterating) or proceeding to the next increment. Don't pester the customer with too many test sessions, but do use the test sessions to develop rapport with customer.

- When performing this activity, don't waste a lot of time responding to minor changes (like colors, placement, and such). Listen to the feedback and get back to work.

Verification

- Not applicable.

Example(s)

Not applicable, since UI Prototype is an executable program.

References

- Good arguments for rapid prototyping are offered in [Connell89]. Although it is not specific to object-oriented technology, many general principles still apply.

- A general discussion of principles and guidelines for Graphical User Interface (GUI) design can be found in [Mayhew92].

Importance

Optional, although very important for UI-intensive applications and applications oriented to the general public (for example: banking, library, event kiosks, exhibitions, lobby facilities).

13.0 Design Work Products

The Design portion of the project workbook details those work products that are created during the design phase of the project.

Object-oriented design is the process of determining the Architecture for and specifying the classes needed to implement a software product. It involves making global and local decisions about a planned implementation based on constraints, Nonfunctional Requirements, and available alternatives.

During analysis we focused on problem-domain objects; however, during design we focus on solution domain objects. During design, the emphasis is on defining a solution [Monarchi92].

The problem domain classes encountered during analysis are refined during design. New objects and classes are created during design as shown in Figure 13-1.

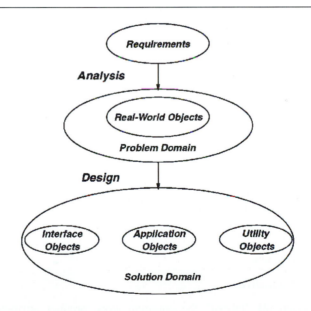

Figure 13-1. The Relationship Between OO Analysis and OO Design.

As part of the design activity, the system is partitioned into subsystems to make the design process more manageable.

In summary:

- Object-oriented design transforms the analysis model into the design of a software solution

- Definition of the overall software architecture (global decisions) is done during design.

- Attributes, operations, and algorithms are defined for all design objects during design.

- New objects, not domain-derived but implementation-oriented, are defined during design process.

The boundary between design and implementation work products is both flexible and subjective. The goal of design is to achieve sufficient agreement on interface definition and internal structure that implementation work may then proceed independently in parallel teams. The amount of design detail that is needed will depend on many factors including the size of implementation groups relative to the size of the project, the degree of coupling between the team components, and the like. In practice this means that each project must decide for itself exactly where to draw the line. Wherever that is, the following work products are relevant, but projects must choose the degree of detail to include in each. As mentioned above, this decision is project-dependent but is by no means arbitrary. The amount of detail is chosen to enable independent parallel implementation of the design after it has been completed and reviewed.

The design section of the project workbook consists of the following work products:

- Design Guidelines
- System Architecture
- Application Programming Interfaces (APIs)
- Target Environment
- Subsystem Model
- Design Object Model
- Design Scenarios
- Design Object Interaction Diagrams
- Design State Models
- Design Class Descriptions
- Rejected Design Alternatives

These work products all "inherit" the common work product attributes described on Section 8.1, and they have specialized attributes of their own.

Design Guidelines are a set of rules that help in defining the design deliverables and guiding the design process and as such have an impact on most of the other design work products.

System Architecture is the set of broad design principles that allows the system design to be coherent and consistent. It, too, has an impact on most of the other design work products.

The Application Programming Interfaces (APIs) are a set of visible classes and their interfaces that enable the system to be used without the need to understand its internal details.

The Target Environment defines the environment(s) in which the system is intended to operate. This is typically part of the Nonfunctional Requirements or at the least is impacted by that work product. This can have a big impact on the System Architecture.

The Subsystem Model partitions a system into smaller entities and delegates certain system responsibility to those entities. The main benefit of this is the breaking up of large, complex systems into more manageable entities. Each Subsystem will have its own set of design work products such as Design Object Model, Design Scenarios, and Design Object Interaction Diagrams.

The Design Object Model is a static model that represents the structure of the classes and their relationships with each other in the implementation of the system.

Design Scenarios enumerate the possible assumptions and resultant outcomes (starting and ending states) for each intended behavior of the planned system.

Design Object Interaction Diagrams graphically depict the collaborations between objects that is required to support the Design Scenarios.

Design State Models represent the dynamic behavior of design classes and are done for all classes that have strong state-dependent object behavior.

Class Descriptions contain all of the information known about a class at the design level. They provide the starting point for implementation work on a class.

Rejected Design Alternatives provided a repository of those major design directions that were considered but rejected. They are valuable when the need arises to revisit design decisions as often happens in complex system development projects.

The work products and their specialized content are defined and discussed in more detail in the following sections.

13.1 DESIGN GUIDELINES

Description

Design Guidelines are the set of rules intended to define the design deliverables and to guide the design process of a particular development project. In this respect they are similar to the Analysis Guidelines (Section 11.1), but are broader in scope to reflect the greater diversity of the design deliverables. Similarly to Analysis Guidelines, Design Guidelines may be divided into work product guidelines and process guidelines.

Analysis Guidelines must address object, scenario, and state modeling, and the processes to perform these. Design Guidelines must address these too. For the common aspects, the Design Guidelines can probably just refer to their analysis counterparts. Some additional notational concerns that are relevant at design time are those of concurrency, distribution, and association directionality. Notational extensions should be defined to indicate process boundaries and to make distinctions between synchronous and asynchronous messaging on Design OIDs. The particular process for deciding upon process boundaries and message types should be described in the guidelines also.

The other work products that are unique to design, such as System Architecture, Subsystem Model, and Application Programming Interface also need guidelines to assure that their documentation is consistent and useful. For example, the API for a subsystem might be documented as a set of figures, tables, and descriptive text, or as a collection of programming "header files," or as both formats. The Design Guidelines must make it clear what is expected of all the participants. Contracts between subsystems are also useful documentation that the guidelines might insist upon.

A very important part of the design process is the way in which it treats design Issues and their resolution. The Design Guidelines should provide guidance on this matter.

Purpose

Both Analysis and Design Guidelines are important, but for slightly different reasons. Analysis Guidelines are required primarily to agree on notation and to help the team get going, particularly if the team includes novices to object-oriented software development. Design Guidelines are used much more to guide the development process. In analysis, freedom is encouraged because the emphasis is on understanding the requirements, documenting and analyzing them, and verifying them with the customer. The nature of design demands a disciplined approach to process and documentation.

Participants

The Analysis and Design Guidelines will probably be written by the same people, perhaps the team leader and the architect. Considerable experience is required of both software engineering in general and object-oriented software development in particular.

Timing

The Design Guidelines must be completed before design can begin. They must, therefore, be written either during the first analysis cycle, or earlier.

As is the case for Analysis Guidelines, Design Guidelines and team education are interdependent. What is special to object-oriented design (as opposed to structured design) is principally in the realm of process. It is therefore the design process that is concentrated on in the Design Guidelines, and in the educational effort targeted at design. This dependency means that the Design Guidelines might have to be agreed upon even before design education has begun.

Technique

Beg, steal, or borrow some existing design guidelines from existing object-oriented projects. Customize these and review them with your project. Interview experienced developers to check that the guidelines are still reasonable and complete. Consider asking a mentor for advice on Design Guidelines, or to comment on those that have already been assembled.

Strengths

Design Guidelines ensure common style and consistency among the various design work products.

Weaknesses

None.

Notation

Design Guidelines take the form of check lists and/or templates addressing each work product, process, and tool intended to be used by the developers.

Design guidelines are usually organized by work products.

Traceability

This work product has the following traceability:

Impacted by:
- Intended Development Process (p. 127)
- Project Workbook Outline (p. 132)
- Quality Assurance Plan (p. 147)
- Reuse Plan (p. 158)
- Test Plan (p. 164)
- Issues (p. 176)

Impacts:
- Project Workbook Outline (p. 132)
- System Architecture (p. 257)
- APIs (p. 265)
- Target Environment (p. 272)
- Subsystems (p. 274)
- Design Object Model (p. 281)
- Design Scenarios (p. 293)
- Design OIDs (p. 298)
- Design State Models (p. 306)
- Design Class Description (p. 311)

Advice and Guidance

- The guidelines should be minimal though sufficient to ensure that the design work products are understandable, usable, and consistent.

- Use existing guidelines where they are available and appropriate. Modify these only as necessary.

- If your guidelines are novel, publish them for others to evaluate and use.

- Use work product templates where relevant.

- Harvest good templates from the workbooks of other projects.

- Use the guidelines as entry criteria to design reviews.

Verification

- Check that guidelines exist for the process, notation, and tool usage for each anticipated type of work product.

- Check that guidelines exist for the usage of all tools, where appropriate.

- Check that the guidelines provide for maximal integration of design work products. For example, are the Design Class Descriptions being generated automatically from the Design Object Model and other models? Is API documentation being generated directly from the Design Object Model?

Example(s)

Sample Design Guidelines might be:

Process	The design process is scenario-driven. That is, design proceeds by incrementally transforming the analysis OIDs into design OIDs, each transformation being the result of a design decision.
API	The Application Programming Interface should include C++ header files for each subsystem.
Scenarios	The first few scenarios chosen for transformation should be central to the business of the application. These scenarios are used to drive out the main architectural features of the application. These initial scenarios are modeled by the entire design team under the leadership of the project architect.
	Subsequent scenarios may be designed by subteams, but the architect must be consulted if a subteam is being forced to make a generic design decision. A generic design decision is one that has implications beyond the single scenario. Daily design meetings are to be held at which the evolving Architecture is presented and discussed.
	If there is significant doubt as to how a scenario is to be designed, a formal Issue is opened and tracked. An Issue is specified as a problematic scenario and a list of alternative OIDs. The Issue is resolved by selecting one of the OIDs, and documenting the decision including the rejected alternatives.
Issues	Issues are to be tracked by the architect.

Figure 13-2. Example of Design Guidelines.

References

None.

Importance

Formal Design Guidelines are optional, but useful in guiding the design process for a development project.

13.2 SYSTEM ARCHITECTURE

Description

In order for a design to be coherent and for the design process to be efficient, it is necessary for certain broad design principles to be established in advance. This agreed-upon set of underlying principles is the System Architecture. Restated with a slightly different emphasis, the System Architecture is the set of global, projectwide design decisions.

A System Architecture can be broad, encompassing many aspects of design, or it can be narrow. Any design statement can be considered to be architectural if it is agreed that it is to have general applicability. The "obvious" areas of architectural interest are the following.

- Structure, the way in which the software is to be layered or partitioned
- The key communication patterns between components of this structure
- Communication (interprocess communication for example)
- Distribution
- Persistence
- Security
- Error Handling
- Recovery
- Debugging
- The use or reuse of specific, existing hardware and software configurations.

Within these and other areas, architectural statements may be strong, imposing a well-defined structure on designs, or they may be weak, insisting on only a minimal structure.

A System Architecture may prescribe new structures, or may insist that the application must use particular, existing class libraries or frameworks.

A distinction exists between the *problem domain* explored during analysis and the *solution domain* defined during design. The solution domain can often be subdivided usefully into the following subdomains.

- Application subdomain
- Application support subdomain
- Utility subdomains

The application subdomain consists principally of (design versions of) those classes identified during design. The application support subdomain consists of application-specific classes that the application classes will need in order to deliver their functionality. The utility subdomain consists of those support classes that are application-independent. A number of utility subdomains might be defined according to subject matter such as collections, communications, and the like. Within the context of a banking application, an example of an application subdomain class is Account; an example of an application support subdomain class is CreditStrategy; an example of a utility subdomain class is ISequence.

The definition of the application, the application support, and the utility subdomains, and the mapping of problem domain classes onto classes in these subdomains is what design, as a whole, is all about. It is the global design decisions of the *System Architecture* that provide a framework within which this mapping can take place in a coherent and consistent manner. The architect must balance the need to guide designers with the need to keep the actual design separate from the statements of the principles that underlie the design, the System Architecture. In practice this usually means doing the following.

- Identifying the utility subdomain class libraries.
- Identifying the broad structures and communication patterns of the application support subdomain.
- Providing guidelines to help designers map the problem domain classes into the solution domain.

As discussed below, it is in response to the various kinds of Nonfunctional Requirements that these decisions are made.

Purpose

If the process of design takes place in the absence of a strong System Architecture, design decisions will tend to be *ad hoc* and unrelated. Furthermore, all design decisions must be made from scratch, which is very time consuming. Successful projects tend to be characterized by System Architectures that are simple, strong, coherent and that have been enforced throughout the project.

As the design process proceeds, more and more people gradually become involved. Initially only the architect works on the design. At a certain point individuals and then teams begin to work in parallel. The System Architecture serves to capture those global design decisions that have to be made centrally by the architect before parallel work begins. After this point, making global design decisions is much more difficult and much less efficient.

A good technique for driving the design process as a whole is scenario-driven design, see Section 18.7, which uses bundles of scenarios as the requirements for each cycle of an iterative and incremental development schedule. A potential problem of the technique, however, is that it is so requirements-driven that software developed in this way may be brittle; changes in the requirements might be difficult to implement. The solution to this problem is to perform scenario-driven development within the context of a System Architecture driven not only by project-specific Nonfunctional Requirements, but also Nonfunctional Requirements related to good software engineering principles, such as modularity, anticipating changes, and reuse. The need to balance scenario-driven design in this way is another factor motivating the development of a strong System Architecture.

Participants

A System Architecture is usually the work of one person. Committees lack the focus to develop the required simplicity and coherence. The project architect is responsible for the System Architecture and for ensuring that its principles are followed.

Timing

System Architecture definition is usually the first activity to be performed in the design phase. All other design work may be thought of as mapping the analysis model onto the System Architecture.

Even in the context of an iterative and incremental development process, it usually pays to develop the bulk of a System Architecture very early. Architectural decisions can and should be tested in development increments, of course, and if necessary adjusted in the light of experience, but right from the beginning of design there must be an architectural vision of how the whole system will work. If this is not done, the necessary rework may be too expensive. Iterative rework is to be expected, but it should be as localized as possible. Reworking a System Architecture, or imposing one after the design and implementation is well advanced, will require the kinds of large-scale changes which most projects will not be able to afford. The most likely results of such an attempt will be a weak System Architecture and a complex design lacking coherence.

Having said that a System Architecture must be defined early, the *implementation* of the architectural ideas can happily be spread over a number of development increments, in a risk-driven manner of course. Initial increments might, for example, ignore persistence and distribution, although parallel, early prototyping activity might test proposed resolutions to persistence and distribution issues.

Technique

In the way that the functional requirements (best expressed as a use case model and a set of scenarios) drive the analysis phase, the Nonfunctional Requirements drive the design phase. It is the constraints of the Nonfunctional Requirements that force design decisions. As the System Architecture consists of those design decisions that must be made globally, architectural design is driven by those Nonfunctional Requirements that have a global impact. Selecting a System Architecture, therefore, uses the following iterative process, however formally or informally.

1. List Nonfunctional Requirements that have a global impact

2. Make whichever design decisions must be taken at a global level to meet these Nonfunctional Requirements

3. Assess the effect of these decisions by transforming a representative sample of OIDs in the light of this candidate System Architecture

4. Iterate

Note that the Nonfunctional Requirements addressed by a System Architecture must include not only those that appear explicitly in the requirements document. These requirements capture constraints related to performance, availability, persistence, distribution, security, et cetera. In addition to these *external* constraints, a System Architecture must also address two further categories of Nonfunctional Requirements: software engineering requirements and *internal* requirements. A System Architecture must address the Nonfunctional Requirements that stem from the need to perform good software engineering. These include requirements related to modularity, anticipating changes, and simplifying future reuse of the software. Reuse will not happen unless it is planned and designed to happen. Nonfunctional Requirements such as these are often not surfaced during requirements gathering which, by definition, focuses on the external system constraints. If not, then they should be made explicit as part of the architectural design activity. A System Architecture must also address such *internal* Nonfunctional Requirements as error recovery, naming conventions, messaging, data integrity, heterogeneous environments, multiplatform dependencies, multiple vendors, wrappering, languages, tools, hardware configurations and dependencies, et cetera. These Nonfunctional Requirements too will typically not be surfaced during requirements gathering. In short, all design topics for which global solutions are required should be addressed by the System Architecture.

Strengths

A System Architecture makes explicit the underlying principles of the design. By doing this, the principles can be applied uniformly, and their appropriateness checked. Factoring out design decisions and making them globally prevents the development team reinventing the wheel and ensures a degree of application consistency.

Weaknesses

Developing a strong System Architecture is challenging. It consumes scarce resources when the architect is probably under pressure to allow the project developers to start to do something.

Notation

A System Architecture takes the form of free format text augmented by design and/or code structures and diagrams of hardware and software configurations. To enhance the traceability of the architectural decisions, it helps to pair (or reference) the Nonfunctional Requirements with the corresponding architectural decision. Other than that, you should organize the System Architecture (grouping the decisions) by category, such as persistence, error handling, recovery, and so forth.

Traceability

This work product has the following traceability:

Impacted by:
- Nonfunctional Requirements (p. 106)
- Prioritized Requirements (p. 111)
- Reuse Plan (p. 158)
- Project Dependencies (p. 173)
- Issues (p. 176)
- Design Guidelines (p. 253)
- Target Environment (p. 272)
- Subsystems (p. 274)

Impacts:
- APIs (p. 265)
- Target Environment (p. 272)
- Subsystems (p. 274)
- Design Object Model (p. 281)
- Design Scenarios (p. 293)
- Design OIDs (p. 298)
- Design State Models (p. 306)
- Design Class Description (p. 311)
- Rejected Design Alternatives (p. 316)
- User Support Materials (p. 341)

Advice and Guidance

- The temptation exists to define very generic, abstract System Architectures that will solve whole categories of problem. It is good for a System Architecture to be generic but it is more important that it supports and facilitates actual application development. The simplest way of keeping a System Architecture with its feet on the ground is to insist that it is always related to a particular application and not developed in a vacuum.

- Only explicit architectural statements can be policed.

- If the System Architecture does not address a particular design issue, the architect must accept that no uniform resolution to that issue will necessarily be adopted by the design teams.

- The stronger a System Architecture, the greater the independence of design teams.

- Remember to address the requirement to anticipate changes. Likely modifications or additions to both functional or Nonfunctional Requirements should be considered. Addressing these requirements for change in the System Architecture is a matter of achieving decouplings of some form or another. Use [Gamma95] as a source of decoupling techniques.

- Include statements of the design trade-offs that have been assumed in the System Architecture. These will help people understand the basis of the System Architecture, assist developers design and implement consistently with the architectural trade-offs, and enable the trade-offs to be reviewed at a later date.

- Developers need not remain idle or unassigned while a System Architecture is being developed. There is considerable work to be done setting up the Development Environment and performing prototyping or basic implementation work. Consider using a depth-first development strategy (see Section 17.1) to get developers up to speed with the development techniques, tools, and domains, in parallel with further development of the System Architecture.

- A System Architecture is often developed iteratively together with a Subsystem Model as these are closely related.

Verification

- Check for completeness by developing a list of topics and issues relevant to System Architecture, such as the one at the beginning of this section. Check the System Architecture work product against each item listed.

- Check that anticipated changes to the design are addressed in the System Architecture.

- Check that all design decisions that require global coordination across the project are included in the System Architecture work product.

- For each architectural statement, can a framework (reusable subsystem) or a component of a framework be used to enforce it automatically?

- Check that the System Architecture is driven by the requirements of an application and that it has not been designed "in a vacuum."

- Check that all design decisions that involve risk are documented appropriately in the Risk Management Plan, see Section 10.7, and that adequate, timely prototyping activity has been scheduled to check the decisions.

- Check that the System Architecture has used existing components and technologies where this is feasible and appropriate.

Example(s)

The following example relates to the image processing system whose Subsystem Model is shown in outline in Figure 13-7. The Nonfunctional Requirement from which each architectural statement is derived appears first in italics. This is done here to show the dependencies between System Architecture and Nonfunctional Requirements. Traceability back to Nonfunctional Requirements as explicitly and at such a fine granularity as this may not always be done. Flat lists of architectural statements and diagrams under headings such as *Structure, Error Handling, Reuse*, et cetera, are frequently used.

Table 13-1 (Page 1 of 2). Example of System Architecture.

Nonfunctional Requirement: *Utilize existing C functions to perform basic image processing operations.*
Derived architectural decision: The basic image processing functions are implemented by a component consisting solely of the legacy C code. An interfacing subsystem invokes the legacy functions. This involves extracting images from the image database, placing them in memory in the format expected by the legacy functions, interpreting their return values, returning images to the image database, and the like.

Nonfunctional Requirement: *Use familiar, off-the-shelf technology to distribute images between image processing nodes, at least in early development cycles.*
Derived architectural decision: Store images one per file and distribute images using NFS.

Table 13-1 (Page 2 of 2). *Example of System Architecture.*

Nonfunctional Requirement: *Reuse as much as possible of this application in similar applications that also exploit image processing technology.*
Derived architectural decision: There is an image processing System Architecture that is independent of the specifics of the application itself. The image processing System Architecture provides a distributed image database, and access to image processing functions.

Nonfunctional Requirement: *Enable the basic image processing functions to be switched on the fly.*
Derived architectural decision: The legacy image processing functions are encapsulated within a subsystem that metamodels the interface to these functions to enable interfaces to new functions to be created dynamically.

Nonfunctional Requirement: *Anticipate new kinds of images. The algorithms to manipulate these new images must be added on the fly.*
Derived architectural decision: The *singleton* and *abstract factory* design patterns [Gamma95] are used to create families of objects related to particular kinds of images. A singleton registry of concrete image factories is maintained. New image code is provided in the form of a DLL that contains the new concrete image factory class and the classes related to the new image that the new factory instantiates. On being loaded, the DLL instantiates a singleton concrete factory and registers it. Image classes are instantiated by means of the appropriate factory obtained from the registry.

Nonfunctional Requirement: *The image processing System Architecture should provide test-bed facilities to enable experimentation with different database access algorithms.*
Derived architectural decision: The *strategy* design pattern [Gamma95] is used to define different database access strategies and to associate them dynamically with image objects.

Nonfunctional Requirement: *Employ uniform error handling mechanism.*
Derived architectural decision: Use C++ exception handling throughout to flag exceptional conditions. Legacy image processing functions currently employ a standard set of return codes. All application-specific exception classes are to be derived from a common class that encapsulates a return code. Legacy code wrappers must check return codes and throw exceptions as appropriate.
Conditionally include code to check all method preconditions identified during design. Preconditions should be coded as protected methods of the invoked class. Preconditions of subclass methods should invoke superclass method preconditions before performing any subclass-specific checking. Do not encode postconditions or invariants.

Nonfunctional Requirement: *Extensible architecture.*
Derived architectural decision: The subsystems will be allocated to the hardware as shown in Figure 13-3.

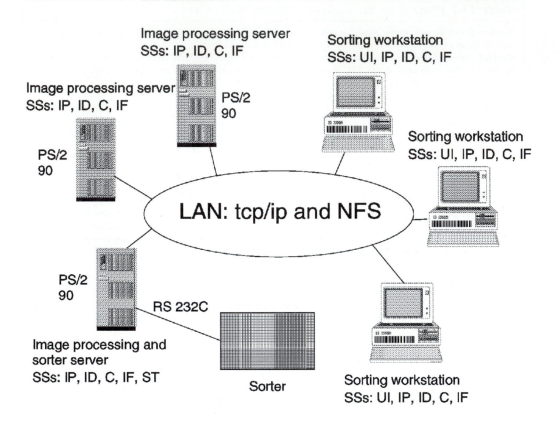

Figure 13-3. Example Architecture Diagram Showing Hardware and Software Configurations.

The software structure of an image processing server is as shown in Figure 13-4.

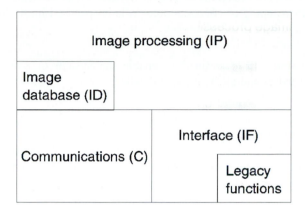

Figure 13-4. *Example Architecture Diagram Showing Software Layers.*

References

[Booch94] discusses Architecture.

Importance

Essential for ensuring that the design process does not become ad hoc.

13.3 APPLICATION PROGRAMMING INTERFACES (APIS)

Description

The term "API" actually stands for Application Programming Interface, but more accurately it refers to an Architected Program Interface. The point of this pun is to emphasize that APIs need not be interfaces to end-user applications, and that an API needs to be designed. An API work product documents an internal or external API provided by the system.

In object-oriented terms, an API is simply a set of visible classes and their interfaces. It also includes associated global types, data, and functions but these, hopefully, are kept to a minimum if they cannot be eliminated entirely. The classes that appear in an API are a subset of those contained in the subsystem to which the API is an interface. An API can, therefore, be considered to be a particular *view* or *filter* of subsystem classes.

As described previously in Section 2.4, a workbook can describe either a whole system or a subsystem. API work products, therefore, relate either to a whole system or to a particular subsystem depending on the workbook of which they form a part. The Subsystem Model, see Section 13.5, defines subsystems and their interdependencies in terms of

contracts that are coherent collections of responsibilities. It is subsystem APIs that implement contracts. This mapping of contracts onto APIs is specified in the Subsystem Model.

Purpose

A system or subsystem API is defined to enable the system or subsystem to be used
without the need to understand all its internal details.

Participants

Each API, if it is not prescribed completely by the system requirements, has an owner who
is responsible for its integrity. In accordance with the workbook approach, the API owner
is responsible for documenting it into this work product. The API owner is likely to be a
designer or developer.

Timing

APIs are usually defined shortly after subsystem partitioning, as the APIs often provide
access to individual subsystems. The need for a particular API usually becomes apparent
during the construction of the Use Case Model but its details can only be provided considerably later.

Technique

In the sense that an API is a filtered view of subsystem classes, at least part of the documentation of an API should be obtainable by using the filtering and documentation facilities of a design tool or class browser.

An API cannot be developed entirely independently of the classes that support that API.
The need for a particular API often arises from a particular Use Case that Scenarios elaborate into a collection of related system behaviors. The triggers for these Scenarios are
implemented by calls to the methods that form the API.

If it is a subsystem being described, as opposed to a system, then Use Cases may not
have been defined, although there is no reason why they should not have been, particularly
if the subsystem is intended to be reused. If Use Cases do not exist then the driver of an
API is the set of Scenarios for that subsystem, or a clustering of those Scenarios into *contracts*. If Scenarios do not exist either, then an API is driven directly by the contracts that
define the interdependencies between subsystems.

Strengths

Precise documentation of APIs enables design work to be done in parallel. Subsystems
depend on each other and if subsystem interfaces are not defined, no autonomous subsystem work is possible, since the internals of each subsystem will have to be developed
simultaneously. Subsystem interfaces modularize a solution.

Weaknesses

None.

Notation

In addition to bare-bones type signatures, such as what C++ header files provide, API documentation should include references and information to permit the API to be understood independently of the system design. The degree of independence will depend, of course, on the intended audience for the documentation: It might be appropriate for API documentation to assume knowledge of the system, or it might not. If the API documentation is to be completely stand-alone, and if it is complex, then an object model and perhaps a set of OIDs should be provided to enable the reader to understand the semantics of the interface. Sample client code is often a good way of illustrating usage while hiding the internal details that OIDs would expose. If the audience for the API documentation might be expected to customize the interface, customization OIDs and/or code should also be included.

The structure of a document describing an API might take the following form:

Chapter 1: Purpose of API
Chapter 2: API structure
Chapter 3: Class interfaces
Chapter 4: Usage scenarios

The motivating Use Case should be used to guide the content of the introductory chapter. The API structure chapter might contain an Object Model together with a textual walk-through of the model. See the example below for a suggested format for documenting class interfaces. Each usage scenario should contain a description of the scenario, statements of assumptions and outcomes, and an OID and/or sample code.

Traceability

This work product has the following traceability:

Impacted by:
- Nonfunctional Requirements (p. 106)
- Issues (p. 176)
- Design Guidelines (p. 253)
- System Architecture (p. 257)

Impacts:
- Source Code (p. 334)
- User Support Materials (p. 341)
- Test Cases (p. 346)

Advice and Guidance

- APIs should be defined in development increments as early as possible.

- Consider using the *facade* design pattern [Gamma95] to encapsulate the interface or to provide alternative, simplified interfaces.

- Exploit the capabilities of your toolset to generate as much as possible of the API documentation automatically.

- A minimal API document obviously lists just the type declarations relevant to client programmers. The degree of additional documentation: usage scenarios, method descriptions, and the like, should be scaled according to the intended audience and usage of the API.

Verification

- Check API for conformance to Coding Guidelines.

- Check the documentation of APIs intended for publication for conformance with appropriate publication guidelines.

- Depending on the intended audience for the API and its complexity, check that documentation includes Scenarios and sample code showing how the API may be used.

- Check API for appropriate levels of completeness and extensibility.

- Check API for unnecessary exposure of internal data representations.

Example(s)

Here is an example of some documentation that was written to describe a simple C++ database server API. The document as a whole followed the structure outlined earlier. The excerpt that follows is from a section documenting the *DbSession* class interface. Note that this documentation is intended for writers of *client* code, not *customization* code. It is for this reason that only the public class interface is described. Note also that the documentation is intended for object technology novices. For this reason the names and short descriptions of inherited methods are included in the description of each class interface. This would not normally be done, but it was felt that this audience would expect to find all methods relevant to a particular class documented there.

Definition

A DbSession is an object representing a database session. FileProxies for database files are created by DbSession methods; the contents of the files are then accessed by means of FileProxy methods without further direct reference to the DbSession.

DbSessions *know* the FileProxies that are associated with them, and deletion of a DbSession object causes deletion of its FileProxies. To ensure that FileProxy construction and deletion only occur at the correct time (and not, for example, when a DbSession object is copied), copy and assignment operations are not part of the DbSession public interface.

Public methods

Static methods:

ApplicationManagerInstance   Get the DbSession initiated by the application manager

New methods:

OpenFile   Open an existing database file

NewFile   Create a new database file

OpenBinarySegmentFile   Open an existing binary segment database file

NewBinarySegmentFile   Create a new binary segment database file

OpenVoiceSegmentFile   Open an existing voice segment database file

NewVoiceSegmentFile   Create a new voice segment database file

GetHandle   Get the database server handle for this session

GetPath   Get the path used by the database server as the database file directory

Inherited, overridden, or instantiated methods:

None

Special methods:

Constructor   Create a DbSession

Destructor   Delete a DbSession

Descriptions of new methods

ApplicationManagerInstance

Purpose   Get the DbSession instance that represents the database session initiated by the application manager. If the instance does not yet exist, the method will construct it.

Format   `static  DbSession&  ApplicationManagerInstance(const  GsiName gsiName)`

Parameters

gsiName The NetBIOS name of the GSI for which the session is being used.

Notes   The method wraps the vmsfopen function.

OpenFile

Purpose   Open a database file and return a reference to a proxy for it.

Format

```
virtual FileProxy& OpenFile(
     const FileName fileName,
     const DbSession::AccessMode accessMode = DbSession::READ_ONLY )
```

Parameters

fileName   The name of the file to be opened.
accessMode   The access mode of the new file proxy.

Notes

NewFile

Purpose   Create a new database file and return a reference to a proxy for it.   The underlying semantics of the method are those of CreateDA in the existing API.

Format

```
virtual FileProxy& NewFile(
     const FileName fileName,
     const int keyLength,
     const int recordLength,
     const int degree = 32 )
```

Parameters

fileName   The name of the file to be created.
keyLength   The length of the key. Possible values are 1 through 49.
recordLength The length of the record (both key and data).
degree   Parameter influencing database index creation algorithm; default 32. Use the default unless otherwise instructed.

Notes   The new file proxy is read-write.

Constructor

Purpose Create a DbSession object.

Format

```
DbSession(
     const ClientName clientName,
     const GsiName gsiName,
     const PVOID ioArea = 0,
     const int ioAreaLength = 0,
     const int timeout = 0,
     const int sessionCount = 3,
     const IBoolean dllServer = False,
     const int adapter = 255 )
```

Parameters

clientName	The NetBIOS client name.
gsiName	The NetBIOS name of the GSI with which the session is being opened.
ioArea	A pointer to the area to be used for GSI requests and responses; default 0. If the pointer is zero (0), the API allocates the storage, but in that case the storage will be overwritten by each GSI request via this session.
ioAreaLength	The length of the user-supplied ioArea.
timeout	The time allowed, in seconds, for a response from the LAN; default 0. The maximum value is 127. A value of zero (0) specifies that no timeout is to be used.
sessionCount	Only relevant if a real network is being used. The number of network sessions opened for the process; default 3. Only the sessionCount parameter for the first session (of any kind) created for each process is used.
dllServer	Whether or not the call is made from a DT/2 DLL server; default False.
adapter	The LAN adapter number as defined to OS/2 system configuration; default 255. Possible values are 0 through 3 (LAN) or 255 (local). If an adapter has not been installed, use value of 255, which means that all operations take place locally.

Exception codes   As for OpnSesDAE.

Notes

Supporting declarations

enum AccessMode {
  READ_ONLY, READ_WRITE }

References

None.

Importance

API work products are optional but may be essential if your project has numerous Application Programming Interfaces or may be required by your customer. APIs work products are important for allowing a system or subsystem to be used without the need for a complete understanding of that system or subsystem.

13.4 TARGET ENVIRONMENT

Description

The target environment is the environment in which the application will operate. The specification of the Target Environment usually comes from the Nonfunctional Requirements and it has a strong influence on the System Architecture. It should specify hardware platform, operating system, and the runtime environment. In a distributed or a client/server system, a Target Environment may describe more than one physical system.

Purpose

It is critical that the environment in which the application will operate is clearly specified. The purpose of this documentation is to ensure that both the end user and system architect share a common understanding of the that operating environment. A change of the Target Environment may result in a selection of a different System Architecture, therefore, its documentation is important.

Participants

The specification of the target environment may come from a customer requirement or a decision by system architects. The architect of the project or project planner should document the Target Environment of the application.

Timing

The information concerning the Target Environment is collected and documented at requirements gathering time. At times, this information may be elaborated during design.

Technique

Any customer or user input to the choice of Target Environment should be obtained and validated like any other Nonfunctional Requirements. If the selection of Target Environment is made by system architects, this specification should be sent to the customer to verify their agreement with the selection.

Strengths

The strength of this work product is to document clearly the operating environment of the system or application.

Weaknesses

None.

Notation

The Target Environment is usually documented as free format text with diagrams as appropriate.

Traceability

This work product has the following traceability:

Impacted by:
- Nonfunctional Requirements (p. 106)
- Issues (p. 176)
- Design Guidelines (p. 253)
- System Architecture (p. 257)

Impacts:
- System Architecture (p. 257)
- Coding Guidelines (p. 322)
- Physical Packaging Plan (p. 326)
- Development Environment (p. 330)
- User Support Materials (p. 341)

Advice and Guidance

It is important that the environment for the application is clearly specified. All the known information on the environment should be recorded in this work product, namely, hardware platforms, operating systems, network protocol, language system runtime requirements, and so forth.

Verification

- Check if the target environment specification is complete with respect to all operational dependencies.

- If more than one system is involved, check to make sure all target environments are specified.

Example(s)

The following are examples of Target Environment specifications.

- The target environment is RISC System/6000 running AIX version 3.2.

- The target environment is ES/9000 running CICS/ESA version 3 and LE/370 version 1 release 2 under MVS/ESA SP version 5.1.

- The target environment for the client is IBM PC running OS/2 WARP and the server is RISC System/6000 running AIX version 3.2.

Figure 13-5. Examples of Target Environment.

References

None.

Importance

The Target Environment is essential since it has a major impact on the System Architecture.

13.5 SUBSYSTEM MODEL

Description

A Subsystem Model is a partitioning of a system into subsystems, and a delegation of system responsibilities to the subsystems. The term "subsystem" is used in this book to refer to *any* large design component. A database management system can, therefore, be a subsystem, as can a user interface component or an application framework. Subsystems, because they are large structures at the design level, must take into account the System Architecture.

This definition of the term "subsystem" is similar to that used by Booch [Booch94]. OMT [Rumbaugh91a] uses the term differently: a logical grouping of classes. This is more of an analysis concept than design, and we prefer to distinguish the two kinds of partitioning. Both analysis and design need a means of clustering, but the goals of analysis and design clustering are not the same, and hence analysis and design cluster divisions may not coincide. We use the term "subsystem" solely for design clustering in order to avoid confusion.

Our definition also differs from what Shlaer and Mellor call "domains" [Shlaer88] which are horizontal partitions each consisting of all the classes of a system in a particular Subject Area. Shlaer and Mellor domains are similar to the "layers" of Booch. Domains are used in a very definite manner by Shlaer and Mellor.

Another design concept that is not necessarily identical to that of the subsystem is the unit of work allocated to a team of developers. There is no reason why units of work need necessarily be aligned with subsystems, although pragmatic constraints may insist that this is the case in particular projects.

A subsystem is not necessarily a design for a particular physical component. The design of physical components will probably be expressed in terms of subsystems, but not all subsystems represent physical components. Some subsystems may contain nested subsystems.

A Subsystem Model identifies existing subsystems that are to be reused as well as those that need to be constructed.

Purpose

The principal reason why a system is subdivided into subsystems is that the system is too complex or too large to understand or to be worked on as a whole; it needs to be partitioned into smaller units to be manageable.

This rationale has two implications. Firstly, each subsystem must be understandable in isolation. Otherwise, no understanding would be gained by partitioning the system. This means that each subsystem must have its own Object Model, its own Scenarios, and its own OIDs. This does not mean, for example, that a class cannot appear in more than one subsystem's Object Model, but the ownership of classes by subsystems must be clear. Secondly, the public subsystem interfaces must be clearly and fully described. This is done so that the developers of one subsystem need not know about the internal structure of other subsystems to use them. If this were not the case, the benefits of partitioning the system would be much reduced.

Another important reason for constructing a system from subsystems is reuse. It may be possible to reuse existing components or to identify problem-independent functionality that can be "harvested" for subsequent reuse. In either case, there is a need to structure the system into large, isolated, design components.

Participants

The architect is responsible for the definition of the subsystems. The project manager must also be involved, as the subsystem partitioning may affect the way in which work can be assigned to teams and the dependencies between the teams.

Timing

Subsystem partitioning is usually done iteratively together with the development of an Architecture, as a result of addressing Nonfunctional Requirements related to defining physical boundaries, achieving modularity, reusing existing components, and designing for further reuse. Both the System Architecture and the Subsystem Model are revised iteratively as design proceeds.

A large system may, however, be partitioned into subsystems at an earlier stage, before analysis, in order to address logically separate aspects of the system independently. Sometimes, parts of previous System Architectures and Subsystem Models can be reused for new systems.

Technique

How to partition a system into subsystems depends on when the partitioning is performed. If it is decided to partition before analysis then a clear idea of how the system can be cleaved into subsystems must already exist; otherwise, such an early partitioning would not be attempted. These lines of cleavage may be those of an existing application that is being re-engineered, or they may be based on the boundaries of existing systems that are being integrated. If the system is completely new, then an early partitioning may stem from a domain analysis, see Section 18.1, which has surfaced a clear separation of concerns in the domain.

If a subsystem partitioning is performed as an initial design step, then it will be based on knowledge gained during analysis, an awareness of the components available for reuse, and physical boundaries. The analysis model might naturally have generated some clusterings of classes that are obvious candidates for encapsulation as subsystems. Physical packaging requirements may reinforce this initial partitioning, or they may impose additional demands of their own. If a project is distributed then the system partitioning must to a certain extent correspond to geography.

If a system is partitioned into subsystems only after an initial Design Object Model and Design OIDs exist, then the partitioning can be performed by clustering the classes of the (system) Object Model and splitting the (system) OIDs into separate OIDs for each of the newly created subsystems. When splitting off a subsystem OID in this way it is often appropriate to represent other subsystems by *Facades* (in the sense of the Facade design pattern of [Gamma95]). A Facade is an object that encapsulates a whole subsystem. In this way the use of subsystem interfaces is emphasized, and the internals of one subsystem hidden from others. The messages sent to a Facade form the interface to that subsystem. Facades are useful when constructing subsystem OIDs irrespective of when subsystem partitioning is performed.

Whenever the partitioning is performed, some heuristic for clustering must be used; a rule of thumb is that subsystem partitioning should minimize the dependencies between subsystems. Obviously, the clustering must also take into account physical boundaries, reused and reusable components, and architectural principles.

In addition to identifying subsystems, a Subsystem Model must also document the way in which subsystems depend on each other. Individual methods or responsibilities are, however, usually too fine-grain to be used as the basis for documenting relationships between subsystems. It is necessary to cluster the responsibilities of a subsystem into *contracts* and to use these to show the links between subsystems. A contract is a coherent collection of related responsibilities. (This is the definition of a contract used in [Wirfs-Brock90].) A subsystem is dependent on a contract of another subsystem, if it employs the responsibilities of that contract to deliver its functionality. It is these subsystem-contract connections that are shown on the subsystem diagram described below.

Each subsystem that is identified is, in principle, treated as a system in its own right. As described earlier in Section 2.4, Workbook Structure, a separate logical workbook is devoted to each subsystem. By giving each its own workbook, the structure exists to manage, gather requirements for, analyze, develop, and test each subsystem independently. Of course, subsystems will not always be developed quite so autonomously or formally, although deriving separate requirements and analysis work products for certain subsystems will greatly assist the understandability and future reuse of these subsystems. If requirements gathering for a subsystem is performed, then a subsystem Use Case Model will be produced. There is a correspondence between a subsystem Use Case Model and contracts in the Subsystem Model of the enclosing system. The contracts presented by a subsystem are the reasons why the subsystem is needed in the Subsystem Model; the subsystem Use Case Model captures the requirements on the subsystem. The subsystem Use Case Model must, therefore, support the subsystem contracts that are implemented by subsystem APIs.

Strengths

The Subsystem Model is an extremely important design document. It straddles the earlier, systemwide design and the later per-subsystem design. To a certain extent it summarizes the System Architecture of the application. When design teams communicate, it is at the subsystem level of abstraction; therefore, it is very important that the subsystem level of design is well documented to satisfy the varied goals of the subsystem partitioning process.

A Subsystem Model provides a basis for identifying reusable or harvestable design components.

Weaknesses

None.

Notation

Logically, each subsystem has its own workbook similar to that used for the system as a whole. Physically, the subsystem workbooks may be parts of the system workbook or they may be separate, as appropriate to the development team size and structure. If the subsystems are in turn broken down into subsubsystems, the latter, too, have their own subsystems.

The work products of the individual subsystems, including the APIs that define the subsystem interfaces, their object models, their code, and the like, belong, therefore, to the subsystem workbooks. What is important in the parent system workbook is to indicate which subsystems exist and how they are interrelated. All other information is delegated to the subsystem workbooks.

The following template may be used for each subsystem identified in the Subsystem Model:

Subsystem name	_____
Description	_____
Workbook	_____
Contracts	_____
	_____
	_____

The *Workbook* slot is used to identify the workbook in which the subsystem is documented. All further documentation of the subsystems is delegated to the subsystem workbooks.

> **Contract name** _____
> **Description** _____
> **API** _____
> **Notes** _____
> _____
> _____

The *API* slot is used to identify the subsystem API that implements the contract. All documentation of the API is delegated to the relevant API work product of the subsystem workbook. In addition to the use of the above templates, a summary diagram showing the subsystems and the contractual dependencies between subsystems is frequently helpful. The form of a subsystem diagram is shown in Figure 13-6.

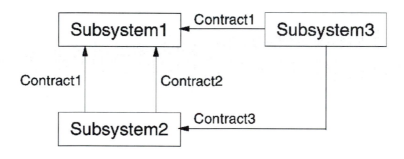

Figure 13-6. *The Form of a Subsystem Diagram.*

Each box of the subsystem diagram represents a subsystem. The arrows connecting the subsystems represent dependencies between subsystems with the arrows pointing towards the server subsystems. The names on the arrows are those of the contracts of the server subsystem being depended upon by the client subsystem.

Traceability

This work product has the following traceability:

Impacted by:
- Nonfunctional Requirements (p. 106)
- Reuse Plan (p. 158)
- Project Dependencies (p. 173)
- Issues (p. 176)
- Design Guidelines (p. 253)
- System Architecture (p. 257)
- Design Object Model (p. 281)

Impacts:
- System Architecture (p. 257)
- Physical Packaging Plan (p. 326)

Note: The Subsystem Model also impacts lower level subsystem work products, most notably Use Case Models and APIs.

Advice and Guidance

- The subsystem partitioning is likely to change from time to time. This is inevitable as experience is gained of system responsibilities.

- Reduce dependencies between subsystems as far as possible.

- Make subsystems problem-independent, if possible, to increase the chance of the subsystem being reused.

- The (logically) multiple subsystem Object Models will almost certainly be represented as divisions within a single model maintained by a design tool.

- After a subsystem partitioning, OIDs may need to be reworked to reassign responsibilities to optimize subsystem decoupling.

Verification

- Check that all subsystem APIs are, or will be, defined in time to enable them to be used by the developers of other subsystems.

- Check the subsystem partitioning for optimal decoupling of subsystems. (This is not necessarily the same as maximal decoupling.)

- Check the frequency and size of intersubsystem communications.

- Check the subsystem partitioning for reuse opportunities; both the reuse of existing components, and the future reuse of new work products.

- Check that the boundary of the system to be built is explicitly represented in the Subsystem Model diagram.

Example(s)

Figure 13-7 shows a subsystem diagram for an image processing architecture. An important design goal for this System Architecture was to develop subsystems that were reusable in several image processing applications. The *Image functions* subsystem consist of many, large legacy functions written in a non-OO language that are to be reused without change. To enable this, the *Image processing* subsystem is responsible for extracting the images from the image database, placing them in memory as expected by the legacy functions, invoking the legacy functions, and interpreting their return values.

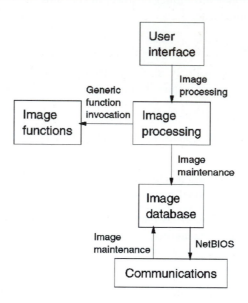

Figure 13-7. *An Example of a Subsystem Diagram.*

The description of the image database subsystem might be as follows:

Table 13-2. *Example of Subsystem Description.*

Subsystem name	Image database
Description	A distributed image database
Workbook	IPA_ID
Contracts	Image maintenance

The description of this contract may be as follows:

Table 13-3. Example of Contract Description.

Contract name	Image maintenance
Description	An API for maintaining a distributed image database.
API	IM
Notes	1. All image processing operations are implemented by subclasses of the *Image* abstract class.
	2. By default, images are stored in the local node.
	3. Dynamic load balancing may result in images being moved, but that is functionally transparent.
	4. Images may be accessed from any node, regardless of where the image is stored.
	5. A mapping from C++ pointers to unique system image IDs is maintained within the subsystem, but is not exposed.

References

- [Booch94] describes subsystems.

- [Wirfs-Brock90] describes contracts.

Importance

The Subsystem Model is optional in small and medium sized projects but essential in large projects. Developing a Subsystem Model provides a means for partitioning a system into more manageable units.

13.6 DESIGN OBJECT MODEL

Description

The Design Object Model is a structural representation of the software objects (classes), that comprise the implementation of a system or application. A Static Model is comprised of design object classes and their attributes, responsibilities, operations, and interrelationships, expressed as association, aggregation, and inheritance links. The object model is a key object-oriented design work product.

Purpose

An Object Model is the fundamental way to document the static aspects of an object-oriented solution to a problem. The focus of the Object Model during design is the structure of the software system as opposed to the structure of the problem domain during analysis (Section 11.3, Analysis Object Model).

The objects in object-oriented design are called "design objects" (vs. "problem-domain objects" in object-oriented analysis). Classes of problem-domain objects can be mapped to one or more classes of the corresponding design objects, depending on the underlying

System Architecture. For example, class *Folder* may be mapped to two classes *Folder* and *FolderView* in design (see examples on page 291). The architectural mechanism here is the Model-View-Controller framework for a system with graphical user interfaces. In this case, the real-world *Folder* object becomes two objects in the solution-domain: The *Folder* data and behavior is part of the "Model," but its graphical representation and on-screen behavior is part of the "View" domain.

Many new classes are invented at this phase, as architectural and design decisions are applied. This is one of the most creative phases of the object-oriented development life cycle. Programmers should have a very clear knowledge of how to proceed with implementation of the system when all the design work products are defined.

Participants

The Design Object Model is created by architects, designers and developers.

Timing

The Design Object Model is primarily developed during the design phase, but it will need to be maintained during the implementation phase as design and implementation decisions are worked out.

Technique

The best way to develop a Design Object Model is to start with the Analysis Object Model and expand it into a design model. The steps to doing this are:

1. Start with a copy of the Analysis Object Model.

2. Add new classes from the solution domain, for example, view and utility classes (identified while developing Design Object Interaction Diagrams).

3. Validate and assign responsibilities from Design OIDs and Design State Models in terms of:

   - attributes (for structural aspects)
   - methods or operations (for behavioral aspects)

4. For every class and association in the model, consider the operations that can result in an instance being created or deleted [D'Souza95].

5. Optimize the object model for performance and reuse. Introduce new associations or modify existing ones to optimize access based on Nonfunctional Requirements (e.g., fast look-up). Consider making associations that were thought to be permanent features of the class into temporary links between objects that are either passed as arguments in methods or created as temporary objects within a method body.

6. Eliminate or collapse structures representing unnecessary information, for example, those not substantiated by Design OIDs.

7. Add metaclass if your implementation language is Smalltalk or SOM. A metaclass is a class whose instances are themselves classes [Booch94]. Metaclasses enable classes to be manipulated as objects in their own right.

8. Transform generalization (or inheritance) structures to delegation when appropriate in order to decouple elements of the design. If a subclass does not pass the substitution (Is-A) test, change Is-A to Uses or Has.

9. Determine which classes will be persistent (for example, based on some startup reference or update Design OID).

10. Specify the accessibility of operations:

   - *Public*: any class can invoke the operation
   - *Protected*: only subclasses can invoke the operation
   - *Private*: no other class can invoke the operation

   If your implementation language has no support for *Private* or *Protected* use Coding Guidelines to enforce them, for example, *Protected* could be expressed in SOM by using the `private` IDL brackets and the `private` emitter switch.

11. Specify the implementation details of associations:

   - Directionality (cf. `using` in Booch [Booch94]). Remember that during analysis associations were bidirectional.
   - Name, visibility, and mutability of the attribute implementing the association.

12. Determine the implementation of the "many" ends in associations:

   - A collection class as an attribute in the "from" object
   - A custom class (usually a subclass of a collection class or an aggregate including a collection class object) as an attribute in the "from" object
   - A reference to an association class that contains one or more attributed references to other objects.
   - No implementation (if the link will not be used in that direction).

13. Determine ownership (Who creates or instantiates objects of a class? Who deletes them?)

   - Determine which aggregations (in particular) represent lifetime encapsulation. That is, the lifetime of the aggregate completely encloses the lifetime of the component (cf. `server binding` in [Coleman94]). Ownership usually implies lifetime encapsulation.

14. Establish the kind of reference (cf. `physical containment` in [Booch94]) to be used by the attributes implementing associations and aggregations:

   - By *reference*: contains a pointer or a reference
   - By *value*: contains an object (applicable only for aggregations at the design level of abstraction. During analysis, reference/value distinctions are usually ignored)

- By *key*: contains a key that can be converted into a reference by some means (for example, a "name resolution mechanism").

15. Determine scope of associations:

- *Operation Scope* (dynamic reference): when an object A gets a reference to an object B through a method parameter or by a local variable of a method

- *Class Scope* (persistent reference): reference from object A to object B needs to persist between method calls

16. Determine mutability: The *mutability* of a reference indicates whether it can be reassigned after initialization [Coleman94]. The `const` adornment can be used to indicate immutability. An attribute can be declared as mutable, that is, the value of the attribute can be changed after initialization, for objects declared as constant, when the `const` adornment applies to the entire object.

17. Determine placement of class operations and class attributes (those that do not apply to specific objects, i.e., instances of the class). In many cases they become attributes and operations of a collection class. For example, the extension of a class, namely, the set of all instances, could be maintained in a class attribute (`static data member` in C++) that is a collection class.

18. Determine special or advanced properties of classes and operations (for example, C++'s template, virtual, inline, const, friend, et cetera). Advanced properties are normally implementation language dependent.

19. Determine the types of all attributes.

Strengths

The Design Object Model is a key deliverable for capturing and communicating solution domain understanding to the development team and other interested parties. Its ability to be simple or richly adorned, capturing all static design information, allows it to be extremely useful throughout the development life cycle. Its clear intuitive notation makes it a favorite work product of all analysts, designers, and developers.

Weaknesses

- A Design Object Model only shows the static relationships.

- It needs to be maintained over time. Neglect of the Design Object Model often stems from the (incorrect) assumption that program Source Code supersedes the design documentation.

Notation

The Design Object Model notation enhances the Analysis Object Model notation (Section 11.3), with the emphasis on architecture and design class description. The enhancement includes:

Directionality

Associations should show the direction(s) of reference between the objects. Association classes and n-ary associations should be transformed to show how they will be implemented (e.g., by containment of a collection class of references, or by reference to a directory of associations).

Class adornments

Whether a class is abstract or parameterized could be shown in the Design Object Model.

Attribute and accessibility adornments

The accessibility of attributes and methods, such as whether they are public, private, or protected, should be shown explicitly in the Design Object Model.

Aggregation and association adornments

Whether associations are "by reference" (owner or not) or "by value" should be shown explicitly.

Visibility dependency

Argument dependency and temporary variable dependency need to be represented in Design Object Diagram, for example, by a dotted line with an arrow head. A class has an argument dependency on another class if one of its methods refers to the other class when defining its formal parameters. On the other hand, a class has a temporary variable dependency on an other class, if it instantiates the class as a local temporary variable (See Figure 13-8).

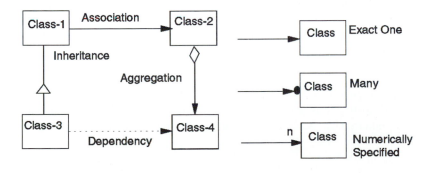

Figure 13-8. Design Object Model Notation.

Traceability

This work product has the following traceability:

Impacted by:
- Nonfunctional Requirements (p. 106)
- Issues (p. 176)
- Analysis Object Model (p. 192)
- Screen Flows (p. 237)
- Screen Layouts (p. 242)
- Design Guidelines (p. 253)
- System Architecture (p. 257)
- Design OIDs (p. 298)

Impacts:
- Subsystems (p. 274)
- Design OIDs (p. 298)
- Design State Models (p. 306)
- Design Class Description (p. 311)
- Glossary (p. 355)

Advice and Guidance

- If you are using an object-oriented CASE tool, copy the relevant part of the Analysis Object Model into a new file (keep separate versions of the Analysis Object Model and the Design Object Model).

- Design Object Model diagrams can become complicated and cluttered. We recommend layering the diagram to reduce clutter and having separate views that focus on particular topics, for example, one with associations but no attributes or operations, and another that focuses on class attributes and operations.

- Not all class dependencies should be depicted as direct associations. An object can be referenced by another if it is passed as an argument to an operation of the other class. When this happens, it is better to model it as a *visibility dependency* between these two classes.

- There is no "association class" in design. Association classes should be converted into normal classes (perhaps derived from or containing a collection class) having direct associations with the other classes.

- Some languages, including C++, permit subclasses to hide inherited services. This is not considered good style. In an inheritance hierarchy a subclass should support all the services provided by its superclass, so that it can be used anywhere the superclass is used. This is known as the substitutability principle[11], i.e. that objects of the subclass are substitutable for objects of the superclass.

- Used properly, inheritance is a key means to achieve object-oriented designs that have well-formed abstractions and whose class structures are reusable and extensible. The misuse of inheritance, however, can lead to designs that are brittle and applications

---

[11] The concept of substitutability also covers the semantic relationships between services, i.e. "require no more, promise no less." See Chapter 10 "Proper Inheritance" in *C++ FAQs*[Cline95] .

that are error-prone and difficult to understand and modify. When designing inheritance structures, a number of process guidelines should be considered:

- Verify the class hierarchy has structural and behavioral conformance. Type-safe use of inheritance considers the conformance of client-server object interactions. Structural conformance concerns the client's expectations of the supplier's properties and relationships with other classes. Behavioral conformance concerns the client's expectation of the supplier's behavior. When accessing properties or navigating relationships or invoking behavior, the client should not need to know if it is dealing with a supplier that is an instance of a class or one of its subclasses.

- Use abstract classes for interface reuse—to enforce common interfaces across subclasses.

- Use structural composition and operational delegation instead of structural subclassing and operational inheritance if the only reason for inheritance was "sharing" of code. Factor-out classes into more atomic behaviors so that large hierarchies become "forests" of trees.

- Consider replacing inheritance with aggregation and states (an object *Has-A* state that determines its behavior) when objects are expected to change types during their life cycle (see "State design pattern" in [Gamma95]).

- Limit the depth of inheritance hierarchies to a maximum of 4 to 5 levels. Deep inheritance hierarchies are a conceptual burden, cause maintenance problems, and can make it extremely difficult to reuse or extend a design.

- Design the Inheritance Hierarchy consistently with Design Patterns. Many design patterns exploit abstract superclasses and inheritance-based relationships, for example Adapter, Bridge, Builder, Composite, Iterator, Mediator, Proxy and Strategy. The underlying principles are often collaborations between superclass and subclass methods using so-called "template" and "hook" methods [Pree95].

- Document the intent of Inheritance. If inheritance is used for code reuse—to "borrow" methods from superclasses—then class hierarchies quickly loose semantic cohesion. Document cases where inheritance is not behaviorally or structurally conforming and how the design would have to change to preserve conformance.

• Document your design decisions (including rejected ones).

• Look for design pattern opportunities. The chosen architecture template may already advocate the use of certain design patterns but many others will come from the discovery of how to use patterns in innovative ways. For example, looking for recurring patterns of interaction among analysis objects often suggests design patterns that will structure the solution.

- Use design patterns to insulate the design of the subsystem. When considering collaborations with other design levels (subsystems) do not bring components from other levels into your design directly. Adopt a design pattern that allows you to access the other level yet protects your system's design against changes to that other level, for example: *facades, adapters, proxies*, and *mediators.*

- Apply design patterns that ease the reuse of an asset. Do not constrain the design session by imposing asset interfaces that seem either wrong, inadequate, or unnatural for the current system; the Adapter pattern helps you to maintain design elegance in the face of unnatural asset interfaces.

- Apply design patterns that protect the reuser against changes to the reused component. If the component is a major concept in the model, widely used, and is likely to change, then apply the *Bridge* pattern. The cost of changing components that reference the asset component is likely to be greater than that of applying the *Bridge* pattern. If the new component needs only a subset of the capabilities of the existing one, introduce a new component using the *Adapter* pattern [Gamma95].

- The following questions can help you to decide on visibility and ownership for aggregations:

  - Is the identity of the contained object used outside of the containing object?

  - What is the cardinality of the containment relationship?

  - Are there other containing objects that contain the same component?

  - Should the contained object know its containing object?

  - Is the lifetime of the components bounded by the containing object or not?

- External Agents are normally out of scope in design (although as part of the problem domain their presence in the analysis model is justifiable).

- Use a "managed pointer" whenever it is not obvious who and when will delete the objects referenced (for example one object is referenced from entries in two different collections).

- Attributes implementing superclass associations should be declared as `Protected.`, or as `Private` with `Protected` accessor operations.

- Use a Reuse-based Approach. Further structuring of the solution arises from requirements that the design presents to itself—for example, objects that coordinate or mediate the activities of other objects and objects that organize queues and manage events.

  - Generate Requirements During Design. As the design proceeds new requirements emerge for the design itself. These should be formulated as design specifications and used to guide the search for reusable assets and candidate design patterns.

- Use Frameworks. A framework stipulates how specific application subclasses should behave. Abstract classes and deferred methods require subclasses to fulfill expectations of 'template' methods. Other methods and classes of the framework should be left well alone.

- Use standard utility classes where possible. Many of the productivity and quality benefits of object-orientation stem from the reuse of libraries and frameworks. We should always approach the design task by being knowledgeable about what already exists and that should shape the way we solve problems.

• Once the object model stabilizes and there is confidence in the completeness of the requirements, you should inspect the classes to look for opportunities to refactor the design.

- Consider removing classes that are leaves or orphans of the inheritance structure, that is, those that are not instantiated nor inherited from. It can be the case that these classes are poor abstractions that should be reformed either by creating a more general concept, introducing a missing superclass or by reallocating their behavior.

- Consider merging classes that have related responsibilities. Small classes should be inspected as candidates for features that have a common generalization. By being combined they might offer a more useful abstraction.

- Consider splitting those classes that have too many attributes or methods. Large classes often exhibit a bias towards a procedural rather than behavioral decomposition of the system. Factor out common behavior and attributes to a superclass. Look for disjoint subsets of coupling between attributes and methods as an obvious way to split the class. Refactor on the basis of behavioral consistency with other parts of the system. Inspect behavior within the class and consider design patterns that can restructure the class.

Verification

See the checklist for an Analysis Object Model, Section 11.3, which is also appropriate here (with the obvious exception of "check for design artifacts").

• Check that Object Model documentation indicates where, how, and why design patterns have been used, where this is appropriate.

• Check the *intent* of design patterns that are used.

• Check that internal representations of classes may be changed independently of other classes, except where explicit dependencies exist. That is, check that knowledge of internal representations is localized as much as possible.

• For all inheritance links, check that public inheritance always implies substitutability, i.e., that objects of the subclass are substitutable for objects of the superclass; that superclass assertions are honored by redefined methods and that deep inheritance hierarchies are designed correctly, particularly regarding flexibility and the advisability of avoiding downcasts.

- Check that there is no intensive communications around one class. If one class dominates the communication pattern, it may have too many responsibilities and knows too much about too many parts of the system. This could become a fragile part of the system: If any of the parts it knows about changes, it may have to change. If it is a large and complex component, then the chances of introducing an error or propagating changes is higher.

- Check that there are no unnecessary intensive communications between classes. Two classes communicating with each other intensively evidently need to know a lot about each other. Perhaps they should be one component or there is a third abstraction waiting to be found.

- Check that there is no redundant or duplicated behavior. Are there classes with the same behaviors? Are there behaviors that can be merged? Are there behaviors that could be removed either by moving the behavior to other methods or by elimination altogether?

- For each class, verify that names are unique and descriptive and, where necessary, a stereotype has been given and overrideability has been specified. Verify that attributes and operations are functionally coupled—there are no disjoint cut sets that could suggest splitting of the class into new classes. Check how instances are created and destroyed.

- For all operations, verify that operation names are descriptive and expressive of their purpose and, where relevant, an overrideability attribute has been defined; that operations are conceptually the same across classes that have the same names; that the types of all arguments and any return results are defined and that the constraints relating to referential integrity, attribute values, preconditions, and postconditions of operations are implemented.

- For all attributes, check that their names are descriptive; that there are no attributes that represent the same thing; that the types of all attributes are defined, either explicitly, as for C++, or using a signature-style for Smalltalk and that the attribute represents a value-based property and is not an object reference that is implied by an association/aggregation or that represents a missing association/aggregation.

- For all relationships, verify that the relationship is named descriptively, that multiplicity and directionality of references has been specified, and that the relationship is always true. Check that associations do not reference too specific an object; that they do not warrant becoming classes in their own right; and that they should not be modeled as aggregations.

- For all aggregations, review visibility and ownership. Is the identity of the contained object used outside of the containing object? If so, then verify that existence constraints are properly observed outside of the containing object. Are there other containing objects that contain the same component? If so, are multiple owners responsible for controlling the existence of the contained object? Are these owners members of the same class? If so, then indicate that the aggregation itself has a multiplicity of "many" by placing a "dot" next to the aggregation diamond. Should the contained object know its containing object? If so, then indicate that visibility is bidirectional.

Example(s)

The example shows a snapshot of the Object Model at the design level for the Library system example previously introduced in Figure 13-9. By comparing the same Object Model at the analysis level (Figure 11-7), it can be found that many *view* classes and directed associations have been added to this model. On the other hand, *User* class has been removed, since it is not within the system scope. By incorporating directed associations, the Object Model at the design level reflects the principle, derived from the `Observer` pattern (cf. Model-View-Controller mechanism) that "only view objects know model objects, but not vice versa."

The key part of the model-view used in the example is the *Observer* design pattern [Gamma95]. This pattern helps determine how to map the classes defined in analysis to those in design. In the example here, only part of that pattern is shown with the assumption that a certain superclass will handle the notification.

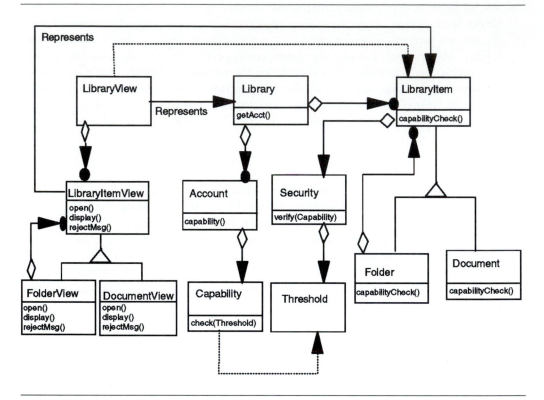

Figure 13-9. *Example of a Design Object Model.*

Associations representing conceptual links are dropped in the Object Model at the design level. The analysis association between classes Capability and Security represent a conceptual link as is shown in Figure 11-7. It is replaced in the design by an association of operation scope. This can be documented in the definition part of the class specification at the design level as a "Class Visibility Dependency" clause. At run time, objects of Capability can be passed to objects of Security for security checking, through a method parameter. There is an argument dependency from class Security to class Capability. In other words, Capability is visible to Security. The argument dependency is captured in the OIDs (see Figure 13-12) and can be added to the Design Class Description, it is not normally shown in the object model. The designers of the Library application have decided to explicitly show in the object model the other two argument dependencies: LibraryView to LibraryItem and Capability to Threshold. Account and Security also have views; however, they are not shown in this diagram because they belong to another subsystem.

References

- How to build a Design Object Model is documented in *Object-Oriented Modeling and Design* [Rumbaugh91a] and in various papers by J. Rumbaugh.

- Object visibility and class adornments are well documented in *Object-Oriented Analysis and Design with Applications* by G. Booch [Booch94].

- A good classification of visibility relationships can be found in *Object-Oriented Development: The Fusion Method* by D. Coleman, et al. [Coleman94].

- Design patterns are described in *Design Patterns: Elements of Reusable Object-Oriented Software* by E. Gamma, et al. [Gamma95].

- Proper inheritance is discussed in *C++ FAQs* by M. Cline and G. Lomow [Cline95].

Importance

The Design Object Model is absolutely essential during design. It is a fundamental way to document the static aspects of a system.

13.7 DESIGN SCENARIOS

Description

Analysis Scenarios define required systems behaviors at an abstract level; Design Scenarios define systems behaviors at a concrete level. In particular, they refer to design rather than analysis objects in describing their behavior, assumptions, and outcomes, and they include information about how to trigger the scenarios. In all other respects they are like Analysis Scenarios (see Section 11.4).

Design Scenarios can be used to define either systems behaviors or subsystems behaviors depending on whether they are used in the workbooks of systems or of subsystems.

A Design Scenario specifies a Design Object Interaction Diagram (OID) in the sense that it states formally what a Design OID must do, and how the behavior of the Design OID is triggered.

Purpose

Many projects require a complete set of functional specifications that define the externally-visible behaviors of a system—the *behaviors* and not just the interfaces that trigger those behaviors. Design Scenarios fill that role. If the Design Scenarios are part of a subsystem workbook then they will, of course, provide a functional specification of that subsystem.

If OIDs are used as a vehicle for discussing design alternatives, documenting design decisions, and validating Object Models, then the assumptions and outcomes of these OIDs must be defined precisely. Design Scenarios define the assumptions and outcomes of Design OIDs.

The approach to design advocated in this book is to transform the analysis models taking design considerations into account in an incremental manner. One way to do that is to take the Analysis OIDs, transform them incrementally and then transform their corresponding Analysis Scenarios (in order to create Design Scenarios that capture the design-level assumptions and outcomes of the new Design OIDs). An alternative is to take the Analysis Scenarios, transform them incrementally, and only then transform their corresponding Analysis OIDs, before performing internal design by continuing to transform the new Design OIDs. The former approach focuses on the development of *mechanisms* to drive design; the latter approach focuses on the development of *interfaces* to drive design. Both approaches are valid. Both have a requirement for Design Scenarios.

Participants

Design Scenarios are written by designers. If the Design Scenarios are part of a subsystem workbook then they will be written by the designers responsible for that subsystem.

Timing

Design Scenarios are written after the System Architecture and the Subsystem Model have been defined.

If Design OIDs are the key vehicle for design, then Design Scenarios will be written immediately after the Design OIDs as a way of capturing their assumptions and outcomes. An alternative is to write the Design Scenarios first, modify (or construct) the Design OIDs next, and then to proceed with design by continuing to transform the Design OIDs. A Design Scenario is the external abstractions of a system behavior, whereas a Design OID captures the internal details. The Design OID needs a Design Scenario to establish its function, and starting and ending states, but Design OIDs often discover missing assumptions and outcomes that need to be added to the Design Scenarios.

In any case, the Design Scenarios, like all other design work products, will have to be revisited whenever design issues force design rework.

Technique

Design OIDs are the key vehicle for performing design. If Design OIDs are written before Design Scenarios, then when a Design OID is produced, its corresponding Design Scenario is then created or updated. The new Design Scenario takes into account the previous version of the Design Scenario (or the corresponding Analysis Scenario if no Design Scenario previously existed), and the design issues that the Design OID was forced to address. Writing the Design Scenario involves reflecting these design issues in the description of the system behavior that the Design Scenario represents. This might, for example, involve replacing an abstractly expressed outcome by one that specifies the result of the scenario on newly-introduced design objects that the Design OID has just surfaced.

If Design Scenarios are written before Design OIDs, the change is that instead of reflecting a design decision that has been made while the Design OID was written, the design decision must be made now. Making that decision involves deciding how the

Design Scenario's specification of system behavior has to change in order to accommodate the design issue under consideration. This might, for example, involve introducing new design objects to set up the scenario. This will involve (at least) adding or changing the assumptions of the Design Scenario to refer to the new objects.

A Design Scenario states the way in which the system behavior specified by the Design Scenario and depicted in the Design OID is to be triggered. A Design Scenario is usually triggered by a method call or a user action. In the case of a user action, user interfacing standards, styles, et cetera. obviously have to be taken into account. See Section 12.0, User Interface Model Work Products for further details. In the case of a method call, the first object shown in the OID is usually the one whose method is called to trigger the behavior. Only this object's class and method declaration are described as the Design Scenario trigger; not the object that invokes the method.

Strengths

Just as Analysis Scenarios are a very good way to formalize the functional *requirements* imposed on a system, so do Design Scenarios provide a functional *specification* of the system (or subsystem). The functional specification includes details that are omitted in the more abstract functional requirements. Documenting behaviors in this way supports the use of OIDs as a design vehicle. It enumerates all the variations that Design OIDs must deal with and establishes the starting and ending states for each OID. Precise subsystem functional specifications facilitate the parallel and independent development of subsystems. The enumeration of Design Scenarios provides another concrete metric for use in project estimation and tracking.

Weaknesses

Writing Design Scenarios is a lot of work. The temptation will exist to use only Design OIDs as a vehicle for design. Worse, you may be tempted to skip both Design Scenarios and Design OIDs due to the work involved. Without a formal language of design, however, it is difficult to control the process of building or maintaining large systems or components.

Notation

Similar to Analysis Scenarios (see Section 11.4) except that the scenario trigger must additionally be described. The following template may be used:

Table 13-4 (Page 1 of 2). *Example of a Design Scenario Notation Template.*
Scenario name _____
Trigger _____
Assumptions _____
_____
Outcomes _____

Table 13-4 (Page 2 of 2). *Example of a Design Scenario Notation Template.*

Notes _____
  _____
  _____

The trigger is either a method declaration or a description or a user action. User actions can be described by free-format text, perhaps including a reference to a User Interface Model work product.

Traceability

This work product has the following traceability:

Impacted by:
- Nonfunctional Requirements (p. 106)
- Issues (p. 176)
- Analysis Scenarios (p. 203)
- Design Guidelines (p. 253)
- System Architecture (p. 257)

Impacts:
- Design OIDs (p. 298)
- Design State Models (p. 306)
- Glossary (p. 355)

Advice and Guidance

Design Scenarios differ from Analysis Scenarios in that their assumptions and outcomes are specified in terms of starting and ending states of design objects versus analysis objects, that is, objects and states from the Design Object Model (DOM) vs. the Analysis Object Model (AOM). Often however, scenarios can be carried over from analysis to design when the referenced objects and states are carried over from AOM to DOM. In this case, Design OIDs can be started from Analysis Scenarios and OIDs. If and when new assumptions or outcomes are discovered during Design OID development, the Design Scenarios can be explicitly documented.

So, although Design Scenarios can be documented before starting on Design OIDs, developers often find it more efficient to discover and record them while developing the Design OIDs.

Care should be taken to distinguish between discoveries affecting simply the design versus those that truly affect the analysis work products. For example, if it is "discovered" that there is a "requirement" that the system must interface with some external software system, it should be questioned to determine whether it is a functional or a nonfunctional requirement.

- If it is determined that the requirement was functional and contractual, for instance "send the transaction and its completion status to the XYZ Audit System," then that should be recognized as an Actor affected by the system and be recorded in the Use Case Model, Analysis Scenarios, Analysis Object Model, State Models, and Class Descriptions.

- If, however, it is determined that the "requirement" was nonfunctional, for instance "use the internal transaction journalizer from the previous system," then that should be recognized as a design decision and result in Design Scenarios whose collaborations or outcomes reflect that design.

In the latter case, the analysis work products are not affected, because the function of the system, the nature of the problem, was not affected.

Verification

- Check that the Design Scenarios cover all anticipated changes to requirements. This might mean reworking the Analysis Scenarios but it is most easily checked by reference to the Design Scenarios.

- Check that all assumptions and outcomes refer to design objects, their states, and their attributes, and not to the analysis model.

- Check the completeness of Design Scenarios by checking how the opposite assumptions are dealt with (play "what if" games).

- Whenever an object state is mentioned in a Design Scenario assumption, check whether the other possible states of the object are adequately addressed by Design Scenarios.

Example(s)

This example refers to the image processing subsystem shown in Figure 13-7. One of the scenarios discovered at design time for this subsystem is that of *Invoke basic image processing function*. This Scenario is purely internal to the image processing architecture. In particular it is architecture-specific. The public interfaces to image processing applications do not know about the basic image processing functions. For both these reasons, the scenario cannot appear in the list of Analysis Scenarios: It is a subsystem scenario identified at design time as a result of projecting a system scenario onto the *Image processing* subsystem. Note that this scenario is used by *all* system scenarios that require usage of the built-in image processing functions.

Table 13-5 (Page 1 of 2). Example of a Design Scenario.

Scenario name	Invoke basic image processing function
Trigger	The scenario is triggered by a request to invoke a particular basic image processing function on the local node.

```
ISequence<IfResult> Image::perform(
        IfParms legacyFunctionParameters )
```

Assumptions	• The specified image processing function is implemented locally.
	• The images on which the function is to operate are currently stored in the image database, but not necessarily all locally.

Table 13-5 (Page 2 of 2). Example of a Design Scenario.

Outcomes	• The image processing function is invoked. • The result images (if any) are stored in the image database. • The return values (if any) are returned to the caller. These may include references to the ids of any result images.
Notes	The images specified as parameters to the function must be retrieved from the image database.

References

- [Jacobson92] has extensive discussion on Use Cases.

- [Spivey88] defines behavior in terms of assumptions and outcomes.

Importance

Design Scenarios are essential for creating Design Object Interaction Diagrams. Sometimes, Design Scenarios are created during Design OID construction as new assumptions and outcomes are discovered relating to design artifacts while working from Analysis OIDs or Scenarios. If you don't create Design Scenarios explicitly, you will have to create them before completing Design OIDs.

13.8 DESIGN OBJECT INTERACTION DIAGRAMS

Description

A Design Object Interaction Diagram (OID), used for *dynamic modeling* in the object-oriented design, is a graphical representation of object collaborations in a Design Scenario either derived from analysis or for design only, in terms of design objects and their interactions.

It is the result of transforming the corresponding Analysis Object Interaction Diagram, if one exists. The driving force behind the transformation is the System Architecture.

One major difference between a Design OID and its analysis equivalent (see Section 11.5) is its emphasis on those design classes intended for implementation. Some of these are directly derived from problem domain classes found in analysis, and others are invented or reused in design to provide control, interface, communication, distribution, and storage function.

The analysis-to-design transformation, of which writing Design OIDs is a vital part, is architecture-driven. For example, if a system has a client/server architecture, some analysis objects will be mapped into the design ones on the client side, some on the server side, and some mapped on both sides.

Purpose

The flexibility and the extensibility of a system depend on an adequate allocation of identified behaviors in terms of coupling and cohesion. A good allocation of behaviors leverages the reusability and interchangeability of objects. The strength of Design OIDs are their intuitive expressiveness for representing the end-to-end dynamic control and information flows among objects, under one specific System Architecture.

Modeling with Design OIDs is an effective driver of the development process. It is the main vehicle for allocating responsibilities to objects, discovering problems, holding design discussions, and considering design alternatives.

The dynamics of a System Architecture can be expressed well using Design OIDs. Knowledge of how objects interact is vital to the definition of an Architecture.

Dynamic modeling with Design OIDs is one of the most important steps. It directly impacts most implementation work products. Any design Issue should be resolved at the Design OID level.

Design OIDs are a means to:

- Decide and graphically depict the design objects' behaviors and responsibilities.
- Discover, present, and understand the function to be accomplished by each object.
- Visualize the distribution of system responsibilities among objects.
- Realize the conversion of classes of the Analysis Object Model into those of the Design Object Model.
- Identify, apply, and present patterns for structuring the design.

The following consequences could result from failing to conducting the Design OID modeling:

- Inconsistent use of design principles, design mechanisms, and the reuse of design patterns.
- Failure to discover opportunities for component and framework reuse.
- Inadequate identification of trade-offs between reusability, modifiability, and efficiency.
- Failure to preform commonality and variability analysis across subsystems.
- Incomplete refactoring the design for better resilience to change.
- Incomplete and erroneous specification of classes to be implemented.
- Potential miscommunication and misunderstanding among development team members.

Participants

Developing Design OIDs is the task of system architects, designers, and developers, led by a system architect. It is very important to have key programmers participate in this step, since they understand well the system constraints, environment, and language limitations. These factors must be reflected in the Design OIDs.

Timing

Design OIDs should be developed as soon as a primitive Design Object Model exists, and the system boundary and Architecture is defined in the design phase. The Design OIDs might be used as a vehicle to drive the development of the system structure. Both the Analysis Object Model and Analysis OIDs provide the basis for those at the design level. When a primitive Design Object Model is ready, it is time to develop the Design OIDs for the system objects. In the Design OID modeling process, more design objects are usually created.

In an iterative and incremental process, design modeling, especially Design OID modeling, should be carried out in each development cycle. Even in the implementation, Design OIDs are often referenced or modified for new design or architecture ideas.

Technique

The Design OIDs are developed by transforming those at the analysis level while considering the underlying Architecture, frameworks, design patterns, and system constraints. Usually, the contents of Design OIDs are more detailed, since they serve as part of the specification for subsequent coding. When an Architecture is in place, Design OIDs are used to assign responsibilities to design classes. For example, if the Model-View-Controller architecture is used, an analysis class is transformed into two design classes, a view class and a model class. The former captures the knowledge of end-user interface, and the latter possesses the business logic. When a persistent layer is used for a multilayer architecture, an analysis class can be transformed into another two design classes: a persistent class and a model class. The former is used only for handling the database interface. Developing a Design OID involves the following:

- Start with Use Cases, Analysis and Design Scenarios, and Analysis OIDs. Identify their corresponding Design OIDs and related design classes.

- Find the object responsibilities identified in the Analysis Object Model. Its corresponding design object may take over some of the responsibilities with additional ones from the System Architecture.

- Analyze the interactions of design objects. Examine the responsibilities for dependencies. For example, if an object is responsible for a specific action, but does not possess all the knowledge needed to accomplish that action, it must collaborate with objects defined in other classes that do possess the knowledge. Any two objects that have direct collaboration should have a directional association or a visibility dependency between their corresponding classes defined in the Design Object Model.

- Identify collaborations by asking the following question for each responsibility of every class: Are the class's objects capable of fulfilling this responsibility itself? If not, what does it need? From which other class can it acquire what it needs? Each responsibility that you decided to share between classes also represents a collaboration between their objects. Check what other objects need the result or information, and make sure that each object that needs the result collaborates with the one getting it.

- Make sure the parameters are well defined for messages including method return values, so that data flow and storage is explicitly documented.

- Add threading and control information, defined in the notation subsection, into your Design OID to show when, where, and how an object behavior is performed or waits for a response.

Strengths

Strengths of Design OIDs are their intuitiveness and expressiveness for representing dynamic interactions between objects, and System Architecture. It is a powerful and effective tool to enable developers discussing design Issues in depth before and during implementation.

Weaknesses

Limitations of Design OIDs are similar to those at the analysis level. A Design OID can only specify the execution of a system for one Scenario. A system can consist of hundreds of Scenarios under different assumptions. The amount of work required to create OIDs for each Design Scenario is daunting. Even if all Design OIDs are written, their number tends to defeat their objective of providing a clear understanding of system dynamics. The solution to this problem is to focus on Design OIDs that are effective in the sense that they impact either the System Architecture or system key function. Avoid those Design OIDs which do not contribute to the system understanding or design.

Notation

Design OID notation is mostly the same as the analysis counterpart (See *Notation* in Section 11.5, "Analysis Object Interaction Diagrams" on page 208).

The additional notation in Design OIDs is architectural, and includes:

- Focus-of-control
- Multitasking
- Process and subsystem boundary.

A focus-of-control shows whether an object is active. It is either in the state of execution, or in the blocking state waiting for a returning message. It is represented by a long rectangle box on the concerned object line time. In a complex system, process and subsystem boundaries as well as multithreading execution can be explicitly represented in the Design OIDs. The Design OID can demonstrate which process and which subsystem an object is in, how many threads the object has at one time point, and what activity one thread is engaged in. One notation format is shown in Figure 13-10.

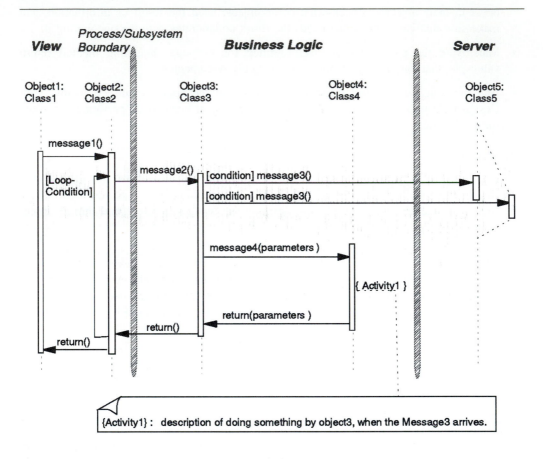

Figure 13-10. *Format of a Design Object Interaction Diagram.*

Traceability

This work product has the following traceability:

Impacted by:
- Nonfunctional Requirements (p. 106)
- Issues (p. 176)
- Analysis OIDs (p. 208)
- Screen Flows (p. 237)
- Screen Layouts (p. 242)
- Design Guidelines (p. 253)
- System Architecture (p. 257)
- Design Object Model (p. 281)
- Design Scenarios (p. 293)
- Design State Models (p. 306)

Impacts:
- Design Object Model (p. 281)
- Design State Models (p. 306)
- Design Class Description (p. 311)

Advice and Guidance

- Consistency should be maintained between the Design Object Model and Design OIDs. If object A sends a message to object B in a Design OID, either A's class has an association (including aggregation) directed to B's class, or there is an argument or typing dependency from A's class to B's class. The latter happens when B is passed to A through method parameters. Both cases should be reflected in the object model. Also, class attributes and operations referenced in the Design OIDs should appear in the Design Object Model.

- Due to the fact that a system may involve hundreds of Scenarios, it is suggested that only the major Scenarios are documents and developed into Design OIDs. Frequently, exceptional conditions are documented as notes at the bottom of each Design OID.

- The System Architecture impacts Design OIDs and should be expressed explicitly.

- Distribute responsibilities evenly among design objects.

- Avoid overly passive objects and overly active objects. The design may fall back to structured System Architectures.

- Determine the frequency of interobject message exchanges to identify any possible system bottleneck, to find ways to improve system performance.

- Check that every message arrow is named and has specified the required parameters.

- Check that the Scenario assumption/start-state is used/needed and that the expected outcome occurs.

- The integration test cases should be the direct result from the Design OID, while the system test cases should closely follow the Design Scenarios.

Verification

See the checklist for Analysis OIDs, Section 11.5, which is also appropriate here.

- Check that all navigations from object to object implied by a Design OID are in practice made possible by the appropriate attributes, parameters, and operations.

- Check that the frequency of interprocess communications is acceptable.

- Check the adequacy of all message parameter lists.

- Check whether the System Architecture is represented in Design OIDs.

Example(s)

We use the same example presented in the Analysis Object Interaction Diagram section, and the Design Scenario is derived from the one used in the corresponding Analysis OID (Section 11.5).

This example is about a library system in which users can access its library items. A user has an account associated with each library that has a unique level security capability. Each library item's security object will check whether the user is permitted to access the current library item.

- **Design Scenario**: A user wants to access a library item.

- **Trigger**: The scenario is triggered by the current user who clicks the mouse on the view icon of the library item to be accessed.

- **Assumption**: The user has already logged into the library system and his or her identity is established within the library.

- **Outcome**: A library item is permitted to be viewed if the user passes the security checking for this library item.

- **Description**: When a library item gets a request from a user for access, it first finds the account information from the library and passes the user's information to its own security object to check whether the user is permitted access. If the user has the proper authorization, the item will display its own content. Otherwise, request is rejected.

Figure 13-11. Example of a Design Object Interaction Scenario.

The Design OID example for this Scenario (Figure 13-12) shows a 2-tier System Architecture that separates the *view* classes from *business-logic* or *model* classes, so that view classes take care of presentation only. The messages are passed one way from view classes to the business-logic classes. In other words, the dependency is unidirectional, as is also shown in its corresponding Design Object model.

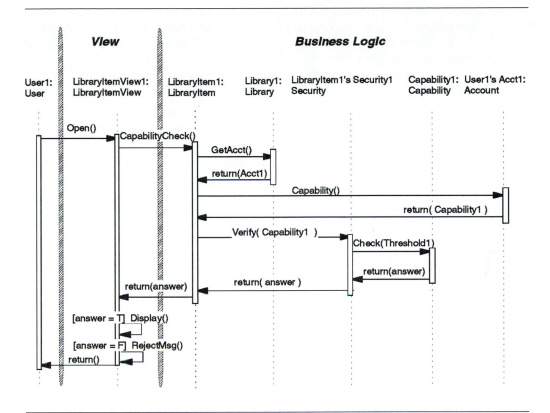

Figure 13-12. *Example of a Design Object Interaction Diagram.*

Comparing this Design OID (Figure 13-12) with the Analysis OID in Figure 11-11, one can find that this one is specified with much more design detail and extra design decisions. These design decisions reflect the Model-View-Controller architecture with separated concerns. In this architecture, the view objects are responsible for presenting the graphics and passing information from users to the model objects. The model objects are those possessing the business logic. One part of the business logic presented here is how to verify a user's security for the tasks she or he is allowed to perform.

References

Jacobson et al [Jacobson92] were the first group employing Use Cases and Object Interaction Diagrams (OID) in object-oriented dynamic modeling. Rumbaugh's OMT [Rumbaugh95b] and Booch's method [Booch94] have very similar work products. For example, OMT has OID-like constructs, called "Event Trace Diagrams" that are used for analysis. We define both Analysis OID and Design OIDs to be a far more expressive work product, by separating the notation for problem abstraction (Analysis OID) from the one for solution representation (Design OID), and adding concepts such as *conditions*, *loops*, *message synchronization*, and *process boundaries*. We also notice that the Unified Modeling Language [Booch96] begins to address issues related to conditions, processes, and message synchronization.

Importance

Dynamic modeling with Design OIDs is essential to specify the system object behaviors and it should be one of the major activities of the design phase. It is the key step to identify and specify methods for each class.

For one Scenario, several alternative Design OIDs may be produced. Each of these represents a different design solution. Modeling with Design OIDs forces solutions to be complete and brings to the surface Issues that must be resolved during system design. It is difficult to do object-oriented design without this form of system dynamics.

13.9 DESIGN STATE MODELS

Description

A Design State Model is a representation of the dynamic object behaviors for design classes. The Design State Model can use the same notation as one in the Analysis State Model (see Section 11.6), even if their contexts are different.

It should be emphasized that only a few key classes with strong state-dependent object behaviors need to be described by the State Model. Dynamic modeling with Design Object Interaction Diagrams (OIDs) is sufficient to express most object interaction and behavior.

For classes with complex states, design state modeling is the place to identify whether the *State* design pattern [Gamma95] can be used.

Purpose

A State Model can show the specification of object behaviors related to each class based on State Diagrams, Tables, or Matrixes. It is easy to understand the life cycle for one object through this mechanism. A State Model provides a convenient, visual means of understanding the life cycle of an object.

Design OIDs often provide clues for building a Design State Model. When a message is sent from one object to another, two things happen. First, the message-sending object will take an *action* in its particular state to accomplish this message sending. Second, an event is formed and arrives at the message-receiving object. This prompts the receiving object to perform some action and potentially change its state.

Participants

At the design level, State Models should be defined by system architects and designers. It is very important to have some key programmers participate this activity, to ensure that the design can be efficiently implemented. Architects should help verify whether the specification meets the requirements described in the State Models at the analysis level.

Timing

Design State Modeling is usually performed iteratively together with the development of a Design Object Model and Design OIDs.

Technique

During design and implementation phases, it may be necessary to develop State Models for certain classes whose dynamic behavior needs to be better understood. The difference between building a State Model for analysis vs. for design is that the design model can be impacted by System Architecture, frameworks, environment, and system constraints. The key objective here is to specify how to accomplish the responsibilities assigned to the object.

Strengths

The strength of State Models is their capability to describe the life cycles and state-dependent behavior of design objects clearly and efficiently. It is also a centralized place to model the behavior for one object.

Weaknesses

State models can be very trivial for some classes, and it is tedious to develop a state diagram for every class. A State Model describes a single class but not interactions between classes and their states. Thus State Models should be built selectively.

Notation

A State Model at the design level uses the same notation as an Analysis State Model (Section 11.6).

Traceability

This work product has the following traceability:

Impacted by:
- Nonfunctional Requirements (p. 106)
- Issues (p. 176)
- Analysis State Models (p. 219)
- Screen Flows (p. 237)
- Screen Layouts (p. 242)
- Design Guidelines (p. 253)
- System Architecture (p. 257)
- Design Object Model (p. 281)
- Design Scenarios (p. 293)
- Design OIDs (p. 298)

Impacts:
- Design OIDs (p. 298)
- Design Class Description (p. 311)
- Glossary (p. 355)

Advice and Guidance

It is wise to present the State Models in such detail that the tough design decisions can be easily discussed. Often, developers hesitate to make design decisions until the coding phase. This is a hidden danger to a project, since if a wrong decision is made by a particular programmer without being fully discussed at the design level, the system might not be built in its best form.

- Classes whose state dependencies have been explored in an Analysis State Model do not necessarily need to have their dynamics explored further in a Design State Model. Design State Models may be written either for newly introduced design classes or for already identified analysis classes as considered appropriate. The criterion is whether the writing of a Design State Model would add significantly to system understanding.

- Once a Design State Model is stable, ensure that it is consistent with the other design work products, in particular, the Design OIDs, the Design Object Model, and the Design Class Descriptions. How this will be done will be dependent on the way it is decided to implement the state-dependent behavior of the target class. In general, there are two ways: directly or by using the State design pattern (see [Gamma95]).

- If a Design State Model is to be implemented using the State design pattern, the following must be done:

  - Classes representing each of the states must be identified and defined. Each of these state classes will implement the services and data relevant to their substate; all services inapplicable to the state are also provided, but their implementation suggests that an exceptional situation has arisen. Default exceptional implementations can be inherited from a common state superclass. The common state superclass can also define any non-state-changing services that are common to all states.

  - All the services of all the states are part of the interface of the target class, and these are delegated to the current state. The target class has an attribute that maintains the current state.

    – State-changing logic is provided either by the target class or by the state classes, as considered appropriate. Do not create new state objects on each state change; reuse existing state objects where possible, both for efficiency and to implement state-specific data that must persist from state to state. If no state-specific data are required, then state objects may be instantiated using the *Singleton* design pattern.

Implementations with state patterns expand the number of classes implemented slightly, but they separate concerns of different states and avoid repetitive code that tests state variables. A key advantage of the state pattern is that adding a new state or changing the details of an existing state, becomes a local and simple change.

- If a Design State Model is to be implemented directly, then all services and state variables are implemented directly by the target class. Each service must, if it is state-dependent, test the state variables and act accordingly. State transitions that are ruled out by the Design State Model are excluded by service *preconditions*, which must be identified and implemented for each service.

Verification

See the checklist for Analysis State Models, Section "Verification" on page 222, which is also appropriate here.

- Check for black holes: A group of states which, once entered, cannot be exited (as a group). Note that not all black holes suggest modeling errors.

- Check the state transition table. Even if the table is not explicitly produced, check each possible combination of states for a possible transition.

- Check for the absence of race conditions.

- Check semantics of absent transitions. An absent transition denotes a behavior that should not happen. Check that this prohibition is enforced. Absent transitions correspond to method preconditions; they should be documented as such.

- Check that each State Model contains initial and final states.

- Check that every noninitial state has at least one incoming transition.

- Check that every nonfinal state has at least one outgoing transition.

- Check that every transition is labeled with the event that triggers it.

- Check the events of all outgoing transitions from each node for completeness: Is another event possible in these circumstances?

- Check that every state is named.

- Check that the State Model identifies the class to which it refers.

- Check the consistency between Design OIDs and their related objects' State Models. If there is a message received by an object in a Design OID, the message should be interpreted as an event occurring in that object's State Model. The object should experience a state change.

Example(s)

The TCP connection can be modeled using Design State Model. A TCP connection has three states, closed, listen, and established. With different events coming to different states, the connection reacts differently. The state diagram for a TCP connection is shown in Figure 13-13.

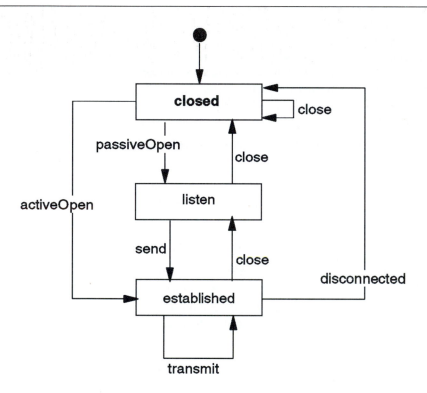

Figure 13-13. *Example of Design State Model.*

References

Sally Shlaer and Steve Mellor [Shlaer92] discuss using state modeling techniques for system analysis and design. Other references for this section are the same as those in the Analysis State Model (see Section 11.6).

Importance

Design State Models are optional but extremely useful for understanding the life cycle of objects with much state-dependent behavior.

13.10 DESIGN CLASS DESCRIPTIONS

Description

Design Class Descriptions are containers of all the information known about a class at the design level. Comments written about Analysis Class Descriptions in Section 11.7 are valid here too, and will not be repeated. Two points should be noted, however, when comparing analysis and Design Class Descriptions.

- They are different work products, although the Design Class Description will refer to its analysis counterpart if one exists. This is because the definition of the design class may be slightly different from that of the analysis class. For example, an analysis class may have been split into several design classes, perhaps to separate the model and view aspects of the class.

- The main audience for Design Class Descriptions is an implementation team. This must be borne in mind when planning the Design Class Description format.

Design Class Descriptions are likely to be generated automatically by the toolset responsible for maintaining the object model, the state models, et cetera.

Purpose

Design Class Descriptions are needed for the same reasons as Analysis Class Descriptions (See Section 11.7) and also serve the vital purpose of providing the starting point for class implementation work.

Participants

The designer who owns a class has the responsibility to maintain its Design Class Description.

Timing

Design Class Descriptions are opened as soon as the need for that design class is identified. The Class Description then serves as a repository for class oriented summary information as the design modeling activity proceeds.

Technique

As soon as the need for a particular class has been identified in a modeling session, a class description is opened for the class. It is a reasonable assumption that most of the analysis classes will become design classes, so an initial design activity might be the creation of Design Class Descriptions from Analysis Class Descriptions. The updating of class descriptions should be one of the activities performed after each design modeling session. Class Descriptions, Glossary entries (see Section 16.1), and the Design Object Model should be integrated, with a tool taking care of consistency and eliminating redundancy.

Use the Design Class Descriptions as a place to document any class or method design decisions that cannot be expressed more succinctly using one of the other design work products. Class invariants fall into this category, as do informal implementation notes on class design.

Strengths

Design Class Descriptions are vital starting points for the implementation of the classes. They organize all known information about each class and often record information that fits nowhere else.

Weaknesses

There is a danger that Class Descriptions may overlap in a redundant manner with other work products such as the Object Model and State Models. Redundancy may lead to inconsistency and a waste of resources. The solution is to ensure that the Class Descriptions are integrated into the chosen toolset so that information need to be entered and maintained only once. This should be considered to be an important criterion for tool selection.

Notation

Design Class Descriptions drive low-level design activity in the subsequent implementation phase. The format of the descriptions must, therefore, be appropriate to support that activity. Design Class Descriptions are necessarily sensitive to the target programming language. The class description template should, therefore, be tailored to that language. The following template is specific to C++; a Smalltalk template would differ only slightly.

A suitable Design Class Description template might be the following. There is no need for a "Name" slot in the template as each class description is expected to be an individual work product in its own right. All work products *inherit* the common work product attributes (defined in Section 8.1), including an identifying name.

Table 13-6 (Page 1 of 2). *Example of a Design Class Description Template.*

Description _____

States   1._____

Table 13-6 (Page 2 of 2). Example of a Design Class Description Template.

Relationships	1._____
	2._____
Public members	1._____
	2._____
Protected members	1._____
	2._____
Private members	1._____
	2._____
Notes	1._____
	2._____

Class invariants, if they are used, can be documented in an additional "Invariant" slot in the template.

At the design level it is assumed that defined operations will specify concrete types for parameters and results. Depending on the development method, the division of the design, the implementation phases, et cetera, it may be considered useful or necessary to provide pseudo-code for each operation. "Notes" can also include any free-format notes, hints, or implementation instructions.

Depending on tool support, the Design Class Descriptions should either include all design information relevant to a particular class, or the detailed information should be easily accessible from the class descriptions.

Traceability

This work product has the following traceability:

Impacted by:
- Issues (p. 176)
- Analysis Class Descriptions (p. 227)
- Design Guidelines (p. 253)
- System Architecture (p. 257)
- Design Object Model (p. 281)
- Design OIDs (p. 298)
- Design State Models (p. 306)

Impacts:
- Source Code (p. 334)

Advice and Guidance

- Use Design Class Descriptions as a place to hold method specifications or pseudo-code if appropriate.

- The degree of detail to be entered in Design Class Descriptions is dependent on the development process used. In general, however, the Design Class Descriptions should define the various interfaces of the classes, and provide enough information to allow the class to be coded autonomously. Design Class Descriptions should be uniform in their level of detail.

- If provided automatically by tool support, do not copy information, for example associations, from other design work products into the Design Class Descriptions.

- A class should be defined independently of its subclasses. The subclass relationships are, however, included in the Design Class Descriptions in order to complete the picture of the class. Once again, good tool support is assumed in order to ensure that this transfer of information from the Design Object Model to the Design Class Descriptions is automatic.

- Tool support should include the visualization of inheritance class structures.

Verification

See the checklist for Analysis Class Descriptions, Section 11.7, which is also appropriate here.
- Check that each Design Class Description is an adequate basis for coding the class.
- Check that each Class Description is consistent with the agreed coding guidelines.
- Check that all methods are defined in adequate detail.
- Check that all attributes, parameters, and returns have types.
- Check that all key attributes and relations have been identified in the class descriptions.
- Check that all n-way associations have been (or will be) implemented by a collection class of the appropriate type.

Example(s)

The following example is for a system that was developed in C++.

Table 13-7 (Page 1 of 3). Example Showing Design Class Descriptions.

Name
> BankAccount

Description
> An agreement between a bank and a customer that enables the customer to deposit funds in the bank and, within certain limits, to withdraw funds.

States
- Active
- Withdrawn (substate of Active)
- InCredit (substate of Active)
- Suspended
- Open
- Closed (no account is ever destroyed)

Relationships
- Subclasses: CheckingAccount, SavingAccount
- Association: ownedBy(Customer)

Public members

Table 13-7 (Page 2 of 3). Example Showing Design Class Descriptions.

Several other public member functions, like constructors, destructor, uninteresting accessor functions, and others have been omitted here.

- `virtual bool isCreditWorthy( Amount creditAmount) const`

Check if this account can be granted a credit of the amount specified. Returns true if the account is creditworthy.

- `virtual TransactionResult modifyOverdraftLimit( Amount overDraftAmount )`

Modify the limit by which this account can be overdrawn. If the amount specified is positive, the limit is increased. If the amount specified is negative, the limit is decreased. The new limit cannot become negative, it will be zero in this case. Returns OK, if the overdraft limit was modified successfully, otherwise a TransactionResult that indicates the reason for failure.

- `virtual TransactionResult replaceCustomerDetails( CustomerDetails* customerDetails)`

Replace the details that are kept for the customer owning this account with the details specified. Returns OK, if the customer details were replaced successfully, otherwise a TransactionResult that indicates the reason for failure. The customer details are passed as pointer to also allow objects of concrete subclasses to be passed in without object slicing. Account is adopting the new customerDetails object and will delete it on its own destruction or if it is replaced again.

- `virtual const CustomerDetails& queryCustomerDetails() const`

Return the details that are kept for the customer owning this account. The customer details are returned by reference to also allow objects of concrete subclasses to be returned without object slicing.

- `virtual TransactionResult`
`addGuarantee( BankAccount& guarantor, Amount guaranteedAmount )`

Add to this account the guarantee provided by the specified account. This additional guarantor will provide a guarantee up to the amount specified. Returns OK, if the guarantee was added successfully, otherwise a TransactionResult indicates the reason for failure.

- `virtual TransactionResult removeGuarantee( BankAccount& guarantor)`

Remove the guarantee provided for this account by the account specified. Returns OK, if the guarantee was removed successfully, otherwise a TransactionResult indicates the reason for failure.

- `virtual TransactionResult addSignatory( const Customer& additionalSignatory )`

Add to this account the customer specified as additional person with the rights to sign. Returns OK, if the signatory was added successfully, otherwise a TransactionResult indicates the reason for failure.

- `virtual TransactionResult removeSignatory( const Customer& additionalSignatory )`

Remove the authorization to sign for this account for signatory specified. Returns OK, if the guarantee was removed successfully, otherwise a TransactionResult indicates the reason for failure.

- `virtual TransactionResult close() = 0;`

Close this account. Returns OK, if the account was closed successfully, otherwise a TransactionResult indicates the reason for failure. This is an abstract member function that needs to be overridden by the derived concrete classes, because closing an account must involve different actions depending on the concrete account type (checking, saving, et cetera).

- `virtual State state() const;`

Return the state of the account.

Protected members

Table 13-7 (Page 3 of 3). *Example Showing Design Class Descriptions.*

Most other set/get accessor functions for private attributes have been omitted here ...

- `virtual void state( State newState)`
  Set the state of the account.

Private members
- AccountCode accountCode
- Name name
- Address address
- Date creationDate
- AccountBalance currentBalance
- CreditArrangement overdraftFacilities

Notes
- **BankAccount is an abstract base class.**

References

See [Wirfs-Brock90], [Rumbaugh91a], and [Booch94] for examples of Class Description formats.

Importance

Design Class Descriptions are essential as a starting point for class implementations.

13.11 REJECTED DESIGN ALTERNATIVES

Description

Rejected Design Alternatives are those design decisions that were considered but, for one reason or another, were rejected. The mainstream design work products document the decisions that *were* taken; this work product documents those that were *not* taken.

Purpose

Documenting the Rejected Design Alternatives is very important, because without them a design is disconnected from its history and from the effort that was required to construct the design. The practical implication of not documenting rejected alternatives is that this information will be lost, either because the members of the design team have changed, or because the details of the issues have simply been forgotten. This matters because design decisions need to be reviewed from time to time. Perhaps the pattern of communication between objects, as shown in Object Interaction Diagrams (OIDs) for example, has become unbalanced, and a design review has suggested that alternatives be considered. Perhaps the project requirements have changed, a not uncommon occurrence, and design trade-offs have to be evaluated anew. Sometimes the need to review a design decision arises informally: A designer wants to be convinced that a decision is correct. In all these cases, if the history of a design decision has been lost, the various alternatives must be rediscovered and reevaluated. This duplication of effort is, of course, an undesirable overhead.

The effort required to consider design alternatives seriously affects the success of an iterative and incremental development process. If considering alternatives, and hence switching to alternatives, is too expensive then design decisions will tend to carry themselves along by their own momentum: "We don't know why a decision was made but it would be too time-consuming to find out." This is not intended to imply that actually making a design switch is trivial or cheap, but that without access to the history of a design decision the switch frequently won't even be considered.

Documenting design alternatives also improves communications between members of design teams. Questions of why something is the way it is can often be answered by a referral to the documented alternatives.

This problem of documenting design decisions can be tackled in one of two ways: one positive and one negative. The positive approach is to capture each design decision that is made and to document it together with its alternatives and their trade-offs. Desirable though this approach is in theory, it is, in practice, very difficult, because design decisions are being made continuously during the design process. What should be documented? How many design decisions does a single OID embody? Many: Design is a matter of continual decision-making, sometimes major, frequently minor.

The negative approach is to capture design alternatives that were rejected for some reason: to state them and to explain why they were rejected. In practice this turns out to be more feasible than a positive documentation approach. The process of design generally flows forward, but occasionally there are problems. Progress halts when alternatives are considered, weighed, and a decision made, perhaps after constructing some prototypes to evaluate the alternatives. This is the time to document what has happened: The facts are recorded as a set of Rejected Design Alternatives. By recording only negative decisions, there is an automatic filtering of the mass of minor decisions that were "obvious" and that would simply clutter the workbook and reduce progress if they were documented. The minor decisions are not recorded because they did not result in any serious consideration of alternatives. If positive decisions are recorded, it is in practice difficult to perform this filtering.

The reason why remembering the history of design decisions is more important than remembering that of analysis decisions is that analysis decisions are usually made in order to capture domain knowledge, or for reasons of modeling "goodness." When performing analysis, we deliberately ignore factors of efficiency, System Architecture, the Target Environment, et cetera. Analysis decisions are, therefore, much less exposed than design decisions to reconsideration. The exception is the case of a requirements change or a change in domain understanding, but in these cases the reworking of the analysis will reflect the new requirements, and alternative ways of modeling the old requirements will be of secondary importance. This is not to say that recording rejected analysis decisions is not sometimes useful, but it is not as vital as it is for design.

Participants

The team leaders, designers and architects who own the design work products are responsible for recording and documenting the alternatives that were considered and that were ultimately rejected.

Timing

Rejected Design Alternatives are documented as the design proceeds, as soon as practically possible after the design decision has been made. Design details are often highly complex and the facts will be forgotten if designers are told to document rejected alternatives only after the design has been completed.

Technique

The common work product structure, see Section 8.1, includes an Issues attribute. The raising of an issue often triggers the consideration of design alternatives. At some point the issue will be resolved by the taking of a decision and the rejection of alternatives. The rejected alternatives are then documented and cross-references made between the relevant work products, the Rejected Alternatives, and the issues that generated them. Not all rejected decisions stem from matters raised as explicit Issues however.

Strengths

Recording Rejected Design Alternatives enables a design team to backtrack without the overhead of rediscovering and reevaluating design alternatives.

Weaknesses

Recording Rejected Design Alternatives imposes an overhead on the project that must be recognized and budgeted. This work is an investment in future rework and will not pay in the very short term. It can be thought of as a form of reuse: reuse of design decisions. The benefits of any form of reuse are often difficult to quantify and sometimes difficult to justify.

Notation

The format in which Rejected Design Alternatives can be documented is very similar to that of design patterns [Gamma95].

Table 13-8. *Example of a Rejected Design Alternative Template.*

Description	_____
Context	_____
Assumptions	_____
Alternatives	1._____
	2._____
Considerations	_____
	_____
Decision	_____

The design alternatives documented in the above template can be described using either text or OIDs.

Traceability

This work product has the following traceability:

Impacted by:
- Issues (p. 176)
- System Architecture (p. 257)

Impacts:
- Historical Work Products (p. 359)

Advice and Guidance

- Record Rejected Design Alternatives as soon as possible.

- Include or refer to rejected Scenarios, OIDs, Object Models, et cetera. if these are relevant.

- The documentation should focus on enabling another designer in the future to return to this design decision and to reevaluate the alternatives, possibly with a different set of assumptions.

- A work product design review should briefly review the rejected alternatives that relate to the accepted design.

- The documentation should be relatively self-contained. References to other work products are fine, but the Issue, its context, and its assumptions should be understandable by someone reading this documentation alone.

Verification

- Review documented decisions to check that they are still reasonable.

Example(s)

In an application to configure distributed computer systems in a centralized manner, the following design issue arose:

Table 13-9. Example of Rejected Design Alternative.

Description	Representation of collected configuration data.
Context	Actual configuration data can be collected from the target nodes, and defined configuration data can be specified by a user. The actual and defined configuration object models have a common structure, as both represent the various alternative ways in which this operating system can be configured. The question is whether the same object model should be used for both actual and defined cases or whether two separate object models should be used.
Assumptions	1. While there are operations that are common to both actual and defined data, there are operations that are only applicable to one. For example, it is only valid to check defined data (against actual nodes), and it is only valid to validate actual data (for consistency). 2. There is an import method that turns valid actual data into defined data.
Alternatives	1. Represent actual and defined configuration data using two separate object models. This permits each of these object models to be as simple as possible, with only those alternatives and operations that are valid. 2. Represent actual and defined configuration data using the same object model. Where necessary, configuration objects use the state pattern to distinguish between the two kinds of representation. The subclasses of the state objects have interfaces that permit only operations appropriate to that state. The state pattern can also be used to distinguish between validated and unvalidated actual data.
Consider-ations	1. The first alternative involves simpler structures and fewer classes. 2. The replication of structure implicit in the first alternative will make the design less modular and more difficult to maintain. 3. The use of the state pattern in the second alternative enables the design to deal with other issues (distinction between validated and unvalidated data) by means of the same mechanism.
Decision	The second alternative was selected.

References

The format for design patterns that also works for Rejected Design Alternatives can be found, along with a complete discussion of design patterns in [Gamma95].

Importance

Recording Rejected Design Alternatives is optional, but we recommend that it be done as it makes revisiting of design decisions much easier.

14.0 Implementation Work Products

The purpose of the implementation phase is to construct the deliverable components of the product based on the plans detailed in the design work products. For software products, the most obvious deliverables are the executable form of the software (a.k.a. binaries) and the User Support Materials (a.k.a. documentation). But it is not a simple task to transform design work products into those deliverables. Since the final step in producing software and documentation is an automated one (e.g., compilation, formatting), we need to focus on the development of the intermediate work products that lead up to that step.

The implementation section of the project workbook consists of the following work products:

- Coding Guidelines

- Physical Packaging Plan

- Development Environment

- Source Code

- User Support Materials

These work products all "inherit" the common work product attributes described in Section 8.1 and have specialized attributes of their own. The work products and their specialized content are defined and commented on in the following sections, but let's briefly describe them here.

Before dispatching scores of programmers to generate millions of lines of code whose quality affects your company's health and whose maintenance defines your future liability, it is a good idea to have some Coding Guidelines. The nature and value of these guidelines is best understood by veteran programmers who have endeavored to extend or maintain someone else's source code.

Since source code files, libraries, and executables are organized and managed in the Development Environment for ease of development and testing rather than for ease of installation and use by a product user, a plan is needed that shows how all the deliverable components will be collected and packaged for delivery and installation. This is known as the Physical Packaging Plan.

The collection of tools, processes, conventions, and organizational infrastructure that a programming shop needs to establish to carry out the implementation of software defines a very complex "environment." A significant part of that involves setting up and running the configuration management and version control system. The Development Environment is often called "that well-oiled machine" because it is big, important, and requires a lot of care to set up and keep running. The Development Environment work product attempts to define that environment.

Source Code is the contents of files directly created by the developers. When processed through the Development Environment and organized according to the Physical Packaging Plan, it is transformed into the deliverable software. Source code is not limited to program files that lead to executable software. It can also be declarative information that is either delivered with the product (e.g. header files in C and C++, IDL[12] , message files, resource files), or files that define how the source code is to be processed in the Development Environment (e.g. makefiles). Since many products today boast of having millions of lines of Source Code configured for different versions of multiple Target Environments, and multiple releases of each, Source Code is probably the most complex and valuable work product discussed.

User Support Material, which describes the different aspects of working with the product, from evaluation to installation, operation, and maintenance, is also large and complex. Today User Support Material means a lot more than a set of manuals. Documentation can take the form of books, compact disks, on-line help, World-Wide Web pages on the Internet, or even last minute "readme" files.

The following sections will explain how to develop these implementation work products in more detail.

14.1 CODING GUIDELINES

Description

Coding Guidelines take the form of a set of documented rules (must do) and recommendations (should do) addressing the programming style to be used within a software development project. They usually cover things that are not detected by the compiler but that cause errors or problems associated with maintenance, portability, performance, simplicity, clarity, conflict, et cetera.

Typical topics covered by Coding Guidelines include:

- File naming conventions
- File structure
- File and function prologues (security and copyright)
- Identifier naming conventions
- Global names
- Class/structure layout
- Initialization
- Use of types within language
- Calling conventions and return types

---

[12] IDL stands for Interface Definition Language as defined by the Common Object Request Broker Architecture (CORBA) of the Object Management Group (OMG).

- Cohesion, encapsulation, binding
- Memory management
- Exception and error handling
- Use of language specific features
- Terseness of expression
- Performance
- Portability
- Formatting

Purpose

Reviewing, discussing, using and enforcing Coding Guidelines significantly reduce common programming errors. Also, the development of a project style of programming leads to a higher quality product with greater consistency. The common style also makes it less distracting when programmers review, inherit, or debug each other's code.

Participants

The team leader (the overall team leader in multiteam projects) or a designate usually gets the job of selecting, documenting, and maintaining the project's Coding Guidelines. However, every member of the implementation team should review, discuss, and suggest extensions and changes to the guidelines.

Timing

Coding Guidelines should be decided on before the start of the implementation phase for the first iteration within a project. If coding education is to be supplied, then the guidelines must be in place sufficiently in advance of the course that they can be taught.

Technique

If a project is totally without Coding Guidelines, it might look for Coding Guidelines from other organizations in the company or it may choose to start with some taken from an external source such as a published book. This can serve as a starting point for the intended Coding Guidelines.

The whole project should review the project's intended Coding Guidelines together once (perhaps in a meeting) at the start of the project and adopt them as a starting point. The process for enforcing the guidelines (code inspections) and improving the guidelines should also be reviewed with the team at this time. Coding Guidelines are eminently reusable from project to project. On project completion, the guidelines should be reviewed in the light of experience gained during the project.

A good approach for improving or adding to the Coding Guidelines is to use a Defect Prevention Process (DPP), see [Mays90]. For example, a group's DPP may consist of holding Causal Analysis meetings aimed at looking at defects to determine if there was a preventable cause and to see if some change in the project's processes and procedures can prevent similar problems from occurring again. At such a meeting it might be discovered that implementing a new Coding Guideline would remove the cause of a class of defects. An Action Team member would then be charged with including the new guideline into the project's Coding Guidelines.

Strengths

Having an accessible, documented, understood, and accepted set of project Coding Guidelines with rationale and examples makes it much easier to implement a high quality product with a high level of consistency. It also makes it easier to bring new programmers into the project and have them fit in and understand how the rest of the group operates. They will also understand the reasons why the group writes the way they do.

Weaknesses

It is not always easy to get programmers to change their coding style to meet the project's guidelines. Checking conformance to guidelines is usually a manual review performed by peers (labor intensive), though new automated tools are starting to appear, for example, ProLint™ from Productivity Through Software PLC (Cheshire, England) and CodeCheck™ by Abraxas Software (Portland Oregon).

Inconsistencies can develop as the project evolves its Coding Guidelines and does not apply the changes to code already written. The investment of reworking the code in this way is often hard to justify.

Notation

Coding Guidelines should be organized for easy reference and perhaps summarized on one to two pages (to pin to wall). In the guidelines document, each guideline should be formatted with:

Table 14-1. *Example of Coding Guidelines Notation Template.*
Guideline: _____   **Reason:** _____   **Example:** _____

Traceability

This work product has the following traceability:

Impacted by:
- Intended Development Process (p. 127)
- Project Workbook Outline (p. 132)
- Quality Assurance Plan (p. 147)
- Issues (p. 176)
- Target Environment (p. 272)

Impacts:
- Project Workbook Outline (p. 132)
- Source Code (p. 334)

Advice and Guidance

Start off using common guidelines or a previous project's guidelines and tune them to your needs. Review all Coding Guidelines with the implementation team before coding begins, and make sure everyone understands and agrees to the guidelines. Make adjustments as early as you can.

For improved comprehension, explain the reasoning behind each Coding Guideline and give an example of its use.

Verification

- Ask a developer experienced in the programming language to review the guidelines for completeness and correctness.

Example(s)

The following example is from a set of guidelines that we have developed and used with the projects we have mentored.

Rule 11.9 **Do not return a pointer or reference to local data from a function.**

Reason   If a reference to local data is passed back from a function the reference will end up pointing to data that has had its storage deallocated upon termination of the function.

Example

```
int& func()
{
  int i=10;
  return i;//i is local to func()
}

void func2()
{
  int& number = func();
  number = 20; //Oh!Oh! The storage pointed to by number has been
              //deallocated.  This would cause a runtime error.
}
```

Note: Most new C++ compilers will produce a warning regarding this error.

Figure 14-1. Example of Coding Guidelines.

References

For C++:

Some excellent sources of C++ Coding Guidelines are:

- *Taligent's Guide to Designing Programs: Well Mannered Object-Oriented Design in C++* [Goldsmith94]

- *C++FAQS:frequently asked questions* [Cline95]

- *Effective C++: 50 Specific Ways to Improve Your Programs and Designs* [Meyers92]

- *More Effective C++: 35 New Ways to Improve Your Programs and Designs* [Meyers96]

  For Smalltalk:

- A very good, easy-to-follow book that provides a minimal set of guidelines to facilitate the reading and writing of Smalltalk is: *Smalltalk with Style* [Skublics95].

Importance

Essential. You should decide on your Coding Guidelines before you start implementation. Those projects that don't do it up front end up doing it later when it is too late and they end up regretting it.

14.2 PHYSICAL PACKAGING PLAN

Description

A Physical Packaging Plan contains decisions about the physical structure of the product deliverables (for example, the executables). It also contains decisions about the physical structure of the data that are used in a build process to create those deliverables (for example Source Code files). Together with those decisions it also documents the requirements leading to the decisions and the trade-offs made.

Deliverables are:

Executables	(for example `.exe` files on OS/2)
Load libraries	(for example `.dll` files on OS/2)
Screen Layouts	(for example `.res` files on OS/2)
Messages	(for example `.msg` files on OS/2)
Runtime images	(for example, the `.vkg`, `.exe`, `.dll` and image files that comprise a VisualAge application on OS/2)

Data from which to build the deliverables are:

Source files	(for example `.cpp` and `.hpp` files for C++, CORBA IDL, `.class` for Java)
Link control files	(for example `.def` files on OS/2)

Screen sources	(for example `.rc` files on OS/2)
Message sources	(for example `.src` files on OS/2)
Visual builder files	(for example `.vbb`, `.cpv` and `.hpv` files on OS/2)
SOM files	(`IDL` and `bindings`)
Build files	(for example `makefiles`)
Development images	(for example, the `image` files of IBM Smalltalk and VisualAge on OS/2)

Typical decisions and considerations to be made and documented are:

• Which classes go into what dynamic link libraries?

Considerations are:

– Subsystem boundaries should be reflected.
– Too many small dynamic link libraries lead to longer load times.
– Unrelated code (for example from different subsystems) going into one library makes the build processes interdependent.
– The installation process to be used may impose limitations on size and structure.
– The Development Environment, the version control system and existing build processes may handle certain file structures and processes better than others.

• How are those runtime executables supplied, which are not part of the product but are required to run it?

Considerations are:

– Will the dynamic load libraries be binary compatible from release to release?
– Binding all together avoids the problem of synchronizing updates to the product and updates to the executables it bases on.
– Binding all together might lead to unreasonably large install images.

• How are the deliverables named?

Considerations are:

– The corrective service process may impose restrictions on structure and names.
– What naming standards (internal, external, de facto) are applicable?

Purpose

Many decisions about the physical packaging must be made. Providing a separate work product ensures that these decisions are not overlooked and then made ad hoc, at the last minute, by the person doing the build. Capturing the considerations and trade-offs made will help when revising the decisions from release to release in a changing environment. It almost never happens that the physical packaging remains unchanged over all releases of one product.

Some of the decisions and considerations will be worth reusing. This will not happen unless they are documented.

Participants

The team leader or a developer should be assigned responsibility for the physical packaging. This team member will create and maintain the Physical Packaging Plan. For this task a good understanding of the following areas is required:

- Target environment
- Installation process
- Maintenance process
- Technologies used (Database, Object Request Broker, VisualAge, et cetera)
- Development Environment
- Version control system

In other words, the owner of the Physical Packaging Plan needs a broad technical understanding of the project.

Timing

The Physical Packaging Plan should be done in parallel with the end of the design activities and the start of the implementation activities.

Technique

The hardest part usually is understanding the target environment, installation process, et cetera. The best starting point is to study projects that have already gained experience with some of the new areas. Discussing the considerations, making the decisions and writing them down will be easy after these areas are understood.

Strengths

A Physical Packaging Plan ensures that physical packaging information does not fall into the gap between design documentation and code. It also highlights the fact that somebody in the team has to understand it enough to be in control.

Weaknesses

A Physical Packaging Plan has considerable influence on the build process and can duplicate information that is already kept in build procedures. This duplication should be avoided.

Notation

The Physical Packaging Plan is best kept as plain text. To avoid duplication of information the Physical Packaging Plan can refer to automated build procedures (makefiles) or the automated build procedures can extract information from the Physical Packaging Plan.

Traceability

This work product has the following traceability:

Impacted by:
- Reuse Plan (p. 158)
- Project Dependencies (p. 173)
- Issues (p. 176)
- Target Environment (p. 272)
- Subsystems (p. 274)
- Development Environment (p. 330)

Impacts:
- Source Code (p. 334)
- User Support Materials (p. 341)

Note: The Packaging Plan also impacts:

- Build procedures (written or executable)

- Install procedures (written or executable)[13]

Advice and Guidance

- Be sure to document all the information relating to Physical Packaging Plan. If you think that your project is not complex enough to call for a separate document, append the Physical Packaging Plan to the design documentation.
- Record the reasons for decisions and rejected alternatives. This seems an additional burden initially but will likely pay off in the second release.
- Try to minimize build time dependencies between subsystems, especially when these are developed from different groups that are geographically apart.

Verification

- Check that all deliverables are addressed.

Example(s)

None.

References

Booch's Module Diagram [Booch94] is related to Physical Packaging Plan.

Importance

Optional but very useful for maintaining control over the physical structure of the product deliverables.

---

[13] Not described in this book.

14.3 DEVELOPMENT ENVIRONMENT

Description

Ideally, the Development Environment would span all phases of development without ever requiring us to enter the same data more than once, even if multiple tools are used. Such ideal systems were envisaged since the eighties at least. Their status today is that the most complete and seamless tools support is found for the implementation phase. A minimum Development Environment contains tools to edit, compile or interpret, run and debug Source Code.

The Development Environment must not only support the creation of new work products, but also their controlled change and customization: "Versioning" or "Version Control" capability allows you to keep different versions in parallel and access them independently. "Change Management" capability allows you to control and track the changes to work products. "Configuration Management" capability allows you to maintain different configurations in parallel and use them independently. The Development Environment components for controlled change and customization must be tightly coupled and are often integrated. For example, the "IBM Smalltalk and VisualAge Team Development Environment" has integrated version control and the "IBM SDE Workbench/6000" can be used together with CMVC, a version control system with integrated change management and problem tracking.

The Development Environment must be selected, installed, tailored, documented, taught to the users, and continuously supported.

Procedures to build the final product must be developed and continuously supported. Preferably these build procedures should run without manual intervention.

Purpose

We may be able somehow to capture analysis and design work products without a tool. It is obvious that writing executable code without tools (compilers, interpreters) would not work.

Typical projects will rarely use the default installation of development tools. What local adaptations have been made, what rules of usage apply for the project, what additional utilities exist must be documented. This is knowledge that all developers need to have and new members joining the team must be able to acquire.

Participants

Definition of the Development Environment is done by a member of the development team, usually in cooperation with the tools support group. Once this definition has been done, the responsibilities for installation, customization, teaching, and maintaining must be negotiated between the development team and the tools support group. No matter how the work split is made, one team member needs to be responsible for the project's usage of the Development Environment. This team member will at least define project specific tailoring and will act as an interface for tracking old and placing new requirements.

Timing

Installing, adapting, understanding, and using efficiently a new Development Environment may take considerable amount of time (months). The Development Environment must, therefore, be addressed as early as possible. The earliest point is when the target environment is known. Architectural decisions made during the design phase will usually place additional requirements on the Development Environment. In the same way the Development Environment can pose restrictions on the Architecture decisions.

Technique

The selection of the best Development Environment for a new project starts with studying the available systems that support the target environment, the selected implementation language, and maybe even related activities (design, documentation, problem tracking, et cetera). If help from a local tools support organization is required, the support team should be involved from the start.

Reading the overview and planning documentation of candidate systems brings an initial understanding. The fastest way to enhance that understanding is to interview current users of the candidate systems.

The decision on the Development Environment must also consider what hardware and tools are installed already. The expected productivity advantages must be balanced against the cost for new equipment and also the cost of training developers to use new tools.

Once the decision on the Development Environment has been reached, responsibilities must be negotiated between the development team and the tools support group. Next, the system must be installed, tailored and verified with small samples. The local adaptations must be documented. The team members must be introduced to the development environment, perhaps through a short course together with a short starter document ("Primer").

It is important that everybody understands responsibilities such as who will have a backup when data are lost, who should be called when a given tool does not seem to work correctly, who will define which version of what classes will be in what driver, et cetera.

Strengths

The productivity of the entire development team is dependent on the Development Environment and on the skill of the team to exploit it. Errors injected during the build process, for example, may cost several days to understand and repair and can sometimes lead to schedule overruns. Spending 100 percent of one person's time on the Development Environment may save 30 percent of the time of 10 developers.

Weaknesses

The responsible persons sometimes consider tools and Development Environments the goal and not the means to develop the product. If that happens, the effort invested will not always pay off.

Notation

The Development Environment is best described in plain text. We recommend to make this text available in printed form and in on-line viewable form.

Traceability

This work product has the following traceability:

Impacted by:
- Issues (p. 176)
- System Architecture (p. 257)
- Target Environment (p. 272)

Impacts:
- Physical Packaging Plan (p. 326)

Note: The Development Environment also impacts Build procedures[14]

Advice and Guidance

If a new Development Environment is needed, it will take considerable amount of time to install and understand. Almost every project will use at least some components of its Development Environment for the first time. Start as early as possible. Allow for enough lead time. The part of the Architecture leading to requirements on the Development Environment and the determination of the target platform should be done as early as possible.

Plan for the learning curve for all team members. If you do not want to have an explicit plan item "Learning new Development Environment" for every developer, then plan for an "Iteration 0" that achieves only minimal function but that represents all the major physical product components and uses all parts of the Development Environment.

---

[14] Not described in this book.

Verification

- Ask a developer experienced in the programming language to check the selected toolset and its configuration.

- An "Iteration 0," which we recommended for learning, is also a very good opportunity to uncover problems with the toolset, its configuration, and its documentation and on line help.

Example(s)

As an example of the kind of information to provide, we are showing the table of contents of a document describing the "Workstation Development Environment" (WDE) used in IBM's Boeblingen (Germany) Programming Lab for software targeted to workstations. WDE uses standard components together with the usual local modifications and glue code.

Build Process with WDEBuild

- What is the Build Process?

  - Objectives for Build Process
  - Concepts of Build Process
  - Providing one Build Process for all Projects
  - Prerequisites

- How does WDEBuild Implement the Build Process?

- How to use WDE Build Process

  - Developer's Tasks
    — Create or Update a Dependency File
  - Driver Build Tasks
  - "wdebuild"
    — Requirements
  - "wdemake"
  - Environment
  - Related Files
    — Structure of a .dpd file
      - Subcomponents
      - Overall Target of Component
      - Runtime Environment of Tools
      - Local Compile and Link Options
    — Linker Script File
    — Structure of a .rul file
  - Common Rules
  - Restrictions

- Internals of "wdebuild"

  - Required Products and Tools
    — Requirements for "make"
    — Requirements for the Generation of Dependencies

Figure 14-2. Example of a Development Environment.

References

For an example of an integrated Development Environment see [IBM94a].

Importance

Optional. While the work product itself is optional all projects will have a development environment of some kind, and it needs to be well thought out to ensure it meets the project needs.

14.4 SOURCE CODE

Description

Source Code is the actual implementation of the application design in a programming language. Depending on the selected programming language and environment, there may be several different types of code files for a given class. These files may contain lines of program code in the programming language of implementation, and one or more files containing a definition of the class attributes and methods. These class definitions will be processed by a compiler or precompiler.

Purpose

Source Code is the ultimate implementation of the designed solution. Once the code implementing the entire design is translated to a machine executable form, the resulting software should provide the solution to the initial Problem Statement. Of course, testing must be done to verify that the implementation indeed satisfies the system requirements.

Participants

Responsibility for implementing the code is distributed at the class level. The developer owning each class will write the code to implement it. After development, the librarian is often considered the "owner" of the source code (files).

Timing

If the project is using a breadth-first or waterfall approach, where each phase of the project is complete before beginning the next, the code will be created after the design has been completed. With a depth-first approach, code will be created after an initial design is completed for the class. See Section 17.1 for a discussion of depth-first development.

Technique

The functionality of the class is implemented in the coding language.

Source Code is usually created in one of three ways:

1. All of the Source Code is manually created using a text editor.
2. Part of the Source Code, for example the interface declarations and the function stubs, are generated by a design tool or from other source forms, for example the Interface Definition Language of some Object Request Broker such as IBM's System Object Model (SOM).

   The rest of the Source Code, usually the function bodies, is filled in by hand using a text editor.
3. All of the Source Code is generated by a tool from other descriptions, be they a higher level form of source, or complete specifications together with design and architecture descriptions. This fully automatic code generation is not a common approach today.

Strengths

Source Code is required to generate any executable program to meet the requirements.

Weaknesses

None.

Notation

The coding notation is dependent on the coding language selected. Whatever the language, the team should agree on and follow a set of Coding Guidelines (See Section 14.1).

Traceability

This work product has the following traceability:

Impacted by:
- Reuse Plan (p. 158)
- Issues (p. 176)
- APIs (p. 265)
- Design Class Description (p. 311)
- Coding Guidelines (p. 322)
- Physical Packaging Plan (p. 326)

Impacts:
- None.

Advice and Guidance

- Use a Source Code repository that supports versioning. This will provide a way to manage the constant changes to the code files. Differences between versions of a code file can be captured without maintaining multiple physical version files for the same code file.

- A versioning tool that also supports release information is most desirable. A release can be frozen when a code shipment is made. This allows the development team to respond to customer problems by testing on a known code base.

Verification

Verification of Source Code should not be completely left to Test Cases. As is true not only for object-oriented programming, code review and walk-through are very valuable to detect immediate problems, potential problems, and shortcomings in readability and maintainability. In addition to these benefits code reviews help to raise the level and awareness of newer team members.

In the following we give examples of points to check during verification of C++ code:

- If there are any pointer attributes in the class, check:

  - The rule of the "big three" (if any of a destructor, a copy constructor, or an assignment operator exists, then all three should exist)

  - Ownership: Which object creates the referent object and which object deletes it?

  - Are there exceptions that would bypass the necessary destruction?

- For each function signature, check:

  - What is returned: pointer/reference/value? Should it be const?

  - What is passed in: pointer/reference/value? Should it be const? whether the method is a const member? If not, should it be?

- Check that any explicit casts are really necessary.

- If there is state-dependent behavior, how is it documented?

- What are the methods' preconditions? Are they documented, checked, and enforced? What happens if they are violated?

- Are the postconditions documented?

- In the case of overloading, is the rule of "require no more—promise no less" respected?

- Could the object end in an illegal state if a method fails halfway?

- Is there code that could be executed concurrently? If so, what serialization or locking is there to protect it?

Example(s)

Following are examples of some C++ code extracted from a real project.

butwligh.hpp

```
/* $TITLE: Button with Light for OrlandoDemo */
#ifndef BUTWLIGH_HPP
  #define BUTWLIGH_HPP
/***********************************************************************
**   module name = butwligh.hpp                                        *
**   description = A button with a control light.  The light can be    *
**                 set and queried and the button can be pressed.      *
**   status =  SCCS: %W% %I% %D% %T%                                   *
**   module type = Include file in  C and C++ source code modules      *
**   processor = CSET++                                                *
**   restrictions = this module produces no executable code           *
**   comments   =  none                                               *
**   CHANGE-ACTIVITY = 01/20/96 - Gerald Kreissig                      *
**                     Creation                                        *
***********************************************************************/


/*------------------------ Includes ----------------------------*/
#include "ipdef.h"
#include "ifprcunt.hpp"
#include "ifevent.hpp"
#include "mobject.hpp"
#include "ifioadr.hpp"


//---------------------------------------------------------------------
//                     MOButtonWithLight
//---------------------------------------------------------------------
class MOButtonWithLight : public MOPressedAndReleasedButton
{
  public:
    MOButtonWithLight( const IFIOAddress& lineNr,
                       LineState initial,
                       IFControl* const controlObject = (IFControl*)NULL);
    MOButtonWithLight( const IFIOAddress& lineNr,
                       ObjectEventId objectEventId,
                       LineState initial,
                       IFControl* const controlObject = (IFControl*)NULL);

      // Return the status of the line controlling this button's light.
    LineState queryLight();

      // Set the status of the line controlling this button's light.
    void setLight( LineState value );

  protected:
    void buttonClicked( ); // called when the button was pressed and released

  private:
    MOLight associatedLight;
    IFEvent buttonEvent;
};
#endif
```

orlando.hpp

```
/* $TITLE: ORLANDO - OrlandoDemo, Interface */
#ifndef ORLANDO_HPP
  #define ORLANDO_HPP
/************************************************************************
** module name = orlando.hpp                                          *
** description = Run a simple demo with four buttons                  *
**               An object of this class can be used within the       *
**               framework.                                           *
** status =  SCCS: %W% %I% %D% %T%                                    *
** module type = Include file in  C and C++ source code modules       *
** processor = CSET++                                                 *
** restrictions = this module produces no executable code             *
** comments   -  none                                                 *
** author = Gerald Kreissig                                           *
** CHANGE-ACTIVITY = 01/20/96 - Gerald Kreissig                       *
**                   Creation                                         *
**                   01/21/96 - Gerald Kreissig                       *
**                   Orlando case for EIP88888 message*               *
**                   03/12/96 - Gerald Kreissig                       *
**                   Change enum off to OFF                           *
************************************************************************/

/*------------------- Includes -----------------------*/
#include "ipdef.h"
#include "ifprcunt.hpp"
#include "ifevent.hpp"
#include "mobject.hpp"
#include "ifioadr.hpp"

const ULONG NUMBER_OF_BUTTONS = 4;

class OrlandoDemo : public IFProcessingUnit
{
  public:
    OrlandoDemo();
     OrlandoDemo();

  protected:
     // Start the demo.
     void start();
     // Process all Framework events.
     void process( const IFEvent& event );

  private:
    MOButtonWithLight* buttonsffiNUMBER_OF_BUTTONS";
};
#endif
```

butwligh.cpp

```
/* $TITLE: Button with Light for OrlandoDemo */

// Standard File Prolog omitted here ...

//************************************************************************
```

```
// MOButtonWithLight::MOButtonWithLight - Constructor
//*********************************************************************
MOButtonWithLight::MOButtonWithLight( const IFIOAddress& lineNr,
                                      LineState initial,
                                      IFControl* const controlObject )
  : MOPressedAndReleasedButton( IFIOAddress(lineNr.getAddress(),0 ),
                                controlObject ),
    associatedLight( IFIOAddress(lineNr.getAddress(),1 ), initial ),
    buttonEvent( this, MOButton::CLICKED )
{ } /* end MOButtonWithLight::MOButtonWithLight( ... ) */


//*********************************************************************
// MOButtonWithLight::MOButtonWithLight - Constructor
//*********************************************************************
MOButtonWithLight::MOButtonWithLight( const IFIOAddress& lineNr,
                                      ObjectEventId objectEventId,
                                      LineState initial,
                                      IFControl* const controlObject )
  : MOPressedAndReleasedButton( IFIOAddress(lineNr.getAddress(),0 ),
                                objectEventId, controlObject ),
    associatedLight( IFIOAddress(lineNr.getAddress(),1 ), initial ),
    buttonEvent( this, MOButton::CLICKED )
{ } /* end MOButtonWithLight::MOButtonWithLight( ... ) */


//*********************************************************************
// MOButtonWithLight::queryLight - returns the state of the light
//*********************************************************************
LineState MOButtonWithLight::queryLight()
{
  return associatedLight.queryLine( );
} /* end MOButtonWithLight::queryLight( ... ) */


//*********************************************************************
// MOButtonWithLight::setLight - sets the state of the associated light
//*********************************************************************
void MOButtonWithLight::setLight( LineState value )
{
  associatedLight.setLine( value );
} /* end MOButtonWithLight::setLight( ... ) */


//*********************************************************************
// MOButtonWithLight::buttonclicked - toggles the light and sends the
//                                    event clicked
//*********************************************************************
void MOButtonWithLight::buttonClicked()
{
  associatedLight.setLine( (associatedLight.queryLine() == ON ? OFF : ON) );
  signalEvent( buttonEvent );
} /* end MOButtonWithLight::buttonClicked( ... ) */
```

orlando.cpp

```cpp
/* $TITLE: ORLANDO - OrlandoDemo, Implementation */

// Standard File Prolog omitted here ...

/*------------------------- Includes ----------------------------*/
#include "orlando.hpp"

const ApplicationId idApplication = 29;
const PSZ configFile = "ORLANDO.INI";

OrlandoDemo::OrlandoDemo()
{
  LineState initLine = ON;
  for ( ULONG i=0; i<NUMBER_OF_BUTTONS; i++ ) {
    buttons[i] = new MOButtonWithLight( (IFIOAddress)(i+1), i+1, initLine );
    initLine = (initLine == ON) ? OFF : ON;
  } /* endfor */
} /* end OrlandoDemo::OrlandoDemo */

OrlandoDemo:: OrlandoDemo()
{
  for ( ULONG i=0; i<NUMBER_OF_BUTTONS; i++ ) {
    delete buttons[i];
  } /* endfor */
} /* end OrlandoDemo:: OrlandoDemo */

void OrlandoDemo::start()
{
  for ( ULONG i=0; i<NUMBER_OF_BUTTONS; i++ ) {
    // send the initial value to the host
    trace(1, (IFString)(ULONG)((buttons[i]->queryLight() == ON ) ? (i+1) : -(i+1)) );
  } /* endfor */
} /* end OrlandoDemo::start(...) */

void OrlandoDemo::process( const IFEvent& event )
{
  switch ( event.getEventId() ) {

    case MOButton::CLICKED:
      { ULONG button = event.getObjectEventId();
        // send the id of the button with its value to the host
        trace(1, (IFString)(ULONG)((buttons[button-1]->queryLight() == ON )
                          ? button : -button) );
        if ( button == NUMBER_OF_BUTTONS )
          terminate();
      };
      break;

    default:
      break;
  } /* endswitch */
}
```

References

The number of good books covering the major object-oriented languages is enormous today and still increasing steadily.

- For Smalltalk, you can get started with [Goldberg83].

- [Stroustrup92] is a good introductory book for C++.

- [Flanagan96] is a good introductory book for Java.

Importance

Essential, as this is the implementation of the solution to the original problem statement.

14.5 USER SUPPORT MATERIALS

Description

User Support Materials generally fall into the classification of customer documentation. The various pieces of documentation must serve different purposes and most likely will be delivered in different forms (on different media), e.g., hardcopy, softcopy, on-screen help, messages, and tools (planner).

End user documentation supports different categories of customer tasks associated with your product:

Evaluation: describes the product's features, limitations, and resource requirements that will help the customer decide whether to buy the product.

Planning: describes choices that should be made before installing the product that would make it easier to use or administer.

Installation: describes how to install the product.

Administration: describes how to manage the product and its resources to meet the needs of the organization.

Operation: describes how to start and stop the product (e.g., server), check on its operation, record its status, and react to abnormal events.

Customization: describes how to enhance or extend the product.

Application Programming: describes how to design, code, compile, execute, debug and test programs that use the product.

Diagnosis: describes how to identify and report problems with the product.

End use: describes how to use the product for its intended purpose.

Sometimes, especially for small, simple products, you can combine some of the task categories into fewer books. For example, you might have a "product brochure" (evaluation), a "planning, installation, and customization guide," an "administration, operation, and diagnosis guide," and a "user's guide."

Purpose

User Support Documentation is usually stipulated in the contract for new products. It is needed by the customer to evaluate, plan, install, administer, operate, customize, program, diagnose, and use the product.

Although you might argue that a full set of books is not needed for every product, some form of User Support Materials is always needed—there is no reason why you would ever produce a product with no User Support Materials.

If there is no User Support Material, the product provider may be forced to perform all the aforementioned tasks. This may sound like a great commercial opportunity for services, but if that was the intent, then the product was really just a service that happened to use hardware and software.

Participants

User Support Material is usually developed by technical writers (information developers) with the assistance of development team leaders and developers. Customers may be involved with its planning and evaluation.

Timing

Planning for User Support Material should start early, during the requirements and project management phases. Although some overview documents can start being developed during the analysis phase, most other documents will be written during the user interface and design phase (e.g., operations documentation). The remaining documentation can be written during implementation and test phases (e.g., application programming, customization, diagnosis).

Technique

Start creating User Support Material as an outline using the task categories listed above and then hierarchically add more and more specific details to the outline. Populate the outline with general tasks first, then recursively break each task into its subtasks. Do not write the prose, but insert notes to the eventual writers to provide hints, essential topics, and points not to miss.

When the outline is complete, divide it into the books (or other formats) you plan to deliver. Assign one or more technical writers to each book to fill in the technical prose for each article.

Strengths

Good User Support Material is generally a sign of high quality products. It is often an explicitly required deliverable. The best products and features can only be used if the customer knows that they exist and knows how to use them. Good products depend on good User Support Material.

Weaknesses

Doing too much or the wrong kinds of User Support Material can not only be a waste of resources, but also a source of confusion and burden on the customer. Good User Support Material needs to be correct from the beginning and maintained as the product evolves—the more you have the more it costs to maintain.

Notation

The structure of the set of User Support Material has already been listed under "Description." Each category should be structured to move the user from general to specific topics. The media or delivery mechanism should be considered when analyzing who will use this material in what situation. For example, a vibrant but detailed product brochure could be used for marketing and customer evaluation. A planning tool (as opposed to a book), might better help a customer determine how to install and configure the product. A hypertext help tool with a CD-ROM might eliminate the need for a user manual.

User Support Material should start off as an outline using the task categories listed above and then hierarchically add more and more specific details to the outline. Eventually, the outline will be populated with many tasks organized by the general topics and leading progressively into very specific tasks. The "leaf" articles are constructed of technical prose.

Template: Each category or document will take on an organization particular to the type of document that it is:

- Guide: comprehensive, primer, layered, minimal, procedural, tutorial

- Reference: hardcopy, softcopy, hypertext

   In any case, each document should address the requirement it was intended to satisfy:

- Who will be using it?

- What will they be doing?

- What environment or situation will they be in?

Traceability

This work product has the following traceability:

Impacted by:
- Problem Statement (p. 93)
- Use Case Model (p. 96)
- Nonfunctional Requirements (p. 106)
- Issues (p. 176)
- Screen Flows (p. 237)
- Screen Layouts (p. 242)
- System Architecture (p. 257)
- APIs (p. 265)
- Target Environment (p. 272)
- Physical Packaging Plan (p. 326)

Impacts:
- None.

Advice and Guidance

- Start User Support Materials planning and development early in the product development cycle.

- Involve the technical writing staff (information developers) in the requirements phase of the project.

- Review the User Support Materials outline with the customer at key customer approval checkpoints.

Verification

User Support Materials should be reviewed by the technical writing staff (peer review) for editorial consistency. They should also be reviewed by the product development team for technical accuracy and by the customer, or surrogate, for usability and completeness. The latter review might be part of the acceptance test.

Example(s)

For an example just pick up the documentation that came with any of your favorite software products!

References

Some of the material for this section was inspired by *Information Development Guideline: Task-Oriented Information* [IBM Corp.91].

Importance

Essential. It is hard to imagine creating any software that has no User Support Material. Even trivial software needs a help file or option to explain what it does. Complex systems will need a great deal of User Support Material.

15.0 Test Work Products

Testing is an integral part of the project development cycle. It is a formal, planned, and documented activity that, on a project time scale, follows various development activities. In this section we are defining testing to mean the traditional testing of the executable project code.

But, we recognize that there are other important activities that are, in essence, a form of test. Two of the more important of these activities in our approach are the validation and verification of work products. They are discussed in Section 8.3 and there is also information presented on the verification of each work product in the work product description sections. Even though we are describing testing somewhat traditionally for purposes of this book, the testing of the executable code can be thought of as verification against the design work products, and validation against the analysis work products. So, this means the validation and verification approach holds across the entire development life cycle.

Testing is performed on each increment, and on final deliverables, and thus has a dual mission to:

- Detect eventual problems as early as possible, thus providing a stabilizing feedback.
- Verify the correctness of each element of the product by itself and in relation to the rest of the already completed elements. This is essential for delivery of products of the highest quality.

In a waterfall development process, testing is performed after the development activity, typically by members of a testing department. Separation of testing and development departments is well suited to the waterfall development process with its long phases, each of which concentrates on different aspects of the product (design, implementation, quality, et cetera).

The iterative and incremental development process is intrinsically different. It allows software to be developed in a very natural, evolutionary way, through iterations and increments. Increments represent the target software at different levels of completeness, with each increment adding new features, properties, and functions, to fulfill the requirements *incrementally*. The *iterative* nature of the process ensures that each increment preserves the consistency and integrity of work products, and provides a solution for the issues, errors, and problems identified in preceding iterations. This is achieved by making testing a part of every iteration, rather than a distinct phase, as happens in the waterfall development process. The iterative and incremental development process allows more freedom in scheduling of testing, allowing various kinds of testing to be performed much earlier, thus lowering the risk of discovering project-impacting problems too late. This in turn is also very cost-effective because the earlier the problems are identified, the cheaper it is to correct them.

Testing in an environment with a strong software development process produces very good results guaranteeing the software to any required quality level. The required quality level must be known and agreed on before the testing begins. Without knowing the required quality level it is impossible to know how much resource should be allocated for testing, or assessing the results of testing.

It also is important to understand that testing is not a substitute for a weak software development process. No amount of testing can make up for sloppy development, lack of organization, bad communication among team members, or mismanagement. Organizations truly concerned with quality consider testing an integral part of their development process and environment. For them testing serves as a way to discover the root causes of their problems so that it can be eliminated.

Organizations that do not take quality issues seriously, and view testing as a formality that, when schedule problems arise can be "skipped," run a risk of reaching their targets with unattractive and unusable products that disappoint customers. For commodity products this translates "only" into economic losses (direct and indirect), but for mission critical systems, it may lead to loss of human life, and may be subject to criminal prosecution in the court of law.

The Test work products section consists of the following work product:

- Test Cases

This work product "inherits" the common work product attributes described in Section 8.1, and has specialized attributes of its own which are described in the next section.

Test Cases are simply used to verify the correctness of the executable code.

It is worth mentioning that a Test Plan could easily be put into this chapter of the workbook. We have chosen to place it into the Project Management section because a Test Plan is a critical but often neglected item. Testing should be considered very early in the planning stages of the project to ensure that adequate time and resources are devoted to it.

15.1 TEST CASES

Description

Test Cases are units of testing used to verify some aspect of code. They might test function, performance, various constraints, et cetera.

Purpose

Test Cases are used to assert and verify the correctness of code to ensure its required quality level. As a potentially infinite number of Test Cases are required to test the code exhaustively, it is impossible to develop and execute them all. To achieve a fair confidence in results, it is necessary to execute a statistically sufficient number of Test Cases, relative to the complexity of the code, and to the required quality level.

Participants

Test Cases for code testing are developed, executed and maintained by testers in close cooperation with developers. Analysts, designers, and customers also provide input for Test Cases via Analysis and Design Scenarios and Acceptance Tests, respectively.

Timing

Depending on the development process, Test Cases are either developed throughout development, as in the iterative and incremental development process, or during the testing phase in the traditional "waterfall" development process.

Technique

Rules and recommendations for writing Test Cases are the same as for writing of code itself. To ease planning, reporting, tracking, and managing of testing, the Test Cases should be under the same version control and naming convention as code. This is even more important from the reuse point of view, when future users will likely want to reuse a set of Test Cases together with the code they want to test (to see if it can be reused), just as happens with benchmark Test Cases today.

One approach to building Test Cases is to exploit the fact that scenarios are used to define the requirements of each increment. Scenarios are statements of the desired system behaviors defined in terms of assumptions and outcomes. A Test Case, based on a scenario, should consist of the following:

- Establish the assumptions of a scenario (test set-up)

- Invoke the scenario

- Check the documented outcomes of the scenario

Should the test results show serious variations or feasibility problems, these should be either fixed immediately or addressed in the analysis and design phases of the next iteration.

Strengths

- Determines the quality of the code

- Repeatable, can be used (reused) as many times as necessary

- Scalable, can be used in small and large development efforts alike

Weaknesses

- Affected by code changes

- May require resources far greater than those of the initial project

Notation

Test Cases for testing of code can be built in a number of ways. They can be written as plain text instructions for manual test execution and verification. They can be written in the same programming language as the code and executed as necessary. They can also be written in a language specific to a tool that will automatically generate test cases. Test Cases also have set-up instructions, statements of what is being tested, lists of prerequisite actions, descriptions of expected behavior and results, and many times the test results themselves, if it is required to store the results. The format of Test Cases depends on the code being tested and on the Development Environment. In some organizations Test Case related information is written in files, while in others it resides within the Development Environment.

Traceability

This work product has the following traceability:

Impacted by:
- Test Plan (p. 164)
- Issues (p. 176)
- APIs (p. 265)

Impacts:
- Issues (p. 176)

Advice and Guidance

1. Maintain all Test Cases uniformly so that common techniques (and maybe tools) can be used to report on them, store them, track them, et cetera.

2. For each issue identified during analysis and design develop a set of Test Cases. This helps to ensure that the rejected alternatives are correctly resolved, and that the selected solution, the one being tested, is in fact the best solution.

3. The quality requirements for the Test Cases are greater than, or at least equal to, the quality requirements for the code being developed. The Test Cases must be carefully designed and carried out to provide a credible assessment of the code's quality level.

4. Separate the testing of line function from user interface testing. It is much easier to automate the testing of line function by invoking APIs. Once this is out of the way, any problems when testing the user interface are almost certain to be user interface problems rather than errors in the code that the user interface invokes.

Verification

- Does each Test Case set up the test correctly?

- Check for Test Case coverage.

Example(s)

Two examples are shown below, one for written instructions for manual execution and verification of the tests, and one for test cases programmed in C++.

The written instructions for manual testing are from a network management product. The part shown here focuses on the timer event handling. The instructions refer to the Design Object Interaction Diagram `TIMERPOP1.OID`, that was used during design. Part of `TIMERPOP1.OID`, is shown in Figure 15-1.

```
F)  TIMER POP  -  TIMERPOP1.OID - 3

    1)  No Domains reach timeout status
        Agent:  Sees timer & sets retry counts to 0 and quits
    2)  A Domain reaches timeout status
        After 5 timer pops, count goes to 0, creates a Timeout Event
        Agent sends:  Alert with HAVEDATA to host
    3)  Domain reaches threshold and declared Domain lost
        After exhausting all 3 retries, Domain Lost    See Figure 15-1
        Agent:  Deletes the Domain, resets BQM, no more timer pops
    4)  After retrys, host responds with something, Agent Resets
        timeout and retry counters to 0.
        Agent sends:  Resets Timeout & Retry counters, process request
    5)  Send HAVEDATA alert to multiple domains, one responds, one
        doesn't, Timeout & Retry are created for just one domain
        Host sends:

        ...
```

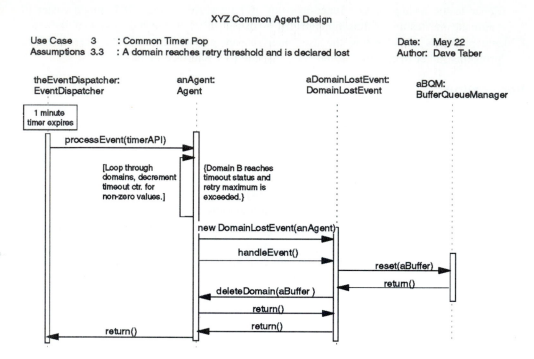

Figure 15-1. TIMERPOP1 Design Object Interaction Diagram.

The following example is from the test cases for collection classes (Set, KeySet, Sequence, Queue, ...). Those test cases use a combination of a few macros and several templates to test all different collections with as little unique code as possible. The code shown here deals with tests for the cursors in those collections. Prologs, include statements, and other similar items have been omitted here to keep the example suitably small.

The sample shown here verifies that the status of a cursor ("valid" or "invalid") is correctly set. Cursors are pointing to elements contained in a collection. They are used in combination with locate commands, which set the cursor to the element that was located, or in combination with iterations over the elements in the collection (for this reason another commonly used name is "Iterator" [Gamma95]). A cursor is called "valid" if it is correctly set to an element in the collection. It is "invalid," if it was not set yet, if it was invalidated explicitly, or if it was last used in an operation (locate, iteration, et cetera) that failed.

Figure 15-2 shows how the test classes are organized into a class hierarchy that mirrors the class hierarchy of the collections to be tested. For each collection there exists a specific tester derived from the class template ICollectionTester<Collection, Element, Cursor> if the collection is not ordered, and from IOrderedCollectionTester<Collection, Element, Cursor> if the collection is ordered.

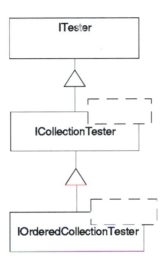

Figure 15-2. *Class Hierarchy for Test Classes.*

ncsvalid.tst: In the file ncsvalid.tst, which contains all test cases for new cursors and their validity:

```
template < class Collection, class Cursor,class Element>
int TEST_CLASS < Collection, Cursor, Element > :: newCursorValidInvalidate ()
{
  // Setup of some local variables is not shown here ...

  IBoolean r;
  ICursor *s = c.newCursor (); // not set yet: so cursor *s is invalid

  reset ();
                              // Check that an OutOfMemory exception is
                              // thrown if there is not enough memory.
  startCheck ("ICursor::invalidate, isValid: test 1");
  memoryCounter.lock ();      // Overloaded new:  will make next new fail.
  CHECK_EXC (IOutOfMemory, ICursor *s1 = c.newCursor ();)
  memoryCounter.unlock ();    // Back to normal new behavior.

  startCheck ("ICursor::invalidate, isValid: test 2");
  setState (r, True);
```

```
        CHECK_OK (r = s->isValid ();)  // Cursor *s has still not been set yet.
        checkState (r, False);

        startCheck ("ICursor::invalidate, isValid: test 3");
        setCursorInvalid (*s);          // Cursor *s is set to invalid now.
        setState (r, True);
        CHECK_OK (r = s->isValid ();)
        checkState (r, False);

        // More tests for behavior of new cursors are not shown here ...
}
```

itst.h: In the file itst.h there are - among others - following macros defined:

```
                        // Execute an operation 'op' and catch any
                        // exception that might result.
                        // Expected result: No exception.
    #define CHECK_OK(op) \
      try { op } \
      catch (...) { cout << ">> error in " << testCaseName \
                        << " : unexpected exception" << endl; \
      }


                        // Execute an operation 'op' and catch any
                        // exception that might result.
                        // Expected result: An exception of type 'exc'.
    #define CHECK_EXC(exc, op) \
      try { op \
            cout << ">> error in " << testCaseName; \
            cout << " : exception expected, but not thrown" << endl; } \
      catch (exc) { } \
      catch (...) { cout << ">> error in " << testCaseName \
                        << " : unexpected exception" << endl; }
```

Later in file itst.h the class ITester is declared:

```
    class ITester {

    public:
      ITester ();
      void reset ();
      void startCheck (char *name);
      void checkSummary (char *name);
      void setState (IBoolean &b, IBoolean v);
      void setState (INumber &n, INumber v);
      void checkState (IBoolean b, IBoolean v);
      void checkState (INumber n, INumber v);
      void checkState (void* p, void* v);

    protected:
      int checkCount;

    private:
```

```
        char *testCaseName;
};
```

itst.cpp: File `itst.cpp` contains the implementation of the member functions of class `ITester`:

```
void ITester::
reset ()
{ checkCount = 0;
  testCaseName = "unknown check";
}
void ITester::
checkState (IBoolean b, IBoolean v)
{ if (b != v) {
     cout << ">> error in " << testCaseName
          << ": expected boolean being = " << v << endl;
  }
}
// The rest of the ITester member functions is not shown here ...
```

icolltst.h: In file `icolltst.h` after prolog, include guards and dependencies, we find the declaration of the class template `ICollectionTester`, that is inheriting from `ITester` and is parameterized with three arguments, the collection type, the cursor type and the element type:

```
template < class Collection, class Cursor, class Element >
class ICollectionTester : public ITester
{
public:
  void setEmpty (Collection &c);
  void setCursorInvalid (ICursor &cursor);

  // many other public member functions are not shown here ...

  void setCollectionState (Collection &c, int i1, int j1);
  void checkElementInvalid (Element const &e);

  static long compareFunction (Element const&, Element const&);
};
```

icolltst.c: In file `icolltst.c` we find the definitions of the template member functions:

```
template < class Collection, class Cursor, class Element >
void ICollectionTester < Collection, Cursor, Element >::
setEmpty (Collection &c)
{ c.removeAll ();
}

template < class Collection, class Cursor, class Element >
void ICollectionTester < Collection, Cursor, Element >::
setCollectionState (Collection &c, int i1, int j1)
{ c.removeAll ();
  c.add (testElement (i1, j1));
}
```

```
template < class Collection, class Cursor, class Element >
void ICollectionTester < Collection, Cursor, Element >::
setCursorInvalid (ICursor &cursor)
{ cursor.invalidate ();
}

// The rest of the many template member functions are not shown here ...
```

References

- See [Siegel96] for detailed information on object-oriented software testing.

- See [Binder94] for a status report on issues and research on object-oriented testing.

- See [Pressman92] for a general discussion of software testing strategies.

Importance

Essential for verifying the correctness of the implementation.

16.0 Appendix Work Products

There are some work products that don't fit cleanly into the project phases that are defined in this book and are the basis for our recommended organization of the project workbook. Yet, it is important to maintain them, so we suggest that they be kept in an appendix of the workbook.

The Appendix of the project workbook consists of the following work products:

- Glossary

- Historical Work Products

These work products all "inherit" the common work product attributes described in Section 8.1, and have specialized attributes of their own.

The Glossary work product promotes common understanding across the project development team by defining all terms that are used within the project.

The Historical Work Products work product provides a repository of previous versions of work products. This is useful in cases where the resolution of issues or problems requires an understanding of how the work product evolved and why it evolved in a particular direction.

These work products are described in more detail in the following sections.

16.1 GLOSSARY

Description

A project Glossary defines all the terms used during the project. For each term it provides a short definition entry. Normally only class and actor names are included in the Glossary, although in principle the Glossary could be used to describe key associations, attributes, operations, and even jargon from the problem domain. A Glossary is conceptually separate from class descriptions, but information may be shared between them and they may be implemented by a common tool.

A Glossary is used to record design and analysis definitions.

Purpose

The purpose of a Glossary is to achieve common understanding. It is very easy for analysis discussions in particular to be either vague or ambiguous. This is often only discovered after much frustration and misunderstanding. For example, some team members might be thinking of a *User* as a customer while others might be thinking in terms of a clerk, and still others in terms of a GUI. Can a *User* be a company? By defining terms as they are used, and agreeing to the definitions, misunderstandings are quickly surfaced and resolved.

A separate justification, the more traditional one for a Glossary, is to enable it to be used to remind people of meanings, or to assist newcomers to understand project documentation.

Participants

One of the team members should be given responsibility for maintaining the Glossary. This should, initially at least, be one of the analysts.

Timing

The Glossary should exist and be maintained throughout the project.

Technique

All classes, even those that are still only "candidate" classes, should have a Glossary entry. As soon as a class is proposed, a Glossary entry for it should be agreed upon.

A draft object model may be created using the Transcribe and Converge technique (see Section 18.3). This technique helps to achieve consensus on definitions by transcribing conflicting definitions into object models, converging the object models, and reflecting the agreed class relationships in a modified definition. Transcribe and Converge has the effect, therefore, not only of producing a draft object model but also definitions for the key classes.

Strengths

A Glossary is a vital tool to limit misunderstandings. It is a highly-accessible, reader-oriented, view of project work products. It provides a fast path to understanding for workbook readers who are new or external to the project.

Weaknesses

Defining all terms as they are used slows progress initially. Maintenance has costs proportional to the detail and scope of Glossary entries. Because of this cost, Glossary maintenance is often neglected. Unfortunately, it is detail and scope that enhance the usefulness of a Glossary as a set of highly readable work product views.

Inconsistent definitions reduce usefulness and confidence. Obsolete entries are distracting.

Notation

Any simple definition format can be used.

Traceability

This work product has the following traceability:

Impacted by:
- Problem Statement (p. 93)
- Issues (p. 176)
- Analysis Object Model (p. 192)
- Analysis Scenarios (p. 203)
- Analysis State Models (p. 219)
- Design Object Model (p. 281)
- Design Scenarios (p. 293)
- Design State Models (p. 306)

Impacts:
- None.

Advice and Guidance

- Agreeing on a definition is sometimes surprisingly difficult. The transcribe and converge technique (see Section 18.3) is frequently very useful to help achieve consensus.

- If failure to agree on a definition has halted modeling progress, or slowed it unacceptably, use whatever definition is possible, record the matter as an Issue to resolve, appoint someone responsible for resolving the Issue, and continue. This obviously requires good facilitation and considerable tact.

- The process of formulating and agreeing on a definition often changes the way that people think about the term. As a result the name of the term might have to be changed to reflect the new understanding.

- Review the Glossary whenever the object model changes significantly.

- Modeling style varies. You might want to keep Glossary entries as short as possible to solely identify and distinguish concepts, or you might use the Glossary to record very full definitions. If the short and quick strategy is used, be prepared to use a technique such as Transcribe and Converge if confusion or conflict arises, and to record the converged definition in the Glossary.

- Use the Glossary. Refer to it when there is doubt about the meaning of a term. If the definition looks wrong or out of date, update it. Alternatively, it may be the object model or an OID that is wrong. In this way the Glossary can serve as a validation tool.

- A single projectwide Glossary is usually sufficient. If more convenient, however, separate analysis and design glossaries can be maintained.

- Avoid defining a class solely in terms of its properties, for example, *an account has a name, number, and balance*. Instead, try to capture the purpose of a class, for example, *an account is an agreement that enables a customer to deposit funds in a bank and, within certain limits, to deposit funds.* By all means refer to the attributes of a class, the ways that the class is related to other classes, or object states if this is helpful, but these should augment and not replace a statement about the purpose of the class.

- Use whatever means is appropriate to record the Glossary. A flip chart works well in the initial stages of analysis. Analysis/design tools can usually be used conveniently to store the object model, the class descriptions, and the Glossary in a nonredundant form.

- Review relevant Glossary definitions with domain experts, customers, and potential end users.

- If work products change in such a way that some Glossary entries are now irrelevant, these entries should be placed in the appendix historical Glossary (one of the Historical Work Products).

Verification

- Are all the Glossary entries current?

- Check that all Glossary entries define an abstraction and not a collection of operations or attributes.

- Check completeness of Glossary.

Example(s)

The following is a partial glossary for a banking system:

Account	An agreement between a bank and a customer that enables the customer to deposit funds in the bank and, within certain limits, to withdraw funds.
Branch	Physical premises used by a bank under the direction of a manager to provide services to the public during published opening times.
Clerk	A bank employee authorized to perform certain transactions relating to accounts.
Customer	A person or other legal entity wishing to use the services of the bank.
Manager	A bank employee capable of authorizing exceptional loans up to a limit related to the status of the manager.

Figure 16-1. Example of a Glossary.

References

See the OMT data dictionary format used in [Rumbaugh91a] pages 156-157.

Importance

Essential for ensuring a common language understanding across a project team.

16.2 HISTORICAL WORK PRODUCTS

Description

This is the repository for all Historical Work Products. All versions of all work products should be retained for future reference.

Purpose

It is frequently a requirement to go back and see how things have evolved over time—this may be in response to an open Issue or a "bug." Therefore, it is important to save all work products and to ensure that they are dated.

Participants

The entire team should be engaged in this activity. The project manager should ensure that it is done.

Timing

Throughout the duration of the project.

Technique

This is basically a collection exercise. Ensure that old copies of work products are preserved in a place from which they can be retrieved.

Strengths

The preservation of Historical Work Products provides an audit capability.

Weaknesses

This activity requires time to perform and therefore may be perceived as nonproductive overhead by members of the team.

Notation

Preserve all of the work in its original form.

Traceability

This work product has the following traceability:

Impacted by:
- Issues (p. 176)
- Rejected Design Alternatives (p. 316)

Impacts:
- None.

Advice and Guidance

- In the absence of CASE tools, it is adequate to keep Historical Work Products in a file folder in a filing cabinet. The key is that they can be found should they be required.

- The team should be aware of how to retrieve historical copies of work products.

- It is possible to be extremely formal concerning historical work. Where warranted a team may choose to document the following concerning all changes:

  - Activity causing change
  - Responsible team member
  - Results
  - Rejected alternatives

  Not all projects need to go to this level of detail. The degree of anticipated change would be a key determiner here. For example, a project with an anticipated short life span would not need to preserve artifacts to the same degree of detail as would a key corporate application expected to run for years and go through many changes.

- Another means of preserving history is to keep a copy of old Project Workbooks.

Verification

Not applicable.

Example(s)

Please refer to the case study for an example (page 590).

References

None.

Importance

Optional. Maintaining Historical Work Products allows the development team to be able to revisit the evolution of the project so, while optional, you should consider whether it might be useful to your project to do this.

Part 4. *Work Product Construction Techniques*

This section describes some of the techniques that we have found to be useful in support of the approach to object-oriented software development described in this text.

This is by no means a complete set of possible techniques but is rather a collection of those techniques that either have been frequently used by us or that our experiences show have the most general applicability for persons using an object-oriented approach to software development.

Previously in this text, when discussing individual work products, we provided some advice and guidance on how to construct those work products. This section describes some alternative approaches to work product construction that we sometimes use during project engagements. We view this as a tool kit of additional techniques that a project using our approach to object-oriented development has at its disposal.

The techniques are classified into groups:

1. Project Management (Section 17.0)

2. Development (Section 18.0)

3. Reuse (Section 19.0)

The techniques sometimes span multiple work products and phases (for example, Section 17.1, A Depth-First Approach to Software Development) or may be used to help with the initial development of work products discussed earlier in this text (such as Section 18.2, Getting Started with Semantic Networks or Section 18.3, Building a Draft Object Model Using Transcribe and Converge). If you find that these additional techniques confuse the issue for you then using the advice provided earlier in the text may be a better option for you. They are presented here to give you more options when undertaking a project and also to illustrate the point that while our approach is explicit on the definition of work products, it is very flexible about which techniques are used to construct those work products.

17.0 Project Management Techniques

This section presents some Project Management techniques that the authors have found useful in their mentoring practice. These are considered to be project management techniques since they effect things like the Intended Development Process, the Quality Plan, and the Risk Management Plan.

The Project Management Techniques presented in this chapter are:

- A Depth-First Approach to Software Development

- Iterative and Incremental Development

- Selecting Object-Oriented Modeling Tools

- Prototyping as a Risk Management Technique

The Depth-First Approach is a scenario-driven special case of an iterative and incremental approach to software development. It consists of identifying a small slice of the project and taking it through implementation with frequent iterations between analysis and design and between design and implementation.

The Iterative and Incremental Development section provides more discussion on the iterative and incremental software process that we recommend be used with the approach to object-oriented software development advocated in this book.

Advice and guidance on how to approach the choice of a CASE tool for object-oriented development is presented in Section 17.3.

Finally, the section on Prototyping discusses how the use of prototypes as learning vehicles, to answer specific technical questions, or to solicit customer input can help to reduce risk in the project.

17.1 A DEPTH-FIRST APPROACH TO SOFTWARE DEVELOPMENT

Description

A depth-first approach is a software process model in which developers replace the initial development increment with a series of shorter minicycles. The approach focuses on the steps within the first normal increment in a product development life cycle.

A depth-first approach is scenario-driven and a special case of an iterative and incremental process. The series of initial depth-first minicycles are controlled in such a way that visible results and tangible experiences can be achieved in a very short time period.

Purpose

Even if a project as a whole is incremental and iterative, its constituent increments are usually waterfall internally. That is, every step in planning, requirements, analysis, design, implementation and testing must be followed one after another. This increment can last as long as five to six months. For the purposes of this discussion, this is referred to as a *breadth-first* approach. This constitutes a risk for many projects, particularly if they are deploying an object-oriented approach for the first time. The breadth-first approach works fine when the system requirements are well defined and developers have a good understanding of the problem domain, a good understanding of concepts such as object-oriented analysis and design, and a good feel for the overall object-oriented development process.

Unfortunately, many projects don't have those advantages. It is unusual for system requirements to be fully understood at the beginning of analysis. Many architecture and design teams are not staffed with members who have sufficient expertise in both the domain and object technology.

The result is that many problems can occur during the project. Common problems are the struggle to determine the boundary between analysis and design leading to the over-analysis of the problem (analysis paralysis). Another example is the overdesign of the system without knowing whether it is practical to implement the design, or necessary to descend into such a level of detail in design (design paralysis). Thus, the breadth-first approach to analysis and design is often ineffective in dealing with systems with vague requirements, less well understood domains, weak object technology knowledge, and complex environments.

Another common problem is the management of increments. Dividing projects into functional increments is important to the object-oriented approach described in this text and is a concept that is not an integral part of most business as usual approaches to software development.

An alternative to the traditional breadth-first process is: a *depth-first* approach to object-oriented development. The depth-first approach aims to produce quick results with a small slice of analysis and design core work products, totally based on Use Cases and their Scenarios. It is accomplished by working on a number of key Use Cases and their Scenarios with short analysis, design, and implementation cycle times, and with frequent iterating between analysis and design, or between design and implementation. The initial resulting work products may be incomplete or imperfect, but the goal is to develop experience through an early exposure to the entire life cycle.

Some of the benefits of using a depth-first approach are:

- Ability to make quick progress early in the development effort.
- Confidence gained by developers in understanding both what needs to be done (analysis) and how to accomplish it (design and implementation) in a short period of time. Also, developers tend to gain confidence in the viability of their project and their ability to employ object technology. This can lead to their ability to do subsequent increments more quickly.

- Analysis paralysis is avoided, and the analysis and design boundary can be better defined by the team once it has a better understanding of both analysis and design.

Participants

The whole project development team should participate in this process. The manager and the team leader would typically be the ones deciding to use this approach.

Timing

This is a process for performing the first major development increment.

Technique

The depth-first approach tries to take advantage of the good domain knowledge that most development teams have by taking *a small slice* of analysis work products from analysis to high-level design to implementation very early in the development life cycle of the project.

We assume a project usually goes through about three major increments before the final shipment, following an iterative and incremental model. Each major increment consists of planning, analysis, design, implementation, and testing. The depth-first approach is applied to the first major increment.

Next, we will discuss the major activities happening within each phase in the depth-first process.

Phase One: Initial Modeling: The initial modeling starts with identifying a core set of Use Cases and their key Scenarios. These Use Cases and Scenarios must be significant to the system users. Along with Use Cases and Scenarios, a set of key classes in the problem domain are identified and described in both an Analysis Object Model and Analysis Object Interaction Diagrams (OIDs). Key classes are those that involve the basic concepts of the problem domain and are often directly derived from the key Scenarios. These Scenarios serve as the drivers for the development cycles. The subclasses, derived from these key classes, can be included in the initial modeling, but are not counted as any of these key classes. For example, in a bank application, class *Account* is considered a key class, while its subclasses *SavingAccount*, *CheckingAccount*, and *ChristmasAccount* may be included but are not considered key classes.

The analysis phase work products are used here. This phase is shown as the first phase in Figure 17-1. The following are the major tasks within this phase.

Major Activities:

- *Strategy*:   Identify a set of key Use Cases, and select five to nine Scenarios from them. These scenarios should be selected carefully, so that they can help bring out major analysis classes.
- *Use Case Modeling*:   The depth-first approach starts with a general analysis brainstorming session on Use Cases and their Scenarios.

- *Dynamic Modeling with Analysis OIDs*: Analysis Object Interaction Diagrams (OIDs) are produced for five to seven Scenarios based on the requirements Use Cases to demonstrate the interactions among real-world objects. The selection of key Scenarios is based on whether their Use Cases are representative of the system requirements.

- *Object Modeling*: When conducting the above dynamic modeling, analysis classes, their attributes, and their relationships are discovered. These identified classes, attributes, and relationships form the initial object model at the analysis level. Class descriptions at the analysis level are produced at the same time.

  Many short increments between object modeling and dynamic modeling take place in this phase.

- *Analysis Reviews*: Reviews must be conducted so that experiences can be shared and errors can be found and corrected on a timely basis.

- *Project Management*: This initial modeling phase should take about *five percent* of the time planned for the first development increment. The models developed in this phase will be revisited many times later in the process. Avoid getting hung up on a few issues at this stage, since they can be resolved later when a better understanding of the problem exists.

Most models at this stage are likely to be incomplete and inaccurate with both analysis and design classes present, due to a limited understanding of the system at this early stage. The key here is not to produce complete analysis work products, but to get started and to think about the whole system from top to bottom with a small slice of classes and Scenarios.

We have observed that many developers are not very comfortable with modeling at this level, since their mind-set is usually on how a system works not on how real-world objects interact. This phase is designed in such a way that developers can get exposure to both analysis and design for their problem, so that they can understand why the analysis is necessary, and the positive impact it can have on design.

Phase Two: *Object-Oriented Design Modeling*: Having built an understanding of a slice of classes and their object interactions, the next step is to move into design to develop precise definitions of how objects in the system interact with each other. The second phase in Figure 17-1 represents this. Tasks at the design level are as follows.

Major Activities:

- *Strategy*: With the slice analyzed, further identify the most challenging part of the system to design and implement. This part could impact the whole project.

- *Architecture Designing*: Use the analysis models as the basis for the system structure while considering architecture, frameworks, design patterns, processes, algorithms, and system constraints. The structure developed here is only a partial solution while the complete one will be fully explored in phase four.   It is important to avoid "architecture-paralysis" or overdesigning the architecture.

- *Object Modeling*: Derive an object model at the design level by representing the physical links between objects more explicitly with directed associations. Discuss the possible interactions among objects.

- *Dynamic Modeling*: Use the Scenarios and their OIDs at the analysis level to develop OIDs at the design level. Usually, more design classes will be derived, and many design issues will surface during this activity.

- *Method and Class Description*: In dynamic modeling, some method specifications can be derived through OIDs. Document them under class descriptions. New attributes and new links should also be put into the class descriptions during this phase.

- *Model Validation and Mini-increment*:   Modify the object model at the design level. When one or more design-level OIDs are completed, it is a good time to go back to the object model to validate whether the object and dynamic models are consistent. This mini-increment can be repeated until the object model and the dynamic model are consistent.

- *Iterating back to Analysis*: Work products can now be checked to determine whether there is a good separation between analysis and design. In particular, the analysis work products should not embody any design decisions.

- *Design Reviews*: The design must be reviewed to check whether it is adequate for the first implementation.

- *Project Management*:   The time spent in the modeling phase should be about *seven to ten percent* of the time planned for the first development increment.

Phase Three: Implementation or "Quick Coding": With the design models developed in phase two, it is time to move into an implementation phase with the classes of the system objects that have been designed so far. We sometimes call this phase "Quick Coding" to show that the emphasis is on a quick introduction to the issues of implementation in an object-oriented environment.

Major Activities:

- *Developing Code*:   The code to be developed establishes a starting point for the whole system. The final product is its extension, perhaps after the initial design and code has been reworked in the light of experience. It is also the time to get familiar with the implementation environment, the User Interface (UI), and some system application programming interfaces (APIs) that will be used. In order for the depth-first coding time to be short, some object behaviors can be simulated or omitted, instead of providing a full implementation.

- *Integration and Testing*: The integration is to glue all the components together to show that the developed system can fulfill part of the systems' required features. Testing is performed against the Scenarios defined for those pieces of the system that have been implemented.

- *Resolving Risks*: This Quick Coding cycle is also a risk management technique. The implementation at this stage can be focused on those parts that might potentially be show-stoppers or those about which there is uncertainty as to how to build them.

- *Demonstrating the System and Getting Early Feedback*: Early feedback can be obtained by checking whether the environment and libraries can be well utilized, and whether the code meets users' expectations.

- *Code Reviews*: Experiences can be shared quickly by conducting code reviews, especially for the object technology novices.

- *Project Management*: The time spent on this phase should be about *ten to fifteen percent* of the time planned for the first development increment.

Phase Four: Increments with Object-Oriented Analysis and Design: After executable code is built for a core set of Scenarios, it is time to consider the whole requirements for the full increment. The following work should be performed during this phase.

Major Activities:

- *Architecture Designing and Adapting*: It is time to complete the architecture design for the whole system. First, define the architecture rules for the whole system. Then, make decisions on the structure for the system, based on the underlying architecture, frameworks, design patterns, and system constraints. Define the architecture rules, to provide a structure for both static and dynamic modeling.

- *Introducing More Requirements*: Starting from analysis, investigate more possible Use Cases and Scenarios. Build OIDs for these Scenarios at the design level when they are fully understood.

- *Iterating*: Having quickly moved from analysis to design and Quick Coding, the development team should have a much better feel for their system. This is the time to revisit analysis and design work products to check that analysis and design information is well separated. Next, add the next wave of new classes and Scenarios, and continue dynamic modeling for both analysis and design. Every OID needs to be refined several times during development.

- *Work Products*: At the end of this phase, class interfaces should be well defined. In C++, they can be defined in H files; and in Smalltalk, they can be defined at the level of class and method names with comments. Implementation details should be kept out of any work products introduced in this phase.

- *Design Reviews*: A relatively complete review should be conducted with clients, analysts, designers and developers to get consensus on the first increment.

- *Project Management*:   This phase should lay out the planning for implementation, and should take about *ten to fifteen percent* of the overall time planned for the first development increment.

Phase Five: Low-Level Design: Low-level design is a distinct phase in this process, distinguished from the previous design phase by a focus on utility domains, environments, and language implementation issues. This activity is driven both by the design needs of phase four, and the initial coding experience obtained in phase three. Code interfaces are defined for classes across all the major domains, especially those in the low level utility domain. Phase Four and Five can be merged together, since most likely there is no clear boundary between the two.

Major Activities:

- *Conducting Low-Level Design*: Having built a comprehensive high-level design, it is time to let every developer complete their major low-level design for the classes they own. During this phase, any low-level implementation issues discussed before are fully explored.

- *Work Products*: Work products are the same as those in Phase Four, except the defined classes are in lower level domains.

- *Project Management*: This phase should take less than *five percent* of the overall time planned for the first development increment.

Phase Six: Coding and Integration for the First Increment: After the low-level design phase, it is the time to expand the code produced earlier in Phase Three to the real system. The new system will incorporate the new Scenarios and other design decisions made in Phases Four and Five.

Major Activities:

- *Coding and Code Review*: All the developers should participate in this coding phase by doing either coding or code reviewing. Coding implements the design work products and extends the previously-implemented code into the real product. The class descriptions and design OIDs are the major vehicles for developers to communicate with each other.

    Code review mainly serves four purposes here. One is to check whether the program follows the design. The second is to check whether the design is adequate to guide the implementation. The third is to share coding experiences among developers. The fourth is to help increase code reusability, by sharing common code. Some of the above purposes, especially the second and fourth, can also be achieved in design reviews.

- *Iterating*:   Many iterations between design and implementation should happen with issues raised listing alternative designs. Issue resolution should happen and is simply the selection of one of these alternatives.

- *Unit Testing*:   Before this phase is complete, code unit testing should also be completed. It is wise to associate testing methods with each class. The unit testing is presumably done before code review, and certainly before Function Verification Testing.

- *Fine-Tuning*:   Time should be allocated to fine tune the working system. The purpose is to improve the system performance through reorganization of classes and reassignment of responsibilities.   Precautions must be taken so that the basic system architecture based on the analysis models is not broken. Fine-tuning can happen during the unit testing.

- *Function Verification Testing (FVT)*: Time should be allocated in this stage to perform a FVT and overall integration.   The code can be released for the alpha user test in order to get early feedback from users.

- *Project Management*:   This phase should take around *fifty to sixty percent* of the overall time planned for the increment.   This breaks down to *thirty to forty percent* for coding and unit testing, and *twenty percent* for integration and FVT.

In this discussion, we have not described system testing in the depth-first approach. When system testing is added into the approach, it should be in *Phase Seven*.   The time allocated for each phase should be changed appropriately.

   This "miniprocess" can be graphically represented as in Figure 17-1.

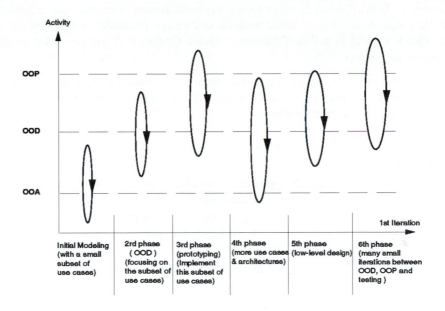

Figure 17-1. A Process for Depth-First Development.

Strengths

One strength of this approach is that it helps developers to more quickly get into the heart of a project in order to identify the risks and potential challenges of the project. This works especially well for those teams using an object-oriented software development approach for the first time as it gives them an earlier introduction to the whole process.

Weaknesses

This approach is designed for use by small teams. For a project larger than 25 person-years, it is advised that the large team be decomposed into smaller ones, and the depth-first approach be applied within each team. A depth-first approach to development is particularly useful during a project's first increment. As the team's understanding of object technology increases, more breadth can be added to the increments as appropriate.

Advice and Guidance

- Getting to Quick Coding in order to test the basic assumptions and base architecture is the key item here. Try to avoid analysis and design paralysis so that you can get to the Quick Coding in a timely fashion. Quick Coding will tell you a lot about your analysis and design.

- The second round of design and coding from Phase Four to Phase Six is where you should focus on making the system work fully and correctly, with regard to the requirements for the first increment.

Example(s)

We often utilize the depth-first approach to resolve high risks in a project. One such project was to utilize the Distributed Computing Environment (DCE) to support System Network Architecture (SNA) stacks. How to utilize an unstable beta DCE as the environment to prove the design concept was a challenge. The team spent three months and completed a working version of the system with two Scenarios. Then in four more months, the whole system was completed with 20 Scenarios successfully implemented.

References

George Yuan's article, [Yuan95], is the source for this approach.

17.2 ITERATIVE AND INCREMENTAL DEVELOPMENT

Description

The iterative and incremental development model is a software process that combines two development models: iterative and incremental. The model is a general one. It can be adapted to fit into different project development processes. For example, the scenario-driven process described in Section 18.7 and the depth-first approach described in Section 17.1 are examples of the iterative and incremental development model applied to the object-oriented paradigm. The iterative model assumes

- Initial requirements and design will change over the development cycle
- Partial implementation can be done from partially-known requirements
- Software can be developed in a repetitive way by building product iterations
- Changes are expected and encouraged at specific points in the process
- Partially-completed design and code are transformed into iterations of working code instead of being thrown away
- Iterations are used to help define remaining requirements
- Each iteration forms the base for the next iteration.

The overall iterative development cycle includes three major phases:

Pre-Iterative—Gather Requirements, Plan Project, Start Analysis

Iterative

- Plan increment of development for a set of requirements
- Execute that plan through analysis, design, and implementation phases
- Assess quality via unit and integration tests and through defect analysis

Post-iterative—System test, package, and ship

The incremental development model is defined in the IEEE Standard Glossary of Software Engineering Terminology as:

A software development technique where requirements, definition, design, implementation, and testing occur in an overlapping, iterative (rather than sequential) manner, resulting in incremental completion of the overall product.

The incremental model

- Relies on incremental problem partitioning based on both functional and Nonfunctional Requirements
- Plans the number and content of increments in advance
- Refers to increments as drivers
- Solves a subset of the problem with the initial implementation
- Intends increments to be final parts of the final products

In summary, iterative development is a process of refining and reworking previously implemented components, while the incremental development is a process of working on one part of the problem during one pass of the development cycle. The iterative and incremental development model combines both these activities. In this process, every iteration consists of both refining previously implemented components and adding new solutions into the system.

An iterative and incremental development process will focus on the following:

- High risk items
- Early feedback on key design points
- Tangible deliverables at every stage of development
- Establishment of an end-to-end software development framework.

Each increment in the iterative and incremental development process has a full waterfall process model within its bounds including all the standard quality checkpoints such as design reviews, and code inspections. Each increment should have well-defined requirements and objectives. An increment should cover a short time period, so that it can be estimated with a high degree of accuracy.

Purpose

Using a predefined process is an important project management technique. A good process:

- Provides guidance through well-defined sequences in an orderly way
- Identifies the knowledge dependencies
- Decomposes a complicated task into well-organized activities
- Provides a consistent framework for project adjustment
- Enhances development productivity and quality
- Enables efficient and effective product management

Traditionally, we use either a waterfall or a code-fix model. The waterfall model sets development into sequential activities with no or few iterations. The code-fix model is intended to start the code when the requirements are ready. The code is tested and fixed during the entire process to meet the requirements. These models are only good when the developers have a very good understanding of requirements that will be stable throughout the development, or for small projects.

This is not the case in most software development projects meaning that project teams face major challenges:

- **Changing Requirements**: In today's business environment, companies must evolve to meet changing economic and marketing challenges. Thus, almost every project's requirements evolve during development.
- **Changing Environments and Technologies**: Application architectures in today's computing environment cannot be assumed to be stable over the short term. New products come to the market almost every day to enhance development productivity, product functionality, performance, and user-friendliness.   Areas that can impact software development projects include:
  - Client/Server Architectures
  - Operating Systems
  - End User Interface (EUI) Standards and Graphical User Interface (GUI) Builders
  - Software Infrastructures
  - Libraries
  - Frameworks
  - Databases
  - Data Distribution and Management
- **Increasing Product Complexity**: Computers are currently used everywhere in our lives, and software is becoming more and more complex while trying to handle a variety of applications.

- **Effective Project Management**: In the competitive product market, developing a product economically and quickly with superior quality is necessary for success.

Traditional processes often do not allow software companies to meet the above challenges.

Participants

The development process should be defined by project managers and team leaders.

Timing

A process must be defined for every project at the project planning phase. The process should be continuously adjusted when the project is in progress, so that any major defects in the process can be corrected in a timely fashion.

Technique

Defining an iterative and incremental process for a project involves the following work.

- Identifying the requirements and objectives for each increment

- Selecting the items to work on in each increment

- Sorting out the Project Dependencies

- Determining the number of increments. It is usually affected by:

  - Size of the project
  - Stability of requirements and environments
  - Complexity of the problem domain
  - Resource and productivity.

  The number of increments:

  - A typical number of increments is about 2 to 4.
  - If less, the process is essentially a waterfall process
  - If more, the length of each increment tends to be shortened. The overhead of project management could be too high in comparison with the development effort. For instance, shorter increments means more planning, scheduling, resourcing, testing, and reviewing per unit time to write code.

- Planning the increment length:

  - A typical increment length is about 6 to 12 weeks
  - If longer, the process becomes weighted too much toward a waterfall model
  - If shorter, project management outweighs the development effort.

The length of an increment also depends on the project. Sometimes, one increment can take longer than expected, because of the high expectation of functionality, unfamiliarity of domain and new technology, and the large size of the project (coordination and inter-team communication can become the bottleneck).

Strengths

Strengths of the iterative and incremental development process include:

- Overlap of development activities
- Incremental product release
- Rapid operational capability
- Efficient use of resources
- Reduced risk of product disaster
- Quick feedback on design decisions
- Easier adjustment to changing requirements and environments
- Easier changes in architecture and design
- Developers can learn as they go
- Reduction of risk by reducing uncertainty
- Improvement of quality by continuous testing during the evolution
- More visible reuse opportunities

Weaknesses

The iterative and incremental development process also has its weaknesses and challenges:

- Additional project management and process complexity
- Difficulties in identifying the components for each iteration
- Difficulties in prioritizing the risks
- Subsequent iterations may affect the work done in the earlier ones
- Coordination of teams working in different stages
- Additional management for change control
- Possible ignorance of long-range architectural and usage consideration
- Lack of complete specification that can make initial estimation less accurate
- Numerous trivial changes occurring during iterations

Notation

The software development process is instantiated in the project Schedule. During planning and scheduling, the iterative and incremental process should be determined for that particular project, in terms of *number of increments*, and *length of each increment*.

Advice and Guidance

In object-oriented software development, using an iterative and incremental process can be a crucial aid to completing the project on time and with good quality.

We highly recommend using a scenario-driven approach where scenarios are used to partition the problems and measure the work needed to be accomplished within each increment.

Example(s)

See Table 17-1 on page 377 for an example increment plan.

Table 17-1. Example Increment Plan.

Name	Duration	Purpose
Preincremental	2 months	Gather requirements, develop project plans kick-off, initial object-oriented analysis
Increment 0	4 weeks	Learn object-oriented process, tools, development environment, implement 2 simple scenarios
Increment 1	10 weeks	Implement Scenarios 12-22 & 28-33
Increment 2	12 weeks	Implement Scenarios 1-8. 23, 26, 27; adds GUI & persistence
Increment 3	10 weeks	Implements rest of scenarios, adds distribution and rest of GUI
Postincremental	2 months	Packaging, System testing, deployment
Buffer	4 weeks	Contingency, dependencies delay, et cetera

References

P. DeGrace and L. Stahl [DeGrace90] present a good discussion on process models.

Importance

Adapting the iterative and incremental model is essential to effective object-oriented software development.

17.3 SELECTING OBJECT-ORIENTED MODELING TOOLS

Description

An object-oriented modeling tool provides mechanical support for preparing the various kinds of work products required for analysis and design. Modeling tools capture a single, integrated model of an analysis or design, and provide many views of that model that can be browsed or edited. Examples of views are the Object Model and Object Interaction Diagrams (OIDs).

Purpose

Although a word processor and graphic editor can be used to record the analysis and design work products, it is extremely inefficient to maintain the information in this way. It is much easier to use a tool that is specifically targeted at the notation being used.

Participants

The team leader typically chooses the modeling tool with input from other team members.

Timing

Before the project starts.

Technique

The decision of the choice of method and tool may be influenced by corporate or local dictates as well as specific project requirements. Since most methods and tools are still maturing and new versions of methods and tools appear on the market at frequent intervals, we will not make any specific suggestions here. Instead we present a checklist for evaluating tools below.

Ease of use

- Is it intuitive to use, i.e. if you are familiar with the method can you enter information easily without resorting to help?
- Does the tool fully support the notations used by the method?
- Have gaps and problems in the published method been addressed?
- Is the method the tool supports stable?
- Does the vendor use the method and tool in the development of the tool?
- Is the tool transparent, so that it allows you to concentrate on the business problem, not problems with the tool or method?
- Does it support direct manipulation, i.e. an object action style of interface?
- When you need help, is it easy to find and is it useful?
- Does it perform adequately?
- Can it operate on a laptop easily?
- Does it support multiple users? If so what is the granularity of locking of items in the model?
- Is the tool based on a unifying metamodel of the artifacts of object-oriented analysis, design, and implementation? Is it just a set of intelligent drawing editors or is there an underlying model so that changes in one diagram will change the underlying model, and cause the changes to appear automatically in other views?
- Can it be tailored, so that deficiencies in the tool or method can be addressed?
- Can the model be animated (for simulation purposes)?

Documentation

- Does the tool create documentation that meets project documentation standards?
- Is the output easy to produce and tailor?

Printing—Does it support:

- Standard operating system supported printers?
- Postscript output?
- Standard graphic file format?

Platforms— Does it support the platforms on which the project will be working?

Open interfaces—Does it:

- support the Common Data Interchange Format (CDIF)?
- Have a published export format?
- Provide an API for accessing the database of information?
- Integrate with other tools such as a word processor?
- Support data interchange interfaces on the supported platforms, i.e. DDE, OpenDoc, OLE?
- Have library control support?

Process—Does the tool:

- Integrate with tools that are required for other parts of the development process?
- Produce metrics?
- Provide versioning or configuration management?
- Provide code generation?
- Support reverse engineering, i.e. if changes are made at the implementation phase which affect the analysis or design, can these changes be easily fed back into the analysis or design models in the tool?
- Support notations and data interchange formats compatible with those of projects with which you will want to collaborate?

Other—Also consider:

- Cost
- Vendor stability and longevity (will they be around in the future?)

These are some of the requirements you might have in the use of an object-oriented analysis and design tool. They have not been ranked because the relative importance of these requirements will vary from project to project.

Strengths

The use of a dedicated object-oriented CASE tool is an important contributor to project efficiency. It is essential for easy maintenance of analysis and design models, which leads to higher quality projects.

Weaknesses

Tools and tool usage education are not cheap, but if you think education is expensive, ignorance is even more expensive.

An inconvenient tool might actually hinder a project. If the tool does not have good multiuser support, for example, then updating the design models will become a serious bottleneck.

Overeager use of tools sometimes slows down modeling work. Modeling tools are usually best employed to document the results of (white board or paper) modeling sessions, not for the modeling sessions themselves.

Notation

Most methods support four types of diagram

- Object Models

- Object Interaction Diagrams

- Class category or Domain charts

- State models.

Some tools support just one notation for representing these diagrams. Others permit alternative notations to be used.

References

- An evaluation of 14 tools is presented in [Church95].

- A discussion of object-oriented case tools and the considerations in choosing one is presented in [Williams95].

17.4 PROTOTYPING AS A RISK MANAGEMENT TECHNIQUE

Description

Often, development projects identify risks that no reasonable amount of analysis, modeling, or research can resolve. These risks usually involve untested interactions among participants. The most efficient way to address these risks and understand the characteristics of a potential solution is to "try it out" or perform an experiment. A simple experiment might be considered research, but as the experiment begins to deal with a recognizable portion of the solution to a problem, we usually call it a prototype.

Prototypes are produced in order to answer specific questions or to solicit feedback. They are commonly developed to understand usability, performance, reliability, resource requirements, cost, and the like.

Prototypes are learning vehicles that allow us to understand some aspect of a solution in the context of the real problem. Although some or all of a prototype may find its way into a production system, the terms "prototype" and "production" are commonly used to contrast the completeness, robustness, and purpose of a particular work product.

Prototypes are usually discarded after the production system is working. But so too are previous development iterations. So how are they different? They differ primarily by their intent. An iteration is an attempt to solve a problem, whereas a prototype is an attempt to resolve a risk, or more simply, to answer a project-threatening question.

As a risk management technique, prototyping is a broad-scaled, contextual experiment that directly addresses the Issue at risk.

Purpose

If your software development project plan contained no risks, then prototyping would be a waste of time and resources.

Risks that warrant prototyping are those for which modeling, study, analysis, and review (customer or peer) yield further uncertainty. For example, a customer review of requirements may result in his agreement that they are complete (enough), yet a customer interaction with a prototype might yield missing function, nonintuitive interaction, or a better understanding of response time requirements.

Participants

Prototyping should be managed by the project manager. The risks that warrant prototyping may be identified by anyone on the project at any time. The actual prototype development is performed by experts in that facet:

- Human Factors experts and customers for user interface risks

- Designers and developers for performance risks

- Architects and Domain experts for domain/subsystem unknowns

- Information Developers for information presentation and description unknowns.

Timing

Prototyping activities should be planned as soon as the risk that requires them has been identified. The actual prototyping work should be scheduled for completion in time for its results to be exploited by the project. The bigger the risk, the more concerned the project manager should be with resolving it.

Often, while a project is just getting started and is still in the requirements or planning stage, significant risks are uncovered that can't be answered from available knowledge. During this time, projects often keep key developers busy between projects with process/environment improvement and technical vitality activities. This available talent can be used to address those risks before the project "gets off the ground." Not only will the talent be put to good use, but also project knowledge and skills will be enhanced while the risks are being addressed.

Technique

Prototyping is a risk resolution technique that involves

1. Identifying the risk to be resolved.

2. Determining whether prototyping is the most appropriate technique to resolve the risk. See Section 10.7.

3. Determining the objectives of the prototype and the minimum scope that needs to be developed to resolve the risk.

4. Determining the importance of this risk. How much is riding on the outcome of the prototype?

5. Determining the effort, resource, and schedule that should be allocated for the prototype.

6. Establishing whether the prototype will be discarded, elaborated, or used in the product.

7. Determining the development process and degree of discipline that will be used during prototype development.

8. Developing the prototype according to the established process and within the determined resource constraints.

9. Exercising the prototype to resolve the risk.

10. Evaluating the results against the objectives and documenting the findings, recommendations, and resolution/decision.

Strengths

Often, prototyping is the only technique that can be used to resolve a risk. The development and exercising of a prototype is a microcosmic "proof" of the feasibility, cost, performance, et cetera, of some area of concern. When prototypes are focused and controlled, they efficiently answer the questions they were created to answer. When "showstoppers" are discovered early, prototyping can save the time that would have been wasted dealing with a problem when it is too late. At best it can shut down an infeasible project before resources are wasted on it.

Weaknesses

The most common failures of prototyping activities are:

- Not identifying the need early enough.

- Not defining the problem/question to be answered.

- Not establishing a rigid schedule and effort budget.

- Putting so much into the prototype that someone decides to ship it.

Notation

Prototypes are developed using a design notation and a programming environment as is the case for production development. There is no need for prototypes and products to use the same tools and languages.

Advice and Guidance

Some common risks that lend themselves to resolution via prototyping are:

- End-user Interface Usability

    - GUI layout, use of widgets, sequence of panels
    - Help
    - Intuitiveness of user interface
    - Validity of functional requirements
    - API completeness and consistency
    - Documentation structure and format

- Performance

    - Algorithmic efficiency
    - Storage management (overhead, fragmentation, paging)
    - Resource contention
    - Distributed function communication delay

- Architecture/Design Technique

    - Distributed (client/server) vs. Replicated (cached)
    - Speed/space/flexibility trade-offs
    - Relational Database Management Systems (RDBMS) versus Object-Oriented Database Management System (OODBMS)
    - Object-oriented versus non-OO
    - Alternative design patterns

- Skill/Education/Tools

    - Do we have enough education and skill to use this new technique or process?
    - Is this an appropriate technique or process for this situation?
    - Are the tools and environment sufficient to do the job?

References

- See [Boehm88] for an excellent discussion of risk resolution within the spiral development process.

- [Boehm89] is a collection of papers on software risk management.

18.0 Development Techniques

This section discusses techniques that can be useful in building some of what can be termed the development work products. That is, the work products that are produced during the Analysis, Design, and Implementation phases.

The Development Techniques presented are:

- Performing a Domain Analysis

- Getting Started with Semantic Networks

- Building a Draft Object Model Using Transcribe and Converge

- Interfacing with Non-OO Systems

- Wrapping Legacy Code

- Object-Oriented Implementation in a Non-OO Programming Language

- Scenario-Driven Development

- Design Patterns

- Providing Object Persistence

- Interfacing to Relational Data

- Visual Programming

- Problem Determination

Performing a Domain Analysis discusses how to do a broad but shallow analysis of the system as a means for achieving a common understanding of a domain, pinpointing requirements, or enhancing an existing application.

Getting Started with Semantic Networks describes a technique for capturing some initial, high-level information on the domain.

Building a Draft Object Model Using Transcribe and Converge describes a technique for developing a form of Object Model while helping the project development team to gain a common understanding of the domain.

Interfacing with Non-OO Systems and Wrapping Legacy Code discuss means of dealing with the need to do object-oriented implementations without throwing away legacy systems.

Object-Oriented Implementation in a Non-OO Programming Language discusses approaches for using object-oriented principles even if, for some reason, a language which supports object-oriented constructs cannot be used.

Scenario-Driven Development discusses an approach for transforming Analysis Scenarios into Design Scenarios.

Design Patterns discusses how to reuse design ideas in order to reduce the amount of invention needed to solve a problem.

Providing Object Persistence discusses techniques for making the lifetime of objects extend beyond the lifetime of the program which creates them.

Interfacing to Relational Data discusses approaches for communicating between an object-oriented application and a relational database.

Visual Programming discusses the graphical construction of applications.

Problem Determination is the process of understanding why an application is not doing what you think it is supposed to. This section discusses some approaches to problem determination.

18.1 PERFORMING A DOMAIN ANALYSIS

Description

A domain analysis is an object-oriented analysis like any other, but it is much shallower and broader than the application-level analysis described in the body of this book. The work products of a domain analysis are for this reason considerably less detailed than those of an application analysis. The sole domain analysis work products are usually an object model and a brief Glossary of definitions.

An *application* analysis is performed in order to achieve understanding of the particular application which is about to be built. The scope of an application analysis is therefore that of the application. That is, the Analysis Object Model includes only those objects which are relevant to the application. By contrast, the scope of a *domain* analysis is much wider. A domain analysis attempts to capture domain knowledge without reference to a particular application.

It is useful in practice for a domain analysis to have a focus. The domain analysis work may otherwise be undirected or, at worst, never-ending. This focus is provided by a textual statement of the analysis aim which indicates why the domain analysis is being performed. It serves a similar role during domain analysis to that of a project Problem Statement during later requirements gathering.

Purpose

A domain analysis may be performed for various reasons.

- To achieve a common understanding of the domain, and a common terminology, among the members of the development team, and between the development team and the customer/users.

    An object model is frequently a good medium for representing domain knowledge and hence for understanding domains, for exactly the same reasons that it is a good medium in which to perform application analyses. By this it is meant that much domain knowledge can be captured by identifying classes and documenting the relationships between the classes. An object model permits domain knowledge to be represented in a simple manner that can be readily understood and validated by domain experts. The process of agreeing to class definitions, relationships between classes, and the names for the classes and relationships, is often a very effective way of achieving the common understanding and terminology mentioned above.

It frequently happens that when developers begin the application-level analysis, and formalize problem domain concepts for the first time, it transpires that things are not quite as they thought. Formalization has a habit of causing embarrassing questions to be asked. Performing a domain analysis during the requirements gathering process has the effect of smoothing the path from requirements to analysis, and of closing the gap between customer and development team.

In short, a brief and shallow domain analysis is often a good way to prepare for an application analysis. It serves the purposes described above, and provides assistance in firming-up requirements as outlined below.

- To help determine the requirements of an application.

It is frequently the case at the start of a project that requirements are vague. A common cause of this is that the customer has never before thought systematically and abstractly about the problem to be solved. As a result, the customer is not able to be definite about requirements without descending into design details. Perhaps the customer does not know exactly what an existing, manual system does. Perhaps the customer is only dimly aware of the different ways in which a new system could assist. In both of these cases, a good solution is to model the relevant part of the problem domain. This is a joint exercise done by developers and the customer.

Domain modeling of this kind is used initially to gain domain understanding, but once the details and issues have been surfaced, the decision must be taken of what exactly the application will be. Once a domain analysis is in place, deciding on the boundaries of the application consists of drawing a line in the object model diagram around those classes to be implemented by the system. The classes left outside but which communicate with the classes inside the circle become the actors of the requirements Use Case Model (see Section 9.2). The object model of the internal classes form the starting point of the subsequent application analysis. In this way domain analysis provides assistance to requirements gathering, and is linked directly to the later analysis modeling activity.

- To plan enhancements to an application.

Once an application exists, or even while an application is being planned, it may be appropriate to plan enhancements. These frequently involve extending the application to refer to "new" parts of the domain: parts of the domain that had previously been outside the scope of the application and hence not modeled within the context of application development. The solution to this problem is of course to widen the scope of the analysis beyond the borders of the existing or planned application. In this way the boundaries of the application are explored, and various kinds of enhancements can be discussed.

A variation on this theme is that if a suite of applications is planned, then the inter-workings of each program of the suite may be discussed by performing a domain analysis and showing the position (in terms of clusters of classes) of each program.

It should be noted that a domain analysis is eminently reusable. Not only is it free of design details, it is also free of application boundaries. A good domain analysis is one of the key assets that a company might hope to build, maintain, and reuse in virtually every application within this domain.

Participants

As domain analysis is often performed as part of the requirements gathering activity, it is usually done by the team responsible for the requirements work products. Domain analysis formalizes domain knowledge, and it is therefore important that domain experts, users, customers, et cetera, are involved in the effort, centrally if possible, but in a validation role at least.

Timing

Domain analysis is most frequently performed at an early stage in requirements gathering, although it could be used whenever it is necessary to formalize domain knowledge.

Technique

All the analysis techniques described elsewhere in this book are applicable to the construction of a domain analysis. Domain analysis is, however, only an enabling technique: its work products will not be used directly for application development. It is, therefore, less formal than application analysis, frequently consisting solely of the identification of classes, their definition in a Glossary, and the identification of relationships between the Classes.

If domain analysis is being used to understand a business process prior to automation, then it is appropriate to model the process as one or more scenarios. The dynamics of a domain analysis are usually otherwise ignored.

Domain analysis may be done as part of a Joint Application Development (JAD) session. That is, JAD techniques are used to elicit agreement on domain details and on application requirements. An object model, and maybe scenarios too, may be used as the formalism in which to express the information discussed during the JAD sessions. This kind of object-oriented JAD technique will inevitably produce a domain analysis as an intermediate deliverable.

Strengths

The power of a domain analysis is that it can capture both the dynamics and the structure of a domain, but is simple enough for it to be understood by users and by other kinds of domain experts. As such it forms a precise but intelligible medium of communication between the development team and others. What distinguishes it from an application analysis is that it is performed before requirements are finalized, and hence before the application boundaries are known.

Weaknesses

Performing a domain analysis must not be used as an excuse for delaying work on the application itself. It should be used only to support the mainstream application requirements gathering activity.

Another danger is analysis paralysis. That is, the requirements team might spend an inordinate amount of time performing the domain analysis. One way to avoid analysis paralysis when performing application-level analysis is to insist that analysis is only done where it is directly helpful to understand the meaning of the application Use Cases. During domain analysis, however, Use Cases do not yet exist. Special care must therefore be taken to avoid domain analysis becoming undirected. The textual statement of the analysis aim is a tool to guide and limit the scope of the analysis.

Notation

Standard analysis work products and notation are used. These are augmented by a short textual statement of why the analysis is being done.

Advice and Guidance

- Keep domain analysis work products few and simple; there is often no need to model dynamics at all.

- Keep syntax to a minimum to enable customers and end users to participate fully.

- Use the modeling notations informally, as a way of sketching domain knowledge as it is revealed by domain experts.

- Continually ask domain experts to validate the analysis.

- Define the analysis aim as precisely as possible; formulate it as a question to be answered by the analysis. An example of an aim might be "Where are the boundaries of the application?" or "How is this application related to the existing XYZ application?" Use this question whenever there is doubt about what should be analyzed, and how deeply.

Example(s)

Figure 18-1 on page 390 shows a domain analysis for a fax decoding application. Only the object model of the domain analysis is shown: The full domain analysis would additionally include a Glossary and Class Descriptions. The object model shows the classes and relationships in the domain of fax decoding. A wider domain could have been chosen, for example, "communications," but the intent of the analysis was to help determine the boundaries of the application and for this the chosen domain was considered adequate.

The object model is a domain analysis model rather than an application analysis model, because no decision has yet been taken about where the boundaries of the application will be.

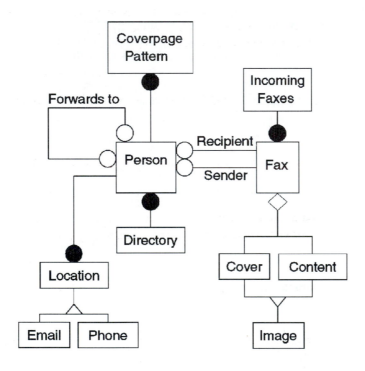

Figure 18-1. An Example of a Domain Object Model.

References

Business Language Analysis discussed in [McDavid96] offers some advice for performing a Domain Analysis.

18.2 GETTING STARTED WITH SEMANTIC NETWORKS

Description

This is a brainstorming technique to do an initial capturing of domain information.

Purpose

It is a simple and informal means of gaining an initial big picture of a problem domain. From this it is possible to identify candidate objects for initial modeling (such as Section 18.3, Building a Draft Object Model Using Transcribe and Converge).

This is a useful alternative to the CRC (class responsibility collaborator) technique.

Participants

An analyst leads the session, but the entire team participates. If there are too many attendees, then restrict participation to persons with knowledge of the problem area.

Timing

It is preferable to do this before you have read the Problem Statement. This is because the Problem Statement may constrain the participants' thinking. It is useful to have an unconstrained view of the domain.

Technique

1. The drawing should be done on a white board or flip chart so that everyone can see what is being written down

2. Write down anything about the business area in circles (such as objects, participants, processes, et cetera).

3. Draw connections between things (and label arcs)

   - is a
   - has
   - actions (verbs)

4. Don't be concerned about correctness, redundancy, and the like, on the first pass.

Strengths

- Good for initial analysis, broad prospective

- Good for identifying objects, attributes, relationships/connections

- Useful for working with groups

Weaknesses

- Very informal and unstructured

- Incomplete

Notation

- "Things" go in circles.

- "Connections" are labels on arcs between the circles.

Advice and Guidance

- Semantic Networks should always be done with people who know the domain.

- It can be used for quick identification of possible domain subsets.

- Semantic Networks should be retained for validation (to see if anything has been left out) later on in the project. While this work product is not maintained, it can be useful to refer to later in the project.

- It should be done in free-form, noncritical brainstorming fashion.

- If possible, find someone with a Joint Application Development (JAD) background to chair/lead the session.

Example(s)

The following figure shows a portion of a semantic network for a retail bank lending application.

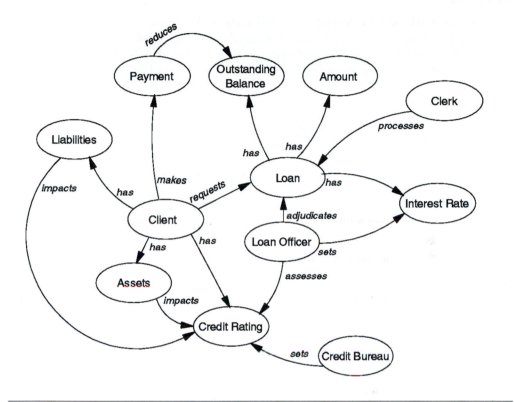

Figure 18-2. *Semantic Network for a Bank Loan.*

References

[Bekke92] uses numerous examples to discuss semantic data modeling principles

18.3 BUILDING A DRAFT OBJECT MODEL USING TRANSCRIBE AND CONVERGE

Description

This technique develops a work product that is very similar to the Object Model: object classes and their relationships are stressed. The main difference is that this diagram shows only classes and does not show their attributes or responsibilities (a box contains only the class name). In fact, attributes may be shown as classes at this stage of things.

Purpose

This technique is used to develop an initial view into a domain—it yields classes and relationships. It is also very useful as a means of achieving common understanding about the domain among the team (and surfacing issues and areas of disagreement). The result of this process is a draft Analysis Object Model (or a fragment of one) and Issues.

Participants

Analysis team, including domain experts and customers.

Timing

Early in analysis or when terms come up where there is lack of consensus.

Technique

1. Select a key word for everyone on the team to define, for example Book.

2. Everyone writes an English definition without disclosing their definitions to the other participants.

   For example, two definitions of "book":
   a. A book is a document written by an author for a reader.
   b. Books are things found in libraries and bookstores and read by readers.

3. Transcribe into the notation described by the following rules (each person transcribes their definition):

   Rule 1: Generalization: is-a or is-a-kind-of

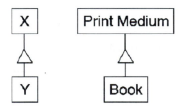

   Rule 2: Aggregation: has-a (contains)

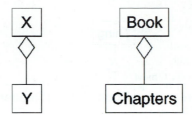

Rule 3: Association: other than is-a or has-a

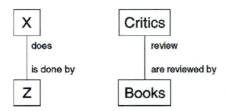

Note: Defer cardinality (for now), assume one to one (1:1).

Applying the rules found in step 3 to the definitions given in step 2 yields the following:

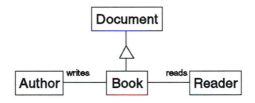

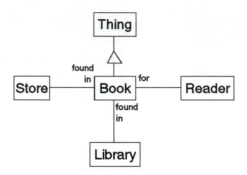

Each person should be able to read his or her diagram with equivalent meaning to his or her original definitions (or intention).

4. Converge the models that everyone created.

Have each person write his or her definition and model on a foil. Show each foil. While covering the written definition, read the model and say the implied definition. Compare this spoken definition with the written definition. Do this for all foils.

Start with one (doesn't matter which). Review the model. Let the author change his or her model, then let the rest of the group suggest changes. This becomes the initial converged model.

Repeat with the second model. Compare with the first. Note and resolve the differences. Merge the second model with the first. Stop when the author is satisfied that the converged model contains his or her meaning.

Based upon the definitions from step 2 and the models from step 3, the converged model is:

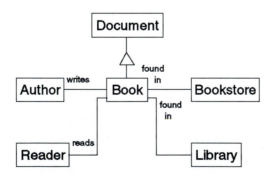

Iterate against other definitions until all definitions are covered.

Note: If no consensus, don't get bogged down. Leave it where most agree, log it as an Issue and move on.

Now write new definitions from the converged model to replace the original definitions. These should go in the Glossary.

Add cardinality.

Strengths

- Achieves early consensus on domain understanding

- Identifies some initial objects and their relationships

- Gives an initial structure

- Identifies issues of disagreement

- Gives some indication concerning the amount of agreement among the team

Weaknesses

- Time-consuming

- Takes time to learn (worth the effort however)

Advice and Guidance

- When doing Transcribe and Converge, if the discussion deals with an object that is not the primary object (the one for which you did the written definition) you may need to stop and do a transcribe and converge of this secondary object. For example, while the client generated an object diagram for the term "SQL statement," another object, "tool" was put on it. As the discussion processed, we began to debate what a "tool" was. At this point, we should have stopped the discussion and done a transcribe and converge on the term "tool."

- A broader initial Object Model may be created by performing this technique repeatedly for the key concepts of the domain, and connecting or merging the individual Object Models.

A key to this joining is to find a common term that can serve as an "anchor." The two models can then be hung off of this common term.

- The Object Model produced can serve as a reference when building Object Interaction Diagrams.

References

This technique is used by the authors in their mentoring practice. This book is the only reference material on the technique.

18.4 INTERFACING WITH NON-OO SYSTEMS

Description

Systems that are object-oriented often need to interface with systems that are not object-oriented (we refer to such systems as non-object-oriented). By *interfacing*, we mean that methods defined in object-oriented classes may need to invoke functions implemented in non-object-oriented programming languages and non-object-oriented functions may need to invoke methods of classes implemented in object-oriented programming classes. There are two issues in interfacing with non-object-oriented systems:

* Meshing diverse paradigms (object vs. procedure orientation), and
* Inter-language programming (Fortran, COBOL, C, C++, Smalltalk, Eiffel, ...).

There are also two different kinds of problems:

1. Object-oriented applications using non-object-oriented services
2. Non-object-oriented applications using object-oriented services

The first kind is not too difficult to handle. Since object-oriented programming has been built on top of non-object-oriented legacies and contemporaries (operating systems, services/facilities, and even other language services), most object-oriented programming languages have provided for accessing non-object-oriented services. This is accomplished via inter-language calls (as from C++) or by adding other primitives to the language to provide this access.

The second kind is usually more difficult to handle because most object-oriented programming languages have private mechanisms to handle. Some of the issues are:

* Determination of which implementation to use for an incoming message to a particular class instance (a.k.a. method resolution)

* Determination of which implementation to use based on the number and type of passed arguments (a.k.a. method overloading, selectors)

* Passing to the implementation a reference to the message receiver (a.k.a. `this`, `self`)

* Initialization of static objects and the runtime environment

* Storage layout of aggregates (classes)

Purpose

The whole world is not object-oriented, so there remains a need for applications to use, or reuse, services whether the application or service is object-oriented or not. Software assets are too valuable to ignore or to lose access to just because they use a different paradigm or programming language.

Participants

Designers, architects, and programmers (developers) usually decide whether and how to interface with non-object-oriented systems. The designers and architects may be addressing Nonfunctional Requirements or Reuse Plan concerns. Programmers may decide to interface with non-object-oriented systems as a low-level design decision to ease programming or enhance reuse. The decision of how to accomplish it might be deferred to the programmers by the designer.

Timing

The decision to:

- Use non-object-oriented services from an object-oriented application, or
- Use object-oriented services from a non-object-oriented application

is usually made during the design phase, based on the designer's or implementer's desire to use (reuse) available solutions.

This differs from the decision to

- Develop object-oriented services to be used by both object-oriented and non-object-oriented applications,

which is usually made much earlier as part of a Business Case or resolution of a risk involving a Nonfunctional Requirement.

Technique

For the case of object-oriented applications using non-object-oriented services, there are two approaches to choose from:

Direct   If the non-object-oriented functions or procedures exhibit good modularity (high cohesion, low coupling), object-oriented method writers might choose to simply invoke the non-object-oriented functions directly via an inter-language call.

Indirect   If the non-object-oriented functions or procedures exhibit poor modularity (low cohesion or high coupling), or if they will be used often in this or other object-oriented applications, create object-oriented wrappers for the sets of functions. The implementation of the wrappers would use the direct interfacing approach (see 18.5, Wrapping Legacy Code).

For the case of non-object-oriented applications using object-oriented services, you must create *glue code*. In C++, the glue code would be a nonmember function declared with `extern "C"` linkage that interfaces with the target object on behalf of the non-object-oriented requestor. It needs a reference to the target object as one of its parameters. Any returned object reference should be seen by the C program simply as a `pointer-to-struct`.

Note: If the interface is also a process boundary, which is often the case, then there is need for the concept of an InstanceId, and a mechanism to handle the mapping between InstanceId and object reference.

The System Architecture should also specify how to map between exceptions and return codes. Most C code communicates failures via return codes or ERRNUM, whereas newer C++ code uses exceptions. Wrappers might need to throw exceptions when non-object-oriented functions return nonzero return codes. Glue code might need to catch exceptions and return nonzero return codes to non-object-oriented callers.

Using these "reverse wrappers," glue code that convert classes to a collection of functions, is not enough. The object-oriented services must assume that static objects and the runtime environment have been initialized properly. If static objects are needed by the object-oriented services, the designers could define package initialization and termination functions to construct and destruct those objects. If resource reclamation and cleanup is not of concern for the static objects' destruction, then the designers might choose to use the *Singleton* design pattern [Gamma95] to manage the static objects in order to forego the need for package initialization and termination functions.

Note: OS/2 and Windows have automated DLL initialization and termination facilities. Good C++ compiler systems, like VisualAge C++, exploit these to automatically initialize and terminate the C++ environment of C++ code delivered as a DLL, even when the DLL is used from C code. For dynamically loaded C++ DLLs, you may have to code the _DLL_InitTerm routines. AIX does not have this automatic initialize/terminate feature for its shared libraries.

Strengths

On the bright side, interfacing with non-object-oriented systems:

- Increases application developer productivity through reuse

- Can increase the market for object-oriented or non-object-oriented services

- Can exploit object-oriented and non-object-oriented language features and libraries

Weaknesses

On the dark side, interfacing with non-object-oriented systems:

- Can make for messy, complicated interfaces

- Increases maintenance and integrity of interface header files

- Can impact performance if glue code is hit frequently and wrapped function is small

Notation

Although a strategy for interfacing with non-object-oriented systems should be specified in the System Architecture, most of the real work is specified in programming language-specific terms.

Advice and Guidance

Do not interface with non-object-oriented systems, unless there is an obvious advantage (reuse, increased market, ...).

When wrapping non-object-oriented services, take care to find useful and appropriate abstractions as the basis for the class wrapper. For example, package the operating system `mutex` services in a `ResourceLock` class (abstraction).

For C/C++, use `extern "C"` to specify C linkage for C++ functions.

Use the System Architecture, Design Guidelines, and Coding Guidelines to specify how all object-oriented/non-object-oriented interfacing will be accomplished—don't leave it to individual programmers.

Example(s)

An example of using non-object-oriented functions from object-oriented code (C++):

```
#include <string.h>
/*-------------------------------------------------------------------
** Constructor: Creates a String from C-string
**-----------------------------------------------------------------*/
String::String(const char* cs) {
        ivLength  = strlen(cs);      // uses C String function: strlen
        ivCapacity = ivLength;
        ivText = new char[ivCapacity+1];
        strcpy(ivText,cs);           // uses C String function: strcpy
}
```

In this example, the use of low-coupling, high-cohesion functions like the C string functions `strlen` and `strcpy` is done directly. The `string.h` include file is a wrapper, of sorts, which specifies a linkage of `extern "C"` for all functions defined in the library to enable C++ to C interlanguage invocations.

The following example shows a snippet of how a C++ object is made available to C clients:

```
/* -------------------------------------- */
/* String.h  a C/&pp. (bilingual) interface */
/* -------------------------------------- */
#include <string.h>
#ifdef __cplusplus
 class String {
    public:
       String(const char* s);   // see previous example
       int length()  {return ivLength;}
       ...
    private:
       char *ivText;
       int  ivCapacity;
       int  ivLength;
};
#else
   struct String;
#endif
#ifdef __cplusplus
   extern "C" {
#endif
   extern struct String* StringCreate(char* s);
   extern int  StringLength(struct String* p);
#ifdef __cplusplus
   }
#endif

/* -------------------------------------- */
/* String.C  implementation of String class*/
/*           and C interface             */
/* -------------------------------------- */
#include "String.h"
// ... skipping the C++ implementation here
// see previous example for constructor implementation

struct String* StringCreate(char* s) {
  return new String(s);
}
int  StringLength(struct String* p) {
  return p->length();
}


/* -------------------------------------- */
/* stringtest.c  a tiny test program to   */
/*           demonstrate C using C++ object*/
/* compile this with a C compiler _BUT_   */
/* link it with  a C++ link command       */
/* -------------------------------------- */
#include "String.h"
int main() {
   struct String *s;
   s=StringCreate("Hello World");
   return StringLength(s);
}
```

In this trivial example, we have provided C++ glue code (StringCreate, StringLength) to allow a C client (stringtest.c) to create and access C++ objects. The interface for the C++ class was defined with a bilingual interface header file (String.h) which exploits the C++ predefined macro variable: `__cplusplus` and C++'s linkage specification for C (`extern "C"`).

References

- FAQs 388-394 in *C++ FAQs: Frequently Asked Questions*[Cline95] addresses inter-language linkage with C.

- The Singleton design pattern and others relevant to hiding non-object-oriented services are described in *Design Patterns: Elements of Reusable Object-Oriented Software* [Gamma95].

18.5 WRAPPING LEGACY CODE

Description

"Wrapping Legacy Code" is a design technique whereby existing (legacy) code (algorithms, function libraries, data structures, database interfaces, et cetera) is wrapped, or encapsulated, inside classes. It is a means of both insulating the users from the legacy code and improving the nature of the interface and function provided by that code. Wrapping is a form of reuse which hides and often improves on the code being wrapped (reused). Legacy code is simply code that you inherited from previous software products (versions or releases) that you have created or used in your application environment. Since this book is about developing object-oriented software, we'll assume that the legacy code is probably not object-oriented. Wrapping Legacy Code, therefore, is one technique to handle the situation of interfacing object-oriented and non-object-oriented code. See Section 18.4, Interfacing with Non-OO Systems to understand the other concerns and to learn about other related techniques.

Purpose

Wrapping is done for several reasons:

- To provide an object-oriented interface to a non-object-oriented resource (for language consistency, better interfacing, improved usability, et cetera).

- To reuse valuable code (reduce development time by using existing high quality high function code).

- To insulate new clients (using programs) from a dependency on the old (legacy) code.

- To add function to an existing package without changing the existing package.

- To integrate existing applications or services into an evolving object-oriented environment.

Participants

Wrapping is done by application and system designers and programmers who are developing code in domains where previous generations of programmers have developed valuable function needed by the object-oriented system under development.

Timing

Considerations for wrapping legacy code would normally arise during:

Project planning   Affects project cost, schedule, dependencies.

Domain analysis   Besides the code, legacy systems may provide a source for mining concepts, approaches, and hidden requirements.

Architectural design   This is where most of the wrapping will be done. Classes and collaborations are designed to mimic, extend, or hide concepts provided in the legacy system.

Implementation   Legacy data definitions, resources, and functions are used by the object-oriented implementation.

Technique

During project planning, determine whether some of the requirements for the new system have already been designed or implemented in an existing (legacy) system. Determine whether it is technically and financially desirable to reuse code, designs or conceptual models from the previous system. Factor into your Business Case the costs and benefits of reuse (learning curve, schedule, development cost, dependency/maintenance cost, ...).

During analysis, use the legacy system's concepts as a source of hidden requirements and for developing customer requirement checklists (for example, do you need cascaded menus? shading? journaling?).

During architectural design, design classes and collaborations that mimic, extend or hide the features and concepts of the legacy system depending on your reason for wrapping. If you're wrapping to provide language consistency, more rigorous interfaces, et cetera, then mimicking features minimizes the cost of your wrappers. If you're wrapping to enhance the function or scope of the legacy system, then selectively extending legacy features and hiding others could give you the best compromise of reuse, encapsulation, and future freedom. If you're trying to change the paradigm or central legacy concepts, then hiding legacy features frees you from supporting undesired concepts now and frees you to replace the wrapped code in the future.

During implementation, simply use the data definitions, functions, and resources provided by the legacy system in your implementation code. You will probably want to hide or permanently adopt features of the legacy system in your wrapper interfaces. Legacy code can be wrapped at various levels:

Source   Imbed legacy code in member functions of the wrapping class. For example, imbed your old TCP/IP socket connect code inside a `Socket::connect(...)` member function.

Object   Invoke legacy functions from member functions of wrapping class. For example, invoke the ANSI C string functions from your own String class methods.

Executable "Shell out" to legacy commands from member functions of wrapping class. For example, invoke CMVC File commands from inside your own version management class's member functions.

Strengths

Wrapping legacy code provides all the benefits of reuse along with the encapsulation and object modeling benefits of using an object-oriented interface. It can reduce your development schedule, development costs, and maintenance costs.

Weaknesses

Wrapping legacy code may incur dependencies that either you or the owner of the legacy code don't wish to create. If the legacy code does not have the desired qualities, adding those qualities to your wrappers may be difficult and the result may be unwieldy. If the legacy function is shallow, the wrapper overhead may adversely affect performance. If the legacy function is deep, it may be difficult to hide all of its artifacts (for example, the legacy function may create files by its own conventions that you have no control over).

Notation

At the architecture and subsystem definition levels, it would be appropriate to use the contract notation for contracts (services) provided by the legacy system and for contracts (interfaces) provided by the wrapper objects. See 13.5, Subsystem Model and [Booch94].

Advice and Guidance

Wrapping legacy code can significantly reduce product development schedules, development costs, and maintenance costs while including and extending the original high quality function with new interfaces that insulate new clients (of the wrappers) from dependencies on the legacy code. For these reasons, it is a worthwhile activity to pursue.

But since there's no such thing as a free lunch, one has to decide whether wrapping is right in all situations. It is not worth wrapping code that has poor quality, has an uncertain maintenance future, or is conceptually too far away from the desired system. Putting lots of code or effort into wrapping something of modest value (or cost) may also be a waste of time (perhaps, reusing the design or copying code fragments may be more suitable).

Putting light-weight wrappers around heavyweight code is efficient but creates conceptual and maintenance dependencies on your system that you might not be able to afford (now or later).

When wrapping non-object-oriented services, take care to find useful and appropriate abstractions as the basis for the class wrapper. For example, package the operating system `mutex` services in a `ResourceLock` class (abstraction).

Example(s)

A common example of wrapping legacy code is a C++ String Class that acts as a wrapper for the full ANSI C String function library (nearly 40 functions) and then extends the functionality by providing character buffer management and perhaps buffer sharing (via substrings and/or reference counting). Depending how it is done, this may be a very thin wrapper (just mapping method names to string functions) or it may be very thick (managing shared character buffers and providing higher level string transformations (for example, `changeAll(str1,str2); parse(delim);)`

Another example is wrapping a GUI (graphic user interface) function library inside a window class library or GUI framework (of classes).

Yet another could be wrapping a communications function library inside a class library which portrays ports, sockets, connections, messages and message queues as the key concepts.

References

- See [Dietrich89] for saving legacy code with objects.

- See [Barton94] for an example of how to wrap the BLAS (numerical) subroutine library in C++.

18.6 OBJECT-ORIENTED IMPLEMENTATION IN A NON-OO PROGRAMMING LANGUAGE

Description

Sometimes you can do object-oriented analysis and object-oriented design but cannot use an object-oriented programming language. When this happens, you suddenly realize all that the object-oriented programming language compiler does for you. Some of the issues you need to consider are:

encapsulation   (also known as data hiding) How will you restrict the visibility and access to attributes and operations and at the same time provide information for allocation (size) and provide the required performance?

inheritance   (also known as subclassing) How will you provide for extensions to the representation and behavior of an object to define a specialization of it? How will the subclass access the superclass's internal attributes and behavior? How will you provide for substitutability, using a subclass object where its superclass is called for?

dynamic binding (related to method resolution and polymorphism) How will you provide for dynamically invoking the correct subclass's method when the compiler only knows the superclass's type?

other features   Do you need to select the appropriate method based on parameter signature (sequence of parameter types)? Do you need to support instantiation of generic classes?

Purpose

Usually the reason for implementing an object-oriented system in a non-object-oriented programming language is because none exist for the target environment. This is sometimes due to it being a specialized environment supported by a limited set of developers (compiler development or porting might not be cost effective).

Another reason might be that although an object-oriented programming language compiler is available, there are reasons not to use it:

* Lack of language skill
* Desire not to proliferate languages used in system
* Desire not to let object-oriented programming language features be exposed (interfacing constraints)
* Customer/client stipulates (non-object-oriented) implementation language

Participants

Since programming in a non-object-oriented programming language is an implementation decision that usually impacts design, the decision of which language, which middleware, and which technique involves the development architects, designers, and implementation team leaders.

Timing

Depending on how it is done, the decision to implement an object-oriented system in a non-object-oriented programming language may be risky. If so, during the project management phase a development team should be assigned the responsibility of determining the technique and developing any needed mechanisms. These should be verified via a prototype in order to resolve any risks that were identified.

Technique

There are several ways to address this. Each has different capabilities, costs, risks, and implications:

1. Implement in a language that SOM supports.

   If SOM is supported by the target language and environment, this might be the most expedient way to implement with object-oriented programming techniques. Beware, though, that SOM does not lend itself to fine-grain usage (i.e. it is less efficient than an object-oriented programming language). It places significant management and runtime burden on the project. SOM is most useful for architectural interfaces, which is where the SOM features of binary compatibility and distribution are aimed.

   A common compromise is to do object-oriented "in the large" by using System Object Model at, say, subsystem interfaces, but using non-object-oriented techniques internally to each subsystem.

2. Create your own dynamic method dispatching mechanism.

   This is difficult but others have done it. The advantage is that you determine how much capability and sophistication you want—you are the limiting factor. The disadvantage is that the result will be nonstandard, not as seamless as an object-oriented programming language compiler would be, and you've reinvented the wheel.

   This technique usually starts with prototyping and designing efficient method-table data structures and method-dispatching code. Most developers who have gotten this far see the need to hide the details of these artifacts and make it easier to code in their environment. Most begin by defining C preprocessor macros to hide the details. However, since the C preprocessor is very limited, it is often augmented or replaced by more powerful text processors. The choice will depend on what is available on your development platform:

Unix	awk/sed/grep, ksh/perl, lex/yacc
IBM	REXX (MVS, VM/CMS, AIX, OS/2)
Other	BASIC, ported Unix utilities

3. Forego true inheritance.

   Limit your technique to encapsulation. Mimic subclassing via composition (subclass is composed of base class plus extensions). Mimic inheritance and dynamic method dispatch via delegation (subclass either overrides base class method or just invokes it).

   What is missing here is dynamic binding and polymorphism. With this simple technique you must know the exact type (class) of the object before you send it a message (invoke a method).

4. Cross-platform language translation.

This technique assumes that you have an object-oriented programming language to non-object-oriented programming language translator on another available platform. For example, if you have the C++ to C translator known as `cfront` from Unix Systems Laboratories (USL) on another platform, you could edit/translate your code on that platform and download the resultant C code to your target platform for compiling and linking.

The weakness with this technique is that it is cumbersome and you must not have dependencies on the C++ runtime environment. This means that you cannot have static objects or static members of objects (in C++ terminology) and you cannot use class libraries that come with the `cfront` package. The `iostream` package is probably the most regrettable loss.

This technique also makes source level debugging difficult since the source files, needed by the debugging tool, don't exist on the target (execution) platform.

Also since `cfront` works after the preprocessor expands `includes`, you will need to point the preprocessor at the target `include` libraries (directories) rather than the default native ones from the platform where `cfront` is running. This may be tricky.

Note: Check the `cfront` license agreement before you contemplate this technique.

Strengths

The main advantage of using one of these techniques is that you can do some level of object-oriented programming when you don't have an object-oriented programming language. Another advantage is that you can implement only as many object-oriented programming features that you will need and use, and may be able to avoid some unnecessary burdens.

See the individual techniques listed under *Technique* for each technique's strengths.

Weaknesses

The major weakness of all of the techniques is that none are as good as using a complete solution provided by a compiler for a standard object-oriented programming language. Another weakness is that you need to support and maintain the extensions you created in your development environment and in your runtime environment. The more you created, the more you need to maintain (and live with).

See the individual techniques listed under *Technique* for each technique's weaknesses.

Notation

The particular notation or syntax you use will depend on the target language and how much you extend it with your own preprocessing.

A simple (encapsulation only) technique targeting the C language might adopt a syntactic convention for invoking methods that looks like:

```
RT  CCCCmmmm(C* c, ...);   /* member function prototype */
```

```
where:
    RT      is any return type
    CCCC    is a prefix assigned to all methods of a particular class
    mmmm    is the method name
    C* c    is a pointer to the receiver object
    ...     are other method parameters
```

```
example:
    // in ZString.h ...
    /* prototype */  ZString* ZSTRcreate(int maxLen);
    /* prototype */  int    ZSTRlen(ZString* s);

    // in myPgm.C ...
    /* usage    */  ZString* myString=ZSTRcreate(80);
    /* usage    */  if (ZSTRlen(myString)==0) ...;
```

Depending on how strongly you need to support encapsulation (hiding representation), you could declare the objects one of three ways:

- For complete hiding, just declare a `pointer to struct` and use it. This does not allow containment by value or stack allocation:

```
    // in ZString.h ----------------------------------
        typedef struct ZString ZString;

    // in myPgm.C ----------------------------------
        ZString *myString;
```

- For content/representation hiding declare a dummy struct of the right size. This does allow containment by value and stack allocation:

```
    // in ZString.h ----------------------------------
        struct ZString { void* dummy[3]; };
        typedef struct ZString ZString;

    // in myPgm.C  ----------------------------------
        ZString myString;
        ZSTRinit(&myString, 80);  // initialize object
    // or
        ZString *myStringP=ZSTRinit(0, 80); // allocate and initialize
```

- For public or semipublic class representations declare the struct and use it. This allows containment by value, stack allocation, and inline accessors (and more).

```
// in ZString.h ------------------------------------------
   struct ZString {
     size_t capacity;
     size_t length;
     char*  text;
   };
   typedef struct ZString ZString;
// inline-like functions
   #define ZSTRcapacity(s) s.capacity
   #define ZSTRlength(s) s.length
   #define ZSTRasCharPtr(s) s.text
// true functions
   ZString* ZSTRassign(ZString *left,ZString *right);
   ZString* ZSTRload  (ZString *left,char    *right);

// in myPgm.C -------------------------------------------
   ZString myString;
   ZSTRinit(&myString, 80);  // initialize object
   ZSTRassign(&myString, &yourString);
   OSwrite(ZSTRasCharPtr(myString),ZSTRlength(myString));
```

Advice and Guidance

- Use an object-oriented programming language if you can.

- Use SOM if it is supported by your language and environment. SOM is best suited to coarse grain objects (subsystem interfaces), so this technique usually leads to hybrid implementations.

- Consider class-based implementation (no true inheritance) using composition (has-a vs. is-a) and delegation (forward the call to the base class) to mimic inheritance. Use naming and coding conventions.

- Before you roll your own dynamic method dispatching mechanism, study the experience of others who have done the same. Try to separate the costs and benefits of their systems versus the academic accomplishments (unless you're doing this for academic credit).

Example(s)

The following example shows a very simplistic style of emulating object-oriented programming in a non-object-oriented programming language (C). The example demonstrates composition, subclassing (emulated via composition and delegation), and an object reference passing convention.

```c
#include <stdio.h>
#define MAXSTR 16
#define ZIPLEN 10
/*-------------------------------------------------------------
** Class: Name
**       HAS-A first, middle and last parts
**       CAN-DO setName(name, first, middle, last)
**              copyName(dest,source)
**              printName(name)
**-------------------------------------------------------------*/
struct Name {char first[MAXSTR], middle[MAXSTR], last[MAXSTR];};
typedef struct Name    Name;
void setName(Name* n, char* f, char* m, char* l) {
    strncpy(n->first ,f,MAXSTR);
    strncpy(n->middle,m,MAXSTR);
    strncpy(n->last  ,l,MAXSTR);
}
void copyName(Name* n1, Name* n2) {
    strcpy(n1->first ,n2->first);
    strcpy(n1->middle,n2->middle);
    strcpy(n1->last  ,n2->last);
}
void printName(Name* n, FILE * fp) {
    fprintf(fp,"%s %s %s\n",n->first ,n->middle,n->last);
}


/*-------------------------------------------------------------
** Class: Address
**       HAS-A street, city, state, and zipcode
**       CAN-DO setAddress(address, street, city, state, and zipcode)
**              copyAddress(dest,source)
**              printAddress(Address)
**-------------------------------------------------------------*/
struct Address{char street[MAXSTR], city[MAXSTR], state[MAXSTR], zip[ZIPLEN];};
typedef struct Address Address;
void setAddress(Address* a, char* s, char* c, char* st, char* z) {
    strncpy(a->street,s,MAXSTR);
    strncpy(a->city  ,c,MAXSTR);
    strncpy(a->state ,st,MAXSTR);
    strncpy(a->zip   ,z,ZIPLEN);
}
void copyAddress(Address* a1, Address* a2) {
    strcpy(a1->street,a2->street);
    strcpy(a1->city  ,a2->city);
    strcpy(a1->state ,a2->state);
    strcpy(a1->zip   ,a2->zip);
}
void printAddress(Address* a, FILE * fp) {
    fprintf(fp,"%s\n%s, %s %s\n",a->street,a->city,a->state,a->zip);
}
```

```
/*------------------------------------------------------------
** Class: Customer
**         HAS-A Name, Address
**         CAN-DO setCustomer(Customer, first, middle, last,
**                            address, street, city, state, and zipcode)
**             setCustomerName(Customer, first, middle, last)
**             setCustomerAddress(Customer, street, city, state, zipcode)
**             copyCustomer(dest,source)
**             printCustomer(Customer)
**------------------------------------------------------------*/
struct Customer {
      Name name;
      Address address;
};
typedef struct Customer Customer;
void setCustomer(Customer* c,char* f, char* m, char* l,
                             char* s, char* ci, char* st, char* z) {
   setName(&(c->name),f,m,l);
   setAddress(&(c->address),s,ci,st,z);
}
void setCustomerName(Customer* c,char* f, char* m, char* l) {
   setName(&(c->name),f,m,l);
}
void setCustomerAddress(Customer* c,char* s, char* ci, char* st, char* z) {
   setAddress(&(c->address),s,ci,st,z);
}
void copyCustomer(Customer* c1, Customer* c2) {
   copyName(&(c1->name),&(c2->name));
   copyAddress(&(c1->address),&(c2->address));
}
void printCustomer(Customer* c, FILE * fp) {
   printName(&(c->name),fp);
   printAddress(&(c->address),fp);
}

/*------------------------------------------------------------
** Class: Date
**         HAS-A month, day, year
**         CAN-DO setDate_mmddyyyy(Date, month, day, year)
**             copyDate(dest,source)
**             printDate(Date)
**------------------------------------------------------------*/
struct Date {
      short month, day, year;
};
static char* MONTH[] = {"JAN","FEB","MAR","APR","MAY","JUN",
                        "JUL","AUG","SEP","OCT","NOV","DEC"};
typedef struct Date Date;
void setDate_mmddyyyy(Date* d, short mm, short dd, short yyyy) {
   d->month = mm;
   d->day   = dd;
   d->year  = yyyy;
}
void copyDate(Date* d1, Date* d2) {
   d1->month = d2->month;
   d1->day   = d2->day;
```

```c
    d1->year  = d2->year;
}
void printDate(Date* d, FILE * fp) {
    fprintf(fp,"%s %d, %d",MONTH[(d->month)-1],d->day,d->year);
}

/*--------------------------------------------------------------
** Class: Member
**        IS-A  Customer
**        HAS-A service expiration Date
**        CAN-DO everything customer can do ... and
**              makeMember(Member, Customer, expirationDate)
**              printMember(Member)
**------------------------------------------------------------*/
struct Member {
      Customer customer;
      Date serviceExpiration;
};
typedef struct Member Member;
void makeMember(Member* m,Customer* c,Date* exp) {
    copyCustomer(&(m->customer),c);
    copyDate(&(m->serviceExpiration),exp);
}
void setMember(Member* m,char* f, char* mi, char* l,
                         char* s, char* ci, char* st, char* z, Date* exp) {
    setCustomer(&(m->customer),f,mi,l,s,ci,st,z);
    copyDate(&(m->serviceExpiration),exp);
}
void setMemberName(Member* m,char* f, char* mi, char* l) {
    setCustomerName(&(m->customer),f,mi,l);
}
void setMemberAddress(Member* m,char* s, char* ci, char* st, char* z) {
    setCustomerAddress(&(m->customer),s,ci,st,z);
}
void printMember(Member* m, FILE * fp) {
    printCustomer(&(m->customer),fp);
    fprintf(fp,"\nExpiration Date: ");
    printDate(&(m->serviceExpiration),fp);
    fprintf(fp,"\n");
}

/*--------------------------------------------------------------
** Sample program to show usage of Customer, Member, and Date classes
** implemented in plain C (non-object-oriented)
**------------------------------------------------------------*/
void main() {
    Customer c1, c2;
    Member m1;
    Date today;

    setDate_mmddyyyy(&today,8,6,1996);

    setCustomer(&c1,"Jane","","Doe","111 Maple St.","San Jose","CA","95123");

    setCustomerName(&c2,"John","Q.","Public");
    setCustomerAddress(&c2,"123 Main St.","Sunny Beach","Florida","33431");
```

```
    printCustomer(&c1,stdout);
    printf("\n");

    makeMember(&m1,&c2,&today);
    printMember(&m1,stdout);
}
```

References

None.

18.7 SCENARIO-DRIVEN DEVELOPMENT

Description

At the end of the analysis phase of an increment, an object-oriented model exists. This model has both static and dynamic aspects. There are two main reasons why this model is an analysis model and not a design model. Firstly, the analysis only models those objects that are part of the problem domain: those objects that end users will recognize. The task of design is to extend the analysis model into the solution domain to encompass additional internal objects that implement communications, storage, user interfacing, et cetera, which are needed to turn the analysis into an executable program. Secondly, the analysis modeling work has deliberately been done without regard to the Nonfunctional Requirements of the system: performance, reliability, et cetera. The design modeling work must take these constraints into account. A design technique that helps in both these directions is *scenario-driven design*. The technique dovetails well with Use Case-driven requirements gathering and scenario-driven analysis. The common theme behind all three is that statements of dynamic end-user functionality drive the development process.

Scenario-driven design consists of taking each Analysis Scenario Object Interaction Diagram (OID) in turn and treating it as a candidate for being a design OID. The OID, considered as a design OID, will almost certainly be deficient in some obvious ways. For example, its concept of user interfacing may consist of messages sent to and from a *user* object. In the design, this idealization must be replaced by messages sent to and from objects that form a user interface, probably a graphical user interface (GUI). Another example is that the analysis OID will have blithely assumed that all objects live forever and that no further mechanism for persistence is necessary.

Each of these deficiencies constitutes an *Issue* that the design phase must resolve. Resolving a design issue of this kind involves considering alternatives, other designs, books, personal experiences, et cetera, and finally deciding how to implement this particular kind of analysis-to-design transformation. The resolution of an issue may take time to develop, but once it has been decided upon it can be applied, more or less as-is, in other scenarios. It is therefore important that the issue and its resolution are adequately documented. For example, it might be decided that a model-view paradigm will be used to implement user interfacing, that view GUI objects will be generated by a particular visual

GUI builder, and that a particular mechanism will be used to maintain consistency between views, et cetera. This could be considered to be a *design pattern* [Gamma95] which is then available to be applied in other scenarios that, in their analysis form, also involve communication with *user* objects. Applying this design pattern to scenarios moves the scenario one step from being an Analysis Scenario towards being a Design Scenario. Scenario-driven design consists of repeatedly transforming analysis OIDs until they become satisfactory design OIDs. A side effect of scenario-driven design is a set of design issues, and their resolution in the form of design decisions. Another side effect is a Design Object Model, which is created by updating the Analysis Object Model to take account of the design decisions.

What has effectively happened in the above example is that a messaging pattern in the Analysis Scenario has been recognized as inappropriate, and replaced by another. This replacement, the deletion of some objects and the introduction of others, is the general rule in scenario-driven design when adding new internal structure to an evolving design. The introduction of a database to deal with data persistence, the introduction of a communications class library to deal with interprocess communications, the introduction of collection classes to manage aggregations of objects, and the introduction of mechanisms to provide client-server facilities are other examples that might be dealt with similarly.

A slightly different example is that of an optimization issue. For example, an Analysis Scenario might involve accessing several objects in order to discover the identity of a particular object, and reaccessing the intermediate objects every time the identity is required. The analysis model might do this in order to simplify the static structure of objects. At design time, this situation may not be satisfactory; it may be decided instead to cache the references at the source object. This design decision changes the messaging pattern in the scenario and, once again, makes the scenario slightly more realistic.

A third example is that of process boundaries. Almost certainly, the analysis model will have ignored the concept of process, making the assumption that all communications will be synchronous, and without any messy local/remote communication distinctions. This may all have to change at design time for a variety of reasons. Process structure constitutes one of the major design-time decisions; it will probably be met on the very first scenario that is considered at design time. Indeed, completely transforming the first one or two Analysis Scenarios into Design Scenarios will probably establish the core of the application architecture. This is one reason why the first increment of an iterative and incremental development project should deal with only a very few scenarios: to generate feedback on the effectiveness of the Architecture as soon as possible. The decision about where to place process boundaries, and the nature of interprocess communications (synchronous vs. asynchronous, message passing vs. remote procedure call, ...) and their implementation in terms of class libraries, subsystems, et cetera, will result in new objects, perhaps new subsystems, and new messaging patterns in the scenario. This is a very complex issue, but one that is quickly surfaced by the technique of scenario-driven design.

Applying the technique is no substitute, of course, for the hard design work required to make design decisions. Scenario-driven design does, however, offer assistance when trying-out design alternatives. Tentative resolutions of any particular design issue that has been surfaced by scenario-driven design can be tried out by modifying the scenario in line with the trial resolution. Perhaps a particular process boundary is placed in a particular position. The effect of this decision can be assessed by applying the decision to this and maybe other scenarios. If the messaging pattern that results is inefficient or inappropriate then another resolution can be tried. If necessary, executable prototypes can be constructed to exercise the alternatives further before a decision is made.

It is possible to drive the whole of the design phase in this way: All design decisions are made and applied within the context of scenario-driven design activity. If this is done then the Architecture, components, subsystems, et cetera, of the solution will all emerge and evolve during the scenario-driven design work. This design process is sometimes inappropriate. For example, it may be known in advance that the application architecture will be client-server, that it will use a relational database, that it will use a model-view user interface paradigm, et cetera. This Architecture may either be a given, or it may be wished to decide these issues separately at the very start of the design phase. In that case, scenario-driven design may still be used, but a set of initial transformations to take this architecture into account must first be made to the Analysis Scenarios before the technique starts to generate design issues of its own. Transforming the Analysis Scenarios in line with an Architecture is likely, however, to surface problems and opportunities that were not envisaged when the Architecture was devised.

All scenario-driven design is likely to contain both depth-first design as well as breadth-first. That is, the basic technique consists of transforming the first Analysis Scenario completely, before beginning on the second. It is in practice useful, however, before deciding on a particular issue resolution, to try the resolution out on a few other scenarios to see whether the proposed solution seems to work in a variety of cases.

Design issues and their resolutions should be documented separately from their application for two reasons. The first has been mentioned above: to aid the application of the decision in other scenarios. A second reason is that the collected set of design decisions constitutes an important body of effort that should be reviewed in its own right, and perhaps reused by other projects, at least in part.

Purpose

Design must be done in a directed manner, otherwise it will be difficult to manage and it will probably be very wasteful in terms of time. Some form of design technique must therefore be used: It is not good enough simply to tell a design team to take analysis work products and to use them to produce the design work products. Scenario-driven design is one such technique that has been applied successfully to a wide variety of problems.

There are good reasons for design to be scenario-driven. It has been explained elsewhere (Section 9.2, Use Case Model) why it is appropriate to express functional requirements by means of Use Cases, and to perform analysis by deriving Scenarios from these Use Cases. Scenario-driven design extends the same ideas into design. The benefits of an iterative and incremental development process have also been explained elsewhere (Section

17.2), where it has been suggested that the requirements on particular development iterations are defined in terms of particular scenarios. If these ideas are followed, then by driving design from the scenarios that define the current iteration, all design activity is directly traceable back to requirements. Not only does this guarantee relevance, but it also strongly encourages progress: Design does not happen in a vacuum but in order to implement the scenarios of the iteration. In practice, scenario-driven design enables rapid and very directed progress.

Participants

Scenario-driven design is relevant to all members of the design team, but the initial scenarios may be transformed by an architect or by an architectural team. After these have been completed, the Architecture is likely to be in place, or the use of a predefined Architecture has been validated.

Timing

Scenario-driven design is done during the design phase. As mentioned above, either the whole of design can be approached in this way, or the technique can be used after the Architecture has been decided upon.

Technique

As described above, scenario-driven design takes Analysis Scenarios one by one and incrementally transforms them into Design Scenarios. This is done by identifying aspects of the scenarios that require optimization or further development. Each such scenario transformation constitutes a design decision, or an application of a previous design decision. Changing the scenarios in this way will almost certainly require parallel changes in the object model, the state models, et cetera.

It is important that scenario-driven design is not an excuse for "design by special cases" in which ad hoc design decisions are taken to satisfy the needs of individual scenarios. This can be avoided by trying out the consequences of design decisions not only on the current scenario, but on a range of others too.

When an opportunity for optimization or development is spotted in a scenario, and if it is not an obvious case of applying a previous design decision, an issue is opened. The issue states the design problem, its different aspects, its implications, and the relevant trade-offs. The Scenario that gave rise to the issue is an important part of the documentation of the problem. Various alternatives are then proposed, and formalized in terms of new scenarios. Perhaps after the construction of one or more executable prototypes to test the alternatives further, one of the alternatives is chosen as the resolution of the issue. The decision is documented, along with the rejected alternatives and the reasons for rejection and acceptance, and the process of scenario-driven design is continued on the transformed scenario. When the scenario has been completely transformed into one that satisfies all the design criteria, the next scenario is considered.

Strengths

The technique is highly focused and generates design activity that is directly traceable back to requirements. It is an integrated part of an approach to development that is scenario-driven from requirements gathering to testing although it can, if necessary, be used in isolation.

Weaknesses

There are three potential dangers with scenario-driven design. The first is that if scenarios are considered in isolation, a global view will be lost. In practice this is rarely a problem, particularly if the initial scenarios chosen for development are simple yet typical. The remedy for narrow vision is to try out design decisions on more than one scenario, and to be prepared to accept changes if subsequent scenarios indicate that they would improve the overall design. In parallel with developing scenarios, the implications of the evolving design decisions in terms of the Architecture, Subsystem Model, communications patterns, et cetera, should be noted, and used to guide future decisions.

The second danger is that it will not be clear when to stop developing a scenario. That is, it will not be clear how much detail to include in a Design Scenario. This is in fact not a problem introduced by the technique of scenario-driven design: It is inherently present in any design activity. The task of the design phase is to perform sufficient design that implementation teams can then complete the design and coding in a completely independent manner. If this guideline is used as a touchstone for determining the detail that should appear in a Design Scenario, then this problem too should be avoidable.

The third danger is that exclusive reliance on the scenario-driven technique might lead to a design that is so driven by requirements that it is brittle to changes in those requirements. The solution to this problem is to balance scenario-driven design with the development of a strong Architecture that addresses the software-engineering principles of modularity, anticipation of changes, and reuse, see Section 13.2, System Architecture.

Notation

The principal notation of scenario-driven design is that of object interaction diagrams. These have been described in Section 11.5. In addition, the design decisions that have been used to transform the scenarios should be documented separately. The format of design patterns [Gamma95] can be used as a guide for this, although the intent of a design pattern, and hence its form, is slightly different to that used here for design decisions. What is important is that the context, trade-offs, alternatives, and rationale are documented, in addition to the final decision.

Advice and Guidance

- Always bear in mind that design decisions will be subject to review and change in the future, and document accordingly.

- Choose a very few scenarios to tackle in the first development cycle, and use a scenario-driven design of these to surface the central architectural issues, and to resolve them.

- Select "mainstream," relatively simple scenarios before more complex variations. Similar to object modeling, scenario-driven design should focus on the business model. The scenarios chosen first to drive design should be those that exercise the business model in obvious ways.

- There is no need to consider scenarios in chronological order, but at some point prototypes will be built, and code drivers must be tested. Startup and shutdown scenarios should therefore not be neglected for long.

- A particular development cycle might well make simplifying assumptions, for example not to consider persistence. These assumptions should be borne in mind when developing scenarios: Never design ahead of requirements.

- Express design alternatives as alternative Design Scenarios, and document them as such.

- Prototype where useful.

- Try out design decisions on different kinds of scenario to verify their appropriateness.

- Ensure that Design Scenarios are traceable both to their analysis roots and to the design decisions responsible for their transformation.

- Ensure traceability from a design decision back to the rejected alternatives. The rejected OIDs should be preserved and documented as rejected design alternatives (see Section 13.11).

References

- See [Jacobson92] for a very full presentation of the way in which Use Cases and Scenarios can be used to drive the whole development process.

- See [Gamma95] for a discussion and presentation of design patterns.

18.8 DESIGN PATTERNS

Description

Design patterns are reusable design ideas used to solve common problems. They refer to abstract configurations of collaborating objects, addressing specific design intents, to solve particular problems. These standard patterns of design have names which encourage describing designs using a higher level of abstraction. Design Patterns are categorized by the problems they solve, how they solve them, and the consequences of their solutions.

As a design technique, using "design patterns" implies using standard solutions, written up in the form of patterns, to solve common recurring problems.

Purpose

Using design patterns reduces the amount of invention required to solve a problem and increases the consistency and commonality of solution. Using known and understood design patterns by name allows designers to raise the level of abstraction and increase the understanding in design discussions. Using a catalog of cross referenced design patterns makes the designer aware of issues, alternatives, and situations that might not have been considered otherwise.

Participants

Software designers use design patterns when deciding how best to solve a problem with object-oriented software.

Analysts might also recognize and use "design patterns" in analytic models when the parts of the pattern come from the problem domain (real world). Examples here are limited, but the *proxy* and *composite* patterns come to mind. A Proxy object stands in for another object that might not be directly accessible. Composite objects have common part-whole characteristics (for example, folder contains folders and documents).

Programmers (developers) can also use design patterns when the design given to them allows for programmer detailing.

Timing

The application of design patterns is mostly done during the design phase, where concrete mechanisms are introduced to the model to describe how a particular facet of the system will be implemented. They help the designer implement or work with various design constraints in their solution. Examples of design constraints that can be handled with design patterns are: access control, instance control, persistence, communication, state dependent behavior, dynamic (changing) behavior, storage and performance.

Design patterns can also be introduced during design reviews or re-engineering activities.

Technique

First, gain a familiarity with some known design patterns by reading a book on the subject. An excellent reference is [Gamma95].

To do it in an ad hoc way:

- Recognize in your design a common problem solved by a known design pattern.
- Copy the pattern into your design.
- Customize it to suit your problem.

To be exhaustive:

- For each known design pattern

    – Determine the problem solved by the design pattern.
    – For each place in your design where that problem exists:
       — Copy the pattern into your design.
       — Customize it to suit your problem.

Strengths

Design patterns have many strengths:

- Use of design patterns is a form of reuse that exploits the experience, ingenuity, and trials of other software designers. This is evidenced as improved designer productivity.

- Using a catalog of design patterns affords software designers alternatives and considerations that they might not otherwise consider.

- Conducting design discussions using commonly understood design patterns by name improves the efficiency and accuracy of those discussions (raises level of abstraction).

- Using design patterns results in greater consistency and commonality in the resultant design. Designers pick up a common, well-crafted style.

- Using design patterns makes designers more aware of common patterns of their own design. When they can't find a pattern to solve a problem, designers will solve it themselves. When they see the same (or similar problem) later, they will want to capture the newly discovered pattern (and perhaps get the privilege of naming it).

Weaknesses

It is possible to misapply, force-fit, or overuse design patterns. If any of these things are done, the results might be worse than if design patterns were not used. Because design patterns are elegant in an abstract sense, to the unfamiliar programmer (maintenance) the concrete code may be less understandable than if it were more simply implemented.

Notation

It is important to refer to design patterns by their exact name and source (where documented). For example, "we are using the `Proxy` design pattern from *Design Patterns*, by Gamma et al."

Design patterns are usually documented using notation that shows relations, inheritance, and aggregation. The notation is often elaborated with instances and implementation notes. See the examples below and [Gamma95].

Advice and Guidance

Read all the introductory material in [Gamma95] and study the design patterns. Be patient—go slowly while introducing design patterns to a new group.

When reading Design Pattern descriptions, focus on the intent rather than the structure. Many patterns have similar structures but very different intentions.

Don't overengineer your design.

Example(s)

- The Proxy design pattern provides a surrogate (proxy) object to control access to the intended object. The proxy object has the same interface as the intended object which it knows about. Common situations for the Proxy pattern are:

  - A remote proxy stands in for an object in a different address space. The proxy and its remote counterpart communicate object interaction messages and reconstitute them in the remote location.

  - A virtual proxy stands in for an object whose instantiation is deferred because it is expensive or rare. The proxy defers full instantiation of the object until it is needed. Partial instantiation is possible in the proxy (for example, the bounding box for an image may be prefetched because it is needed to determine whether the image is visible in the current view).

  - A protection proxy stands in for an object that may have limited access based on locks, context, requestor, et cetera. The proxy checks whether the request is allowed before passing it on to the intended object.

  - A smart reference is a stand-in for a plain pointer to an object. The smart reference is a special proxy that acts like a pointer to the intended object but also provides additional function during every access to the object (for example, reference counting/garbage collection, deferred instantiation of real object, access serialization). Smart references only need to implement reference operators (in C++, —> and *), constructors, and destructors.

  The general structure for the Proxy pattern is

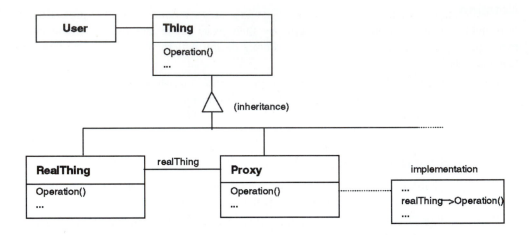

Figure 18-3. *Structure for the Proxy Pattern.*

- The following is a simple usage of the Proxy pattern that assumes that sound files require lots of storage or are slow to load. It also assumes that the sound duration can be obtained quickly (say, from the beginning of the file).

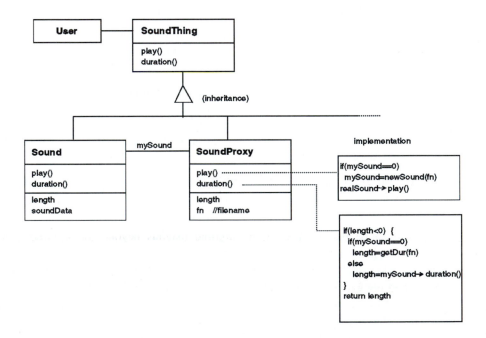

Figure 18-4. *Structure for the SoundProxy Pattern.*

- Alternatively, replacing the SoundProxy with a smart reference (limited proxy) would yield:

```
class Sound {
  public:
    void play();
    long duration();
  ...
};
class SoundPtr {
  public:
    SoundPtr(const char* filename) : fn(strdup(filename)) {}
    ~SoundPtr()          { free(fn); delete mySound; }
    Sound* operator->()  { return  loadSound(); }
    Sound& operator*()   { return *loadSound(); }
  private:
    Sound* loadSound() {
      if (mySound==0) mySound = new Sound(fn);
      return mySound;
    }
    char * fn;
    Sound* mySound;
};
int main(){
// -----------------------------
// Sample usage
// -----------------------------
    SoundPtr tune("Yankee.doo");
    ...
// sometime later ... if the user wins the game ...
    tune->play();  // load and play tune
}
```

References

The essential book describing the subject of design patterns and providing many examples is [Gamma95].

18.9 PROVIDING OBJECT PERSISTENCE

Description

An object is said to be persistent when its lifetime extends beyond the lifetime of the program that creates it. A persistent object can be created by one program and accessed by another. A persistent object is usually stored on an external storage device, such as a disk, that does not lose its memory when the power of the computer is turned off.

Purpose

By making objects persistent, objects created by one application can be shared and maintained by other applications.

Participants

The selection of a specific object persistence mechanism is the responsibility of a designer or a project architect. The selection criteria may be impacted by Nonfunctional Requirements of the project such as performance or access to legacy data.

Timing

The selection of a persistence mechanism is normally done during the design phase of the project. Usually it is covered in the architecture section. It is possible that the selection of a particular mechanism may require some prototyping work to understand the characteristics of a particular persistence mechanism and how it matches with the project requirements.

Technique

There are many ways of making objects persistent. In generally, we can divide the back-end technology for persistence into three categories by how objects are stored and retrieved in the storage media. They are:

- Flatten Object Approach

- Direct Object Approach

- Object-RDB Mapping Approach

The Flatten Object approach is to flatten the in-memory representation of objects into byte streams, so that they can be stored on external storage devices, such as disks. Each time when they are retrieved from disks, they will be converted back to the in-memory representation of objects for applications to use. Typically, the transformation between the in-memory representation of an object and the byte stream representation is not trivial. Many people develop classes to do this kind of conversion. The Persistence Framework of SOMobjects Toolkit is an example of this approach.

The Direct Object approach is to store and to retrieve objects directly. A mapping is provided to maintain objects' in-memory representation on external storage devices. This approach is sometimes referred to as single-level storage mechanism. This approach requires some kind of pointer swizzling in order to preserve the in-memory address of objects. There are no explicit operations for storing and retrieving the objects. An application that employs this approach does not have to be cognizant of the retrieval of objects. Persistent object access is transparent to the application. This is the approach taken by some object-oriented database (OODB) vendors including ObjectStore from ODI.

Lastly, the Object-RDB Mapping approach is to maintain a mapping between objects and relational tables. In the simplest case, an object class can be mapped to one relational table. Many database vendors offer schema mapping tools to facilitate this mapping work. It is relatively straightforward when there is no class hierarchy involved in the mapping. IBM's Database Access Class Library of VisualAge C++ and VisualAge as well as ODI's DBconnect are examples of this approach.

The three approaches discussed above deal with the back-end technology for persistence. In addition to the back-end technology, there is also the front-end technology to consider. In general, there are two front-end methods for making objects persistent in a program. One is based on a persistence class. A class obtains the persistence capability by inheriting from a persistence class. All objects of a persistence class are persistent objects. A second method of making an object persistent is to make an object persistent at the time of object creation. By invoking a special method, a persistent object is created. Otherwise a transient object is created. (For the purpose of discussion here, a transient object is an object that is not persistent.) With this method, objects that belong to the same class may or may not be persistent.

Strengths

The lifetime of a transient object is the same as the application that creates it. Both of them come to an end when the application terminates. By making objects persistent, objects created by one application can be used by that application at a later time or shared and maintained by other applications. For most applications, object persistence is a requirement. It is not a matter of choice. The choice for a project lies in how to provide persistence.

Weaknesses

For most applications, persistence is a requirement. However, the selection of a particular persistence mechanism can be difficult and often requires prototyping.

Notation

There is no standard notation for object persistence. It will depend on the specific tool or product used for the project.

Advice and Guidance

The selection of a persistence strategy needs to be determined at the system level in most projects. Essential data can be lost due to the chaos that will result from each developer making persistence decisions based on their limited view of the system.

The first decision to be made in considering object persistence is to determine whether an object or data should even be persistent. It may not be necessary to make all objects persistent. Once the decision is made that objects should be persistent, then the decision of which persistence mechanism to use is based on the trade-off between cost, access time, capacity, and reliability.

Each approach has its strengths and weaknesses. There are situations that are suitable for each approach. The selection of which approach to take requires careful examination of the requirements and trade-offs. Is there a requirement to access relational data? What is the performance criterion for accessing objects? In addition to studies and analysis, this subject is a good candidate for prototyping work.

The strength of the Flatten Object approach is that conceptually it is relatively simple and straightforward. It can be implemented with regular file systems. The disadvantage of this approach is that it may not be the most efficient way of handling persistent objects. Most likely this approach is not suitable for a large scale project without significant amount of work on the part of the designer.

Generally speaking, the Direct Object approach is the most efficient way of handling persistent objects. From the programming perspective, it is simpler as well since there is no explicit storing or retrieving object operation involved. The application is free from the management of the in-memory persistent objects.

Typically, the Object-RDB Mapping approach is used when there are existing data stored in relational databases, such as DB2, which need to be accessed by new object-oriented applications. The advantage of this approach is that it allows object-oriented application to access relational data. Another advantage of this approach is the fact that relational database technology is well established, reasonably mature and standardized. Relational database technology is especially strong in the areas of query and security, where the other two approaches are weak in these areas. In addition, many people are familiar and comfortable with this technology.

Two critical issues remain with the Object-RDB Mapping approach:

- Complexity of mapping objects to relational tables
- Mapping of object identity to relational data fields.

Many implementations suggest the use of primary key for object identity and one relational table for each class of objects. The difficulty arises when the mapping of class hierarchy (or class inheritance) to relational tables is necessary. There is no agreement on how it should be done. Different products may offer different solutions for the problem. Without the inheritance capability, object-oriented design is restricted.

Depending on the implementation, the Object-RDB Mapping approach is probably not the most efficient approach for handling persistent objects; however, it is a common approach taken by many projects. It is likely due to the fact that RDBMS technology is more mature.

The question of how objects will be used by different applications should also be an important consideration for determining which persistent approach to take. Will there be multiple users accessing the same objects at the same time? How will data integrity be maintained under this environment? Should some people be blocked from accessing certain objects? How will an application navigate through objects? And lastly, what about the query capability? These are typical questions concerning the selection of a database management system. They will also have an impact on the selection of a persistent object mechanism.

There are several standards related to object persistence. SQL3 is the relational database standard with some object extensions. In the area of object-oriented database management systems (OODBMS), there is the ODMG-93 from the Object Database Management

Group (ODMG) consortium. In addition, Object Management Group's (OMG) persistence services and other related OMG services may have some impact on the decision of which persistent mechanism to use for the project.

Example(s)

Please refer to the reference manuals of ObjectStore from ODI for examples of the Direct Object approach and VisualAge C++ Open Class Library manuals for examples on Object-RDBMS approach.

References

• *Object Databases—The Essentials,* by Mary E. S. Loomis is a good introduction to Object Databases. [Loomis95]

• *Object Data Management* by R. Cattell is a good introduction to Object Data Management related issues. [Cattell94a]

• *The Object Database Standard - ODMG-93,* by R. Cattell, is the published standard for ODMG. ODMG is a consortium from OODB vendors. [Cattell94b]

18.10 INTERFACING TO RELATIONAL DATA

Description

An object-oriented interface to relational, persistent data is a layer between an object-oriented application and data stored in a relational database management system (RDBMS). It consists of classes that from the point of view of the object-oriented application are just like any other classes, while from the point of view of the relational database management system they are normal SQL interfaces that access relational tables. With these classes, persistent objects can be stored or retrieved in an RDBMS.

Purpose

An object-oriented interface is built to provide seamless integration of object-oriented applications into an existing suite of traditional applications built around a relational database management system. This is done in order to protect current investments in relational technology, while enabling transition towards object-oriented technology in a manner that is as unobtrusive as possible.

Participants

The object-oriented layer can be provided by a RDBMS vendor, a language vendor, or a third party. If it is not provided, it can be developed by the project that needs it, which means it would be the task of designers and developers. However, the selection of which interface to use may be the task of an architect or a designer. Some examples of a vendor-provided object-oriented layer are DBtools.h++ from Rogue Wave and Database Access Class Library(DACL) in IBM's VisualAge C++.

Timing

Very often this interface is developed before the design of an application. Regardless of who provides the object-oriented layer to a RDBMS, its structure affects the Architecture of the application, and should therefore be known at the beginning of the design of the application.

Technique

There are two levels of concerns with regard to this interface framework. One is to build an object-oriented interface framework to the RDBMS and the other is to use a vendor-supplied RDBMS interface framework.

Building a generic object-oriented RDBMS interface framework can be done by using a RDBMS's code level APIs wrapped in framework classes. To achieve generality, the problem of object-oriented interfacing should be considered in the context of RDBMS's, in general, and not just a particular one. This is important especially when the application is targeted to be used with several different RDBMSs.

A good place to start is by studying the code level APIs that describe RDBMS access and manipulation routines from procedural languages such as C. Typically, there are three different categories of commands, that do the following:

- Establish and close connections to the database server

- Prepare and send queries and retrieve results

- Work with error conditions, messages and recovery actions.

For example, class databaseServer would store information relevant to establishing connections to the database server in its attributes, while its methods would correspond to functions from the RDBMS's API. Those arguments that appear as attributes would not need to be present in the methods' signatures. This makes an object-oriented interface simpler than the initial code level API, as well as easier and less error prone to use.

When building or using object-oriented RDBMS interfaces, there are several RDBMS-related issues that have to be addressed, and the way they are resolved will greatly influence the system's Architecture. The decisions to make are:

- How to map the RDBMS representation (tables, views, et cetera) to objects

- Where to put the responsibilities for security

- How to organize transaction management in order to provide the ACID (Atomicity, Consistency, Isolation and Durability) properties

- How to do object queries.

The answers to the above questions depend on the reasons behind providing an object-oriented interface to a RDBMS and on Nonfunctional Requirements. First of all, mapping relational tables to objects is not always an easy task. There is some discussion on this subject in Section18.9, Providing Object Persistence.

As for issues related to security, transactions, and queries, there are at the least two alternatives. One simple way of approaching this problem is to leave them in the traditional RDBMS. There won't be new classes defined for each service. The object interface will simply pass these requests to the RDBMS. In other words, the underlying RDBMS will be somewhat visible. An application taking this approach needs to be aware of cursor, table, et cetera, and the mapping of objects to tables when transactions or queries are involved. Another possibility is to follow the Object Management Group (OMG) approach that is to provide object-oriented classes for these services. A client of these classes will not see the underlying RDBMS, so there will be some new APIs to invoke these services. However, this approach does not preclude the possibility that these services could be implemented on top of the traditional RDBMSs. It is foreseeable that some vendor-provided object services (such as IBM's SOMObjects) can be used in conjunction with the object-oriented interface.

Strengths

- Uniform object-oriented interfaces across products increases their interoperability.

- Since all the interaction with the actual RDBMS is hidden behind the object-oriented interface, the applications are insulated from changes in the actual RDBMS, which makes support for several different RDBMSs easier.

- Insulating RDBMS code in object-oriented interfaces relieves object-oriented developers of having to learn and deal with the relational paradigm. They can use native object-oriented constructs (in Smalltalk, C++, et cetera), rather than learning SQL and particular RDBMS programming constructs.

- An object-oriented interface allows a smooth transition from a traditional procedure-oriented system to an object-oriented system.

Weaknesses

- Object-oriented interfaces from different vendors are not standardized and they may not support the desired RDBMS. In addition, there could be some inter-operability problems among different vendor's products.

- If the mapping between object-oriented classes and relational tables is not carefully designed, there may be some negative performance impacts on the application. For example, a class that involves more than one table should be carefully examined.

- Different RDBMSs have different sets of code level APIs, so it might be difficult to devise an object-oriented interface that will be equally well suited for all of them (especially if they do not have code level APIs available).

Notation

Developing an object-oriented interface to a RDBMS is done in a programming language or through visual tools, such as the Data Access Builder in IBM's VisualAge C++ product.

Advice and Guidance

Following are some considerations and steps for building an object-oriented interface to relational databases:

1. Identify several major RDBMSs

2. Identify the common set of their code level APIs

3. Design a framework with services common to all RDBMS's APIs

4. Encapsulate the specifics of certain RDBMS in its own extension of the base framework (using inheritance).

There are different choices for using this object-oriented interface. The first decision to make is the mapping of relational tables or views to classes. Map one table to one class if possible, but this does not always match with the Design Object Model. If a class consists of more than one table, it will have a significant performance impact because of the JOIN operation. As for where to put the responsibility for security and transactions, et cetera, each approach has its pros and cons. Keeping most responsibilities in the RDBMS is a simpler solution to build, but users of these services will need to be RDBMS-sensitive, and will suffer from any changes in the RDBMS, thus defeating the purpose for using them. Putting these services into the object-oriented classes is more difficult, but it pays off in the long run in two ways. First, this approach hides the underlying RDBMS, so the application that uses this service does not have to know about the RDBMS. Second, these classes are more resilient to change and thus more reusable.

Typically the steps involved for using this API are:

1. Create a mapping between object classes and relational tables

2. Build the application using these object classes for persistent objects.

Example(s)

Building an object-oriented interface in C++ for DB2/6000. Classes for DB2/6000 services were built using the DB2/6000 Call Level Interface (DB2/CLI) for C. *IBM DATABASE 2 AIX/6000 Call Level Interface Guide and Reference* explains in detail how DB2/CLI works in the C environment.

The choice of classes to encapsulate the DB2/CLI services was based on the fact that some functions in the DB2/CLI are effective for an entire application, whereas other functions are oriented toward single SQL statements:

- The class *dbserver* encapsulates functions that provide services for the whole application (for example, establishing and releasing the connection to DB2/6000).

- The class *dbstmt* encapsulates DB2/CLI functions that provide SQL services. They all have an SQL statement handle (a variable of *SQLHSTMT* type) as the first parameter in their parameter list (except SQLAllocStmt, which allocates a new statement handle).

- The class *dberror* serves for C++ error handling using throw/catch mechanism.

The member functions have the same names as the corresponding DB2/CLI functions. The parameters are in the same order, except that parameters that are known to the class are omitted.

Class dbserver

This is a top level class used to connect our application to the DB2/6000 database.

```
class dbserver
{
  public:
    dbserver(const char* serv_name,
             const char* user_name,
             const char* password) throw(dberror);

    virtual ~dbserver(void) throw(dberror);
    SQLHENV gethenv(void) const;
    SQLHDBC gethdbc(void) const;

  protected:
    typedef enum
    {
      NAME_LEN    = 20,
      STATE_LEN   =  6
    } info;

    SQLHENV    henv;   // environment handle
    SQLHDBC    hdbc;   // connection handle
    SQLRETURN  rc;     // return code

    SQLCHAR    server_name[NAME_LEN+1],
```

```
                  user_name[NAME_LEN+1],
                  password[NAME_LEN+1] ;

};

// implementation of dbserver constructor

dbserver::dbserver(const char* server_name,
                   const char* user_name,
                   const char* password) throw(dberror)
{
  // copy parameters into internal storage
  strncpy((char *)server_name,server_name,NAME_LEN);
  strncpy((char *)user_name,user_name,NAME_LEN);
  strncpy((char *)password,password,NAME_LEN);

  // allocate the environment and required structures
  // they are 'hidden' behind henv variable
  rc = SQLAllocEnv(&henv);

  // if allocation failed, throw an exception
  if (rc != SQL_SUCCESS)
    throw(dberror(this,"dbserver::dbserver SQLAllocEnv"));

  // connect to the database
  // and get the communication structures initialized
  rc = SQLAllocConnect(henv,&hdbc);

  // if connect failed, throw an exception
  if(SQL_SUCCESS != rc)
    throw(dberror(this,"dbserver::dbserver SQLAllocConnect"));

  // logon to the database
  rc = SQLConnect(hdbc,
                  server_name,SQL_NTS,
                  user_name, SQL_NTS,
                  password, SQL_NTS);

  // if successful, do nothing, otherwise indicate the information
  // or throw an exception in case of failure
  switch(rc)
  {
    case SQL_SUCCESS:
      break;
    case SQL_SUCCESS_WITH_INFO:
      cout << dberror(this,"dbserver::dbserver SQLConnect info").msg();
      break;
    default:
      throw(dberror(this,"dbserver::dbserver SQLConnect"));
  }
}
```

Class dbstmt

```
class dbstmt
{
  public:
    dbstmt(dbserver* ds) throw(dberror);
    virtual ~dbstmt(void) throw(dberror);

    void SQLAllocStmt(void) throw(dberror);
    void SQLFreeStmt(SQLSMALLINT option=SQL_DROP) throw(dberror);

    void SQLPrepare(SQLCHAR* sql_string) throw(dberror);

    void SQLSetParam(SQLSMALLINT     par_no,
                     SQLSMALLINT     par_type,
                     SQLSMALLINT     col_type,
                     SQLINTEGER      col_length,
                     SQLSMALLINT     par_scale,
                     SQLPOINTER      data_ptr,
                     SQLINTEGER*     data_size) throw(dberror);

    void SQLExecute(void) throw(dberror);

  ⋮

  protected:
    SQLHSTMT     hstmt;      // SQL statement handle
    dbserver*    dbserver;   // pointer to dbserver object
    SQLRETURN    rc;         // for return code
};

// implementation of dbstmt constructor, destructor and
// dbstmt::SQLAllocStmt method
// other methods designed analogously

dbstmt::dbstmt(dbserver* ds) throw(dberror) : dbserver(ds)
{
  // allocate and initialize required structures
  SQLAllocStmt();
}

dbstmt::~dbstmt(void) throw(dberror)
{
  // deallocate the acquired structures
  SQLFreeStmt();
}

void dbstmt::SQLAllocStmt(void) throw(dberror)
{
  // allocate and initialize required structures
  rc = ::SQLAllocStmt(dbserver->gethdbc(),&hstmt);

  // if successful, do nothing, otherwise indicate the information
  // or throw an exception in case of failure
  switch(rc)
  {
```

```
    case SQL_SUCCESS:
      break;
    case SQL_SUCCESS_WITH_INFO:
      cout << dberror(dbserver,"dbstmt::SQLAllocStmt
info").msg();
      break;
    default:
      throw(dberror(dbserver,"dbstmt::SQLAllocStmt"));
  }
}
  :
```

Class dberror

```
class dberror
{
  public:
    dberror(dbserver* dbserver,const char* init_text);
    virtual ~dberror(void);

    const char*     msg(void);

  protected:
    typedef enum
    {
      MSG_ID_LEN    =  30,
      STATE_LEN     =  10
    } info;

    dbserver*     dbserver;
    SQLRETURN     rc;

    SQLCHAR       sqlstate[STATE_LEN];
    char*         errmsg[SQL_MAX_MESSAGE_LENGTH+MSG_ID_LEN];
    SQLINTEGER    sqlcode;
    SQLSMALLINT   errmsglen;
};

// implementation of the constructor of dberror

dberror::dberror(dbserver* dbserver,const char* init_text) :
                dbserver(dbserver)
{
  static SQLCHAR  errmsg[SQL_MAX_MESSAGE_LENGTH+20];
  static SQLCHAR  tmpmsg[SQL_MAX_MESSAGE_LENGTH+20];
  SQLSMALLINT       errmsglen;
  SQLRETURN ret;

  // copy the initial text into the message
  sprintf((char *)errmsg,"[%s]",init_text);

  // retrieve the error text and information
  ret = SQLError(dbserver->gethenv(),
                dbserver->gethdbc(),
```

```
                SQL_NULL_HSTMT,
                sqlstate,&sqlcode,errmsg,
                SQL_MAX_MESSAGE_LENGTH-1,
                &errmsglen);

// format the results
switch(ret)
{
  case SQL_NO_DATA_FOUND:
    sprintf((char*)tmpmsg," SQLError - No error found\n");
    break;
  case SQL_SUCCESS:
  case SQL_SUCCESS_WITH_INFO:
    sprintf((char*)tmpmsg,"\nSQL state: %s SQL code: %d\n%s",sqlstate,
                                                   sqlcode,
                                                   errmsg);

    break;
  default:

    sprintf((char*)tmpmsg,"SQLError failed with rc= %d\n",ret);
}
// create the final message text = initial + findings
```

The following example demonstrates the steps involved in building an application using the Data Access Builder of VisualAge C++ 3.0.

First, we will build the mapping between the object classes and the relational database tables. In this process, we need to decide which object classes need to be persistent, which classes map to which tables, and the mapping between attributes and columns. Not all columns from a table need to be mapped to an attribute in the corresponding object.

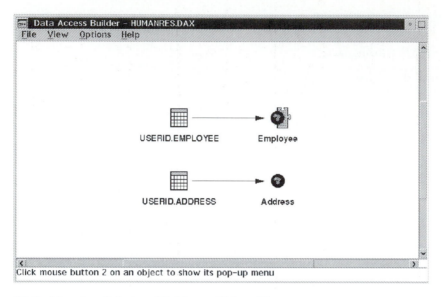

Figure 18-5. *Mapping Relational Tables to Object Classes.*

Figure 18-5 shows the mapping of relational tables to object classes done by using a visual tool like Data Access Builder.

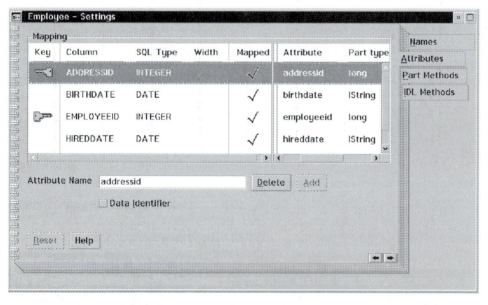

Figure 18-6. *Mapping Table Columns to Object Attributes.*

Figure 18-6 shows that the mapping between tables and classes can be customized via this visual tool to fit the needs of the application.

Once the mapping is done, the corresponding C++ header files and libraries necessary for the application can be generated. Once these files are generated, they can be used by applications to access relational data. In general, a client program will need to do the following in order to access the relational database.

1. Connect to the database

2. Access the database tables

3. Commit or rollback the transaction

4. Disconnect from the database.

The following sample code shows part of a C++ header file generated by VisualAge C++ 3.0 on OS/2.

```cpp
#ifndef _EMPLOYEE_
  #define _EMPLOYEE_


//***********************************************************************
// This code is generated by IBM VisualAge C++ Data Access Builder.
// WARNING: User modifications will be lost on next code generation.
//***********************************************************************


//***********************************************************************
// FILE NAME:Employe.hpp
//
// DESCRIPTION:
//    Declaration of the class(es):
//     Employee - EmployeeClass
//
//***********************************************************************


class _Export Employee: public IPersistentObject
{
public:
  friend class EmployeeManager;
  Employee();
  Employee(const Employee& partCopy);
virtual
   ~Employee();

  Employee& operator= (const Employee& aEmployee);
Boolean
  operator == (const Employee& value) const,
  operator != (const Employee& value) const,
  operator <  (const Employee& value) const,
  operator == (const Employee* value) const,
  operator != (const Employee* value) const,
  operator <  (const Employee* value) const;
```

```
virtual IString  asString () const;

//***************************************************************************
// Methods for addressid
//***************************************************************************
virtual long addressid () const;
const IString addressidAsString() const;
virtual Employee& setAddressid (long aaddressid);
virtual void setAddressid (const IString& aaddressid)
     { setAddressid((long) aaddressid.asInt()); };
Boolean isAddressidNull() const;
Employee& setAddressidToNull(Boolean nullState=true);
Boolean isAddressidNullable() const;


//***************************************************************************
// Methods for birthdate
//***************************************************************************
virtual const IString& birthdate () const;
virtual Employee& setBirthdate (const IString& abirthdate);
Boolean isBirthdateNull() const;
Employee& setBirthdateToNull(Boolean nullState=true);
Boolean isBirthdateNullable() const;


//***************************************************************************
// Methods for employeeid
//***************************************************************************
virtual long employeeid () const;
const IString employeeidAsString() const;
virtual Employee& setEmployeeid (long aemployeeid);
virtual void setEmployeeid (const IString& aemployeeid)
     { setEmployeeid((long) aemployeeid.asInt()); };
Boolean isEmployeeidNull() const;
Employee& setEmployeeidToNull(Boolean nullState=true);
Boolean isEmployeeidNullable() const;


//***************************************************************************
// Methods for hireddate
//***************************************************************************
 ⋮


//***************************************************************************
// Methods for name
//***************************************************************************
virtual const IString&  name () const;
virtual Employee&  setName (const IString& aname);
Boolean  isNameNull() const;
Employee& setNameToNull(Boolean nullState=true);
Boolean isNameNullable() const;

virtual Employee &add ();
virtual Employee &update ();
virtual Employee &del();
virtual Employee &retrieve ();
virtual Employee &setReadOnly (Boolean flag = true);

 ⋮
```

```
protected:
  virtual Boolean makeConnections();
private:
  long         iaddressid; // column name=ADDRESSID;
  const Boolean iaddressidIsNullable;
  Boolean      iaddressidIsNull;
  IString      ibirthdate; // column name=BIRTHDATE; length = 4
  const Boolean ibirthdateIsNullable;
  long         iemployeeid; // column name=EMPLOYEEID;
  const Boolean iemployeeidIsNullable;
  IString      ihireddate; // column name=HIREDDATE; length = 4
  const Boolean ihireddateIsNullable;
  IString      iname; // column name=NAME; length = 30
  const Boolean inameIsNullable;
  Boolean      inameIsNull;
};

class _Export EmployeeManager: public IPOManager
{
public:
  EmployeeManager ();
  EmployeeManager (const EmployeeManager& partCopy);
virtual
   ~EmployeeManager ();

  EmployeeManager& operator= (const EmployeeManager& aEmployeeManager);
Boolean
  operator == (const EmployeeManager& value) const,
  operator != (const EmployeeManager& value) const,
  operator <  (const EmployeeManager& value) const,
  operator == (const EmployeeManager* value) const,
  operator != (const EmployeeManager* value) const,
  operator <  (const EmployeeManager* value) const;

virtual IVSequence <Employee*> *items () const;
virtual EmployeeManager &refresh ();
virtual EmployeeManager &select (const IString& clause);
  ⋮

protected:
  virtual Boolean makeConnections();

private:
  virtual EmployeeManager  &clearItems();
  virtual EmployeeManager  &setItems (IVSequence <Employee*> * aItems);
  virtual EmployeeManager  &setItems (const IVSequence <Employee*>& aItems);
  IVSequence <Employee*> * iItems;
};
#endif
```

References

- See [Rumbaugh91a] Chapter 17 for some discussions on object-oriented application and relational databases.

- Chapter 10 of [Booch94] shows an example of developing an object-oriented application with relational databases.

- [Martin95] offers a good discussion about different paradigms (object-oriented, relational, et cetera) and how to cross them.

18.11 VISUAL PROGRAMMING

Description

Visual programming is a technology that allows application developers to graphically construct applications. Using a visual programming tool, a developer manipulates "parts" on the screen to define the application behavior. Parts are reusable software components and may be either visual or nonvisual. An example of a visual part is a push button. A nonvisual part might be a customer object. Composite parts can be built by combining existing parts.

There are tools available that aid in the creation of graphical user interface (GUI) windows but do not provide any ability to define any application logic. For this reason, we are not considering these tools to be visual programming tools, and they will not be considered in this section. These tools are often called "GUI builders."

Different tool vendors have different paradigms for visual programming. Some tools support an object-oriented paradigm for application development while others use traditional methods. The features provided by different tools may vary greatly. In this section we will discuss the impact of visual programming on a development project. Although most of this discussion applies to most visual programming tools, IBM's VisualAge family of tools will be the focus. VisualAge is a visual programming tool that supports object-oriented programming. Other object-oriented visual programming tools include VisualSmalltalk and VisualWorks, both from ParkPlace-Digitalk Inc., and Visual C++ from Microsoft.

Each visual programming tool has a particular programming language that it supports. Currently, the VisualAge suite of tools support Smalltalk, C++ and COBOL, each through a separate tool. After using the tool to create parts, code may be generated in the target language or the tool may provide a runtime environment to support the application. Experience in the target programming language is required although perhaps not as much as if the application were to be created by manual coding.

Visual programming tools aid in the creation of the executable program but their use does not preclude the need for analysis and design work products. As analysis is the study of the problem domain, the use of a visual programming tool has a limited effect on that phase. Only when it is used to create a prototype intended to solicit more or clearer requirements and scenarios from the customer does it affect the requirements and analysis phases. The design phase is affected by the selection of a visual programming tool in that it steers the GUI design into the user interface style chosen by the tool's designer and the application design into using the tool-chosen class libraries. The tool also determines the design patterns and subsystem contracts that become part of the application's architecture. The tool's impact on user interface design and system architecture should not be taken lightly. It must be addressed early in the design phase.

The implementation phase is also dramatically affected when using a visual programming tool. Some classes that have been designed will be implemented as parts with the tool rather than as Source Code with a text editor. But there will still be a need to create parts with manual methods as not all required parts can be drawn from the tool. These parts will either be coded with a external text editor and their interface be imported into the tool, or their code will be entered via a tool-provided script editor.

The VisualAge products provide multiple views for parts under construction. The composition editor shows the visual parts, nonvisual parts, and connections between them. This is the graphical depiction of the part where most of the visual programming will take place. The public interface editor shows the attributes, actions, and events that make up the part interface. This is the main view for constructing and editing nonvisual parts. VisualAge C++ has an additional tool that is the class editor that allows the developer to select the names of the Source Code files to be generated and allows the specification of any external code that should be included.

Purpose

Using a visual programming tool can reduce the development time required to deliver an application. This of course is dependent on the skill level of the team members in both traditional programming methods and in the use of the visual programming tool. As with any tool, there is a learning curve associated with understanding the tool and the visual programming paradigm.

Creating the visual component of the application is much more intuitive with a visual programming tool than by hand coding source code. It is much easier to visually place controls on a window than to try to hand code the correct window position. When hand coding views, it is common to recompile the view part numerous times, each time making some adjustments in the control position.

Although some understanding of the underlying graphics class library must be understood when using a visual programming tool, much less expertise is required than if the code were to be written by hand. This allows a visual programming tool to be used by a less experienced programmer to build a majority of the code supporting the application's user interface, and allows more experienced programmers to focus on more complex user interface and business model problems. A GUI designer may not necessarily be an expert in the target programming language and the tool helps in facilitating this specialization.

When code is generated by a visual programming tool, the code will have a consistency that is often difficult to achieve on a project with many developers. VisualAge C++ generates C++ code using the IBM Open Class Library and its event notification framework. This not only supports the model view separation but enforces it by implementing the Observer design pattern [Gamma95] automatically. This is a powerful pattern that many developers may not implement if coding by hand.

Still, there is a need for coding standards for the code that must be manually written and naming conventions for classes, methods, attributes, and files that the tool will generate.

Another use of a visual programming tool is constructing a GUI prototype. User feedback can be solicited for the look and feel of the application being built. This is much more effective than producing static representations of the views to be built, because the users can execute the prototype and have a better feel for the usability of the system. The designer building the GUI Prototype will probably still sketch out Screen Flows and the more complicated Screen Layouts before getting wrapped up using the visual programming tool. We still recommend developing Screen Flows and Screen Layout work products since they act as a work outline for the series of visual programming tool sessions that lead to the prototype or the real application.

The GUI Prototype usually has only a simple underlying model that enables data to persist from screen to screen. While some of the views may be reused in the final application, the underlying model will most certainly be replaced by the model constructed during the design phase.

Participants

If the project is creating a GUI Prototype, the visual programming tool will be used by the designer responsible for the GUI.

When implementing the real application, responsibility for implementing the parts in the visual programming tool is usually distributed at the class level amongst several developers. Each developer owning a class will be responsible for creating the parts and adding custom code as necessary. The designed classes will include visual and nonvisual parts and utility classes. Each of these can be assigned to developers with the required skill.

Timing

A visual programming tool may be used during the construction of a GUI Prototype (see Section 12.4) and during the implementation phase for the real application.

Construction of the GUI Prototype can begin after some analysis work has been completed. User feedback from the prototype may provide insight into the problem analysis. Also, additional analysis will affect the prototype. Through the use of the GUI Prototype, the users can verify that the analysts have a good understanding of the problem domain.

The visual programming tool may again be used in the construction of the real application. Many of the visual parts from the GUI Prototype may be reused, but the underlying model that the visual parts support must be designed outside the tool, using the design work products defined in this book. During the implementation phase, the model objects will be entered into the visual tool as nonvisual parts. Nonvisual parts will be required to support the architectural decisions such as object persistence and communication. Connections will be made between the visual parts and the nonvisual parts in the visual programming tool.

Technique

The details of tool use presented in this section are specific to the VisualAge family of tools. If a different tool is being used, these details may not apply, but the ideas will be relevant.

If using the visual programming tool for GUI prototyping, the *composition editor* is used to construct the necessary visual parts (e.g. windows, fixed text, text input fields, buttons). These parts are based on the classes defined in the analysis phase. The purpose of the GUI Prototype is to demonstrate the user's interaction with the system but not the underlying model, which carries out the business function. Nonvisual parts are required to allow information to flow from screen to screen but no complex processing should be defined for these parts. Treat the nonvisual parts as throwaway parts used only to support the prototype. The look and feel of the prototype can be iteratively modified as the analysis progresses, and the user's conceptual model is better understood.

When constructing visual parts, try to keep each one simple to promote its reuse. For example, an address part may have fields to enter the street, city, country, and zip code. This part may be reused in many contexts, both within the application and in other applications. This visual address part can then be included in a more complex part, for example, a customer information visual part. This is the concept of construction from parts.

After design has been completed, at least for a particular subsystem, implementation of the application (or subsystem) can begin. Again, the scope of the implementation phase is the same with or without the aid of a visual programming tool. An iterative and incremental process is recommended for the development cycle. Additional views of the same model classes may be implemented in later increments if an incremental process is followed.

If a GUI Prototype exists, many of the visual parts may be reused in the construction of the application. The nonvisual parts that were created to support the prototype will need to be replaced by nonvisual parts created from the Design Class Descriptions.

Many classes from the design phase will become nonvisual parts in the visual programming tool. Some classes from the design phase are required to support the implementation of nonvisual parts and are not parts themselves. These utility classes cannot be directly manipulated in the composition editor window but are used from within the handwritten implementation code. The first step in creating a nonvisual part is defining its *attributes* through the *public interface editor*. Attributes in VisualAge are slightly different from the normal object-oriented definition. Although an attribute is still a property of an object, it does not necessarily need to be stored in the class. For example, a part may have two attributes: age and birthYear. Age may be calculated by subtracting the stored birthYear from the current year. Age is considered a derived attribute of the part. Entering an attribute in the public interface editor can generate any number of the following:

- A get method
- A set method
- A "changed" event
- A data member in the part

In the example with the age and birthYear, we may choose to generate the getAge and setAge methods whose implementations would query and modify birthYear.

Events are also entered in the public interface editor. Events are triggered when something has happened that other collaborating objects may be interested in knowing about. These parts can subscribe to be notified when a desired event occurs. Often, events are triggered by state changes in an object, but they may also be triggered by external events, such as a visual part acquiring the keyboard focus. Not all parts have events. If a class has interesting state dependent behavior, a State Model may have been created for the class during the design phase.

The remaining part of the part's public interface is the *actions* that it supports. Actions are the methods that invoke the object's responsibilities. For example, a file part may have an open "action." Actions may require parameters and may return values. The action name, parameter types, and return type are all entered through the public interface editor for the part.

Once the parts are defined in the visual programming tool, *connections* between parts can be made. There are several types of connections that can be made between parts:

- *Attribute-to-attribute connections*: These connections are used when two attribute values are to have the same value. When one attribute changes, the attribute at the other end of the connection is also changed.

- *Event-to-attribute connections*: This allows an attribute to be changed when a specific event is triggered. Parameters will likely need to be added to the connection to provide the value that the attribute should be set to.

- *Event-to-action connections*: This is used to invoke a part's action when a specified event occurs. It is common for these connections to require parameters also. Any parameters that need to be passed to the part subscribing to the event notification must be explicitly passed. That is, there are no implicit parameters passed.

- *Event-to-member function connections*: This is similar to an event-to-action connection but a nonpublic member function can be called. This is used in VisualAge C++ and the member function called must also be on the part providing the notification. Therefore, this notification is internal to a part.

- *Attribute-to-action connections*: When an attribute changes, an action is invoked. This is similar to an event-to-action connection but the attribute value is passed by default to the action. This parameter can be overridden if required.

- *Attribute-to-member function connections*: When an attribute is changed, a member function on the part containing the attribute is invoked.

- *Custom logic connections*: These connections can be triggered by attribute changes or events. When the trigger occurs, custom code is executed. The custom code is written in the target programming language. This can be useful when many actions must be taken when an event occurs. For example, when a "Clear" pushbutton is pressed, all entryfields on the view should be cleared. This one custom logic connection can replace all the simpler connections to each entryfield. The custom logic would be a function that made calls to each entryfield. This reduces the connection overhead and the clutter in the composition editor.

- *Parameter connections*: These connections are used to supply parameters where appropriate to the above kinds of connections.

By making connections within and between the visual and nonvisual parts, the logic of the application is specified to the visual programming tool.

Strengths

Using a visual programming tool can reduce the development effort required to deliver a graphical application, particularly the visual components. Most visual programming tools are shipped with a good selection of primitive visual parts that can be assembled to create composite parts. This changes the development paradigm from one of custom development to one of construction from parts. Some code will still need to be written to implement parts that are not shipped with the tool or are available from other sources.

Weaknesses

There is a considerable learning curve associated with understanding the operation of the selected tool. Time must be allocated to learning how to use the tool properly. As with any new technology, time spent learning it may impact the schedule for the first project where the tool is used and the benefits may not be manifest until subsequent projects. On the other hand, learning to use a visual programming tool may have a smaller learning curve than that posed by learning to hand code a GUI application if those skills are not available.

As most of the available tools are still fairly new, some of the features expected may not be available. For example, although VisualAge Smalltalk supports a team development environment with versioning built in, VisualAge C++ does not. This may not be as big of a problem as it may seem though. As this tool generates C++ code, the standard revision control systems can be used. But as some of the Source Code is generated from the part files, these part files are the ones that need the version management the most. Unfortunately, there is no API (e.g. from a command line) for a build process (e.g. make) to generate the code for a part. This facility would be of considerable value for a build process. In its absence, both the part files and the generated source must all be entered into a revision control system.

A visual programming tool will not likely support all GUI features provided by the underlying class library and programming language. To implement some application features, such as drag-and-drop, the developers may need to provide handwritten code.

As application complexity increases, the composition editor becomes more and more cluttered with connections. It is difficult to understand the application logic from viewing the composition editor. It can be simpler to follow logic in Source Code than in a graphical representation of the application. Here, the tool has limited benefit to the maintenance of the application.

Notation

The representation of parts within a visual programming tool is dependant on the tool being used. Generally, there is a part palette where a part type can be selected and dropped onto a composition editor through a drag and drop interface.

If the tool generates some form of Source Code, the code will follow the syntax rules for the target programming language. Any custom code that is added to the application will also follow these syntax rules.

Advice and Guidance

Using a visual programming tool can be valuable in creating both a GUI Prototype and the actual application. Although some design patterns may be implemented by the tool, completing the analysis and design of the application is outside the tool's scope and cannot be ignored. The work products described in this book are as applicable to an application developed with a visual programming tool as they are to an application developed without one.

Do not assume that programming language skills will not be required on the team when doing development with a visual programming tool. Although the tool will generate much of the code required, there will always be functionality that must be hand coded. Besides an understanding the target programming language, an understanding of the underlying class libraries is also required. For example, in VisualAge C++, the underlying class library is IBM's Open Class Library. These skills must be available to the team as a whole, though they are not required by every team member.

Although much of the code will be generated by the visual tool, there is still a need for coding standards for the code that must be manually written, and for naming conventions for classes, methods, attributes and files that the tool will generate. Each part defined through the composition editor should be named according to an agreed naming convention. Not only will this aid in reading generated code, but also these names will be visible within the composition editor when editing the part.

The VMT method (see reference below) provides some guidelines for creating composite parts. These guidelines help to keep the parts simple to understand:

- A composite part should contain no more than five to eight subparts.

- Try to keep the number of connections within a composition editor screen to twelve.

- Position connection lines to avoid line crossing whenever possible.

But keep in mind that guidelines must be adjusted to your project's goals and objectives. For instance, when designing user interfaces for expert users, there is an absolute need to reduce the number of interactions to accomplish a task. This often translates into a trade-off favoring richer (more complex) user interface panels over the need for reusable parts.

Example(s)

Following is an example of using VisualAge C++ Composition Editor to build the Logon View of the Portable-Client:

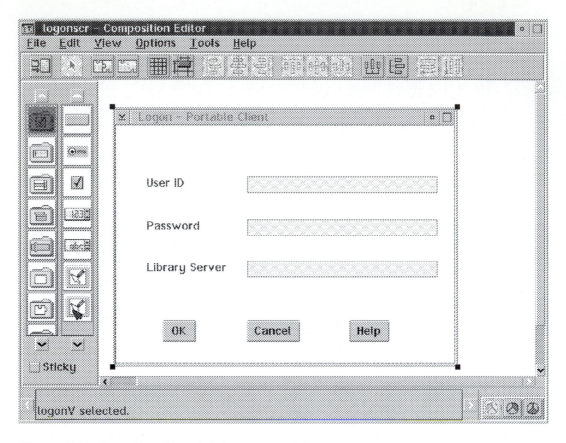

Figure 18-7. Using VisualAge C++ Composition Editor.

References

- See [IBM Corp.95] for a good overview of construction from parts in VisualAge C++.

- See [Fang94] for a description of the Visual Modeling Technique (VMT) with examples in VisualAge Smalltalk.

- For IBM's Common User Access (CUA) Guidelines, see [IBM94b].

- [Mayhew92] discusses principles and guidelines for Graphical User Interface (GUI) design in general.

18.12 PROBLEM DETERMINATION

Description

Problem Determination is the process of understanding an unintended behavior or defect in software, with the goal of changing the unintended behavior to the intended. This activity takes place mainly during the implementation phase, even though the problems might have roots in earlier phases (design for example). Problem Determination to a large degree depends on the programming languages used. Typical activities of Problem Determination are debugging, trace generation and analysis, and dump analysis.

Purpose

The primary objective is to make the software behave as intended. A secondary objective is to learn from the defect in order to look for similar problems in other parts of the software and to prevent future defects of the same kind.

Participants

The developer of the software in which the problem is occurring is often responsible for performing Problem Determination. In some organizations, function and system testers may also have some Problem Determination responsibility.

Timing

Whenever problems surface during development and testing or in the maintenance phase.

Technique

To the largest degree the techniques for Problem Determination are not unique to object-oriented programming. Problem Determination in object-oriented software differs from Problem Determination in procedural software mainly because of two reasons: the better structure of object-oriented software and the dynamic binding of object services. Data encapsulation and the packaging of services with the data they operate on, makes the understanding and observation of object-oriented software easier. The more flexible dynamic binding of code can make it harder to predict what version of code will be executed. Overall, these differences (for example between finding a problem in a C program versus in a C++ program) are much smaller than the differences in the debugging and tracing support offered by the operating system (host system versus workstation or PC) and the tools like source level debuggers.

To narrow down a problem requires experience with the programming languages used as well as with the technologies used (databases, communication protocols, and object request brokers just to name a few). We have used and observed several techniques for Problem Determination. Which technique is used depends on the particular situation as well as on the preferences of the practitioner. The techniques can range from pure reliance on experience (in the following we refer to "experience with and knowledge of the programming language, the tools, the application and the domain" by simply calling it "experience") on one extreme to systematic hard work on the other, with several mixtures in between:

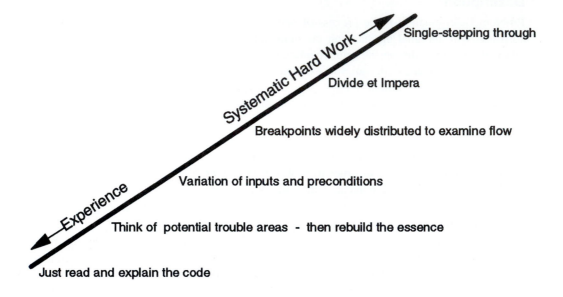

Figure 18-8. *Various Problem Determination Techniques.*

Just and explain the code: This Problem Determination technique, if it succeeds at all, is usually the fastest method, because it would not require the building of a special debug version of the executable nor the manual intervention required by setting break points, single-stepping through code, and other such labor-intensive techniques.

Try to explain the code instead of just reading it. When you explain the code you are forced to better understand it. Therefore, explaining the code to yourself is more effective than just reading. Explaining to somebody else who will ask questions is even more effective. The most important question is "What unexpected event might occur in this operation here"? After a while you will anticipate the next questions and ask them yourself.

Experience is needed to quickly focus your review of the code on those areas that might be critical. To imagine what could have gone wrong requires some intuition and, more importantly, lots of experience. It can happen that you read and explain the code without detecting the problem. If you can not think of areas to review, or if you did not spot anything, there are still the following more systematic techniques at your disposal.

Think of areas that might be problematic: Think of potential trouble areas and try to build the simplest possible model having a similar unintended behavior.

With enough knowledge and observation of the software, you might be able to suspect what the problem area is from the very beginning of Problem Determination. In this case it is often the most efficient strategy to model the situation with a very small example ignoring all unnecessary detail. If the small model demonstrates the same undesirable behavior, then the necessary analysis can be bounded by this simple example.

The advantage of this method is especially obvious when the problem is a defect in a software or language system that you reused. In this case the example is also the best means for you to communicate the defect to the owner of the reused part or system.

Some initial considerations in trying to guess where the problem areas are include:

- Are there any major constructs or services that you have never used before?
- Are there areas where you were not comfortable with the documentation of the function that you used?
- Are there usage circumstances in your software that might be rather unexpected? Could a developer of a service you use be surprised by the way you use it?

This technique does require a lot of experience and knowledge of the internals. Therefore, it can happen that you do not have any idea where to start. If that is the case, you might have better luck with one of the following techniques.

Vary the input and watch the variation of behavior: Sometimes you will have observed that the problem is data dependent. In this case you might be able to bound the problem at least partially by using variations on the input data and observing the corresponding variations of the behavior.

To apply this method requires experience in order to devise the most effective variations and to draw conclusions from the observations.

Use widely distributed breakpoints to monitor the flow: This technique is applicable when, with the problem at hand, you lack experience and inspiration. You do not really need a suspicion or hypothesis to get started. While you proceed on this more labor intensive route, you may begin to develop some questions and ideas that will help you to succeed. For every breakpoint that is reached, ask following questions:

- Did you expect the execution to proceed to this point at this time?
- Did the program flow skip a part that you had expected to execute?
- Is the call stack (the chain of callers) at every breakpoint as you expected?
- Are the objects involved at the states that you would expect here?

Typical examples where this technique is the first choice are situations where the initialization of objects might contribute to the problem. To examine the initialization the obvious spots for breakpoints are the entry and exit of the initialization functions (the constructors in C++). In general the entries and exits of functions ("member functions" in C++, "methods" in most other languages) are the first choices to set breakpoints. Breakpoints in functions that are called very often result in more observations. If the main execution path is part of your source code then you might want to set breakpoints there to follow the overall flow. If the main execution path is outside of your source code this is not an option. You encounter the latter when you build your software from individual object services that are called by frameworks.

A variant of this technique that is supported by some debugging tools is to set a monitor for certain data and have the execution halted the data get changed.

In multithreading situations this technique is usually not feasible. Then you must use traces instead of break points. This is not as handy as the use of an interactive debugger of course.

Divide and Conquer: Another technique that can be used with limited experience and in the absence of any hints or suspicions, is to divide and conquer the program. This technique is often used to narrow down spurious abends. Sometimes with C++, this technique is even used to find out compile time errors that are impossible to understand given the compiler messages (missing or excessive parentheses or curly braces for example).

Try to remove or disable about half of the function of your program and check whether the problem persists. If it does, try to disable another half of the remaining part. If it does not, continue with the previously disabled part. Continue until the problem is narrowed down sufficiently. This recursive division of the remaining part into two parts of nearly half size is well known from the "Binary Search" algorithm for fast lookup in sorted tables.

While very simple to perform, this technique is often not feasible because it might not be possible to reasonably run a part of the program without the rest. Also it is usually less effective with object-oriented programming because, in contrast to procedural programming, functions are often too short to be worthwhile for splitting. If the "Divide and Conquer" technique can not be applied, probably the closest alternative is the monitoring of the program at widely distributed breakpoints.

Single-step through: The most desperate method of Problem Determination is to step through the execution in single steps. Since this single step execution is very time consuming, you should try to limit it to a small portion of the program and possibly combine it with one of the other techniques. Set a breakpoint well before the occurrence of the problem and start the step execution. While you do so, check for the following:

- Examine the call stack and the state and data of the objects used (local variables, instance variables).
- Is everything as you would expect?

If you reach the occurrence of the problem and did not observe anything unexpected, restart the process at an earlier point in the execution.

The disadvantages of this method are that it can not be used in a multithreading situation and that it might take considerable time to perform. The advantage is that usually it will help you to generate ideas and suspicions while you go. Once you got an inspiration, leave the step-by-step execution and apply one of the other techniques described above.

In multithreading situations or in time critical software, where it is not possible to arbitrarily halt execution, you can use traces instead, that record important or all execution steps and important intermediate results.

Strengths

Problem Determination is a mandatory step for defect removal.

Weaknesses

Problem Determination is not a process that creates something novel. Rather it consists mainly of understanding an existing situation. This can be as exciting as watching an espionage movie. However entertaining Problem Determination might be, applying good discipline to prevent most of this activity and the need for it is in general more cost effective.

Notation

Usually the result of Problem Determination is a problem solution that consists of a change to the implementation. We recommend that the problem itself be recorded to support the goal of defect prevention and causal analysis. Recording can best be done using free text. How to organize the problem information for retrieval and evaluation will not be discussed here.

Advice and Guidance

We have described several individual techniques for problem determination. You can use these techniques in isolation as well as in a combination. For example you can start with "Divide and Conquer" to narrow down the problem to a smaller area that you then investigate with distributed breakpoints or code reviewing.

The techniques require different levels of experience and knowledge and involve different amounts of manual processing. Usually you will resort to the more labor intensive techniques only if a less laborious technique would not work well in your situation. In most cases the mere reviewing of the code is the technique that requires the least work and the most experience. If it can be done it is preferable.

If you spend hours or days in applying the above described Problem Determination techniques and in the end find out that you could have determined and solved the problem with much simpler actions, this will be a frustrating experience. Therefore, consider the following easy actions first. If you are using a compiled language:

- Make sure that you installed the latest updates to your compiler and class libraries if the symptoms could be explained by problems in these components.

- Make sure that you have rebuilt everything. This also needs to be done for template instantiations in case you used C++ templates.

- Carefully examine all compiler warnings. You always should do this, but this sometimes is forgotten.

With languages that offer pointers (C++, but not Smalltalk or Java) you can encounter problems caused by an overwriting of storage. With languages that do not have garbage collection (C++, but not Smalltalk or Java) you can encounter "storage leaks."

Overwritten Storage: One of the most common problems in C++ is that storage gets overwritten unintentionally. This happens mainly if data are written using pointers that are not pointing properly. These problems are especially nasty because the symptoms often lead to areas far away from the area that is causing the trouble. To narrow down these problems is an art that Marshall Cline and Greg Lomow called "Voodoo Debugging" in their book on C++ frequently asked questions [Cline95].

Besides using breakpoints and examining data and objects at the breaks a storage debugger can help here. Storage debuggers can be interactive, such as "HeapView" in the "IBM CSet++" C++ development environment on AIX, or they can write traces to standard error, such as the storage debugger in "IBM VisualAge C++" on OS/2.

Storage Leaks: A storage leak occurs when storage is never given back after it is no longer in use. These leaks can best be detected using a storage debugger.

Note: We have seen C++ projects that did not check for storage leaks. Storage leaks might exist unnoticed until the software is executed repeatedly for a long time. Therefore it is necessary to check for storage leaks explicitly as part of the standard testing.

References

We are not aware of any books that discuss Problem Determination in great detail. Several books on programming languages such as [Cline95] give some hints.

19.0 Reuse Techniques

Reuse is a very broad topic, spanning all aspects of software development. A primary goal of reuse is to minimize the overall effort one has to expend in developing software. We would like to be able to develop software by assembling as many existing assets (parts, components, class libraries, frameworks, et cetera) as we can and gluing them together to meet our specific needs. To accomplish that, reusable pieces need to exist or be built. This section discusses some issues regarding using and building assets.

The following topics are addressed in this section:

- Reuse in General

- Using Assets

- Making Project Parts Reusable

- Creating Truly Reusable Assets

The Reuse in General section provides some definitions for various reuse terms, categorizes the different types of reusable assets, covers the motivation for building and reusing components and discusses other general reuse topics.

The Using Assets section talks about developing a solution based on existing assets. For most projects, which are typically time constrained, using assets is a more likely scenario than creating reusable assets. But even the use of existing assets requires careful planning and preparation to use an existing asset successfully.

The section, Making Project Parts Reusable, covers issues surrounding the creation of parts as part of your development effort. These kinds of parts would typically be intended for informal reuse. That is reuse by the project team or closely associated project teams with some modification.

The final section, Creating Truly Reusable Assets, discusses the effort required to create assets that have extremely high quality and that can be reused without modification. This is the highest level of reuse we will discuss and the one that provides for the most benefit.

19.1 REUSE IN GENERAL

Description

Reuse is typically defined as the use of an asset in the solution of different problems or different versions of a problem. Our usage expands this definition beyond the implied direct reuse of an asset to include indirect reuse and the reuse of ideas and knowledge.

In the software world, object technology is the most effective enabler of reuse though reuse is by no means limited to reuse of object-oriented code. As a recurring activity, reuse can help to eliminate effort in every phase and activity. For example, a development team might be able to eliminate the development of entire subsystems by reusing code, or they might be able to use an existing Users Guide to save time considering appropriate format and coverage.

The following questions are used to further explore this topic.

What are reusable assets?

Reusable assets are elements that are used directly on a project. They include, but are not limited to, code (objects, class libraries, frameworks), models, tools, environments, and test cases. These assets are typically a primary focus, because they can help project teams to avoid particular work activities.

Experience assets are information about projects or how to perform projects. They include, but are not limited to, project summaries, design patterns, technical reports, lessons learned, and methods. These assets help project teams to be more productive in their work activities but don't necessarily allow the complete avoidance of activities.

How are Black Box and White Box reuse different?

"Black Box reuse" is done when a part can be used without having to modify its internals. It is accessed through a well defined interface. Black Box provides for "delegation of ownership" and "raising the level of abstraction."

1. Delegating ownership simply means that a reusable asset is designed, implemented, maintained, and supported by an owner. This frees the project team to use, but not worry about, the asset.
2. Raising the level of abstraction gives you intellectual leverage. This allows you to use terminology and thought processes that are rooted in the problem domain without the need to understand implementation details. For example, a reusable asset for banking applications may have methods like "deposit" and "withdraw" of a reusable "Account" class. A developer can readily understand and invoke these methods without understanding the technical details of what the method does.

Reusable class libraries are examples of black box reuse.

"White Box reuse" is done when the user of an asset needs to understand and possibly modify it. There are some savings in doing this, but this really implies that a new (though similar) part is being created and it sacrifices the benefits of "delegation of ownership." This form of reuse might better be called "recycling." For example reusing a design falls into this category. The result is a unique version of the design that has to be implemented, tested, and maintained.

[Karlsson95] introduces *"Grey Box reuse"* that is conceptually between White Box and Black Box reuse. It consists of reusing a component by applying a *few* changes to the component to customize it. Such adaptations of an asset can include renaming variables, changing method calls, and changing an implementation part. Inheritance can be used to modify the component definition or behavior by overloading. The negative side is that any changes to the code means that there is a new maintenance "load." Grey box reuse does not achieve work elimination in downstream processes such as testing, documentation, and maintenance.

What are the kinds of reusable assets?

Classes are one of the most basic reusable entities. They yield the benefits of abstraction and information hiding by encapsulating function and data and by providing a controlled access to the internal structures.

Class libraries or frameworks provide the most benefit, because they allow the reuse of code in a complete form. With this kind of reusable part, true "delegation of ownership" and "black box reuse" are attainable.

Parts are software components which have been packaged using component technology such as OpenDoc. The benefits are comparable to the benefits for using frameworks or class libraries.

Other Reusable Assets Things other than classes, class libraries, frameworks, and parts can also be reused, typically in a "white box reuse" sense. For example, an analysis work product might be reused, but it will not provide a clear boundary encapsulating a major part. In fact the user will have to understand the entire work product to be able to do design and produce code from the analysis work product.

Design patterns are a very reusable form of design artifacts. To make such work products reusable they have to follow the same construction criteria as listed for reusable libraries.

What Types of Reuse are there?

"Reuse" usually implies the *acquisition and modification of some artifact*. That is, a developer has a particular set of work products to produce, some of which are executables and some of which are things such as design or documents. The developer, knowing that he or a friend developed something similar to what is now needed, finds it, determines what changes are needed, does the modifications, and takes ownership of this new entity.

Today, the emphasis on *reusing components without modifying them* is growing. A successful, complete transition to this model requires that an adequate set of supported reusable assets be available, easy to find, and easy to understand and use.

Another view of reuse is the *purposeful creation of assets to meet a determined market need*. Most assets are developed as the result of a specific project that is being done to meet some specific market need. The asset may have value outside the project for which it was developed but additional work on it and additional experiences in using it are likely necessary before it can be considered to be generally reusable in a particular market niche.

In this book we make a distinction between creating reusable assets during a development activity and ***creating assets in a separate parts center***. In practice it often happens that an asset is developed as part of a development project initially but that later someone is found to build a generalized version of the asset.

Purpose

Reuse can lead to work avoidance and the following benefits:

- Improved time to market (some function already exists, so its development time is eliminated)

- Reduced development costs that can increase profitability

- Increased customer satisfaction with improved quality and reduced cycle times between project enhancements

Participants

Anyone involved in the development of software can be involved in reuse activities. But different reuse aspects have to be addressed and carried out at different levels in the organization:

- Standards and architectures should be set at the highest level of an organization and should be cooperatively supported across organizations

- Project managers must evaluate whether the product can be built while using or creating certain reusable assets

- Reuse experts should help technical leaders to find and understand existing assets

- Specific people might be assigned to develop reusable assets as some kind of parts center

- Project teams look for reuse opportunities throughout all phases of development

Timing

Reuse is an ongoing activity. It affects everybody at all times. Reuse needs to be planned for at the very earliest stages of the project and attention to reuse continues throughout the rest of the development cycle.

Technique

There are usually two approaches for building a repository of reusable classes:

1. Install a reuse repository and collect reusable classes.
   This approach will inevitably lead to a flea market of parts: It is easy to fill, you "can" find everything, but, what you find may be an "unknown" quantity in function, quality, and support.
2. Define an Architecture for a given domain and build a complete, designed class library. This approach requires investment but is the best way to build a well structured repository of parts.

An Architecture must cover the following areas:

- Business domains
- System Architectures (for example, client/server, data stores, system types, networking structures)
- Language environments (Smalltalk, C++, selection of class libraries, et cetera)
- The form of the asset

Management aspects

Outside the responsibilities of a single project or parts center, there are important aspects that need to be addressed:

- Understanding markets and targeting selected segments for reuse
- Understanding the market's customers and opportunities and using the available resources for creation and use of assets in the market segment
- Doing architecture definition and domain engineering for reuse across a market or multiple markets
- Developing guidelines for creating reusable assets
- Providing infrastructure elements such as reuse repository development and operations

Strengths

Improved time to market, reduced development cost, higher profit margins, and increased customer satisfaction.

Weaknesses

Reuse requires time, planning, investment and commitment. If immediate results are expected, disappointment will surely follow.

Notation

In the various areas of reuse you will use different notations: Free form text for process descriptions and notations as described in this book for different development work products.

Advice and Guidance

- Management commitment is critical. Reuse always needs some form of investment (time and money) which can only be made from management.

- Don't expect quick results without prior significant investment.

References

- [Korson92] define criteria for reusable class libraries.

- Martin Griss describes in [Griss93] an approach developed at Hewlett-Packard that is similar to the notion of "application foundries."

- [Karlsson95] is a book on all aspects of reuse. Its contents are based on the results of a European Community ESPRIT project on "Reuse Based on Object-Oriented Techniques" (REBOOT).

- [Tracz95] gives a good overview of a number of reuse related topics.

19.2 USING ASSETS

Description

The concept of using assets is very straightforward. It involves the inclusion of artifacts into a system that were not produced as part of that development effort. That seems very simple, but in fact does involve some very careful planning and preparation by a development team. They must find assets that fit into their design and not try to fit the design into an existing asset. The assets should be simple to use and ideally require no modification to be used. This is not always a simple feat.

Purpose

Reusing software is generally accepted to be the best way to improve productivity in software development.

Participants

Anybody developing software. This includes normal software developers and can also include architects, information developers, and other software personnel.

Timing

Activities related to using assets occur throughout the development cycle and particularly in the early phases of development. The next section will explain this in more detail.

Technique

The goal is to make design decisions that will allow you to reuse existing parts.

The basic steps for reuse during projects follow a pattern. This pattern can be viewed as a template to apply at each phase and increment during the development process. The template below is taken from [Karlsson95] and has the following elements:

- Identification of component requirements
- Searching
- Plan
- Understanding
- Investigating possible adaptations
- Selection
- Adaptation - Integration
- Reporting

Figure 19-1. *Pattern for Using Assets.*

This pattern can be followed for a single work product. It could help in producing a specific work product more quickly.

But instead of focusing on a single work product (a plan or a model, for example) it would be better to reuse a complete component or subsystem of the product or solution being built. This will increase productivity across the entire project, since it can help the avoidance of portions of work in several development phases. For example, by reusing existing class libraries time can be saved during implementation, design, test, and maintenance.

In the following list we will step though the pattern assuming a project desires to reuse a complete component or class library.

The early phases in the life cycle are the most critical for reuse. It is here where decisions are made that enable the reuse of existing frameworks or other products.

- **Identification of component requirements:** In early planning and analysis stages requirements must be identified.

- **Searching:** In early planning and analysis the development team must become familiar with the available resources. They should look for assets or raw material that has potential.

- **Plan:** Using an asset generally requires effort to be expended. This can include efforts for understanding an asset or for negotiating usage and support with the asset owner.

- **Understanding:** Reusable assets should provide documentation that tell about function, constraints, or usage prerequisites of the asset. This must be studied and understood. Use a prototype or a "depth-first cycle" with the assets that are candidates for being used and organize education about the assets.

- **Investigating possible adaptations:** "Adaptation" here addresses two areas:

  1. *Adapting the reused asset*. It would be nice to do "black box reuse." But often changes are needed. It would be nice if the owner of the asset would make the changes but, if not, the project team might have to consider modifying the asset themselves.
  2. *Adapting the System Architecture*. To be able to use an asset the project's System Architecture might have to change.

- **Selection:** Select the asset that will best fit project needs.

- **Adaptation/Integration:** During design there are some particularly important aspects:

  - *Architecture:* Define an Architecture which follows an existing Architecture. When doing design or defining the Architecture a close look is needed at the capabilities and Architecture of an asset. For example, verification is needed to see if it fits the architectural decisions the project team has made or those decisions may need to be modified to better support the chosen libraries (though it is certainly far better if the parts meet the architecture). Typically the assets "dictate" how you can use them. For example, they will have made design and implementation choices that the user will simply have to accept.
  - *Subsystem Model:* Split the overall system into subsystems where subsystems match existing subsystems. Note that a subsystem here is a boundary for a framework/asset.

- **Reporting:** Provide feedback to the owner of the asset about the project's usage.

Strengths

- Using assets improves productivity and quality.

- When assets are reused "expert knowledge" that may help the performance and quality of the application is reused as well.

Weaknesses

- Reusing an asset adds dependencies to a project. The team using the asset relies on the availability of and support for the asset.

- Any "generally" reusable asset will force a compromise, meaning you will accept not getting the optimal solution for your specific usage.

Advice and Guidance

- Class libraries (or in a special form, frameworks) are a collection of logically related classes. Class libraries are considered the best form of "reusable software." Stand alone classes, or code fragments are far less beneficial. See "Interoperability and Class Library Design" in Section Class Library Evaluation Criteria for more discussion on this.

- The biggest danger is to find out very late that the asset has severe restrictions that will force the user to move to a different library or to abandon the reuse effort all together. The documentation may not completely list all assumptions or limitations. Time must be invested before a commitment to an asset is made to reduce this risk. How much time is spent should be directly related to the severity of the possible risk. Use the class library in a prototype or at least in early increments.

- During prototyping and coding it is important that you use the asset correctly. Assets may offer choices on usage.

- Expect that assets will change or may have to be replaced. Prepare for such changes.

- If a part that "almost" fits a project's needs, can not be used, then an effort should be made to get these assets improved by their owner. It is counterproductive to create many similar assets.

- Though everyone should have reuse in mind, it is advisable that one person be assigned responsibility for reuse. This person can search for reusable parts, identify parts that can be made reusable, and build and maintain the Reuse Plan (see Section 10.8, Reuse Plan).

- Using assets in a "white box" fashion by copying and changing the source, follows the same pattern. The main differences are:
  - Information that allows the understanding and modification of the asset is needed.
  - Copying, changing, and maintaining the asset will not generate the same savings that "black box reuse" would.

References

- C Set ++ Class Library references [IBM93] describe the class libraries shipped with VisualAge C++.

- [Karlsson95] discusses developing with reusable assets.

- [Poulin93] discusses efforts to define the savings gained by reuse.

19.3 MAKING PROJECT PARTS REUSABLE

Description

This section describes what a normal project can do to make portions of its deliverable functions available as assets that can be used in the future for informal ("white box") reuse by the project team or closely related project teams. Normal projects will usually not be able to create and support high quality reusable assets as described in Section 19.4, Creating Truly Reusable Assets. However, the effort to make parts of a system reusable for the future within the same project can be small. In fact most activities just require the practice of good software engineering principles that are of immediate benefit to maintainability and extensibility of the project.

Purpose

Ideally, one would like to have access to assets that are reusable with little or no effort required by the user to change them. If such assets are not available, it would be good to be able to get raw material that is at least reusable in some form. Such material is not only valuable when used in projects but is also very important for use in building high quality reusable assets.

Participants

The project manager and the project architects will have the biggest roles to play. The project manager allocates resources and the architect makes the technical decisions that enable reuse. It is likely that other members of the project team will participate as designers, implementers, or users of the assets.

Timing

Activities related to reusing parts happen during all development stages. It must be planned for early in the project and executed throughout the analysis, design, and implementation phases.

Technique

Making a part reusable involves:

- **Partitioning**: meaning that a part needs to be "extractable" from its context. A class, a class library, or a piece of a model needs to be isolated from its context and should have few dependencies on other parts.
- **Generalization**: meaning that a part needs to be applicable outside the context it was developed for. This includes abstraction (of terms and functions) and additions (of functions). Subsystems should be independent and should use syntax and semantics that are not tied to the current problem.

The following describes a pattern for making parts reusable:

- **Identification of component requirements:** Find requirements that go beyond the requirements of the current project. This should be both functional requirements (additional capabilities) and Nonfunctional Requirements (additional platforms supported, additional flexibilities, use of different kinds of middleware, et cetera).

- **Searching:** Look around for reusable parts or usable raw material. Ideally parts that can be reused (perhaps with some adaptations) will be found so that we will not have to create another part. It should be the first goal to reuse or improve an existing part.

- **Understanding:** Gain an understanding of reusable parts and of architectures and related parts. This is necessary to ensure that what is created can be used (after some generalizing effort) in a different context.

- **Generalization:** Possibly the only real additional effort that is beyond the activities that any project following good software engineering principles would do. Additional requirements that allow the generalization of portions of the solution should be sought.

- **Adaptation/Integration:** Design is the most important phase for reuse, particularly the creation of the following two work products:

  - *Architecture:* When defining the Architecture one should be looking closely at the capabilities and architecture of other assets. Define an Architecture that follows an existing Architecture.
  - *Subsystem Model:* Split the overall system into subsystems where subsystems match existing subsystems or the boundary of existing assets.

- **Reporting:** Communicate that there is material to be made reusable.

Strengths

- Efforts to make portions of the project reusable are good project management, analysis, and design practices. The project can benefit greatly from that effort later in the project cycle or in future releases of the product.

- Other projects will be able to use material that was developed by this real project.

Weaknesses

- The project manager and architects have to make sure that there will be a good, well-documented system architecture. Such efforts often get neglected.

- There may be the misconception that parts are directly reusable without any modifications. It must be clear that to make something truly reusable, additional effort will be needed.

Advice and Guidance

- Before developing a work product that is similar to an existing part make an effort to get this part improved by its owner. If necessary, provide resources such as money or people. It is counterproductive to create many similar parts.

- See Section 13.2, System Architecture and Section 13.5, Subsystem Model for advice on how to build a good architecture and to create subsystems.

- Base your architecture on existing architectures.

- Consider requirements that go beyond the concrete requirements of your project. These should include in particular Nonfunctional Requirements such as additional platforms, additional flexibility, and potential support of other middleware or compilers.

- Make sure all essential work products are carefully created. This will allow the next project to use this material more efficiently.

References

- [Schafer94] discusses key business and technical issues regarding reuse.

19.4 CREATING TRULY REUSABLE ASSETS

Description

Truly reusable assets are components that can be used without modification by other project development teams. These are called "black box" assets and are superior to the reusable parts, discussed in the previous section, in that you need not know anything about the implementation details. This section will discuss how they are created.

Purpose

Reuse is generally accepted to be the best way to improve productivity. The less a reusable asset needs to be modified by the user, the better the user's productivity.

Participants

Theoretically there are two sources for assets:

- Product-related projects
- Parts Centers (stand-alone or in cooperation with normal projects)

Experience shows that in normal projects there is little time for the additional effort required to build truly reusable assets. Creating truly reusable assets is expensive. These costs are seldom justifiable by a single project. The recommended source for truly reusable assets are teams of people with the sole mission to build such assets. These teams are often called parts centers.

This does not mean that normal projects should forget about making their code reusable. A project can work together with a parts center to make portions of their product reusable. If this is not possible, then a project should apply good software engineering practices that will make sure that work products are designed and built so they may be the raw material for the creation of a truly reusable asset.

Timing

There are several possibilities:

- **Build assets after first developing some applications:** Key parts of existing applications are collected and truly reusable assets are built based on these parts.
    - *Advantage:* Asset fragments may be collected and used as a base for a fully reusable asset allowing the reuse of previous work and experience.
    - *Disadvantage:* It is a large effort to turn "fragments" into a truly reusable asset. There are unrealistic expectations about the effort needed to make a truly reusable asset. Experience shows that making code reusable takes three times longer than to develop than "normal" code. This means you have to expect to add twice as much time to make the code truly reusable as was spent to build it.

- **Build assets before applications:** For example, assets are built on strategic decisions. When you know you need to develop client/server solutions, it may be a good idea to invest in client/server services.
    - *Advantage:* Applications can be built with the truly reusable assets.
    - *Disadvantage:* It takes additional effort to obtain real experiences and new requirements through uses of assets by projects.

- **Parts centers build assets in cooperation with real projects:** Instead of building assets "for the shelf" people from the parts center build reusable assets in cooperation with a real project.
    - *Advantage:* Synergy between a parts center and the project. Members of the project and the parts center work together to build an asset that is useful and truly reusable.

- *Disadvantage:* There is a danger that the asset will be too project specific. There may be pressure to meet the project's requirements and to neglect the abstraction that is necessary to make the asset truly reusable.

  The project Schedule may not allow time for the thorough analysis and design which is needed to make a component reusable.

In practice a combination of all three variants is possible. A parts center may start investigations and work on domain modeling and architecture based on existing material. Concrete design and implementation can be done with a real project.

Technique

An asset has to be constructed like any other product. All phases and activities of a normal project life cycle are applicable with perhaps additional emphasis on:

- Business Case
- Gathering requirements
- Domain Modeling
- Generalization
- Architecture
- Stability of the APIs
- Documentation.

Strengths

- Investments in assets will pay off in future development through improved productivity and quality.

Weaknesses

- Lack of standards and coordination to ensure interoperability between assets.
- Need for additional up front investment in parts centers or their equivalent.

Notation

Assets are just work products as defined in this book. For each work product the appropriate notation will be used.

Advice and Guidance

- Have a separate group (parts center) perform this activity. As suggested above only a parts center is likely to have the resources, skills, and mission to build a strong asset.

- Asset development needs to be driven as a business:

  - Development of parts has to support an organization's business strategy in some way.
  - Based on that strategy there should be a targeted asset portfolio.

- Just like for any other product, assets should be built when there is a "business justification."

- Do a domain assessment when considering building reusable parts. During a domain assessment decide for which domain you should build reusable assets. Aspects that influence the decision include stability of the domain, strategic importance of the domain, understanding of domain, and the availability of existing material in this domain that might be a useful starting point for assets.

- Do not expect to get good assets as a side effect of your normal product cycle.

- Use existing experiences and raw material.

  - Include past projects, users, documentation, et cetera
  - This is a source for additional requirements
  - This makes possible the building of a more stable architecture

- Before you decide to write a framework, you should write an application in the domain first. Newcomers to object technology or the domain should not start their first project by trying to write a framework. Experience and domain knowledge is critical before tackling a generic solution.

- Since assets are used in other products their interfaces and function have to be very stable. This requires that special effort be spent in analysis and design.

- Class libraries (or, in a special form, frameworks) are a collection of logically related classes. Class libraries are considered the best form of "reusable software." Stand-alone classes or code fragments are far less beneficial.

- Good assets should have certain attributes including:

  - Specification
  - Consistency
  - Usability
  - Power
  - Performance
  - Robustness
  - Extensibility
  - Domain Coverage
  - Genericity
  - Completeness
  - Support

- Assets can be built incrementally with early releases providing opportunities for rapid deployment and feedback.

- Provide support as you would for a product. To a large extent a truly reusable asset is like a product. And just as for a product, there has to be available support, ranging from usage support such as help desks, to maintenance such as upgrades to new compiler levels or bug fixes. It is not sufficient to spend the short-term effort building assets. There has to be long-term commitment to supporting the assets as well.

Class Library Evaluation Criteria

The following is a list of attributes and characteristics of good class libraries. This list was developed based on experiences in developing and using class libraries in IBM and from [Korson92].

The attributes and characteristics are intended to represent criteria that reflect the overall quality of a class library. They have been selected and defined independent of the function of the library.

Specification

Capabilities are summarized independent of implementation

The specification of the capabilities of a library is one of the most significant attributes affecting reuse. Each capability must be specified completely to allow use without reference to the actual code. Each capability specification should summarize what each unit does and its expected inputs and outputs without burdening the user with the details of the internal implementation.

Consistency

Follows rule of least surprise

For a library to exhibit consistency, it must be homogeneous in its structure, especially as it is presented to the user (both the program developer and the end user of the product). All declarations should be of the same form. All invocations of capabilities should be the same except where, by nature of their function, they have to be different. If the library has the feel of being conceived out of one mind with care to its form, it is probably consistent.

Usability

Knowledge gained can be easily used and extended

For a library to exhibit high usability requires attention to both its presentation and its form. Presentation affects initial learning and application. Form affects the ability to extend base knowledge.

The presentation is related to the documentation, including "help" capabilities, but also includes the initial level of knowledge necessary to use the library, the ability to integrate its resources into programs, and any other support for working with the library.

Usability includes the initial use of the library, the ease of extension of the library, the library's interoperability with other resources, and its ease of assimilation into the program using it.

Power

Supplies significant leverage

The leverage associated with the use of libraries is related to the amount of capability that is used divided by the effort to use it. As an example, the number of instructions used from the library units divided by the number of instructions necessary to be written to use each unit is an indication. This can be called physical leverage. The savings associated with the general distance between the abstraction and the implementation in complexity will be called the logical leverage. In the sense of logical leverage, a library that supplies simple support for complex environments (for example, shielding the user from the underlying structure as in Use Interface enabling routines) has high logical leverage.

In summary, leverage is a measure of effort saved divided by effort expended for each use.

Performance

Uses assets well, affords alternate trade-offs

Performance is more than efficiency of execution path. It includes utilization of all resources from time to memory to input and output.

Since not all uses of a library's resources require the same trade-off on utilization of various resources, the ability to substitute various implementations for the same abstraction is very valuable. The abstraction focuses on what the unit does; the implementation selects a specific trade-off in utilization of that capability.

Robustness

No unexpected behavior

For a library to exhibit robustness, there should be no unexpected behavior. Each capability supplied should work on its specified set of data values. This includes such attributes as being total functions (for example, it is defined across the entire range of possible input values) or partial functions where the illegal input values are explicitly specified. An example of a partial function is a square root routine that is only specified on positive numbers. An example of a related total function is a square root routine that, in addition to the square root (when the input is positive), returns a code: BadInput for negative input numbers, GoodInput for positive input numbers.

Extensibility

Additional capabilities can be easily added

A library's extensibility is associated with how easily a user can extend the capabilities originally supplied, or add new implementations for supplied capabilities. This also may include how easily the library's capabilities may be assimilated into programs in the sense that when the supplied capabilities are not quite what is required, how easily can the gap between them and the program's needs be closed through mechanisms such as inheritance or wrapping.

Domain Coverage

Covers the domain completely and consistently in knowledge standard to domain

A library should be specific to a particular area of application: a domain. It should package knowledge regarding that domain to allow implementers to build systems at the abstract application layer without undue reference to the details below. The intent is to supply, in a complete and consistent manner across the domain, capabilities that approximate a very high-level problem-specific implementation language for that domain.

Areas that are not covered or inconsistencies in the level of coverage require the user to learn the implementation level details associated with the domain and decrease the effectiveness of the library. An example is a library to support development of banking applications that omits capabilities to manage accounts.

Customizability

Parameterized abstractions

Libraries should supply generalizations that can be refined by the user. Such generalizations may be packaged in a variety of ways, but the property of binding details to generalities will be evaluated as the attribute of customizability.

For a library to exhibit customizability it must be easily adaptable to a variety of system and application environments. It should package the common information and parameterize the uncommon.

Completeness

Complete abstractions

Complete abstractions are necessary to ensure that the leverage supplied by a library can be exploited. An example of an incomplete abstraction would be a data structure that supplied capabilities to add, delete, and search the structure but none to reset the structure to empty. To implement this capability when needed, the user has two choices, neither of which are good: Implement it in the supplied capabilities, thereby losing efficiency or modify the library unit to add the missing capability, thereby losing leverage.

For a library to exhibit completeness, all units must be total abstractions with no missing common or universally useful capabilities.

Support

Support structure in place

For a library to exhibit support, there must be a responsibility and strategy in place to support each user. This support must include maintenance of errors at a minimum, with such things as enhancements and efficiency upgrades being desirable.

For a library to exhibit good support, it must treat each user as a customer.

Example(s)

IBM's Open Class Library is just one example of a truly reusable asset.

References

- Development guidelines can be found in:

    - Taligent's Guide to Designing Programs [Goldsmith94].
    - The IBM Open Class Library documentation as an example for documentation style [IBM93].

- Class Library Design Guidelines can be found in [Karlsson95] discusses development for reuse.

Part 5. *Video Store Case Study*

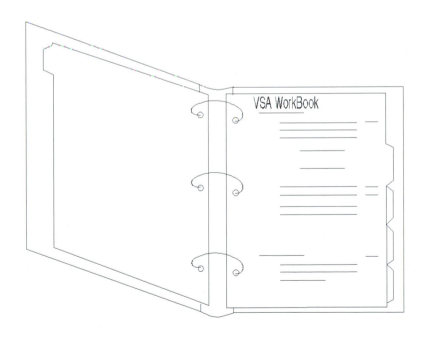

20.0 Introduction to the Case Study

This section presents a case study that is included to illustrate what work products and a project workbook might look like for a project using the approach presented in this book.

We knew that including such a case study could be very useful in strengthening the points made in this text, but there was much discussion on whether we should include a subset of a project workbook from a real project or whether to use an invented example.

While there is much to be said in favor of using a real-world example, there are also problems: Many of the domains are difficult to understand unless the reader has a background in the domain; or they are proprietary (our clients would not wish their workbooks to be made publicly available).

We opted for an invented example, in general, and the Video Store problem in particular, because:

- It is a domain that can be readily understood by most readers, as most persons working in software development have some familiarity with renting videos (or a Public Library which is a very similar domain).

- The authors have used this problem as a teaching example during numerous analysis and design workshops and have found great success with it.

- The problem contains some of the situations that are encountered in real-world applications:

  - There is some confusion between physical and conceptual objects (such as the physical video cassette and the conceptual record about the video that is kept in the store's files).

  - The distinction between a video movie and a copy of the video represents a challenge during analysis modeling. [15]

So while this is not a perfect case study, we trust that it will improve the user's understanding of what the work products discussed in this book really are, improve understanding of what is meant by a project workbook, and enhance understanding of the object-oriented software development life cycle presented in this book.

---

[15] Also known as the *type* problem, for example: Product and Product Type, Course and Course Type, et cetera.

20.1 CASE STUDY ASSUMPTIONS

There is an assumption that the Video Store problem is a 9-month project from requirements gathering to product delivery.

Another assumption is that the project is using an iterative and incremental process as
advocated in this book.

There is also an assumption that a fictional software company called ACME has been
contracted to develop the Video Store Administration (VSA) software system for a chain of
video rental stores.

With those assumptions in mind, the material included in this Case Study would be
representative of that produced at the end of 2 months of work on the project.

20.2 CASE STUDY FORMAT

We've chosen to structure this case study as if it were an actual project workbook, see
Figure 20-1. That is, it is our view of what a project team that is using this approach
would have in their project workbook two months into their development cycle.

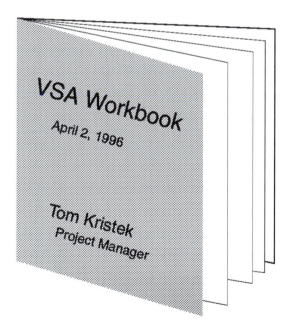

Figure 20-1. Video Store Administration (VSA) Workbook.

So, you will see work products from the various life cycle phases (Requirements, Analysis, User Interface Model, Design, Implementation, Testing, and Appendix) as they would look in the project workbook of the Video Store development team.

Within many of the workbook sections you will see boxes labeled **Author's Commentary**. Within these boxes, we present "editorial comments" on things such as why the team has done the things it has done, or why they haven't done things that maybe they should have done, or other advice and guidance that will aid the reader in understanding what we are presenting.

You will note that not all work products described in this book are contained in this Case Study. This is because not all work products are produced in every project and many are not needed in this one.

We have also chosen to present the Common Work Product Attributes as an appendix of this Case Study rather than presenting these data within each work product. This is done in order to focus attention on the content of the work products rather than the form. We are also seeing more clients who use Lotus Databases to store project workbooks, and they typically are keeping the common attributes information separate from the technical content of each work product.

21.0 Case Study: Requirements Work Products

21.1 PROBLEM STATEMENT

> **Author's Commentary**
>
> The Problem Statement in this case comes directly from the customer and was not written by the software development team that is implementing the project.
>
> The Video Store management team also included "Project Objectives" and "Success Criteria" in the Problem Statement.

The "Express Video" chain is having great success in the marketplace.

However, we are encountering growing pains and serious problems with customer satisfaction. Since the video rental business is very competitive, our company's management is concerned. We have begun to record their major concerns. These concerns, which we consider our Problem Statement, include:

1. We only have two categories of films: *classics* and *new releases* and this has led to numerous customer complaints about not being able to find titles on the shelves.

2. The current inventory system was written in dBase by a summer student. It is hard to maintain and does not allow for the definition of new categories.

3. Our clerks are overworked and are unable to effectively help the customers locate titles. Profit margins are such that we cannot hire additional staff.

These problems are compounded by the fact that we would like to vigorously expand the number of stores that we operate in the near future, but, we are afraid to do so under the current mode of operation.

The company has a vision of eliminating these problems through exploitation of the *Information Highway*. We would like to see functions such as:

- A customer kiosk to allow a customer to query the video catalogue

- A reservation system

- More subject matter categories

- Customer access from home

21.1.1 Project Objectives

- Improve customer satisfaction

- Continue to grow market share

- Help customers (and staff) to know what videos are currently available.

21.1.2 Success Criteria

- It is anticipated that rentals should increase by about ten percent once the system is in place.

  Statistics will be gathered prior to implementation for comparison with a similar period after the new system is installed.

- Improved employee satisfaction.

  It hasn't yet been determined if an employee survey will be conducted to measure the impact of the system

21.1.3 Video Store Requirements

┌─── **Author's Commentary** ───────────────────────────────────

These requirements are a free form list that the development team has received directly from its customer, the Video Store's management. These requirements, along with interviews performed by the development team will be used to create the Use Case Model and the list of Nonfunctional Requirements.

└──

In addition to the Problem Statement the following requirements have been identified by our store managers.

System

- The system must be able to administrate the rental of video movies. This must be done in a user-friendly way.

- The system should have a graphical user interface, with icons.

- The clerk should be able to find out if a movie is in, rented, missing (meaning it is lost), not carried by this store, or not carried by this store but available at another store.

- The system should be able to print a list of all rentals that are overdue by more than a specified number of days. The default value should be one day. For example, a movie that was supposed to be returned yesterday is one day late. The list should be sorted with the longest overdue movies first.

- The system should be able to print a list of all customers who have overdue movies, which movies they are, and how overdue they are.

- The system should be able to collect some statistics:

  - How many times a movie has been rented.
  - What are the most popular rentals.
  - A list of "poor performers," i.e. movies that are not getting enough rentals to justify the shelf space.

Customers

- The system must be able to handle several kinds of customers. This includes adding, updating, and removing them from the system.
- Customers get a discount if they buy a membership. They don't need to show an identification when they rent a movie, but then they must be able to show their membership card.
- Nonmembers may rent videos, but they must pay a deposit of $60.00 per movie. They must show an identification at time of rental.
- A customer who has not returned a movie that is due will not be allowed to rent additional movies until the overdue movies are returned and any late charges are paid.

Rentals

- Each rental agreement can handle several movies, but only one date of return.
- A customer can have several rental agreements at the same time.
- The rental agreement should contain information on who rented what movie, at what time it was rented, when it should be returned, and the amount paid.
- The system must be able to print the rental agreement for signature.
- For lost or damaged video, a fine will be charged.

Reservations

- It should be possible to extend the system such that members can call and make reservations for movies, whether they are rented or not. If the movie is not rented, then the clerk should go out to the shelf and remove the video so that no one else can claim it. If the movie is rented, then the customer is added to the queue for that movie. When the movie is returned, the system should look up the reservations and notify a clerk to call the customer who is next on the queue.
- If a reserved video is not collected after 2 days, the reservation is canceled and a fee will be charged.
- A week after the reservation, if the video is still unavailable, a clerk apologizes (mail or phone may be used) to the Member and asks if the reservation should be maintained.

- If Member does not answer back within one week and the video is still unavailable, the reservation is canceled.
- A video cannot be reserved for some future date.
- Reservations are currently free, but a possible future change in requirements is that reservations that are canceled (other than due to nonavailability of the video) will be charged.

Customer Kiosk

- Customers should be able to browse the store's video catalogue via a kiosk in the customer floor area. This would allow for customers to make queries like "show me a list of films directed by Woody Allen" or "show me comedies in which Sharon Stone appears."

- The Kiosk could have a multimedia capability and be able to display video clips.

- A selective group of members will be allowed to access the catalogue through the Internet.

Videos

- The system must be able to handle a database of movies. This includes adding, updating, and removing them from the system.

- The system must be able to handle categories of movies; for example, action, comedy and children's movies. Each movie can only belong to one category. Each category should have an age limit. People younger than the age limit for a category will not be allowed to rent movies in that category.

- Each cassette should be marked with a bar code that contains a system-recognizable identifier for the cassette.

- Each movie has a title and a suggested rental price.

- A cassette that is already rented cannot be rented again until it is returned. A movie cassette can also be recorded as "missing."

Vendors

- The shop buys movies from vendors.

- The system must maintain a database of vendors that track information on what movies are purchased from which vendors.

- The system must be able to produce a list of vendors and how much money each one should receive per time period.

21.2 USE CASE MODEL

Note: The use cases were collected during a brainstorming session with Store Managers. They are represented in the form in which they were collected, Actor: Use Case—tuples

1. Customer rents video

2. Customer returns video

3. Customer applies for membership

4. Member reserves video

5. Member claims reserved video

6. Manager purchases video from video supplier

7. Manager or Clerk adds video to inventory

8. Manager or Clerk removes video from inventory

9. Manager reviews rental statistics

10. Manager requests list of overdue videos

11. Customer browses video catalogue

12. Manager or Clerk requests video information

13. Manager requests list of all videos on rental

14. Customer pays outstanding fees (for example, late return)

15. Customer enquires about availability of a certain title

16. Clerk shelves video

17. Clerk sells a video (removes from inventory)

18. Customer loses video

19. Manager sends rental statistics to head office

20. Manager hires Clerk

21. Clerk views customer's rental history

22. Clerk calls customer with overdue video

23. Customer reports lost membership card

24. Customer requests replacement membership card

Author's Commentary

Brainstorming sessions are useful for identifying use cases. Of course this is only the first step. The analysis team has to study each suggested use case, decide if it will be included in the Use Case Model (it may not be in scope), and, document it in detail as is shown below.

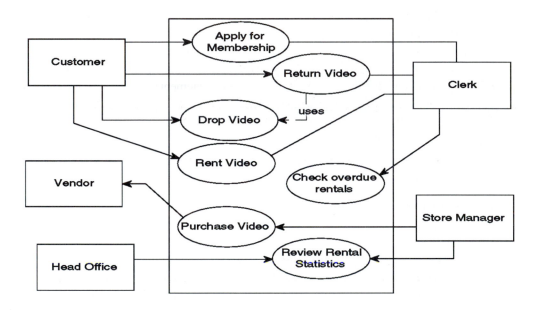

Figure 21-1. *Use Case Model.*

The center box represents the Video Store Administration (VSA) system to be constructed. Inside this box are the named use cases (ovals) that are supported by the system. The actors are represented by named rectangles outside the box. The direction of the links between actors and use cases indicates who initiates the communication.

Author's Commentary

From the list of use cases captured during the brainstorming session and the material provided by the customer (Problem Statement and requirements list) the VSA team developed a Use Case Model that is partially shown in Figure 21-1.

The team followed the use case model notation recommended in this book. An actor may be linked to many use cases, and a use case may be linked to many actors. More than one actor (or use cases) can initiate the communication. Links without an arrow indicate the existence of a nonprimary communication. For example one could think of an interface (for example, Internet) where customers could apply for membership. In that case the Clerk would not be involved or would not have a communication link with the use case. In order to defer those issues for the design phase the VSA team opted for links without arrows for all nonprimary communications.

The model expresses top-level functional requirements from the list supplied by the Video Store management (see Section 21.1, Problem Statement). For example, "Customer Rents Video" identifies a customer as the initiator of the use case and makes a statement on where the boundary of the system is.

Some sample definitions of use cases are as follows.

21.2.1 Use cases

1. Customer Rents Video

Definition: This use case involves a customer who wishes to rent a particular video. If successful, the customer will rent the video and the video store will note this fact. Rental requires validation of the customer's membership and availability of a suitable video copy.

Notes:

- Each rental agreement can handle several videos, but only one date of return.
- A customer can have several rental agreements at the same time.
- The rental agreement should contain information on who rented what video, at what time it was rented, when it should be returned, and the amount paid.
- A member gets a discount.
- A customer who is not a member, pays a deposit of $60.00 per video, shows an identification, and pays full fee.
- If rental is successful, rental agreement is printed, customer signs it, and grabs video.
- A customer who has not returned a movie that is due will not be allowed to rent additional movies until the overdue movies are returned and any late charges are paid.

- A cassette that is already rented cannot be rented again until it is returned.
- The requested video may be unavailable due to outstanding reservations.
- If unavailable, the customer should be offered the possibility of reserving the video.
- Membership validation may be initiated by scanning a membership card or by manual entry of personal details such as name and address.

Actors:

- Clerk
- Customer
- Member
- Nonmember

2. **Customer returns video**

Definition: The action of returning a rented video. For lost or damaged video, a fine will be charged. Members may drop off the video cassette in a drop box outside the store, or hand it to a clerk. The clerk marks the video as returned and the cassette is returned to the shelf.

Notes:

- If member and late, will have to pay a penalty for overdue period.
- If nonmember, deposit (minus penalty for overdue period) is returned.

Actors:

- Clerk
- Customer

3. **Customer applies for membership**

Definition: This use case involves a customer who wants to become a member. The customer provides all the information required and must produce an identification, such as a driver's license or passport. The customer pays the initial fee. Club membership is local to a store. The customer is added to this store's member list. The customer gets a membership card.

Notes:

- Check if the customer has ever been a member and in that case, access his/her past record.
- Check if the customer is a member in another store (in the chain).

Actors:

- Clerk
- Customer

4. **Member Reserves Video**

Definition: This use case involves a customer who wishes to reserve a particular video. If successful, a reservation for that video will be made in the name of this customer and the customer will subsequently be informed when a copy of this video becomes available. The customer will then have a period of time (2 days) in which to rent the video before the copy reverts to being generally available.

If the movie is not rented, then the clerk should go out to the shelf and remove the video so that no one else can claim it. If the movie is rented, then the customer is added to the queue for that movie. When the movie is returned, the system should look up the reservations and notify a clerk to call the customer who is next on the queue.

Notes:

- Making a reservation involves membership validation.
- A week after the reservation, if the video is still unavailable, a clerk apologizes (mail or phone may be used) to the member and asks if the reservation should be maintained.
- If the member does not answer back within one week and the video is still unavailable, the reservation is canceled.
- All reservations are "current." That is, a video cannot be reserved for some future date.
- Reservations are currently free, but a possible future change in requirements is that reservations that are canceled (other than due to nonavailability of the video) will be charged.

Actors:

- Clerk
- Manager

5. **Member claims reserved video**

   Definition: After being advised that the reserved video has become available, the member collects the video within 2 days.

   Notes:

   - See Use Case `Customer rents video`

   Actors:

   - Clerk
   - Manager

6. **Manager purchases video**

   Definition: The manager purchases a set of video copies from a vendor.

   Notes:

- New vendors are added to the store's vendor list.
- For each copy received: see Use Case `Manager or Clerk adds video to inventory`.

Actors:

- Manager
- Vendor

7. **Manager or Clerk adds video to inventory**

Definition: This use case involves a Manager or Clerk who will add a recently received video copy to the inventory. Each cassette is marked with a bar code that contains a system-recognizable identifier for the cassette.

Notes:

- The system must be able to handle categories of videos (i.e., action, comedy, and children's movies).
- Each category should have an age limit. People younger than the age limit for a category will not be allowed to rent movies in that category.
- Each video can only belong to one category.
- Each video has a title and a suggested rental price.

Actors:

- Clerk
- Manager

8. **Manager or Clerk removes video from inventory**

Definition: This use case involves a Manager or Clerk who will remove a video from the inventory. Removal of video copies and video movies must be approved by the store manager. Broken, disposed, or missing tapes should be removed from the system. The manager may decide to remove movies that are "poor performers."

Notes:

- A video movie should not be removed from the system as long as there are video copies on the shelves.

Actors:

- Clerk
- Manager

9. **Manager requests rental statistics**

Definition: This use case involves the manager who wants to obtain statistical information about movies. The manager may want to know how often a video has been rented or to obtain a report of the most popular rentals. These statistics will help the manager to decide whether to purchase more copies of the most popular rentals and/or to remove "poor performers."

Notes:

- These statistics will have to be displayed/printed in a way to help the manager to easily make decisions on which one to add and which one to remove.

Actors:

- Manager

10. **Manager requests list of overdue videos**

Definition: This use case involves the manager who wants to obtain a list of rentals that are overdue in order to validate sending of reminders to customers.

Notes:

- The system should be able to print a list of all rentals that are overdue by more than a specified number of days.
- The default value of this parameter is one day, but the manager can ask the system to produce reports for different values of this parameter.
- The list should be sorted with the longest overdue video first.
- The system should be able to print a list of all customers who have overdue videos, which videos they are, and how many days they are overdue.

Actors:

- Manager

11. **Customer browses video catalogue**

Definition: This use case involves a customer who wishes to browse the video catalogue. This would allow for customers to make queries such as "show me a list of films directed by Woody Allen after 1990 of which you have copies."

Notes:

- A customer kiosk in the floor area is under consideration.
- A selective group of members will be allowed to access the catalogue through the Internet.

Actors:

- Customer
- Member

12. **Manager or Clerk requests video information**

Definition: This use case involves a Manager or Clerk who wishes to obtain information about a video. This would allow clerks or the manager to find out if a movie is in, rented, missing (meaning it is lost), not carried by this store, or not carried by this store but available at another store.

Notes:

- The system should be able to show information for a particular tape, for a movie, or for all copies of that movie.

Actors:

- Clerk
- Manager

13. **Manager requests a list of all videos on rental**

Definition: This use case involves the manager who wishes to obtain a list of all videos on rental. This request is usually done at the end of each day.

Notes:

The system should be able to display or print this list at manager's request.

Actors:

Manager

21.2.2 Actors

The following is a partial list of actors identified so far:

Clerk: A Clerk answers customer questions, checks out videos rented by Customers, and checks in videos when they are returned. The Clerk will also maintain the inventory by adding new arrivals and removing lost, broken or 'poor performer' videos with the approval of the Manager. The Clerk is also responsible for making the calls to Customers for overdue videos.

Customer: A person the store does business with. A customer can become a member if he/she wants to use these services on a regular basis and at a member's rate. A customer may also choose to remain a nonmember and occasionally use these services at the full rate.

Manager: The Manager is in charge of tracking the performance of the VideoStore and its Inventory. The Manager makes the decisions on which videos to add or remove and how to price and promote them by setting various pricing policies.

Member: A customer who has a membership card. Only members can reserve videos. Becoming a member requires a driver's license or a passport and a credit card (Amex, Visa, Diners Club, or Mastercard) in order to receive membership.

Nonmember: A customer who does not have a membership card. Nonmembers cannot reserve videos. Becoming a member requires a driver's license or a passport and a credit card (Amex, Visa, Diners Club, or Mastercard) in order to receive membership.

Vendor: A person or company the store purchases videos from.

21.3 NONFUNCTIONAL REQUIREMENTS

The following Nonfunctional Requirements have been identified:

- Maximum of eight checkout workstations per store, each connected to a database server
- One kiosk with multimedia capabilities (display video clips) per store
- Internet access for selected customers
- Up to 100,000 titles
- Stores have dial-up link to head office
- Up to 12 months rental information kept in store
- Up to 50 staff per store
- Up to 5,000 transactions per day
- Less than 20 seconds per transaction (locate, retrieve, handle payment)
- As of 3/96, the chain consists of 11 stores. By year-end 1996, it will be 19 stores and by year-end 1997, over 40. Currently all existing and planned stores are located within 50 miles of the head office. Before expanding beyond this distance, the owner wants the Head Office support system in place.
- An intuitive graphical user interface (GUI) is required for all workstations and kiosks
- Fast (under 20 seconds) lookup of reservations for a particular customer (members may phone the store and ask for the status of their reservations)
- Fast lookup of reservation for a particular movie

Additionally, the following Nonfunctional Requirements have been identified from the project Quality Assurance Plan:

- The system must be available 100 percent of the time during normal store operating hours.

- The system should be able to be used error-free by a noncomputer literate clerk after 2 hours of training with the system.

- A clerk using this system should be able to process a customer in no more than 3 minutes.

Author's Commentary

   This list was developed by the project team from the original Problem Statement and list of requirements from the customer, the project Quality Assurance Plan, and interviews of customer representatives. The list was then reviewed with the customer, updated appropriately, and finalized.

21.4 PRIORITIZED REQUIREMENTS

For each requirement below, its urgency and importance uses the following scale:

Importance   1 (vital), 2 (important), 3 (would be nice)

Urgency   1 (immediate need), 2 (pressing), 3 (can wait)

Table 21-1. *Prioritized Requirements.*

Requirement	Importance	Urgency
Customer rents video	1	1
Customer returns video	1	2
Customer applies for membership	1	2
Member reserves video	2	3
Member claims reserved video	2	3
Manager purchases video from video supplier	3	3
Customer browses video catalogue	3	3
Manager sends rental statistics to head office	2	3

Author's Commentary

   The Prioritized Requirements list above represents input from the store managers. It was written as part of the process of requirements gathering.

21.5 BUSINESS CASE

> **Author's Commentary**
>
> This project is a service engagement for a specific customer, so there will be no traditional business case as would have been done for a product.
>
> The customer will have found a reason to go out and have a service company work on a solution for his problem. The justification for the customer could be the owner's concern about the reliability of his current system. In addition, he may see this as a springboard for his long-term expansion plans. A make vs. buy study may have been undertaken that concluded that no off-the-shelf system was available that met the client's needs.
>
> The service organization would have done a bid on the solution. Depending on the business model of the service provider (and what the customer is looking for), this bid could have been based on "time and material," or it could be a fixed-price offering. For a fixed-price offering the service provider could try to recover all costs plus make a profit, or the service provider could use this engagement to build up some assets that could be used in similar future projects.
>
> To make it simple we assume that the project will not try to make a profit (but rather build up experience) but will try to recover all costs. And the bid will be a fixed-price offer.

Costs for the overall project.

Development effort	$834,000 (for 78 person months)
Expenses for external training and consulting	$50,000
Expenses for additional hardware and software	$50,000
Expenses for 35 test videos and 2 VCRs	$2000
Support after installation for one year	$50,000
Contingency	$50,000
Total	$1.036 million

The effort is based on the Resource Plan. The bid to the customer will be made at some amount over this total cost.

21.6 ACCEPTANCE PLAN

The criteria that this application must meet are:

- Usability

  - The application must be easily used by a store clerk requiring no more than 2 hours of training to accomplish basic video rental, return, and purchase.
  - Advanced functions such as clearing fines, making reservations, and the like will be done by more experienced clerks.
  - Customers should not be able to crash the Customer Kiosk.

- Performance

  - Requirements must be met for volumes as outlined in the Nonfunctional Requirements.

- Reliability

  - While 100 percent integrity is not a requirement, the system should be designed to not lose any information.

- Availability

  - The clerk system must have 100 percent availability during business hours.
  - The customer kiosk should be available 80 percent of the time during business hours.
  - The manager's workstation should be available 60 percent of the time It is anticipated that most of its functions will be performed outside of normal store business hours.

- Backup/Recovery

  - The current plan is for a weekly backup of the inventory and a daily backup of the day's rentals.

The customer is responsible for final definition and execution of the Acceptance Plan. ACME may provide staff to assist with this, provided they are at arm's-length from the application development team.

Author's Commentary

Acceptance criteria is crucial of course, and that's what is reflected here. However; the really important piece is how the system will be tested and measured against those criteria. The project team has left that to the imagination by saying it is the responsibility of the customer. That is true of course, but it might be possible to guess that the customer will want to do some trial run testing of the system during hours that the stores are closed with a variety of experienced and new clerks acting as guinea pigs. They would probably want to simulate their real environment by having "pretend customers" participate. Or, better yet, ask real customers to participate and offer them free rentals as payment for their help.

This would allow assessment of the usability and performance of the system against the criteria, and at least some insight into how the system is meeting its reliability and availability criteria.

Time has been built into the schedule for an acceptance testing period.

22.0 Case Study: Project Management Work Products

22.1 PROJECT WORKBOOK OUTLINE

The following list shows the outline structure of the VSA's Project Workbook:

- Requirements
  - Problem Statement
  - Use Case Model
  - Nonfunctional Requirements
  - Prioritized Requirements
  - Business Case
  - Acceptance Plan
- Project Management
  - Project Workbook Outline
  - Intended Development Process
  - Resource Plan
  - Schedule
  - Release Plan
  - Quality Assurance Plan
  - Risk Management Plan
  - Reuse Plan
  - Test Plan
  - Metrics
  - Dependencies
  - Issues
- Analysis
  - Guidelines
  - Object Model
  - Scenarios
  - Object Interaction Diagrams
  - State Models
  - Class Descriptions
- User Interface Model
  - User Interface Guidelines
  - Screen Flows
  - Screen Layout
  - User Interface Prototype
- Design
  - Guidelines

- System Architecture
- Application Programming Interfaces
- Target Environment
- Subsystem Model
- Object Model
- Scenarios
- Object Interaction Diagrams
- State Models
- Class Descriptions
- Rejected Design Alternatives
- Implementation
  - Coding Guidelines
  - Physical Package Plan
  - Development Environment
  - Source Code
- Testing
  - Test Cases
- Appendix
  - Glossary
  - Historical Work Products

22.2 INTENDED DEVELOPMENT PROCESS

- Use the workbook and basic techniques described in the book *Developing Object-Oriented Software: An Experience-Based Approach.*

- Use a combination of a waterfall and an iterative and incremental process. Requirements gathering, initial project planning, analysis, and architectural definition phases are performed in a waterfall manner, followed by a series of incremental development cycles. The work products of these initial phases, like all others, are subject to iterative improvement during the life cycle of the project

> **Author's Commentary**
>
> This is a critical component to successful object-oriented development processes and to our approach.

- Use conventional estimation techniques to provide initial project sizing estimates. From the end of the analysis phase, estimate total classes (including utility and graphical user interface) in the ratio of one (1) analysis class to six (6) final implementation classes. Use an initial estimate of 1 person-month per implementation class for all project phases through to delivery. (This is an estimate for experts. For people with intermediate skills use 2 person-months per implementation class; for novices use 3 person-months per implementation class.) Use these figures to update the original estimate of project size.

> **Author's Commentary**
>
> Metrics and estimating object-oriented projects remain a fuzzy area and this team has no real object-oriented development experience on which to base their planning. So, they wisely use what they do have; their past experience with projects that were not object-oriented. Most projects can get by doing this.

- The incremental part of the development process follows a seven-month release schedule. Each release consists of three eight-week increments, followed by a four-week system test cycle, culminating in the release.

- Each increment has three distinct phases of two weeks each:

  - Design and interface development
  - Implementation and documentation
  - Integration, final verification test (FVT), metric data analysis, process adjustment, and plan adjustment

  Further, the activities associated with the first two phases include a week of developing the work products followed by a week of review and iterative rework. As an estimate, a person can design, implement, and document the solutions to five scenarios throughout the two-week cycle (including the review and iteration).

- The very first development increment follows a depth-first approach consisting of a series of four minicycles of two weeks' duration each. The goals of these minicycles are to establish the Development Environment, to give all team members a taste of all development phases, and to establish the Architecture.

> **Author's Commentary**
>
> In real life don't forget to factor education time into your schedule if you have no object-oriented experienced people on your team.
>
> The first increment should probably have less technical content than subsequent increments as it will more than likely be the slowest increment as the team adjusts to the use of an object-oriented approach to software development.
>
> The depth-first technique, described in Section 17.1, A Depth-First Approach to Software Development, is a good way to establish the team's confidence and ability with object-oriented software development. In addition to the benefits stated in the team's Intended Development Process work product, it can also allow an early deliverable (which in some cases can be useful in keeping a project funded), and it allows the opportunity to sanity check estimates and adjust them as needed.

22.3 RESOURCE PLAN

- ACME Software has been selected as the prime contractor for this project. The client has no IT shop and currently has no plans for one.

- The client will provide our development team access to domain expertise.

- System operations will be performed by store management and staff.

- ACME hardware will be used for development. ACME will provide the resulting system on a server connected to point-of-sale terminals.

- The project is estimated to utilize 87 person-months to complete.

- The development effort budget is $834,000 for the project.

- The target availability date is November 15, 1996.

22.3.1 Planned Staff:

Table 22-1. *Project Team.*

Staff member	Initials	Project Role(s)
Tom Kristek	TK	Project Manager
George Yuan	GY	Architect, Designer, Team Leader
Dave Livesey	DL	Analyst, Designer, Developer, Tester
Tom Guinane	TG	Analyst, Designer, Developer, Tester
Frank Seliger	FS	Analyst, Architect, Designer
John Barry	JB	Analyst, Designer
Thomas Wappler	TW	Designer, Developer, Tester
Guillermo Lois	GL	Developer, Tester, Librarian
Tom Bridge	TB	Developer
Paul Fertig	PF	Developer
Daniel Hu	DH	Developer

Author's Commentary

Note that most staff members have multiple roles. This is typical in small projects. In larger projects, the Resource Plan may be split up across several resource owners and coordinated by the project manager.

22.3.2 Staff Availability

Team members are scheduled to be on the project for the following time periods:

Staff Member	1996											
	Jan	Feb	Mar	Apr	May	Jun	Jul	Aug	Sep	Oct	Nov	Dec
TK												
GY												
DL												
TG												
GL												
FS												
JB												
TW												
TB												
PF												
DH												

Author's Commentary

The staff availability schedule above is at a very high level for this project. Many project management tools provide a finer grain tracking for each staff member that allows planning for vacation, education, et cetera. Some of these tools also hook directly to the schedule and other charts so that impact analysis can be done should staff interruptions occur.

22.4 SCHEDULE

Activities	# Weeks	1996											
		Jan	Feb	Mar	Apr	May	Jun	Jul	Aug	Sep	Oct	Nov	Dec
Initiate	2	▭											
Staff	2	▭											
Tool/Methodology	2		▭										
Train	4		▭										
Requirements	6		▭										
Project Kickoff				△									
Analysis	4				▭								
Analysis Model Review					△								
Architecture	2				▭								
Application Design	1				▭								
Build Cycle 1	8					▭							
Iteration 1	3					▭							
Iteration2	3						▭						
Iteration3	2						▭						
Build Cycle 2	9							▭					
Iteration 1	4						▭						
Iteration 2	2							▭					
Iteration 3	3								▭				
Build Cycle 3	7									▭			
Iteration 1	3								▭				
Iteration 2	4									▭			
System Test	3										▭		
Install and Train	1											▭	
Acceptance Test	1											▭	
Product Acceptance	1												△

Legend:

▭ projected date range
▬ actual date range
▬ completed actual date range
△ projected single date
♦ actual single date

Author's Commentary

The first four items of this schedule (Initiate, Staff, Tool/Methodology, Train) are outside of the actual product development life cycle that we discuss in this book, but they are critical nonetheless.

Projects need to be aware of the need to do each of these things and need to have them reflected in their overall project Schedule.

Initiate: This deals with the recognition that there is a project to begin, negotiating with the customer, identifying the organization that will be doing the work, identifying the manager that will be running the project, et cetera.

Staff: This deals with developing the initial Resource Plans (how many people? what skills? et cetera), identifying positions, and filling those positions. In many projects, it will be impossible to complete all staffing as neatly as is shown here, but it is important to get an initial core of leadership on the project up front, and to have a detailed Resource Plan that addresses when other positions need to be filled in order to maintain the plans and schedules.

Tool/Methodology: This is in recognition that there will need to be time spent up front (especially with a first time object-oriented project) in determining what development approach will be followed and what tools will be used. Education can then be built around these decisions and they also can dictate the project management and technical approaches that will be followed for the rest of the life cycle.

Again, it is likely that some refinements of these selections will take place throughout the early stages of the project. However, some important decisions (on process or on the use of class libraries for example) which affect the scheduling approach or the design approach should be made as early as possible.

Train: Recognize, that in this case, some training in object-oriented analysis, design, the IBM Open Class Library, IBM's System Object Model (SOM), and Distributed System Object Model (DSOM) technologies, and C++ are needed by certain members of the team.

22.5 RELEASE PLAN

This project has been divided into three releases. Currently, only Release 1 is firmly planned.

- Release 1, which is scheduled to be released 8 months after completion of the requirements phase) will address:

    - All "stand-alone" requirements except for customer kiosk multimedia support. This means all functions related to the operation of one store will be included.

- Release 2, which would tentatively be released 12 months after Release 1, currently is targeted to include:

  - The Head Office support system.

  - Multiple store support system.

- Release 3, which would tentatively be released 12 months after Release 2, currently is targeted to include:

  - Customer Kiosk multimedia support.

Author's Commentary

This is obviously a simplistic Release Plan. The more detailed the plans are in terms of exact function that will be delivered, the better. Each functional item needs to be weighed against the team's ability to develop it, test it, and perform all other related quality and support efforts.

22.6 QUALITY ASSURANCE PLAN

The development team and the customer working together have established a Quality Assurance Plan, as described in this section.

22.6.1 General Quality Goals

The following are the key quality goals for the project:

- **Availability:** The system must be available 100 percent of the time during normal store operating hours

- **Code Quality:** The system must be shipped with no more than 0.5 Total Valid Unique Problems per thousand lines of code (KLOC). Code in this case is shipped source instructions.

- **Usability:** The system should be able to be used error-free by a noncomputer literate clerk after 2 hours of training with the system.

- **Performance:** A clerk using this system should be able to process a customer in no more than 3 minutes

---
Author's Commentary

In this case, these goals come directly from customer requirements.

22.6.2 Validation and Tracking

The customer and the development team have decided on the following approach for validating and tracking the adherence to the Quality Assurance Plan and its stated goals.

- **Work Product Validation:** During all phases of development, work products will be validated per the advice and guidance prescribed in this book. Formal reviews, to which the customer will be invited, will be held to perform this validation.

   At the end of the initial Analysis phase, an analysis model review will be scheduled. This will involve bringing in a senior ACME consultant who is not a member of the development team (someone who is arm's length and who has not directly participated in the project), to lead a review of the analysis work products.

Author's Commentary

   The agenda for such a review will normally consist of walking through the Object Model with the analysis team and reviewing selective Object Interaction Diagrams.

   The focus of such a review is both semantic and syntactic—you want to ensure that the domain is modeled correctly (i.e. the content is a true reflection of the users' needs) and that the models say what is meant (e.g. aggregation is used correctly).

- **Problem Severity:** Each problem will be recorded and assigned a severity from one (crashes system) to five (extremely minor). All problems will be assigned an owner and will have to be fixed within a designated amount of time. All severity 1, 2, 3, and 4 problems must be fixed before delivery of the system to the customer.

- **Causal Analysis:** Each Severity 1 and 2 problem will be analyzed by the development team and reviewed with the customer. The emphasis will be on finding and fixing any global problems with the process or the requirements that may lead to errors.

- **Quality Reviews:** Meetings will take place weekly between the customer and the development team (management and technical leads) to review progress in the project and all aspects of the quality plan and the progress toward achieving the overall quality goals.

- **Test Plan:** A Test Plan, described elsewhere, will be created and implemented.

22.6.3 Defect Removal

A project Defect Removal Model has been created. This has been reviewed with, and approved by, the customer.

Previous project development experiences indicate that there will be 50 Defects per thousand lines of shipped source instructions (KLOC) discovered during the life of this project. This is based on historical data and it, along with an understanding of the development process and quality goals, has led to the development of the Defect Removal Model that follows. Each figure represents the number of valid defects that are expected to be found and eliminated at each phase of the development cycle. These represent an accumulation of errors found in various iterations. For example, a problem found at design time is counted in the design number regardless of whether it was found during iteration 1 or iteration 2 or later.

```
        Requirements:   3.0 / KLOC
            Analysis:  18.0 / KLOC
              Design:  11.0 / KLOC
      Implementation:   7.5 / KLOC
       Function Test:   6.0 / KLOC
         System Test:   4.0 / KLOC
 Remaining in product:   0.5 / KLOC
```

Author's Commentary

Don't read too much into this please. This defect removal model is made up. It is fairly reflective of a business as usual defect model and would have been based directly on the development group's prior experiences with non-OO projects.   As is expected with a heavy emphasis on analysis and design (and reviews of those work products), the error removal is weighted toward "front-end" steps. But, problems can and will be introduced/removed at the other steps in the life cycle as well.

Expressing error rates in terms of lines of code is acceptable in this C++ project. A Smalltalk effort might prefer something like errors per function point.

During the weekly quality reviews with the customer, the number of actual errors found will be compared to this model. Any significant deviation from the model will be analyzed and any action necessary to assure that project will attain its overall quality goals will be taken.

22.6.4 "Global" Quality Aspects

The following decisions have been made between the customer and the development team in order to ensure the overall quality of the project.

- **Customer involvement:** This project is aimed at a particular customer with a particular, and mostly firm, set of requirements. The customer will be involved in the validation of requirements (Use Case Model), Nonfunctional Requirements, Schedule, and this Quality Assurance Plan. The customer will also provide clerks for early testing and validation of early iterations of the project.

- **Process:** Both the customer and the development team have agreed that the use of object technology and the approach presented in this book will provide the basis for developing a high quality, easy-to-maintain system.

Author's Commentary

As with many first time object-oriented projects, the overall quality approach, including error estimates, taken by this development team are based on its business as usual historical data. They have wisely not assumed that using object technology will bring any significant reduction in the overall error rate that is used in the Defect Removal Model. They do believe, however, that the use of object technology and this approach will allow them to identify and remove a significant number of errors early in the development cycle and will allow them to fix errors more efficiently than in the past.

They are also strongly focused on validating work products formally and analyzing and fixing the causes of any critical errors.

Their focus on customer involvement from the requirements phase through the testing of the product also gives them confidence that they will deliver the product the customer wants. And it is this that is their key quality measurement.

22.7 RISK MANAGEMENT PLAN

The risks we have currently identified are:

1. **Usability might not be adequate for unskilled users**

   - **Description**—There is a concern as to how easy the system will be to use for the store clerks who do not have extensive computer training.
   - **Owner**—GY.
   - **Deadline**—07/31/96.
   - **Likelihood of occurrence**—high.

- **Cost of occurrence (without applying strategy)**—large, as it may cause a major redesign in the user interface and possibly in other areas as well.
- **Cost of applying strategy**—1 person-month for developing a user interface prototype and running a test.
- **Cost of occurrence (when strategy is applied)**—low, as feedback on usability early in the development process will not cause major problems.
- **Priority**—high.
- **Management Strategy**—Develop a user interface prototype.

2. **Performance may not be adequate**

- **Description**—There are some Nonfunctional Requirements on performance. Early in the development cycle we need to verify that the Architecture is such that these requirements can be met.
- **Owner**—GY.
- **Deadline**—06/15/96.
- **Likelihood of occurrence**—medium.
- **Cost of occurrence (without applying strategy)**—high, as improving performance will most likely require changes in the Architecture, which would cause changes in the design and code.
- **Cost of applying strategy** - 0.25 person month for a stress test to simulate a high load situation.
- **Cost of occurrence (when strategy is applied)**—medium, as feedback on performance early in the development will not cause major problems, although some of the design and code may have to be redone.
- **Priority**—high.
- **Management Strategy**—Select performance critical scenarios for Build Cycle 1 and include a stress test as well.

Author's Commentary

The project has identified two risks (so far) that both could be addressed in separate prototypes: one to simulate the user interface and one to verify the Architecture for performance.

To verify usability, a special user interface prototype will be built.

Rather than developing a performance prototype, the VSA team decided to use the first "driver" to verify some of the performance aspects. This is a reasonable decision because, performance tests should be as "real" as possible.

22.8 REUSE PLAN

1. **Reused Assets:**

   - **Open Class:** The project will use the class libraries that are shipped with VisualAge C++ (Open Class).
     Effort: Three members of the development team need training for the use of the class libraries early in the project, so that design can be done with those class libraries in mind. This will include a one-week class and we must allow some time for the "learning curve." One member of the team already has some experience; we hope that the remaining people will be able to learn enough "on the job."

     > **Author's Commentary**
     >
     > The project has probably made a compromise by not training all people that have no experience with Open Class. This may not be optimal but is not uncommon. At least it was recognized that it is important to train some people on these class libraries in order to avoid problems during design and implementation.

     Justification: Rewriting graphical user interface classes or collection classes would destroy the Business Case for the project.

   - **DSOM:** Distribution will be done through DSOM in a future release.
     Effort: Two members of the team need training for SOM/DSOM. This will include a one week class and we must allow some time for the "learning curve." There is no experience with SOM/DSOM in the team, but we hope to get some help from (or through) consultants or colleagues in other projects. This is not critical since SOM/DSOM will not be used in this release, but the team has decided to build up some skills soon to be able to influence the design in this release.
     Justification: Rewriting distribution services would destroy the Business Case for the project.

     > **Author's Commentary**
     >
     > Note that the team "hopes" to get help from consultants (or other people). This is a risk and a dependency that need to be addressed properly.

   - **n-n relationship class:** We are using and modifying a piece of code from another project. The code implements n...n relationships. We have adapted this code to "reservations" and will do the same for "rentals" in the next increment.
     Effort: There will be only minimal effort involved in learning this class. There is some impact on our design, because we adapted the design to the piece of code we wanted to reuse.

Justification: there will be only small savings by using the design and code of this class, but since there are no significant costs involved in learning and adapting the code and no future dependencies on its owner, there will still be savings of several person days.

- **Application specific reusable parts:** After a brief survey, we couldn't find any reusable parts in the application domain, although we are sure that similar applications must exist.

Author's Commentary

This is a common problem. We must assume that there are similar applications built already, but we don't have time to find them. Thorough searches of resources available should really be made a priority by management, as the time spent on these searches can often yield something useful and might save a lot more time in development costs than it requires for the search.

---

2. **Future reuse opportunities:** For future releases when we are adding multimedia functions, we will have more opportunities for reuse.

3. **Building Reusable Assets:** There are two potential areas for reuse that will be looked at:

- **Expanding the application to other rental items.**
  The video store may in the future also rent video games or VCRs. The solution could be built in a way that would allow extensions such as this to be done by reusing major portions of the solution without modification.

- **Using parts of the solution for other customers.**
  Video stores or other rental stores are very common. The solution should be built so that major portions are reusable in potential future customer engagements. This would include other video store chains or other rental stores.

Due to our schedules, no major activities to support this direction are planned. But the structure of the system is such that it can be modified without a major effort to support the expansion of the application or use of parts for other applications.

Author's Commentary

This is another common problem. It would have been easy to make some parts of the solution more reusable. The parts would not be documented or tested differently, but at least some design decisions could have been made differently. Again, management should not accept such a statement if they have a genuine interest in achieving some level of reuse.

22.9 TEST PLAN

The current test plan consists of the following elements:

- At the end of each Build Cycle, user testing will be performed.

- User acceptance test criteria will need to be defined for final acceptance test.

- Test Cases based on the most common Use Cases will be used to define test scripts for use in the ACME test lab (and in store testing).

  As completion of development approaches, testing will be done in phases:

- Internal testing at ACME.

  The customer has asked us to "mock up" a store environment to test function, installation procedures, and performance. Some store staff will also be trained in the test lab.

- Off-hour testing at a selected test site store.

  Once the internal testing is complete, a test site will be selected near the ACME development site (to allow for improved on-site support). The system will then be installed and tested during off-hours (i.e. when the store is closed between midnight and 7 A.M.).

- Live testing for two weeks at the selected test site store.

  Once the off-hours testing is complete, the system will be installed, the store's staff trained and the system transferred into production.

- General roll-out to all stores.

  When no severity one or two problems remain, and 98 percent of all test cases have run successfully general roll out to all stores can occur.

22.10 METRICS

Our client is not particularly concerned about Metrics.

  We will use our normal metrics that are:

- Number of Use Cases

- Number of Scenarios at analysis and design

- Number of Object Interaction Diagrams at analysis and design

- Number of Classes at analysis, design, and implementation

- Number of Methods per class at analysis, design, and implementation

- Lines of code per class

- Error metrics (as per Quality Assurance Plan)

Author's Commentary

The team will use a simple metrics tool to provide the metrics related to the code, namely, number of classes as well as number of methods and lines of code per class. The number of OIDs can be easily obtained from the CASE tool the team is using. Only the first two metrics in their list will be collected manually. Metrics collection will take place at the end of each increment.

22.11 DEPENDENCIES

Dependency #   1

Abstract   Test environment at a video store

Explanation   For off-hour testing we need access to a video store with a complete environment including equipment that is completely set up, dummy videos, and customer databases. We also need a clerk at the site.

Responsible   Tester

Date Required   05/05/96

Tracker   Planner

History/Status   01/20/96 - contacted the customer
02/06/96 - customer confirmed availability of a store and gave a name

Dependency #   2

Abstract   Classroom and class material

Explanation   Prior to delivery and prior to the live testing we need to train the video store personnel. They are very unskilled; therefore, we need excellent training material including real hardware for hands on exercises.

Responsible   Information Developer

Date Required   09/30/96

Tracker   Planner

History/Status   01/20/96 - contacted the customer
02/06/96 - customer confirmed availability of a store and gave a name

Dependency #   3

Abstract	C++ advanced education and training for the IBM Open Class Library
Explanation	The developers have only limited C++ skills and no experience with the VisualAge Open Class Library. We need to arrange for some training.
Responsible	Developer
Date Required	03/15/96
Tracker	Planner
History/Status	01/20/96 - contacted ACME for education
Dependency #	4
Abstract	SOM/DSOM education and training
Explanation	The developers have limited knowledge of the System Object Model (SOM) and Distributed SOM (DSOM) which is being used to provide distributed support. We need to arrange for some training.
Responsible	Developer
Date Required	03/15/96
Tracker	Planner
History/Status	01/20/96 - contacted ACME for education
Dependency #	5
Abstract	Support for n-n relationship class
Explanation	We are reusing a piece of code from another project. The code implements n...n relationships. We have adapted his code to "reservations" and will do the same for "rentals" in the next increment. The dependency is that we need access to this code developer during development.
Responsible	Team Leader
Date Required	03/31/96
Tracker	Planner
History/Status	01/15/96 - contacted project manager class library owner 02/07/96 - got agreement for support during development
Dependency #	6
Abstract	Domain skills

Explanation   The architect and designer of the video store have only limited skills in the domain. None of them owns a Video Cassette Recorder (VCR). It was decided that both should get a VCR and rent at least two videos per week for the duration of the project.

Responsible   Analyst

Date Required   02/29/96

Tracker   Planner

History/Status   02/08/96 - bought two VCRs on project expenses, picked up two applications for memberships and two copies of Fanny and Alexander (one the Swedish original).

22.12 ISSUES

> **Author's Commentary**
>
> The VSA team probably keeps the issues in a database. Issues can then be sorted by status, assignee, or due date. In this section a subset of the identified issues is presented in three tables:
>
> - 22-2 contains information on Open Issues.
>
> - 22-3 contains information on Closed Business Decision Issues.
>
> - 22-4 contains information on Closed Technical Decision Issues.
>
>   For presentation reasons (in order to get one table per page), the *Activity Log* is not included in the tables.

Table 22-2. Open Issues.

Issue ID	Title	Owner	Asgn	Status	Description	Classification	Prty	Open Date	Close Date	Due Date	Action Plan	Decision
4	Customer policy	TG		U	What is policy for customers who dispute late charges?	Requirements	Low	2/15		4/6	1	
6	Reservation responsibility	DL	DL	A	How do we decide whether or not a reservation can be made (ask the video or the catalogue or the inventory)?	Design	Med	2/15		4/6		
9	Reservation request	DL	TG	A	When do we not accept a reservation request & what is the criteria?	Requirements	High	2/15		4/6	1	
14	Damaged videos	TG	TG	A	Can we repair damaged videos (or do we just trash them)? If we repair them, do we give the customer a rebate of some sort on their penalty?	Requirements	High	2/22		4/6	1*	
18	Common membership list	TW	TW	A	What are the implications of having a common membership list? This would allow for a single card to be valid at all store locations. However, this could increase costs. Leased line? More DB access?	Requirements & Design	Med	2/22		4/26	1	
20	Connections with Head Office	TB	TB	A	Who initiates connections with Head Office? Is the Head Office using LAN Distance? Or does the store dial into the Head Office? The advantage of LAN Distance is that the Head Office could manage the store's network remotely.	Design	Med	2/22		4/26	1	
23	UI standard	GL	JB	A	What user interface standards are we going to adopt?	Management	High	3/15		6/19	2	
25	Drag and drop	GL	TG	A	What is the customer's view of drag and drop on the clerk's desktop?	Requirements	Med	3/15		6/19	1	
26	Rental duration	TB	TB	A	What is rental duration (days)?	Requirements	Med	3/15		6/19	1	

Note:

Legend: A - Assign; U - Unassigned; 1 - Ask Customer; 2 - Discuss with Customer

Table 22-3. Closed Issues—Business Decisions.

Issue ID	Title	Status	Description	Classification	Prty	Owner	Asgn	Open Date	Close Date	Due Date	Action Plan	Decision
1	Video rental policy	Clsd	Who is allowed to rent videos?	Requirements	High	TG	TG	2/15	3/15	4/6	1	Only members can rent videos. However, nonmembers will be allowed to rent provided they make a deposit. The amount of the deposit will be a sum greater than the purchase price of the video (in order to deter theft).
2	Reservation policy	Clsd	Who is allowed to make reservations?	Requirements	High	FS	FS	2/15	3/15	4/6	1	Reservations can be made by members only.
5	Rewind fee policy	Clsd		Requirements	Low	GY	GL	2/15	4/6	4/6	1	There is no tape rewind fee.
7	Tape insurance	Clsd		Requirements	High	TK	TG	2/15	4/6	4/6	1	There is no tape insurance fee.
8	Reservation policy	Clsd		Requirements	High	GL	GL	2/15	4/6	4/6	1	A customer who fails to pick-up a reservation will have his/her reservation privileges suspended for 1 month.
11	Bar code	Clsd		Requirements & Design	Low	DL	PF	2/15	4/6	4/6	1	Physical videos are bar coded.
12	Video location	Clsd		Design	High	DL	PF	2/22	3/15	4/26		Physical videos sit on shelves (and not behind a service desk with clerks acting as gophers).
13	Customer Kiosk	Clsd		Requirements & Design	Low	TK	GL	2/22	3/15	4/26	1	A customer kiosk will be provided for customers to query the video catalogue.
15	Rental agreement	Clsd		Requirements	Low	DH	DH	2/22	4/6	4/26	1	Every rental transaction (which may involve more than one video) will involve the printing of a video rental agreement that the member will be required to sign.

Note:

Legend: A - Assign; U - Unassigned; 1 - Ask Customer; 2 - Discuss   with Customer

Table 22-4. *Closed Issues—Technical Decisions.*

Issue ID	Title	Owner	Asgn	Status	Description	Classification	Prty	Open Date	Close Date	Due Date	Action Plan	Decision
17	**Scanner**	DH	DH	Clsd		Requirements & Design	Med	2/22	4/6	4/26	1	Scanners are used to scan video bar codes and membership cards.
19	**Video states**			Clsd		Analysis	Med	3/15	4/26	4/26		Video states **"Late"** is a substate of rented **"Stolen"** is a substate of unavailable.
21	**Reservation management**	TW	TW	Clsd	Which class will be responsible for managing reservations?	Design	High	3/15	4/26	4/26		Video Movie manages reservation request. Considered delegating this to the video catalogue, but was rejected because this class is already overloaded. Also considering creating a reservation manager class.
22	**Video cassette**	PF	PF	Clsd	The Physical Video Tape class should not be part of the analysis object model, because it does not exhibit any interesting behavior from a real-world analysis perspective. It is a passive object—although it could do things like report on its contents (done by the Video Movie class) or its state (handled by the Video Copy class). There is a 1-to-1 relationship between the Physical Video Tape and the Video Copy class.	Analysis	Low	3/15	4/26	4/26		Keep the cassette class in the model. This is a subjective opinion made by two members of the analysis team and supported by the domain expert.
24	**Membership card**	PF	PF	Clsd	Should we have a MemberCard class in the model?	Analysis	High	3/15	4/26	4/26		While members are issued with membership cards, it is not part of the model for similar reasons to the case of the physical video

Note:

23.0 Case Study: Analysis Work Products

23.1 ANALYSIS GUIDELINES

The following analysis work products will be produced:

- Scenarios

- Object Interaction Diagrams

- Object Model

- State Models

- Class Descriptions

> **Author's Commentary**
>
> Analysis guidelines are the set of rules intended to document the way in which analysis is to be performed on the Video Store Administration project (VSA). The point of Analysis Guidelines is to ensure that the analysis deliverables and process are planned in advance, and that team members are consistent in their application of the process to achieve the deliverables. There are, in general, two kinds of Analysis Guidelines that are enforced: work product guidelines and process guidelines.

23.1.1 Work Product Guidelines

The syntax used will be that described in *Developing Object-Oriented Software: An Experience-Based Approach.*

> **Author's Commentary**
>
> The work product guidelines describe the nature of the analysis work products which are to be produced. In this case, the analysis team has decided to produce scenarios, OIDs, an object model, state models, and class descriptions.
>
> Because the project is rather small, the analysis team decided to leave Subject Areas out and not divide the analysis work into parts.

Work Product Tools

We will use the Rational Rose tool to document the graphical work products and the word processor Word Pro to produce the textual work products and the project workbook.

Rose

Rose is used to design and draw the diagrams, i.e. class, object interaction, and state transition diagrams. The diagrams are exported as Encapsulated Postscript files (EPS) for inclusion into Word Pro. The diagrams are documented in Word Pro.

Word Processor Word Pro

Word Pro is used to document the diagrams, the scenarios, and the class descriptions. When necessary, explanations for the notation used will be added after the figures representing the diagrams.

Working Directories

The work products exist on the project LAN disk with alias VSA. Use the logical drive H: to access the disk (gime VSA H:).

The project uses the following working directories:

- Rose project files for analysis

    H:\VSA\Model\Analysis

- Rose exported EPS files

    H:\VSA\Model\Analysis

- Work product Word Pro documents

    H:\VSA\Docs

Author's Commentary

No tool set currently provides automated support for the complete set of work products the VSA team is about to produce. A common strategy is to use a CASE tool for the work products the tool supports (normally diagrams) and a word processor for textual information. This was also the choice of this project (see Appendix C, Tool Support) for a discussion on tools selection). It was nothing particular that motivated the use of Rose and Word Pro; the team happened to own a couple of Rose and Word Pro licenses.

23.1.2 Object Model Guidelines

Rules

The following rules apply to object model documentation:

- Use the Rose tool to draw the object model diagram.

- Name the Rose diagram that contains the object model as *Cfaaaaaa*

  - *"C"* stands for the type of diagram (Class Diagram)
  - *"f"* is the modeling phase, and should be "A" for analysis or "D" for design
  - *"aaaaaaa"* is an arbitrary chosen abbreviation for what it describes
  - The same name will be used for the encapsulated PostScript file when you export it to Word Pro. "EPS" is used as extension.

- Every Class Diagram should have a title that you update with **Browse →Class Diagram →Rename**

- Class name should start with an uppercase letter. Each consecutive word should be uppercase as well. The name may contain blanks.

- Every class should have a three-letter unique abbreviation for usage where convenient.

- In order to not assign the same abbreviation to two classes, all abbreviations used should be entered in the glossary.

- Export the diagram from the Rose as an EPS file. Use the same file name and extension EPS.

- Import the file into the Word Pro document using the option **File →Import Picture...** and the Encapsulated PostScript format.

- Describe the diagram in the Word Pro document.

Format

Use a free text (Word Pro style Body text) to describe the object diagram imported from Rose.

Responsible Persons

The chief architect, project analyst, and the component owners.

When to Update the Work Product

Primarily during analysis but it needs to be maintained during design or implementation if domain understanding changes.

23.1.3 Scenarios Guidelines

Scenarios are a textual description of tasks or events that occur in the context of the application domain.

Rules

The following rule applies to documenting scenarios:

- References to object states should be used when appropriate for assumptions and outcomes. To differentiate an object state from the rest of the text the `Bookman` font should be used.

Format

Use the following format for describing the scenarios:

```
1.1.1. Use case: Use case name        (Word Pro style Heading 3)
1.1.1.1 Scenario: Scenario name       (Word Pro style Heading 4)
Assumptions:                          (Word Pro style Body head 2)
Assumption 1                          (Word Pro style Unord list 1)
Assumption 2
Outcomes:                             (Word Pro style Body head 2)
Outcome description                   (Word Pro style Body text)
Object Interaction Diagram            (Optional. Word Pro style Body head 2)

    <<< insert OID here >>>

Figure x: The Object Interaction Diagram

OID description follows here          (Word Pro style Body text)
1.1.1.2 Scenario: New scenario for the same use case
```

Responsible Persons

The chief architect, project analyst, and the component owners.

When to Update the Work Product

Early in analysis after the use cases have been identified.

23.1.4 Object Interaction Diagrams Guidelines

Rules

The following rules apply to documenting OIDs:

- Use the Rose tool to draw the OIDs.

- Name the Object Interaction Diagram (OID) as *OfCCCaaa.EPS*, where:
    - *"O"* stands for Object Interaction Diagram
    - *"f"* is the modeling phase, and should be "A" for analysis or "D" for design
    - *"CCC"* is the abbreviation for the class receiving the first message in the OID
    - *"aaa"* is chosen arbitrarily
    - *"EPS"* extension is used when you generate a PostScript file for inclusion into Word Pro.

- The Object Interaction Diagram is limited when it comes to describing the methods, for example, specifying what happens when an object receives a message. Describe briefly the message flow on the left side of the diagram or for wide diagrams use footnotes. Enter more detailed description in the Word Pro document under the imported OID diagram.

- Sometimes a message to an object results in complex communication with many other objects. In this case you might want to create a new OID with the operation as parent. This is also a way of partitioning a "cluttered" OID. Export the OID from the Rose as EPS file. Use the same file name and extension EPS. Import the exported OID file into the Word Pro document using the option **File →Import Picture...** and the EPS format. Describe the OID in the Word Pro document.

- Rose has no notion of return messages. Avoid using return messages unless you need one for clarity. In that case turn the message numbering off and add the return message as a new event.

Format

Use a free text (Word Pro style Body text) to describe the OID imported from Rose.

Responsible Persons

The chief architect, project analyst, and the component owners.

When to Update the Work Product

OIDs at the analysis level should begin to be developed at the early analysis phase. In an iterative process, it will be performed continuously throughout development to represent the evolving understanding of the real-world objects.

23.1.5 State Models Guidelines

Rules

The following rules apply to state model documentation:

- Use the Rose tool to draw the state transition diagrams.

- Name the Rose diagram that contains the state model as *Sfaaaaaa*

    - *"S"* stands for the type of diagram (State Diagram)
    - *"f"* is the modeling phase, and should be "A" for analysis or "D" for design
    - *"aaaaaaa"* is an arbitrary chosen abbreviation for what it describes
    - The same name will be used for the encapsulated PostScript file when you export it to Word Pro. "EPS" is used as the extension.

- Every Class Diagram should have a title that you update with **Browse →Class Diagram →Rename**

- State name should start with uppercase letter. Each consecutive word should be upper-case as well. The name may contain blanks.

- Export the diagram from Rose as EPS file. Use the same file name and extension EPS.

- Import the file into the Word Pro document using the option **File →Import Picture...** and the Encapsulated PostScript format.

- Describe the diagram in the Word Pro document.

Format

Use a free text (Word Pro style Body text) to describe the state diagram imported from Rose.

Responsible Persons

The chief architect, project analyst, and the component owners.

When to Update the Work Product

Primarily during analysis, but it needs to be maintained during design or implementation if domain understanding changes.

23.1.6 Class Description Guidelines

Analysis class descriptions are summaries of all the information known about a class at the analysis level. Class-related information exists in several places in the analysis chapter of the project workbook; for example, in different parts of an object model, in scenarios, and Object Interaction Diagrams (OIDs). For each class, a class description provides a concentrated summary.

Rules

No special rules are enforced.

Format

Use the following format to describe analysis level classes:

```
1.2.1 Class Class Name          (Word Pro style Heading 3)
Description                      (Word Pro style Body head 2)
Class description               (Word Pro style Body text)
Responsibilities                (Word Pro style Body head 2)
Responsibility 1                (Word Pro style Unord list 1)

Attributes                      (Word Pro style Body head 2)
Attribute                       (Word Pro style Def title)
Attribute description           (Word Pro style Body text)
Services                        (Word Pro style Body head 2)
```

```
Service                           (Word Pro style Def title)
Service description               (Word Pro style Body text)
```

Responsible Persons

The owner of a class has the responsibility of maintaining the Analysis Class Description for the class.

When to Update the Work Product

Whenever the class description changes.

23.1.7 Process Guidelines

The Video Store Administration uses the Object Modeling Technique (OMT), by Rumbaugh et.al. as the main methodology to perform object-oriented analysis and design.

In addition we use the process guidelines described in *Developing Object-Oriented Software: An Experience-Based Approach.* by the IBM Object-Oriented Technology Center as a reference document for defining the Video Store Administration work product documents.

23.2 ANALYSIS OBJECT MODEL

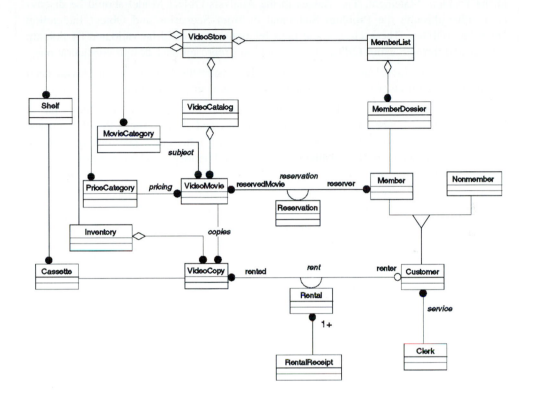

Figure 23-1. *Analysis Object Model.*

Author's Commentary

An Analysis Object Model is a static model of the part of the problem domain relevant to the Problem Statement. The classes in the Analysis Object Model should be discovered either through the Problem Statement or from Scenarios and Object Interaction Diagrams (OIDs). These classes and their relationships should be validated by domain experts and through using OIDs. They should not represent any design considerations.

It is useful to model an association as a class when the links between classes need to participate with other objects or when links are subject to operations.

Figure 23-1 shows several relationships between classes. A VideoStore has a VideoCatalog, a MemberList, zero or more Shelves, and zero or more PriceCategories. A Shelf can have zero or more Cassettes. There is an inheritance relationship between Customer, Member, and Nonmember classes. Both Member and Nonmember are subclasses of the Customer class .

An association represents a structural relationship between objects of different classes. In Figure 23-1, Reservation is an association class between VideoMovie and Member classes. Every instance of the Reservation class represents a 1-1 link relationship between a VideoMovie object and a Member object. In other words, a Reservation shows the relationship of a VideoMovie and a Member. A Member may have zero or more Reservations, thus zero or more VideoMovies reserved through those Reservations. A VideoMovie, on the other hand, may be reserved by zero or more Members through Reservations.

In addition, we see different roles between a Member and a VideoMovie. A Member can be a "reserver" to a VideoMovie, and a VideoMovie can be a "reservedMovie" to a Member.

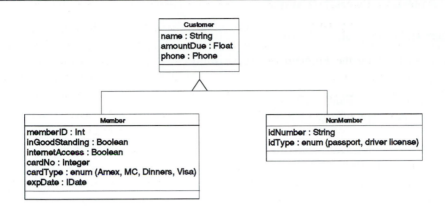

Figure 23-2. Analysis Object Model: Customer Related Classes.

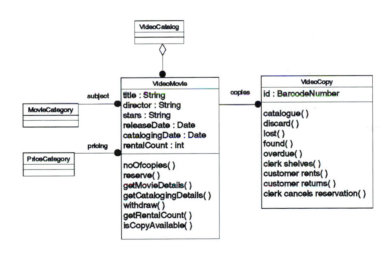

Figure 23-3. Analysis Object Model: VideoMovie Related Classes.

23.3 ANALYSIS SCENARIOS

Use Case 1: *Customer Rents Video*

- Scenario 1.1: Member Rents Video (successfully)

  Assumptions:
  - Member is `InGoodStanding`
  - A video copy of requested movie is `Available`

  Outcomes:
  - Member rents successfully
  - Video is `Rented`
  - A rental is created
  - Rental counter for this movie is incremented

- Scenario 1.2: Customer Rents Video (successfully)

  Assumptions:
  - Customer `HasFinesOutstanding`
  - Customer agrees to pay fine
  - A video copy of requested movie is `Available`

  Outcomes:
  - Customer rents successfully
  - Customer is `InGoodStanding`
  - Video is `Rented`
  - A rental is created
  - Rental counter for this movie is incremented

- Scenario 1.3: Member Rents Video (fines)

  Assumptions:
  - Member `HasFinesOutstanding`
  - Refuses to pay fine

  Outcomes:
  - Member `Suspended`

- Scenario 1.4: Member Rents Video (has reserved)

  Assumptions:
  - Member is `InGoodStanding`
  - Video movie is `Reserved` by this member
  - Requested video for rental is the `Reserved` one
  - A video copy of requested movie is `Available`

  Outcomes:
  - Video is `Rented`
  - A rental is created
  - Rental counter for this movie is incremented

- Scenario 1.5: Member Rents Video (reserved & not picked up)

  Assumptions:
  - Member is InGoodStanding
  - Video is Reserved by this member
  - Member fails to pick up reserved video within 2 days
  Outcomes:
  - Reservation is Canceled
  - A fee is charged for canceled reservation

- Scenario 1.6: Customer Rents Video (Pays deposit)

  Assumptions:
  - A video copy of requested movie is Available
  - Customer is not a member
  Outcomes:
  - Customer pays 2-day rental fee, cash tally updated
  - Video is Rented
  - Rental counter for this movie is incremented
  - A rental is created

Use Case 2: *Customer Returns Video*

- Scenario 2.1: Customer Returns Video (on time)

  Assumptions:
  - Video is returned on time
  Outcomes:
  - Customer receives deposit back, cash tally updated
  - Video rental deleted
  - Video is Available

- Scenario 2.2: Member Drops Video (late)

  Assumptions:
  - Video is dropped in a box outside the store late
  Outcomes:
  - Late charge calculated
  - Video rental deleted
  - Video is Available
  - Member HasFinesOutstanding

Use Case 3: *Customer Applies for Membership*

- Scenario 3.1: Customer Becomes Member

  Assumptions:
  - Customer produces valid identification and credit card
  - Customer pays membership fee

Outcomes:
- Customer becomes Member
- Customer receives a membership card

Use Case 4: *Member Reserves Video*

- Scenario 4.1: Member Reserves Video (successfully)

  Assumptions:
  - Member is `InGoodStanding`
  - No video copies are `Available`

  Outcomes:
  - Video reservation created successfully
  - Video is `Reserved`

- Scenario 4.2: Member Reserves Video (unsuccessfully)

  Assumptions:
  - Member `HasFinesOutstanding`
  - Member refuses to pay

  Outcomes:
  - Member is `Suspended`

Use Case 5: *Member Claims Reserved Video*

- Scenario 5.1: Member Claims Reserved Video (successfully)
  See Scenario 1.4: Member Rents Video (has reserved)

- Scenario 5.2: Member Claims Reserved Video (unsuccessfully, maintains reservation)

  Assumptions:
  - Member is `InGoodStanding`
  - Video movie is `Reserved` by this member
  - Requested video for rental is the `Reserved` one
  - A video copy of requested movie is not `Available`

  Outcomes:
  - Video is `Reserved`

Use Case 11: *Customer Browses Video Catalogue*

- Scenario 11.1: Member Browses Video Catalogue (successfully)

  Assumptions:
  - Member has Internet connection
  - Member is `Authorized`

  Outcomes:
  - Browse counter is increased

23.4 ANALYSIS OBJECT INTERACTION DIAGRAMS

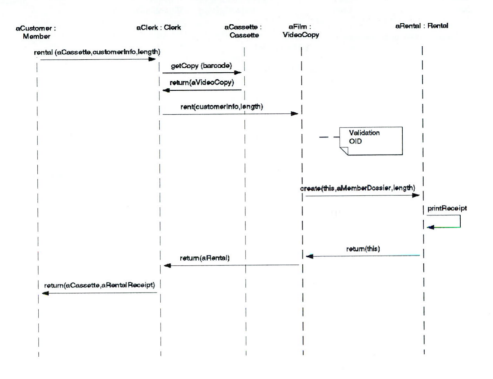

Figure 23-4. *Analysis Object Interaction Diagram.*   Member rents a video successfully (Scenario 1.1).

Author's Commentary

The analysis team had a set of working sessions. Domain experts from the video store attended some of those sessions and made an invaluable contribution to the understanding of the problem domain.

During the working sessions real instance names from the problem domain were used. This facilitated the reasoning and helped the domain experts to "recognize themselves." Some of the OIDs with real instance names are recorded in Section 28.2, Historical Work Products. General instance names were used to document the result of the Analysis Object Interaction Diagrams as recommended by the authors.

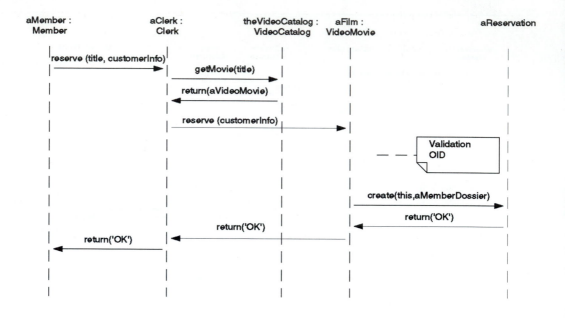

Figure 23-5. *Analysis Object Interaction Diagram.*   Member reserves a video (Scenario 4.1).

Note: The tool does not support dotted lines for return messages.

> **Author's Commentary**
>
> The OIDs in Figure 23-4 and Figure 23-5 show the walk-through of the "physical" and "abstract" objects. The analysts decided to include in the analysis OIDs "actors" and other "physical" objects, such as the videocassette. This approach facilitates the participation of domain experts. They can easily map the model components to the reality they confront every day.
>
> However, this caused other problems to the analysts; `customerInfo` cannot be specified in more concrete terms without making *design* decisions.
>
> The OIDs should be interpreted in a declarative way by the UI and design teams. This means that they have the freedom to change the order in which things are done. However, there is a message to the designers here: Whatever solution you invent, please keep the work required of the clerk as small as possible. In other words, the system should do as much work as possible, and the clerk should do as little as possible. This is why both OIDs show a minimum number of messages from the clerk.

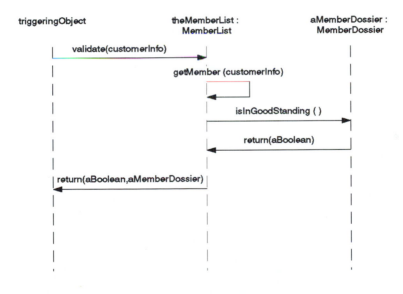

Figure 23-6. *Validation OID.* Used in several Analysis OIDs.

Author's Commentary

The analysis team soon discovered common "patterns" of object interactions. One of them was the validation of members before renting or reserving a video. In early versions of the OIDs "cut & paste" was used. Keeping consistency among the various diagrams was time-consuming. The team decided to use *subOIDs*.

Figure 23-6 is used by several OIDs that need to validate members.

23.5 ANALYSIS STATE MODELS

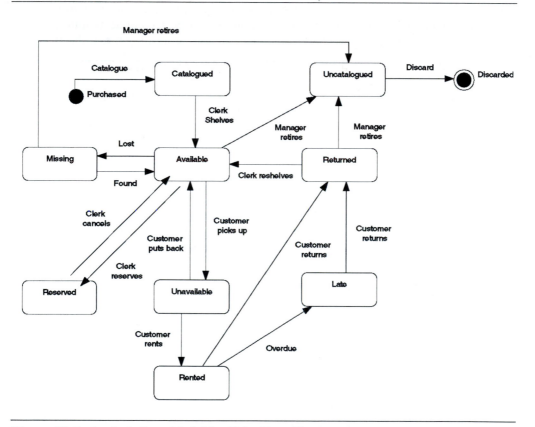

Figure 23-7. Analysis State Model for VideoCopy Class.

> **Author's Commentary**
>
> For objects that have a life cycle, for example, VideoCopy, the Analysis State Model brings out a lot of behavior and the variation of behavior dependent on state. The analysts updated this work product several times as they uncovered new states (Missing and Returned). Each new state identified new events, actions, and transitions. Their current result is shown in Figure 23-7.
>
> The analysts chose to leave off details such as actions, event names, and event parameters to keep the diagram easier to understand for the client. These details will become important during design.
>
> Some thought was given to making Missing, Reserved, Rented, and Late substates of Unavailable. At this point, the value of doing it was not clear, so it was not modeled that way.
>
> Compare this with Section 25.9, Design State Models and the State Design Pattern in Section 25.11, Rejected Design Alternatives.

23.6 ANALYSIS CLASS DESCRIPTIONS

23.6.1 VideoMovie Analysis Class Descriptions

This class description was automatically generated by Rational Rose 3.0 then edited by the team.

```
Class name:
   VideoMovie

Documentation:
   A catalogued movie, copies of which are held by the
   video store.

Hierarchy:
   Superclasses:    none

Associations:

        reserver : Member in association reserve
        <no rolename> : PriceCategory in association pricing
        <no rolename> : VideoCopy in association copies
        <no rolename> : VideoCatalog
        <no rolename> : MovieCategory in association subject

Public Interface:
   Operations:
            noOfcopies
```

```
                  reserve
                  getMovieDetails
                  getCatalogingDetails
                  withdraw
                  getRentalCount
                  isCopyAvailable

Protected Interface:
   Attributes:
                  title : String
                  director : String
                  stars : String
                  releaseDate : Date
                  catalogingDate : Date
                  rentalCount : int


Operation name:
   noOfcopies

Public member of:   VideoMovie
Return Class:    int


Operation name:
   reserve

Public member of:   VideoMovie
Return Class:    void
Arguments:
     customerInfo
Semantics:
   Object diagram: Reservation OOA




Operation name:
   getMovieDetails

Public member of:   VideoMovie
Return Class:    String




Operation name:
   getCatalogingDetails

Public member of:   VideoMovie
Return Class:    String




Operation name:
   withdraw
```

```
Public member of:    VideoMovie
Return Class:    void
Documentation:
    Withdraw all copies of this movie and delete the
    catalog entry.



Operation name:
    getRentalCount

Public member of:    VideoMovie
Return Class:    int



Operation name:
    isCopyAvailable

Public member of:    VideoMovie
Return Class:    Boolean
```

23.6.2 VideoCopy Analysis Class Descriptions

This class description was written by hand before we started using Rational Rose 3.0.

- **VideoCopy**
- *Definition:* VideoCopy is a copy of a video movie owned by the video store.
- *Operations:*
    - Catalogue
    - Discard
    - Clerk shelves
    - Customer rents
    - Customer returns
    - Clerk Reserves
    - Clerk cancels reservation
    - Lost
    - Found
    - Overdue
- *Key attributes:*
    - Id: a unique id for this copy (matches bar code)
- *Relations:*
    - Copy of VideoMovie (which has the description)
    - Rented by Customer
    - Represents (physical) Cassette
- *States:*

- – Available
- – Catalogued
- – Late
- – Missing
- – Rented
- – Reserved (on reserve shelf)
- – Returned
- – Unavailable
- **Documentation:** VideoCopy is the primary unit of inventory at the video store. It represents a cassette. Since there may be millions of these, VideoCopy should be small and efficient—just enough to relate the bar code to the unit of inventory, its description (VideoMovie), and any rental agreements.

Author's Commentary

It is interesting to see the difference a layout can make for the Class Descriptions. The first Class Description, VideoMovie, was automatically generated by a tool (Rational Rose 3.0) and then filtered down because it had lots of distracting trivia. The second Class Description, VideoCopy, was manually generated using a 'fill-in the blank' template. Although it was very quick to create and looks better, it will have to be manually maintained as changes are made.

24.0 Case Study: User Interface Model Work Products

24.1 USER INTERFACE GUIDELINES

The project will follow IBM's Common User Access (CUA) 91 standard for developing graphical user interfaces on OS/2.

A touch screen interface may be considered.

24.2 SCREEN FLOWS

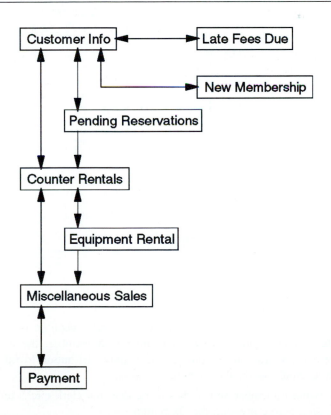

Figure 24-1. *Partial Screen Flow for Video Rental.*

Author's Commentary

Since the Human Factors team planned to create Screen Layouts for each screen in the Screen Flow, only the name of the screen and none of its contents were shown. If no Screen Layouts were to be done, "thumbnails" or outlines of each of these could have been drawn into the Screen Flow.

24.3 SCREEN LAYOUTS

24.3.1 Customer Info

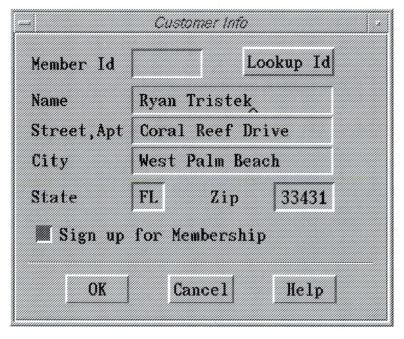

Figure 24-2. *Customer Info Screen Layout.*

The *Customer Info* screen is the first screen that the clerk sees when he is about to service a customer wishing to rent a video. If the customer is a member, the clerk enters the Member Id number and presses enter or presses the Lookup Id button to fill in the rest of the screen. The clerk should verify the customer address.

   If the customer is not a member and wishes to be one, the clerk clicks on the Sign up for Membership button before pressing the OK button.

24.3.2 Late Fees Due

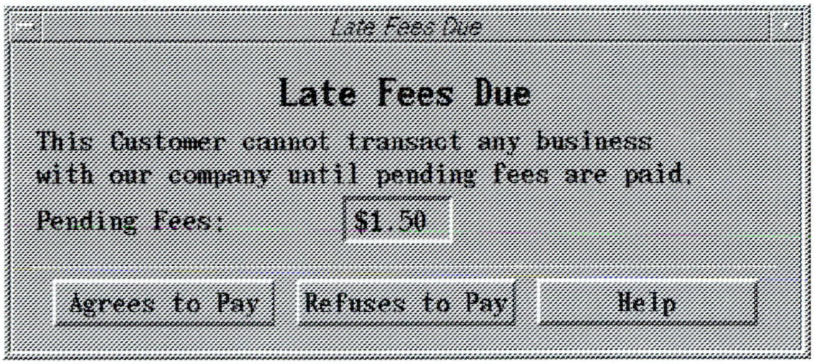

Figure 24-3. *Late Fees Due Screen Layout.*

The *Late Fees Due* screen is the next screen that the clerk sees after pressing OK button on the *Customer Info* Screen if the customer returned a video via the depository slot outside the store. If the customer agrees to pay, the fee will be added to the bill for this transaction. If the customer refuses to pay, the transaction is terminated, and the Customer record is marked for legal processing.

Note: If customer brings a late rental to the counter and offers to pay, the clerk will process that transaction via the *Late Return* screen.

> — **Author's Commentary** —
>
> Although the target system is OS/2, the Human Factors team was using an RS/6000 machine with AIX with Motif. The screen images are slightly different, but the purpose, to assess the Screen Layout and content, was satisfied nevertheless.

24.4 USER INTERFACE PROTOTYPE

Video Store Case Study User Interface Prototype can be exercised remotely if you have an X-server and telnet capability from your workstation. Telnet into the Human Factors team's server using the guest userid, go to the videostore project, and run UIproto:

```
$ telnet HFserver.westpalm.ibm.com
$ login: guest
$ cd project/videostore
$ UIproto
```

Send comments and feedback to `hf_feedback@HFserver.westpalm.ibm.com`. and refer to "video store."

Author's Commentary

Notice that even though the team's target and development platforms did not include Motif and X-Windows, that by including the special Human Factors team, another development (prototype) platform was introduced. This worked out in this case, since all the interested parties were able to exercise the UI Prototype from their X-servers and TCP/IP running on their OS/2 Warp workstations.

25.0 Case Study: Design Work Products

25.1 DESIGN GUIDELINES

- Do not anticipate the design requirements of future development increments.

- Use the Rational Rose tool to capture the evolving design. The key Rose views are its class diagrams, message trace diagrams (Object Interaction Diagrams), and state diagrams.

- Use the Rose model as a design source with Rose code generation as an integral part of each build. Place the Rose work products under configuration management and version control.

- Beware that Rose code generation properties are *not* solely related to code generation: They affect the semantics of the model. For example, The fact that a method is `static` or `virtual` is a code generation property.

- Consider the Rose properties file as an architectural work product. Establish ownership of it and ensure that components override it substantially only after consulting the properties file owner.

- Be aware that some Rose actions, such as reordering a method parameter list, can best be done by editing the model file by hand.

- Only represent method returns explicitly in the Rose message trace diagram if data are returned, and if the depiction of this data return contributes to the understanding of the diagram.

- Partition subsystems, if possible, into categories whose class diagram can be viewed on one screen.

- Assign class ownership at the category level.

- Employ a common design pattern to implement many:many associations that need to be navigated in both directions.

- Maintain message trace diagrams and state models even though they do not influence code generation.

- Use the Analysis Scenarios as Design Scenarios, overriding or supplementing them only when needed to add design detail or to specify subsystems.

- Use the analysis class diagrams and message trace diagrams as initial design work products.

25.2 SYSTEM ARCHITECTURE

The Architecture of the video store is built to satisfy the system requirements based on the technologies that we must use.

- Persistence
  - Persistent data will be maintained in DB2
- Communication
  - TCP/IP is assumed
- Distribution
  - Not addressed in this release. Distributed System Object Model (DSOM) is being considered for future releases
- Platform
  - Clerk workstation will be an IBM PC with Warp Connect
- Error Handling
  - C++ exception and error logging techniques
- Languages
  - Application will be written in VisualAge C++ Version 3.0
- Client/Server
  - A 3-tier topology will be deployed in future releases with communications built on TCP/IP and DSOM.
- Platform Configurations
  - Customer Kiosk
    — PowerPC with multimedia capability (for future release)
  - Clerk Workstation configuration
    — IBM PC
    — Each workstation has a bar code scanner and every two workstations share a printer (to print video rental agreements)
  - Manager workstation
    — IBM PC—with hard-drive as required
  - Store data server
    — IBM PC Server—with hard-drive as required
  - Head Office server
    — To be determined—either a large model IBM PC Server or a RISC machine depending on load requirements
- Security
  - Not addressed in this release
- Backup/Restore
  - Not addressed in this release

The graphical representation of the Layered Architecture Model for the Video Store Application is shown in Figure 25-1 on page 551.

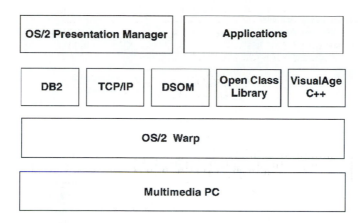

Figure 25-1. *The Layered Architecture Model for VSA.*

The 3-tier topology Architecture is shown in Figure 25-2.

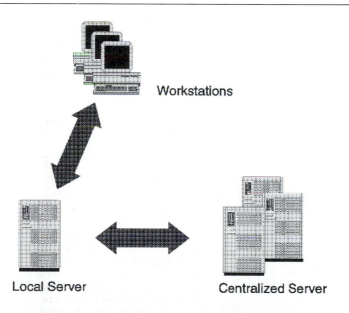

Figure 25-2. *The 3-tier Topology Architecture Model.*

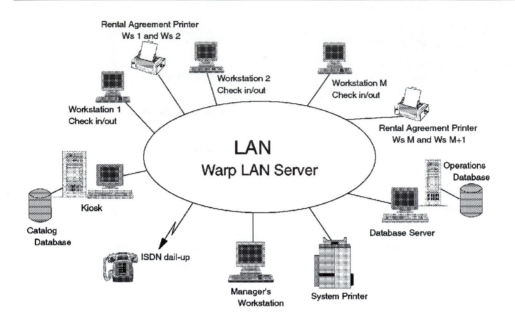

Figure 25-3. *The Hardware Architecture Model for VSA.*

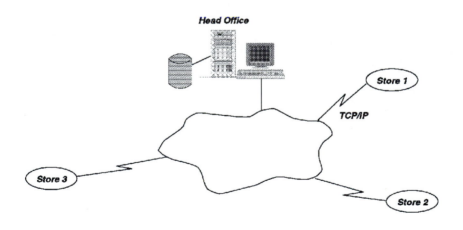

Figure 25-4. *VSA Distributed Environment.*

Author's Commentary

The VSA architect has decided to address future release requirements in the architectural model diagrams. This facilitates communication with the Video Store management by showing the "state of direction". The team still has the freedom to change the components of the architecture during the future releases after gaining more insight on the system.

Another advantage of having "cross-release" decisions in the architecture is to ensure that first release design decisions will not lead to a dead-end path (for example, the use of a class library that is incompatible with DSOM).

25.3 APPLICATION PROGRAMMING INTERFACES (APIS)

This work product is not applicable to this project, as the product does not need to be accessible to "external" software through programming interfaces.

25.4 TARGET ENVIRONMENT

The Video Store system is a system that is based on the client/server architecture. There are two kinds of servers. One is the Store data server and the other is the Head Office server. For both of them, the target environment is OS/2 WARP running on an IBM PC Server with DB2/2, TCP/IP, Distributed System Object Model (DSOM), and LAN Server installed.

There are two kinds of clients in this system as well. The first one is the Clerk Workstation and the second one is the Customer Kiosk. For both clients, the target environment is an OS/2 WARP on an IBM PC with DB2 DAE/2, WARP Connect with TCP/IP and DSOM installed.

25.5 SUBSYSTEM MODEL

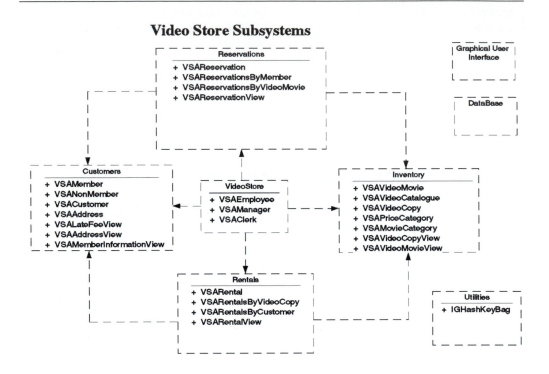

Figure 25-5. *Subsystem diagram for Video Store.*

Author's Commentary

An earlier version of the Subsystem Diagram looked more like a "pigeon-holing" of classes into categories. Here though, the shape of the system and its natural partitioning into subsystems is becoming clearer. The team decided to use the Rational Rose "category" notation (top-level class diagram) instead of the tool's "subsystem" notation (top-level module diagram), because the former showed the classes that were members of the subsystems. This also implies that the diagram needs to be maintained, but since a tool keeps and draws the information, the burden is limited to remembering to regenerate the picture.

25.5.1 Subsystem Contracts

Subsystem Name   Inventory

Definition   Manage the videocassette stock condition, price, and availability

Contracts

1. Stock condition

2. Rent-buy price

3. Availability

Contract Name   Stock condition

Definition   Manage the number, condition, and reordering of stock

Public Operations

```
int              VSAVideoMovie::numOfCopies()
Cost&            VSAVideoMovie::orderCopies(int)
VSAVideoCopy&    VSAVideoMovie::mostUsed()
int              VSAVideoCopy::numOfUses()
bool             VSAVideoCopy::isAvailable()
int              VSAReorderStrategy::reorder(VSAVideoMovie&)
```

Author's Commentary

Notice that the prefix VSA is showing up in these design work products. Normally, adding prefixes to global namespace names is deferred until the implementation phase. This team started prototyping some of their ideas in C++ code and hit the problem early. As they used *reverse engineering* and *round-trip engineering* they decided early to standardize on using prefixes so they wouldn't have to add/remove them during the round-trips between code and design models.

25.6 DESIGN OBJECT MODEL

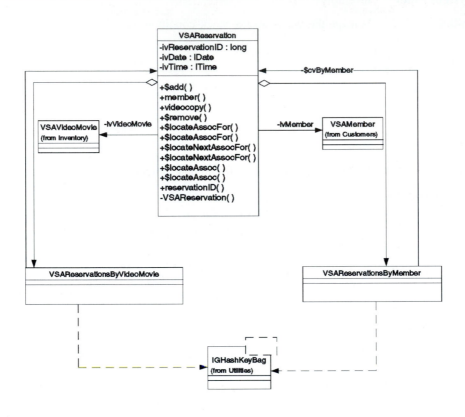

Figure 25-6. *Design Object Model: Reservation Related Classes.*

Figure 25-6 shows part of the Design Object Model that is related to the Reservation class. IGHashKeyBag is a parameterized class with two instantiated classes, namely VSAReservationsByVideoMovie and VSAReservationsByMember. Both ivMember and ivVideoMovie are private members of the VASReservation. cvByMember and cvByVideoMovie are static private members of the VSAReservation.

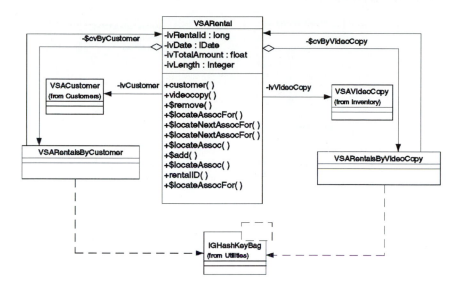

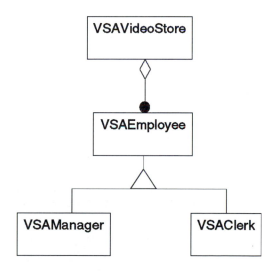

Figure 25-7. *Design Object Model: Rental Related Classes.*

Figure 25-8. *Design Object Model: Video Store Related Classes.*

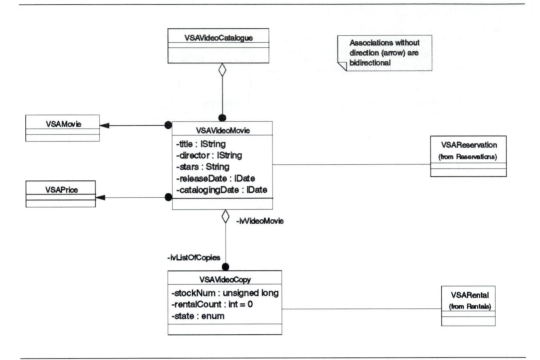

Figure 25-9. *Design Object Model: Inventory Related Classes.*

┌───┐

Author's Commentary

A key difference between the Analysis Object Model and the Design Object Model is that these design objects either represent the refinement of analysis objects (such as `VideoCopy` and `Rental`) or are invented to address design decisions (such as `ReservationsByVideoMovie`). They do not come from the problem domain directly. In general, they are directional and have accessibility adornments.

During analysis the team had assumed that a member is a specialization of a customer (see Figure 23-2). Consequently, the first design had an inheritance relation from class Member to class Customer. With this approach the transition from a customer to a member can not be done in the most direct way. In C++ objects can not change their type. Therefore, the transition must be performed by creating a new member copying all customer information into it and deleting the customer object. This transition would be easier when the State Design Pattern (see [Gamma95]) is used to model Member and Nonmember as states of a customer. However, this transition will happen very infrequently in comparison to all other transactions in the system. Therefore, the team decided not to optimize for that rare case at the expense of the more frequent cases.

Normally, there should not be any prefix before any class names. The VSA prefix here is the result of round-trip engineering.

└───┘

25.7 DESIGN SCENARIOS

No new (nonanalysis) Design Scenarios have been defined. The system is currently small and the Analysis Scenarios serve to document design requirements adequately. The requirements of each subsystem can be inferred from the system-level Analysis Scenarios and the definitions of each subsystem. If and when the system grows to the point at which requirements need to be defined formally for individual subsystems, then these will be expressed in terms of Design Scenarios. That point will come when the high-level design of the whole system can no longer be done by a single, small team.

25.8 DESIGN OBJECT INTERACTION DIAGRAMS

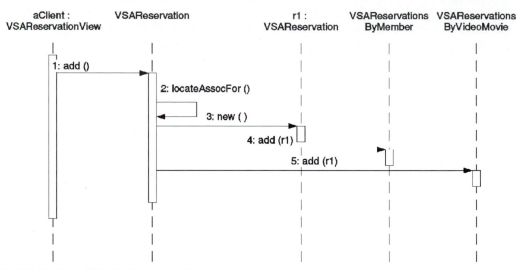

1: add (aMember, aVideoMovie, unsigned long)
2: locateAssocFor (aVideoMovie, aReservationCursorForVideoMovie)
3: new (aMember, aVideoMovie, aRentalID)

Figure 25-10. Create a Reservation.

The assumption in the "Create a reservation" OID is that the object does not exist, i.e the combination member/videoMovie is not in the static member collections (ReservationsByVideoMovie and ReservationsByMember).

Two instances, *r1* and *aClient* and three classes participate in the OID. The *Create a reservation* OID does not assume invocation from the user interface, i.e. the client instance can be replaced by the "main" of a test program.

The message *new()* is actually the invocation of the constructor of class Reservation. It will result in the creation of r1:Reservation.

The messages *add()* and *locateAssocFor()* invoke class operations. (static member functions).

Author's Commentary

The design OID *Create a reservation* focuses on the internal behavior of the system and assumes the existence of an instance of Member and VideoCopy, in contrast to the analysis OID *Member reserves a video* (see Figure 23-5) where the focus was on the external behavior. One could consider the OID in Figure 25-10 as a refinement of one of the messages in the analysis OID, namely the create(this,aMemberDossier) message from an instance of VideoMovie to Reservation. One can also notice that the designers moved the responsibility of creating a reservation from VideoMovie to the Reservation class. This responsibility will be fulfilled by the class operation add().

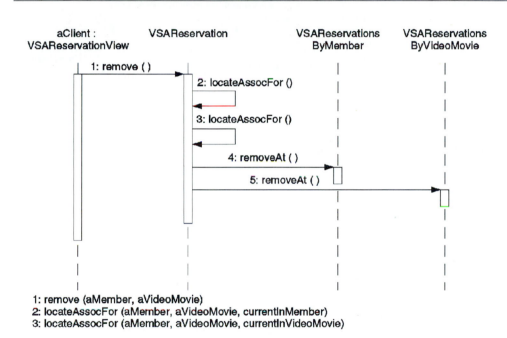

Figure 25-11. *Remove a Reservation.*

The assumption for the "Remove reservation" OID is that both static member collections are in sync, i.e. if the reservation is in one collection then it is also in the other one. The implementer may use an exception to deal with the unexpected situation.

25.9 DESIGN STATE MODELS

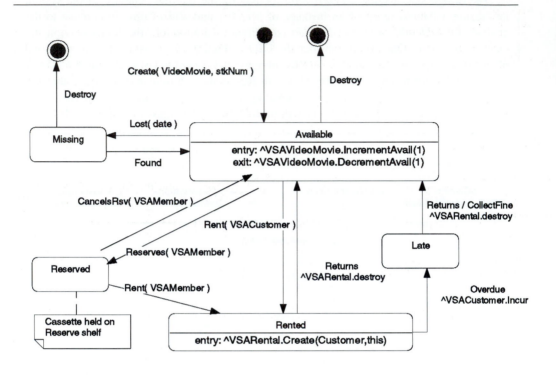

Figure 25-12. *Design State Model for VideoCopy Class.*

--- Author's Commentary ---

The designers had an easy start with this Design State Model. They "seeded" it from the Analysis State Model and removed states that related to the *physical* cassette but not to the *logical* VideoCopy (the system's representation of it). For example, the system does not know if a customer picks up, walks around the store with, then returns a cassette to the shelf. Although the cassette was unavailable, the system did not know it. The designers removed other "real world" clutter too by simplifying the event names.

The designers also added information to the State Model in the form of event parameters, conditions, actions, and sent events to other targets. This really made the model "talk." For example, it pointed out that the Available state was responsible for telling VideoMovie to adjust its available count.

Compare this with Section 23.5, Analysis State Models and the State Design Pattern in Section 25.11, Rejected Design Alternatives.

25.10 DESIGN CLASS DESCRIPTIONS

25.10.1 VSAReservation Class Description

This is an edited version of the *model specifications* generated by Rational Rose 3.0.

```
Class name: VSAReservation

Subsystem:              Reservations
Description:
    Each reservation instance simply relates one
    video movie with one member and has a unique id. The
    class VSAReservation keeps two private static keyed
    collections of reservations, so that you can ask
    VSAReservation for a specific reservation by member
    or by video movie.

Hierarchy:
    Superclasses:    none

Associations:
    -ivMember : VSAMember in association
    -ivVideoMovie : VSAVideoMovie in association
    -$cvByMember : VSAReservationsByMember in association
    -$cvByVideoMovie : VSAReservationsByVideoMovie in association

Public Interface:
    Operations:
                    add
                    member
                    videocopy
                    remove
                    locateAssocFor
                    locateAssocFor
                    locateNextAssocFor
                    locateNextAssocFor
                    locateAssoc
                    locateAssoc
                    reservationID

Private Interface:
    Attributes:
        ivReservationID : const unsigned long = (reservationId)
        ivdate : IDate
```

```
            ivTime : ITime

    Operations:
            VSAReservation

Operation name: add
Return Class:       IBoolean
Description:
    Add to all reservations one for the given member
    and the given video movie.
    Return True if the reservation was added, False otherwise.
Arguments:
        const class VSAMember&    member
        const class VSAVideoMovie&        videomovie
        unsigned long    reservationID

Operation name: member
Return Class:       const class VSAMember&
Description:
    Return the member that holds this reservation.

Operation name: videocopy
Return Class:       const class VSAVideoCopy&
Description:
    Return the video copy that this reservation is for.

Operation name: remove
Return Class:       IBoolean
Arguments:
        const class VSAMember&    member
        const class VSAVideoMovie&        videomovie
Description:
    Remove from all reservations the one for the given member
    and the given video movie.
    Return True if the reservation was removed, False otherwise.
    Remove is a class operation (static).
```

Operation name: locateAssocFor
Return Class: IBoolean
Arguments:
    const class VSAVideoMovie&   videomovie
    VSAReservationCursor<class VSAVideoMovie>&   cursor
Description:
    Locate a reservation for the given movie. If a matching
    reservation is found, True is returned and the cursor is
    set to the first matching reservation. Otherwise False
    is returned and the cursor is undefined.
    locateAssocFor is a class operation (static).

Operation name: locateAssocFor
Return Class: IBoolean
Arguments:
    const class VSAMember&   member
    VSAReservationCursor<class VSAMember>&   cursor
Description:
    Locate a reservation for the given member. If a matching
    reservation is found, True is returned and the cursor is
    set to the first matching reservation. Otherwise False
    is returned and the cursor is undefined.
    locateAssocFor is a class operation (static).

Operation name: locateNextAssocFor
Return Class: IBoolean
Arguments:
    const class VSAVideoMovie&   videomovie
    VSAReservationCursor<class VSAVideoMovie>&   cursor
Description:
    Locate the next reservation for the given movie. The search
    starts at the position determined by the given cursor.
    If a matching reservation is found, True is returned and
    the cursor is set to the found reservation.
    Otherwise False is returned and the cursor is undefined.
    locateNextAssocFor is a class operation (static).

Operation name: locateNextAssocFor
Return Class: IBoolean
Arguments:
    const class VSAMember&   member
    VSAReservationCursor<class VSAMember>&   cursor
Description:
    Locate the next reservation for the given member. The search
    starts at the position determined by the given cursor.
    If a matching reservation is found, True is returned and
    the cursor is set to the found reservation.
    Otherwise False is returned and the cursor is undefined.
    locateNextAssocFor is a class operation (static).

Operation name: locateAssoc
Return Class: IBoolean
Arguments:
    const class VSAMember&   member
    const class VSAVideoCopy& videocopy
    VSAReservationCursor<class VSAMember>&   cursor
Description:
    Locate the reservation for the given member and movie.
    If a matching reservation is found, True is returned
    and the cursor is set to the found reservation.
    Otherwise False is returned and the cursor is undefined.
    locateAssoc is a class operation (static).

Operation name: locateAssoc
Return Class: IBoolean
Arguments:
    const class VSAMember&   member
    const class VSAVideoCopy& videocopy
    VSAReservationCursor<class VSAVideoCopy>&   cursor
Description:
    Locate the reservation for the given member and movie.
    If a matching reservation is found, True is returned
    and the cursor is set to the found reservation.
    Otherwise False is returned and the cursor is undefined.
    locateAssoc is a class operation (static).

Operation name: reservationID
Return Class: unsigned long
Description:
    Returns the ID of this reservation.

Operation name: VSAReservation
Return Class: VSAReservation
Arguments:
    const class VSAMember&   member
    const class VSAVideoCopy& videocopy
    unsigned long   reservationId
Description:
    Construct a new reservation for the given member and movie.
    This function is used by add(...) only and is not
    accessible outside of the reservation class.

25.10.2 VSAVideoCopy Class Description

This is an edited version of the *model specifications* generated by Rational Rose 3.0.

Class name: VSAVideoCopy

Subsystem: Inventory
Description:
    A videoCopy represents a videocassette, which is a
    copy of a video movie. The copy points to the movie for
    its description but by itself it simply has identity
    (stock number) and state (available, rented, reserved,
    lost, late).

Hierarchy:
    Superclasses: none
Associations:

        -ivVideoMovie : VSAVideoMovie in association
        -ivVideoCopy : VSARental in association

Public Interface:
    Operations:
            Create
            Destroy
            Lost
            Found
            Rents
            Returns
            Overdue
            Reserve
            CancelRsv

Private Interface:
    Attributes:
            stockNum : unsigned long

                              Unique stock number for the
                              VideoCopy (cassette)

            rentalCount : int = 0
            state : enum

Implementation:
    Operations:
                available
                unAvailable

Operation name: Create
Arguments:
    unsigned long   stockNum
    VideoMovie&   movie

Operation name: Destroy

Operation name: Lost
Arguments:
    IDate dateLost
Description:
    Can't rent or reserve it if it is lost.
Semantics:
    state=lost

Operation name: Found
Description:
    Now we can rent or reserve it again.
Semantics:
    state=available

```
Operation name: Rents
Arguments:
    VSACustomer&   customer
Description:
    The videoCopy is rented to a customer.
Semantics:
    state=rented;  rental=new VSARental(movie,customer)

Operation name: Returns
Description:
    The customer returns the video copy
Semantics:
    rental.destroy()

Operation name: Overdue
Description:
    Used to signal that a fine is to be collected and for
    report on overdue videos.
Semantics:
    state=overdue;

Operation name: Reserve
Arguments:
    VSACustomer&   customer
Description:
    Clerk moves cassette from regular shelves to reserved
    shelf.
Semantics:
```

```
    state=reserved

Operation name: CancelRsv
Arguments:
    VSACustomer    customer
Description:
    Cancels a customer reservation.  Clerk moves cassette
    from reserve shelf to regular shelves.
Semantics:
    state=available

Operation name: available
Description:
    When videoCopy becomes available, tell videoMovie to
    increment its count of available copies
Semantics:
    movie.incrementAvail(1)

Operation name: unAvailable
Description:
    When videoCopy is unavailable for any reason (lost,
    rented, reserved), tell videoMovie to decrement its
    count of available copies.
Semantics:
    movie.decrementAvail(1)
```

Author's Commentary

It appears that the team filtered the output from a tool (Rational Rose) because its output was too voluminous or distracting. The nice part is that, other than filtering, this output Class Description was automatically generated from the other work products developed with the tool. With a better filtering and reformatting, it might even look better and be easier to read.

25.11 REJECTED DESIGN ALTERNATIVES

1. VideoCopy was going to manage reservations but it was decided that this wasn't a natural responsibility. As a result the reservation class was added to the model.

2. The VideoCopy Design State Model was going to be designed into the Design Object Model using the State Design Pattern from the "Design Patterns" book by Gamma, et al. The states from the Design State Model would be concrete subclasses of class `VideoCopyState`. The `VideoCopy` class would always have a pointer, of type `VideoCopyState*`, to the current concrete state class (`VideoCopyAvailable`, `VideoCopyRented`, `VideoCopyLate`, et cetera). `VideoCopy` would delegate all state-dependent operations to the concrete state classes via the superclasses interface, i.e. via virtual functions. Each delegated operation would also set the next state in `VideoCopy` before returning. A typical state-dependent operation in `VideoCopy` would look like:

```
inline
void VideoCopy::returns() { state->returns(this); }
```

And in a concrete state class it would look like:

```
/* virtual */
void VideoCopyLate::returns(VideoCopy* vc) {
    payLateFee(vc);
    vc->nextState(videoCopyAvailable);
}
```

This would avoid all the conditional logic for testing: was it late? was it reserved? was it rented? was it available? et cetera, as well as determining the next state.

This idea was rejected, because the designers already had the nonstate machine design figured out, and they were considering removing the reservation aspect from VideoCopy entirely.

Note: In fact, after this Rejected Design Alternative was recorded, all reservation responsibility was assigned to the Reservation class. VideoCopy only needed to know it was "waiting on the shelf," i.e. it could not be rented.

If that were done, the remaining states of interest (Available, Rented, Late) did not warrant the creation of four extra (state) classes, dozens of virtual functions in state classes, and a state variable (and set function) in VideoCopy.

The diagram associated with this rejected design alternative is kept in Historical Work Products (see Figure 28-4).

Author's Commentary

Notice that by keeping this Rejected Design Alternative, the designers can quickly come back to this scheme if reservations turn out to be a complicated design aspect of VideoCopy.

26.0 Case Study: Implementation Work Products

26.1 CODING GUIDELINES

Author's Commentary

Many projects get guidelines from somewhere else and modify them to their specific project needs. Please see the references portion of Section 14.1 for pointers to good sources of coding guidelines.

From the over one hundred rules and guidelines for the VSA project three rules are shown here as an example.

Rule 4.3   **A file name prefix that indicates the owning component of the file must be adopted. In the VSA project we use the prefix "VS." for all files.**

Reason   A file name prefix that establishes a relationship between source code and executable allows a developer to easily obtain all source files necessary to build any executable in the project. Advanced revision control systems allow a developer to establish this relationship independent of any naming convention. However, if one ports the application to another platform where this revision control system may not exist, then a more archaic form of source code control may have to be used. Thus it would have been helpful to have established this executable-code relationship through a file naming convention.

Example

The files containing the reservation class are named:

```
vsreserv.h
vsreserv.cpp
```

Rule 10.2   **Do not modify an lvalue with the postfix ++ or -- operators and then use that lvalue in the same expression.**

Reason   We are only guaranteed that the lvalue that the postfix ++ or -- operators act on will be altered by end of the expression. The value of the lvalue within the expression will be unknown until the expression has executed.

Example

```
void func()
{
  int i, j;
  int array[20];

  ....

  array[i++] = array[j++]; //this is fine!

  array[i] = array[i++]; //the lvalue i is undefined, don't do this!
}
```

Rule 15.1   **Data that must be known only to all instances of a particular class should be a static data member of that class.**

Reason   By moving global data into the class, we are reducing the pollution of the global name space and encapsulating the data.

Example

A common use of a static class member is to generate a unique object id for every instance of the class.

```
class A
{
  public:
    A():thisObjId(objId++){}//increment static and initialize this objId
    //... other member functions
  private:
    //... other members
    int thisObjId;
    static int objId;
};

int A::objId = 0;//member initialized at file scope
```

26.2 PHYSICAL PACKAGING PLAN

This will be added during our next increment.

26.3 DEVELOPMENT ENVIRONMENT

- Rational Rose is used for documentation of Analysis and Design work products.

- Word Pro is used for documentation of textual work products.

- DB2/2 tables and views needed for the application will be set up by a Database Administrator (DBA). Proper authorization will be given by the DBA for client access.

- VisualAge C++ is used for the development of C++ as well as the mapping of object classes to DB2 tables.

- Make files are used for creating and maintaining the executable and library files.

- CMVC/2 is used for configuration management, version control, change control, and problem tracking of the Source Code. CMVC/2 can also provide access control to the Source Code.

- Code and unit test is done on the team members 755 Thinkpads running Warp Connect and Warp Server for server machines. Function and system tests will be done using the same machine model and configuration as encountered in the Video Store.

26.4 SOURCE CODE

Author's Commentary

The source code shown here is representative of what the code would look like roughly four months after the start of the project. Throughout the rest of this case study, the assumption is that the work products shown are what would exist roughly two months into the project. Since this project would not have completed any source code after two months, we've bent the rules a bit in order to show an example of source code for the VSA project.

This source code is only the portion that deals with the reservation. Further, parts of the code that consist of constructs similar to those shown earlier are not shown. Those skipped parts are indicated by a symbol, **0**, where the number in the symbol points to a comment in Section 26.4.7, Comments on the code. The comment explains what parts are not shown, and why they are not interesting. The comments also contain other points of interest.

A reservation is an association between a member (class VSAMember declared in file VSMEMBER.H, not listed here) and a video movie (class VSAVideoMovie declared in file VSVDOMVI.h, not listed here).

This version of the code reflects some short cuts taken for the first iterations. For example all possible exceptions are directly raised as instances of the exception base class IException. At a later time this will be changed to group all executions into appropriate subclasses. Another example is that some messages are hard coded. They will eventually be put into a separate messages file and accessed from there. This facilitates translation into other national languages.

Reservations form an n-n association between members and video movies (see Figure 23-1). This explains the occasional occurrences of the stem Assoc in some names in the code. We can speculate that at a later time in this project, or in another project trying to reuse this code, a generic n-n association will be created. Very likely this generic association will be a class template, with two template arguments that correspond to the types VSAMember and VSAVideoMovie used here.

The part of the static Design Object Model implemented with this code is shown in Figure 25-6. The parameterized class IGHashKeyBag is from the IBM Open Class library. It offers KeyBags, which store elements in a way optimized for access by key. More than one element with the same identical key can be contained in the KeyBag.

26.4.1   VSRESRV.H

```
/*----------------------------------------------------------------*
 |  File:     VSRESRV.H              Type: Interface              |
 |  Classes:  VSAReservation                                     |
 |  Description:                                                 |
 |            Each reservation instance simply relates one       |
 |            video movie with one member and has a unique id. The|
 |            class VSAReservation keeps two private static keyed |
 |            collections of reservations, so that you can ask    |
 |            VSAReservation for a specific reservation by member |
 |            or by video movie.                                 |
 |  Project:  Video Store Administration  Management System      |
 |  Owner:    Frank Seliger                                      |
 |  History:  96-05-15   FS, Creation                            |
 |            96-06-07   FS, Added reservationID                 |
 *----------------------------------------------------------------*/

#ifndef VSRESRV_H
#define VSRESRV_H

        // For the collections used to maintain all reservations
        // we include only forward declarations:                   ■1
#include <vsresrvc.hf>

#pragma info(none)
#include <icursor.h>
#pragma info(restore)

class VSAMember;
class VSAVideoMovie;

class VSAReservation
{
public:

template <class Element>
friend class VSAReservationCursor;  // Our own Cursors are our friends.  ■2

    // Add to all reservations one for the given member and the given
    // video movie.
    // Return True if the reservation was added, False otherwise.
    static IBoolean                                        // ■3
    add     (VSAMember const&  member,
             VSAVideoMovie const& videomovie,
             unsigned long memberId);

    // Remove from all reservations the one for the given member
    // and the given video movie.
    // Return True if the reservation was removed, False otherwise.
    static IBoolean
    remove  (VSAMember const& member,
             VSAVideoMovie const& videomovie);

    // Locate a reservation for the given movie.  If a matching    ■4
    // reservation is found, True is returned and the cursor is set
```

```
// to the first matching reservation.  Otherwise False
// is returned and the cursor is undefined.
static IBoolean
locateAssocFor  (VSAVideoMovie const& videomovie,
                 VSAReservationCursor<VSAVideoMovie>& cursor);
//  5


// Locate a reservation for the given member.  If a matching
// reservation is found, True is returned and the cursor is set
// to the first matching reservation.  Otherwise False
// is returned and the cursor is undefined.
static IBoolean
locateAssocFor  (VSAMember const& member,
                 VSAReservationCursor<VSAMember>& cursor);


// Locate the next reservation for the given movie.  The search
// starts at the position determined by the given cursor.
// If a matching reservation is found, True is returned and
// the cursor  is set to the found reservation.
// Otherwise False is returned and the cursor is undefined.
static IBoolean
locateNextAssocFor  (VSAVideoMovie const& videomovie,
                     VSAReservationCursor<VSAVideoMovie>& cursor);


// Locate the next reservation for the given member.  The search
// starts at the position determined by the given cursor.
// If a matching reservation is found, True is returned and
// the cursor  is set to the found reservation.
// Otherwise False is returned and the cursor is undefined.
static IBoolean
locateNextAssocFor  (VSAMember const& member,
                     VSAReservationCursor<VSAMember>& cursor);


// Locate the reservation for the given member and movie.
// If a matching reservation is found, True is returned
// and the cursor is set to the found reservation.
// Otherwise False is returned and the cursor is undefined.
static IBoolean
locateAssoc  ( VSAMember const& member,
               VSAVideoMovie const& videomovie,
               VSAReservationCursor<VSAMember>& cursor);


// Locate the reservation for the given member and movie.
// If a matching reservation is found, True is returned
// and the cursor is set to the found reservation.
// Otherwise False is returned and the cursor is undefined.
static IBoolean
locateAssoc  ( VSAMember const& member,
               VSAVideoMovie const& videomovie,
               VSAReservationCursor<VSAVideoMovie>& cursor);


// Return the member that holds this reservation.
VSAMember const&
member () const;


// Return the video copy that this reservation is for.
```

```
        VSAVideoMovie const&
        videoMovie () const;

         // Return the ID of this reservation.
        unsigned long
        reservationID () const;

         // Compare two reservations for equal.
        friend Boolean
        operator== (VSAReservation const& lhs, VSAReservation const& rhs);

private:
        // Construct a new reservation for the given member and movie.
        // This function is used by add(...) only and is not accessible
        // outside of the reservation class.
        VSAReservation  (VSAMember const& member,
                         VSAVideoMovie const& videomovie,
                         unsigned long reservationID);

         // Instance data members
        const VSAMember     *   ivMember;
        const VSAVideoMovie *   ivVideoMovie;
        const unsigned long     ivReservationID;

         // Class data members
        static VSAReservationsByMember       cvByMember;
        static VSAReservationsByVideoMovie   cvByVideoMovie;

};

//-----------------------------------------------------------------------
// Inline implementations
//-----------------------------------------------------------------------

inline VSAReservation::VSAReservation (VSAMember const& member,
                                       VSAVideoMovie const& videomovie,
                                       unsigned long reservationID )
:    ivMember (&member), ivVideoMovie (&videomovie),
     ivReservationID(reservationID)
{
}

inline Boolean
operator== (VSAReservation const& lhs, VSAReservation const& rhs)
{      // Equal is defined as the Member/VideoMovie pointed to
       // being the identical same, not their contents being identical.
    Boolean equal;
    if (lhs.ivMember == rhs.ivMember
    &&  lhs.ivVideoMovie == rhs.ivVideoMovie)
       equal = 1;
    else
       equal = 0;
    return equal;
}
```

```
inline VSAMember const&
VSAReservation::member () const
{ return *ivMember;
}

inline VSAVideoMovie const&
VSAReservation::videoMovie () const
{ return *ivVideoMovie;
}

inline unsigned long
VSAReservation::reservationID () const
{ return ivReservationID;
}
#endif /* VSRESRV_H */
```

26.4.2 VSRESRV.CPP

```
/*-------------------------------------------------------------------*
 |  File:      VSRESRV.CPP          Type: Implementation             |
 |  Classes:   VSAReservation                                        |
 |  Description:                                                     |
 |             Each reservation instance simply relates one          |
 |             video movie with one member and has a unique id.      |
 |             For a description of the interface see VSRESRV.H.      |
 |  Project:   Video Store Administration  Management System         |
 |  Owner:     Frank Seliger                                         |
 |  History:   96-05-16   FS, Creation                               |
 |             96-06-07   FS, Added reservationID                    |
 *-------------------------------------------------------------------*/

#include <vsresrvc.h>
#include <vsresrv.h>
#include <vsrescur.h>


      // Define our static data members:
VSAReservationsByMember  VSAReservation::cvByMember;
VSAReservationsByVideoMovie  VSAReservation::cvByVideoMovie;


IBoolean
VSAReservation::add     (VSAMember const&  member,
                         VSAVideoMovie const& videomovie,
                         unsigned long reservationID )
{
    VSAReservationCursor<VSAMember> current;
    IBoolean wasContained = locateAssoc(member, videomovie, current);

    if (wasContained == False)
    {
      VSAReservation* eap
         = new VSAReservation (member, videomovie, reservationID);
      cvByMember.add(eap);
      cvByVideoMovie.add(eap);
```

```
          // What else could have gone wrong here except OutOfMemory?
          // Let the caller catch and handle the exception for that.
      }
      return (!wasContained);
}


IBoolean
VSAReservation::remove  (VSAMember const& member,
                         VSAVideoMovie const& videomovie)
{
      VSAReservationCursor<VSAMember> currentInMember;
      VSAReservationCursor<VSAVideoMovie> currentInVideoMovie;

      IBoolean wasContainedInMember
        = locateAssoc(member, videomovie, currentInMember);
      IBoolean wasContainedInVideoMovie
        = locateAssoc(member, videomovie, currentInVideoMovie);

      if ((wasContainedInMember == True)
      != (wasContainedInVideoMovie == True))
      {     // This could happen only as a consequence of a programming
            // error, that most likely is in this class itself.
         IException e(
           "The reservation to be removed is contained only partially.");
         throw e;
      }

      if (wasContainedInMember == True)
      {
         VSAReservation* p =  // We need to delete it after all removes.
            cvByMember.elementAt(currentInMember.asMemberCursor());

         cvByMember.removeAt(currentInMember.asMemberCursor());
         cvByVideoMovie.removeAt(currentInVideoMovie.asVideoMovieCursor());
         delete p;
         return True;
      }
      else
         return False;
}


IBoolean
VSAReservation::locateAssocFor (
                         VSAVideoMovie const& videomovie,
                         VSAReservationCursor<VSAVideoMovie>& cursor)
{
      // This is in gray area between pure encapsulation and breakage
      // of encapsulation for faster performance: We plan to have the
      // collection cursor set, that is contained in the reservation
      // cursor 'cursor.'
      // Therefore 'current' is a reference to 'cursor.'
      VSAReservationsByVideoMovie::Cursor& current
        = cursor.asVideoMovieCursor();
```

```
        // The following locate will set the VideoMovie cursor,
        // that is contained in 'cursor':
    return cvByVideoMovie.locateElementWithKey(videomovie, current);
}

// 6


IBoolean
VSAReservation::locateAssoc (
                        VSAMember const& member,
                        VSAVideoMovie const& videomovie,
                        VSAReservationCursor<VSAVideoMovie>&
cursor)
{
    IBoolean wasContained(False);

        // This the shady area between pure encapsulation and breakage
        // of encapsulation for faster performance: We plan to have the
        // collection cursor set, that is contained in the reservation
        // cursor 'cursor.'
        // Therefore 'current' is a reference to 'cursor.'
    VSAReservationsByVideoMovie::Cursor& current
        = cursor.asVideoMovieCursor();

    IBoolean rc        // Find the first reservation for the given movie
        = cvByVideoMovie.locateElementWithKey(videomovie, current);

                    // Check the other reservations for given movie
                    // until we find the one for the given member.
    while ((rc == True)  &&  (wasContained == False))
    {
        if ((*(cvByVideoMovie.elementAt(current))->ivMember) == member)
            wasContained = True;
        else
            rc = cvByVideoMovie.locateNextElementWithKey( videomovie,
                                                          current);
    }

    return (wasContained);
}
```

26.4.3 VSRESCUR.H

```
/*------------------------------------------------------------------*
|  File:     VSRESCUR.H         Type: Interface and inline implem.  7 |
|  Classes:  VSAReservationCursor  class template                   |
|  Description:                                                      |
|           The template VSAReservationCursor is providing cursors  |
|           that operate on all reservations.  When this template   |
|           is instantiated for type VSAMember, its internal        |
|           cursor is operating on the collection that allows for    |
|           fast and efficient retrieval of a reservation by member.|
|           When this template is instantiated for type             |
```

```
|              VSAVideoMovie, its internal cursor is operating on the   |
|              collection that allows for fast and efficient           |
|              retrieval of a reservation by video movie.              |
| Project:    Video Store Administration  Management System            |
| Owner:      Frank Seliger                                            |
| History:    96-05-16    FS, Creation                                 |
*----------------------------------------------------------------*/

#ifndef VSRESCUR_H
#define VSRESCUR_H

#include <vsresrvc.h>
#pragma info(none)
#include <icursor.h>
#pragma info(restore)

template <class Element>
class VSAReservationCursor : public ICursor
{
 public:

      // Construct a cursor for reservations.  This cursor can be used
      // to work with all reservations (which are maintained by class
      // VSAReservation).
    VSAReservationCursor ();

    ~VSAReservationCursor ();

      // Set this cursor to the first of all reservations.
      // If the cursor is set successfully, True is returned.
      // Otherwise False is returned and the cursor is undefined.
      // This function is declared by ICursor.  We must override it.
    IBoolean
    setToFirst ();

      // Set this cursor to the next reservation.
      // If the cursor is set successfully, True is returned.
      // Otherwise False is returned and the cursor is undefined.
      // This function is declared by ICursor as a pure virtual function,
      // so we must override it.
    IBoolean
    setToNext ();

      // If the cursor is valid (on a valid reservation),
      // True is returned.
      // Otherwise False is returned.
      // Pure virtual function from ICursor.  We must override it.
    IBoolean
    isValid () const;

      // Set the the cursor status to invalid.
      // Pure virtual function from ICursor.  We must override it.
    void
    invalidate ();

      // Copy the given cursor to this cursor.  This cursor then
```

```cpp
    // points to the same reservation as the given cursor.
    // Pure virtual function from ICursor.  We must override it.
  void
  copy (ICursor const& otherCursor);

    // Pure virtual function from ICursor.  We must override it.
  IBoolean
  operator == (ICursor const& rhs) const;

    // Pure virtual function from ICursor.  We must override it.
  IBoolean
  operator != (ICursor const& rhs) const;

    // Return the reservation that this cursor refers to.
  VSAReservation const&
  assoc() const;

    // Return this cursor's internal cursor that operates on the
    // reservations by member.  This internal cursor can be modified,
    // which is trading off encapsulation for better efficiency.
  IGHashKeyBagCursor< VSAReservation*, VSAMember,
                      VSAReservatKeyOps<VSAMember> > &
  asMemberCursor ();

    // Return this cursor's internal cursor that operates on the
    // reservations by member.  This internal cursor can not
    // be modified.
  IGHashKeyBagCursor< VSAReservation*, VSAMember,
                      VSAReservatKeyOps<VSAMember> > const&
  asMemberCursor () const;

    // Return this cursor's internal cursor that operates on the
    // reservations by movie.  This internal cursor can be modified,
    // which is trading off encapsulation for better efficiency.
  IGHashKeyBagCursor< VSAReservation*, VSAVideoMovie,
                      VSAReservatKeyOps<VSAVideoMovie> > &
  asVideoMovieCursor ();

    // Return this cursor's internal cursor that operates on the
    // reservations by movie.  This internal cursor can not
    // be modified.
  IGHashKeyBagCursor< VSAReservation*, VSAVideoMovie,
                      VSAReservatKeyOps<VSAVideoMovie> > const&
  asVideoMovieCursor () const;

private:

    // Our internal cursor
  IGHashKeyBagCursor< VSAReservation*, Element,
                      VSAReservatKeyOps<Element> > ivCursor;
};


//----------------------------------------------------------------------
// Inline implementations
//----------------------------------------------------------------------
```

```
inline  VSAReservationCursor<VSAMember>::VSAReservationCursor ()
: ivCursor(VSAReservation::cvByMember)
{
}

inline  VSAReservationCursor<VSAVideoMovie>::VSAReservationCursor ()
: ivCursor(VSAReservation::cvByVideoMovie)
{
}

template <class Element>
VSAReservation const&
VSAReservationCursor<Element>::assoc() const
{ return *ivCursor.element();
}

inline
IGHashKeyBagCursor< VSAReservation*, VSAMember,
                    VSAReservatKeyOps< VSAMember > > &
VSAReservationCursor<VSAMember>::asMemberCursor ()
{ return ivCursor;
}

inline
IGHashKeyBagCursor< VSAReservation*, VSAMember,
                    VSAReservatKeyOps< VSAMember > > &
VSAReservationCursor<VSAVideoMovie>::asMemberCursor ()
{ throw IException(
      "VideoMovie Cursor can not be converted to Member Cursor.");
}

inline
IGHashKeyBagCursor< VSAReservation*, VSAMember,
                    VSAReservatKeyOps< VSAMember > > const&
VSAReservationCursor<VSAMember>::asMemberCursor () const
{ return ivCursor;
}

// 8

// 9

template <class Element>
inline IBoolean
VSAReservationCursor<Element>::isValid () const
{
  return ivCursor.isValid();
}

template <class Element>
inline void
VSAReservationCursor<Element>::invalidate ()
{
  ivCursor.invalidate();
}
```

```
inline void
VSAReservationCursor<VSAMember>::copy (ICursor const&
cur)
{
  operator=( (VSAReservationCursor<VSAMember>const&) cur);
            // Explicit cast, dangerous as always!
            // Worst case could be that during memberwise assignment
            // our internal cursor throws an exception, or that
            // we get exception "Cursor is not for this collection"
            // during a following access.
}

inline void
VSAReservationCursor<VSAVideoMovie>::copy (ICursor const& cur)
{
  operator=( (VSAReservationCursor<VSAVideoMovie>const&) cur);
            // Explicit cast, dangerous as always!  See previous copy.
}

inline IBoolean
VSAReservationCursor<VSAMember>::operator == (ICursor const& rhs) const
{
  return ( ivCursor ==
           ( (VSAReservationCursor<VSAMember>const&) rhs)
           .asMemberCursor()
       );   // Another dangerous explicit cast.  If "rhs" was not the
            // same type as ours, our calling of asMemberCursor() on it
            // could bring havoc.  We have no way of preventing.
            // This is one of the cases where RTTI will help a lot.
}

inline IBoolean
VSAReservationCursor<VSAVideoMovie>::operator == (ICursor const& rhs) const
{
  return ( ivCursor ==
           ( (VSAReservationCursor<VSAVideoMovie>const&) rhs)
           .asVideoMovieCursor()
       );   // Another dangerous cast.  See previous operator==
}

template <class Element>
inline IBoolean
VSAReservationCursor<Element>::operator != ( ICursor const& rhs) const
{
   return ! operator==(rhs);
}

#endif
```

26.4.4 VSRESRVC.H

```
/*----------------------------------------------------------------*
 |  File:     VSRESRVC.H          Type: Interface                 |
 |  Classes:  VSAReservation Collections                          |
 |  Description:                                                   |
 |            The collections declared here as instantiations of   |
 |            collection class templates are used to maintain      |
 |            the set of all reservations.  There are two collections |
 |            used to provide very fast access by either one of the |
 |            elements associated by a reservation, the member, and |
 |            the video movie.                                      |
 |  Project:  Video Store Administration  Management System        |
 |  Owner:    Frank Seliger                                        |
 |  History:  96-05-17    FS, Creation                             |
 |            96-05-24    FS, Changed AVL tree to hash table KeyBag |
 *----------------------------------------------------------------*/

#ifndef VSRESRVC_H
#define VSRESRVC_H

        // Include the forward declarations.  They are redundant here,
        // but in case they are not consistent, the compiler will tell.
#include <vsresrvc.hf>

        // Include the "element operations" that the collections can
        // use to manage the elements of type member and video movie.
#include <vsresrvo.h>

        //
        // Keep the collection type used here in sync with VSRESRVC.HF !
        //
#include <ihshkb.h>  // Hash Table KeyBag

#endif /* VSRESRVC_H */
```

26.4.5 VSRESRVC.HF

```
/*----------------------------------------------------------------*
 |  File:     VSRESRVC.HF         Type: Interface Forward Declarations|
 |  Classes:  VSAReservation Collections                          |
 |  Description:                                                   |
 |            The collections declared here as instantiations of   |
 |            collection class templates are used to maintain      |
 |            the set of all reservations.  There are two collections |
 |            used to provide very fast access by either one of the |
 |            elements associated by a reservation, the member, and |
 |            the video movie.                                      |
 |            This file contains only forward declarations.  The   |
 |            advantage is that clients of VSAReservation can be    |
 |            decoupled from the collections and their templates.   |
 |  Project:  Video Store Administration  Management System        |
 |  Owner:    Frank Seliger                                        |
```

```
|  History:    96-05-17    FS, Creation                      |
|              96-05-24    FS, Changed AVL tree to hash table KeyBag  |
*-------------------------------------------------------------------*/

#ifndef VSRESRVC_HF
#define VSRESRVC_HF

        // Include the abbreviations of collection names for shorter
        // link symbols.  This is tricky: If we do not include the
        // abbreviations already here, the compile will fail.
        // Probably, the macro substitution is too late after the
        // typedefs below.
#include <iabbrev.h>

class VSAReservation;
class VSAMember;
class VSAVideoMovie;

template < class Element > class VSAReservatKeyOps;

//
// Keep the collection forward declared here in sync with VSRESRVC.H !
//
template < class Element, class Key, class Operations >
class IGHashKeyBag;
                                                    //  1
template < class Element, class Key, class Operations >
class IGHashKeyBagCursor;

typedef IGHashKeyBag< VSAReservation*,
                      VSAMember, VSAReservatKeyOps< VSAMember > >
      VSAReservationsByMember;

typedef IGHashKeyBag< VSAReservation*,
                      VSAVideoMovie, VSAReservatKeyOps< VSAVideoMovie > >
      VSAReservationsByVideoMovie;

#endif /* VSRESRVC_HF */
```

26.4.6 VSRESRVO.H

```
/*-------------------------------------------------------------------*
|  File:     VSRESRVO.H          Type: Interface and inline implem.  |
|  Classes:  VSAReservatKeyOps    class template                     |
|  Description:                                                       |
|          VSAReservatKeyOps is a class template that provides        |
|          all "element operations" that are needed by the           |
|          collections of reservations to maintain and access the    |
|          elements associated by a reservation, the member, and     |
|          the video movie.                                          |
|  Project:  Video Store Administration  Management System           |
|  Owner:    Frank Seliger                                           |
|  History:  96-05-17    FS, Creation                                |
*-------------------------------------------------------------------*/
```

```
#ifndef _VSRESRVO_H_
#define _VSRESRVO_H_

#include <isynonym.hpp>
#include <iptr.h>
#include <istdops.h>

#include <vsmember.h>
#include <vsvdomvi.h>

#include <vsresrv.h>

class VSAReservation;

// Functions to copy and destruct the elements in the collections must
// not be provided here.  We store pointers in the collections and
// for the basic data type pointer those operations are built-in.

template <class Key>                                    // 10
class VSAReservatKeyOps : public IStdMemOps
{
public:
                // We delegate assignment to the assignment defined for
  void          // the basic datatype pointer.
  assign (VSAReservation*& lhs, VSAReservation* const& rhs) const
  {
   lhs = rhs;
  }


                // Key Access
  Key const&
  key(VSAReservation* const& element) const;

  class KeyOps // Operations on the key
  {
  public:
                // Compare two keys for equal
      IBoolean
      equal (Key const& k1, Key const& k2) const
      {
        IBoolean result = (k1 == k2);
        return result;
      }

                // Hash a key into a long integer between 0 and n.
      unsigned long
      hash (Key const& k, unsigned long n) const;

  } keyOps;
};


//----------------------------------------------------------------------
// Inline implementations
//----------------------------------------------------------------------
```

```
      // For key access we have to use specialized template functions.
inline VSAMember const&
VSAReservatKeyOps<VSAMember>::key(VSAReservation* const& element) const
{ return element->member();
}


inline VSAVideoMovie const&
VSAReservatKeyOps<VSAVideoMovie>::key(VSAReservation* const& element) const
{ return element->videoMovie();
}

      // Global hash function for any kind of IString.
      // Let's hope that nobody else defined one yet.
inline unsigned long
hash (IString const& s, unsigned long n)
{ size_t len = s.length();
  if (len == 0)
    return 0;
  else {
    unsigned long result = ((s [0] + s [len-1] + s [len/2]) % n);
    return result;
  }
}

      // The Key Hash Function for VSAMember uses the member name,
      // which is an IString.
inline unsigned long
VSAReservatKeyOps<VSAMember>::KeyOps::hash ( VSAMember const& member,
                                             unsigned long n) const
{ return ::hash(member.name(), n);
}


      // The Key Hash Function for VSAVideoMovie uses the movie title,
      // which is an IString.
inline unsigned long
VSAReservatKeyOps<VSAVideoMovie>::KeyOps::hash (
                                    VSAVideoMovie const& vMovie,
                                    unsigned long n) const
{ return ::hash(vMovie.title(), n);
}

#endif
```

26.4.7 Comments on the code

1   This technique to use forward declarations instead of the full declarations wherever possible has several advantages. It minimizes the dependencies. In the case here, where the collections used are templates, the compile time (and often code size as well) for unnecessary template instantiations can be saved.

2   Cursors are pointing to elements contained in a collection. They are used in combination with locate commands, which set the cursor to the element that was located, or in combination with iterations over the elements in the collection (for this reason another commonly used name is "iterator" [Gamma95]. They must access the internal structure of the collection and therefore be `friend` of the collection. John Vlissides, one of the authors of [Gamma95], has called this "controlled breakage of encapsulation."

3   The add, remove, and locate member functions are declared `static.` because they do not operate on an instance of a reservation. The add member function, for example, creates a new reservation and adds it to all reservations. Bear in mind that class `VSAReservation` has two important roles: to provide the master plan for the data and services of reservation objects and to maintain collections that provide different ways of accessing all reservations in the system. The `static` member functions perform the latter role.

4   This project decided to have the class and function descriptions that came out of the design, in the source code header files. The advantage is that a programmer using the class can work with the header file only and have most of the information at hand. The disadvantage is that the header files can get large and bulky. Also, keeping the description synchronized between design and code is almost impossible when the design tool does not provide support for this.

5   A better name (one that makes more sense for the clients of this class) would be `locateReservationFor`. The `Assoc` came from the fact that a reservation is an association between members and video movies.

6   Several other locate functions are not shown here since they are using the same concepts as the locate function shown above and below.

7   The question of what to `inline` is to a certain degree a matter of taste. The most common strategies are either not to inline at all unless an execution performance measurement (profiling) determines a function to be critical, or to inline all trivial functions, such as those setting or returning a data member. This team here followed the latter approach to inlining, which can lead to storage size problems when overdone.

8   The five remaining `as...Cursor` functions are not shown here.

9   Also not shown are some overridden functions that were declared by the base class ICursor and are implemented by delegating them directly to the internal cursor as in the functions below.

10   Key is VSAMember or VSAVideoMovie in our case.

27.0 Case Study: Testing Work Products

27.1 TEST CASES

The integration and unit testing cases are developed at a lower level to validate each unit and subsystem. The set of test cases below are developed based on the design scenarios that are derived from analysis scenarios. The following system testing level test cases for the use cases "Customer rents video" and "Member reserves video" have been identified (partial list):

- Test case 1.1: Member Rents Video (successfully)

  - *Objective*: This test must demonstrate that the system can successfully rent video tapes to those members in good standing.
  - *Requirements*:
    — Hardware: The network, client/server configuration must be ready.
    — Software: Database, database connections, and front client subsystem must be ready having proper database authorization for each client access.
  - *Assumed Input*:
    — The customer is a member in good standing.
    — A copy of the movie is available.
  - *Execution Step: (manual)*
    — The clerk inputs the cassette's bar code into the system.
    — On the input screen, the clerk must enter the customer information and renting information.
  - *Output:*
    — The system will confirm the renting and print out a receipt.

- Test case 1.2: Member Rents Video (successfully)

  - *Objective*: This test must demonstrate that the system can successfully rent video tapes to those members who are not in good standing but paid fine at the point of sale.
  - *Requirements*:
    — Hardware: The network, client/server configuration must be ready.
    — Software: Database, database connections, and front client subsystem must be ready, having proper database authorization for each client access.
  - *Assumed Input:*
    — The customer is a member in good standing.
    — A copy of the movie is available.
  - *Execution Step: (manual)*

— The clerk inputs the cassette's bar code into the system.
— On the input screen, the clerk must enter the customer information and renting information.
— The system gives a warning sign and displays the fine owed.
— The clerk inputs the payment matching the fine amount.
  – *Output:*
— The system will confirm the renting and print out a receipt. The customer is in a good standing status again.

• Test case 4.1: Member Reserves Video (successfully)

  – *Objective*:   This test must demonstrate that the system can successfully reserve video tapes for those members in good standing.
  – *Requirements*:
— Hardware: The network, client/server configuration must be ready.
— Software: Database, database connections, and front client subsystem must be ready having proper database authorization for each client access.
  – *Assumed Input:*
— The customer is a member, in good standing.
  – *Execution Step: (manual)*
— The member must input his/her membership information first.
— The member searches and selects a movie name in the system. The system will play a short introduction of the movie, with its clips.
— On the input screen, the member must enter the reserve button.
— The system gives a confirm sign when the transaction is completed.
  – *Output:*
— The system will confirm the reservation.
— The member will be notified of the availability of the movie.

Author's Commentary

This list was developed by the test team starting with the identified scenarios. There are, of course, many test cases very closely associated with nonsuccessful return, which are not fully shown in the list above, such as:

• Member wants to rent a video, but cassette has wrong or damaged bar code

• Member wants to rent cassette, but clerk misspells customer's name

Test cases have to check for every branch/outcome. Scenarios usually cover only the interesting flow.

28.0 Case Study: Appendix Work Products

28.1 GLOSSARY

Bar code A unique inventory control number assigned to each video copy.

Category Type of video; Action, Comedy, Children, et cetera.

Customer A person the store does business with (sales and/or rentals).

Customer Kiosk A view of the video catalog in the store that would allow customers to browse and make queries of existing videos.

Member A customer who has a membership card. Only members can reserve videos. A member requires a drivers license and a credit card (Amex, Visa or Mastercard) in order to receive membership.

Rental agreement A transaction that indicates video(s) have been checked out by a customer. It states the title of the movie(s), customer, date and time rented, date due to be returned, and price.

Reservation A request from a customer to either hold a stocked video for one day or to go into a queue for a checked-out video.

Receipt A printed rental agreement.

Shelf Racks in the store where videos are stored.

Shop/Store A location where videos are rented and sold.

Vendor A person or a company the store purchases videos from.

Video catalogue A list of available videos the store owns.

Author's Commentary

The team is using a project glossary to ensure that the development team develops and maintains a common understanding of the terms that are important to the Video Store domain. Since they are not, themselves, the domain experts, the decision to have a glossary is an important and wise one.

28.2 HISTORICAL WORK PRODUCTS

> **Author's Commentary**
>
> The team has decided to set aside early versions of the object model, some Analysis Object Interaction Diagrams, and some of the rejected design alternatives. This will allow the team to review the evolution of the work products should they begin to question why certain decisions were made later in the process. This happens regularly in software development, of course.

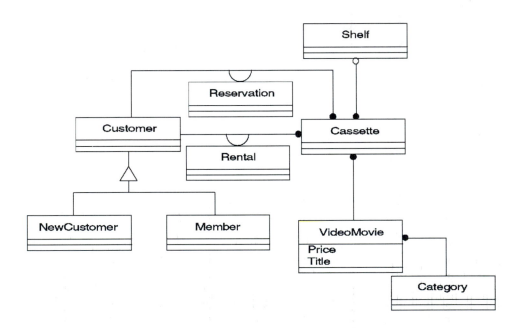

Figure 28-1. *Early Draft of Video Store Object Model.*

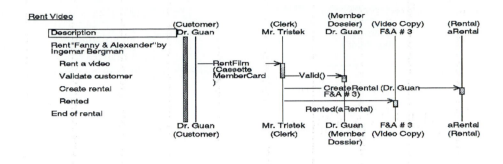

Figure 28-2. *Early Draft of Analysis OID (From Working Sessions).*   Member rents a video successfully.

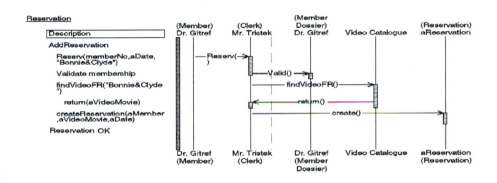

Figure 28-3. *Early Draft of Analysis OID (From Working Sessions).*   Member reserves a video (Scenario 10.1).

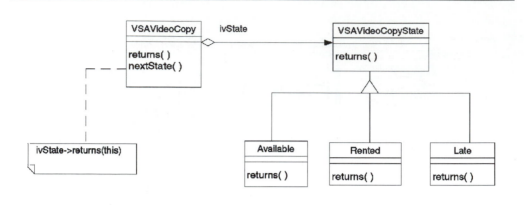

Figure 28-4. *Design of VideoCopyState (Rejected Design Alternative).* Member reserves a video (Scenario 10.1).

28.2.1 Semantic Network

This was developed during a brainstorming session at the start of the project. Users were asked to discuss the world of video stores, before they had seen the Problem Statement.

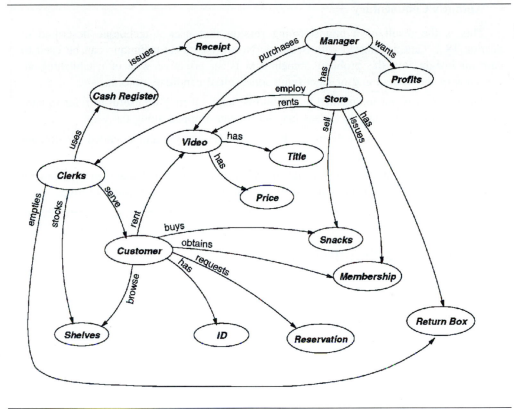

Figure 28-5. *Semantic Network.*

From the above diagram we have identified the following candidate classes:

- Customer
- Video
- Clerk
- Membership
- Reservation
- Receipt

Author's Commentary

This is the result of a brainstorming session that uses a technique described in Section 18.2, Getting Started with Semantic Networks. This technique can be used to gain an insight into the problem domain and is an effective way of establishing an overview of the system and of identifying some initial candidate objects.

The diagram is not maintained but should be kept. It may be useful to refer to later in the project to see if any key ideas may have been dropped along the way.

The session would have been led by an ACME analyst and attended by domain experts.

The candidate classes were selected from the diagram by the team after reviewing the Problem Statement. It is pretty much an educated guess at this point in time.

28.3 COMMON ATTRIBUTES

Author's Commentary

Table 28-1 is used by the development team to maintain common attributes of work products, see Section 8.1. Using this method keeps the work products themselves focused on content and allows for quick reference of important common attributes of work products, such as ownership.

Table 28-1 (Page 1 of 3). Common Attributes of Work Products.

Work Product	Identifier	Date	Author	Owner	Status	Issues	Metrics	Traceability (impacts)	Change History
							Common Attributes of Work Products		
Problem Statement (1)	PS01	1/12	TB	TB	done	See Issues WP	identified 4 actors, 14 objects	Seeded Glossary	updated 1/9, 1/10, 1/11
Use Case Model	UCM	1/12	PF	PF	started		24 Use Cases		
- Use Case	UC01	1/12	PF	PF	done		n/a	AS01.1-1.5	
- Use Case	UC02	1/12	PF	PF	done		n/a	AS02	
- Use Case	UC03	1/12	PF	PF	done		n/a	AS03.1	updated 1/10
- Use Case	UC04	1/12	TB	TB	done		n/a	AS04	
- Use Case	UC05	1/12	TB	TB	done		n/a	AS05	
- Use Case	UC06	1/12	TB	TB	done		n/a	AS06	updated 1/9, 1/10
- Use Case	UC07	1/12	PF	PF	done		n/a	AS07	
- Use Case	UC08	1/12	PF	PF	done		n/a	AS08	
- Use Case	UC09	1/12	GL	GL	done		n/a	AS09	
- Use Case	UC10	1/12	GL	GL	done		n/a	AS10.1	updated 1/11
- Use Case	UC11	1/12	TB	TB	done		n/a	AS11	
- Use Case	UC12	1/12	PF	PF	done		n/a	AS12	
- Use Case	UC13	1/12	GL	GL	done		n/a	AS13	
- Use Case	UC14	1/12	GL	GL	done		n/a	AS14	
- Use Case	UC15	1/13	PF	PF	done		n/a	AS15	
- Use Case	UC16	1/13	PF	PF	done		n/a	AS16	
- Use Case	UC17	1/13	GL	GL	done		n/a	AS17	updated 1/12
- Use Case	UC18	1/13	PF	PF	done		n/a	AS18	
- Use Case	UC19	1/13	GL	GL	done		n/a	AS19	
- Use Case	UC20	1/13	PF	PF	done		n/a	AS20	
- Use Case	UC21	1/13	GL	GL	done		n/a	AS21	
- Use Case	UC22	1/13	PF	PF	done		n/a	AS22	updated 1/11
- Use Case	UC23	1/13	TB	TB	done		n/a	AS23	
- Use Case	UC24	1/13	TB	TB	done		n/a	AS24	
Nonfunctional Requirements	NFR01	1/12	PF	PF	started	Y	15 NFRs	Impacts ARCH01	
Business Case	BC01	1/12	PF	PF	done			RSC01, SCHD01, REL01	
Acceptance Plan	AP01	1/12	PF	PF	done		5 categories	TP01	
Intended Development Process	IDP01	1/12	PF	PF	done			SCHD01, REL01, AG01, DG01, CG01	updated 1/10
Resource Plan	RSC01	1/26	TK	TK	done	Y	11 on-board	SCHD01, REL01	
Schedule	SCHD01	1/12	TK	TK	done	Y	24 activities	RSC01, REL01	
Release Plan	REL01	1/12	TB	TB	done		3 releases planned	SCHD01, RSC01	

Table 28-1 (Page 2 of 3). Common Attributes of Work Products.

Work Product	Identifier	Date	Author	Owner	Status	Issues	Metrics	Traceability (impacts)	Change History
Quality Assurance Plan	QAP01	1/26	TK	TK	done			SCHD01, TP01, AG01, DG01, CG01	updated 1/11, 1/14
Risk Management Plan	RMP01	2/16	PF	PF	ongoing		2 risks	UIP01, ARCH01	updated 1/24, 1/31, 2/7
Reuse Plan	REU01	2/16	TW	TW	done		2 classlibs	ARCH01, DG01	
Test Plan	TP01	2/16	TG	TG	started	Y	3 phases	SCHD01, RSC01, REL01	
Metrics	MET01	1/12	TK	TK	done	Y	7 metrics chosen	AG01, DG01, CG01	
Project Dependencies	PD01	1/26	TG	TG	done		6 determined	RMP01, REL01, SCHD01	
Issues	ISU01	1/12	TB	TB	started		26 issues	everything	
Analysis Guidelines	AG01	2/26	PF	PF	started		5 WPs	all Analysis WPs	updated 2/7
Analysis Object Model	AOM01	2/26	GL	GL	started	Y	16 Classes		
Analysis Scenarios	AS	2/26	TB	TB	started	Y	8 Scenarios		
- Analysis Scenario	AS01.0	2/26	TB	TB	started	Y		AOID01.0	
- Analysis Scenario	AS01.1	2/26	TB	TB	started	Y		AOID01.1	
- Analysis Scenario	AS01.2	2/26	TB	TB	started	Y		AOID01.2	updated 2/14, 2/15
- Analysis Scenario	AS01.3	2/26	TB	TB	started	Y		AOID01.3	
- Analysis Scenario	AS01.4	2/26	TB	TB	started	Y		AOID01.4	
- Analysis Scenario	AS01.5	2/26	TB	TB	started	Y		AOID01.5	
- Analysis Scenario	AS03.1	2/26	TB	TB	started	Y		AOID03.1	
- Analysis Scenario	AS10.1	2/26	TB	TB	started	Y		AOID10.1	
Analysis OIDs	AOID	2/26	GY	GY	started	Y	3 OIDs		updated 2/24
- Analysis OID	AOID01.0	2/26	GY	GY	started	Y	5 Obj, 5 Msg		
- Analysis OID	AOID10.1	2/26	GY	GY	started	Y	5 Obj, 4 Msg		
- Analysis OID	AOIDVL	2/26	GY	GY	started	Y	3 Obj, 3 Msg	AOID01.0, AOID10.1	
Analysis State Models	ASM01	2/26	TB	TB	started	Y	9 states, 16 transitions		
Analysis Class Descriptions	ACD	2/26	PF	PF	started		2 ACDs		
- Analysis Class Description	ACD-Movie	2/26	PF	PF	started		7 methods		updated 2/17
- Analysis Class Description	ACD-Copy	2/26	PF	PF	started		10 methods		
User Interface Guidelines	UIG01	3/8	PF	PF	done				
Screen Flow	SF01	3/8	JB	JB	done	Y	9 screens	SL01-09	
Screen Layouts	SL	3/8	JB	JB	started		2 screens		updated 2/28
- Screen Layout	SL01	3/8	JB	JB	started				
- Screen Layout	SL01	3/8	JB	JB	started				
User Interface Prototype	UIP01	3/8	HF team	HF team	started				
Design Guidelines	DG01	3/15	PF	PF	started	Y	13 guidelines		

Table 28-1 (Page 3 of 3). Common Attributes of Work Products.

Work Product	Identifier	Date	Author	Owner	Common Attributes of Work Products				
					Status	Issues	Metrics	Traceability (impacts)	Change History
Architecture	ARCH01	3/15	PF	PF	started	Y			
APIs	AP01	3/15	PF	PF	started				updated 3/11
Target Environment	TE01	1/12	DH	DH	done				
Subsystems	SUBS01	3/15	PF	PF	started		8 subsystems		
Design Object Model	DOM01	3/15	GL	GL	started	Y	17 Classes		
Design Scenarios	DS	3/15	PF	PF	started	Y	8 Scenarios		
- **Design Scenario**	DS01.0	3/15	TB	TB	started	Y		DOID01.0	
- **Design Scenario**	DS01.1	3/15	TB	TB	started	Y		DOID01.1	updated 3/12
- **Design Scenario**	DS01.2	3/15	TB	TB	started	Y		DOID01.2	
- **Design Scenario**	DS01.3	3/15	TB	TB	started	Y		DOID01.3	
- **Design Scenario**	DS01.4	3/15	TB	TB	started	Y		DOID01.4	
- **Design Scenario**	DS01.5	3/15	TB	TB	started	Y		DOID01.5	
- **Design Scenario**	DS03.1	3/15	TB	TB	started	Y		DOID03.1	updated 3/12
- **Design Scenario**	DS10.1	3/15	TB	TB	started	Y		DOID10.1	
Design OIDs	DOID	3/15	GY	GY	started	Y	8 OIDs		
- **Design OID**	DOID10.1	3/15	GY	GY	started	Y	5 Objs, 5 Msgs		updated 3/10
- **Design OID**	DOID10.2	3/15	GY	GY	started	Y	4 Objs, 5 Msgs		
Design State Models	DSM01	3/15	GY	GY	started	Y	5 states, 11 transitions		
Design Class Descriptions	DCD	3/15	PF	PF	started		2 classes		
- **Design Class Description**	Reservation	3/15	PF	PF	started		11 methods	VSRESRV.H/CPP	
- **Design Class Description**	VideoCopy	3/15	PF	PF	started		9 methods	VSVDOCOP.H/CPP	updated 3/13
Rejected Design Alternatives	RDA01	3/15	PF	PF	started		2 RDAs		
Coding Guidelines	CG01	1/12	JB	JB	done				
Development Environment	DE01	2/16	FS	FS	done				
Source Code	SC	3/15	FS	FS	started		3 classes, 2 utility classes, 8 files		updated 3/14
- **Source Code**	VSAMEMBER.H	3/15	FS	FS	started		23 LOC		updated 3/14
- **Source Code**	VSVDOMV1.H	3/15	FS	FS	started		22 LOC		updated 3/14
- **Source Code**	VSRESRV.H/CPP,	3/15	FS	FS	started		174 LOC		updated 3/14
- **Source Code**	VSRESCUR.H, VSRESRVC.H/.HF, VXRESRVO.H	3/15	FS	FS	started		131 LOC + 22 LOC pragma/typedef +29 LOC ops		updated 3/14
Test Cases	TC01	3/15	TG	TG	open	Y	0 test cases		
Glossary	GLOS01	1/12	PF	PF	started	Y	12 terms		
Historical Work Products	HWP01	1/12	PF	PF	started		3 WPs		

Note:
- (1) Provided by the customer

Part 6. Appendixes

Appendix A. Sources and References

[Apple92]   Apple, *Macintosh Human Interface Guidelines*, Reading, MA: Addison-Wesley, 1992.

[Arthur92]   Lowell J. Arthur,, *Improving Software Quality: An Insider's Guide to TQM*, New York, NY: John Wiley & Sons, Inc., 1992. ISBN:0-471-57804-5.

[Barton94]   John J. Barton and Lee R. Nackman, *Scientific and Engineering C++: An Introduction with Advance Techniques and Examples*, Reading, MA: Addison-Wesley Publishing Co.,, 1994. ISBN 0-201-53393-6.

[Bekke92]   J.H. ter Bekke, *Semantic Data Modelling*, Prentice-Hall, 1992.

[Binder94]   Robert V. Binder, "Testing Object-Oriented Systems: A Status Report," *American Programmer*, pp. 22–28,, April 1994.

[Boehm88]   Barry Boehm, "A spiral model of software development and enhancement," *Computer*, vol. 21, no. 5, pp. 61–72, May 1988.

[Boehm89]   Barry Boehm, *Software Risk Management*, Washington, D.C.: IEEE Computer Society Press, 1989. ISBN 0-8186-8906-4.

[Booch94]   Grady Booch, *Object-Oriented Analysis and Design with Applications*, Benjamin/Cummings Publishing Company, Inc., 1994.

[Booch96]   Rational Software Corporation, "The Unified Modeling Language for Object-Oriented Development, July, 1996.

[Cattell94a]   R. G. G. Cattell, *Object data management: object-oriented and extended relational database systems, Revised Edition*, Addison-Wesley Publishing Company, 1994. ISBN 0-201-54748-1.

[Cattell94b]   R. G. G. Cattell, *ed., The Object Database Standard—ODMG-93*, Morgan Kaufmann Publishers, 1994.

[Church95]   Terry Church and Philip Matthews, Evaluation of Object-Oriented Case Tools: the Newbridge Experience, Software Engineering, pp. 4–9, 1995.

[Civelo93]   Franco Civelo, "Roles for composite objects on object-oriented analysis and design," *OOPSLA '93 Proceedings*, pp. 376–393, 1993.

601

[Cline95]   Marshal Cline and Greg Lomow, *C++ FAQs: Frequently Asked Questions*, Reading, MA: Addison-Wesley Publishing Co., 1995. ISBN 0-201-58958-3.

[Coad90]   Peter Coad and Ed Yourdon, *Object-Oriented Analysis*, Englewood Cliffs, NJ: Yourdon Press, Prentice-Hall, 1990.

[Coleman94]   Derek Coleman, et al., *Object-Oriented Development: The Fusion Method*, Englewood Cliffs, NJ: Prentice-Hall, 1994.

[Collins95]   Dave Collins, *Designing Object-Oriented User Interfaces*, Benjamin/Cummings Publishing Company, Inc., 1995. ISBN 0-8053-5350-X.

[Connell89]   J. Connell and L. Shafer, *Structured Rapid Prototyping*, Englewood Cliffs, NJ: Yourdon Press, Prentice Hall, 1989. ISBN 0-13-853573-6.

[Cook94]   Steve Cook and John Daniels, *Designing Object Systems: Object-Oriented Modelling with Syntropy*, Prentice-Hall, 1994. ISBN 0-13-203860-9.

[D'Souza94]   Desmond D'Souza and Petter Graff, "Integration of OMT Models," *Report on Object Analysis and Design*, September 1994.

[D'Souza95]   Desmond D'Souza and Petter Graff, "Working with OMT: model integration," *Journal of Object-oriented Programming*, pp. 23–29, February 1995.

[DeGrace90]   Peter DeGrace and Leslie H. Stahl, *Wicked Problems, Righteous Solutions, A Catalogue of Modern Software Engineering Paradigms*, NJ: Yourdon Press, Prentice Hall, Inc., 1990.

[Demarco79]   Tom Demarco, *Structured Analysis and System Specification*, NJ: Yourdon Press, 1979.

[Derrer95]   Kurt W. Derrer, *Applying OMT: A Practical Step-by-Step Guide to Using the Object Modeling Technique*, New York: SIGS Books, 1995.

[Dietrich89]   Walter Dietrich, Lee Nackman and Franklin Gracer, "Saving a Legacy with Objects," *OOPSLA '89 Proceedings*, pp. 77–83, 1989.

[Fang94]   Walter Fang, Andrew C. So, Alessandro Mottadelli, Daniel Tkach and Thomas K. Donahue, "Object Oriented Application Development with VisualAge in a Client/Server Environment", San Jose, California, USA: IBM International Technical Support Organization, June 1994. Document GG24-4227-00.

[Flanagan96]   David Flanagan, *Java in a Nutshell*, Sebastopol, CA: O'Reilly & Associates, Inc., 1996. ISBN 1-56592-183-6.

[Fowler95]   Susan Fowler and Victor Stanwick, *The GUI Style Guide*, Cambridge, MA: Academic Press, Inc., 1995. ISBN 0-12-263590-6.

[Gamma95]   Erich Gamma, Richard Helm, Ralph Johnson and John Vlissides, *Design Patterns: Elements of Reusable Object-Oriented Software*, Addison-Wesley Publishing Co., Reading, MA, 1995. ISBN 0-201-63361-2.

[Gibson90]   E. Gibson, "Objects—Born and Bred," *BYTE*, October 1990.

[Goldberg83]   A. Goldberg and D. Robson, *Smalltalk-80: The Language and its Implementation*, Addison-Wesley Publishing Co., Reading, MA, 1983.

[Goldberg95]   Adele Goldberg and Kenneth S. Rubin, *Succeeding with Object Technology: Decision Frameworks for Project Management*, Addison-Wesley Publishing Co., Reading, MA, 1995. ISBN 0-201-62878-3.

[Goldsmith94]   David Goldsmith, *Taligent's Guide to Designing Programs—Well-Mannered Object-Oriented Design in C++*, Addison-Wesley Publishing Co., Reading, MA, 1994. ISBN 0-201-40888-0.

[Graham95]   Ian Graham, *Migrating to Object Technology*, Addison-Wesley Publishing Co., Reading, MA, 1995. ISBN 0-201-59389-0.

[Griss93]   Martin Griss, "Software Reuse: from Library to Factory," *IBM Systems Journal*, vol. 92, no. 4, 1993.

[Harel87]   David Harel, "StateCharts: A visual formalism for complex systems," *Science of Computer Programming*, vol. 8, no. 3, pp. 231–274, North Holland, 1987.

[Henderson-S96] Brian Henderson-Sellers, *Object-Oriented Metrics: Measures of Complexity*, Prentice Hall, 1996.

[IBM93]   IBM, IBM CSet++ Collection Class Library Reference, 1993. SC09-1604.

[IBM Corp.91]   IBM Corp., Information Development Guideline: Task-Oriented Information, 1991. Document ZZ27-1971-01.

[IBM Corp.95]   IBM Corp., Building VisualAge C++ Parts for Fun and Profit, 1995. Document S25H-6968.

[IBM94a]   IBM, *IBM Smalltalk & VisualAge Team Development Guide*, IBM SC34-4494, 1994.

[IBM94b]   IBM, *Object-Oriented Interface Design: IBM Common User Access Guidelines*, Que Corporation, 1994. ISBN 1-56529-170.

[Jacobson92]   Ivar Jacobson, Magnus Christerson, Patrik Jonsson and Gunnar Övergaard, *Object-Oriented Software Engineering: A Use Case Driven Approach*, Addison-Wesley Publishing Company, 1992.   ISBN 0-201-54435-0.

[Kaplan95]   Craig Kaplan, Ralph Clark and Victor Tang, *Secrets of Software Quality: 40 Innovations from IBM*, New York, NY: McGraw-Hill, Inc., 1995. ISBN 0-07-911795-3.

[Karlsson95]   Even-Andre Karlsson, *Software Reuse: A Holistic Approach*, West Sussex, England: John Wiley & Sons, Inc., 1995. ISBN 0-471-95489-6.

[Korson96]   Timothy D. Korson and Vijay K. Vaishnavi, *Object Technology Centers of Excellence*, Manning Publications Co., 1996. ISBN 1-884777-16-3.

[Korson92]   Timothy Korson, "Technical criteria for the specification and evaluation of object-oriented libraries," *Software Engineering Journal*, vol. 7, no. 2, March 1992.

[Krasner88]   Glenn Krasner and Stephen T. Pope, "A cookbook for using the model-view-controller user interface paradigm in Smalltalk-80," *Journal of Object-Oriented Programming*, vol. 1, no. 3, pp. 26–49, 1988.

[Kristen94]   Gerald Kristen, *Object-Orientation—The KISS Method—From Information Architecture to Information System*, Addison-Wesley Publishing Company, 1994.

[Loomis95]   Mary Loomis, *Object Databases—The Essentials*, Reading, MA: Addison-Wesley Publishing Co., 1995.

[Lorenz94]   Mark Lorenz and Jeff Kidd, *Object-Oriented Software Metrics*, Englewood Cliffs, NJ: Prentice Hall, 1994. ISBN 0-13-179292-X.

[Malan96]   Ruth Malan, Reed Letsinger and Derek Coleman, *Object-Oriented Development at Work: Fusion in the Real World*, Upper Saddle River, NJ: Prentice-Hall, 1996.

[Martin95]   Robert C. Martin, *Designing Object-Oriented C++ Applications Using The Booch Method*, Englewood Cliffs, NJ: Prentice Hall, 1995. ISBN 0-13-203837-4.

[Mayhew92]   Deborah Mayhew, *Principles and Guidelines in Software User Interface Design*, Englewood Cliffs, NJ: Prentice Hall, 1992. ISBN 0-13-721929-6.

[Mays90]   R. G. Mays, C. L. Jones, G. J. Holloway and D. P. Studinski, "Experiences with Defect Prevention Systems," *IBM Systems Journal*, vol. 29, no. 1, 1990.

[McDavid96]   D. W. McDavid, "Business Language Analysis for Object-Oriented Information Systems," *IBM Systems Journal*, vol. 35, no. 2, pp. 128–150, 1996.

[Meyers92]   Scott Meyers, *Effective C++: 50 Specific Ways to Improve Your Programs and Designs*, Reading, MA: Addison-Wesley Publishing Co., 1992. ISBN 0-201-56364-9.

[Meyers96]   Scott Meyers, *More Effective C++: 35 New Ways to Improve Your Programs and Designs*, Reading, MA: Addison-Wesley Publishing Co., 1996. ISBN 0-201-63371-X.

[Microsoft92]   Microsoft, *The Windows Interface: An Application Design Guide*, Microsoft Press, 1992.

[Monarchi92]   David E. Monarchi and Gretchen I. Puhr, "A Research Typology for Object-Oriented Analysis and Design," *Communications of the ACM*, vol. 35, no. 9, pp. 35–47, 1992.

[Nerson92]   J. M. Nerson, "Applying Object-Oriented Analysis and Design," *Communications of the ACM*, vol. 35, no. 9, pp. 63–67, September 1992.

[OSF93]   OSF, *OSF/Motif Style Guide*, Prentice Hall, 1993.

[Poulin93]   J. M. Poulin, J. M. Caruso and D. R. Hancock, "The Business Case for Software Reuse," *IBM Systems Journal*, vol. 32, no. 4, pp. 567–594, 1993.

[Pree95]   Wolfgang Pree, *Design Patterns for Object-Oriented Software Development*, Addison-Wesley, 1995.

[Pressman92]   Roger S. Pressman, *Software Engineering A Practitioner's Approach*, McGraw-Hill International Editions, 1992. ISBN:0-07-112779-8.

[Rakos90]   J .J. Rakos, *Software Project Management for Small to Medium Sized Projects*, Prentice-Hall, 1990.

[Reenskaug96]   Trygve Reenskaug, Per Wold and Odd Arild Lehne, *Working with Objects: The OORAM Software Engineering Method*, Manning Publications Co., 1996. ISBN 1-884777-10-4.

[Rubin94]   Kenneth S. Rubin, "Object Behavior Analysis (OBA)," in Andrew Hutt, editor, *Object Analysis and Design: Description of Methods*, New York: John Wiley & Sons, Inc., 1994. ISBN 0-471-62366-0.

[Rubin92]   Kenneth S. Rubin and Adele Goldberg, "Object Behavior Analysis," *Communications of the ACM*, vol. 35, no. 9, pp. 48–62, September 1992.

[Rumbaugh95a]   James Rumbaugh, "OMT: The object model," *Journal of Object-Oriented Programming*, January 1995.

[Rumbaugh95b]   James Rumbaugh, "OMT: The dynamic model," *Journal of Object-Oriented Programming*, February 1995.

[Rumbaugh91a]   James Rumbaugh, Michael Blaha, William Premerlani, Frederick Eddy and William Lorenson, *Object-Oriented Modeling and Design*, Prentice Hall, 1991. ISBN 0-13-630054-5.

[Rumbaugh91b]   James Rumbaugh, Michael Blaha, William Premerlani, Frederick Eddy and William Lorenson, *Solutions Manual: Object-Oriented Modeling and Design*, Prentice Hall, 1991. ISBN 0-13-629858-3.

[Schafer94]   W. Schafer, R. Prieto-Díaz and M. Matsumoto, *Software Reusability*, United Kingdom: Ellis Horwood, 1994.

[Schulmeyer90]   G. Schulmeyer, *Zero Defect Software*, New York, NY: McGraw-Hill, Inc., 1990. ISBN 0-07-055663-6.

[Selic94]   Bran Selic, *Real-Time Object-Oriented Modeling*, John Wiley & Sons, Inc., 1994. ISBN 0-471-59917-4.

[Shlaer88]   Sally Shlaer and Stephen J. Mellor, *Object -Oriented Systems Analysis: Modeling the World in Data*, Englewood Cliffs, NJ: Yourdon Press, 1988.

[Shlaer92]   Sally Shlaer and Stephen J. Mellor, *Object Lifecycles: Modeling the World in States*, Englewood Cliffs, NJ: Yourdon Press, 1992.

[Siegel96]   S. Siegel, *Object-Oriented Software Testing: A Hierarchical Approach*, New York, NY: John Wiley & Sons, Inc., 1996.

[Skublics95]   Suzanne Skublics, Edward Klimas and David Thomas, *Smalltalk with Style*, Prentice Hall, 1995. ISBN 0-13-165549-3.

[Spivey88]   J. M. Spivey, *The Z Notation: A Reference Manual*, Prentice-Hall International, 1988.

[Stevens81]   W. P. Stevens, *Using Structured Design*, Toronto, Canada: A Wiley-Interscience Publication, 1981.

[Stroustrup92]   Bjarne Stroustrup, *The C++ Programming Language—Second Edition*, Addison-Wesley Publishing Company, 1992.

[Tracz95]   Will Tracz, *Confessions of a Used Program Salesman Institutionalizing Software Reuse*, Addison-Wesley Publishing Co., Reading, MA, 1995. ISBN 0-201-63369-8.

[Walden95]   Kim Walden and Jean-Marc Nerson, *Seamless Object-Oriented Software Architecture: Analysis and Design of Reliable Systems*, Prentice-Hall, 1995. ISBN 0-13-031303-3.

[Whitten89]   Neal Whitten, *Managing Software Development Projects Formula for Success*, John Wiley & Sons, Inc., 1989. ISBN:0-471-51255-9.

[Williams95]   Tom Williams, "Object-Oriented CASE tools carve a path from concept to code", Computer Design, October 1995. Vol. 3, No. 10

[Wirfs-Brock92]   Rebecca Wirfs-Brock, Object Design, 1992. Class notes.

[Wirfs-Brock89]   Rebecca Wirfs-Brock and Brian Wilkerson, "Object-Oriented Design: A Responsibility-Driven Approach," *OOPSLA '89 Proceedings*, 1989.

[Wirfs-Brock90]   R. Wirfs-Brock, B. Wilkerson and L. Wiener, *Designing Object-Oriented Software*, Prentice Hall, 1990.

[Yuan95]   George Yuan, "A Depth-First Process Model for Object-Oriented Development with Improved OOA/OOD Notations", Report on Object Analysis & Design, May–June 1995. Volume 2, No. I.

Appendix B. Workbook Skeleton

The skeleton shown below can be used to create your project workbook in HTML so that it can be viewed with a World Wide Web browser from your local or distributed file system or via the Internet or via your company's Intranet. We used the HyperText Markup Language (HTML) to do this, but it is simple enough to translate this to any markup language (e.g. GML, SGML), or use similar level headings in any word processor.

Modify the <TITLE>, Release, and Owner fields of each file with your project information.

The first file, named workbook.html, is simply a table of contents that gets the browser to the particular phase or work product of interest. You can think of this as your Project Workbook Outline. If your project decides that certain work products will not be done then simply comment out or delete them from this file.

```
<HTML><HEAD>
<TITLE>XYZ Project Workbook</TITLE>
</HEAD><BODY>
<H1>XYZ Project Workbook</H1>
<P>Release: 1.0
<P>Owner:    (project leader)<BR>
<HR><P><H2>Table of Contents</H2><P>
<P><B><A HREF="reqmnts.html" >Requirements</A></B><BR>
<MENU>
<LI><A HREF="probstmt.html" >Problem Statement</A>
<LI><A HREF="usecasem.html" >Use Case Model</A>
<LI><A HREF="nfreqts.html" >Nonfunctional Requirements</A>
<LI><A HREF="reqtspri.html" >Requirements Prioritization</A>
<LI><A HREF="buscase.html" >Business Case</A>
<LI><A HREF="accplan.html" >Acceptance Plan</A>
</MENU>
<P><B><A HREF="projmgmt.html" >Project Management</A></B><BR>
<MENU>
<LI><A HREF="idevproc.html" >Intended Development Process</A>
<LI><A HREF="wboutlin.html" >Project Workbook Outline</A>
<LI><A HREF="resplan.html" >Resource Plan</A>
<LI><A HREF="schedule.html" >Schedule</A>
<LI><A HREF="relplan.html" >Release Plan</A>
<LI><A HREF="qualplan.html" >Quality Assurance Plan</A>
<LI><A HREF="riskplan.html" >Risk Management Plan</A>
<LI><A HREF="reusplan.html" >Reuse Plan</A>
<LI><A HREF="testplan.html" >Test Plan</A>
<LI><A HREF="metrics.html" >Metrics</A>
<LI><A HREF="projdeps.html" >Project Dependencies</A>
```

```
<LI><A HREF="issues.html" >Issues</A>
</MENU>
<P><B><A HREF="analysis.html" >Analysis</A></B><BR>
<MENU>
<LI><A HREF="anaguide.html" >Analysis Guidelines</A>
<LI><A HREF="asubarea.html" >Analysis Subject Areas</A>
<LI><A HREF="aobjmod.html" >Analysis Object Model</A>
<LI><A HREF="ascenars.html" >Analysis Scenarios</A>
<LI><A HREF="aoids.html" >Analysis Object Interaction Diagrams</A>
<LI><A HREF="astmods.html" >Analysis State Models</A>
<LI><A HREF="aclsdes.html" >Analysis Class Descriptions</A>
</MENU>
<P><B><A HREF="uimodel.html" >User Interface Model</A></B><BR>
<MENU>
<LI><A HREF="uiguide.html" >User Interface Guidelines</A>
<LI><A HREF="uscrflow.html" >Screen Flows</A>
<LI><A HREF="uscrlayo.html" >Screen Layouts</A>
<LI><A HREF="uiproto.html" >User Interface Prototype</A>
</MENU>
<P><B><A HREF="design.html" >Design</A></B><BR>
<MENU>
<LI><A HREF="desguide.html" >Design Guidelines</A>
<LI><A HREF="dsysarch.html" >System Architecture</A>
<LI><A HREF="dapis.html" >Application Programming Interfaces (APIs)</A>
<LI><A HREF="dtargenv.html" >Target environment</A>
<LI><A HREF="dsubsysm.html" >Subsystem Model</A>
<LI><A HREF="dobjmod.html" >Design Object Model</A>
<LI><A HREF="dscenars.html" >Design Scenarios</A>
<LI><A HREF="doids.html" >Design Object Interaction Diagrams</A>
<LI><A HREF="dstmods.html" >Design State Models</A>
<LI><A HREF="dclsdes.html" >Design Class Descriptions</A>
<LI><A HREF="drdesalt.html" >Rejected Design Alternatives</A>
</MENU>
<P><B><A HREF="implemnt.html" >Implementation</A></B><BR>
<MENU>
<LI><A HREF="codguide.html" >Coding Guidelines</A>
<LI><A HREF="ipkgplan.html" >Physical Packaging Plan</A>
<LI><A HREF="idevenvt.html" >Development Environment</A>
<LI><A HREF="isrccode.html" >Source Code</A>
<LI><A HREF="iusrsupp.html" >User Support Material</A>
</MENU>
<P><B><A HREF="testing.html" >Testing</A></B><BR>
<MENU>
<LI><A HREF="testcase.html" >Test Cases</A>
</MENU>
```

```
<P><B><A HREF="appendix.html" >Appendix</A></B><BR>
<MENU>
<LI><A HREF="glossary.html" >Glossary</A>
<LI><A HREF="histwps.html" >Historical Work Products</A>
</MENU><HR><P>
</BODY></HTML>
```

The second file, named reqmnts.html, is simply a table of contents for the Requirements section of your Project Workbook. It is optional, but shown here to complete this style of workbook. If you choose to use it, you will need one file like this for each phase (section) of your workbook. You can cut and paste most of what you need from the workbook.html file. Again, comment out or delete the references to work products that you don't intend to use in this project.

```
<HTML><HEAD>
<TITLE>XYZ Requirements</TITLE>
</HEAD><BODY>
<H1>XYZ Requirements</H1>
<P>Release: 1.0
<P>Owner:   (project leader)<BR>
<HR><P><H2>Table of Contents</H2><P>
<MENU>
<LI><A HREF="probstmt.html" >Problem Statement</A>
<LI><A HREF="usecasem.html" >Use Case Model</A>
<LI><A HREF="nfreqts.html" >Nonfunctional Requirements</A>
<LI><A HREF="reqtspri.html" >Requirements Prioritization</A>
<LI><A HREF="buscase.html" >Business Case</A>
<LI><A HREF="accplan.html" >Acceptance Plan</A>
</MENU>
<HR>Go to
<MENU>
<LI><P><B><A HREF="workbook.html" >
Project XYZ Workbook (Table of Contents) </A></B><BR>
</MENU>
</BODY></HTML>
```

The third file, named probstmt.html, is the template for the Problem Statement work product section of your Project Workbook. It starts off with a table of common work product attributes. After that, fill in your own Problem Statement text. You will need to replicate this section for each work product that you intend to develop. The names of the html files you need to create can be seen in the anchor tag (i.e.<A HREF=...>) of the workbook.html file.

```
<HTML><HEAD>
<TITLE>XYZ Problem Statement</TITLE>
</HEAD><BODY>
<H1>XYZ Problem Statement</H1>
<P>Release: 1.0
<HR>
<TABLE BORDER>
<TR><TD>Identifier       <TD>???
<TR><TD>Date             <TD>???
<TR><TD>Author           <TD>???
<TR><TD>Owner            <TD>???
<TR><TD>Status           <TD>???
<TR><TD>Issues           <TD>???
<TR><TD>Metrics          <TD>???
<TR><TD>Traceability     <TD>???
<TR><TD>History          <TD>???
</TABLE>
<HR>
<P>(Your problem statement text goes here)
<HR>Return to
<MENU>
<LI><P><B><A HREF="workbook.html" >
Project XYZ Workbook (Table of Contents) </A></B><BR>
<LI><P><B><A HREF="reqmnts.html" >
Requirements Phase (Table of Contents) </A></B><BR>
</MENU>
</BODY></HTML>
```

Appendix C. Tool Support

No tool set currently provides automated support for the complete set of work products described in this book. This picture is not likely to change soon. Having said that, current tools provide direct support for many of the work products and the other work products can be produced using general-purpose tools such as text and graphics editing systems. While this situation is not perfect, it is a workable solution. The purpose of this section is to give examples of the types of tools with which the work products presented in this book have been produced by us and our mentoring clients.

The choice of tool set depends on many factors including budget, existing tools, tool experience, development platform, nature and size of the application, team structure, and organizational policies. This appendix is not intended to provide a one-size-fits-all proposal or even a specific set of recommendations for "typical" projects. Instead it is intended to provide some information on which tools have been successfully used with the approach described in this book. The reader should realize that many of the tools listed in these sections are replaceable by his or her own personal favorites.

In the following section you will see a list of the work products defined in this book along with one or two examples of the tools that have been used by us or our mentoring clients to produce the work product.

C.1.1 Example Tool Set Configuration

We and our mentoring clients frequently use:

- Either Rational's Rose product or Select Software Tools Select OMT for the "technical" work products that they are capable of supporting (such as Object Model).

- IBM's Generalized Markup Language (GML), also known as BookMaster, or Lotus's Word Pro for textual work products (such as Business Case), and to provide the top-level workbook structure, using a template such as that included in Appendix B, Workbook Skeleton.

- Lotus Freelance for the graphics to be inserted into work products where appropriate (such as the Use Case diagram of the Use Case Model work product).

Other tools, mentioned below, are also used, but those are the main tools that define the character of the tool set.

The models produced using Rose or Select OMT are themselves logically considered a part of the workbook although it may not be included physically in the workbook document. As including such model documentation in the GML or Word Pro versions of the workbook involves manual operations and is not simple, it is done only for project checkpoints. The Rose or Select OMT models are used directly for intermediate, current work product documentation.

Requirements

Problem Statement	GML or Word Pro
Use Case Model	Freelance for Use Case diagrams GML or Word Pro for textual descriptions
Nonfunctional Requirements	GML or Word Pro
Prioritized Requirements	GML or Word Pro
Business Case	GML or Word Pro
Acceptance Plan	GML or Word Pro

Project Management

Intended Development Process	GML or Word Pro
Project Workbook Outline	GML or Word Pro
Resource Plan	Computer Associates SuperProject
Schedule	Computer Associates SuperProject
Release Plan	GML or Word Pro
Quality Assurance Plan	GML or Word Pro
Risk Management Plan	GML or Word Pro
Reuse Plan	GML or Word Pro
Test Plan	GML or Word Pro
Metrics	GML or Word Pro
Project Dependencies	GML or Word Pro
Issues	GML or Word Pro

Analysis

Analysis Guidelines	GML or Word Pro
Subject Areas	GML or Word Pro
Analysis Object Model	Rose or Select OMT GML or Word Pro for textual descriptions
Analysis Scenarios	GML or Word Pro
Analysis OIDs	Rose or Select OMT GML or Word Pro for textual descriptions
Analysis State Models	Rose or Select OMT GML or Word Pro for textual descriptions
Analysis Class Descriptions	Rose can generate class description text Text can be edited for inclusion in GML or Word Pro document

User Interface Model

User Interface Guidelines	GML or Word Pro
Screen Flows	VisualAge for C++ or Smalltalk
Screen Layouts	VisualAge for C++ or Smalltalk
UI Prototype	VisualAge for C++ or Smalltalk

Design

Design Guidelines	GML or Word Pro
System Architecture	GML or Word Pro
APIs	Rose or Select OMT Text can be edited for inclusion in GML or Word Pro document
Target Environment	Freelance and either GML or Word Pro
Subsystem Model	Freelance and either GML or Word Pro
Design Object Model	Rose or Select OMT
Design Scenarios	GML or Word Pro
Design OIDs	Rose or Select OMT
Design State Models	Rose or Select OMT GML or Word Pro for textual descriptions
Design Class Descriptions	Rose or Select OMT GML or Word Pro for textual descriptions
Rejected Design Alternatives	GML or Word Pro

Implementation

Coding Guidelines	GML or Word Pro
Physical Packaging Plan	GML or Word Pro
Development Environment	GML or Word Pro
Source Code	Editing of text files generated by Rose or Select OMT
User Support Material	Full function document processing applications are normally chosen by a special Information Development organization.

Testing

Test Cases	GML or Word Pro to document manually written code, test scripts, or imbedded test case headers or prologues.

Appendix

Glossary	Rose or Select OMT Text can be edited for inclusion in GML or Word Pro document
Historical Work Products	Physical copies of workbook.

Glossary

A

Acceptance Plan. a work product documenting the criteria that the customer will use when deciding whether to accept the system.

actor. an object representing an external agent, human or mechanical, with which the system must interact.

aggregation. a special type of association that implies ownership or containment.

analysis. act of exploring the problem domain to gain a better understanding of the problem.

API. Application Programming Interface.

application. a software solution. Projects developing system software or class libraries are not excluded from this definition.

application development life cycle. see *software development life cycle*.

application domain. see *solution domain*.

Architecture. set of design principles that a design is based on.

association. a relationship between two classes in which one class "knows about" the other.

association class. a class that defines the properties and behaviors of an

association. For example, a hotel reservation class would be an association that relates a traveler with a hotel.

B

breadth first. a software development approach that uses the waterfall model.

business area. see *problem domain*.

Business Case. a justification for a development project showing costs and benefits. The costs and benefits are not merely financial but include all business concerns.

C

cardinality. a property of one "end" of an association. The cardinality specifies the number of instances of a particular class that may be related to a single instance of the associated class.

change control system. a system to track incremental changes in a work product, particularly Source Code, to enable changes to be reviewed and backed out as necessary.

class. A class is a set of objects that share the same behavior and a common structure. It is a template for a specific kind of object. Examples of a class may be Person, Airplane, et cetera. Each of them represent a class of objects rather than a specific object.

component. see *subsystem*.

contract. (1) a formal agreement between two parties on services to be provided. (2) documentation of the service-level dependencies between subsystems.

customer. the person or group commissioning the work on a project. May also refer to a team member taking the role of customer representative.

D

depth-first. a software development approach where a small, key area of the system is iteratively analyzed, designed, and implemented in isolation as an early project step in order to learn and to reduce risk.

design. the mapping of an analysis onto a selected architecture to create a software solution to a problem.

design pattern. a structured description of a reusable design idea.

Development Environment. a set of tools used in the design and implementation phases of a project. Common tools are compilers, editors, debugging tools, and change control systems.

directionality. specifies which class's instance has knowledge of the related class instances in an association relationship.

domain. a coherent body of knowledge, rules, and definitions, related to a particular subject.

domain expert. a person with knowledge of a particular area of business or technology that is required for a software development effort.

DOU. document of understanding.

DPP. defect prevention process.

DSOM. DSOM stands for Distributed System Object Model. It is part of the SOMobjects Workgroup Enabler product. It allows objects to be accessed in a distributed environment. SOMobjects Workgroup Enabler includes DSOM, SOM Kernel, Interface Repository, and Replication Frameworks. See also *SOMobjects*.

dynamic model. documentation of the dynamic aspects of a domain or system, conveniently represented as a Use Case Model, a set of Scenarios, and a set of OIDs.

dynamic modeling. modeling the interactions and state changes of objects in a domain or system.

E

encapsulation. the separation of a class's external interface from its implementation details. Information hiding.

event. (1) a stimulus to which one or more objects may respond. (2) an observable, logically indivisible real-world behavior within the *problem domain*.

F

finite state machine. representation of a *state model* of a class in terms of a finite set of states, events, transitions, and an initial state.

framework. a class library whose

classes are designed to interact in order to solve a particular problem, as opposed to a conventional class library whose classes are designed to be used primarily in isolation.

functional requirements. requirements reflecting what the system should do, as opposed to how it should be designed.

G

GUI. graphical user interface.

I

implementation. the phase of a project that creates a working solution from a design.

increment. one of a sequence of development cycles in each of which a specified subset of end-to-end system function is designed, incremented, and tested. An increment gives the development team early experience with the development process and the domains that can then be leveraged in later increments.

inheritance. the sharing of structure and function. In object-oriented inheritance hierarchies, subclasses inherit from their superclasses.

interface. the external (public) view of a system or class. This can refer to an API or to a user interface.

Issue. an area of uncertainty or a disagreement that requires resolution. Many Issues take the form of problematic *Scenarios*. Exploration of an issue consists, among other things, of defining several alternative solutions or answers. Alternatives can often be

conveniently represented as *OIDs* each showing a different assignment of system responsibilities. Resolving the issue consists of selecting the alternative that is most appropriate in the given context.

iteration. one of a sequence of development cycles in which work products are evolved from cycle to cycle.

iterative and incremental. a development process consisting of a sequence of *increments* each of which adds new end-to-end function and sets aside time as well for the *iterative rework* of already completed work products. Work items are scheduled on a risk-driven basis.

iterative rework. development work within a development cycle that is devoted to raising the quality of existing function, as opposed to adding new function.

L

LOC. lines of code.

logical partition. a section of the system created by the logical grouping of related classes. Primarily an analysis concept.

M

method. (1) a formal framework for modeling a system from its requirements to its deployed solution. (2) an operation that can be invoked on an object of a particular class.

Metrics. (1) estimated or measured data used in the planning or tracking of a software development effort. (2) the rules for calculating metric data.

model. a representation of a domain or a system from a particular point of view. Models are broadly divided into three kinds: *static models, dynamic models, and state models.*

mutability. the ability of an object to change.

MVC. Model-View-Controller. MVC is a concept introduced in Smalltalk-80. It separates the presentation of the model from the model itself. It is consisted of three kinds of objects. The Model is the application object, the View is its screen presentation, and the Controller defines a subscribe/notify protocol between the Model and the View.

N

notation. a set of standards defining the symbols used when documenting models, particularly graphical ones. Common notations include Booch and OMT.

O

object. An object is an entity that has state, behavior, and identity. It may be something physical or a concept. Examples of an object may be a car, an invoice, or an account. An object is also an instance of a class.

object interaction diagram. A diagram used to represent dynamic system behavior in a sequence of interactions between objects. An object interaction diagram demon-

strates how an *object model* can support the behavior defined by a *Scenario.*

object model. a model identifying classes, their responsibilities, and their static relationships, often represented by a diagram plus supporting documentation.

OID. see *object interaction diagram.*

OOTC. the IBM Object-Oriented Technology Center. A group that supports the internal use of object technology in IBM through offerings such as mentoring, document development, and informal assistance.

P

platform. a hardware and/or software environment.

problem domain. the *domain* that relates directly to a business problem and that captures the business knowledge required to solve the problem. It is the problem domain that is modeled during the analysis phase of a project.

Problem Statement. a statement of the motivation for developing a software system, preferably written by the customer. The Problem Statement provides the reasons for creating the application, as opposed to what the application must do functionally.

process. a template for a project documenting the anticipated work products, the order in which they will be produced, and how work product construction or refinement will be scheduled. A process should be defined, ideally, in terms of *metrics* by which the project can be planned and then tracked.

project. all effort related to the identification and solution of a problem.

project workbook. See *workbook*.

protocol. the interface and associated semantics of a class or subsystem.

prototype. something built or written to answer specific questions or to elicit feedback. An example is a graphical user interface prototype built to invite customer comment, or code written to determine how a particular software package can be used in a certain context. Prototyping is a risk reduction technique.

R

release. a software drop.

resource. staff, budget, training, equipment or services required for a project.

resource exposure risk. a risk that a required resource may not be available at the relevant time.

Resource Plan. a list specifying the resources required for a project. For each required resource, its nature, quantity, date required, and duration are recorded.

reuse. the use of some existing asset in the solution of different problems or different versions of a problem.

risk. anything that may jeopardize the success of a project.

risk management. the identification of risks, and strategies for dealing with them.

S

Scenario. an elaboration of a Use Case into a precisely defined statement of system behavior. A Scenario is represented as a Use Case plus a set of assumptions (initial conditions) plus a set of outcomes. Many Scenarios may be derived from a single Use Case.

scenario-driven. the transformation of a model from analysis to design by focusing on Scenarios. Analysis Scenarios are transformed to Design Scenarios and the required changes are reflected in the design model.

semantic network. a diagram showing a very early conceptual view of the domain. The semantic network is usually the outcome of a brainstorming session with a domain expert and is used in the construction of an initial object model.

service. function provided publicly by a class.

software development life cycle. the states through which a software development project passes from inception to deployment and maintenance.

solution domain. a *domain* relevant to the resolution of a problem, as opposed to the *problem domain* that captures knowledge about the problem itself.

SOM. see *SOMobjects*.

SOMobjects. SOM stands for System Object Model. SOMobjects Toolkit is IBM's implementation of Object Management Group's (OMG) Common Object Request Broker Architecture (CORBA). It includes an Interface Definition Language (IDL) compiler, SOM run-time kernel, and a set of object services defined by OMG, such as persistence, transaction, naming, and security. It enables object-oriented software to be developed and used in a language and platform-independent environment.

state. (1) a binding of all the variables of an object to specific values. (2) the set of all such bindings that each causes the object to behave in the same, identifiable manner. (An "equivalence class" of the space of all possible variable bindings.) (3) a node in a state model that represents such an identifiable set of variable bindings.

state model. documentation of the state-dependent behavior of a class, often represented as a *finite state machine* and/or a *state transition table*.

state transition table. a table showing the response of an object, in terms of state transitions, to each relevant event when in each of its states.

static model. documentation of the static aspects of a domain or system, usually represented as an *object model* plus the class descriptions that consolidate all the information currently known about each class.

static modeling. the production of a *static model*.

Subject Area. a work product representing an analysis-time partition of the *problem domain*.

subsystem. a major design component; a partition of the entire system.

system. the software solution to be delivered.

T

technique. a documented way of creating a particular work product or set of work products.

testing. the checking of work products to determine whether they satisfy specific quality criteria. Testing may be divided into internal *verification* and *validation* against other work products or specifications.

tools. aids to assist in the creation of work products. Examples are drawing packages and code generators.

U

Use Case. a visible and identifiable system behavior associated with one or more *actors* external to the system.

V

validation. ensuring that the correct problem is being solved.

verification. ensuring that the problem is being solved correctly. Checking the internal correctness and quality of a work product.

version. a major release.

W

waterfall. a software development process in which the development life cycle is divided into discrete phases that must be completed in order.

window of opportunity. a period of time in which releasing a product would provide a competitive advantage.

workbook. a logical book with a predetermined structure containing all the work products associated with a project from requirements gathering and project management through analysis, design, implementation, and testing.

work product. any planned, concrete result of the development process; either a final deliverable or an intermediate one. Examples include source code, a design object model, an analysis state model, a use case model, and a project schedule. The set of all project work products constitute the project *workbook*. Work products all have a common structure providing names, dates, description, issues, status, and the like, as well as structure that is work product-specific, for example, an object model diagram.

Index

A

Abraxas Software - CodeCheck   324
Acceptance Plan   119—123, 149
   definition of   617
actor   96—106
   definition of   49, 617
adornment
   aggregation   196, 281
   association   195, 281
   attribute   194, 197
   cardinality   196
   generalizations/specializations   195
   operation   194, 197
   service   194, 197
   subclass   281
aggregation   192
   definition of   617
analysis   69, 181
   Class Descriptions   227—232
   definition of   617
   domain   69
     performing   386—390
   example toolset   614
   Guidelines   131, 183—187
   model   233
   modeling   192
   Object Interaction
    Diagram   208—219
   Object Model   192—202, 248
   paralysis   181—182
   partitions   274
   process   127
   Scenarios   203—208, 238, 248,
   415
   semantic networks, getting
    started   391—393
   separating from design   15
   State Model   219—227
   Subject Areas   187—192, 193

analysis *(continued)*
   transcribe and
    converge   393—398
analyst   192, 238
API   265—272, 429—442
   See also Application Programming
    Interface
Apple Hypercard   244, 247
application
   architecture   257—265, 383, 404
   definition of   617
   development life cycle, definition
    of   617
Application Programming
  Interface   383
   definition of   617
   documentation   265—272
Architecture   257—265, 383, 404,
  464, 467
   definition of   617
assets, using   462
   frameworks   463
association   192, 195, 199, 282
   class, definition of   617
   definition of   617
assumptions   173
   project   173
attributes   445

B

balancing schedule and risks   154,
  380—383, 404
behavior   198
Booch, Grady   xxiii, 5, 7, 8, 191,
  305, 329
breadth-first
   definition of   617
Brooks, Fred   15

X

Y